COUNSELING SEXUAL AND GENDER MINORITIES

Lynne Carroll

University of North Florida

Merrill

Upper Saddle River, New Jersey
Columbus, Ohio

Library of Congress Cataloging-in-Publication Data

Carroll, Lynne.
  Counseling gender and sexual minorities/Lynne Carroll.
      p. cm.
  Includes bibliographical references and index.
  ISBN-13: 978–0–13–171051–1
  ISBN-10: 0–13–171051–6
  1. Sexual minorities—Counseling of.   2.   Sexual minorities—Mental health.   I. Title.
  RC451.4.G39C37   2010
  616.85 '83—dc22

                                                          2008032842

Vice President and Editor in Chief: Jeffery W. Johnston
Publisher: Kevin M. Davis
Acquisitions Editor: Meredith D. Fossel
Senior Managing Editor: Pamela D. Bennett
Senior Project Manager: Mary Irvin
Editorial Assistant: Nancy Holstein
Production Coordination: Rebecca K. Giusti, GGS Higher Education Resources, A Division of
    Premedia Global, Inc.
Art Director and Cover Design: Diane Lorenzo
Cover Image: © Christie's Images/SuperStock, Yurok/iStockphoto
Senior Operations Supervisor and Operations Specialist: Matt Ottenweller
Vice President, Director of Sales and Marketing: Quinn Perkson
Marketing Manager: Jared Brueckner
Marketing Coordinator: Brian Mounts

This book was set in ITC Century by GGS Higher Education Resources. It was printed and bound by Bind-Rite
Graphics. The cover was printed by Bind-Rite Graphics.

Pearson Education Ltd., London   Pearson Education North Asia, Ltd., Hong Kong
Pearson Education Singapore, Pte. Ltd.   Pearson Educación de Mexico, S.A. de C.V.
Pearson Education Canada, Inc.   Pearson Education Malaysia, Pte. Ltd.
Pearson Education—Japan   Pearson Education Upper Saddle River, New Jersey
Pearson Education Australia, Limited

Merrill
is an imprint of

www.pearsonhighered.com

10 9 8 7 6 5 4 3 2 1
ISBN 13: 978-0-13-171051-1
ISBN 10:   0-13-171051-6

For Billy

*If in the twilight of memory we should meet
once more, we shall speak again together
and you shall sing to me a deeper song....*

Kahlil Gibran, The Prophet

PREFACE

Any book written on the psychology of human beings will cause a degree of controversy. Such is the nature and complexity of our makeup that it is rare for the community of helping professionals to voice wholesale agreement on either the causes or the resolutions of our conflicts. So, by definition, a book on the topic of counseling sexual and gender minorities may create volatile reactions.

Additionally, treating sexual and gender minorities is still a relatively new field, certainly in the area of treatment protocols. There are some treatment approaches that seem more appropriate to the Dark Ages. And there are some that are so new they perhaps haven't had the documentation necessary to prove their effectiveness. Although research has expanded in certain areas, some sexual minorities, particularly bisexual women and men, are still largely ignored. Gender minorities remain glaringly absent from behavioral science research. Sexual and gender minority students themselves are too often without affirmative professional mentors and clinical supervisors in their universities and agencies. But one thing is certain: There is a critical need to help this population. The first step in doing so is educating a new generation of therapists about the complex world of counseling options for a highly complex community.

It is not uncommon for novice therapists and students to get a bit rattled at the prospect of talking to a client about his or her identity as a sexual or gender minority. Even with the best of intentions, it is difficult to counsel someone through the twists and turns of a route that to the novice therapist might seem incomprehensible. And what is the ideal destination for the client pursuing such a path as gender transformation?

Throughout my twenty-plus years as a professor, I have watched students grapple with their conflicts when these topics are introduced. At times, students are ready and interested, even excited, to explore this new terrain. For some, it is a relief and an affirmation to hear about themselves or a loved one. But for many, the topic of sexual and gender minority issues and counseling can evoke feelings of disapproval, dissonance, and aversion to the point of revulsion.

For them, I tell the story of a mother. Her 35-year-old son and his wife arranged for a trip for all three of them to meet in New York. After a night at a Broadway show and a late supper, the son ordered a round of brandy and said they had something to tell her. Then her son proceeded to say that he and his wife were getting a divorce and that he was going through sex change to become a woman. "When they said they wanted to tell me something that was going to be difficult, I first thought they were getting a divorce. Then as my son started to talk about his life, I thought he was going to tell me he was gay. The gender transformation was so staggering, I could do little more than listen. I couldn't even think of an intelligent question to ask."

But as the night went on and her son continued to talk, the mother said it was as if puzzle pieces that had been missing all her child's life were suddenly found and being put into place. "I can't explain it other than to say that it all made some sort of crazy sense."

The son is now a woman. It has been 10 years since that fateful night. And in that time, the son—now the daughter—has met and married a man who loves her very much.

From time to time, the mother has offered to speak with parents of children who were anticipating a sexual reassignment. One evening, after having spoken with an irate, totally irrational father of such a child, the woman came to see me. She was frustrated and furious. "He seems to think his kid is going through a phase! Dear God. I told him about my son. He had three years of intense therapy and counseling. He underwent months of hormone injections. He had a painful chin reduction surgery. He had hair transplants. He had the sexual reassignment surgery. He went through the isolating and difficult experience of learning to "pass" as a woman. He lost many of his friends, guys he'd gone all through school with. They didn't understand what he was doing and were repulsed by it. His sister's husband called him some sort of perverted aberration, and for about five years, refused to let him see his beloved nieces."

And she finished by crying, "My God, does that sound like he was 'going through a phase'? Why would someone go through all that excruciating pain if this were a phase!"

Sexual and gender minorities face issues that few people can even begin to imagine. Sometimes, that far out of the mainstream is a pretty lonely, difficult place. To become their best, most genuine selves takes courage, support, and guidance. If this text helps a novice therapist to better understand this community of clients, if it helps a novice therapist offer real compassion and understanding, then I will be deeply grateful.

There is much work yet to be done in understanding the nature, causes, and complexities of sexual orientation and gender identity. In the meantime, we will need to set our sights on developing effective treatment strategies for sexual and gender minorities. I hope we professionals can continue to commit time, talent, research, and compassion to helping our clients deal with—and overcome—some of the harsher realities they face and go on to live full, rich, contributing lives.

UNIQUE FEATURES OF THIS TEXT

This text provides a balance of theory, research, and clinical application. Each chapter opens with the voice of a sexual or gender minority person so readers will first have an opportunity to explore their more personal and sometimes visceral responses to sexual and gender minority issues. Each chapter provides readers with exercises for active learning and self-reflection. Central among these activities is the use of popular films, and sometimes lesser known films. A short synopsis of every movie is provided along with specific questions for further discussion and contemplation. Chapters also contain additional resources to aid you in practical ways with your work as a helping professional.

All chapters are arranged in a sequential fashion. In Chapter 1, readers are introduced to an extensive array of terms and to the theoretical orientation that undergirds this text. Next, readers will become acquainted with the history of clinical approaches used by physicians, psychiatrists, and other helping professionals to treat sexual and gender minorities. Chapter 2 concludes with a snapshot of the current policies, practices, and controversies that surround the treatment of sexual and gender minorities in the helping professions. In Chapter 3, readers will come to appreciate the vulnerabilities and challenges associated with survival in the context of a heterosexually oriented culture. In Chapter 4, readers will become acquainted with the empirical research that has explored counselor behaviors and attitudes toward their sexual and gender minorities. Chapter 5 examines the ways in which sexual and gender minority persons integrate additional aspects of their identities, including race, ethnicity, class, disability status, and religious affiliation. Readers explore possible negative effects of multiple and interlocking oppressions and the unique strengths that often emerge as a result of marginalization. Specific recommendations are offered to aid practitioners in their clinical work with sexual and gender clients, whose identities are complex and interwoven. The second half of the text contains a thorough review of research findings regarding the mental health issues of youth, couples, and families and practical suggestions for counseling these populations (Chapters 6–8). Chapter 9 focuses on the sexual health and substance use patterns of sexual and gender minorities and on the practitioners who treat them. Issues related to employment and workplace discrimination are presented in Chapter 10. Chapter 11 explores the role of helping professionals as advocates for sexual and gender minorities. This chapter contains a number of practical suggestions for readers who are interested in and inspired to become social activists for sexual and gender minorities.

Acknowledgments

I am most grateful to Meredith Fossel, Editor at Merrill/Pearson, for her guidance and supportive feedback and to Emily Rokosch, Lesbian, Gay, Bisexual and Transgender Resource Center at the University of North Florida, for her assistance with securing permissions. I am indebted to Diane Till for her editorial assistance. Heartfelt thanks to Jacquie Fraser and to my family, Bill and Mary Lou, for their unwavering support and encouragement. Thanks also to the reviewers of my manuscript for their thoughtful comments and insights: Tony W. Cawthon, Clemson University; Beverly Greene, St. John's University; Sharon Horne, The University of Memphis; Sakinah Salahu-Din, Florida Gulf Coast; and Amnat Hong-Chittaphong, Sienna College.

ABOUT THE AUTHOR

Lynne Carroll is professor and graduate director of counseling psychology at the University of North Florida. She has been a counselor educator and program director of mental health counseling for several years and has practiced as a psychologist and counselor in private practice and in community and university settings. She is author of numerous articles and book chapters on sexual and gender minority issues.

BRIEF TABLE OF CONTENTS

CONTENTS

NOTE: Every effort has been made to provide accurate and current Internet information in this book. However, the Internet and information posted on it are constantly changing, so it is inevitable that some of the Internet addresses listed in this textbook will change.

CHAPTER 1

Paradigm Shifts
Multiple Sexes, Sexualities, and Genders

INTRODUCTION

This is the reality: Our assumptions about the nature of sex, gender, and sexual orientation are unconscious and tenacious. Most of us consider our status as male or female to be natural or innate and, therefore, an unchangeable aspect of our identities. When confronted with a person who doesn't fit this cognitive map, it is not uncommon for us to assume this person is homosexual. Indeed, even many helping professionals assume that gender minority persons are "repressed homosexuals" who cannot seem to accept their true identities (Fagan, Schmidt, & Wise, 1994).

The following two excerpts give some idea of what it is like to live outside the mainstream. As you read them, check your immediate visceral responses. Your reaction may provide insight into your own assumptions and preconceived notions. In any case, how you react to these paragraphs will likely be instructive.

There is most certainly a privilege to having a gender. Just ask someone who doesn't have a gender, or who can't pass, or who doesn't pass. When you have a gender, or when you are perceived as having a gender, you don't get laughed at in the street. You don't get beat up. You know which public bathroom to use, and when you use it, people don't stare at you or worse. You know which form to fill out. You know what clothes to wear. You have heroes and role models. You have a past. (Bornstein, 1995, p. 127)

Both gay and straight consider it rather weird that I inhabit the social space of "former lesbian." It's a little (just a little) like being a transgendered person, or maybe one of those super-scrutinized mothers on welfare: someone on whom the burden of explanation falls disproportionately. I think people want to know which version of me is real and how to locate other leopards who might be prone to changing their spots. When all's said and done, they are sexually curious, though they hardly have the nerve to come right out and ask, "So what's it like to move from Vaginaland to Penisville?" (Clausen, 1999, p. 11)

Bornstein and Clausen give a sense of what they face as they come to grips with their own realities, living in a world that neither accepts nor understands them. Each defies conventional views of what is considered "normal" and "desirable." Bornstein, a gender minority author and activist, writes about her life in *Gender Outlaw: On Men, Women and the Rest of Us* (1995). She completed a sex change from biological male to female after living in the body of a male and being socialized accordingly until the age of 38.

In the second excerpt, from *Apples and Oranges: My Journey Through Sexual Identity* (1999), Clausen describes the reactions of others—gay as well as straight—when after 12 years of identifying herself as a lesbian, she fell in love with a West Indian male lawyer. As a result of living with a man, she became the subject of both curiosity in heterosexual circles and hostility in the gay and lesbian community.

If both excerpts left you feeling uncomfortable, it would be an understandable response. For those uninitiated in the fluid and challenging world of sex and gender minorities, it's a new and somewhat confusing place.

The cognitive map most of us use to organize and guide our interactions with others probably looks something like this:

Man = Masculine = Heterosexual

Woman = Feminine = Heterosexual

In instances when we encounter persons whose appearance and demeanor are not consistent with the equation above, our map might be revised to look something like this:

Man = Feminine = Gay

Woman = Masculine = Lesbian

These ways of thinking about the world can become so habitual and second nature that we think these notions are actually facts about the world. Alsop, Fitzsimons, and Lennon (2002) nicknamed this phenomenon the "naturalizing trick." After all, it is certainly not uncommon for us to simplify things by generalizing and stereotyping. We live in a fast-paced world. We reach reflexive conclusions, and our reactions are as fast as a text message—abbreviated and to the point.

A guest speaker at one of my graduate counseling courses was a preoperative male-to-female transsexual. She told of growing up as a boy in a small southern town, her years of military service, her marriage to a woman, the birth of her two sons, and her struggle with alcoholism. She disclosed that for many years, she had cross-dressed in secret. Finally, her desire to change her sex from male to female became so overpowering that she sought medical help. Now on a daily regimen of hormones, our guest speaker described her yearlong "test" period of living as a woman (called the "real-life experience"). She told of her upcoming and long-anticipated sex reassignment surgery and her excitement at finally—physically—becoming the sex she was born to be.

The students were fascinated with her story. But there was a good deal of confusion. One student timidly raised her hand. "Well, what is your sexual orientation?" she asked. The speaker said that as a biological male, he had had a history of sexual relationships with women. And now she continued to experience erotic and emotional attractions to women. The student, clearly perplexed, asked, "So, does that make him-her a lesbian?"

A Preview of Chapter Contents

This book explores the realities of the day-to-day lives of sexual and gender minorities and outlines specific therapeutic approaches to helping them. This first chapter offers an overview and looks at the complex interrelationships among sex, gender, and sexual orientation. Specifically, this chapter

- Defines key terms associated with sex, gender, and sexual orientation and discusses the research that has explored these alignments.
- Describes the interpersonal and cultural responses to persons who defy traditional views of biological sex, gender, and sexual orientation.
- Describes helping professionals' use of treatment protocols, especially those that reinforce sociocultural views, with sexual and gender minorities.
- Explores the implications of postmodern, constructionist, and queer theories for social policy, research, and therapy practices related to sexual and gender minorities.

DEFINING TERMS AND DESCRIBING LINKAGES

Sex

Biological sex is defined as the "genetic, hormonal, morphological, chromosomal, biochemical and anatomical factors" that "impact the physiology of the body and the sexual differentiation of the brain" (Lev, 2007, p. 155). Despite our scientific understanding of the biological complexity of the sexual-differentiation process, our determination of a person's sex is based on a doctor's inspection of the newborn's genitals (Kessler, 1998): penis = boy, vagina = girl. According to Fausto-Sterling (2000), a biologist and cultural critic, whenever we make an attribution about a person's sex, we are making a "social decision." In her text *Sexing the Body* (2000), Fausto-Sterling argues that it is our beliefs about gender that determine how we label someone as man or woman.

Biological sex is always described in binary terms—one is either male or female. Sex is a core ingredient of our identities, and sexual dualism is a basic cornerstone of Western culture (Lorber, 2005). It is a decisive factor in how and where we are educated and employed. It is a determinant of our economic status and the distribution of our responsibilities for child care and household duties (Lorber, 2005). It is the basis for most of our social lives and is enforced in all of our major social institutions: family, school, workplace, law, politics, religion, medicine, and psychological theory and its practices.

When the Sexual Binary Doesn't Fit: Intersexed Persons

The reality is that, while statistically unusual, there are some infants who are born with genitals and body types that are in between the extreme ends of the maleness – femaleness spectrum. Historically, they were identified as *hermaphrodites*. Now called *intersexed* or infants with disorders of sex development, these infants are born with markers of biological sex — chromosomes, hormones, genitals, reproductive function, and secondary sexual characteristics—that are not aligned. Currently, the prevalence of intersexuality is estimated to be 1.7% of all live births (Fausto-Sterling, 2000). Fausto-Sterling (2000) posits the following as the most common forms of intersexuality:

- Genetic females who are born with enlarged clitorises or with male genitals (congenital adrenal hyperplasia)
- Genetic males who are born with feminized genitalia (androgen insensitivity syndrome)
- Individuals whose gonads do not develop (gonadal dysgenesis)
- Genetic males whose penile urethra exits other than at the tip of the penis (hypospadias)
- Individuals with unusual chromosome compositions such as XXY (Klinefelter Syndrome) or XO (Turner Syndrome)
- "True hermaphrodites" (infants born with a combination of ovaries and testes)

The Medical Treatment of Intersexed Persons

Because the genital and bodily configurations of intersexed persons transgress gender categories, such persons are thought of as defective and as objects. Fausto-Sterling (2000) has detailed the treatment protocol that "fixes" this "mistake," maintaining gender divisions by requiring that these "unruly" bodies be controlled (p. 6). According to Fausto-Sterling, the practice of interceding at birth through reconstructive surgeries on the genitals of intersex infants began in the 1950s with the advent of refinements in surgical technology. Sexologist John Money developed the standard medical protocol for the treatment of infants born with ambiguous genitalia. Money (1985) proposed that children develop a gender identity during the first two years of life through interaction with their parents, their perception of their own genitals, and biological influences originating in utero, which can be hormonal surges in the fetus. Money's protocol required that the infant with obviously ambiguous genitals undergo chromosomal and hormonal tests by a multidisciplinary team of medical specialists such as geneticists, endocrinologists, and pediatric urologists. These experts would then make a determination as to which sex the infant would be assigned.

Gender reassignment was usually made within 48 hours of birth and was determined by the potential to surgically create nonambiguous, functioning genitals. The determining factor in many cases was the actual size of the penis. In cases where the penis was adequate in size, chromosomal tests were performed. In genetic males (babies with a Y chromosome), phalluses of 2.5 centimeters or less (about an inch) in length were considered to be inadequate. In the case of genetic females (babies lacking a Y chromosome), those born with ambiguous genitalia were assigned as girls. Surgeons considered enlarged clitorises to be "cosmetically offensive" in girls, and surgical reductions were performed (Dreger, 1998).

Over the past 10 years, several factors have led many to call for a moratorium on genital surgeries. A growing and more vocal group of adults reject the practice of infant sex/gender assignment because of the genital scarring, infection, orgasmic incapacity, and emotional trauma they experienced as a result of these medical procedures (Colapinto, 1997). Additionally, many have begun to criticize the lack of scientific research, including long-term follow-up after surgery of intersex persons (Zucker, 2001). Further, there are reports of persons whose initial gender assignment was totally at odds with their later sense of gender identity (Intersex Society of North America, 2006).

As a result of these criticisms, the Consortium on the Management of Disorders of Sex Development has developed a roster of Clinical Guidelines (Intersex Society of North America, 2006). These include the need for a multidisciplinary approach to initial gender assignment, the complete disclosure of test results to parents, and the delay of cosmetic surgical intervention until the child has been able to establish a sense of gender identity and is able to provide input into decisions. The next chapters expand on current treatment approaches with intersex children and their families.

Gender

The term *gender* typically refers to the psychological and social aspects associated with someone's biologically determined sex (Unger, 1979). The phrase *gender identity* commonly refers to a person's subjective sense of identity as either male or female. Like the biological sexes, our gender identities are considered to be dichotomous—that is, either masculine or feminine. Gender identity is a state of mind that exists in each of us regardless of what our genitals look like. The term *gender expression* is sometimes used to characterize ways in which we outwardly display or express our inner sense of gender. We identify ourselves to the world through dress, nonverbal mannerisms, stride, sway, voice, and other behaviors. Basically, our self-identification and our behaviors evolve from social practices whereby human bodies are transformed, usually starting in early childhood, into men and women (Bem, 1993). Cultural definitions of what constitutes masculine and feminine evolve over time.

Think of the social practices that categorize your gender. From an early age, it is the selection of toys and clothes, games, and responsibilities and the clear desirability of certain behaviors, impulses, and feelings. These practices

> program different social experiences for males and females respectively, and they communicate to both males and females that the male-female distinction is extraordinarily important, that it has—and ought to have—intensive and extensive relevance to virtually every aspect of human experience. (Bem, 1993, p. 146)

Gender Minorities

In many instances, we describe persons whose gender identity does not coincide with their biological sex as *transsexual* or, more commonly, as *transgender*. Many prefer the word *transgender* because it is a more inclusive way to describe the full spectrum of people with nontraditional gender identities, including pre- and postoperative transsexuals, cross-dressers, and intersex persons. This text uses the term *gender minority* because it more broadly captures persons whose expression of gender identity differs, or is perceived by others to differ, from what is considered to be the norm in our Western culture.

When Biological Sex and Gender Identity Don't Align: "Policing" Practices

How significant is the relationship between biological sex and gender identity? The answer is surprising. It's a relationship that tends to be completely ignored until we suddenly find ourselves in situations where our way of organizing our perceptions doesn't seem to apply. Social scientists like Kessler and McKenna (1978) claim that every time we encounter a new social situation, the first thing we do is attribute a gender to the people we observe. We also present ourselves to others using culturally established rules, behaviors, mannerisms, and other cues we've been conditioned to associate with members of "our" gender (Lucal, 1999). Goffman (1959) called this phenomenon *gender displays*. On *Saturday Night Live,* comedienne Julia Sweeney created a character named Pat. The whole premise of the skits was that Pat never revealed his/her gender. Dress, voice, and demeanor could go either way. And the hilarity resulted from various ploys used to determine Pat's true gender. Unfortunately, those whose gender (and sexual) identity is ambiguous must deal with a harsher reality. They are often the target of ridicule, verbal and physical harassment, and even hatred.

In the 1970s, feminist scholars challenged the assumption that masculine behaviors were the sole and most desirable traits in men and feminine attributes aligned solely with womanhood. In particular, Bem (1974), a feminist psychologist, argued that masculinity and femininity can be understood as socially constructed, multiple, and changeable, rather than viewed as fixed biological essences.

Feminists such as Brownmiller (1975) and Morgan (1970) questioned the patriarchal nature of Western culture, where women were paid lower wages, had fewer chances at career advancement, and lacked access to political office and leadership positions. They explored ways in which gender roles are "policed" in our culture. Indeed, tremendous social consequences await those who do not conform to gender roles in Western culture (Gagne, Tewksbury, & McGaughey, 1997; Skidmore, Linsenmeier, & Bailey, 2006; Witten & Eyler, 1999). "There is not a single word for people who don't fit gender norms that is positive, affirming, and complimentary" (Wilchins, 2004, p. 38).

Girls/women who exhibit masculine behavioral traits are sometimes labeled "tomboys" and boys/men who exhibit feminine traits are labeled "sissies" or "girlyboys." But "tomboy" is often used as an indulgent, amused term, indicating "she'll grow out of it," whereas the policing practices are far harsher for boys. Quite simply, men and masculine traits are more highly valued in Western culture than are women and feminine traits (Bowers & Bieschke, 2005; Morrow, 2000; Skidmore et al., 2006). Gender-nonconforming boys more than girls tend to suffer rejection by peers and parents, particularly by their fathers (LaMar & Kite, 1998; Landolt, Bartholomew, Saffrey, Oram, & Perlman, 2004; Skidmore et al., 2006). Hatred of feminine attributes in men is considered to be the cornerstone of masculinity in our culture (Herek, 1989, 2002a; Herek & Capitanio, 1996; Kimmel & Mahler, 2003).

When Biological Sex and Gender Identity Don't Align in Children: The Use of Reparative Therapy

The extent to which the alignment between biological sex and gender identity is reinforced in psychological theory and counseling practices is dramatically illustrated in the treatment strategies employed by medicine and psychiatry with children.

The following pages explore the ways in which the psychiatric and medical professions have treated children who either defy our assumptions about the relationship between biological sex and gender identity or have gender dysphoria (defined as psychological discomfort with one's biological sex), often diagnosed as gender identity disorder (GID). Beginning in the 1960s, researchers explored gender variance in children, mostly boys. The leading researchers in this area—Richard Green, John Money, Robert Stoller, and Bernard Zuger—argued that gender-variant children were at greater risk of becoming homosexuals, transvestites, or transsexuals (Bryant, 1996).

A treatment approach used in GID cases to help children accept their biological sex and associated gender identity is termed *rehabilitative treatment* (Hill, Rozanski, Carfagnini, & Willoughby, 2005; Raj, 2002). George Rekers, Susan Coates, and Kenneth Zucker are considered leading proponents of rehabilitative treatment of GID. Supporters of this reparative therapy argue that ultimately it helps defend against the negative effects of the social ostracism that gender-nonconforming children typically experience. Reparative treatment incorporates behavioral techniques (e.g., Rekers, 1995; Zucker & Bradley, 1995). One behavioral strategy known as *play reconditioning* (Rekers & Lovass, 1974) requires children to wear wrist counters when playing with same-sex-typed toys. While playing, they earn points they can exchange for rewards or privileges. "Bug-in-ear" devices are also used to communicate and guide the play of children diagnosed with GID. In this "treatment," professionals who are observing communicate via a transmission device in the child's ear: e.g., "No, Charlie, put down that doll. Pick up the truck." Rekers describes the use of these techniques in *Handbook of Child and Adolescent Sexual Problems* (1995), which was used in the 1990s to assist pediatricians with the diagnosis and treatment of gender identity disorder in children (Burke, 1996).

The diagnosis of GID and the subsequent rehabilitative treatment approaches are certainly not without critics. Interestingly, Burke's fascinating text *Gender Shock* (1996) provides an alternative perspective on the work of Rekers and those who practice aversive approaches to treatment. In her follow-up of Rekers's treatment of "Kraig," the subject of his 1974 article, Burke noted that several years after his treatment, Kraig attempted suicide by ingesting pills. He reportedly attributed his depression and suicidal attempt to the shame and embarrassment he felt over the childhood diagnosis and treatment he received.

In the excerpt below, Scholinski describes her rehabilitative-style treatment during her hospitalization in a psychiatric facility in the early 1980s. Scholinski's autobiography, *The Last Time I Wore a Dress* (1997), chronicles her treatment regimen over a three-year period, including wearing make-up and swinging her hips. Scholinski's words echo those of other gender minority clients who are angered and disillusioned as a result of their treatment in the mental health system.

[Dr. Browning] rolled his pen between his fingers for a moment. He said the other diagnosis was something called Gender Identity Disorder which he said I'd had since Grade 3, according to my records. He said what this means is you are not an appropriate female, you don't act the way a female is supposed to act. I looked at him. I didn't mind being called a delinquent, a truant, a hard kid who smoked and drank and ran around with a knife in her sock. But I didn't want to be called something I wasn't. Gender screw-up or whatever wasn't cool. My foot started to jiggle, I couldn't stop it. He was calling me a freak, not normal. He was like the boys in Little League calling out tomboy, tomboy, and Michelle who pinned me down for the red lipstick treatment. He was like the boys who yelled, *"let me see your titties"* when I rode shirtless on my bike in the wind. (Scholinski, 1997, pp. 15–16)

Critics of reparative treatment approaches argue that there is little research to support the idea that such therapy is effective. Further, they claim that such approaches "disrespect the youth's subjective sense of gender" and cast parents and therapists into the role of "gender police" (Hill et al., 2005, p. 26). Protection against peer ostracism is typically used as a rationale in support of reparative treatment. However, Lev (2005) points out that in most instances in which children are bullied on the basis of race, ethnicity, and physical disabilities, any interventions are directed at the system level and "not on changing children to better fit in to oppressive circumstances" (p. 49).

When Biological Sex and Gender Identity Don't Align in Adults: The Use of Sex Reassignment Procedures

The extent to which the alignment between biological sex and gender identity is reinforced in our culture is dramatically illustrated in the treatment strategies that physicians and psychiatrists have employed to treat transsexual adults. In the 1960s, following the widely publicized news of Christine Jorgensen's successful sex change, Benjamin, a New York endocrinologist, published "The Transsexual Phenomenon" (1967). He clearly advocated sex reassignment surgery as a form of humane and compassionate treatment for persons whose genitals did not match their gender. Three years later Green and Money (1968) published an edited textbook that established a medical protocol for sex reassignment at Johns Hopkins University. Within 10 years, there were more than 40 university-based gender clinics in the United States. The standard treatment protocol in place currently requires persons to seek counseling and adhere to a series of specific procedures. These are outlined in the Standards of Care developed by the Harry Benjamin International Gender Dysphoria Association (Meyer et al., 2001).*

Basically, transsexual persons are diagnosed as having *gender dysphoria* (defined as psychological discomfort with one's biological sex) and as such are considered "sick." The standards dictate that persons seeking hormonal and surgical reassignment receive counseling and obtain official letters of recommendation by qualified mental health professionals. Those interested in surgical reassignment are also mandated to live as their desired gender for approximately one year (called the "real-life experience"). The treatment objective of the medical and psychiatric establishments is for gender dysphoric persons to alter their bodies and adapt a new gender presentation so they can "pass" (conceal the fact that they are

---

*Now known as the World Professional Association for Transgender Health (http://www.path.org).

differently gendered) successfully and not be "read" or discovered. In most instances, the costs of treatment are covered by insurance only if the patient has been diagnosed with gender identity disorder as defined in the text revision of the fourth edition of the *Diagnostic and Statistical Manual of Mental Disorders* (*DSM–IV–TR*; American Psychiatric Association, 2000). Currently, the *DSM–IV–TR* deems cross-dressing a "fetish" and transsexualism a gender identity disorder.

Current treatment protocols for transsexuals place helping professionals in the unique and awkward position of being potential gatekeepers to their clients. Even in the days of increasing use of cosmetic surgery, there are no other instances in which therapists are required to sanction surgical interventions. Many transsexuals are able (with the aid of hormonal and surgical interventions) to successfully pass as their desired gender without detection. However, it is important to note that others are less successful in doing so. Either the medical procedures are too costly and painful, or their basic body morphology makes their attempt to transition more noticeable to others.

Some gender minorities advocate for a future in which a multiplicity of genders, sexes, and sexualities might be possible. Based on his extensive interviews with persons with nontraditional gender identities, Hill (1997) noted the majority preferred to identify themselves as transgendered and did not want to "reedit" their biographies or to "pass" in mainstream society. Transgender activists like Riki Anne Wilchings, Kate Bornstein, Pat Califa, and Holly Devor advocate that transsexual persons "come out" and identify themselves as transgendered and, in so doing, "begin to write [themselves] into the discourses which have been written [about them] (Stone, 1991, p. 299). As Feinberg (1998) stated: "We are oppressed for not fitting these narrow social norms, and we are fighting back" (p. 5). Bockting (1997) observed that by affirming their identities as either transsexuals or transgendered persons, persons with nontraditional gender identities could alleviate the shame, isolation, and secrecy that often accompany attempts to pass as a desired gender.

Outside of academic circles, a growing number of young people do not believe that sex and gender are necessarily dichotomous. For example, some members of Generation X are more comfortable than previous generations with tattooing and piercing their bodies, dressing more androgynously, and labeling themselves as bisexual (Elkins & King, 2002; Herdt, 2001). Some see themselves as somewhere in the middle of the gender continuum and define themselves as neither male nor female but as "other." Evidence of a new acceptance of sexual and gender diversity is clear in the proliferation of labels: queer, butch, dyke, androgyne, ambigendered, two spirited, bigendered, transgenderist, genderqueer, gender variant, and gender outlaw. In contrast, baby boomers whose activism required their ability to "stand up and be counted" as gay and lesbian seem more uncomfortable with using such labels when referring to themselves. Anthropologist Herdt (2001) sees this phenomenon among younger age cohorts as evidence of a future with diverse sexual cultures and gender minorities, the byproduct of which is an increasing resistance to heteronormativity.

Sexual Orientation

The term *sexual orientation* is broadly used to refer to a type of erotic and affiliative attraction toward potential romantic partners based on their natal or biological sex. Just as we think of biological sex in binary terms, as either male or female, sexual orientation is conceptualized in binary terms, as either heterosexual or homosexual. Heterosexuality has long been deemed universal, desirable, and healthy. Rich (1980), a feminist poet, challenged this thinking in the early 1980s by arguing that heterosexuality is compulsory in nature. Ingraham (2005) described heteronormativity as akin to the idea of "thinking straight," or assuming that everyone is heterosexual. The converse of this is "thinking bent," which is to explore the lives of people who are marginalized and question to the practices that render them invisible. How strongly entrenched dichotomous categorizations of sexuality are in social science research and therapy practice can be illustrated by considering the status of bisexuality.

When the Sexual Binary Doesn't Fit: Bisexual Persons

While the existence of bisexuality received empirical support in the late 1940s with the publication of Alfred Kinsey's research, most sexologists and researchers perceived bisexuality as an illegitimate form of sexual expression. The Kinsey research found that a large number of men who labeled themselves as heterosexual had had sexual desire for and sexual contact with other males during adolescence and young adulthood (Kinsey, Pomeroy, & Martin, 1948). Nonetheless, bisexuality has typically been defined by researchers, therapists, and laypersons as

- A "phase" on the path toward determining one's true identity as a homosexual or heterosexual
- A form of fence-sitting, an avoidance of making a commitment to any one person
- A form of denial of one's true homosexual nature (MacDonald, 1981)

These views of bisexuality have had obvious implications for researchers and clinicians. Indeed, there has been only limited research on bisexual issues and bisexual identity development. In their quantitative analysis of psychological research documented in the PsycInfo database and published over a 27-year period, Lee and Crawford (2007) reported studies of bisexual persons accounted for less than 0.20 percent of the research. They also reported that while there had been an increase over time in research on gay men and lesbians, the amount of research incorporating bisexual men and particularly bisexual women has remained small. And there are few models that take into account multiple minority statuses such as ethnicity and bisexuality (Collins, 2004).

Later chapters of this text explore the implications of cultural views for the work of helping professionals, some of whom categorize their bisexual clients as less mature, are essentially homophobic, and assume that nonmonogamy is evidence of immature and unhealthy development (Dworkin, 2001). Only in the past decade have researchers and clinicians begun to question the view of bisexuality as immature and transitory and to argue that it may be indicative of more cognitive flexibility (Konik & Crawford, 2004) and creativity (Brown, 1989). Eve Kosofsky Sedgwick raised the question of why researchers have neglected to explore the role that other personal qualities, including intelligence and compassion, play in sexual and emotional attraction. Many bisexuals, for example, maintain their choice of romantic partner is based on their attraction to a specific person and not to a specific gender. These critiques of bisexuality have resulted in newer and more interesting models that take into account dimensions of sexual attraction other than biological sex (i.e., Rust, 2000).

When Gender Identity and Sexual Orientation Don't Align

Persons deviating from normative gender roles are likely to experience negative repercussions, ranging from accusations of homosexuality to violence (Bem, 1993). In Western culture, genitals, gender, and sexuality are aligned. For many, the terms *man, masculine,* and *heterosexual* are synonymous, as are *woman, feminine,* and *heterosexual.* Men who are considered effeminate and women who are viewed as hypermasculine are labeled as homosexuals (Herdt, 1991). Those who are gender nonconforming in appearance and behavior are perceived to be homosexual (Hill, 2003).

One interesting laboratory experiment sought to test this observation. Madson (2000) showed photographs depicting physically androgynous persons (those with "a combination of physical characteristics that make it difficult to categorize their gender," p. 149) and clearly gendered persons (women who appeared "feminine" and men who appeared "masculine") to undergraduate research participants. After viewing randomly assigned photographs, participants were asked to answer a series of questions about the subjects' sexual orientations. As was anticipated, the physically androgynous people in the photographs were more often perceived as homosexuals than were the clearly gendered persons.

The threat of being accused as homosexual in and of itself has served to reinforce compulsive heterosexuality (Bohan, 1996). When confronted with persons whose genitals don't seem to match our expectations about gender expression and behavior or with those who don't seem to fit the schema outlined above, it is not uncommon for us to assume they are gay or lesbian.

Consider the sense of bewilderment one experiences when confronted with a male-to-female transgendered person who identifies herself as lesbian. In this context, all alignments among genitals, gender, and sexuality are arrested. Typically, gender minority persons who have transitioned from males at birth to women are described as lesbians if they are sexually attracted to other women. Alternately, persons who are identified as anatomical females at birth and presently identify themselves as men are described as gay if they are sexually attracted to other men (Tarver, 2002). When genitals, gender identity, and sexual orientation are conflated, they are difficult to disentangle.

While many gender minorities are comfortable defining themselves as gay or lesbian, there are many who are not. Preliminary research demonstrates that gender minorities are sometimes more fluid in their sexual attractions (e.g., bisexual) (Denny, 2007). However, the gender minority population comprises persons who identify themselves in many ways, including heterosexual, gay, lesbian, and queer.

CHANGING THEORIES, CHANGING TIMES

Academics and practitioners have shifted in their framework for understanding sex, gender, and sexual orientation over the past 20 years, as our traditional binary notions of sex, gender, and sexual orientation have become increasingly complex. Many describe the paradigm used to understand gender identity and sexuality as essentialism. An essentialist perspective represents sex, gender, and sexual orientation as stable and biologically determined (Lorber, 1994). Essentialists believe that homosexuality has existed, with the same meaning, regardless of cultural context or historical time. The dominance of the essentialist paradigm in psychology has impacted the types of research questions posed as well as the methodologies employed. More research money is being spent now on trying to explain why people are homosexuals than at any other time at our history (Wilton, 2000).

Many theories exist about the causes of homosexuality. Ones that remain popular suggest that homosexuality is a consequence of hormonal events in utero (Mulaikal, Migeon, & Rock, 1987), an atypical brain structure (LeVay, 1993), and a genetic predisposition (Bailey & Pillard, 1991). In perhaps the most highly publicized findings, LeVay discovered through autopsying the cadavers of men who had died with AIDS that the medial preoptic region of the hypothalamus was smaller in gay men and heterosexual women. However, as critics (Wilton, 2000) point out, the determination of sexual identity had been made through an inspection of clinical records. If the mode of HIV infection was through sexual activity with men, the cadaver was deemed gay. What is problematic here is that research has indicated many men who have sex with other men do not think of themselves as gay or bisexual and often live basically heterosexual lifestyles. The studies that have reported some genetic or biological difference between homosexual and nonhomosexual persons have not as of yet been replicated successfully (Garnets & Kimmel, 2003).

Since the late 1970s, several identity models that depict the development of same-sex sexual orientation (Cass, 1979, 1984; Coleman, 1982; Troiden, 1979, 1988) have been generated. Most of these models are based on the assumption that sexuality is relatively fixed at an early age but is marked by a developmental progression in which persons move initially from a gradual sense of self-awareness of their same-sex feelings, thoughts, or behaviors to ultimately a sense of self-affirmation as being homosexual. Many of these models are still being incorporated in texts and references dealing with gay and lesbian issues. Such approaches suggest that fluctuations in the ways individuals define their sexual identities are indicative of immaturity (Rust, 2000). These contemporary models of "coming out" are also premised on the idea that sexual orientation is a major component of personal identity.

Such models tend to fall short when addressing the experiences of people of color who are also struggling with issues of sexual identity. As psychologist Greene (2000) argued, the concept of identity is usually explored by splitting up varying aspects of the self (usually the white middle-class self) and studying these in isolation instead of as a complex, interrelated whole. The consequence of these practices is that we have developed models that don't fit or adequately account for the experiences of persons of color, persons with disabilities, and persons who are economically disadvantaged. Lorde (1984) is right on point as she describes her own inner struggle:

> As a Black lesbian feminist comfortable with the many different ingredients of my identity, and a woman committed to racial and sexual freedom from oppression, I find I am constantly being encouraged to pluck out one aspect of myself and present this as a meaningful whole, eclipsing or denying the other parts of self. But this is a destructive and fragmenting way to live. (p. 120)

The Birth of Constructionism

More-contemporary notions of gender and sexual orientation have been generated over the last 20 years. These notions have often originated from academic disciplines other than psychology, such as philosophy, anthropology, and sociology. The term *postmodern* is often used to describe the particular historical era we live in, one that has rejected the view that "truth" can be uncovered through the use of objective, scientific methods. The origins of postmodernism are said to be found in the work of French philosopher Jacques Derrida, who lived through the Nazi death camps and the destruction of Hiroshima and Nagasaki. Derrida argued that Western culture has overvalued language, and he deemed its use transparent.

Beginning in the 1980s, in many disciplines, including education, literature, political science, and sociology, popular models and methods were critiqued or deconstructed. Within the field of psychology, Gergen (1985) critiqued science, arguing against its insistence on objective truths. Gergen maintained that the degree to which any model, method, or theory is viewed as accurate is determined by its political usefulness rather than its validity and, further, that our models and methods are developed through social interaction. As such, these models are forms of social actions and, therefore, always have political consequences.

In order to better comprehend what *postmodern* really means, it is helpful to explore its origins. Sociologist McIntosh, an early and influential figure in social constructionist theory, wrote in 1968 of homosexuality as a social role characterized by complex and hidden social interactions rather than a basic aspect of personality identity. McIntosh indicated the view of sexual orientation as a static, core attribute forces us to ask the "wrong" questions, including what causes homosexuality and whether or not one is "truly" homosexual. By her definition, homosexuality was conceived as a label, albeit a stigmatized one. McIntosh proposed that the more one identifies with the label "homosexual" and the more negatively stigmatized that identity is, the more difficult it becomes to disown the label.

Foucault (1978), a French social critic, advanced the notion that language can be used as an instrument of power by social institutions in industrialized societies in order to exert control over bodies and sexuality. He asserted that people internalize the stories or narratives that are promulgated by those who are deemed to have expert knowledge, like teachers, doctors, psychologists, and clergy. These narratives are assumed to be "truths." Foucault noted the term *homosexual* was first applied by the judicial and medical establishments in the 1800s to categorize persons whose sexual behavior was considered abnormal:

> The nineteenth-century homosexual became a personage, a past, a case history and a childhood, in addition to being a type of life, a life form, and a morphology, with an indiscreet anatomy and possibly a mysterious physiology. . . . Homosexuality appeared as one of the forms of sexuality when it was transposed from the practice of sodomy onto a kind of interior androgyny, a hermaphrodism of the soul. The sodomite had been a temporary aberration; the homosexual was now a species. (Foucault, 1978, p. 43)

Foucault objected to labels or categories because they are often used to subjugate some and privilege others. In the case of psychiatry and medicine, diagnostic labels and treatments have resulted in the marginalization of persons and have influenced social policy and civil rights (Lev, 2005). For example, in the late 1800s African slaves who tried to escape enslavement were described as suffering from a mental illness called *drapetomania* (Kutchins & Kirk, 1997, as cited by Lev, 2005). This diagnosis was later used as a rationale for slavery (Kutchings & Kirk, 1997). Other examples where a diagnosis has been used as a weapon or a method of social control include homosexuality and gender identity disorder.

Queer Theory

The analyses described above and the subsequent emergence of "queer studies" opened up new possibilities for academics to challenge traditional binary notions of sex/gender. Queer theorists advocated that we aggressively critique labels and categories. The term *queer*, for example, has been reclaimed by many gay, lesbian, bisexual, and transgender persons and used to describe people who transgress culturally imposed norms of heterosexuality and gender. Although the word *queer* is still often an abusive epithet when used by heterosexuals, many queer-identified people have taken back the word to use it as a symbol of pride and affirmation of difference and diversity.

It was not until the end of the twentieth century that researchers began to question our dichotomous view of gender identity. Several texts (Brown, 1998; Jacobs, Thomas, & Lang, 1997; Roscoe, 1998) have, for example, detailed instances where members of North American Indian tribes who assumed multiple gender roles, "two-spirit people," were actually revered and considered to be prophets and visionaries. Butler, author of the text *Gender Trouble* (1990), is perhaps one of the most influential contemporary queer theorists. She argues against the assumption that gender is biologically determined and observes that gender is enacted and that "feminine" and "masculine" behaviors are "performed." According to Butler, sexual identity is performed at the level of tacit and mundane activities: dress, gesture, walk, mannerisms, and the like. Butler, who studied drag performers, seems to be saying that when drag queens put on panty hose and high heels, they perform societal constructions of what women are like, just as women who dress in these garments do. So, much like RuPaul's (1995) motto, "you're born naked and all the rest is drag," there is no essential woman (or man) and no deep sense of self that every woman (or man) has that influences what she (or he) does; there is no fixed relationship among one's anatomy, identity, and sexuality.

In a similar fashion, theorists are exploring ways in which heterosexuality is both a "constructed identity" and a "performance" that is "not necessarily linked to sexual acts" (Baca Zinn, Hondagneu-Sotelo, & Messner, 2005, p. 231). A good example of this is provided by the Internet, where people can meet in cyberspace and assume alternative sexual and gender identities.

The Current Status of Social Constructionism

Postmodern feminist, queer, and cultural theorists continue to advance increasingly complex explanations of identity, sex, gender, and sexual orientation. According to these theorists, sexual orientation and gender identity are continually renegotiated in the context of competing cultural messages and discourses (Butler, 1990; Lorber, 1994). Holloway (1989) defined discourse as a "system of statements which cohere around common meanings" and as "a product of social factors, of powers and practices" (p. 231). Labels we use to describe ourselves, such as homosexual, heterosexual, and bisexual, are produced or determined by specific contexts and cultures. According to Richardson (2003), the meaning individuals give to their sexual fantasies, desires, and behaviors can change over time through the aging process, situational experiences, and wider social changes. For example, sometimes they reconstruct their pasts in accordance with their current sense of who they are. A woman who has been in a heterosexual marriage for 30 years and who enters a same-sex sexual relationship may conceive of her present self as her "real" self and look on her past as a byproduct of the suppression of her lesbianism. Basically, the social constructionist perspective proposes that our sense of ourselves changes over time and that the names or labels we use to describe ourselves may change as well. Ultimately, of course, the labels themselves do not really fully describe what they purport to name.

It is perhaps tempting to oversimplify the meaning of social constructionism in reference to sexual orientation. However, Rust (2000) warns against the assumption that social constructionism means that we choose our sexual orientation. According to Rust (2000), we do not choose our sexuality any more than we chose the particular family we were born into:

> Social constructionism focuses not on the ways in which a person is socialized into, or chooses a particular sexuality but on the cultural factors that create a concept of that form of sexuality that individuals can use to describe themselves and this experience and on the ways those individuals use social constructs to create themselves. (p. 47)

Interestingly, current research is supportive of the social constructionist perspectives of sexuality, particularly with regard to women. Social psychologist Baumeister's (2000) systematic review of an extensive body of literature concluded that women's sexuality is more malleable or fluid than that of men and more susceptible to the influence of social and situational influences. As absurd as this sounds, there is a body of research (the National Health and Social Life Survey by Laumann, Gagnon, Michael, and Michaels, the results of which were published in 1994) that claims the simple act of graduating from college doubles the likelihood that men self-identify as gay or bisexual. And for women college graduates, there is a 90% increase in the likelihood that they identify as lesbian or bisexual. According to Baumeister, women were more apt to change their sexual patterns, including sexual preference. Women also evidenced less consistency between their sexual behaviors and attitudes, including interest in or desire for same-gender sex. Research on adolescent girls seems to suggest that girls' sexuality is also more fluid and situationally determined. One of the strongest determinants of same-sex sexual behavior for young women was the presence of an emotionally intense relationship with another female (Diamond & Savin-Williams, 2003).

The Implications of Social Constructionism for Social Policy, Research, and Therapy Practices

A postmodern world is said to be "a place in which so much is happening to so many so fast that no story or theory is sufficient to correspond fully to its subject matter" (Parry & Doan, 1994, p. 10). Even if counseling and social work practitioners are fortunate enough to be exposed to research about sexual and gender minorities in their graduate studies, most undoubtedly it has been written from an essentialist perspective. Treatment approaches for gender and sexual minorities have emanated from an essentialist perspective. And yet results prove that such a framework has not been sufficient to account for the diverse ways in which people define themselves. Most therapists in Western culture have been taught that a person's sex and sexuality are stable and major components of his or her identity (Richardson, 2003). In the past, a person who experienced gender dysphoria was often depicted as someone whose "true" inner sense of gender did not match his or her genitals. The typical narrative goes that people who experienced gender dysphoria were "trapped in the wrong bodies." Given this, it seems impossible to envision a future in terms of counselor training that doesn't question some of our most fundamental assumptions about sexual and gender identities.

In the words of Weinberg, Williams, and Pryor (1994), we are being challenged to adopt an "open gender schema" or an intellectual perspective that disconnects biological sex, gender identity, and sexual orientation. Imagining a world without gender is not just fodder for science fiction. Several authors have attempted this with rather intriguing results. For example, Califia, a transgender author and activist, asked readers in *Sex Changes: The Politics of Transgenderism* (1997) to imagine existence in a world where gender is not the first thing that one ascertains about others. Lorber (2005) asked her readers to fantasize about the possibility of inhabiting a "degendered world" where the genitalia of newborns are irrelevant to parents' choices of names, clothing, and playthings and where "child announcements read "A child is born to . . .'" (p. 167).

Largely because of the influence of feminism, multiculturism, and queer theories, helping professionals are being challenged to think more critically about the nature and use of power in our culture and how the absence of power relates to mental health issues. In other words, they are now being challenged to ask more probing questions about the impact of being underprivileged because of sex, race, ethnicity, gender identity, religion, economic standing, and the like on mental status—and to ask whether or not a particular therapy practice or strategy replicates the belief that people who do conform to sex, gender, and sexual orientation standards and norms are personally defective.

Politics and Policies

The assumption that sexual orientation is biologically determined, or at least fixed at a very early age, has been adopted by many who advocate for gay, lesbian, bisexual, and transgender rights. If sexual orientation and gender identity are fixed and not freely chosen, then how could sexual and gender minorities be considered morally reprehensible? Many sexual and gender minorities fear that from a political perspective, they will lose valuable ground they have gained in the area of civil rights by arguing that sexual orientation is a choice. Feminists, for example, assume that women can differ by sexual orientation, ethnicity, class, age, and so on but that there are still commonalities based on gender that unite them (Alsop, Fitzsimons, & Lennon, 2002). Alsop et al. (2002) ask, "How do we challenge the structural and material inequalities that many women face if we do not operate on some basis at least with the category 'women,' even if while utilizing the term we remain cognizant of its factious and unstable foundations?" (p. 232). Indeed, a number of gay and lesbian activists voice concern about adopting such a stance:

> If one of the goals of a postmodern politics is to provide social spaces for
> greater individual democracy and freedom, then to assume a uniform fluidity

is equally as narrow and restrictive as enforcing a uniform essentialism. To assume that all women want their sexuality to be fluid and elusive is unwarranted. For some identities provide an anchor and stability that is welcomed, as well as a potential basis for political mobilization. (Esterberg, 1997, p. 171)

Postmodern and social constructionist perspectives emphasize the power of social interaction in generating meaning (Gergen, 1985). In the past, helping professionals have been criticized for their failure to account for the daily realities of those who seem to transgress culturally cherished assumptions about sex, gender, and sexual orientation. With that said, most of us inhabit a heterosexist culture where all of our social institutions—families, schools, churches, and temples—teach us that homosexuality is "abnormal" and "wrong." According to heterosexual respondents in the American National Election Studies in 1996, gay men and lesbians are rated the lowest of all groups on a 101-point feeling thermometer (Yang, 1997). In our Western culture, those who refuse to do what it takes to fit into the traditional gender binary are marginalized and punished through verbal and physical harassment, hate crimes, housing and employment discrimination, lack of access to health care, and so on. The plight of those who challenge rules of gender expression was graphically and painfully illustrated in the popular film *Boys Don't Cry* (Peirce, 1999). The film depicted the experiences of Brandon Teena, a biological female, who lived as a male and was brutally raped and murdered after two male acquaintances discovered her biological sex was female.

A major paradigm shift in the counseling profession calls for practitioners to move beyond the goal of transforming the lives of sexual and gender minorities. Instead, the goal must be to help transform the cultural context in which we all live (Lee & Walz, 1998; Speight & Vera, 2004). According to Lorber (2005), "It is up to those who practice gender within the basic institutions of a society to start the process of degendering by challenging the binary gender system in work organizations, families, schools, religions, cultural institutions, and politics" (p. 13). Thus, an important role for helping professionals who work with sexual and gender minorities is one of advocacy and social action. Traditionally, most helping professionals have defined themselves as advocates for their individual clients. Now they will need to make a commitment to social justice at the global level and, as a result, will need to learn new skills and competencies. This text will outline in greater depth the kinds of skills and competencies necessary to advocate for sexual and gender minorities.

Research

The result of postmodern and social constructionist models has been a radical change in the research process itself. For many years, the experimental sciences was considered the only legitimate research method in the social sciences. Postmodern and social constructionist perspectives have generated radical changes in the ways the research process is currently being conceptualized. The process is no longer conceived of as a neutral one. Researchers now attend to the ways in which traditional methods tended to marginalize different groups by making them the passive object of inquiry (Marshall & Rossman, 2006). In particular, qualitative methods such as action research, narrative, and discourse analyses are being favored because they permit researchers to explore the meaning of experiences, particularly for those who are marginalized. For example, discourse analysis focuses on how people use language (organized into discourses) to construct their social worlds (Coyle, 2000). Language, according to those who use the discourse analytic methodology, is not a "neutral transmitter for relaying dispassionate descriptions of something that has occurred or was experienced" (Drew, Dobson, & Stam, 1999, p. 193).

The postmodern and social constructionist models have brought about changes not only in research processes but also in the nature of the topics that are studied. For many years, psychological and biological researchers have been preoccupied with explaining how people become gay. This focus on causation of homosexuality implied that heterosexuality is natural and, therefore, requires no explanation. Research attention has shifted from a psychopathological perspective on homosexuality to studies that explore strengths and resiliency inherent in sexual and gender minorities (Lee & Crawford, 2007).

Therapy Practices

Our disciplines—psychology, counseling, and social work—have taken the notion that the biological categories of male and female are natural and "normal" and made it the basis of scientific fact. Research has shown that gay, lesbian, and bisexual (GLB) persons experience similar forms of discrimination from mental health professionals as they do from the general population (Garnets, Hancock, Cochran, Goodchilds, & Peplau, 1991; Mohr, Israel, & Sedlacek, 2001). Obviously, this lack of sensitivity on the part of clinicians must have potentially devastating effects on GLB clients. Despite the large numbers of clinicians who work with sexual minority clients (Haldeman, 2002; Murphy, Rawlings, & Howe, 2002), only a small percentage report having had any graduate training in GLB issues (Pilkington & Cantor, 1996). More distressing still is the extent to which gender minority issues are ignored in research and graduate training (Cole, Denny, Eyler, & Samons, 2000; Gainor, 2000).

In working with sexual and gender minorities, helping professionals in training face a world of confusing possibilities. A helping professional likely encounters clients who are comfortable with labels (gay, lesbian, bisexual, transgender) and clients who are not as well as those who believe their sexual orientation is a central aspect of who they are and those who believe their race or ethnicity figures much larger in their identities. Richardson (2003) addressed the social pressure people feel to label themselves; she points out that practitioners can sometimes get caught up in this. The implication of social constructionism for therapy is that neither therapist nor client is "right"; therefore, this relationship must be conceived of as a collaborative one. This means that helping professionals may have to be more critical and reflective in their use of labels. In other words, there are persons for whom gender and sexual orientation feel fixed and inherent. Such persons describe themselves differently (e.g., "I've always felt myself to be gay") than others whose sense of themselves is more fluid. Consider Bohan's (1996) wise words of advice:

> The task of the therapist here is not to help clients arrive at a firm and fixed identity, but to support an awareness of their own flexibility and to affirm that as a healthy identity in its own right. The therapeutic task is complicated by the intersection between what might (or might not) be genuine and healthy fluidity and the individual's need to construct a personal understanding that matches cultural understandings (even if those diminish the potential richness of her or his identity). (p. 230)

According to Broido (2000), helping professionals must also be prepared to help clients cope with the consequences of not fitting into socially constructed categories as well as the important loss of support systems when they experience shifts in sexual orientation.

Social constructionism became an important catalyst for the development of narrative therapy in the 1980s by Michael White and David Epston. Impacted by the ideas of Foucault and of feminists and cultural anthropologists, this approach considers the ways that societal oppressive negativity impacts human beings and often drives them to therapy. It also questions the assumptions in therapy that may inadvertently be reproducing oppression in the larger society. In addition, narrative therapy critiques the role of the therapist as expert and encourages therapists to engage in "radical listening" (Weingarten, 1998) and to adopt a questioning style (White, 1995).

Constructionist and narrative therapy approaches (Laird, 1999) may be particularly helpful when working with sexual and gender minorities. As a later chapter explains, these approaches do not assume that problems are "in people" or "in their relationships" as much as they are embedded in a particular point of view about others and their situations (Nichols & Schwartz, 2005). These approaches enable clients to tell their own stories, unburdened by assumptions of what the therapist may think and feel about gender and sexuality. Basically, clinicians create an atmosphere in which the larger cultural narratives concerning heterosexism and gender are deconstructed. As Laird (2000) argues, the most important requirement for a counselor is a willingness to challenge traditional assumptions about gender and sexuality and to consider the ways in which these have supported or constricted the lives of their sexual and gender minority clients.

Summary

Despite the large numbers of clinicians who work with sexual minority clients (Murphy et al., 2002), only a small percentage report having had any graduate training in GLB issues. And helping professionals will likely encounter at least one transgendered client at some point in their professional careers (Ettner, 1999) and won't have sufficient knowledge or skills. What's more, many therapists may operate out of a homophobic/biphobic/transphobic frame of reference (Carroll, Gilroy, & Ryan, 2002).

Recently, with the advent of postmodern theory, many have challenged the essentialist view of sexual orientation as biologically determined and immutable. Current theories about sex, gender, and sexual orientation are shifting away from dichotomous views of these phenomenon to continuum models that advance multiple views of identities. An alternative theory, social constructionism, posits that persons actively construct their identities and that these constructions are determined by historical and social contexts. Research indicates that a substantial number of people live with the fact their sexual identity and sexual behavior do not match (Davies & Neal, 1996; Fitzpatrick, McLean, Boulton, Hart, & Dawson, 1990), and further, many persons may change their sexual identity over the course of a lifetime (Diamond & Savin-Williams, 2003; Whisman, 1996; Wilton, 2000). The proliferation of postmodern, constructionist, and queer theories has important implications for social policy, research, and therapy practices. Just as social activists argued against the view in psychiatry of homosexuality as a sickness, activists now demand that mental health treatment center on assisting gender dysphoric persons not in their adjustment to their new gender but rather in their acknowledgment of a unique transgender identity (Bockting, 1997). The use of therapeutic theories/techniques, such as feminist, constructionist, and narrative therapies, is particularly suitable with sexual and gender minorities because these enable clients to tell their own stories (Laird, 1999).

Personal Reflection

Jan Clausen is the author of several books. She is a highly successful writer and was a lesbian feminist activist. In 1987, after a 12-year relationship with a woman, she fell in love with a man. Following this disclosure, she received harsh criticism from her friends and fellow activists in the lesbian feminist community. In 1990, Clausen published an essay entitled "My Interesting Condition," in which she states that she refuses to identify herself as bisexual. Her personal experiences are chronicled in her autobiography, *Apples and Oranges*, written in 1999. The following is an excerpt from a previous article:

It's a shock to find myself once again facing problems I dimly recall from my heterosexual youth, built-in inequities I thought I'd cleverly sidestepped by choosing my own kind. Suddenly, out of two people in bed, I'm the one elected to run the risk of unwanted pregnancy. Out of a pair drawn together by delicious mutual lust, I'm the one who, by physiological laws, will occasionally be left dangling at the moment of someone else's climax.

The emotional disparities are equally unsettling. To judge from my recent experience, that old saying about men not sharing feelings has a lot of truth to it. Or rather, their assumptions about when and how and how much to share are so wildly divergent from women's that the two sexes might have been socialized on different planets. At times this comes as a clear relief to me, after years of analyzing to death every slightest stirring of affect. I am learning other ways to be close but at times it just feels lonely.

I know that I love my lover as a man; to claim that I love him as a "person" would be a transparent evasion, and to say that I'd like him to be who he is only female would be both

nonsensical and a lie. Yet at times when we make love, I feel so close to his pleasure that I have the illusion of experiencing his feeling, and when that happens I say to myself that it's as though I were making love with a woman, and I am very happy. I want my separation and my fusion too.

I miss my ex-lover's body, but that missing is inseparable from all my missing of her. I no longer feel, as I did in my early 20s when I lived with a man following a first brief lesbian affair, that it would be terrible to die without touching a woman again. Sometimes I wonder where that urgency went. For the time being, I take casual erotic interest in members of my sex. I notice myself noticing fems much more, after years of liking butches, and wonder whether indulging my own femminess to the hilt has freed some latent butch impulse. I wonder also about the astonishing malleability of my sexual inclinations: am I some sort of weirdo, or is it just that most people are a lot more complicated than the common wisdom of either gay or straight society encourages us to think? (Source: From "My Interesting Condition" by Jan Clausen (1990). *Journal of Sex Research*, 27, 445–459. Reprinted with permission.)

Self-Reflection Questions

After reading this passage from Clausen's essay, what are your thoughts?
1. Do you agree with Clausen's suggestion that sexual orientation is more malleable than most people think?
2. Clausen seems to be talking about her gender identity when she refers to the "butch" and "fem." What do you think about her analysis? How does this relate to the way that you see yourself in terms of your own gender identity?

3. Clausen indicates that she experiences difficulty fitting into either the lesbian or the heterosexual world. What do you think she might mean by this?

4. As a counselor, how might you respond to her sense of isolation?

Library, Media, and Internet Activities

In the foreign film section of your local video/DVD store, you will find Ma vie en rose *(Berliner, 1997). This poignant and charming film is about a little boy named Ludovic who moves with his parents and three older siblings to the suburbs. It seems that Ludovic is not like other little boys his age. He longs to be a girl, like Pam, a popular television character. Ludovic causes a great deal of commotion when he attends the family's backyard housewarming picnic in a pink dress and red pumps, with make-up and earrings and flowers in his long bobbed hair.*

Discussion Questions

1. What are your impressions of the way that Ludovic's father and mother react to his belief that God gave him the wrong chromosomes?
2. If Ludovic's parents came to see you regarding their son's refusal to be a boy, how might you respond?
3. Reflecting on the material presented in this chapter, do you see Ludovic's story as supportive of an essentialist or a social constructionist theory?
4. What were your reactions to the ending of the film?

References

Alsop, R., Fitzsimons, A., & Lennon, K. (2002). *Theorizing gender.* Malden, MA: Blackwell Publishers.

American Psychiatric Association. (2000). *Diagnostic and statistical manual of mental disorders—Text revision* (4th ed.). Washington, DC: Author.

Baca Zinn, M., Hondagneu-Sotelo, P., & Messner, M. A. (2005). *Gender through the prism of difference* (3rd ed.). New York: Oxford University Press.

Bailey, J. M., & Pillard, R. C. (1991). A genetic study of male sexual orientation. *Archives of General Psychiatry, 48(12),* 1089–1096.

Baumeister, R. F. (2000). Gender differences in erotic plasticity: The female sex drive as socially flexible and responsive. *Psychological Bulletin, 126(3),* 347–374.

Bem, S. L. (1974). The measurement of psychological androgyny. *Journal of Consulting & Clinical Psychology, 42(2),* 155–162.

Bem, S. L. (1993). *The lenses of gender: Transforming the debate on sexual inequality.* New Haven, CT: Yale University Press.

Benjamin, H. (1967). The transsexual phenomenon. *Transactions of the New York Academy of Sciences, 29(4),* 428–430.

Berliner, A. (Director). (1997). *Ma vie en rose* [Motion picture]. France: Sony Classics.

Bockting, W. O. (1997). Transgender coming out: Implications for the clinical management of gender dysphoria. In B. Bullough, V. L. Bullough, & J. Elias (Eds.), *Gender blending* (pp. 48–52). Amherst, NY: Prometheus Books.

Bohan, J. S. (1996). *Psychology and sexual orientation: Coming to terms.* New York: Routledge.

Bornstein, K. (1995). *Gender outlaw: On men, women and the rest of us.* New York: Vintage Books.

Bowers, A. M. V., & Bieschke, K. J. (2005). Psychologists' clinical evaluations and attitudes: An examination of the influence of gender and sexual orientation. *Professional Psychology: Research & Practice, 36(1),* 97–103.

Broido, E. M. (2000). Constructing identity: The nature and meaning of lesbian, gay, and bisexual identities. In R. M. Perez, K. A. DeBord, & K. J. Bieschke (Eds.), *Handbook of counseling and psychotherapy with lesbian, gay, and bisexual clients* (pp. 13–33). Washington, DC: American Psychological Association.

Brown, L. B. (1998). *Two-spirit people: American Indian lesbian women and gay men*. New York: Haworth Press.

Brown, L. S. (1989). New voices, new visions: Toward a lesbian/gay paradigm for psychology. *Psychology of Women Quarterly. Special Issue: Theory and Method in Feminist Psychology, 13,* 445–458.

Brownmiller, S. (1975). *Against our will: Men, women, and rape.* New York: Simon & Schuster.

Bryant, K. (1996). Making gender identity disorder of childhood: Historical lessons for contemporary debates. *Sexuality Research & Social Policy: Journal of NSRC, 3(3),* 23–39.

Burke, P. (1996). *Gender shock: Exploding the myths of male and female.* New York: Anchor Books/Doubleday.

Butler, J. (1990). *Gender trouble: Feminism and the subversion of identity.* London: Routledge.

Califia, P. (1997). *Sex changes: The politics of transgenderism.* San Francisco: Cleis.

Carroll, L., Gilroy, P., & Ryan, J. (2002). Counseling transgendered, transsexual, and gender-variant clients. *Journal of Counseling & Development, 80(2),* 131–139.

Cass, V. C. (1979). Homosexual identity formation: A theoretical model. *Journal of Homosexuality, 4(3),* 219–236.

Cass, V. C. (1984). Homosexual identity formation: Testing a theoretical model. *Journal of Sex Research, 20(2),* 143–167.

Clausen, J. (1990). My interesting condition. *Journal of Sex Research, 27,* 445–459.

Clausen, J. (1999). *Apples and oranges: My journey through sexual identity.* New York: Houghton Mifflin.

Colapinto, J. (1997, December). The true story of John/Joan. *Rolling Stone, 54–97,* 92–97.

Cole, S. S., Denny, D., Eyler, A. E., & Samons, S. L. (2000). Issues of transgender. In T. Szuchman & F. Muscarella (Eds.), *Psychological perspectives in human sexuality* (pp. 149–195). New York: Wiley.

Coleman, E. (1982). Developmental Stages of the Coming Out Process. *Journal of homosexuality, 7(2/3),* 31.

Collins, J. F. (2004). The intersection of race and bisexuality: A critical overview of the literature and past, present, and future directions of the "borderlands." *Journal of Bisexuality, 4(1/2),* 99–116.

Davies, D., & Neal, C. (1996). *Pink therapy: A guide for counselors and therapists working with lesbian, gay, and bisexual clients.* Bristol, PA: Open University Press.

Denny, D. (2007). Transgender identities and bisexual expression: Implications for counselors. In B. A. Firestein (Ed.), *Becoming visible: Counseling bisexuals across the lifespan* (pp. 268–284). New York: Columbia University Press.

Diamond, L., & Savin-Williams, R. (2003). Explaining diversity in the development of same-sex sexuality among young women. In L. D. Garnets & D. C. Kimmel (Eds.), *Psychological perspectives on lesbian, gay, and bisexual experiences* (2nd ed., pp. 130–148). New York: Columbia University Press.

Dreger, A. E. (1998). A history of intersexuality: From the age of gonads to the age of consent. *Journal of Clinical Ethics, 9,* 345–355.

Drew, M. L., Dobson, K. S., & Stam, H. J. (1999). The negative self-concept in clinical depression: A discourse analysis. *Canadian Psychology. Special Issue: Women and Depression: Qualitative research approaches, 40(2),* 192–204.

Dworkin, S. H. (2001). Treating the bisexual client. *Journal of Clinical Psychology. Special Issue: Working with gay, lesbian, and bisexual clients, 57(5),* 671–680.

Elkins, R., & King, D. (Eds.). (2002). *Blending genders: Social aspects of cross-dressing and sex changing.* New York: Routledge.

Esterberg, K. G. (1997). *Lesbian and bisexual identities: constructing communities, constructing selves.* Philadelphia: Temple University Press.

Ettner, R. (1999). *Gender loving care: A guide to counseling gender-variant clients.* New York: Norton.

Fagan, P. J., Schmidt, C. W., & Wise, T. N. (1994, August 22 & 29). Born to the wrong sex. *The New Yorker,* 15.

Fausto-Sterling, A. (2000). *Sexing the body: Gender politics and the construction of sexuality.* New York: Basic Books.

Feinberg, L. (1998). *Trans liberation: Beyond pink or blue.* Boston: Beacon Press.

Fitzpatrick, R., McLean, J., Boulton, M., Hart, G., & Dawson, J. (1990). Variation in sexual behavior in gay men. In P. Aggleton, P. Davies, & G. Haret (Eds.), *AIDS: Individual, cultural and policy dimensions* (pp. 121–132). London: Falmer Press.

Foucault, M. (1978). *The history of sexuality: An introduction* (Trans). New York: Random House. (Original work published 1976).

Gagne, P., Tewksbury, R., & McGaughey, D. (1997). Coming out and crossing over: Identity formation and proclamation in a transgender community. *Gender & Society, 11(4)*, 478–508.

Gainor, K. (2000). Including transgender issues in lesbian, gay, and bisexual psychology: Implications for clinical practice and training. In B. Greene & G. L. Croom (Eds.), *Education, research, and practice in lesbian, gay, bisexual, and transgendered psychology: A resource manual* (pp. 131–160). Thousand Oaks, CA: Sage.

Garnets, L., Hancock, K. A., Cochran, S. D., Goodchilds, J., & Peplau, L. A. (1991). Issues in psychotherapy with lesbians and gay men: A survey of psychologists. *American Psychologist, 46(9)*, 964–974.

Garnets, L. D., & Kimmel, D. C. (2003). Part 1: The meaning of sexual orientation. In L. D. Garnets & D. C. Kimmel (Eds.), *Psychological perspectives on lesbian and gay experiences*, (2nd ed., pp. 23–29). New York: Columbia University Press.

Gergen, K. J. (1985). The social constructionist movement in modern psychology. *American Psychologist, 40*, 266–275.

Goffman, E. (1959). *The presentation of self in everyday life*. Garden City, NY: Doubleday.

Green, R., & Money, J. (Eds.). (1968). *Transexualism and Sex Reassignment*. Baltimore: Johns Hopkins Press.

Greene, B. (2000). Beyond heterosexism and across the cultural divide: Developing an inclusive lesbian, gay, and bisexual psychology: A look at the future. In B. Greene & G. L. Croom (Eds.), *Education, research, and practice in lesbian, gay, bisexual, and transgendered psychology: A resource manual* (pp. 244–262). Thousand Oaks, CA: Sage.

Haldeman, D. C. (2002). Therapeutic responses to sexual orientation: Psychology's evolution. In B. Greene & G. L. Croom (Eds.), *Education, research, and practice in lesbian, gay, bisexual, and transgendered psychology: A resource manual* (pp. 244–262). Thousand Oaks, CA: Sage.

Herek, G. M. (1989). Hate crimes against lesbians and gay men: Issues for research and policy. *American Psychologist, 44(6)*, 948–955.

Herdt, G. (1991). Commentary on status of sex research: Cross-cultural implications of sexual development. *Journal of Psychology and Human Sexuality, 4(1)*, 5–12.

Herdt, G. (2001). Social change, sexual diversity, and tolerance for bisexuality in the United States. In A. R. D'Augelli & C. J. Patterson (Eds.), *Lesbian, gay and bisexual identities and youth* (pp. 267–283). New York: Oxford University Press.

Hill, D. (2003). Genderism, transphobia, and gender bashing: A framework for interpreting anti-transgender violence. In B. C. Wallace & R.T. Carter (Eds.), *Understanding and dealing with violence: A multicultural approach* (pp. 113–136). Thousand Oaks, CA: Sage.

Hill, D. B., Rozanski, C., Carfagnini, J., & Willoughby, B. (2005). Gender identity disorders in childhood and adolescence: A critical inquiry. *Journal of Psychology & Human Sexuality, 17(3/4)*, 7–33.

Holloway, W. (1989). *Subjectivity and method in psychology: Gender, meaning, and science*. London: Sage.

Ingraham, C. (2006). Thinking straight, acting bent. In K. Davis, M. Evans, & J. Lorber (Eds.), *Handbook of gender and women's studies* (pp. 307–321). Thousand Oaks, CA: Sage.

Intersex Society of North America (2006). Clinical guidelines for the management of disorders of sex development in childhood. Consortium on the management of disorders of sex development. Retrieved October 10, 2007 from www.dsd guidelines.org

Jacobs, S. T., Thomas, W., & Lang, S. (1997). *Two-spirit people: Native American gender identity, sexuality, and spirituality*. Urbana: University of Illinois Press.

Kessler, S. (1998). *Lessons from the intersexed*. New Brunswick, NJ: Rutgers University Press.

Kessler, S. J., & McKenna, W. (1985). *Gender: An ethnomethodological approach*. Chicago: University of Chicago Press.

Kimmel, M. S., & Mahler, M. (2003). Adolescent masculinity, homophobia, and violence. *American Behavioral Scientist, 46*, 1439–1458.

Kinsey, A. C., Pomeroy, W. B., & Martin, C. E. (1948). *Sexual behavior in the human male*. Philadelphia: Saunders.

Konik, J., & Crawford, M. (2004). Exploring normative creativity: Testing the relationship between cognitive flexibility and sexual identity. *Sex Roles, 51(3/4)*, 249–253.

Kutchins, H., & Kirk, S. (1997). *Making us crazy: DSM: The psychiatric bible and the creation of mental disorders*. New York: Free Press.

Laird, J. (1999). Gender and sexuality in lesbian relationships: Feminist and constructionist perspectives. In J. Laird (Ed.), *Lesbians and lesbian families: Reflections of theory and practice* (pp. 47–89). New York: Columbia University Press.

Laird, J. (2000). Gender in lesbian relationships: Cultural, feminist, and constructionist reflections. *Journal of Marital & Family Therapy, 26*(4), 455–468.

LaMar, L., & Kite, M. (1998). Sex differences in attitudes toward gay men and lesbians: A multidimensional perspective. *Journal of Sex Research, 35*(2), 189–196.

Landolt, M. A., Bartholomew, K., Saffrey, C., Oram, D., & Perlman, D. (2004). Gender nonconformity, childhood rejection, and adult attachment: A study of gay men. *Archives of Sexual Behavior, 33*(2), 117–128.

Laumann, E. O., Gagnon, J. H., Michael, R. T., & Michaels, S. (1994). *The social organization of sexuality: Sexual practices in the United States.* Chicago: University of Chicago Press.

Lee, C. C., & Walz, G. R. (1998). *Social action: A mandate for counselors.* Arlington, VA: American Counseling Association.

Lee, I-C., & Crawford, M. (2007). Lesbians and bisexual women in the eyes of scientific psychology. *Feminism & Psychology, 17*(1), 109–127.

Lev, A. I. (2005). Disordering gender identity: Gender identity disorder in the DSM-IV-TR. *Journal of Psychology & Human Sexuality, 17*(3/4), 35–69.

Lev, A. I. (2007). Transgender communities: Developing identity through connection. In K. J. Bieschke, R. M. Perez, & K. A. DeBord (Eds.), *Handbook of counseling and psychotherapy with lesbian, gay, bisexual, and transgender clients* (pp. 147–175). Washington, DC: American Psychological Association.

LeVay, S. (1993). *The sexual brain.* Cambridge, MA: MIT Press.

Lorber, J. (1994). *Paradoxes of gender.* New Haven, CT: Yale University Press.

Lorber, J. (2005). *Breaking the bowls: Degendering and feminist change.* New York: Norton.

Lorde, A. (1984). Age, race, class, and sex: Women redefining the difference. In A. Lorde (Ed.), *Sister outsider: Essays and speeches* (pp. 114–123). Freedom, CA: Crossing Press.

Lucal, B. (1999). What it means to be gendered me: Life on the boundaries of a dichotomous gender system. *Gender & Society, 13*(6), 781–797.

MacDonald, A. P. (1981). Bisexuality: Some comment on research and theory. *Journal of Homosexuality, 6*(3), 21–35.

Madison, L. (2000). Inferences regarding the personality traits and sexual orientation of physically androgynous people. *Psychology of Women Quarterly, 24*(2), 148.

Marshall, C., & Rossman, G. B. (2006). *Designing qualitative research.* Thousand Oaks, CA: Sage.

McIntosh, M. (1968). The homosexual role. *Social Problems, 16*(2), 12–22.

Meyer, W., Bockting, W., Cohen-Kettenis, P., Coleman, E., DiCeglie, D., Devor, H., et al. (2001). The standards of care for gender identity disorders, sixth version [Electronic version]. *International Journal of Transgenderism, 5*, 1. Retrieved October 23, 2003 from www.symposion. com/ijt/soc_.05.htm

Mohr, J. J., Israel, T., & Sedlacek, W. E. (2001). Counselors' attitudes regarding bisexuality as predictors of counselors' clinical responses: An analogue study of a female bisexual client. *Journal of Counseling Psychology, 48*(2), 212–222.

Money, J. (1985). The conceptual neutering of gender and the criminalization of sex. *Archives of Sexual Behavior, 14*, 279–290.

Morgan, R. (1970). *Sisterhood is powerful: An anthology of writing from the women's liberation movement.* New York: Random House.

Morrow, S. L. (2000). First do no harm: Therapist issues in psychotherapy with lesbian, gay, and bisexual clients. In R. M. Perez, K. A. DeBord, & K. J. Bieschke (Eds.), *Handbook of counseling and psychotherapy with lesbian, gay, and bisexual clients* (pp. 137–156). Washington, DC: American Psychological Association.

Mulaikal, R. M., Migeon, C. J., & Rock, J. A. (1987). Fertility rates in female patients with congenital adrenal hyperplasia due to 21-hydroxlase deficiency. *New England Journal of Medicine, 316*(4), 178–182.

Murphy, J. A., Rawlings, E. I., & Howe, S. R. (2002). A survey of clinical psychologists on treating lesbian, gay, and bisexual clients. *Professional Psychology: Research & Practice, 33*, 183–189.

Nichols, M. P., & Schwartz, R. C. (2005). *The essentials of family therapy* (2nd ed.). Boston: Allyn & Bacon.

Parry, A., & Doan, R. E. (1994). *Story re-visions: Narrative therapy in the postmodern world.* New York: Guilford Press.

Peirce, K. (Director). (1999). *Boys don't cry* [Motion picture]. United States: Fox Searchlight Pictures.

Pilkington, N., & Cantor, J. (1996). Perceptions of heterosexual bias in professional psychology programs: A survey of graduate students. *Professional Psychology: Research & Practice, 27*(6), 604–612.

Raj, R. (2002). Towards a transpositive therapeutic model: Developing clinical sensitivity and cultural competence in the effective support of transsexual and transgendered clients [Electronic version]. *International Journal of Transgenderism, 6*, 1–59. Retrieved October 23, 2003 from http://www.symposion.com/ijt/ijtvo06no02_04.htm

Rekers, G. A. (1995). Assessment and treatment methods for gender identity disorders and transvestism. In G. A. Rekers (Ed.), *Handbook of child and adolescent sexual problems* (pp. 272–289). New York: Lexington Books.

Rekers, G., & Lovass, I. (1974). Behavioral treatment of deviant sex-role behaviors in a male child. *Journal of Applied Behavior Analysis, 7*, 173–190.

Rich, A. (1980). Compulsory heterosexuality and lesbian existence. *Signs, 5*, 631–660.

Richardson, D. (2003). Recent challenges to traditional assumptions about homosexuality: Some implications for practice. In L. D. Garnets & D. C. Kimmel (Eds.), *Psychological perspectives on lesbian, gay, and bisexual experiences* (pp. 117–129). New York: Columbia University Press.

Roscoe, W. (1998). *Changing ones: Third and fourth genders in native North America.* New York: St. Martin's Press.

RuPaul. (1995). *Lettin it all hang out: An autobiography.* New York: Hyperion.

Rust, P. C. Rodriguez (2000). Alternatives to binary sexuality: Modeling bisexuality. In P. C. R. Rust (Ed.), *Bisexuality in the United States: A social science reader* (pp. 33–54). New York: Columbia University Press.

Scholinski, D. (1997). *The last time I wore a dress.* New York: Riverhead Books.

Skidmore, W. C., Linsenmeier, J. A. W., & Bailey, J. M. (2006). Gender nonconformity and psychological distress in lesbians and gay men. *Archives of Sexual Behavior, 35(6)*, 685–697.

Speight, S. L., & Vera, E. M. (2004). A social justice agenda: Ready, or not? *Counseling Psychologist. Special Issue: The Fourth National Counseling Psychology Conference: Houston 2001, 32(1)*, 109–118.

Stone, S. (1991). The empire strikes back: A posttranssexual manifesto. In J. Epstein & K. Straus (Eds.), *Body guards: The cultural politics of gender ambiguity* (pp. 280–304). New York: Routledge.

Tarver, D. E. (2002). Transgender mental health: The intersection of race, sexual orientation, and gender identity. In B. E. Jones & M. J. Hill (Eds.), *Mental health issues in lesbian, gay, bisexual, and transgender communities* (pp. 93–108). Washington, DC: American Psychiatric Association.

Troiden, R. R. (1979). Becoming homosexual: A model of gay identity acquisition. *Psychiatry: Journal for the Study of Interpersonal Process, 42(4)*, 362–373.

Troiden, R. R. (1988). *Gay and lesbian identity: A sociological analysis.* Dix Hills, NY: General Hall.

Unger, R. (1979). Toward a redefinition of sex and gender. *American Psychologist, 34*, 1085–1094.

Weinberg, M. S., Williams, C. J., & Pryor, D. W. (1994). *Dual attraction: Understanding bisexuality.* New York: Oxford University Press.

Weingarten, K. (1998, Spring). The small and the ordinary: The daily practice of the postmodern narrative therapy. *Family Process, 37(1)*, 3–15.

Whisman, V. (1996). *Queer by choice: Lesbians, gay men and the politics of identity.* London: Routledge.

White, M. (1995). *Re-authoring lives: Interviews and essays.* Adelaide: Dulwich Centre Publications.

Wilchins, R. (2004). *Queer theory, gender theory: An instant primer.* Los Angeles: Alyson Press.

Wilton, T. (2000). *Sexualities in health and social care: A textbook.* Philadelphia: Open University Press.

Witten, T., & Eyler, E. (1999). Hate crimes and violence against the transgendered. *Peace Review, 11(3)*, 461–468.

Yang, A. (1997). The polls—trends: Attitudes toward homosexuality. *Public Opinion Quarterly, 61(3)*, 477–507.

Zucker, K. J. (2001). Biological influences on psychosexual differentiation. In R. Unger (Ed.), *Handbook of the psychology of women and gender* (pp. 101–115). New York: Wiley.

Zucker, K. J., & Bradley, S. J. (1995). *Gender identity disorder and psychosexual problems in children and adolescents.* Hoboken, NJ: Guilford Press.

CHAPTER 2

Policies, Practices, and Controversies in the Treatment of Sexual and Gender Minorities

INTRODUCTION

The excerpts below contain first-hand accounts of two men who sought treatment in order to change their sexual orientation. Both men experienced different outcomes. In the first, Jeffrey Ford describes his experience undergoing a form of behavioral therapy called aversion therapy.

I got married at the age of 20 to try to be "normal," with great hopes of becoming straight. I withheld the truth about my sexual orientation from my wife for the first year and a half of our marriage. I gave up a good-paying job, and my wife and I moved to Minnesota where I began seeing a psychologist who believed that by using electric shock he could cure me of my homosexuality. I decided to tell my wife about it since it was for both of us. I went through 40 or more sessions twice a week during which the psychologist strapped electrodes to my arms and hooked me up to a "penile plythysmograph" (an instrument that, when attached to the penis, can measure blood engorgement).

I can still remember the horror I felt every time I sat in the chair. I can still feel the shame and embarrassment of having wires hooked to my arm and penis while looking at pictures of naked men. Intermittently, the psychologist would give an electric shock that would involuntarily catapult my arm several inches into the air. When leaving his office, I always felt embarrassed and tried to hide the two red burn marks the electrodes left on my arm. My wife and I both hoped and prayed for my "healing." After the completion of the sessions, I found myself several hundred dollars poorer and still gay. (Ford, 2000, p. 8)

After undergoing therapy, Jeffrey Ford eventually divorced his wife and now lives as an openly gay man. He is currently a licensed psychologist.

Ben Newman's experiences in treatment are quite different.

My first order of business on my first visit with Matt was for me to sign the "Consent to Treat" form. It is required by the clinic, as a result of the American Psychological Association's resolutions that discourage this type of treatment. Reparative therapy was unproven, the form said; the APA's official stance was that it didn't believe it was possible to change sexual orientation; attempting to do so might even cause psychological harm.

Yeah, right, I thought, as if the double life I was living was not causing psychological harm enough.

Too, I resented the suggestion that the only "correct solution" (politically correct, anyway) for me was to abandon my wife and children and throw myself into the gay life. That was not what I wanted. I had had the chance to do that before I met Diane and had children with her, when the stakes were much lower—and I realized then that that wasn't what I wanted. While dating men, adopting a gay identity and throwing myself into the gay lifestyle had been exhilarating at first, it had soon felt like it was killing my spirit, alienating myself from my goals in life, from God and a sense of high purpose. I had realized then that I didn't want to be affirmed as gay; I wanted to be affirmed as a man. (Newman, 2004)

Newman is still married to Diane and refers to himself as an "ex-gay," a label used to denote persons who experience same-sex sexual attractions and make efforts to change these largely due to religious reasons.

A Preview of Chapter Contents

The treatment approaches described by Ford and Newman are called reparative or conversion therapies and are part of an increasingly visible controversy (Luo, 2007). This chapter explores the controversy and the arguments that have been proposed to support and negate the use of such therapies. It reviews the research methods and outcomes on the efficacy of such practices, and in addition, it looks at the helping professions from three distinct vantage points:

- It explores the medical and behavioral interventions employed by physicians, psychiatrists, and other mental health professionals to "cure" homosexuality from the early 1800s to the present

- It discusses current laws regarding the treatment of sexual minorities as well as the practices and profession guidelines followed by members of the American Psychological Association (APA), American Counseling Association (ACA), National Association of Social Work (NASW), American Mental Health Counselors Association (AMHCA), and American Association for Marriage and Family Therapy (AAMFT)
- It explores the current medical and psychiatric protocols for use with persons who are gender variant and wish to change or modify their gender presentation and the controversies that surround such practices

A BRIEF HISTORY OF THE TREATMENT OF SEXUAL MINORITIES

The previous chapter explored current meanings and distinctions among the concepts of *sex*, *gender*, and *sexual orientation*. Historically, medical and psychiatric treatments of sexual and gender minorities made no such distinctions; gender minorities were considered to be gay or lesbian. Physicians who provided treatment to sexual and gender minority patients assumed that sexual orientation and gender were interrelated, biologically determined, and unchangeable. Prior to the 1800s, same-sex sexual behaviors and gender-nonconforming behaviors were considered morally reprehensible and worthy of punishment in Western culture. For example, in the period before the American Revolution gay men were put to death, and later such men were given lengthy prison sentences for engaging in same-sex sexual activities (Katz, 1976).

The promulgation of scientific views of homosexuality and transgenderism was attributed to several key historical figures, including Karl Heinrich Ulrichs, Richard von Krafft-Ebing, Magnus Hirschfeld, and Havelock Ellis. Each of these men was instrumental in generating the dramatic paradigm shift from interpreting transgenderism and homosexuality as moral perversities to viewing them as medical/psychiatric "conditions" worthy of treatment. These early sexologists were considered essentialists because they viewed homosexuality and transgenderism as biologically determined phenomena.

Prior to the 1800s, the term *homosexual* was nonexistent. In pioneering efforts to try to understand or explain sexual and gender identity issues, Karl Heinrich Ulrichs introduced the labels *uring* to describe men who had sex with men and *urningin* for women who had sex with women, based on references in Plato's *Symposium*. The term *homosexual* was introduced later by Karl Maria Kerbeny, who campaigned for the abolition of Prussia's laws that criminalized sexual relations between men (Miller, 1995). Ulrichs perceived homosexuality as the result of the abnormal development of the fetus. In the case of the male *uring*, the body of the fetus developed as male and the mind developed as female. In a similar fashion, female *urningins* were born with the sex of the female body and the mind of a male. Ulrichs perceived *urings* and *urningins* as neither totally male nor totally female but rather as a third sex.

Another influential figure at this time was Richard von Krafft-Ebing, a neurologist and professor of psychiatry, whose 1893 text *Psychopathia Sexualis* included categorizations of sexual deviance. He categorized people who were attracted to persons of their own sex and persons who experienced gender dysphoria under the broad umbrella of "homo-sexual." He posited four levels of homosexuality, the third and fourth levels of which were characterized by the experience of bodily sensations of the opposite sex and the full-blown belief they had become the opposite sex. He cited specific cases in which such persons dressed in opposite-sex clothing.

Magnus Hirschfeld, a physician and advocate for homosexual rights during the 1920s and 1930s, viewed sexual orientation as determined in utero. He believed there were neural centers in the brain that determined sexual attraction. In the case of male same-sex sexual attraction, the center of attraction to women regressed, while the center of attraction to males developed. Hirschfeld also viewed gay men and lesbians as a third sex or a mosaic of male and female elements. Later in his career, Hirschfeld noted that homosexual persons sometimes possessed physical characteristics of the opposite sex and speculated that some "inverts" were hermaphroditic in terms of their reproductive physiology. Hirschfeld believed the urine of gay men contained menstrual blood and the vaginal secretions of lesbians contained spermatozoa (LeVay, 1996). Hirschfeld is credited with coining the term *transvestite* to describe cases in which men dressed as women and vice versa.

Havelock Ellis, a famous sexologist during the early 1900s, departed slightly from previous accounts of homosexuality. In his 1897 text *Sexual Inversion*, Ellis presented 33 case studies, many of which involved personal acquaintances, including his wife. Unlike his predecessors, Ellis noted that male inverts did not necessarily act like women. He also more narrowly defined male homosexuality in terms of the choice of romantic objects. It is important to note, however, that Ellis held a more traditional view of lesbians (Miller, 1995). He observed that female inverts were discernable by their "brusque, energetic movements, the attitude of the arms, the direct speech, and the inflections of the voice, the masculine straight-forwardness and sense of humor" (Ellis, 1940, p. 250). While Ellis thought of most homosexuals as having anatomically nonambiguous genitals, he used the term *psycho-sexual hermaphrodite* to describe what we now refer to as a bisexual person.

Early Medical Cures for Homosexuality

During the 1800s, physicians and psychiatrists employed an amazing array of behavioral, chemical, and surgical techniques to "cure" those who experienced same-sex sexual desire (Murphy, 1992). Most of these early cures were applied to male patients. In her historical analysis *How Sex Changed* (1992), Meyerowitz noted that the medical treatments for homosexuality, such as electroshock treatment and aversive conditioning, were sometimes imposed on patients without proper consent. In the United States, one of the earliest recorded treatments to remedy homosexuality was physical exercise. In 1892, Dr. Graeme Hammond prescribed excessive bicycle riding in response to a 24-year-old man's fear of "committing acts which were naturally abhorrent to him"; other alternative cures that were prescribed at that time were rest and relaxation, visits to prostitutes, and forced marriages (Murphy, 1992).

One of the earliest attempts to convert homosexuals through the use of chemical substances occurred in 1899, when Dr. Denslow Lewis injected female patients who were attracted to women with cocaine-solution bromides and strychnine. Injections of testosterone (Sansweet, 1975) were also used, as were chemicals like Metrazol, to induce grand mal convulsions (Murphy, 1992). In one notorious case reported in the British publication *Medico Legal Journal* (cited in Sansweet, 1975), a male homosexual referred to as W.T. was given apomorphine (a morphine derivative), emetine (a main ingredient of ipecacuanha, used to treat amoebic dysentery), and tincture of ipecacuanha in order to produce nausea. W.T. subsequently died as a result of emetine poisoning.

Louis W. Max, a physician, employed aversive behavioral techniques in the mid-1930s (Sansweet, 1975). Max claimed his use of high-intensity electric shock to treat a homosexual male patient was a success. Olfactory aversive techniques were also utilized, including the administration of potent diuretics prior to the introduction of ammonium sulfide, butyric acid, and ammonia while patients simultaneously fantasized about a homosexual encounter. The combined smells of rotten eggs, "dirty underwear," and ammonia were followed by a reward of a cold drink, provided the "patient's penis responds to female slides" (Sansweet, 1975, p. 78).

The use of aversive behavioral techniques in the treatment of homosexuality continued for several years beyond the 1973 declassification of homosexuality as a psychiatric disorder by the American Psychiatric Association. Shidlo and Schroeder (2001) interviewed gay men who had received treatments as late as 1992 that combined electric shocks to fingers and genitalia, a bowl of feces, and photographs of Kaposi's Sarcoma lesions on gay men living with AIDS.

The Talking Cures

Starting with Sigmund Freud, psychoanalytically trained psychiatrists emphasized environmental causations rather than biological explanations of homosexuality and advocated "talking cures" as opposed to medical intervention. Freud (1905) posited that homosexuality represented some form of arrested development. As to the reasons that such a fixation occurred, Freud offered differing interpretations, including a family dynamic in which the mother is seductive and the father is weak. Interestingly, later in his career Freud expressed pessimism regarding a cure for homosexuality. After his death, psychiatrists like Rado (1940) and Bieber et al. (1962) offered alternative, psychoanalytically oriented theories of causation and treatment.

The Dawn of a New Era in the Treatment of Homosexuality

Efforts to change sexual orientation became less popular as the data from several studies were made public. First, in 1948, Alfred Kinsey and his colleagues' research suggested sexuality was more fluid than previously thought. For example, some participants in his research indicated that while in heterosexual relationships, they had experienced sexual attraction for same-sex persons. Hooker's work in 1957 was also highly influential in terms of suggesting that homosexuals were not psychologically disturbed. She administered the Rorschach inkblots to 30 gay men and 30 straight men; the two groups were matched in terms of age, IQ, and educational levels. Test results were given to three independent judges, who conducted "blind" interpretations of their responses. The finding of no differences between the two groups was instrumental in challenging prevailing views of homosexuality as a sickness.

In 1973, the American Psychiatric Association declassified homosexuality as a mental disorder. Despite this move, the third edition of the *Diagnostic and Statistical Manual of Mental Disorder (DSM-III)*, published in 1980, contained the listing *ego-dystonic homosexuality*, which was finally removed in 1987 with the publication of the revised third edition (*DSM-III-R*). As many have commented (e.g., LeVay, 1996), this decision was not entirely attributed to science. The involvement of several gay and lesbian activists, including gay psychiatrists, was certainly an important influence. Protests were held at the American Psychiatric Association conventions in 1971 and 1972. At the 1972 convention symposium in Dallas, Texas, a psychiatrist named "Dr. Henry Anonymous" appeared in mask and wig and used a voice-altering microphone to give a speech about how he was one of 200 gay psychiatrists who was forced to live a double life. Following a vote by the membership of the American Psychiatric Association to remove homosexuality from the *DSM-III*, a Philadelphia newspaper announced the historic event with the following headline: "20 Million Homosexuals Gain Instant Cure."

A BRIEF HISTORY OF THE TREATMENT OF GENDER MINORITIES

Early Medical Cures for Transsexualism

In contrast to the aversive and behavioral techniques used in the treatment of homosexuality, the majority of attempts to "cure" gender minorities were surgical in nature (Sansweet, 1975). Many of these surgical interventions were the result of strong demands by the patients themselves. In Meyerowitz's text *How Sex Changed (2002)*, she noted that physicians were mostly sympathetic toward these persons and "showed an unusual tolerance for their patients' unconventional cross gender behavior" (p. 107).

One of the first recorded surgical attempts to alter sex in the United States occurred in 1902; Earl Lind loathed his genitals so much he actually convinced a doctor to castrate him in hopes that he would be less masculine. In the early 1900s, sex change experiments were more prevalent in Europe, particularly in Germany. In the 1910s, Viennese endocrinologist Eugen Steinach at the University of Vienna received international acclaim for his transplantations of testes and ovaries in guinea pigs and rats. Influenced by Hirschfeld's ideas, Steinach proposed that the testicular secretions in gay men were abnormal and drove brain development in a female direction. In 1917, he reported on the results of transplanting a testicle from a heterosexual man into a gay man. He reported this patient to have been "cured" of his attraction to other men. As LeVay (1996) reported, one German surgeon at the time stated that he had "cured" his uninformed homosexual patient by slipping a piece of testicle into his body during a hernia operation. The surgeon later reported that his patient developed heterosexual desires and wanted to marry.

Magnus Hirschfeld, who founded the Institute for Sexual Science in Berlin, completed the first genital transformation of Dorchen Richter. Richter was a biological male who had begun cross-dressing as a child and had attempted, at the age of six, to rid himself of his penis and scrotum by tying a cord around them (Bullough, 1994). He underwent castration in 1922 and had his penis removed and a vagina surgically constructed in 1931. Denslow Lewis also performed genital surgeries on patients like Richter to control what he termed *hyperesthesia* in patients; cauterizations of the neck, lower back, and loins; and castration.

After World War II, Drs. David Oliver Cauldwell and Harry Benjamin studied the work of Steinach and Hirschfeld in an attempt to introduce their American colleagues to these works. Cauldwell (1949) adopted the word *transsexual*, which was first coined by Hirschfeld to describe the case of a girl who wished to change her sex. In the 1920s and 1930s, Benjamin offered medical treatment to Otto Spengler, who lived and worked at home as a woman but dressed as a man outside the home. At Spengler's request, Benjamin administered an extract of estrogenic hormone and x-rayed his testicles.

Historically, the medical and psychiatric approaches to the treatment of cross-dressers were less well documented. One of the treatments of choice for cross-dressers was behavioral and aversive in nature. In one recorded instance, a team of British psychologists used treatment methods that were modeled after those used with laboratory animals during the early 1960s. Male cross-dressers were escorted to a room with flooring that had been electrically wired and were instructed to dress in women's clothing. These patients were repeatedly administered electric shocks as they dressed in female attire. More than 400 trials were administered to these patients over a six-day period (Sansweet, 1975).

Early treatment approaches used with infants born with ambiguous genitalia were developed at Johns Hopkins University during the 1920s and 1930s by urologist Hugh Hampton Young. Chase (2002) posited that some of Young's patients were not necessarily interested in the surgery he had to offer. She cited the example of Emma T., a young woman with an enlarged clitoris who was sexually attracted to women but who elected not to have surgery for fear she would lose financial support from her husband. Chase speculated that the policies requiring postnatal intervention for intersexed infants that were in place at Hopkins in the 1950s were developed, in part, because parents were more amenable to surgery on their ambiguously sexed infants than were intersex adults.

The practice of interceding at birth through reconstructive surgeries on the genitals of intersex infants was also made possible in the 1950s because of the improvements in surgical technology. Sexologist John Money of Johns Hopkins developed the standard medical protocol for the treatment of infants born with ambiguous genitalia. The Hopkins model involved the use of a multidisciplinary team of surgeons and endocrinologists, who typically determined the infant's "sex of assignment" and informed the parents afterward of their child's true sex. These decisions were based on the motto "you can make a hole, but you can't build a pole" (Henricks, 1993, p. 10), meaning the penis had to be at least one inch long in order for the infant to be assigned as male, and the clitoris no greater than three-eighths of an inch for female assignment. Additional surgery and hormones were used to make the child's body conform as closely as possible to the sex of assignment.

The Dawn of a New Era in the Treatment of Gender Minority Persons

Meyerowitz (2002) posited that "the medical practice of 'sex change' evolved as transsexual patients insisted on their right to determine their own sex and alter their bodies to fit their minds" (p. 129). In 1948, Harry Benjamin, an endocrinologist, examined his first transsexual patient, a referral made to him by Kinsey. Benjamin had been taking steps to secure sex change surgery for appropriate patients, and it was about the same time in the spring of 1950 that news arrived of Christine Jorgensen (a.k.a. George William Jorgensen). Jorgensen, who worked as a laboratory technician in New York, had secretly self-administered estrogen, acquired women's clothes, and shaved his pubic hair to resemble a female's. He then traveled to Sweden and sought consultation from Dr. Christian Hamburger. In 1952, he underwent castration, and later his penis was removed. What followed was an explosion of media coverage and public fascination. The headline of the *New York Daily News* on December 1, 1952, proclaimed: "Ex-GI Becomes Blonde Beauty." Upon returning to the United States, Jorgensen became one of Benjamin's patients. In 1966, Benjamin published *The Transsexual Phenomenon*, and he advocated humane treatment that consisted of hormone and surgical alteration.

In 1969, Richard Green and John Money developed a medical protocol for sex reassignment based on their work at Johns Hopkins University. Within 10 years, there were more than 40 university-based gender clinics in the United States (Cole, Denny, Eyler, & Samons, 2000), including the one at Hopkins and those at Stanford University, the University of Minnesota, and the University of Oregon (Bullough, 1994). Beginning in 1979, persons seeking hormonal therapy and/or sex reassignment were required to seek counseling and adhere to a series of procedures set out in the Standards of Care developed by the Harry Benjamin International Gender Dysphoria Association (Meyer et al., 2001). These standards dictated that hormonal and surgical candidates receive counseling and obtain official letters of recommendation written by qualified mental health professionals. Those interested in surgical reassignment were also mandated to live as their desired gender for approximately one year (called the "real-life experience") prior to surgery.

In the United States, scientific theories about the origins of transsexuality did not begin to emerge until after the news about Christine Jorgensen's case. Such theories proposed transsexuality might have resulted from bisexuality, psychodynamic processes of personality development, or social learning (Meyerowitz, 2002). For example, Stoller (1967) theorized that male-to-female transsexualism was the result of a detached mother who is typically bisexual and is overly involved with her child during the first two to three years of life.

The psychiatric treatment of cross-dressers was also greatly impacted by the work of Virginia Prince, a biological male who later transitioned to become female. Prince defied the popular opinion at that time that cross-dressers were homosexual men who dressed in women's clothing when she argued that cross-dressers were predominantly heterosexual men. Prince published *Transvestia*, a comprehensive magazine for cross-dressers, and later published the results of her magazine surveys in professional journals (Cole et al., 2000). In 1961, Prince founded the Hose and Heels Club, which was eventually renamed Tri-Ess, standing for the Society for the Second Self. Now an international organization with chapters throughout the United States, Tri-Ess provides cross-dressers and their spouses with education, advocacy, and networking opportunities.

CURRENT POLICIES, PRACTICES, AND CONTROVERSIES IN THE TREATMENT OF SEXUAL MINORITIES

Today a number of practice organizations have developed ethical guidelines and policy statements banning discrimination on the basis of sexual orientation (AAMFT, 1991; NASW, 1996). They have further proposed guidelines for the practice of affirmative therapy with sexual minority persons. In 1997, the APA passed a resolution opposing portrayals of gays and lesbians as mentally ill and in need of treatment, requiring practitioners to provide informed consent and alternative treatment information, and protecting young people from being coerced into treatment by parents or guardians.

In addition to professional ethical codes and position statements that address the treatment of sexual minorities, our judicial system is just beginning to render decisions related to the clinical treatment of sexual minority persons. For example, in 2001 in *Bruff v. North Mississippi Health Services, Inc.*, the U.S. Court of Appeals for the Fifth Circuit upheld the firing of an employee assistance counselor. The plaintiff in this case had asked her employer, North Mississippi Health Services, to be removed from the ongoing treatment of her lesbian client because of religious conflicts that arose when the client requested assistance with her same-sex romantic relationship. In this case, described in detail by Hermann and Herlihy (2006), the plaintiff argued that her employer had failed to accommodate her religious beliefs, as required by Title VII of the Civil Rights Act of 1964.

The judges ruled in favor of the employer on the grounds that the counselor's refusal to provide therapy to address her client's same-sex sexual relationship might "cause emotional harm to the client" (Hermann & Herlihy, 2006, p. 416).

Current Controversies in the Treatment of Sexual Minority Persons

Some of the unusual and frequently bizarre treatment strategies that were used in medicine and psychiatry over 100 years ago to treat sexual and gender minorities seem outrageous, given today's awareness. Yet controversies continue. Treatment efforts to "cure" homosexuals still persist, and debates about whether same-sex sexual orientation can and should be changed have intensified of late (Luo, 2007). While churches and other faith-based organizations established programs to convert homosexuals as early as the 1970s (Cianciotto & Cahill, 2006), the 1990s saw the growth of a movement of clinicians who were determined to offer their clients treatment options for changing their sexual orientations (Haldeman, 2003). The use of therapeutic strategies to promote a change in sexual orientation has been variably named reparative therapy, conversion therapy, and reorientation therapy.

The term *reparative therapy* was coined by Nicolosi (1991, 1993) to describe his psychodynamic therapy approach to changing sexual orientation. Now, more broadly defined, reparative therapies can encompass a wider array of techniques like aversive conditioning, social skills training, visualization, and cognitive therapy (Morrow & Beckstead, 2004).

The 1990s also saw the birth of the National Association of Research and Therapy of Homosexuality (NARTH), a national organization whose membership consists of psychotherapists, licensed psychologists, mental health counselors, social workers, and laypersons. Founded by Drs. Charles Socarides, Benjamin Kaufman, and Joseph Nicolosi, NARTH's mission is to "defend the right to pursue change of sexual orientation" (NARTH, 2006). NARTH currently has a membership of over 1,000.

Professional Organizations' Policies and Guidelines Regarding Conversion Therapy Practices

Nationally, several professional organizations have issued formal statements about the use of conversion therapies. The American Psychiatric Association's Position Statement on Psychiatric Treatment and Sexual Orientation (1998) concluded that "potential risks of reparative therapy are great, including depression, anxiety and self-destructive behavior, since therapist alignment with societal prejudices against homosexuality may reinforce self-hatred already experienced by the patient" (p. 5). In May 2000, the American Psychiatric Association issued the following additional Position Statement for the purpose of elaborating on public and professional concerns about therapies designed to change a patient's sexual orientation:

> As a general principle, a therapist should not determine the goal of treatment either coercively or through subtle influence. Psychotherapeutic modalities to convert or "repair" homosexuality are based on developmental theories whose scientific validity is questionable. Furthermore, anecdotal reports of "cures" are counterbalanced by anecdotal claims of psychological harm. In the last four

BOX 2.1

Anecdote from the Field

A prospective applicant called about my university's graduate program in mental health counseling. I gave him an overview of the program, and he proceeded to fire a whole volley of questions. Clearly, he had done his homework and was well informed about the various degree programs and licensing options. His objective was to become a licensed mental health counselor working with young people. He then said he wanted to specialize in treating clients in a religious setting with the goal of helping them "change" their sexual orientation from homosexual to heterosexual.

I responded by saying that our admissions process was contingent on a number of factors, including "fit" between applicants and the mission of the program. I indicated that our faculty did not endorse and our program did not provide education and training specific to the practice of conversion or reparative therapy. I also said our position was consistent with the ethical codes and position statements of our professional counseling organizations.

How would you have handled the call? How would you have responded to his inquiry? Would you have engaged in the pros and cons of "fixing" people?

decades, "reparative" therapists have not produced any rigorous scientific research to substantiate their claims of cure. Until there is such research available, APA recommends that ethical practitioners refrain from attempts to change individuals' sexual orientation, keeping in mind the medical dictum to first, do no harm. (p. 2)

In 2000, the Board of Directors of the National Association of Social Workers approved a position statement opposing the use of reparative and conversion therapies with lesbian and gay clients. Its National Committee on Lesbian, Gay, and Bisexual Issues (NCLGB, 2000) indicated that "no data demonstrate that reparative or conversion therapies are effective, and in fact they may be harmful" (pp. 1–2).

The 1999 World Conference of the ACA adopted a position statement that specifically opposed the promotion of reparative therapy as a cure for homosexuals (Action by American Counseling Association Governing Council, April 1999).

In a special statement, the Board of Directors of the AAMFT likened a client who requests conversion therapy to a person of color who believes that he or she is "deficient" because of his or her color. The board concluded that it would be "unconscionable not to address that conviction, whether as a moral, philosophical, religious, or scientific issue, as part of treatment" (AAMFT, 2002).

In 2000, the Committee on Lesbian, Gay, and Bisexual Concerns Joint Task Force of the APA's Division 44 published Guidelines for Psychotherapy with Lesbian, Gay, and Bisexual Clients. Guideline 4 states: "Psychologists strive to understand how inaccurate or prejudicial views of homosexuality or bisexuality may affect the client's presentation in treatment and the therapeutic process" (APA Division 44, 2000, p. 1443). While many people interpret this guideline to mean that reparative therapies are blatantly unethical, Schneider, Brown, and Glassgold (2002) assert that it serves more as an "aspirational guide" (p. 265) that focuses on the need for practitioners to obtain full informed consent. Such informed consent should include data about the risks, benefits, and costs of reparative therapy. While the APA may be reluctant to take a firm stance prohibiting reparative therapy, many professional organizations have criticized such therapy, claiming there is a lack of data supporting its efficacy. The newly renamed Committee on Lesbian, Gay, Bisexual and *Transgender* Concerns and Division 44 are currently at work on a revision of the original psychotherapy guidelines for sexual minorities. A separate task force is reviewing research on conversion therapy practises (APA, 2007).

Motivations and Methods of Conversion Therapy

Research suggests that the majority of persons who express a desire to change their sexual orientation are largely motivated to do so because of religious beliefs (Haldeman, 2004; Rosik, 2003; Shidlo & Schroeder, 2002; Tozer & Hayes, 2004). Other motivators include the desire to pursue or maintain a heterosexually based marriage and family, a concern with risky sexual behavior leading to HIV infection, and the perception that homoerotic sexual activity is associated with nonmonogamy (Rosik, 2003).

Nicolosi's texts, *Reparative Therapy of Male Homosexuality* (1991) and *Healing Homosexuality: Case Studies of Reparative Therapy* (1993), described the etiology of male homosexuality and a psychodynamic therapy approach to changing sexual orientation. The premise of Nicolosi's approach was that male homosexuality results when sons fail to bond and to eventually form identifications with their fathers. This failure to identify with the father is attributed to a number of factors, including an absent or emotionally distant father, the presence of a "more rewarding relationship with the mother" (1991, p. 32), and failure to encourage the male child's sense of autonomy because of overprotection or domination. Basically, he argued that same-sex sexual attraction results when males fail to completely develop a masculine gender identity because "gender identity determines sexual orientation" (1993, p. 211). Nicolosi's treatment approach included individual and group psychotherapy, therapeutic dream-work, bibliotherapy, and adjunctive experiences such as nonsexual intimate friendships with men.

In addition to Nicolosi's approach, there are other types of conversion therapies. The majority of these are faith-based, operate independently of secular counseling agencies, and incorporate a variety of change-oriented strategies, including the use of personal testimonies, prayer, Bible reading, and peer support (Ponticelli, 1999). Most incorporate volunteer counselors as opposed to licensed clinicians (Throckmorten, 2002). Examples of religiously based programs include Exodus International (http://exodus); Courage Reparational Group (www.couragerc.net/ReparationalGroup.html), primarily for Catholics; and Jonah (www.jonahweb.org/html), for people of the Jewish faith.

RESEARCHING THE EFFICACY OF CONVERSION THERAPIES

Methodological Challenges

While professional organizations such as the APA, ACA, AMHCA, and AAMFT have insisted that scientific evidence does not support the efficacy of reparative therapy, many (Byrd, 2004; Zucker, 2003) point out that much of the research on both sides of the controversy is methodologically flawed. Some of the methodological problems include inconsistencies both in the kinds of therapeutic techniques that make up conversion therapy and in the ways that *sexual orientation* is defined and assessed. With regard to the latter, a number of studies rely exclusively on the client's self-labeling as "heterosexual" or "homosexual" or the client's history of sexual behaviors, failing to distinguish among behaviors, arousal, fantasies, and attraction.

Many conversion programs include participants who have significant histories of heterosexual behaviors and fantasies and who may, in fact, be more bisexual than gay or lesbian. As a result, conversion efforts may be more successful than would otherwise be the case with participants who have had exclusively homoerotic behaviors and fantasies (Haldeman, 2003).

From a methodological viewpoint, most studies use self-report measures to assess change after reorientation therapy. Such a practice is questionable, given the social desirability and experimental demand effect that can bias participants' self-reports (Haldeman, 2003). Other problems associated with such research are the lack of long-term outcome data and the failure to use comparison or control groups (Morrow & Beckstead, 2004). Lastly, such research tends to rely on samples consisting of predominantly white, male Christians. Lesbians and bisexual women are seldom involved in such programs and/or incorporated in research (Bright, 2004).

Research Results

Perhaps in response to the methodological flaws associated with prior research, as well as the lack of data-based research, in the last several years there has been an increase in data-based research and in publications regarding the efficacy of conversion therapy. For example, Schaeffer, Hyde, Kroencke, McCormick, and Nottebaum (2000) surveyed approximately 250 persons who attended one of the North American conferences of Exodus International during the period from 1993 to 1995. Based on their self-report, participants experienced significant change in their sexual orientation. Further, they reported that their changes were motivated by religion and were not a byproduct of psychotherapy.

Nicolosi, Byrd, and Potts (2000) conducted a survey of beliefs about the impact of conversion therapy on 882 persons who were dissatisfied with their same-sex sexual orientation. The participants were members of ex-gay ministry groups, portions of whom had received therapy from a professional therapist only, from a professional therapist and a pastoral counselor, from a pastoral counselor or friends, from family, and/or from ex-gay ministries. Forty-three percent of participants reported some changes in their sexual orientation. While the majority of respondents viewed their experiences as helpful in terms of self-acceptance, self-esteem, and relationship with God, 7.1% said that they were doing worse after intervention.

A study by Spitzer that was published in 2003 is perhaps the most controversial of those on the efficacy of conversion therapies reported thus far. Spitzer, a psychiatrist, interviewed 200 self-selected participants in structured telephone interviews regarding same-sex attraction, fantasy, yearning, and overt homosexual behavior during a five-year period after participating in reparative therapies. Participating in the research were 143 men and 57 women who met the following minimum criteria: (1) based on self-rating, predominantly homosexual attractions and, in the year before therapy, a self-rating of at least 60 on a scale of sexual attraction (0 = exclusively heterosexual and 100 = exclusively homosexual); and (2) based on self-rating, a minimum change of 10 points for a minimum of five years following therapy toward the heterosexual end of the sexual attraction scale.

Spitzer incorporated 10 self-report assessments of the following: sexual attraction, sexual orientation, self-identity, yearning for romantic intimacy, daydreaming, masturbation frequency, and emotional and physical satisfaction with heterosexual sex. The majority of Spitzer's sample had participated in more than one type of therapy, including seeing a mental health professional and attending an ex-gay or religious support group. The interview questions focused on two specific time periods: one year before the onset of reorientation therapy and one year before the interview itself. The reasons most frequently given to account for their motivation to change sexual orientation were lack of emotional satisfaction from life as a gay person, religious conflict, and a desire to either get married or stay married. Results showed a majority of participants reported some degree of change not only in their sexual orientation identity but in their behavior as well, while complete change was rarely reported; women reported significantly more change than did men.

Spitzer's published findings, along with the reviews of 26 other researchers and practitioners, appeared in the October 2003 issue of the *Archives of Sexual Behavior*. The commentaries noted significant methodology problems that have also been found in other conversion therapy studies. Chief among these was the biased nature of Spitzer's sample, as 23% of his participants were referred by NARTH (Cianciotto & Cahill, 2006).

Shidlo and Schroeder (2002) conducted interviews of 202 clients of sexual orientation conversion therapies over a five-year period from 1995 to 2000. Participants received therapy from licensed mental health practitioners, nonlicensed practitioners, peer counselors, and/or religious counselors. The clinical interventions that participants received included individual therapy, cognitive-behavioral therapy, aversive conditioning, hypnosis, psychotropic medications, and clinical/religious group therapy. Nonclinical interventions consisted of peer groups, Homosexuals Anonymous, and a residential program affiliated with Exodus.

Despite variations in the types of interventions the participants received, they all had in common the application of what Shidlo and Schroeder termed "homosexual behavior management," a collection of techniques from cognitive and behavioral therapists. Such techniques included (1) not engaging in masturbation, (2) using aversive images when experiencing same-sex sexual arousal, (3) using cognitive reframing, (4) working out at the gym, (5) reading the Bible, and (6) praying.

A total of 13% indicated that conversion therapy was helpful in changing their sexual orientation. The remaining 87% of participants perceived themselves as having "failed" conversion therapy. Many of the latter participants believed themselves to be harmed by their experiences and reported increased depression, suicidality, and decreased self-esteem. Some participants who had received aversive conditioning and covert sensitization experienced intrusive flashback-like images associated with serious and long-term sexual dysfunction. One of the criticisms levied against this study was that the participants had to refer back to interventions they received over 12 years prior.

More recently, Jones and Yarhouse (2007) published the results of a longitudinal study of 98 participants seeking conversion through involvement in Exodus. Through the use of standardized measures at various intervals, the researchers reported that the majority of participants experienced either a reduction of same-sex desire through celibacy or a decrease in same-sex desire concomitant with an increase in heterosexual desire.

What Advocates of Conversion Therapy Say

While some advocates of reparative therapy maintain that homosexuality is immoral and sick, a number of supporters argue that clients should have the right to self-determination. They recommend the use of reparative or conversion therapy only after an exhaustive informed consent process has been completed by therapists and their clients. They often cite those professional ethical standards that speak to the need to respect cultural, religious, and other individual differences. Practitioners such as Yarhouse (1998), Rosik (2003), and Throckmorton (1998, 2002) are particularly outspoken about the need to use reparative therapy in certain cases. Throckmorton is a counseling psychologist and former president of the AMHCA. Yarhouse (1998) and his colleague Jones (Jones & Yarhouse, 2007) maintain that counselors are ethically obligated to respect the treatment goals of clients who seek to modify their same-sex attractions and sexual behaviors. Yarhouse points out that as mental health professionals have become more aggressive about the need to integrate spirituality into their clinical practices, they need to recognize that some clients will elect to follow the historical teachings of their religious communities that are resolutely against same-sex sexual behaviors.

What Opponents of Conversion Therapy Say

Many counseling practitioners have argued that not only is reorientation therapy ineffective, but also it is harmful to some clients and should, therefore, not be condoned (Bright, 2004; Drescher, 2001; Haldeman, 2003). Many are concerned as a result of studies that show persons who fail to change their sexual orientation are harmed because the therapy reinforces their self-hatred. After conducting an extensive review of research, Bieschke, Paul, and Blasko (2007) acknowledge that although a small minority of persons report experiencing a shift in their orientation from homosexual to heterosexual, the risk of potential harm leads the authors to conclude "this treatment modality should not be offered" (p. 312).

Opponents of conversion therapy also argue that those who would participate in such practices in the name of clients' right to self-determination ignore the fact that we all live in a culture where heterosexism and homophobia prevail (Tozer & McClanahan, 1999). Haldeman (2003) stated: "Psychology cannot free people from stigma by continuing to promote or tacitly endorse conversion therapy" (p. 696).

Another reason that the practice of reparative therapy is inadvisable is that the boards that regulate counseling and social work licensure in a number of states have adopted the ethical codes of professional counseling organizations (i.e., the APA, ACA, and NASW) (Halpert, 2000). Thus, practitioners who engage in conversion therapy practices that potentially harm clients may face ethical review by their state licensing board.

Integrative Strategies

In a middle-ground approach to the conversion therapy debate, Gonsiorek (2004) proposed an integrative solution: that is, for therapists to aid persons who are religiously conservative and have a same-sex sexual orientation by neither affirming their sexual identities nor denying their religious beliefs. An integrative perspective would require therapists to help clients find a solution to their conflict between homosexuality and religion by finding ways to embrace and integrate both aspects of their identity.

In a similar vein, Beckstead and Israel (2007) advocated for the adoption of a broad-based approach that attends to all aspects of persons' identities, including their religious and cultural orientations. They recommend that for those clients who specifically request conversion therapy, therapists try to assess their clients' external and internal motivations for wanting to change their orientations. They also caution therapists against making referrals to practitioners who engage in conversion therapy techniques, as this may send messages to clients that they are sanctioning such approaches.

Bancroft (2003) recommended that counselors carefully attend to the informed consent process when working with clients who have sexual orientation issues. This means that therapists must be explicit about their values as they pertain to sexual behaviors, sexual orientation, and gender and discuss how these might impact the treatment process so that the client can choose whether to work with the therapist or not. He advocated that therapists disclose their own personal values regardless of what the patient's values or beliefs might be. Bancroft lets it be known that he has no difficulty with bisexual, homosexual, and heterosexual identities and/or behaviors. He advised:

> Make it clear that in order to find out what type of sexual relationship works best, it may be necessary to experience more than one type of relationship, involving partners of either gender. Furthermore, during a lifetime, more than one successful relationship may occur, involving same sex and opposite sex partners at different times. Emphasize the need to take time to work out what is right. The therapist, who is better designated as a counselor in this context, facilitates this process of search and discovery as appropriate. This may involve helping the patient to identify the different "compartments" of his or her sexuality, and how to incorporate them into a sexually rewarding, intimate, and loving relationship. This is more education than therapy. (p. 421)

CURRENT POLICIES, PRACTICES, AND RECOMMENDATIONS REGARDING TREATMENT OF GENDER MINORITIES

Few professional organizations offer policy and practice guidelines and policies specifically for gender minorities. However, in August 2008, the Governing Council of Representatives of the APA passed a resolution banning discrimination on the basis of gender identity. The APA policy statement calls for additional practice guidelines, training and research (APA, 2008). The most popular treatment protocol for gender minorities, the Standards of Care (SOC) for Gender Identity Disorders, was established by the Harry Benjamin International Gender Dysphoria Association (HBIGDA) in 1979. Now in its sixth version (Meyer et al., 2001), the SOC prevails in most places throughout the world. The HBIGDA is an international organization whose membership consists of 500 psychiatrists, psychologists, mental health professionals, and physicians. According to Ekins (2005), the membership of HBIGDA also contains a "significant number of transgendered professionals" (p. 307), many of whom objected to the term *gender dysphoria* and to the assumption of pathology inherent in the treatment guidelines. It was for this reason that the organization voted to rename itself the World Professional Association for Transgender Health (WPATH) in 2006 (*http://www.wpath.org*).

The SOC, which were last revised in February 2001, represent a consensus of opinion about how to provide medical and psychological care to persons with gender identity disorders. The SOC's minimal training requirements for those mental health professionals who work with adults and children include a master's degree and specialized training in the assessment and treatment of gender identity issues. According to these guidelines, mental health professionals must provide documentation letters for hormone therapy or for breast surgery to physicians who will provide medical treatment. Letters of documentation are also required in order for genital surgery, referred to as sex reassignment surgery, to be performed. The SOC also list additional responsibilities that are germane to the work of mental health professionals, including (1) accurately diagnosing gender identity disorder and any other co-morbid mental disorders, (2) discussing the range of treatment options and the risks and benefits associated with these, (3) making an evaluation and formal recommendation to medical personnel, (4) educating family members and others, and (5) conducting follow-up with clients. The SOC also contain eligibility criteria for hormone therapy, including either a real-life experience for three months prior to administration or a period of psychotherapy of not less than three months.

There have been a number of criticisms of the SOC. According to Denny, because the SOC are minimal standards, they have often been inappropriately applied:

> Access to hormones and surgery were oft-promised and seldom delivered, and were, in fact, frequently used like carrots at the end of stick. Some transsexuals were kept in abeyance for years with false promises. Others were required (read forced) to make changes in their sexual orientation, marital status, career, manner of presentation, name, and physical characteristics. Many were required to live full time for extended periods before hormonal therapy. (Denny, n.d., p. 1)

Many believe that the Standards of Care are too restrictive. For example, at the second International Conference of Transgender Law and Employment Policy in 1993, the membership adopted Health Law Standards of Care for Transsexualism. These standards were less restrictive than the HBIGDA/WPATH SOC and stipulated that medical providers who perform hormonal and sex reassignment therapy must also conduct periodic blood chemistry checks and seek informed consent and waiver of liability from their patients (http://www.transgendercare.com/guidance/resources/ictlep_soc.htm).

Another criticism of the SOC is their omission of gender minority persons who do not want hormones or surgery (Martin & Yonkin, 2006). There are increasing numbers of gender minorities who choose not to transition through hormones (NoHo) or surgery and instead employ nonmedical strategies (behavior, dress, and speech) to express their gender identities (Denny, 2006; Lombardi & Davis, 2006; Martin & Yonkin, 2006). There are also increasing numbers of persons who choose to present themselves androgynously (Denny, 2006; Lombardi & Davis, 2006).

> The decision to live in a gender identity that defies traditional notions of male and female (or notions about the medical transition from one sex to another) should be respected as a viable alternative to transitioning to a new gender. (Lombardi & Davis, 2006, p. 355)

Current Controversies

The previous chapter described the use of behavioral treatment strategies (Rekers, 1992; Rekers & Lovass, 1974; Zucker & Bradley, 1995) which have been used with children who are gender nonconforming. The objective of these rehabilitative treatments is to put children "on track" in terms of their gender role behaviors and to ultimately help defend against the social ostracism that such children typically experience (Raj, 2002). Critics of these treatment approaches argue that they make the mistake of conflating gender identity and sexual orientation and raise a number of ethical and treatment-related questions. Chapter 6 explores these issues in greater detail.

The 1990s also saw many changes in the treatment of other segments of the transgender community. The idea that had been promulgated by John Money and his colleagues at the Johns Hopkins School of Medicine in the fifties—that newborns are "neutral" when it comes to gender identity and that the assignment of sex at birth and rearing are the major determinants of gender identity—was strongly contested in the early 1990s (Zucker, 2005). The standard policies for the treatment of intersex newborns were also criticized on ethical grounds. In 1993, what was started by Cheryl Chase as a peer support group for intersexed adults became the Intersex Society of North America (ISNA). The ISNA's goals are to stop the practice of genital surgery in infancy and provide parents and intersex children with professional mental health care. The controversy over this protocol continues even today. In 1997, intersex activists visited Congress to request the Law to Ban Female Genital Mutilation be enforced to protect intersex children as well. The recent APA policy statement and report of the Task Force on Gender Identity and Gender Variance purposefully exclude intersex persons because of the growing division between persons who are born with medical conditions many of whom prefer the label Disorders of Sex Development over intersex and those who alter their bodies through hormones and/or surgery (APA, 2008).

Beginning in the late 1980s and throughout the 1990s, changes in the medical and psychological treatment approaches across all segments of the transgender population have emerged in large measure through the political activism of coalitions formed across the transgender community (e.g., the International Foundation for Gender Education, American Educational Gender Information Service, Renaissance Transgender Association) (Denny, 2006). For example, Tri-Ess, the national organization introduced earlier, for cross-dressers and their spouses, joined other organizations in ratifying the Gender Bill of Rights and developing outreach educational programs for counseling-related organizations such as the American Association of Sex Educators, Counselors, and Teachers (AASECT) and the NASW (Fairfax, 2006).

A number of clinicians (e.g., Rosario, 2004; Seil, 2004) reported that many of those who requested sex reassignment during the 1970s fabricated descriptions of their experiences, often copying the same terminology (e.g., "trapped in the wrong body") over and over again, in order to assure that they qualified under the medical evaluation standards that were used for gender reassignment treatments. Some believe that this practice continues and serves to alienate gender minorities from helping professionals. For example, Spade (2006), a transgender activist, described this experience quite vividly:

> After attending only three discussion group meetings with other trans people, I am struck by the naiveté with which I approached the search for counseling to get my surgery authorizing letters. No one at these groups seems to see therapy as the place where they voice their doubts about their transitions, where they wrestle with the political implications of their changes, where they speak about fears of losing membership in various communities or in their families. No one trusts the doctors as the place to work things out. When I mention the places I've gone for help, places that are supposed to support queer and trans people, everyone nods knowingly, having heard countless stories like mine about these very places before. Some suggest therapists who are better, but none cost less than $50/hr. Most people simply offer different ways to get around the requirements. I get names of surgeons who do not always ask for letters. Someone suggests that since I won't be on hormones, I can go in and pretend I'm a woman with a history of breast cancer in my family and that I want a double mastectomy to prevent it. I have these great, sad conversations with these people who know all about what it means to lie and cheat their way through the medical roadblocks to get the opportunity to occupy their bodies in the way they want. (p. 327)

Summary

Historically, a vast array of medical, psychological, and behavioral treatments has been used to "cure" both sexual and gender minorities. As the psychiatric and counseling professions evolved in their depiction and understanding of homosexuality, the pressure to "cure" gay men and lesbians dissipated. This was especially true in the years following the removal of homosexuality from the *DSM*.

The 1990s saw the growth of multiculturalism in counseling and a growing interest among clinicians in spirituality and religion. The need to preserve the dignity and human rights of all has led some mainstream and secular practitioners to advocate for the advancement of treatment options for clients seeking to change their sexual orientation from homosexual to heterosexual. During the past 15 years, the controversy surrounding conversion or reparative therapy has resurfaced, and so has debate about its ethicality and efficacy. Ironically, while many debate whether it is morally and ethically appropriate to offer conversion therapy, others believe the very notion of changing sexual orientation is itself implausible. Such persons argue from an essentialist point of view because they assert sexual orientation is relatively fixed and biologically determined. As mentioned in the previous chapter, some research supports the view that sexual orientation is a rather continuous, developmentally stable phenomenon that manifests itself during childhood, often with cross-gender behaviors (D'Augelli & Patterson, 1995).

Historically, as medical and psychiatric practitioners began to distinguish between sexual and gender minorities and as sophisticated surgical interventions were developed, the treatment of gender minority persons became increasingly medicalized. Today the World Professional Association for Transgender Health (WPATH) publishes the Standards of Care (SOC) for the treatment of gender minorities. Now in its sixth version, the SOC represent a consensus of opinion about how to provide medical and psychological care to persons with gender identity disorders. The SOC contain minimal training requirements for mental health professionals, service recommendations, eligibility criteria, and guidelines for hormone therapy, breast surgery, and genital surgery. These treatment protocols are becoming increasingly the object of critique from professionals as well as gender minorities themselves.

Personal Reflection

Cheryl Chase is a highly successful intersex activist and the founder of the Intersex Society of North America (ISNA), an organization whose mission is to "end shame, secrecy, and unwanted genital surgeries" (ISNA, 1993–2008) for persons who are born as intersexed. The ISNA also advocates for the sex assignment of children without surgery as well as the provision of mental health services to intersex children and their families. The following narrative is excerpted from her chapter entitled '"Culture Practice' or 'Reconstructive Surgery?' U.S. Genital Cutting, the Intersex Movement, and Medical Double Standards" in *Genital Cutting and Transnational Sisterhood: Disputing U.S. Polemics* (James & Robertson, 2002):

I was born with ambiguous genitals. A doctor specializing in intersexuality deliberated for three days—and sedated my mother each time she asked what was wrong with her baby—before concluding that I was male, with micropenis, complete hypospadisas, undescended testes, and a strange extra opening behind the urethra. A male birth certificate was completed for me, and my parents began raising me as a boy. When I was a year and a half old, my parents consulted a different set of intersex experts, who admitted me to a hospital for "sex determination."

Doctors told my parents that a thorough medical investigation, including exploratory surgery, would be necessary to determine (that is, ascertain) what my "true sex" was. They judged my genital appendage to be inadequate as a penis: too short to effectively mark masculine status or to penetrate females. As a female however, I would be penetrable and potentially fertile. My anatomy having now been re-labeled as vagina, urethra, labia, and outsized clitoris, my sex was next determined by amputating my genital appendage—clitoridectomy. Following doctors' orders my parents then changed my name; combed their house to eliminate all traces of my existence as a boy (photographs, birthday cards, etc.); engaged a lawyer to change my birth certificate; moved to a different town; instructed extended family members to no longer refer to me as a boy; and never told anyone else—including me—just what had happened. My intersexuality and change of sex were the family's dirty little secrets. As an adolescent I became aware that I had no clitoris or inner labia and was unable to experience orgasm. By the end of my teens, I began to research in medical libraries, trying to discover what might have happened to me. When I finally determined to obtain my personal medical records, it took three years to overcome the obstruction of the doctors whom I asked for help. When I did obtain a scant three pages from my medical files, I learned for the first time that I was a "true hermaphrodite" who had been my parents'

son for a year and a half, with a name that was unfamiliar to me.

Nearly fifteen years later, in my middle thirties, I suffered an emotional meltdown. In the eyes of the world I was a highly successful businesswoman, a principal in an international high-tech company. To myself, I was a freak, incapable of loving or being loved, filled with shame about my status as a hermaphrodite, about the imagined appearance of my genitals before surgery (I thought "true hermaphrodite" meant that I have been born with a penis), and about my sexual dysfunction. Unable to make peace with these facts about myself, I finally sought help from a professional therapist, only to find my experience denied. She reacted to each revelation about my history and predicament with some version of "no it's not" or "so what?" I'd say, "I'm not really a woman." She would say, "Of course you are. You look female." I'd say, "My complete withdrawal from sexuality has destroyed every relationship I've entered." She would say, "Everybody has their ups and downs." I tried another therapist and met with similar responses. Increasingly desperate, I confided my story to several friends who shrank away in embarrassed silence. I was in emotional agony and found myself utterly alone with no possible way out. I decided to kill myself. (Source: From *Genital Cutting and Transnational Sisterhood: Disputing U.S. Polemics* (pp. 134–136). Copyright © 2002 by the Board of Trustees of the University of Illinois. Used with permission of the University of Illinois Press.)

Self-Reflection Questions

After reading this passage from Chase's personal story, what are your thoughts?

1. What is your reaction to how Chase's intersex condition was handled by her doctors and her parents?
2. Given the current controversy over surgical sex assignment for intersex infants, do you agree with recent mandates to allow the

intersexed child to decide when he or she reaches maturity?

3. What is your sense of the kind of mental health services and support intersex children and their families might need?

4. As a counselor how might you respond to Chase's sense of desperation?

Library, Media, and Internet Activities

Check your local video/DVD store for three important films.

Kinsey (Condon, 2004)

This film chronicles the life of Alfred Kinsey from his childhood experiences as the son of an engineering teacher and occasional Sunday school preacher father to the years before his death in 1956. The film depicts Kinsey's transition from a biology professor at Indiana University specializing in the study of gall wasps to a world-renowned sexology researcher.

Discussion Questions

1. This film provides a glimpse into Kinsey's research methods, principally, the interview. Kinsey's base interview consisted of 350 items, with additional items numbering up to 521 items, all of which were memorized by the interviewers (Bullough, 2004). How do Kinsey's interviewing techniques compare with postmodern research approaches described in Chapter 1?

2. *Kinsey* depicts the interwoven nature of Kinsey's personal and professional lives. How did Kinsey's research impact his personal life and vice versa?

3. In Kinsey, Pomeroy, and Martin's text *Sexual Behavior in the Human Male* (1948), the theory of a continuum of sexual behavior was presented, as was a seven-point scale that depicted the graduations of human sexuality. Consulting your library and the Internet, review the literature to uncover other measures that have been developed to assess sexual orientation since Kinsey's version.

Hard Pill (Baumgartner, 2005)

This highly provocative film centers on Tim, a single, unhappy gay man who decides to serve as a volunteer in the trial of an experimental drug developed by New Day Industries, which claims the drug changes sexual orientation from gay to straight. The film depicts the personal impact of this decision on Tim and on the lives of his friends and co-workers.

Discussion Questions

1. Imagine that Tim decides to see a counselor before making the final decision to take the "hard pill." You are his counselor. How might you respond to him and his dilemma?

2. *Hard Pill*'s director, Baumgartner, introduces each character at the beginning of the film with a rating on a graphic scale similar to the one that Kinsey developed. How might your assessment of each character at the end of the film compare to those presented at the beginning of the film? What implication does this have for the debate presented in Chapter 1 between the essentialist and social constructionist points of view?

3. Given the current emphasis on psychopharmacology and "better living through chemistry," imagine that the "hard pill" does exist and that it could permit changes in sexual orientation, including moving a person from heterosexuality to homosexuality or bisexuality. Would you counsel someone to take the pill? Why?

Fixing Frank (Selditch, 2002)

This film is based on a stage play written by Ken Hanes. Frank Johnston, a journalist, is urged by his partner, Dr. Jonathan Baldwin, to pose as a client in order to write an exposé about Baldwin's fellow psychologist Dr. Arthur Apsey. Dr. Apsey specializes in conversion therapy. As the story unfolds, Frank reveals himself to Apsey as an investigative reporter and begins to find himself becoming more and more drawn to Apsey, questioning his relationship and his sexual orientation.

Discussion Questions

1. Dr. Apsey states that he does not use aversion techniques in his conversion therapy. How might you describe his approach to working with Frank? What therapeutic methods or theories is he using in his work with Frank?

2. Arthur Apsey and Jonathan Baldwin disclose personal events that seem to impact them on a professional level. What were these events, and how might each have been impacted by them? What underlying assumptions does each psychologist make in the treatment of his clients? Why in your opinion is the issue of bisexuality neglected by either Apsey or Baldwin?

3. Suppose that after the professional board hearing has been completed, Frank is referred to another therapist contracted through the board to help him process his experience. You are that therapist. How might you proceed with therapy?

Group Activity

Evidence of the controversy over conversion therapy was particularly evident in the classroom one evening during the internship supervision seminar with several masters'-level counseling students. A student described her field placement at an agency that was affiliated with a local church. The student told about all the interesting experiences that awaited her as an intern, one of which was the possibility of facilitating a support group for ex-gays. Startled by her enthusiasm for this endeavor, the professor asked students in the seminar what issues they might consider in terms of facilitating such a group. At this point, a lively debate ensued. It went something like this:

JEAN: If some people are gay and don't want to be, I don't see why they shouldn't have the right to ask for counseling to help them change.

HAYDEN: Yes, but are we really free to choose? As long as our government, churches, military organizations, and schools view homosexuality as unacceptable, how could it be a free choice? After all, are there any straight people coming into therapy to change their orientation from heterosexual to gay?

JEAN: Just because a client comes to you as a therapist and wants to not be gay doesn't mean that he or she suffers from internalized homophobia.

HAYDEN: It is hard to believe that those clients haven't somehow internalized messages from our culture that homosexuality is not desirable; otherwise, why would they want to change?

ERIN: Well, maybe homosexuality just isn't okay with their religion? Shouldn't we respect that religion is important enough to some people that they just can't be gay?

CRIS: But I thought way back in 1973 the American Psychiatric Association said that homosexuality is not an illness, so why should we as therapists still be treating it like one? Aren't we as counselors being a bit hypocritical when we try to "cure" somebody of homosexuality at the same time we're saying that homosexuality isn't a pathological condition?

JEAN: If a gay client believes that he or she will be happier and more well adjusted as a heterosexual, why not support him or her in changing?

ERIN: But all of the major professional organizations like the APA and the ACA have discouraged practitioners from counseling people to change. Aren't you as a therapist going against our profession?

Discussion Questions

1. In your opinion, which of the arguments in favor of conversion therapy are most compelling? Why?
2. In your opinion, which of the arguments against conversion therapy are most compelling? Why?
3. Divide your group in half and arbitrarily designate one subgroup as "pro" conversion therapy and one as "anti" conversion therapy, and debate this issue.

Role Play Activity

A 29-year-old, single, Euro-American female, named Anne, presents for therapy at your office with what might be referred to as ego-dystonic homosexuality. She has been an extremely active member of her church for several years and is now serving as a volunteer youth director. Her church is extremely conservative and has taken a firm stance against homosexuality. She is currently pursuing her graduate degree in business administration. She tells you that she is "deeply troubled" because she has found herself to be increasingly drawn to a fellow student in one of her graduate classes who is an "out lesbian." She tells you that she is sexually attracted to her and has even had an erotic dream or two about her. She tearfully says that her faith is the most important thing in her life and that she cannot turn her back on her church and her faith. She tells you, "I want to fix it so that I will no longer have these feelings ever again."

Directions

1. Choose a partner in class and agree for one person to play the role of the therapist in this case and one person to play the role of Anne.
2. Following are questions to ponder in preparation for role playing:
   a. What would you say to Anne as her counselor?
   b. Would you present her with the option of conversion therapy?
   c. How would you do this?

References

American Association for Marriage and Family Therapy. (2002). *Board of Directors statement*. Retrieved March 4, 2005, from http://www.aamft.org/about/boardletter.asp

American Association for Marriage and Family Therapy. (1991) *Code of ethics*. Washington, DC: Author.

American Psychiatric Association. (1980). *Diagnostic and statistical manual of mental disorders* (3rd ed.). Washington, DC: Author.

American Psychiatric Association. (1987). *Diagnostic and statistical manual of mental disorders* (3rd ed., rev.). Washington, DC: Author.

American Psychiatric Association Position Statement on Therapies Focused on Attempts to Change Sexual Orientation (Reparative or Conversion Therapies) (2000, May). Arlington, VA: Author. Retrieved August 25, 2008 from http://www.psych.org/Departments/EDU/Library/APAOfficialDocumentsandRelated/PositionStatements/200001.aspx

American Psychiatric Association Position Statement on Psychiatric Treatment and Sexual Orientation (1998, December 11). Arlington, VA: Author. Retrieved August 25, 2008 from http://www.psych.org/Departments/EDU/Library/APAOfficialDocumentsandRelated/PositionStatements/199820.aspx

American Psychological Association (August 2008). Resolution on transgender, gender identity, and gender expression non-discrimination. Retrieved September 17, 2008, from http://www.apa.org/pi/lgbt/policy/transgender.html

American Psychological Association Division 44, Committee on Lesbian, Gay, and Bisexual Concerns Joint Task Force. (2000). Guidelines for psychotherapy with lesbian, gay, and bisexual clients. *American Psychologist, 55,* 1440–1451.

American Psychological Association Committee on Lesbian, Gay, Bisexual, and Transgender Concerns (2007). Annual Report. Retrieved September 17, 2008, from http://www.apa.org/pi/CLBT_2007_ar.pdf

Bancroft, J. (2003). Can sexual orientation change? A long-running saga. In Peer commentaries on Spitzer. *Archives of Sexual Behavior, 32*(5), 419–421.

Baumgartner, J. (Director). (2005). *Hard pill* [Motion picture]. United States: Fox Searchlight Pictures.

Beckstead, L., & Israel, T. (2007). Affirmative counseling and psychotherapy focused on issues related to sexual orientation conflicts. In K. J. Bieschke, R. M. Perez, & K. A. DeBord (Eds.), *Handbook of counseling and psychotherapy with lesbian, gay, bisexual, and transgender clients* (2nd ed., pp. 221–244). Washington, DC: American Psychological Association.

Benjamin, H. (1966). *The transsexual phenomenon: A scientific report on transsexualism and sex conversion in the human male and female*. New York: Julian Press.

Bieber, I., Dain, H., Dince, P., Drellian, M., Grand, H., Gundlach, R., et al. (1962). *Homosexuality: A psychoanalytic study*. New York: Basic Books.

Bieschke, K. J., Paul, P. L., & Blasko, K. A. (2007). Review of empirical research focused on the experience of lesbian, gay, and bisexual clients in counseling and psychotherapy. In K. J. Bieschke, R. M. Perez, & K. A. DeBord (Eds.), *Handbook of counseling and psychotherapy with lesbian, gay, bisexual, and transgender clients* (2nd ed., pp. 293–315). Washington, DC: American Psychological Association.

Bright, C. (2004). Deconstructing reparative therapy: An examination of the processes involved when attempting to change sexual orientation. *Clinical Social Work Journal, 32*(4), 471–481.

Bullough, V. L. (1994). *Science in the bedroom: A history of sex research*. New York: Basic Books.

Bullough, V. L. (2004). Sex will never be the same: The contributions of Alfred C. Kinsey. *Archives of Sexual Behavior, 33* (3), 277–286.

Byrd, D. A. (2004, November 22). *Former APA president supports NARTH's mission statement, assails APA's intolerance of differing views*. Retrieved January 20, 2005, from http://www.narth.com/docs/perloff.html

Cauldwell, D. O. (1949, December). Psychopathia transexualism. *Sexology, 16,* 274–280.

Chase, C. (2002). "Culture practice" or "reconstructive surgery?" U.S. genital cutting, the intersex movement, and medical double standards. In S. M. James & C. C. Robertson (Eds.), *Genital cutting and transnational sisterhood: Disputing U. S. polemics* (pp. 126–151). Champaign: University of Illinois Press.

Cianciotto, J., & Cahill, S. (2006, March 2). *Youth in the crosshairs: The third wave of ex-gay activism*. Retrieved November 1, 2006, from http://www.

thetaskforce.org/downloads/ reports/reports/ YouthInTheCrosshairs.pdf

Cole, S. S., Denny, D., Eyler, A. E., & Samons, S. L. (2000). Issues of transgender. In T. Szuchman & F. Muscarella (Eds.), *Psychological perspectives in human sexuality* (pp. 149–195). New York: Wiley.

Condon, B. (Director). (2004). *Kinsey* [Motion picture]. United States: Fox Searchlight Pictures.

D'Augelli, R. R., & Patterson, C. J. (Eds). (1995). *Lesbian, gay and bisexual identities over the lifespan: Psychological perspectives.* New York: Oxford University Press.

Denny, D. (n.d.). Dallas Denny on the Standards of Care. Some notes on access to medical treatment: A position paper. Retrieved February 7, 2007 from http://www.my.execpc.com/dummson/ dallasdennySOC.htm

Denny, D. (2006). Transgender communities of the United States in the late twentieth century. In P. Currah, J. M. Juang, & S. P. Minter (Eds.), *Transgender rights* (pp. 171–191). Minneapolis: University of Minnesota Press.

Dreger, A. D. (1998). *Hermaphrodites and the medical invention of sex.* Cambridge, MA: Harvard University Press.

Drescher, J. (2001). Ethical concerns raised when patients seek to change same sex attractions. *Journal of Gay & Lesbian Psychotherapy, 5,* 181–210.

Ekins, R. (2005). Science, politics and clinical intervention: Harry Benjamin, transsexualism and the problem of heteronormativity. *Sexualities, 8*(3), 306–328.

Ellis, H. (1940). Sexual inversion. In H. Ellis, *Studies in the psychology of sex* (Vol. 1, pp. 1–391). New York: Random House. (Reprinted from *Sexual inversion,* pp. 1–391, by H. Ellis, 1897. London: The University Press.)

Fairfax, J. E. (2006). *A brief history of Tri-Ess.* Retrieved February 23, 2007, from http://www.tri-ess.org/ history.html

Feinberg, L. (1996). *Transgender warrior.* Boston: Beacon Press.

Ford, J. (2000). Jeffrey Ford. In *Finally free: Personal stories: How love and self-acceptance saved us from "ex-gay" ministries* (pp. 8–9). Washington, DC: Human Rights Campaign Foundation. Retrieved March 9, 2005, from http://www.hrc.org/Content/ ContentGroups/Publications1/Finally_Free/ FinallyFREE.pdf

Freud, S. (1905). Three essays on the theory of sexuality. In J. Strachey (Ed. & Trans.), *The standard edition of the complete psychological works of Sigmund Freud* (Vol. 7, pp. 123–245). London: Hogarth Press. (Original work published 1905.)

Gonsiorek, J. C. (2004). Reflections from the conversion therapy battlefield. *Counseling Psychologist, 32*(5), 750–759.

Haldeman, D. C. (2003). The practice and ethics of sexual orientation conversion therapy. In L. D. Garnets & D. C. Kimmel (Eds.), *Psychological perspectives on lesbian, gay and bisexual experiences* (pp. 681–698). New York: Columbia University Press.

Haldeman, D. C. (2004). When sexual and religious orientations collide: Considerations in working with conflicted same-sex attracted male clients. *Counseling Psychologist, 32*(5), 691–715.

Halpert, S. (2000). "If it ain't broke, don't fix it": Ethical considerations regarding conversion therapies. *International Journal of Sexuality & Gender Studies, 53*(1), 19–35.

Hendricks, M. (1993). Is it a boy or a girl? *Johns Hopkins Magazine, 45*(5), 10.

Hermann, M. A., & Herlihy, B. R. (2006). Legal and ethical implications of refusing to counsel homosexual clients. *Journal of Counseling & Development, 84*(4), 414–418.

Hooker, E. (1957). The adjustment of the male overt homosexual. *Journal of Projective Techniques, 21,* 18–31.

Intersex Society of North America (1993–2008). Our Mission. Retrieved March 15, 2006 from http:// www.isna.org

James, S. M., & Robertson, C. C. (Eds.). (2002). *Genital cutting and transnational sisterhood: Disputing U.S. polemics.* Champaign: University of Illinois Press.

Jones, S. L., & Yarhouse, M. A. (2007). *Ex-gays? A longitudinal study of religiously mediated change in sexual orientation.* Downers Grove, IL: Intervarity Press.

Katz, J. (1976). *Gay American history: Lesbians and gay men in the U.S.A.: A documentary.* New York: Cromwell.

Kinsey, A. C., Pomeroy, W. B., & Martin, C. E. (1948). *Sexual behavior in the human male.* Philadelphia: Saunders.

Krafft-Ebing, R. v. (1893). *Psychopathia sexualis, with especial reference to contrary sexual instinct: A medico-legal study.* Philadelphia: F. A. Davis.

LeVay, S. (1996). *Queer science: The use and abuse of research into homosexuality.* Cambridge, MA: MIT Press.

Lombardi, E., & Davis, S. M. (2006). Transgender health issues. In D. F. Morrow & L. Messinger

(Eds.), *Sexual orientation and gender expression in social work practice* (pp. 343–363). New York: Columbia University Press.

Luo, M. (2007, February 12). Some tormented by homosexuality look to a controversial therapy [Electronic version]. *The New York Times.* Retrieved February 12, 2007, from http://www.nytimes.com/2007/02/12/nyregion/12group.html?ei=5070&en=1829a43bcd5c

Martin, J. I., & Yonkin, D. R. (2006). Transgender identity. In D. F. Morrow & L. Messinger (Eds.), *Sexual orientation and gender expression in social work practice* (pp. 105–128). New York: Columbia University Press.

Meyer, J. K., & Reter, D. (1979). Sex reassignment: Follow-up. *Archives of General Psychiatry, 36(9),* 1010–1015.

Meyer, W., Bockting, W., Cohen-Kettenis, P., Coleman, E., DiCeglie, D., Devor, H., et al. (2001). The standards of care for gender identity disorders, sixth version [Electronic version]. *International Journal of Transgenderism, 5,* 1. Retrieved May 1, 2004, from www.symposion.com/ijt/soc_.05.htm

Meyerowitz, J. (2002). *How sex changed: A history of transsexuality.* Cambridge, MA: Harvard University Press.

Miller, N. (1995). *Out of the past: Gay and lesbian history from 1869 to the present.* New York: Vintage Books.

Morrow, S., & Beckstead, A. L. (2004). Conversion therapies for same-sex attracted clients in religious conflict: Context, predisposing factors, experiences and implications for therapy. *Counseling Psychologist, 32(5),* 641–650.

Murphy, T. F. (1992). Redirecting sexual orientation: Techniques and justifications. *Journal of Sex Research, 29(4),* 501–523.

National Association for Research and Therapy of Homosexuality. (2006). *Our purpose: Defending true diversity.* Retrieved March 1, 2007, from http://www.narth.com/menus/statement.html

National Association of Social Workers. (1996). *NASW code of ethics.* Washington, DC: Author.

National Committee on Lesbian, Gay, and Bisexual Issues. (2000). *"Reparative" and "conversion" therapies for lesbians and gay men.* Washington, DC: National Association of Social Workers.

Newman, B. (2004, September). *Change of heart: "My two years in reparative therapy."* Retrieved March 11, 2005, from http://www.narth.com/docs/ben.html

Nicolosi, J. (1991). *Reparative therapy of male homosexuality.* Northvale, NJ: Jason Aronson.

Nicolosi, J., (1993). *Healing homosexuality: Case stories of reparative therapy.* Northvale, NJ: Jason Aronson.

Nicolosi, J., Byrd, A. D., & Potts, R. W. (2000). Retrospective self-reports of changes in homosexual orientation: A consumer survey of conversion therapy clients. *Psychological Reports, 86,* 1071–1088.

Ponticelli, C. M. (1999). Crafting stories of identity reconstruction. *Social Psychology Quarterly, 62,* 157–172.

Rado, S. (1940). A critical examination of bisexuality. *Psychosomatic Medicine, 2,* 459–467.

Raj, R. (2002). Towards a transpositive therapeutic model: Developing clinical sensitivity and cultural competence in the effective support of transsexual and transgendered clients [Electronic version]. *International Journal of Transgenderism, 6,* 2. Retrieved June 22, 2005, from http://www.symposion.com/ijt/ijtvo06no02_04.htm

Rekers, G. A. (1992). Development of problems of puberty and sex roles in adolescence. In C. E. Walker & M. C. Roberts (Eds.), *Handbook of clinical child psychology* (2nd ed., pp. 607–622). Oxford, England: Wiley.

Rekers, G. A. (1995). *Handbook of child and adolescent sexual problems.* New York: Lexington Books.

Rekers, G. A., & Lovass, O. I. (1974). Behavioral treatment of deviant sex-role behaviors in a male child. *Journal of Applied Behavior Analysis, 7(2),* 173–190.

Rosario, V. A. (2004). Transforming sex: An interview with Joanne Meyerowitz, Ph.D., author of "How sex changed: A history of transsexuality in the United States." *Studies in Gender & Sexuality, 5(4),* 473–483.

Rosik, C. H. (2003). Motivational, ethical, and epistemological foundations in the treatment of unwanted homoerotic attraction. *Journal of Marital & Family Therapy, 29(1),* 13–28.

Sansweet, S. J. (1975). *The punishment cure.* Oxford, England: Mason Charter.

Schaeffer, K. W., Hyde, R. A., Kroencke, T., McCormick, B., & Nottebaum, L. (2000). Religiously-motivated sexual orientation change. *Journal of Psychology & Christianity, 19(1),* 61–70.

Schneider, M. S., Brown, L. S., & Glassgold, J. M. (2002). Implementing the resolution appropriate therapeutic responses to sexual orientation: A guide for the perplexed. *Professional Psychology: Research & Practice, 33,* 265–276.

Seil, D. (2004). The diagnosis and treatment of transgendered patients. *Journal of Gay & Lesbian Psychotherapy, 8(1/2),* 99–116.

Selditch, M. (Director). (2002). *Fixing Frank* [Motion picture]. United States: Maximum Vacuum.

Shidlo, A., & Schroeder, M. (2002). Changing sexual orientation: A consumer's report. *Professional Psychology: Research & Practice, 33(3)*, 249–259.

Shidlo, A., & Schroeder, M. (2001, November). Attempts to change homosexual orientation: Iatrogenic effects of conversion therapies. Paper presented at the annual meeting of the Association for Advancement of Behavioral Therapy, Philadelphia, PA.

Spade, D. (2006). Mutilating gender. In S. Stryker & S. Whittle (Eds.), *The transgender studies reader* (pp. 315–332). New York: Routledge.

Spitzer, R. J. (2003). Can some gay men and lesbians change their sexual orientation? 200 participants reporting a change from homosexual to heterosexual orientation. *Archives of Sexual Behavior, 32(5)*, 403–417.

Stoller, R. (1967). Etiological factors in male transsexualism. *Transactions of the New York Academy of Sciences, 29(4)*, 431–433.

Throckmorton, W. (1998). Efforts to modify sexual orientation: A review of outcome literature and ethical issues. *Journal of Mental Health Counseling, 20(4)*, 283–304.

Throckmorton, W. (2002). Initial empirical and clinical findings concerning the change process for ex-gays. *Professional Psychology: Research & Practice, 33(3)*, 242–247.

Tozer, E. E., & Hayes, J. A. (2004). Why do individuals seek conversion therapy? The role of religiosity, internalized homonegativity, and identity development. *Counseling Psychologist, 32(5)*, 716–740.

Tozer, E. E., & McClanahan, M. K. (1999). Treating the purple menace: Ethical considerations of conversion therapy and affirmative alternatives. *Counseling Psychologist, 27*, 722–742.

Yarhouse, M. A. (1998). When clients seek treatment for same-sex attraction: Ethical issues in the "right to choose" debate. *Psychotherapy, 35(2)*, 248–259.

Zucker, K. J. (2003). The politics and science of "reparative therapy." *Archives of Sexual Behavior, 32(5)*, 399–402.

Zucker, K. J. (2005). Measurement of psychosexual differentiation. *Archives of Sexual Behavior, 34(4)*, 375–388.

CHAPTER 3

Sexual/Gender Prejudice: Managing Stigma, Treating Trauma, and Healing Shame

INTRODUCTION

Leslie Feinberg is a transgender author and activist for the rights of gender minority persons. Feinberg, who was born a biological female, began taking male hormones but chose not to have genital surgery. Feinberg adapted the term *hir* (pronounced "here") as a form of self-description because it combines the pronouns *his* and *her*. In the following excerpt from hir text *Trans Liberation* (1998), Feinberg recounted hir harrowing personal experience in the emergency room of a hospital:

> From December 1995 to December 1996, I was dying of endocarditis—a bacterial infection that lodges and proliferates in the valves of the heart. One night my lover and I arrived in a hospital emergency room during a snowstorm. My fever was 104 degrees and rising. My blood pressure was pounding dangerously high. The staff immediately hooked me up to monitors and worked to bring down my fever. The doctor in charge began physically examining me. When he determined that my anatomy was female, he flashed me a mean-spirited smirk. While keeping his eyes fixed on me, he approached one of the nurses and began rubbing her neck and shoulder. He told me to get dressed and then he stormed out of the room. When the doctor returned after I was dressed, he ordered me to leave the hospital and never return. I refused until he could tell me why my fever was so high. He said, "You have a fever because you are a very troubled person." (pp. 1–2)

Feinberg wrote about hir experiences in order to raise our awareness of the hate that is often levied against gender minority persons and to promote greater sensitivity on the part of medical and psychiatric professionals regarding transgender health issues. Feinberg's personal experiences are indicative of the pervasive discrimination that exists in our culture toward gender minorities. They are also illustrative of what can happen when the alignments among sex, gender identity, and sexuality are disrupted, when physical appearance and demeanor do not match biological sex.

An anecdote in Chapter 1 described the effect a guest speaker named Joni had on a group of students. Joni, a preoperative male-to-female transsexual openly and frankly told her story, which caused confusion and a lot of curiosity among the students. Was she a lesbian? Would she like men? What was her life like? Well, Joni was extremely active in the gay, lesbian, bisexual, and transgender (GLBT) community; she volunteered at the local GLBT youth drop-in center and served as a role model and inspiration to many. Tragically, her body was discovered just outside her home. Her purse and its contents were intact, a can of mace still unused in her hand. Although a lengthy police investigation was conducted, her murder was never officially categorized by the investigators as a "hate crime," and her murder remains unsolved. Joni's death and the personal experiences of Leslie Feinberg are not infrequent occurrences among gender minorities. Indeed, the incidence of verbal and physical harassment, physical and sexual assaults, and murder are truly alarming (Carroll, Gilroy, & Ryan, 2002).

A Preview of Chapter Contents

Chapter 2 described the evolving nature of theories and treatment practices with sexual and gender minorities as well as current debates and controversies. In this chapter, the focus expands beyond treatment of sexual and gender minorities by helping professionals. It enters a broader cultural arena in order to study the psychology of prejudice toward sexual and gender minority persons. This chapter deals with some of the harsh realities the GLBT community faces:

- Hatred toward sexual and gender minorities is expressed not just through interpersonal relationships.
- Hatred is interwoven in cultural institutions and practices.
- Prejudice is enacted in subtle ways, from avoidance of eye contact to more blatant acts such as verbal harassment, bullying, and violent crimes against those who belong or are perceived to belong to sexual and gender minorities.

To come to grips with the depth and magnitude of such hatred, this chapter will also take an unvarnished look at the following:

- Terms associated with prejudice toward sexual and gender minorities;
- The attitudinal dimensions of prejudice toward sexual and gender minorities;
- The research findings regarding homo, bi, and transphobias;
- The behavioral dimensions of prejudice toward sexual and gender minorities and the empirical research findings;
- The psychological and behavioral consequences of victimization in sexual and gender minorities;
- The determinants of antisexual and gender prejudice and the research on perpetrators of hate crimes against sexual and gender minorities;

- A view of minority stress and the external and internal stressors that accompany the lives of sexual and gender minorities;
- The research findings regarding the psychological consequences of minority stress;
- The various coping strategies used to manage identities in the face of sexual/gender prejudice; and
- Counseling interventions and resources that are considered crucial for the recovery and ongoing survival of victims of hate crimes.

ATTITUDES TOWARD SEXUAL AND GENDER MINORITIES

Phobias

The attitudes toward sexual and gender minorities are evident in the following key terms.

HOMOPHOBIA   Homophobia has been widely adopted to refer to negative reactions toward persons who are gay or lesbian. In its most literal sense, homophobia refers to feelings of aversion toward homosexuality (Weinberg, 1972). Interestingly, many (e.g., Hoffman et al., 2000) take issue with the reference to phobia because this usually connotes a clinically significant fear and avoidance (American Psychiatric Association, *Diagnostic and Statistical Manual of Mental Disorders* or *DSM–IV–TR*, 2000). Yet, in many instances, homophobia is accompanied more by feelings of anger and aggressive behaviors than by fear (Haaga, 1991; Hoffman et al., 2000). Some recommend replacing the term *homophobia* with such alternatives as *homoprejudice* and *homonegativity*. Another closely related term, *heterosexism*, has also been used to describe the assumption that the only healthy and legitimate type of sexual and affectionate relationship is heterosexual (Pharr, 1988).

BIPHOBIA   Biphobia describes the denigration of bisexuality. Like gay men and lesbians, bisexual persons can provoke aversive reactions in others. Various hypotheses have been advanced to explain biphobia, including the notion that bisexual persons are threatening because they challenge the heterosexual/homosexual dichotomy (Ochs, 1996) and the cultural idealization of monogamy (McLean, 2004). Bisexual persons are commonly assumed to be incapable of monogamy, simply confused and in a transitional phase from heterosexuality to homosexuality, or repressed lesbians and gay men who are in denial about their homosexuality (Rust, 2002).

Bisexual persons have also been marginalized and rejected by gay men and lesbians who sometimes view bisexual persons as reverting to heterosexuality to avoid the hardships associated with being openly gay or lesbian (Rust, 2002). Some gay activists view bisexuality and the implication that sexuality is chosen as a threat to the argument that sexuality is inborn and unchangeable (Potoczniak, 2007). Rust (1996) asserts that cultural stereotypes affect bisexual men's and women's experiences, particularly in terms of finding and sustaining relationships. She writes that non-bisexual persons are often hesitant to form relationships with bisexuals and that averse attitudes towards bisexuals may have intensified as a result of the onset of AIDS (Rust, 1996, 2002).

TRANSPHOBIA   The cognitive map presented in Chapter 1 depicted the tenaciousness of the sex = gender equation. Negative emotions, thoughts, and behaviors can be easily provoked when someone's biological sexual and gender identities seem incongruent. Often this incongruence is not physically visible but is experienced internally and subjectively. Early on, many gender minority men articulated the experience as feeling trapped in the wrong body. The term *transphobia* is used (LaFramboise & Long, n.d.; Raj, 2002) to refer to prejudicial attitudes and behaviors directed toward persons who are or appear to be transitioning from their natal or biological sex to their internalized gender identity.

Transphobia can be expressed in a myriad of ways:

- The conviction that gender minority persons are "sick" or psychologically unstable;
- The insistence on referring to gender minorities in ways that are inconsistent with their self-presentation;
- The destructive behaviors, including violence, against transgender persons; and
- The insistence that persons who have hormonally and surgically transitioned are not "true" women/men.

Like bisexual persons, gender minority persons have been marginalized and sometimes rejected by gay and lesbian communities. Female-to-male transsexuals have been especially maligned by lesbians because of fears that these persons will reinforce cultural stereotypes about lesbians wanting to be men (Pearlman, 2006).

Researching These Attitudes

HOMOPHOBIC ATTITUDES   Recent empirical research has sought to identify variables, such as gender, race, ethnicity, political affiliation, and religion, that correlate most closely with homophobic attitudes. The results suggest that the majority of the American public holds negative attitudes toward sexual minorities (Herek, 2000). Further, they seem to converge in suggesting that persons who report negative attitudes toward gay men and lesbians are less educated (Herek & Capitanio, 1996), are religiously and politically conservative (Yang, 1997), are less likely to have close contact with persons who identify themselves as sexual minorities (Herek & Capitanio, 1996), and are more likely to be African Americans (Herek, 2000).

One consistent and compelling finding that emerges from surveys of attitudes toward homosexuality (i.e., Herek, 2002a; Whitley, 2001) is the association among homophobia, sex, and gender. In a meta-analysis of 112 studies, Kite and Whitley (1996) reported that heterosexual men held more negative attitudes toward homosexuality in general and toward gay men in particular than did heterosexual women. Studies in which male participants expressed hypermasculine identifications reported significantly more negative attitudes toward gay men (Davies, 2004; Herek, 2002b; Kite & Whitley, 1996; LaMar & Kite, 1998; Parrott, Adams, & Zeichner, 2002; Theodore & Basow, 2000).

BIPHOBIC ATTITUDES   In contrast to the research on attitudes toward gay men and lesbians, the literature exploring public attitudes toward bisexual men and women is scarce. This gap is not surprising, given the general sense of invisibility many bisexuals experience in our culture. Bisexual persons can potentially shift between gay/lesbian and heterosexual identities, depending on the sex of their partner (Weinberg, Williams, & Pryor, 1994). For example, when a bisexual man becomes romantically involved with a male partner, he is assumed by others to be gay and/or pressured to self-identify as gay. Alternately, should he become romantically involved with a female partner, he feels compelled to self-identify as heterosexual.

In one of the few studies to specifically address beliefs and attitudes toward bisexuality, Spalding and Peplau (1997) asked undergraduate students to read differing versions of vignettes in which the sexual orientations of the partners were randomly assigned. Participants believed that bisexual men and women were more apt to infect others with sexually transmitted diseases, to cheat, and to become bored with and leave their partners than were heterosexual men and women, gay men, or lesbians. More recently, Herek (2002a) reported that among his national sample of 1,335 adults, heterosexual men and women rated bisexuals less favorably than all other social groups except drug abusers.

Many of the variables identified as correlates of homophobia are similar to those connected to biphobia, including being religiously conservative and male (Israel & Mohr, 2004). Eliason (1997) reported that male heterosexual college students were less accepting of bisexual men than of lesbians, gay men, or bisexual women. Likewise, Mohr and Rochlen (1999) conducted extensive research among undergraduates to develop an instrument to assess attitudes toward bisexuality in men and women. In their series of studies, they found evidence that heterosexual men viewed male bisexuals as less moral and tolerable than female bisexuals and that attitudes regarding bisexuality correlated with religious attendance, conservative political ideology, and lack of personal contact with a bisexual person.

TRANSPHOBIC ATTITUDES   Although gender minorities have recently become more visible in our culture, largely through media portrayals (e.g., *Boys Don't Cry*, *The Crying Game*, *Midnight in the Garden of Good and Evil*, *Transamerica*), there has been remarkably little systematic research on the public's understanding of and opinions toward gender minorities. In 2002, the Human Rights Campaign, a national advocacy organization for GLBT persons, commissioned a separate polling group to conduct a national telephone survey of 800 registered voters (Mubarak, 2002). Once surveyors provided respondents with a definition of *transgender*, described as a "person who may do certain things so that their outward appearance fits who they feel they are on the inside" (p. 38), attitudes toward transgender persons became less favorable than without such a definition. Roughly 31% indicated they felt generally "unfavorable" toward transgender people.

In another published study, Ceglian and Lyons (2004) explored undergraduate students' attitudes toward a specific segment of the transgendered population, male crossdressers. The authors invited two heterosexually identified members of Tri-ess, a national organization for men who cross-dress, to come to their classes to speak about their cross-dressing experiences. Male undergraduates in their sample showed a sizeable increase in their acceptance of cross-dressing when assessments of their attitude before and after the classroom visits were compared. Interestingly, their post-visit ratings were similar to the women's scores. Ceglian and Lyons speculated that the dramatic increase in men's acceptance of cross-dressing behaviors might be attributed to the disclosure made in the context of the classroom visits that both cross-dressers were heterosexually married with children.

HARASSMENT AND VICTIMIZATION OF SEXUAL AND GENDER MINORITIES

Homo-, bi-, and transphobias are expressed in multiple ways, including teasing, namecalling, and other forms of verbal harassment; physical harassment; and sexual and physical assaults.

The most commonly reported type of antigay harassment is verbal in nature (Berrill, 1990). In their recent study of homophobic verbal harassment, Silverschanz, Cortina, Konik, and Magley (2008) surveyed over 3,000 college students, including sexual minorities and nonminorities. Of their sample, over 40% reported experiencing direct homophobic harassment (i.e., homophobic names, slurs, and personal remarks) or indirect harassment (i.e., offensive jokes, slurs about gay people in general) at least once within the past year.

Balsam, Rothblum, and Beauchaine (2005) surveyed over 1,000 heterosexual, gay, lesbian, and bisexual siblings to determine the lifetime prevalence of victimization. According to their findings, sexual orientation was a significant predictor of most types of victimization experiences, including sexual, physical, and abuse emotional in childhood and partner abuse in adulthood.

Hate-Related Violence Toward Sexual Minorities

Hate crimes are defined in the United States as physical assault, homicide or attempted homicide, harassment, and property damage on the basis of the victim's in-group status (Dunbar, 2001, 2006). Hate crimes laws generally provide a mechanism for the tracking and recording of violent crimes as well as the training of law enforcement personnel. The incidence of hate crimes targeted at sexual minorities is difficult to determine. Most are probably underreported due to the fact that many jurisdictions do not collect this data and many sexual minorities fear and distrust the police (Kuehnle & Sullivan, 2001; Swigonski, 2006). The incidence of hate crimes among bisexual men and women is particularly difficult to ascertain. In a number of cases, these crimes are categorized as "gay" because of false assumptions on the part of investigating police officers (Miller, Andre, Ebin, & Bessonova, 2007).

Herek, at the University of California at Davis, has been very active in studying hate-related violence against sexual minorities. Herek, Gillis, and Cogan (1999) explored victimization experiences, both hate related and unrelated, in a sample of 2,500 sexual minorities in the Sacramento area. Twenty-five percent of men and 20% of women reported being victimized because of their sexual orientation, and 40% of the men and 50% of the women reported experiencing crimes not associated with their sexual orientation. As might be anticipated, respondents were more likely to report their nonbiased crimes to the police than to report antigay hate crimes. Symptoms related to post-traumatic stress, including depression and anxiety, were more severe after experiencing antigay crimes than after nonbiased crimes.

Herek, Cogan, and Gillis (2002) interviewed 450 sexual minority victims of bias and nonbiased crimes. Most bias crimes could be classified as vandalism or as crimes that occurred in public settings and were perpetrated by multiple persons, predominantly male adolescents or young adults. Herek and his colleagues were interested in how victims make the determination that the crimes perpetrated against them are hate related. Based on the victims' narratives, they identified several categories of responses, including the use of explicit statements by the perpetrators, the occurrence of the crime in a gay and lesbian identified locale (i.e., gay bar), and other contextual cues and inferences made by victims.

Huebner, Rebchook, and Kegeles (2004) explored the incidence of harassment and violence among 1,248 gay and bisexual men in three major cities in the United States over a six-month period. In all, 37% reported experiencing antigay verbal harassment, and 4.8% reported physical violence.

In his analysis of 1,538 hate-related crimes reported in Los Angles during a two-year period, Dunbar (2006) reported that the frequency and severity of hate crimes were significant factors in reducing the probability that survivors would report their crimes to law enforcement. He also noted that sexual minorities with additional identity statuses, including race, ethnicity and sex, were at increased risk for victimization.

Hate-Related Violence Toward Gender Minorities

Gender minority persons are rendered invisible, and violent acts perpetrated against them are ignored, according to Namaste (2000). Hate-motivated violence directed at gender minorities is often misreported as a "gay" hate crime because people who dress or otherwise appear to be gender ambiguous are presumed to be gay or lesbian. Generally, there is a sense that hate-related incidents are vastly underreported, as many gender minorities lack trust in the police and fear being revictimized once their transgender status is made known to authorities (Hill, 2003). Federal hate crimes legislation does not require documentation of such incidents, and most cities do not have legislation to protect gender minorities. According to the National Center for Transgender Equality (2006), only 10 states have hate crimes laws that include gender minorities.

In one of the few published articles on the topic, Lombardi, Wilchins, Priesing, and Malouf (2001) reported on a World Wide Web–based survey conducted over a 12-month period. A total of 19.4% of their sample of 402 gender minorities reported having been physically assaulted, 17.4% reported having had objects thrown at them, and 10.2% reported having been assaulted with a weapon. Approximately 14% reported a rape or attempted rape at some time in their lives.

Kuehnle and Sullivan (2001) analyzed 241 incidents over a three-year period in a city located in the northeastern United States. They found that transgender persons were more likely than gay men or lesbians to sustain serious personal injuries, including those resulting in hospitalization and death, and were more likely to be victimized in their homes by an acquaintance. A recent survey of 182 transgender persons indicated that 51.3% had been physically abused and 53.8% had been forced to have sex (Kenagy, 2005). In a qualitative study of a transgender community in Canada, male-to-female transsexuals were especially vulnerable to sexual assault due to their lack of experience with sexual advances by biological males (Bockting, Robinson, & Rosser, 1998).

While statistics on crimes against gender minorities are grim, the personal stories of persons who have died as a result of hate are especially moving. The death of Brandon Teena, a female-to-male transgendered person, captured the headlines in 1993 and was later the focus of a popular film titled *Boys Don't Cry* (Peirce, 1999). Brandon was brutally raped and murdered after two male acquaintances discovered that he was biologically female. The death of Tyra Hunter, a transgendered woman who was left unattended by paramedics at the scene of a car accident after they opened her pants and discovered that she had a penis (Stine, as reported by Parlee, 1998), horrified and outraged many in the transgender community as well.

The Consequences of Hate Crimes

There is research evidence (i.e., Herek et al., 1999; Herek; Gillis, Cogan, & Glunt, 1997; McDevitt, Balboni, Garcia, & Gu, 2001; Recker, Dunbar, & Sullaway, 1998; Rose & Mechanic, 2002) to suggest that the psychological impact of hate crimes on sexual minorities lasts longer and is more devastating than the impact of similar, nonbiased crimes on the general population. For example, Herek et al. (1997) report that sexual minorities who experience hate crimes exhibit higher levels of depression, anxiety, and other symptoms of posttraumatic stress than do general crime survivors. Sexual minority survivors of hate crimes also report more negative beliefs about the world and about the benevolence of people (Herek et al., 1999).

For most sexual and gender minorities, the effects of victimization are more profound than for the general population because the victimization occurred as a result of the survivors' sexual or gender identity. As Garnets, Herek, and Levy (2003) asserted, victimization of sexual minorities often results in the "intensification of psychosocial problems associated with being gay or lesbian" and can also lead to a further "consolidation of the survivor's gay or lesbian identity and involvement with her or his community" (p. 201). Reactions such as self-blame, which most victims of violent crimes experience, are often exacerbated in sexual and gender minorities.

Determinants of Hate-Motivated Violence

Herek (1990) posits that violence toward sexual minorities is motivated by a desire on the part of perpetrators to

- Affirm personal values (labeled "value expressive").
- Fit in and attain approval from peers (labeled "social expressive").
- Reduce in an unconscious way the anxiety that may originate from the perpetrator's psychological conflict over the probability of being gay or lesbian (labeled "defensive").

Herek's hypothesis that homophobia serves as a defensive function for heterosexual men was supported in a study by Adams, Wright, and Lohr (1996). Adams et al. asked groups of men who were classified as either homophobic or nonhomophobic based on their scores on the Index of Homophobia (Hudson & Rickets, 1980) to view a series of sexually explicit videotapes of encounters between gay men. Both groups were first outfitted with penile plethysmography instruments that measured penile erection. The men who were classified in the homophobic group showed greater physical arousal when viewing the tapes that showed consensual sex between men than did the nonhomophobic men.

Franklin (1998, 2000), a psychologist, has also been interested in the motivations and backgrounds of those who perpetrate hate crimes against sexual minorities. In 2000, she circulated an anonymous survey to students at six community colleges in five counties in California to assess the frequency of various types of antigay behaviors ranging from spitting to hitting. In the sample, 23% reported calling homosexuals by insulting names. The majority of those who admitted verbal harassment were heterosexual men who reported a strong masculine identification. Based on her findings, Franklin identified four types of antigay perpetrators: (1) those who have strong antigay feelings, (2) those who are motivated by a desire to gain peer approval, (3) those who minimize the harm done to victims, and (4) those who perceive their actions as self-defense.

While there is little, if any, empirical research on the perpetrators of antitransgender harassment and violence, Hill (2003) argued that offenders' motivations are similar to those Herek (1990) noted in gay hate crime perpetrators. Hate crimes against gender minorities serve numerous functions, including the affirmation of values, the attainment of social approval from others, and defense against internal conflicts related to the gender identities of the perpetrators.

Gender Policing

Sexual and gender minorities threaten deeply embedded beliefs in our society. At the interpersonal level, gender conformity is regulated by a phenomenon referred to as *gender policing* (Gagne, Tewksbury, & McGaughey, 1997). Boyd (2007) summarizes this aptly when she observes: "When something isn't right with someone's gender, nothing could be more wrong or more important" (p. 33). Gender policing is a process through which social groups enact and reinforce compliance to traditional gender categories and hierarchies (Gagne, Tewksbury, & McGaughey, 1997).

Methods of policing range from subtle behaviors to deliberate acts of aggression. One form of gender policing is bullying, defined as repetitive negative behaviors such as making verbal threats, teasing, spreading rumors, and hitting in the context of relationships marked by inequities in power (Olweus, 1994; Poteat & Espelage, 2005). Bullying is a means by which young people often police masculine and feminine behaviors (Epstein, 2001). Witten and Eyler (1999) consider emotional, verbal, and physical acts of force as forms of *gender terrorism* and perceive these to be motivated by the desire to preserve a social system where the demarcation between the genders is rigidly maintained.

Evidence suggests our gender-policing practices that enforce cultural imperatives about gender and sexuality are harsher for boys and men (Bowers & Bieschke, 2005; Morrow, 2000; Poteat & Espelage, 2005). Fear of feminine attributes in men (O'Neil, 1981) and hatred of gay men (Herek & Capitanio, 1996; Kimmel & Mahler, 2003) are considered by many to be the cornerstones of masculinity in our culture. In childhood, boys are more apt than girls to be rejected by their parents and their peers for gender nonconformity (LaMar & Kite, 1998; Landolt, Bartholomew, Saffrey, Oram, & Perlman, 2004). Both boys and girls learn to use derogatory words to refer to boys who exhibit feminine-like behaviors, often without even knowing what such terms mean (Schiff, 2003). By the time boys reach high school, they learn that being called "girl" or "faggot" is absolutely the worst possible insult (Schiff, 2003).

In their analysis of the life experiences and backgrounds of boys who have committed school violence in the recent past, Kimmel and Mahler (2003) hypothesize that these boys were motivated, in part, by constant gay-baiting (being accused of being gay). They write:

> There is much at stake for boys and, as a result, they engage in a variety of evasive strategies to make sure that no one gets the wrong idea about them (and their manhood). These range from the seemingly comic (although telling), such as two young boys occupying three movie seats by placing their coats on the seat between them to the truly tragic, such as engaging in homophobic violence, bullying, menacing other boys, masochistic or sadistic games and rituals, excessive risk taking (drunk or aggressive driving), and even sexual predation. (p. 1446)

Kimmel and Mahler's assertion that violence is used to police expectations about gender and sexuality has been substantiated in studies of antigay hate crime perpetrators who were more likely to attack men whom they perceived to be gender nonconforming.

Gay men also devalue feminine attributes in themselves and other men despite the fact that gay culture has celebrated drag queen performances and other forms of gender nonconformity. Gay men who experience conflict about their gender roles report higher levels of anxiety, depression, and anger (Simonsen, Blazina, & Watkins, 2000) and lower self-esteem (Szymanski & Carr, 2008).

Taywaditep (2001) describes the rejection of feminine characteristics as *anti-effeminacy prejudice* and maintains that this is common among gay men. He cites research in which Bailey and Zucker (1995) found that a significant majority of gay men exhibit feminine traits during childhood. Taywaditep (2001) argues that beginning in adolescence, gay males make deliberate efforts to defeminize themselves. He supports his thesis about the existence of anti-effeminacy prejudice in gay men with evidence from several studies, including Bailey, Kim, Hills, and Linsenmeier's (1997) analysis of gay men's personal advertisements. These routinely show that effeminacy is considered undesirable in gay men's partnerships. Gay men report a stronger desire to conform to a masculine ideal. For them, being both muscular and thin is more important than it is with heterosexual men. Perhaps as a consequence, gay men have more eating disorders (Kaminski, Chapman, Haynes, & Own, 2005; Martins, Tiggemann, & Kirkbride, 2007). Gay men who develop more traditional masculine self-images have significantly higher levels of self-esteem (Harry, 1983).

MINORITY STRESS IN SEXUAL AND GENDER MINORITIES

Consider the following scenario: A 34-year-old lesbian, Ann, has been employed in a small advertising firm for approximately two years. It is Monday morning and her co-workers are chatting during an impromptu coffee break about their weekend activities. Ann is still reeling from the romantic weekend she had with the woman she has dated for the past six months. She wants to share her news with her co-workers. She is on the verge of disclosing but suddenly asks herself: Should she reveal herself to her colleagues, or should she disguise the nature of her relationship by using a fictional man's name? By the time she resolves her dilemma, the group begins to dissolve, and her co-workers return to their desks. Perhaps this scenario seems trivial. Yet, if one looks at the cumulative impact of daily self-monitoring, censorship, and "little white lies," it requires a lot of energy and causes a great deal of stress.

In 1981, Brooks introduced the term *minority stress* to describe the emotional and physical consequences of being a minority person, living in a world of social prejudice and discrimination. Subsequently, several researchers (Lewis, Derlega, Berndt, Morris, & Rose, 2001; Meyer, 1995, 2003) applied Brooks's concept of minority stress to sexual and gender minorities. These researchers differentiate between externally based stressors, which result from discrimination such as verbal and physical harassment, and internally based stressors. Externally based gay-related stressors are experiences that are considered to be unique to sexual and gender minorities. These differ from the general stress of everyday life. Internally based stressors originate from the internalization of society's negative messages about homosexuality and gender nonconformity.

Minority Stress

Meyer (1995) posits that the consequences of minority stress can be modulated by several factors, including

- The degree to which sexual minorities deal with the expectation of possible discrimination and prejudice,

- The degree to which such persons conceal their same-sex sexual orientation from others, and
- The internalization of negative social attitudes toward sexual minorities.

DiPlacido (1998) observed, for example, that sexual minorities who are "out" are more vulnerable to the stress of social rejection, discrimination, and violence. Yet, while sexual and gender minorities who are "open" about their nontraditional statuses are at risk of social rejection, discrimination, and violence (DiPlacido, 1998), those who are "closeted" are also vulnerable to stress.

Research has identified some of the specific psychosocial stressors that are unique to sexual minorities. In a series of focus groups, Morris, Lewis, and Derlega (1993) asked their participants to identify possible stressors associated with being gay, lesbian, or bisexual. The summarized responses of group members subsequently served as items on a questionnaire administered to an additional sample of over seven hundred sexual minorities. The results of the questionnaires were, in turn, subjected to a factor analysis. The 10 factors or subscales that emerged from this analysis included such stressors as workplace discrimination, disclosing one's sexual orientation to family members, introducing one's partner to family members, visibility in public, and the threat of harassment and violence.

In their subsequent research, Lewis et al. (2001) administered this subscale to 557 gay and bisexual men and 421 lesbians and bisexual women. As the researchers anticipated, gay men reported more stress related to HIV/AIDS and harassment/violence, and lesbians reported more stress over family reactions to one's partner. In additional samples (Lewis, Derlega, Griffin, & Krowinski, 2003), gay-related stress was shown to be a predictor of depressive symptoms in gay men and lesbians.

The impact of minority stress is also compounded in sexual minority persons of color. While minority stress in persons of color will be explored in more depth in Chapter 5, it is important to emphasize that persons of color and those with disabilities who possess "double" and "triple" minority statuses have incrementally more to juggle, especially when membership in these multiple identity groups is a source of conflict (Harper & Schneider, 2003). Persons who are bisexual also experience unique pressures. They are pressured to adopt a lesbian or gay identity when their romantic partners are the same sex and pushed to adopt a non-bisexual identity when their partners are of a different biological sex. Bisexual persons are rendered invisible and socially isolated, and they lack role models (Dodge & Sandfort, 2007; Firestein, 2007; Potocznick, 2007). In a study by Page (2004), 27% of bisexual women and 46% of bisexual men reported that being bisexual was "quite difficult" or "the hardest thing in life."

Comparatively less research has attempted to identify particular psychosocial stressors associated with the experiences of gender minorities. Several authors have noted the pervasive nature of employment, housing, medical, and social service discrimination (Gagne, Tewksbury, & McGaughey, 1998; Nuttbrock, Rosenblum, & Blumenstein, 2002) against gender minorities. Of particular note is the extent to which transgender persons experience discriminatory hiring practices and workplace harassment (Felsenthal, 2004; Gagne et al., 1998).

In a qualitative study of male-to-female transsexual persons, Schrock, Reid, and Boyd (2005) noted their interviewees experienced a number of unique externally mediated stressors—namely, shunning by friends and family members and shaming by uncaring therapists. As is true of sexual minorities, minority stress is mediated by the degree to which transgender persons are "open" about their nontraditional gender status and the extent to which their gender nonconformity is visible to others.

Those gender minorities who want to reconfigure their bodies—typically, transsexuals—are exposed to differing stressors, depending on whether their transition is from male to female or female to male. It has been observed that the process of transitioning from male to female is more "work intensive" than female-to-male transitions (Rubin, 2003). Evidence obtained from Schrock et al.'s interviews lent support for this conclusion, as their participants described what they termed "arduous" efforts to modify their bodily movements and speech, establish different dressing patterns, and reconfigure their bodies through expensive and painful electrolysis and cosmetic and genital surgeries. Simple tasks such as learning how to pick up a fork or smoke a cigarette had to be relearned. Cole, Denny, Eyler, and Samons (2000) also note that male-to-female transsexuals typically experience a drop in social status and earning power after transitioning.

In a series of interviews of transgendered persons in Canada, Namaste (2000) reported a number of psychosocial stressors among her sample, including (1) police officers who refuse to take reports of sexual assault from transsexual and transgender prostitutes; (2) physicians who refuse to treat transgender persons whose desired gender does not fit their body type; (3) refusal to admit transgender persons into homeless shelters; and (4) refusal of health care and social services, especially among transgendered prostitutes.

Mental Health Consequences of Minority Stress for Sexual and Gender Minorities

Research has begun to explore the psychological and physical health consequences of minority stress for sexual minorities. Beginning in the mid-1990s, a series of health-related studies was undertaken in the general population. This research was impacted by the need to assess same-sex sexual behavior and risk factors associated with HIV transmission. Questions that specifically addressed sexual behavior provided a serendipitous means of making comparisons between groups. These studies have shown that sexual minorities are at risk for certain stress-related disorders such as depression, anxiety, and substance abuse (Cochran, Sullivan, & Mays, 2003). Sexual minorities are also more likely to utilize mental health services more often than are nonsexual minorities (Cochran, 2001; Cochran & Mays, 2000).

Accessing data from the national survey in 1995 entitled the MacArthur Foundation National Survey of Midlife Development in the United States (MIDUS), Mays and Cochran (2001) reviewed the responses of approximately three thousand adults. In this population-based sample, participants were interviewed by telephone about their day-to-day life experiences and mental health symptoms. Structured interviews were used to assess depression and anxiety disorders. Results indicated that lesbians, gay men, and bisexual men and women do report more day-to-day occurrences of discrimination than do heterosexuals. But they also showed a "robust" association between discriminatory experiences and psychiatric disorders. They concluded: "It is possible that widespread and pernicious experiences with discrimination lie at the heart of the somewhat greater prevalence of psychiatric morbidity among lesbians and gay men found in recent studies" (p. 1874).

STIGMA CONSCIOUSNESS AND INTERNALIZED HOMO-, BI-, AND TRANSPHOBIAS

Pinel (1999) introduced the concept of *stigma consciousness* to refer to minority persons' anticipation that other people will stereotype them as a result of their minority status. In his research, Pinel found that those with a high degree of stigma consciousness tended to worry more about others' perceptions. Goffman (1963) theorized that in stigmatized groups, the stigmatized attribute, whatever its nature, overshadowed all other aspects of the person and became the single most important and defining characteristic of that person.

Prior research has demonstrated that sexual minorities who have a greater expectation of discrimination and prejudice—who have a higher degree of stigma consciousness—experience correspondingly greater psychological distress (Lewis, Derlega, Clarke, & Kuang, 2006; Lewis et al., 2003). Haldeman (2001) wrote about this phenomenon in gay men and lesbians and coined the term *heterophobia* to refer to the "belief that the dominant heterosexual culture is hostile" (p. 809).

Internalized Homophobia

While Weinberg (1972) was the first to introduce the term *internalized homophobia*, psychologists Allport (1954) and Goffman (1963) had written earlier about the effects of stigmatization. For example, Goffman (1963) wrote extensively about the nature of stigma and defined this as a characteristic or attribute that is devalued and later becomes the basis for shame. Allport (1954) referred to "traits due to victimization" such as social withdrawal, insecurity, personal denial, and self-hatred. Therefore, internalized homophobia generally refers to negative beliefs that exist in the broader social context and that are absorbed by sexual minorities about their identities. These beliefs and associated feelings range from a strong sense of being different to self-loathing (Gonsiorek, 1993; Plummer, 1995; Williamson, 2000).

Several authors (e.g., Cohler & Galatzer-Levy, 2000) have written about the central role that shame plays in the lives of sexual minorities: "Shame is perhaps the most powerful feeling state associated with the experience of a conflicted and socially disvalued identity such as being gay or lesbian" (Cohler & Galatzer-Levy, 2000, p. 265).

Research has explored the negative impacts of internalized homophobia on gay men and lesbians. These have included higher sexual anxiety and guilt (Rowen & Malcolm, 2002), concern about sexual image (Dupras, 1994), and greater HIV-related sexual risk-taking (Huebner, Davis, Nemeroff, & Aiken, 2002; Meyer & Dean, 1998) in gay men and bisexual men. Internalized homophobia has been correlated with lower self-esteem (Allen & Oleson, 1999; Rowen & Malcolm, 2002; Szymanski, Chung, & Balsam, 2001) and greater depressive symptoms (Meyer & Dean, 1998; Shidlo, 1994) in gay men and lesbians.

Internalized Biphobia

The introjection of negative stereotypes about bisexual people, known as *internalized biphobia*, has been related to lower levels of well-being and greater stress in bisexual persons (Bronn, 2001). Ochs (1996) wrote about the struggles of bisexual men who feel they must identify with either the straight or the gay/lesbian community, depending on the sexual orientation of their partners.

Internalized Transphobia

Most of the literature on the concept of *internalized transphobia* is based on retrospective personal accounts of the experiences of gender minorities (Gagne et al., 1997) and clinical observations (Anderson, 1998). In a series of qualitative interviews with male-to-female transgender persons, Gagne et al. noted that the pervasive coping strategy many of the interviewees used in the face of this self-loathing was to develop hypermasculine traits and assume occupations that were traditionally masculine like military service. There is also some evidence that gender minorities are vulnerable to eating disorders because of the prevalence of body dissatisfaction and desire to refashion their bodies, often according to cultural ideals of masculine and feminine (Korell & Lorah, 2007).

Stigma Management Strategies in Sexual and Gender Minorities

Social psychologists have long been interested in how people cope with being stigmatized and have provided us with some interesting and useful insights. Goffman (1963) was especially intrigued with the ways that stigmatized people interact with others in order to avoid being shamed or embarrassed. Allport (1954) was also intrigued by this and proposed that those who are stigmatized develop a sense of vigilance as a defensive strategy. This vigilance or sense of hyperawareness may lead to deception, manipulation, and the wearing of a mask in order to hide the traits that others may judge.

Recently, researchers have also begun to explore the cognitive and behavioral coping mechanisms that sexual and gender minorities use to manage their stigmatized identities. Perhaps not surprisingly, like Allport, most see this as a process that requires attentiveness to environmental cues. Because their source of stigmatization may sometimes be invisible and discreditable, sexual and gender minorities are engaged in a stigma management process that is both complex and ongoing.

"Coming Out" Versus "Being Out" in Sexual Minorities

"Coming out" and "being out" are both evolutionary processes. The first refers to the process of coming to accept one's sexual orientation, whereas "being out" refers to the process of revealing oneself to others as a sexual minority person. The term *coming out* has been used in gay culture to denote a largely internal process of identity formation in which persons move from self-labeling to self-acceptance. In the past, the "coming out" process has been the subject of extensive theorizing and investigation. Several descriptive stage models have detailed the development of homosexual identities (i.e., Cass, 1979; Coleman, 1982). These have appeared extensively in the counseling literature and will be briefly reviewed in a later chapter. Rust (2002) argued from a social constructionist point of view that, while these models seem to resonate with many sexual minorities, they tend to cast bisexuality as a less mature identity and to overlook the fact that "coming out" is a lifelong process. Other limitations of these stage models are the tendencies to assume that there is a final stage of identity and that identity is a static achievement rather than a fluid process. As Rust (2003) indicates:

> Linear models of coming out, both those codified in scientific literature and the popular versions on which these scientific models are based, provide insight into coming out, as it is experienced by some individuals. But they also lend a

moral quality to the process of coming out by casting it as a developmental process leading toward certain forms of sexual identity, thereby privileging these sexual identities over others. In so doing they blind us to the legitimacy of other sexual identities, to the possibility that refusing to adopt a sexual identity might be a healthy choice, and to the reality that for many people, coming out is a lifelong process of recurrent self-creation and self-discovery, not a singular goal oriented process of self-classification. (p. 262)

Chapter 6 takes a more in-depth look at identity models.

In contrast to the concept of "coming out," which describes the singular experience of self-revelation, "being out" refers to an ongoing process of revealing one's sexual minority status to others (Harry, 1993). Harry described this as a complex and continuous decision-making process entailing assessment of the risks inherent in particular situations and of the particular audience for self-disclosure.

It is important to remember that "being out" is not a dichotomous experience; it is a multidimensional and complex process. It can also entail the use of behavioral expressions like wearing a rainbow pin on one's lapel or driving a car with a rainbow sticker affixed to the car's bumper rather than strictly verbal disclosures like "I am gay/lesbian/bisexual/transgender" (Carroll & Gilroy, 2000).

Stigma Management Strategies and Sexual Minorities

The process of managing one's stigmatized identity, also termed *stigma management*, is complex for sexual minorities. If they tell others about their sexual orientation, they run the risk of being charged with "flaunting" their sexuality; after all, heterosexuals do not make such proclamations about their identities. Alternatively, choosing to withhold such information may lead to isolation and loneliness.

Researchers have found that sexual minorities use a broad variety of behavioral strategies in order to manage their identities. These strategies entail elements of concealment and self-disclosure (Cain, 1991) and include censoring oneself, actively preventing others from acquiring personal information, and supplying false information about oneself (Herek, 2003; Zerubavel, 1982). This process often involves performing an internal cost–benefit analysis in which "lesbians, gay man, and bisexuals must constantly decide whether or not to tell, whom to tell, and when to tell" (DiPlacido, 1998, p. 149).

De Monteflores (1986) was interested in the types of behavioral strategies that sexual minorities use to cope with social prejudice. The first of these was termed *assimilation* to refer to "passing" or acting straight so as to escape detection. This requires continual vigilance, accommodation, and fragmentation. A second behavior was termed *ghettoization* and referred to removal of oneself from contexts that are heterosexual. The last of De Monteflores's strategies, *confrontation*, encompassed existence in both heterosexual and gay cultures, with the ability to "be out" in contexts that are not necessarily open and accepting. In their discussion of sexual identity management in employment settings, Chrobot-Mason, Button, and DiClementi (2001) identified behavioral strategies similar to those proposed by De Monteflores such as *avoidance* (eluding personal questions and talking in generalities about one's personal life), *counterfeiting* (altering gender-specific pronouns, fabricating stories about dates or relationships), and *integration* (revealing one's true identity and managing the consequences of this disclosure).

Regardless of the type of coping responses sexual minorities use to manage their identities in a heterosexist context, "constant self-monitoring and vigilance over safety consume a fair amount of psychological energy" (Fukuyama & Ferguson, 2000, p. 99).

Stigma Management Strategies and Gender Minorities

Gender minorities experience similarities to as well as differences from sexual minorities in terms of managing their identities (Gagne et al., 1997). Many sexual minorities have the option of concealing their identities from others, while many gender minorities cannot conceal their identities from others, often because their gender nonconformity is visible to others.

As is true with sexual minorities, gender minorities' stress is mediated by the extent to which their gender nonconformity is visible to others. Gender minorities who want to transition or move to change physical aspects of their bodies are generally more vulnerable to discrimination and to acts of violence. This vulnerability severely limits their ability to go out in public (Felsenthal, 2004). In their qualitative interviews with gender minorities, Gagne et al. (1997) noted the extent to which their sample feared entering public spaces and developed distinct survival strategies for going out into public arenas. For example, many often started very slowly, initially going to public places that were perceived to be "safe zones," like gay bars.

Gender minorities must make the same cost–benefit analysis that sexual minorities do in terms of disclosing their identities. Often they must sift through friendship networks in order to determine whom to avoid and from whom to seek support (Nuttbrock et al., 2002). As Gagne et al. (1997) point out, cross-dressers and gender radicals have greater control over the self-disclosure process than do male-to-female transsexual persons, primarily because the former, as a group, are more limited in their need and desire to publicly enact their feminine selves.

Gender minorities often use the term *woodworking* to describe "blending into the woodwork" as their desired gender (Boyd, 2007). Alternately, *passing* is defined as "presenting clearly as one gender, erasing any trace of multiple or conflicting genders, and avoiding confrontation" (Hill, 2003, p. 125). The intent among many gender minorities is to be able—with the aid of hormones, electrolysis, plastic surgery, voice therapy, and other surgical interventions—to successfully present themselves as their desired gender without detection. For many, once the transition process is complete, they want to be identified in terms of their new gender. In a sense, once the transition process is complete, many become "invisible" as gender minorities. Hill (2003) likens this to the sense of invisibility that many bisexual persons experience.

Sometimes despite their intentions, gender minorities are "read" or identified by others. Perhaps they make conscious decisions to identify outside the gender binary as gender variants, or the medical procedures are too costly and painful, and/or their basic body type makes their attempt to transition more noticeable to others. In the past decade, many transgender activists (e.g., Feinberg, 1998) have advocated that transsexuals and other gender minority persons "come out" and identify themselves as transgendered. In our current era, the focus has shifted from using surgical and hormonal interventions to enable gender minorities to "pass" to affirming the unique identities of transgendered persons. Gagne et al. (1997) observed that despite the emerging trend among some gender minorities to

BOX 3.1

Anecdote from the Field

Many years ago, working as a psychologist in a private practice, I was assigned a male client in his midthirties. He worked in a midlevel management position. He came to therapy seeking assistance with what he termed his difficulties managing "stress." He was socially awkward and emotionally reserved. I experienced difficulty in establishing a rapport with him and getting him to open up about himself. I discussed this predicament at length in clinical supervision. I felt stuck.

One Friday evening about six weeks after beginning therapy with this client, I impulsively decided to stop at the grocery store on my way home from work. As I was walking down a grocery aisle, I noted a shopper walking toward me from the opposite direction. As we passed one another, our eyes met. Something about this person seemed familiar. This was a fashionably attired, meticulously groomed woman with brown shoulder-length hair. In the next instant, I realized that she was my client. While I had received input from my professors and clinical supervisors about how to handle seeing clients in social contexts outside the therapy office, I felt totally unprepared for what had happened. How should I deal with seeing my male client out in public in women's clothing?

At work the following week, I wondered about the implications of seeing my client. I could understand why he seemed so stiff and uncomfortable. This surely was the secret he was protecting. On the plus side, I thought seeing him might provide the basis for a therapeutic breakthrough. As I talked with my supervisor that week, I decided I would wait to see if my client would mention our accidental meeting first. Several minutes passed without mention of the incident, and I decided to broach the topic. I said I thought I had recognized him in the grocery store on Friday evening. In monotone expression, he denied having seen me. He left my office that day, and I never saw him again.

What are your reactions after reading about this incident? How might you have handled this situation? Would you have spoken to him/her in the store? Would you have waited for the client to bring up the incident?

seek free gender expression outside of the gender binary, there are a number of formidable obstacles in doing so:

> To challenge the binary, individuals must overcome a number of interactional, organizational, and structural barriers. They must learn to live and find ways to cope with the discomfort and hostility that others express at not being able to categorize them within an existing gender category. They must find ways to establish themselves as legal and social actors within institutions that recognize only two sexes and two congruent genders. Given these pressures, it is understandable why most transgendered individuals come out quickly and cross over to the "other gender" category. (p. 504)

COUNSELING SEXUAL AND GENDER MINORITIES

Helping professionals need to be responsive to the sense of vulnerability that can result from living at risk of experiencing multiple forms of antigay, antibisexual, or antitransgender harassment and violence. Practitioners need to be aware that the most common forms of antigay harassment are verbal in nature (Berrill, 1990) and that the impact of these behaviors tends to be minimized over and against that of physical assault (Garnets et al., 2003).

Explore the Fear of Femininity in Sexual Minority Men

Helping professionals need to be cognizant of the fact that a great number of sexual and gender minorities have experienced childhoods fraught with shame and rejection, or fear of rejection, by friends and family. In particular, gay and bisexual men have childhood histories of being teased, bullied, and/or otherwise marginalized on the basis of their gender nonconformity. Wood (2004) advocates that the topic of gender oppression be broached, particularly when working with gay men, given the likelihood that they have experienced wounding associated with effeminacy. Helping professionals will likely need to explore the messages that their clients have received about masculinity within their families and from the larger cultural context and to help clients appreciate the losses generated from restrictive male gender roles (Szymanski & Carr, 2008).

Provide Validation and Affirmation

Unfortunately, too many practitioners fail to comprehend the demands of managing one's identity in the context of a society that is generally unaccepting (Bohan, 1996). It is, therefore, essential that they recognize the stigma associated with homosexuality, bisexuality, and transgenderism and provide the validation that is often missing (Goetstouwers, 2006). Given the lack of visible role models, this need for validation is especially important for persons who are bisexual and gender minorities. Maguen, Shipherd, and Harris (2005) found the use of semistructured support groups to be particularly effective for their gender minority clients, given that many of their clients had so few opportunities outside of Internet-based communication to connect with other gender minorities. Their groups also incorporated psychoeducation on such issues as promoting personal safety with regard to sexual practices, HIV prevention, and hormone injections.

Create Stigma Management Strategies

Practitioners can play an important role in aiding their sexual and gender minority clients to manage the stigma associated with their identities. First, there must be sensitivity to the complex and sometimes continual process of negotiating safety and self-disclosure. They can assist clients in the process of evaluating the risks and benefits associated with self-disclosure and help them depathologize the implications of nondisclosure. The process for gender minority clients is especially important. "Clients may use the therapy setting as a source of both 'reality testing' regarding gender-expression decisions and support during the sequential layers of the coming out process" (Cole et al., 2000, p. 179).

A common mistake that many practitioners make is minimizing the complexities and complications concomitant with "being out." This failure to comprehend the reality their clients live with can be dangerous, especially in the context of racial, cultural, and ethnic minority communities. This failure is sometimes reflected in the tendency to encourage all sexual minorities to come out. Bohan (1996) noted the pervasive bias among practitioners that self-disclosure is a necessary prerequisite for psychological health in sexual minorities. Green (2002) recommended that practitioners adopt a "pro-choice" approach to disclosure and respect the choices that clients make regardless of the outcome. Ettner (1999) noted one mistake that counselors make when working with gender minority clients who are in the process of transitioning: They pressure these clients prematurely to come out to others and appear fully transitional as the other gender. In so doing, they inadvertently make their clients more vulnerable to physical harm.

Therapists can assist clients in assessing the risks of self-disclosure in various contexts and the risks in going out in public. For sexual and gender minorities, it is important that practitioners and clients consider the ramifications of "being out" specifically in the context of their unique social situation.

Develop Awareness of Gender/Sexual Orientation Microaggressions

The next chapter deals extensively with the personal responses of helping professionals. This section, however, explores subtle aspects of counselor behaviors. Recently, multicultural researchers (i.e., Constantine, 2007; Sue et al., 2007) have focused on covert forms of racism, termed *racial microaggressions*, that are frequently exhibited in the context of psychotherapy relationships. Racial microaggressions are automatic and sometimes unconscious verbal and nonverbal insults, snubs, and dismissive nonverbal behaviors and tones toward persons of color (Sue et al., 2007). Some common examples of microaggressions include giving preferential treatment to white customers over persons of color, assuming a person of color is a service worker, and assuming that cultural values or communications associated with persons of color are inferior (Sue et al., 2007). It is assumed that microaggressions are levied against sexual and gender minorities (Sue et al., 2007).

Both Sue et al. (2007) and Constantine (2007) have identified several types of subtle forms of racial microaggression that have emerged in therapeutic relationships, including denying or minimizing racial issues, referred to as "colorblindness" (Sue et al., 2007); denying personal racism (Sue et al., 2007); and idealizing and assigning special status on the basis of race. Many of these forms of racial microaggression are similar in nature to the microaggressions that occur in counseling situations with gender and sexual minority clients. The following are some possible examples of gender/sexual orientation microaggessions in therapy:

1. "Relationships are all the same; it doesn't matter if it's two women or two men together."
2. "I am not homophobic; my best friend is gay."
3. "I would never have suspected that you had transitioned" (to a client who has transitioned from male-to-female or female-to-male).
4. "I would never have suspected that you were lesbian/gay" (to a client who is feminine/masculine in appearance).
5. Therapists assume that clients' friendships with ex-lovers are indications of boundary disturbances.
6. Nonminority therapists insist that gender and/or sexual identity does not impact the counseling relationship.
7. Agencies fail to employ openly gay, lesbian, bisexual, or transgendered therapists.

Assess Symptoms Related to Minority Stress

While there is no evidence that a same-sex sexual orientation or a gender variance is a psychopathological condition, the consequences of living in a homo-, bi-, and transphobic culture can result in low self-esteem and feelings of inadequacy. Practitioners need to be attentive to symptoms associated with minority stress, including depression, anxiety, panic, and substance abuse.

It is likely that sexual and gender minority clients will have histories of abuse and may well be at current risk of victimization (Balsam et al., 2005). Because childhood gender nonconformity has been associated with childhood rejection and harassment, helping professionals need to screen for depression, dissociative symptoms, suicidality, substance abuse, and other symptoms. Given the propensity of gender minorities and gay men to experience body shame and eating disorders, it is also important for practitioners to assess for the presence of these symptoms (Korell & Lorah, 2007; Surgenor & Fear, 1998).

Acknowledge Insidious Traumatization

While many of us think of trauma solely in relation to wartime and other catastrophic events, traumatic events are defined as those that are unanticipated and that both exceed an individual's coping strategies and disrupt one's internal frame of reference (McCann & Pearlman, 1990). Root (1992), a feminist author, advanced the concept of *insidious traumatization*, which is particularly useful in the context of understanding the experiences of sexual and gender minorities. Root posited that marginalized persons such as sexual and gender minorities are continually exposed to *subthreshold* traumatic stressors. These can lead to situations where even small events become traumatic stressors, causing more severe symptoms such as flashbacking and numbing. Root cited examples of subthreshold traumatic stressors: hearing news that another sexual and/or gender minority person has been the target of hate violence or harassment and the negative communications or depictions of sexual and gender minorities in the media. Dunbar (2001) observed that even persons who are exposed to ongoing harassment may become habituated to these experiences. The danger in this is that they are less able to evaluate risk effectively in certain situations.

Explore the Ramifications of Rejection from Religious Communities

One area that needs continued research and clinical attention concerns the psychological effects of the rejection that many sexual and gender minorities experience in their faith communities. Negative messages are prevalent in many traditional religions, including Protestantism, Catholicism, Islamism, and Judaism (Clark, Brown, & Hochstein, 1989), and appear to have a significant impact on the psychological health of sexual and gender minorities. The significance of affirmation of spirituality to the emotional well-being of minorities makes it important for practitioners to assist clients in finding alternative faith groups (Lease, Horne, & Noffsinger-Frazier, 2005). One possible avenue for practitioners in the future might be to meet with faith leaders and advocate on behalf of their sexual and gender minority congregants (Lease et al., 2005).

Explore the Use of Alternative Treatment Models for Survivors of Victimization

The aim of therapeutic interventions with victims of hate-motivated violence is to provide sufficient support and emotional validation for victims to reestablish safety and control. To be sure, family members, friends, and clergy can be important sources of support for the victims of hate-motivated crimes. However, in some cases this may be contraindicated, particularly when family and friends are disapproving and rejecting of their loved ones' sexual orientation and gender identity. This section provides readers with some tools to use beyond the more generic crisis intervention skills that are necessary for work with victims of hate-motivated violence.

FEMINIST APPROACHES   Herman (1992), a feminist psychiatrist, noted the presence of underlying themes in persons who have experienced different kinds of trauma with associated feelings of fear and numbness. She referred to the *dialectic of trauma* in which persons often vacillate between shutting down emotionally and being overly aroused and hypervigilant. Herman's therapeutic approach encompasses three stages of recovery: (1) establishment of safety, (2) remembrance and mourning, and (3) reconnection with ordinary life. For Herman, the reconnection occurs to one's own body and one's feelings, to others, and to the world.

COGNITIVE-BEHAVIORAL APPROACHES   Cognitive-processing therapy (CPT) was first introduced by Resick and Schnicke (1992, 1993) as a form of treatment for posttraumatic stress disorder. Its focus is on overgeneralized trauma-related beliefs such as thoughts that one is to blame or that the victim is somehow responsible for the attack. The use of cognitive restructuring techniques that discourage survivors from the frequent experience of negative and self-blaming thoughts about their victimization is recommended. For example, the cognition that "bad things happen because I am gay" can be reformulated to "bad things happen" (Garnets et al., 2003, p. 199). In Kaysen, Lostutter, and Goines's (2005) application of CPT with a gay male victim of a hate crime, they asked their client to write an account of this assault. Their therapy consisted of asking him to examine evidence to support or refute the beliefs that were contained in his first-person account of the crime. Practitioners can also assist survivors with weighing the risks and benefits associated with reporting their experiences to the criminal justice system, while exercising caution in letting victims take the lead in decision making.

Dunbar's (2001) treatment model, which combines cognitive-behavioral and multicultural components, maintains that there are two counseling tasks: to reduce and/or alleviate symptoms, including intrusive ideation, anxiety and numbing, and avoidance behaviors, and to reestablish an adaptive in-group identity. He offered a five-phase model of intervention. Phase 1, containment and safety, entails an assessment of the victim's risk of self or other harm, the current level of functioning, and the potential for retaliation. Dunbar recommends the use of measures such as the Impact of Event Scale (Horowitz, Wilner, & Alvarez, 1979) to aid in this process. In phase 2, the clinician explores the hate crime incident itself as well as the victim's social support network. Phase 3 involves attention to the nature of the therapeutic alliance itself in terms of the clinician's sexual and gender identity, race, ethnicity, age, and so on. In phase 4, acute symptom reduction, the practitioner incorporates empirically validated treatment techniques such as progressive relaxation, role-playing techniques, and pharmacotherapy that are often used with crime and sexual assault victims. Therapy interventions in phase 5, identity recovery and re-formation, are often dependent on pretrauma feelings and identification with sexual and gender minorities prior to victimization as well as the nature, timing, and intensity of the trauma itself. In this phase, the clinician might encourage the client to connect with the experiences of other sexual and gender minority survivors and to explore the resiliency of such persons.

THERAPEUTIC ENACTMENT   Herman (1992) and Dunbar (2001) posit that an important part of trauma treatment involves verbally telling one's story safely in the presence of an affirming therapist. The use of witnesses to form a healing community is also an integral component in the therapeutic enactment approach developed by Westwood, Keats, and Wilensky (2003) and by Hirakata and Buchanan-Arvay (2005). The rationale behind this approach to trauma work is the observation that victims often lack words to translate their experiences because they become so overwhelmed by the physiological arousal and emotions that are reexperienced during the process of retelling their stories. On a neural level, when victims reexperience traumatic incidents, the parts of the brain that are activated are those associated with emotions (Rauch et al., 1996). Concomitantly, the areas of the brain that are associated with language skills show decreased function (Rauch et al., 1996).

Hirakata and Buchanan-Arvay (2005) and Rothschild (2000, 2006) argue that during times of trauma or victimization, the body is impacted at a sensorimotor level, and the memory of these events is also contained within the body, a phenomenon known as *somatic memory*. The therapeutic enactment approach is, therefore, an integrative and body-centered treatment approach. Trained practitioners help clients integrate implicit and explicit memories into a narrative or script of events, aid them in becoming more aware of their body sensations, and help them learn skills associated with self-soothing. As victims "restory their traumatic experience," there are "process memories held in the body at a sensorimotor level" (Hirakata & Buchanan-Arvay, 2005, p. 447). Verbal expression does not adequately capture the complex nuances that are allowed to speak through body posture, gesture, skin tone, and breathing. This process is reminiscent of Dunbar's emphasis on "giving voice" in the presence of a supportive community. Therapeutic enactment is also an action-based approach in which participants are able to physically engage in "corrective re-experiencing" (Hirakata & Buchanan-Arvay, 2005, p. 451).

Advocate for Political Action

While it is important for practitioners to cultivate awareness of the possible implications of minority stress and of internalized homo/bi/transphobias for their sexual and gender minority clients, Russell (2007) and Russell and Bohan (2006) offered a cautionary note. Russell and her colleagues warned that concepts like internalized homophobia have become yet another means by which sexual minority persons can berate themselves and can be "pathologized" by practitioners. Russell (2007) assumed a social constructionist perspective when she argued that it is senseless to make a distinction between the external social world, which promotes homophobia, and the internal world of the self. Russell and Bohan (2006) observed that therapists typically help "clients accept themselves and recognize the social roots of their self-doubt; rarely are they counseled to encourage clients' engaging in political activism targeting that bias (p. 347). Russell and her colleagues believed that practitioners must go further in terms of addressing the sociopolitical factors that create and maintain homophobia. In a similar vein, Garnets et al. (2003) emphasized the importance of encouraging clients who are survivors of hate-motivated violence to direct their anger in active and constructive ways through such activities as political involvement.

Negative perceptions of sexual and gender minorities are institutionalized or fortified in all of our major social institutions, including families, schools, and places of worship, and through media portrayals and governmental regulations (Felsenthal, 2004). Sexual and gender minorities are denied such basic human rights as employment security, health insurance benefits, income tax benefits afforded married couples, options to adopt children or to serve as foster parents, and service in the military without fear of expulsion.

Russell and her colleagues are part of a growing number of psychologists and mental health practitioners (Arredondo & Perez, 2003; Donahue & McDonald, 2005; Goodman, Liang, Helms, Latta, Sparks & Weintraub, 2004) who have adapted a social justice perspective. This perspective means that many of the presenting issues that sexual and gender minority persons bring to therapy are seen not as psychopathology but as byproducts of the consequences of their social experiences. In accordance with this paradigm shift, practitioners, social workers, and psychologists are encouraged to participate in political organizing as well to lobby legislative representatives, write letters to the editors of local newspapers, attend rallies, and the like. Education of law enforcement personnel is particularly needed in many communities in order to respond more effectively and humanely to hate-motivated violence against sexual and gender minorities. There is much that can be done to prevent future violence and victimization of sexual and gender minorities through communitywide education. The strategic use of community meetings, speak-outs, rallies, and vigils following these tragedies can be instrumental in raising awareness and promoting safety. The National Center for Transgender Equality provides an important resource for persons who wish to organize communitywide responses to hate violence, at *www.nctequality.org.* Chapter 11 provides readers with a number of ideas on how practitioners, social workers, and psychologists can advocate for broader social and institutional changes in order to create a more affirmative climate for sexual and gender minorities.

Summary

Social scientists who study hate crimes search for answers as to what motivates perpetrators to harm strangers simply based on the perception that such persons are members of a particular stigmatized group. Most perpetrators don't stop to ask questions of their victims; most assume based on physical appearances and locations that persons are sexual and gender minorities. Most psychologists attribute sexual prejudice, including homophobia, to a cultural context in which gender is dichotomous and heterosexuality is compulsory.

Gender role expectations are policed through everyday social interactions as well as through major social institutions. Antigay hate crimes are forms of "policing" or punishment of those who don't adhere not only to traditionally defined gender roles but also to heterosexual sexual practices. The empirical research seems to suggest that negative attitudes and behaviors toward sexual and gender minorities stem in part from the confluence between sex and gender. Men who are perceived to be feminine are also deemed to be homosexual and are devalued as human beings. Persons who don't conform to normative expectations of gender are punished for their transgressions. Harry (1990) studied the motives and modus operandi of antigay hate crime perpetrators and found that they were more likely to attack persons whom they perceived to be gender nonconforming than those whom they perceived as conforming.

Heterosexism is so firmly grounded in our culture that it serves as a breeding ground for hate crimes to occur (Franklin, 2000; Gagne et al., 1997). As Fone noted in his text *Homophobia* (2000), in our society we are more tolerant of hate speech directed at sexual and gender minorities than we are of racist, sexist, and anti-Semitic remarks. Perhaps, as Fone (2000) suggests, homophobia is the "last acceptable prejudice" (p. 3).

While much of this chapter has focused on the negative consequences of sexual prejudice, readers must bear in mind that sexual and gender minorities as well as all minority group members are not just victims of prejudice and discrimination, but also survivors who are capable of great strength and resiliency (Meyer, 2003; Miller & Major, 2000).

Personal Reflection

Paul Monette was a highly successful author of several novels. His depictions of his experiences growing up gay were the focus of his memoir, *Becoming a Man: Half a Life Story* (1992), for which he won the 1992 National Book Award for nonfiction. Monette also wrote *Borrowed Time* (1988) and *Love Alone* (1988) about his experiences with his life partner, Roger Horwitz, who died of AIDS. After his partner's death, Monette became a national spokesperson for AIDS for several years and later died of AIDS-related complications in 1995. The following is an excerpt from his autobiography:

> *I speak for no one else here, if only because I don't want to saddle the women and men of my tribe with the lead weight of my self-hatred, the particular doorless room of my internal exile. Yet, I've come to learn that all our stories add*

> *up to the same imprisonment. The self-delusion of uniqueness. The festering pretense that we are the same as they are. The gutting of all our passions till we are a bunch of eunuchs, our zones of pleasure in enemy hands. Most of all, the ventriloquism, the learning how to pass for straight. Such obedient slaves we make, with such very tidy rooms. (pp. 1–2).*

Self-Reflection Questions

1. What were your immediate visceral responses as you read Monette's words?
2. What do you think Monette means when he refers to himself as one of the "obedient slaves"?
3. How does Monette's depiction of his experiences growing up gay relate to his later life experiences as a person with HIV/AIDS?

Library, Media, and Internet Activity

Check the documentary section of your local video/DVD store for three important films depicting the lives and tragic deaths of sexual and gender minorities.

The Laramie Project (Kaufman, 2003)

This HBO film recreates the efforts of a New York theater troupe to chronicle the experiences of the townspeople of Laramie, Wyoming, in the wake of the hate-motivated murder of University of Wyoming student Matthew Shepard. This film is based on the acclaimed play whose script was adapted from transcripts of over 200 interviews with the people of Laramie.

Discussion Questions

1. Several townspeople in Laramie reacted in disbelief to the murder of Matthew Shepard. What were your thoughts and feelings as you heard the often repeated comments from various townspeople like "Laramie isn't that kind of town." How is Laramie like your town? How does it differ?
2. Utilizing the concepts of minority stress, stigma consciousness, and stigma management, describe the reactions of several of Laramie's gay and lesbian citizens following Matthew's murder.
3. Respond to the following statement made by one of Laramie's citizens: "Every murder is a hate crime."

The Brandon Teena Story (Muska & Olafsdottir, 1998)

This documentary tells the true story of "Teena Brandon," who captured the headlines in 1993 and was the focus of a popular film titled *Boys Don't Cry* (Peirce, 1999). Brandon was born a biological female. She wanted to pass as a man and attempted to do so without hormonal or surgical intervention. Brandon moved to rural Nebraska and was brutally raped and murdered by two male acquaintances when they discovered that Brandon was a biological female. This documentary contains interviews with Brandon's girlfriend, Lana Tisdel; the murderers, John Lotter and Marvin Thomas Nissen; and actual audiotaped excerpts from Brandon's police interrogations.

Discussion Questions

1. What were your reactions as you heard the audiotaped excerpts of Brandon's interview with Richardson County Sheriff Charles Laux?
2. Using the counseling approaches described in this chapter, how might you work with a gender minority person like Brandon who has experienced multiple traumas?
3. Imagine working with a client who, like Lana Tisdel, appears to have fallen in love with a transgendered person. What kinds of issues might arise for someone who has a relationship with a transgendered person like Brandon?

Soldier's Girl (Pierson, 2004)

This film is based on the true story of Barry Winchell, a soldier in the 101st Airborne Division, who was brutally murdered by a fellow GI on July 4, 1999, shortly after the installment of the "don't ask, don't tell" policy. During a social outing with his fellow soldiers, Barry was captivated by Calpernia Adams, a transgendered entertainer in a local Nashville nightclub. This story focuses on the relationship that developed between them.

Discussion Questions

1. What personal and social factors contributed to Barry's death?
2. Toward the latter part of the film, Barry says to Calpernia, "I don't know what I am." Imagine that Barry is your client. How might you respond to his statement?
3. Discuss the pros and cons of the military's "don't ask, don't tell" policy as a stigma management strategy?

Case Study

You are a mental health counselor in a small community mental health clinic. Janine, a 24-year-old Hispanic preoperative male-to-female transsexual, found her way to your office after being jumped and beaten with pieces of a metal pole by three young males. She came to your office because her friend thought it would be a good idea to talk to someone about the incident. When you asked what happened to her, she replied:

I was walking home from work and three young men passed me. They started yelling "hey faggot . . . you faggot" and then approached me. One of the men began shouting that I was not a real woman and that I should stop trying to deceive people. I'm not sure what happened next because I was hit in the head with something and fell to the ground. I was kicked and spit on repeatedly until two women walking down the street yelled at them to stop. The men only stopped because they wanted to tell the women that I was a faggot and not a real woman. I was able to get up and run to a pay phone and call the police. When the police

came, the men appeared once more and said all they'd done was to verbally harass me. The police took my statement and then took the men's statements. The police wrote down that I had blown kisses at the men. They ignored my side of the story, and most importantly, they ignored the fact that there were two witnesses and the visible bruises and cuts. They told me to go home; there was nothing they could do. But don't feel sorry for me because this stuff happens to people like me.

Discussion Questions

1. What was your reaction after reading Janine's story?
2. In your opinion, was Janine the victim of two hate crimes?
3. What was your response to Janine's request not to feel sorry for her? Given the literature presented in this chapter, how might you come to understand this request? What might your response be to Janine when she tells you not to feel sorry for her?

References

Adams, H. E., Wright, L. W., & Lohr, B. A. (1996). Is homophobia associated with homosexual arousal? *Journal of Abnormal Psychology, 105,* 440–445.

Allen, D. J., & Oleson, T. (1999). Shame and internalized homophobia in gay men. *Journal of Homosexuality, 37*(3), 22–43.

Allport, G. W. (1954). *The nature of prejudice.* Reading, MA: Addison-Wesley.

American Psychiatric Association. (2000). *Diagnostic and statistical manual of mental disorders—Text revision* (4th ed.). Washington, DC: Author.

Anderson, B. F. (1998). Therapeutic issues in working with transgendered clients. In D. Denny (Ed.), *Current concepts in transgender identity* (pp. 215–226). New York: Garland.

Arredondo, P., & Perez, P. (2003). Expanding multicultural competence through social justice leadership. *Counseling Psychologist, 31*(3), 282–289.

Bailey, J. M., Kim, P., Hills, A., & Linsenmeier, J. A. (1997). Butch, femme, or straight acting? Partner preferences of gay men and lesbians. *Journal of Personality & Social Psychology, 73,* 960–973.

Bailey, J. M., & Zucker, K. J. (1995). Childhood sex-typed behavior and sexual orientation: A conceptual analysis and quantitative review. *Developmental Psychology, 31,* 43–55.

Balsam, K. F., Rothblum, E. D., & Beauchaine, T. P. (2005). Victimization over the life span: A comparison of lesbian, gay, bisexual and heterosexual siblings. *Journal of Consulting & Clinical Psychology, 73*(3), 477–487.

Berrill, K. T. (1990). Violence and victimization of lesbians and gay men: Mental health consequences. *Journal of Interpersonal Violence, 5* (3), 274–294.

Bockting, W. O., Robinson, B. E., & Rosser, B. R. S. (1998). Transgender HIV prevention: Qualitative evaluation of a model prevention education program. *Journal of Sex Education & Therapy, 23,* 125–133.

Bohan, J. (1996). *Psychology and sexual orientation.* New York: Routledge.

Bowers, A. M. V., & Bieschke, K. J. (2005). Psychologists' clinical evaluations and attitudes: An examination of the influence of gender and sexual orientation. *Professional Psychology: Research & Practice, 36*(1), 97–103.

Boyd, H. (2007). *She's not the man I married: My life with a transgendered husband.* Emeryville, CA: Seal Press.

Bronn, C. D. (2001). Attitudes and self-images of male and female bisexuals. *Journal of Bisexuality, 1*(4), 5–29.

Brooks, V. R. (1981). *Minority stress and lesbian women.* Lexington, MA: Heath.

Cain, R. (1991). Stigma management and gay identity development. *Social Work, 36*(1), 67–73.

Carroll, L., & Gilroy, P. (2000). Being out: The behavioral language of self-disclosure. *Journal of Gay & Lesbian Psychotherapy 4,* 69–86.

Carroll, L., Gilroy, P., & Ryan, J. (2002). Counseling transgendered, transsexual, and gender-variant clients. *Journal of Counseling & Development, 80,* 131–139.

Cass, V. C. (1979). Homosexual identity formation: A theoretical model. *Journal of Homosexuality, 4*(3), 219–235.

Ceglian, C. M. P., & Lyons, N. N. (2004). Gender type and comfort with cross-dressers. *Sex Roles, 50*(7/8), 539–546.

Chrobot-Mason, D., Button, S. B., & DiClementi, J. D. (2001). Sexual identity management strategies: An explanation of antecedents and consequences. *Sex Roles, 45,* 321–336.

Clark, J. M., Brown, J. C., & Hochstein, L. M. (1989). Institutional religion and gay/lesbian oppression. *Marriage & Family Review, 14,* (3/4), 265–284.

Cochran, S. D. (2001). Emerging issues in research on lesbians' and gay men's mental health: Does sexual orientation really matter? *American Psychologist, 56,* 931–947.

Cochran, S. D., & Mays, V. M. (2000). Lifetime prevalence of suicidal symptoms and affective disorders among men reporting same-sex sexual partners: Results from MHANES III. *American Journal of Public Health, 90,* 573–578.

Cochran, S. D., Sullivan, J. G., & Mays, V. M. (2003). Prevalence of mental disorders, psychological distress and mental services use among lesbian, gay, and bisexual adults in the United States. *Journal of Consulting & Clinical Psychology, 71*(1), 53–61.

Cohler, B. J., & Galatzer-Levy, R. M. (2000). *The course of gay and lesbian lives: Social and psychoanalytic perspectives.* Chicago: University of Chicago Press.

Cole, S. S., Denny, D., Eyler, A. E., & Samons, S. L. (2000). Issues of transgender. In L. T. Szuchman & F. Muscarella (Eds.), *Psychological perspectives on human sexuality* (pp. 149–195). New York: Wiley.

Coleman, E. (1982). Developmental stages of the coming-out process. *Journal of Homosexuality, 7,* 31–43.

Constantine, M. G. (2007). Racial microaggressions against African American clients in cross-racial counseling relationships. *Journal of Counseling Psychology, 54*(1), 1–16.

Davies, M. (2004). Correlates of negative attitudes toward gay men: Sexism, male role norms, and male sexuality. *Journal of Sex Research, 41,* 259–265.

De Monteflores, C. (1986). Notes on the management of difference. In T. S. Stein & C. J. Cohen (Eds.), *Contemporary perspectives on psychotherapy with lesbians and gay men* (pp. 73–101). New York: Plenum.

DiPlacido, J. (1998). Minority stress among lesbians, gay men, and bisexuals: A consequence of heterosexism, homophobia, and stigmatization. In G. M. Herek (Ed.), *Stigma and sexual orientation: Understanding prejudice against lesbians, gay men, and bisexuals* (pp. 138–159). Thousand Oaks, CA: Sage.

Dodge, B., & Sandfort, T. G. M. (2007). A review of mental health research on bisexual individuals when compared to homosexual and heterosexual individuals. In B. A. Firestein (Ed.), *Becoming visible: Counseling bisexuals across the lifespan* (pp. 28–51). New York: Columbia University Press.

Donahue, P., & McDonald, L. (2005). Gay and lesbian aging: Current perspectives and future directions for social work practice and research. *Families in Society, 86*(3), 359–366.

Dunbar, E. (2001). Counseling practices to ameliorate the effects of discrimination and hate events: Toward a systematic approach to assessment and intervention. *Counseling Psychologist, 29,* 279–307.

Dunbar, E. (2006). Race, gender, and sexual orientation in hate crime victimization: Identity politics or identity risk? *Violence & Victims, 21*(2), 323–337.

Dupras, A. (1994). Internalized homophobia and psychosexual adjustment among gay men. *Psychological Reports, 75*, 23–28.

Eliason, M. J. (1997). The prevalence and nature of biphobia in heterosexual undergraduate students. *Archives of Sexual Behavior, 26*, 317–326.

Epstein, D. (2001). Boyz' own stories: Masculinities and sexualities in schools. In W. Martino & B. Meyenn (Eds.), *What about the boys? Issues of masculinity in schools* (pp. 96–109). Philadelphia: Open University Press.

Ettner, R. (1999). *Gender loving care: A guide to counseling gender-variant clients.* New York: Norton.

Feinberg, L. (1998). *Trans liberation: Beyond pink or blue.* Boston: Beacon Press.

Felsenthal, K. D. (2004). Socio-spatial experiences of transgender individuals. In J. L. Chin (Ed.), *The psychology of prejudice and discrimination: Vol. 3. Bias based on gender and sexual orientation* (pp. 201–225). Westport, CT: Praeger.

Firestein, B. (2007). Cultural and relational contexts of bisexual women: Implications for therapy. In K. J. Bieschke, R. M. Perez, & K. A. DeBord (Eds.), *Handbook of counseling and psychotherapy with lesbian, gay, bisexual, and transgender clients* (2nd ed.) (pp. 91–117). Washington, D.C.: American Psychological Association.

Fone, B. (2000). *Homophobia. A history.* New York: Holt.

Franklin, K. (1998). Unassuming motivations: Contextualizing the narratives of antigay assailants. In G. M. Herek (Ed.), *Stigma and sexual orientation: Understanding prejudice against lesbians, gay men, and bisexuals.* Thousand Oaks, CA: Sage.

Franklin, K. (2000). Antigay behaviors among young adults: Prevalence, patterns, and motivators in a noncriminal population. *Journal of Interpersonal Violence, 15*, 339–362.

Fukuyama, M. A., & Ferguson, A. D. (2000). Lesbian, gay, and bisexual people of color: Understanding cultural complexity and managing multiple oppressions. In R. M. Perez, K. A. DeBord, & Bieschke K. J. (Eds.), *Handbook of counseling and psychotherapy with lesbian, gay and bisexual clients* (pp. 81–105). Washington, DC: American Psychological Association.

Gagne, P., Tewksbury, R., & McGaughey, D. (1997). Coming out and crossing over. Identity formation and proclamation in a transgender community. *Gender & Society, 11*, 478–508.

Gagne, P., Tewksbury, R., & McGaughey, D. (1998). Conformity pressures and gender resistance among transgender individuals. *Social Problems, 45*(1), 81–101.

Garnets, L. D., Herek, G. M., & Levy, G. (2003). Violence and victimization of lesbians and gay men: Mental health consequences. In L. D. Garnets & D. G. Kimmel (Eds.), *Psychological perspectives on lesbian, gay, and bisexual experiences* (pp. 188–206). New York: Columbia University Press.

Goetstouwers, L. (2006). Affirmative psychotherapy with bisexual men. *Journal of Bisexuality, 6*, (1/2), 27–49.

Goffman, E. (1963). *Stigma: Notes on the management of spoiled identity.* New York: Prentice Hall.

Gonsiorek, J. C. (1993). Mental health issues of gay and lesbian adolescents. In L. D. Garnets & D. G. Kimmel (Eds.), *Psychological perspectives on lesbian and gay male experiences* (pp. 469–485). New York: Columbia University Press.

Goodman, L. A., Liang, B., Helms, J. E., Latta, R. E., Sparks, E., & Weintraub, S. R. (2004). Training counseling psychologists as social justice agents: Feminist and multicultural principles in action. *Counseling Psychologist, 32*, 793–837.

Green, R. J. (2002). Coming out to family . . . in context. In E. Davis-Russell (Ed.), *The California School of Professional Psychology handbook of multicultural education, research, intervention, and training* (pp. 277–284). San Francisco: Jossey-Bass.

Haaga, D. A. (1991). "Homophobia"? *Journal of Social Behavior & Personality, 6*(1), 171–174.

Haldeman, D. (2001). Psychotherapy with gay and bisexual men. In G. R. Brooks & G. E. Good (Eds.), *The new handbook of psychotherapy and counseling with men* (pp. 796–815). San Francisco: Jossey-Bass.

Harper, G. W., & Schneider, M. (2003). Oppression and discrimination among lesbian, gay, bisexual, and transgendered people and communities: A challenge for community psychology. *American Journal of Community Psychology, 31*, 243–252.

Harry, J. (1983). Defeminization and adult psychological well-being among male homosexuals. *Archives of Sexual Behavior, 12*, 1–19.

Harry, J. (1990). Conceptualizing anti-gay violence. *Journal of Interpersonal Violence. Special Issue: Violence against lesbians and gay men: Issues for research, practice, and policy. 5* (3), 350–358.

Harry, J. (1993). Being out: A general model. *Journal of Homosexuality, 26*, 25–39.

Herek, G. M. (1989). Hate crimes against lesbians and gay men: Issues for research and policy. *American Psychologist, 44(6)*, 948–955.

Herek, G. M. (1990). The context of anti-gay violence: Notes on cultural and psychological heterosexism. *Journal of Interpersonal Violence, 5*, 316–333.

Herek, G. M. (2000). The psychology of sexual prejudice. *Current Directions in Psychological Science, 9(1)*, 19–22.

Herek, G. M. (2002a). Gender gaps in public opinion about lesbian and gay men. *Public Opinion Quarterly, 66*, 40–66.

Herek, G. M. (2002b). Heterosexuals' attitudes toward bisexual men and women in the United States. *Journal of Sex Research, 39*, 264–275.

Herek, G. M. (2003). Why tell if you're not asked? Self-disclosure, intergroup contact and heterosexuals' attitudes toward lesbians and gay men. In L. D. Garnets & D. C. Kimmel (Eds.), *Psychological perspectives on lesbian, gay, and bisexual experiences* (pp. 270–298). New York: Columbia University Press.

*Herek, G. M., & Capitanio, J. P. (1995). Black heterosexuals' attitudes toward lesbians and gay men in the United States. *Journal of Sex Research, 32*, 95–105.

Herek, G. M., & Capitanio, J. P. (1996). "Some of my best friends": Intergroup contact, concealable stigma and heterosexuals' attitudes toward gay men and lesbians. *Personality & Social Psychology Bulletin, 22*, 412–424.

Herek, G. M., Cogan, J. C., & Gillis, J. R. (2002). Victim experiences in hate crimes based on sexual orientation. *Journal of Social Issues, 58*, 319–339.

Herek, G. M., Gillis, J. R., & Cogan, J. C. (1999). Psychological sequelae of hate-crime victimization among lesbian, gay, and bisexual adults. *Journal of Consulting & Clinical Psychology, 67*, 945–951.

Herek, G. M., Gillis, J. R., Cogan, J. C., & Glunt, E. K. (1997). Hate crime victimization among lesbian, gay and bisexual adults: Prevalence, psychological correlates, and methodological issues. *Journal of Interpersonal Violence, 12*, 195–215.

Herman, J. (1992). *Trauma and recovery*. New York: Basic Books.

Hill, D. (2003). Genderism, transphobia, and gender bashing: A framework for interpreting anti-transgender violence. In B. C. & R. T. Carter (Eds.), *Understanding and dealing with violence: A multicultural approach* (pp. 113–136). Thousand Oaks, CA: Sage.

Hirakata, P., & Buchanan-Arvay, M. J. (2005). Into the fire: Using therapeutic enactments to bridge early traumatic memories of childhood sexual abuse. *International Journal for the Advancement of Counselling, 27(3)*, 445–455.

Hoffman, L. G., Hevesi, A. G., Lynch, P. E., Gomes, P. J., Chodorow, N. J., Roughton, R. E., et al. (2000). Homophobia: Analysis of a "permissible" prejudice: A public forum of the American Psychoanalytic Association and the American Psychoanalytic Foundation. *Journal of Gay & Lesbian Psychotherapy, 4*, 5–53.

Horowitz, M. J., Wilner, N., & Alvarez, W. (1979). Impact of event scale: A measure of subjective distress. *Psychosomatic Medicine, 41*, 209–218.

Hudson, W. W., & Rickets, W. A. (1980). A strategy for the measurement of homophobia. *Journal of Homosexuality, 5*, 356–371.

Huebner, D. M., Davis, M. C., Nemeroff, C. J., & Aiken, L. S. (2002). The impact of internalized homophobia on HIV preventive interventions. *American Journal of Community Psychology, 30(3)*, 327–348.

Huebner, D. M., Rebchook, G. M., & Kegeles, S. M. (2004). Experiences of harassment, discrimination and physical violence among young gay and bisexual men. *American Journal of Public Health, 94*, 1200–1206.

Israel, T., & Mohr, J. J. (2004). Attitudes toward bisexual women and men: Current research, future directions. *Journal of Bisexuality, 4 (1/2)*, 117–134.

Kaminski, P. L., Chapman, B., Haynes, S. D., & Own, L. (2005). Body image, eating behaviors, and attitudes toward exercise among gay and straight men. *Eating Behaviors, 6(3)*, 179–187.

Kaufman, M. (Director) (2003). *The Laramie Project* [Motion Picture].

Kaysen, D., Lostutter, T. W., & Goines, M. A. (2005). Cognitive processing therapy for acute stress disorder resulting from an anti-gay assault. *Cognitive & Behavioral Practice, 12*, 278–289.

Kenagy, G. (2005). Transgender health: Findings from two needs assessment studies in Philadelphia. *Health & Social Work, 30*, 19–27.

Kimmel, M. S., & Mahler, M. (2003). Adolescent masculinity, homophobia, and violence. *American Behavioral Scientist, 46*, 1439–1458.

Kite, M. E., & Whitley, B. E. (1996). Sex differences in attitudes towards homosexual persons, behaviors, and civil rights: A meta-analysis. *Personality & Social Psychology Bulletin, 22,* 336–353.

Korell, S. C., & Lorah, P. (2007). An overview of affirmative psychotherapy and counseling with transgender clients. In K. J. Bieschke, R. M. Perez, & K. A. DeBord (Eds.), *Handbook of counseling and psychotherapy with lesbian, gay, bisexual, and transgender clients* (2nd ed.) (pp. 271–288). Washington, DC: American Psychological Association.

Kuehnle, K., & Sullivan, A. (2001). Patterns of antigay violence: An analysis of incident characteristics and victim reporting. *Journal of Interpersonal Violence, 16,* 928–943.

LaFramboise, S., & Long, B. (n.d). An introduction to: Gender, transgender and transphobia. Retrieved December 1, 2000, from http://mypage.direct.ca/h/hrp/gendertr.html

LaMar, L., & Kite, M. (1998). Sex differences in attitudes toward gay men and lesbians: A multidimensional perspective. *Journal of Sex Research, 35*(2), 189–196.

Landolt, M. A., Bartholomew, K., Saffrey, C., Oram, D., & Perlman, D. (2004). Gender nonconformity, childhood rejection, and adult attachment: A study of gay men. *Archives of Sexual Behavior, 33*(2), 117–128.

Lease, S. H., Horne, S. G., & Noffsinger-Frazier, N. (2005). Affirming faith experiences and psychological health for Caucasian lesbian, gay and bisexual individuals. *Journal of Counseling Psychology, 52*(3), 378–388.

Lewis, R. J., Derlega, V. J., Berndt, A., Morris, L. M., & Rose, S. (2001). An empirical analysis of stressors for gay men and lesbians. *Journal of Homosexuality, 42,* 63–88.

Lewis, R. J., Derlega, V. J., Clarke, E. G., & Kuang, J. C. (2006). Stigma consciousness, social constraints, and lesbian well-being. *Journal of Counseling Psychology, 53*(1), 48–56.

Lewis, R. J., Derlega, V. J., Griffin, J. L., & Krowinski, A. C. (2003). Stressors for gay men and lesbians: Life stress, gay-related stress, stigma consciousness, and depressive symptoms. *Journal of Social & Clinical Psychology, 22,* 716–729.

Lombardi, E. L., Wilchins, R. A., Priesing, D., & Malouf, D. (2001). Gender violence: Transgender experiences with violence and discrimination. *Journal of Homosexuality, 42,* 89–101.

Maguen, S., Shipherd, J. C., & Harris, H. N. (2005). Providing culturally sensitive care for transgender patients. *Cognitive & Behavioral Practice, 12,* 479–490.

Martins, Y., Tiggemann, M., & Kirkbride, A. (2007). Those speedos become them: The role of self-objectification in gay and heterosexual men's body image. *Personality & Social Psychology Bulletin, 33*(5), 634–647.

Mays, V. M., & Cochran, S. D. (2001). Mental health correlates of perceived discrimination among lesbians, gay, and bisexual adults in the United States. *American Journal of Public Health, 91*(11), 1869–1876.

McCann, L., & Pearlman, L. A. (1990). *Psychological trauma and the adult survivor: Theory, therapy, and transformation.* New York: Brunner/Mazel.

McDevitt, J., Balboni, J., Garcia, L., & Gu, J. (2001). Consequences for victims: A comparison of bias- and non-bias-motivated assaults. *American Behavioral Scientist, 45,* 697–713.

McLean, K. (2004). Negotiating (non)monogamy: Bisexuality and intimate relationships. *Journal of Bisexuality, 4*(1/2), 83–97.

Meyer, I. H. (1995). Minority stress and mental health in gay men. *Journal of Health & Social Behavior, 36,* 38–56.

Meyer, I. H. (2003). Prejudice, social stress, and mental health in lesbian, gay, and bisexual populations: Conceptual issues and research evidence. *Psychological Bulletin, 129,* 674–697.

Meyer, I. H., & Dean, L. (1998). Internalized homophobia, intimacy, and sexual behavior among gay and bisexual men. In G. M. Herek (Ed.), *Stigma and sexual orientation: Understanding prejudice against lesbians, gay men, and bisexuals* (pp. 160–186). Thousand Oaks, CA: Sage.

Miller, C. T., & Major, B. (2000). Coping with stigma and prejudice. In F. F. Heatherton, R. E. Klect, M. R. Hebl, & J. G. Hull (Eds.), *The social psychology of stigma* (pp. 243–272). New York: Guilford Press.

Miller, M., Andre, A., Ebin, J., & Bessonova, L. (2007). *Bisexual health: An introduction and model practices for HIV/STI prevention programming.* New York: National Gay and Lesbian Task Force Policy Institute, Fenway Institute at Fenway Community Health, and BiNet USA.

Mohr, J. J., & Rochlen, A. B. (1999). Measuring attitudes regarding bisexuality in lesbian, gay male and heterosexual populations. *Journal of Counseling Psychology, 46,* 353–369.

Monette, P. (1992). *Becoming a man: Half a life story.* New York: Harcourt Brace Jovanovich.

Morris, L. M., Lewis, R. J., & Derlega, V. J. (1993). *Development of a measure of homosexual stress.* Paper presented at the meeting in the Virginia Academy of Science, Norfolk, VA.

Morrow, S. L. (2000). First do no harm: Therapist issues in psychotherapy with lesbian, gay and bisexual clients . In R. M. Perez, K. A. DeBord, & K. J. Bieschke (Eds.), *Handbook of counseling and psychotherapy with lesbian, gay, and bisexual clients* (pp. 137–156). Washington, DC: American Psychological Association.

Mubarak, D. (2002, October 15). Transgender breakthrough: People in the United States have a surprising understanding and acceptance of transgender lives, a major survey shows. *Advocate*, Iss. 874, p. 38.

Muska, S., & Olafsdottir, G. (Directors) (1998). *The Brandon Teena Story* [Motion Picture]. United States: Zeitgeist Films.

Namaste, V. K. (2000). *Invisible lives: The erasure of transsexual and transgendered people.* Chicago: University of Chicago Press.

National Center for Transgender Equality. (2006). *Responding to hate crimes: A community resource manual.* Washington, DC: Author. Retrieved March, 2, 2007, from http://www.nctequality.org

*National Coalition of Anti-violence Programs and Horizons. (1995). *Anti-lesbian/gay violence in 1995.* Chicago: Horizons.

Nuttbrock, L., Rosenblum, A., & Blumenstein, R. (2002). Transgender identity affirmation and mental health [Electronic version]. *International Journal of Transgenderism, 6*, 4. Retrieved June 22, 2005, from http://www.symposion.com/ijt/ijtvo06no04_o3. htm

Ochs, R. (1996). Biphobia: It goes more than two ways. In B. A. Firestein (Ed.), *Bisexuality: The psychology and politics of an invisible minority* (pp. 217–239). Thousand Oaks, CA: Sage.

Olweus, D. (1994). Bullying at school: Long-term outcomes for the victims and an effective school-based intervention program. In L. R. Huesmann (Ed.), *Aggressive behavior: Current perspectives* (pp. 97–130). New York: Plenum.

O'Neil, J. (1981). Patterns of gender role conflict and strain: Sexism and the fear of femininity in men's lives. *Personnel & Guidance Journal, 60*, 203–210.

Page, E. (2004). Mental health services experiences of bisexual women and bisexual men: An empirical study. *Journal of Bisexuality, 3(1)*, 53–85.

Parlee, M. B. (1998). Situated knowledge of personal embodiment: Transgender activists' and psychological theorists' perspectives on "sex" and "gender." In H. J. Stam (Ed.), *The body and psychology* (pp. 120–140). Thousand Oaks, CA: Sage.

Parrott, D. J., Adams, H. E., & Zeichner, A. (2002). Homophobia: Personality and attitudinal correlates. *Personality & Individual Differences, 32*, 1269–1278.

Pearlman, S. F. (2006). Terms of connection: Mother-talk about female-to-male transgender children. *Journal of GLBT Family Studies, 2(2/3)*, 93–122.

Peirce, K. (Director). (1999). *Boys Don't Cry* [Motion Picture]. United States: Fox Searchlight Pictures.

Pharr, Suzanne. (1988). *Homophobia: A weapon of sexism.* Inverness, CA: Chardon Press.

Pierson, F. (Director) (2003). *Soldier's Girl* [Motion Picture].

Pinel, E. C. (1999). Stigma consciousness: The psychological legacy of social stereotypes. *Journal of Personality & Social Psychology, 76*, 114–128.

Plummer, K. (1995). *Telling sexual stories.* London: Routledge.

Poteat, V. P., & Espelage, D. L. (2005). Exploring the relation between bullying and homophobic verbal content: The homophobic content agent target (HCAT) scale. *Violence & Victims, 20(5)*, 513–528.

Potoczniak, D. J. (2007). Development of bisexual men's identities and relationships. In K. J. Bieschke, R. M. Perez, & K. A. DeBord (Eds.), *Handbook of counseling and psychotherapy with lesbian, gay, bisexual, and transgender clients* (2nd ed.) (pp. 117–145). Washington, DC: American Psychological Association.

Raj, R. (2002). Towards a transpositive therapeutic model: Developing clinical sensitivity and cultural competence in the effective support of transsexual and transgendered clients. [Electronic version] *International Journal of Transgenderism, 6.* Retrieved on April 7, 2005, from http://www.symposion.com/ijt/ijtvo06no02_04.htm

Recker, N., Dunbar, E. W., & Sullaway, M. E. (August 1998). *The relationship of prejudice to social deviance and psychopathology.* Paper presented at the annual meeting of the American Psychological Association, Los Angeles.

Resick, P. A., & Schnicke, M. K. (1992). Cognitive processing for sexual assault victims. *Journal of Consulting & Clinical Psychology, 60 (5)*, 748–756.

Resick, P. A., & Schnicke, M. K. (1993). Cognitive processing therapy for rape victims: A treatment manual. *Interpersonal violence: The practice series* (Vol. 4). Thousand Oaks, CA: Sage.

Root, M. P. P. (1992). Reconstructing the impact of trauma on personality. In L. Brown & M. Ballou (Eds.), *Personality and psychopathology: Feminist reappraisals* (pp. 229–265). New York: Guilford Press.

Rose, S. M., & Mechanic, M. B. (2002). Psychological distress, crime features, and help-seeking behaviors related to homophobic bias incidents. *American Behavioral Scientist, 46*, 14–26.

Rothschild, B. (2000). *The body remembers: The psychophysiology of trauma and trauma treatment.* New York: Norton.

Rothschild, B. (2006). *Help for the helper. The psychophysiology of compassion fatigue and vicarious trauma.* New York: Norton.

Rowen, C. J., & Malcolm, J. P. (2002). Correlates of internalized homophobia and homosexual identity formation in a sample of gay men. *Journal of Homosexuality, 43*(2), 77–92.

Rubin, H. (2003). *Self-made men: Identity and embodiment among transsexual men.* Nashville, TN: Vanderbilt University Press.

Russell, G. M. (2007). Internalized homophobia: Lessons from the Mobius Strip. In C. Brown & T. Augusta-Scott (Eds.), *Narrative therapy: Making meaning, making lives* (pp. 151–173). Thousand Oaks, CA: Sage.

Russell, G. M., & Bohan, J. S. (2006). The case of internalized homophobia: Theory and/as practice. *Theory & Psychology, 16*(3), 343–366.

Rust, P. C. (1996). Monogamy and polyamory: Relationship issues for bisexuals. In B. A. Firestein (Ed.), *Bisexuality: The psychology and politics of an invisible minority* (pp. 127–148). Thousand Oaks, CA: Sage.

Rust, P. C. (2002). Bisexuality: The state of the union. *Annual Review of Sex Research, 13*, 180–240.

Rust, P.C. (2003). Finding a sexual identity and community: Therapeutic implications and cultural assumptions in scientific models of coming out. In L. D. Garnets & D. G. Kimmel (Eds.), *Psychological perspectives on lesbian, gay, and bisexual experiences* (pp. 227-269). New York: Columbia University.

Schiff, T. (2003). Developing men's leadership to challenge sexism and violence: Working in university settings to develop "Pro-feminist, gay-affirmative and male-positive" men. In B. C. Wallace & R. T. Carter (Eds.), *Understanding and dealing with violence: A multicultural approach* (pp. 161–182). Thousand Oaks, CA: Sage.

Schrock, D., Reid, L., & Boyd, E. M. (2005). Transsexuals' embodiment of womanhood. *Gender & Society, 19*(3), 317–335.

Shidlo, A. (1994). Internalized homophobia: Conceptual and empirical issues in measurement. In B. Greene & G. M. Herek (Eds.), *Lesbian and gay psychology: Theory, research and applications* (pp. 176–205). Thousand Oaks, CA: Sage.

Silverschanz, P., Cortina, L. M., Konik, J., & Magley, V. J. (2008). Slurs, snubs, and queer jokes: Incidence and impact of heterosexist harassment in academia. *Sex Roles, 58*, 179–191.

Simonsen, G., Blazina, C., & Watkins, J. C. E. (2000). Gender role conflict and psychological well-being among gay men. *Journal of Counseling Psychology, 47*, 85–89.

Spalding, L. R., & Peplau, L. A. (1997). The unfaithful lover: Heterosexuals' perceptions of bisexuals and their relationships. *Psychology of Women Quarterly, 21*, 611–625.

Sue, D. W., Capodilupo, C. M., Torino, G. C., Bucceri, J. M., Holder, A. M. B., Nadal, K. L., et al. (2007). Racial microaggressions in everyday life: Implications for clinical practice. *American Psychologist, 82*(4), 271–286.

Surgenor, L. J., & Fear, J. L. (1998). Eating disorder in a transgender patient: A case report. *International Journal of Eating Disorders, 24*, 449–452.

Swigonski, M. E. (2006). Violence, hate crimes, and hate language. In D. F. Morrow & L. Messinger (Eds.), *Sexual orientation & gender expression in social work practice* (pp. 364–383). New York: Columbia University Press.

Szymanski, D. M., & Carr, E. R. (2008). The roles of gender role conflict and internalized heterosexism in gay and bisexual men's psychological distress: Testing two mediation models. *Psychology of Men & Masculinity, 9*(1), 40–54.

Szymanski, D. M., Chung, Y. B., & Balsam, K. F. (2001). Psychosocial correlates of internalized homophobia in lesbians. *Measurement & Evaluation in Counseling & Development, 34*, 27–49.

Taywaditep, K. J. (2001). Marginalization among the marginalized: Gay men's anti-effeminacy attitudes. *Journal of Homosexuality, 42*(1), 1–28.

Theodore, P. S., & Basow, S. A. (2000). Heterosexual masculinity and homophobia: A reaction to the self? *Journal of Homosexuality, 40*(2), 31–47.

Weinberg, G. H. (1972). *Society and the healthy homosexual.* New York: St. Martin's Press.

Weinberg, M. S., Williams, C. J., & Pryor, D. W. (1994). *Dual attraction: Understanding bisexuality*. New York: Oxford University Press.

Westwood, M. J., Keats, P. A., & Wilensky, P. (2003). Therapeutic enactment: Integrating individual and group counseling models for change. *Journal of Specialists in Group Work, 28*(2), 122–138.

Whitley, B. E. (2001). Gender role variables and attitudes towards homosexuality. *Sex Roles, 45,* 691–721.

Williamson, I. R. (2000). Internalized homophobia and health issues affecting lesbians and gay men. *Health Education Research, 15*(1), 97–107.

Witten, T., & Eyler, E. (1999). Hate crimes and violence against the transgendered. *Peace Review, 11,* 3.

Wood, M. J. (2004). The gay male gaze: Body image disturbance and gender oppression among gay men. *Journal of Gay & Lesbian Social Services, 17*(2), 43–62.

Yang, A. (1997). Trends: Attitudes toward homosexuality. *Public Opinion Quarterly 61,* 477–507.

Zerubavel, E. (1982). Personal information and social life. *Symbolic Interaction, 5,* 97–10.

CHAPTER 4

Moving Toward Affirmative Practices With Sexual and Gender Minorities

INTRODUCTION

The excerpts below were written by trainees in the helping professions; the first is from a survey respondent, a graduate student whose lesson from his/her professor seems to be that gay men and lesbians are psychologically unsuitable as parents:

> In a family therapy class, the instructor would only consider heterosexual parents and heterosexual offspring. Any time that a gay/lesbian issue was brought up, the instructor became defensive and stated that "alternative lifestyles" were not part of his class and that there were no gay parents who were happy. (Quoted in Pilkington & Cantor, 1996, p. 607).

In this next excerpt, a counseling intern describes his experience in clinical supervision when he attempted to process personal reactions that surfaced in relation to his client and their shared identities as gay men:

> In another site, I conducted an assessment on a gay man with AIDS. The client's ambivalence about his sexual orientation had emerged from assessment data, and I wanted to talk about this with my supervisor. However I felt uncomfortable discussing sexual orientation issues with her without coming out. I decided to do so in a supervision meeting as I discussed the case. As I did, I said

that I had done so to share this part of my life and to figure out how to integrate my personal and professional identity. Her immediate response horrified me. "Well, if I were you, I wouldn't discuss it at all. I mean, I don't talk about who I sleep with." Blood rushed to my face as feelings of shame, anger, and fear washed over me. However, for the first time, my shame did not silence me. I informed the supervisor that being gay was much more than sexual behavior. "Oh, I know" she said with a wry smile. "I was just kidding." (Quoted in O'Brien, 2005, pp. 97–98)

How do the experiences of these students compare with your own? How have sexual and gender minorities been depicted in your textbooks and in your courses, and how has this impacted you and your emerging identity as a helping professional?

A Preview of Chapter Contents

The previous chapter explored psychological and behavioral aspects of homo-, bi-, and transphobias and their implications for the mental health of sexual and gender minorities. In this chapter, the focus shifts to you and to other helping professionals—in particular, to an exploration of the degree to which societal norms and practices have affected your personal views about your sex, gender, and sexual orientation.

Self-reflection is considered a critical component of training in the helping professions (Corey & Corey, 2007) and is viewed as essential to the practice of ethical psychotherapy with sexual and gender minorities (Biaggio, Orchard, Larson, Petrino, & Mihara, 2003; Morrow, 2000; Phillips, 2000). The exercises in this chapter are designed to serve as catalysts in the process of your own self-exploration. This chapter also provides some concrete examples of affirmative treatment approaches to working with sexual and gender minorities as it

- Defines countertransference and describes its evolution in the literature in relation to practitioners who work with sexual and gender minority clients,
- Reviews research and describes various methodologies used to explore helping practitioners' responses to sexual and gender minority clients (Garnets, Hancock, Cochran, Goodchilds, & Peplau, 1991; Mohr, Israel, & Sedlacek, 2001),
- Cites examples of counseling behaviors that are contraindicated and those that are necessary for practitioners to work affirmatively and effectively with sexual and gender minority clients, and
- Discusses issues related to the educational preparation of helping professionals and provides recommendations to enhance training and practice.

THERAPISTS' RESPONSES TOWARD SEXUAL AND GENDER MINORITY CLIENTS

Researchers have long recognized that therapeutic alliances are an integral part of effective therapy (Stevens, Muran, & Safran, 2003) and that therapists' personal issues and values play a vital role in determining the nature of these relationships. In psychoanalysis, Freud (1959) coined the term *countertransference* to describe a phenomenon in which a patient's projection of unresolved childhood conflicts onto the analyst triggers the analyst's own unresolved conflicts. Since Freud's original formulation, countertransference has been re-defined in numerous ways by researchers from various schools of psychotherapy. This text adopts Hayes's (2004) definition of countertransference: the unconscious and conscious personal conflicts that arise in therapists' responses to their clients. Most researchers agree that countertransference reactions are not signs of pathology in therapists; rather, these reactions are natural and universal. For example, Hayes (2004) "normalizes" countertrans-ference: "Therapists of all theoretical persuasions, by virtue of their humanity, have unre-solved personal conflicts; try though we might, no professional credentials or experience shield us from the human condition" (p. 24).

Hayes (2004) and Hayes and Gelso (1993) posited that countertransference reactions can take various forms. For example, therapists can exhibit countertransference by making cognitive errors such as forgetting important information about clients. And they can ex-perience anxiety and become overly involved emotionally with their clients. Therapists can also engage in avoidance behaviors like redirecting the client by changing topics and prematurely terminating therapy (Liddle, 1996). Frequently, countertransference can be translated into visceral terms through quickened respiration, heartbeat, sweating, and flushing.

One interesting example of cognitive-behavioral transference emerged from a labo-ratory study by Gelso, Fassinger, Gomez, and Latts (1995). Sixty-seven professional practi-tioners completed a paper-and-pencil measure of homophobia and viewed one of two videotaped dramatizations wherein lesbian clients discussed relationship difficulties with their therapists. The videotapes were stopped at six distinct points, and participants were asked to verbally record their own responses to these clients into a recording microphone. At the end of this task, participants were asked to complete a measure of anxiety and to recall contents of the interview. Practitioners' ratings on the homophobia scale correlated with their avoidance behaviors (disapproval, silence, ignoring, mislabeling) with the client.

As a result of differing viewpoints about the definition of countertransference, re-searchers have been challenged to define the best ways to explore this dynamic. It has only been in recent years that researchers have begun to focus on therapists' countertransfer-ence responses toward sexual minority clients. The bulk of research into this topic is based on retrospective accounts by clients of their past therapy experiences, analogue studies that involve the random assignment of case vignettes or videotaped counseling interviews that are identical except for the sexual orientation of the client and/or the therapist, and surveys of practitioners. There are obvious limitations inherent in these studies, including difficulties posed by relying on retrospective reporting, the artificiality of analogue methodology, sampling problems, and response bias.

COUNTERTRANSFERENCE TOWARD SEXUAL AND GENDER MINORITY CLIENTS: RESEARCH FINDINGS

Research on countertransference among helping professionals suggests that partici-pants are less likely to report homophobic attitudes than was the case 20 years ago (Jones, Botsko, & Gorman, 2003). It is difficult to know whether these improvements reflect real changes or represent a desire not to appear homophobic. And despite this overall pattern of improvement, there are still some differences in countertransference responses to sexual minority clients, depending on the demographic characteristics of the therapists.

Numerous researchers (Bieschke, McClanahan, Tozer, Grzegorek, & Park, 2000; Bowers & Bieschke, 2005; Ford & Hendrick, 2003; Jones, Botsko, & Gorman, 2003; Liddle, 1996; Matthews, Selvidge, & Fisher, 2005) report that women therapists, regardless of their training and clinical specialties, report more positive attitudes toward their lesbian and gay clients than do their male counterparts. For example, in a recent study, Bowers and Bieschke (2005) administered counseling vignettes to approximately three hundred licensed practitioners in which the client's gender and sexual orientation (gay, lesbian, bisexual man, bisexual woman, heterosexual man, heterosexual woman) were manipulated. Each vignette contained a description of the client as experiencing moderate depression related to the management of diabetes. Respondents were asked to assess their attitudinal responses to the client depicted in the vignette and to rate his or her overall functioning and degree of personal responsibility for the creation of and solution to his or her problems. Results indicated that female practitioners held more optimistic attitudes and clinical evaluations of all clients than did their male counterparts. Female practitioners perceived all clients as stronger, more active, and less responsible for the cause of their problems than did male therapists. Male participants also perceived lesbian, gay, and bisexual clients as more likely to harm others than did their heterosexual counterparts.

A number of recent studies also report that helping professionals view particular subgroups of sexual minority persons differently. For example, Mohr, Israel, and Sedlacek (2001) explored practitioners' attitudes toward bisexuality in an analogue study. Practitioners were randomly given written descriptions of a bisexual female or a heterosexual client and asked to complete a number of measures. Those practitioners who had more negative attitudes toward bisexuality perceived the fictitious bisexual client as functioning at lower levels than her heterosexual counterpart.

Crawford, McLeod, Zamboni, and Jordan (1999) incorporated an analogue technique to assess psychologists' attitudes regarding gay and lesbian parents. Approximately four hundred psychologists were asked to read one of three vignettes depicting either gay male, lesbian, or heterosexual couples interested in adopting a child. Participants were significantly less likely to recommend granting custody to lesbian and gay male couples seeking to adopt a female child than were participants who rated heterosexual couples.

Hayes and Gelso (1993) and Hayes and Erkis (2000) explored the effects of therapist homophobia in analogue studies with gay men and HIV-positive men. In Hayes and Gelso's (1993) study, therapists' homophobia was predictive of avoidance behaviors toward gay men who were HIV positive. In a related study, Hayes and Erkis (2000) presented vignettes involving a male client who was HIV positive to 425 psychologists. Respondents who were considered homophobic on an assessment of homophobia responded with significantly less empathy and were less willing to work with gay clients who were HIV positive.

While gender minorities have typically been omitted from countertransference research, it is probable that practitioners also exhibit negative cognitive and behavioral responses toward gender minority clients. Because the subject of gender minority issues is even more taboo than sexual orientation (Mallon, 1999), much of our information regarding therapists' attitudes and behaviors is derived from anecdotal reports by therapists themselves and the retrospective accounts of gender minority clients. Perhaps one of the most commonly held beliefs among practitioners is that gender minorities are truly homosexuals who simply cannot face their homosexuality. Many practitioners believe that the origins of transgenderism lie in family dysfunction or childhood sexual abuse (Mallon, 1999). Many still communicate "either-or" messages about sex reassignment surgery by counseling clients out of reassignment procedures because of "somatically inappropriate" body types and facial features (Ettner, 1999). As one therapist reported, "[T]he patient was a 6 foot 5 inch male. It was virtually an inconceivable challenge that due to his size, he could ever pass as female."

GAY-, BI-, AND TRANS-AFFIRMATIVE COUNSELING

Affirmative approaches to counseling sexual and gender minorities do not just entail refraining from clinical practices that might potentially harm sexual and gender minority clients. Rather, affirmative approaches actively value and support sexual and gender diversity (Matthews et al., 2005; Raj, 2002). *Gay-affirmative counseling* is defined as a guideline for the provision of unconditional positive regard for and acceptance of all sexual minorities (Bergh & Crisp, 2004).

Many researchers have attempted to elucidate more clearly the dimensions or behaviors that make up gay-affirmative therapy by identifying its opposite. In a landmark study that explored therapists' behaviors toward their sexual minority clients in counseling, Garnets et al. (1991) conducted a national survey of psychologists. Several thousand surveys were sent to members of the American Psychological Association. Participants were asked to cite examples of discriminatory and exemplary practices with sexual minority clients and to assess the degree to which these practices were perceived as particularly helpful or harmful. Content analysis of the responses yielded a total of 17 themes of biased and inadequate responses ranging from the therapist's belief that homosexuality is a mental disorder to the therapist's abrupt referral to another therapist without emotionally processing the referral with the client. Fourteen themes of exemplary practice included the therapist's recognition of the impact of antigay prejudice and the impact of such bias in terms of creating or contributing to clients' presenting problems.

The list of themes that emerged from the research by Garnets et al. served as a foundation for the development of Guidelines for Psychotherapy with Lesbian, Gay, and Bisexual Clients, later published by the American Psychological Association's Division 44 (2000).

In 1996, Bieschke and Matthews surveyed 106 career practitioners employed in university counseling centers regarding their use of affirming behaviors with their sexual minority career clients. *Affirming behaviors* were defined by Fassinger (1991) as behaviors that validate sexual minorities and that acknowledge antigay discrimination and its consequences. Respondents were given several measures, including a homophobia scale, a measure of organizational climate, and a 30-item affirmative behaviors scale. Bieschke and Matthews (1996) reported that there were two factors that particularly predicted affirmative behaviors. The first was the sexual orientation of the practitioner. The second was the offering of a gay-positive climate by the clinical practice or agency itself.

Dorland and Fischer (2001) explored the impact of therapists' use of heterosexist language on gay, lesbian, and bisexual clients and then analyzed the clients' satisfaction and progress with their therapists. Participants who were exposed to therapists' use of heterosexist language were significantly less comfortable in therapy, less willing to disclose sexual orientation to the counselor, and less likely to return to therapy.

In their survey of addictions practitioners, Matthews et al. (2005) attempted to identify factors that would predict affirmative clinical practice with sexual minority clients. The factor that was statistically significant was the organizational climate of the treatment agency. Matthews et al. noted that "when counseling centers and treatment facilities create a climate of affirmation, the practitioners employed there are more inclined to behave similarly in their work with clients" (p. 63). Such things as the selection of magazines in the waiting area, terminology used in intake forms, artwork and posters, and books on the shelves help define the organizational climate of an agency.

Trans-Affirmative Counseling

A related term, *transpositive practice* (Raj, 2002), refers to practitioners' attitudes and behaviors that convey acceptance of gender minorities. In perhaps one of the very few surveys of gender minority clients' experiences in psychotherapy, Rachlin (2002) sampled 93 participants, 70 female-to-male and 23 male-to-female transsexual persons. Of the respondents, 87% reported that positive change occurred in their lives as a result of psychotherapy. In particular, respondents noted that the therapists' acceptance of and respect for their gender identity, the therapists' flexibility in the treatment approach, and the therapists' referrals to the transgender community were the most helpful aspects of their therapy experiences. Negative experiences were associated with therapists who were perceived by their clients to be extremely passive or distant and not knowledgeable about gender minority issues.

Anecdotal reports of gender minority clients' experiences in therapy have been consistent with Rachlin's results. Gender minority clients often perceived their therapists as being unsupportive, lacking sufficient knowledge, and exhibiting negative countertransference responses toward them (Carroll & Gilroy, 2002; Korell & Lorah, 2007).

EXAMPLES OF GAY/TRANS-AFFIRMATIVE PRACTICE. The following examples of gay- and trans-affirmative practices illustrate the kinds of positive attitudes and behaviors that helping professionals exhibit:

- Recognizes that sexual and gender minorities are stigmatized minorities and that social oppression may play a role in the presenting problems sexual and gender minorities bring to therapy (Bergh & Crisp, 2004; Mallon, 1999; Phillips, 2000);
- Appreciates diversity within sexual and gender minority communities in terms of people of color, sex trade workers, persons with HIV/AIDS, youth, and others (Bergh & Crisp, 2004; Mallon, 1999; Raj, 2002);
- Knows about community resources for sexual and gender minorities (Bergh & Crisp, 2004; Mallon, 1999; Raj, 2002);
- Refers to clients by the names and pronouns that sexual and gender minorities have chosen and prefer (Bergh & Crisp, 2004; Israel & Tarver, 1997; Raj, 2002); and
- Assumes a person-centered approach to gender expression by aiding clients in exploring all their options, including cross-dressing, periodic cross-living, the use of cross-sex hormones, chest/breast surgery, and genital surgery (Bockting, Knudson, & Goldberg, 2006).

EXAMPLES OF NON-GAY/TRANS-AFFIRMATIVE PRACTICE.   The following examples are definitive illustrations of attitudes and behaviors on the part of helping professionals that do not convey acceptance:

- Avoids asking clients about their sexual and gender orientations (Martell, Safren, & Prince, 2004) or changes the topic when a client discusses sexual or gender minority issues (Bergh & Crisp, 2004);
- Voices the view that the client's sexual or gender orientation is a psychopathology (Bergh & Crisp, 2004; Crisp & McCave, 2007; Israel & Tarver, 1997; Mathy, 2001; Raj, 2002; Zandvliet, 2000);
- Displays an excessive curiosity about or fascination with gender and sexual minorities (Zandvliet, 2000);
- Doesn't recognize the psychological impact of homophobia, biphobia, and transphobia (Garnets et al., 1991; Morrow, 2000);
- Minimizes or exaggerates the importance of sexual and gender orientation in terms of the presenting problem (Bergh & Crisp, 2004; Crisp & McCave, 2007) or interprets every client problem as a byproduct of the client's sexual or gender minority status (Zandvliet, 2000);
- Minimizes the differences between heterosexual and same-sex relationships or, conversely, assumes vast differences between heterosexual and same-sex relationships (Garnets et al., 1991; Morrow, 2000);
- Shows discomfort when hearing about a client's same-sex sexual behavior or gender nonconformity (Bergh & Crisp, 2004; Crisp & McCave, 2007);
- Attempts to discourage clients from disclosing details of their sexual behavior or gender nonconformity when the client exhibits such gender-atypical behavior (such as a man with strong feminine characteristics) (Martell, Safren, & Prince, 2004; Phillips & Fischer, 1998)
- Suggests the client may not actually be gay/lesbian/bisexual/transgender but is just going through a "phase" (Bergh & Crisp, 2004);
- Pressures bisexual clients to stay in monogamous, heterosexual relationships (Phillips & Fischer, 1998) or, alternatively, fails to acknowledge that some bisexual clients are polyamorous (pursuing simultaneous romantic relationships with partners who are informed about the nature of these relationships) (Weitzman, 2006);
- Lacks basic knowledge about polyamory and places sexual and gender minority clients in the position of having to educate them (Weitzman, 2006);
- Makes premature assumptions about HIV/AIDS and sexual behaviors when informed the client's identification is bisexual (Goetstouwers, 2006);
- Lacks basic knowledge about sexual and gender minority issues and places these clients in the position of having to educate them (Liddle, 1997; Zandvliet, 2000);
- Lacks knowledge of medical options for gender minorities (Rachlin, 2002);
- Is either overly encouraging about coming out to someone despite the client's assessment of the situation as "risky" or overly discouraging (Garnets et al., 1991; Morrow, 2000);
- Is either overly encouraging or overly discouraging about sex reassignment surgery (Ettner, 1999; Gagne, Tewksbury, & McGaughey, 1997; Raj, 2002; Zandvliet, 2000).

- Believes all gender minorities are fundamentally homophobic and has difficulty accepting their sexual identity as gay or lesbian (Raj, 2002); and
- Bases views about sexual and gender minorities solely on observations of clinical samples of such persons in crises rather than on observations of a normal population (Cole & Meyer, 1998).

GRADUATE/PROFESSIONAL DEVELOPMENT TRAINING: A WORK IN PROGRESS

This section explores issues that are relevant to the educational preparation of helping professionals. Specifically, it contains important recommendations that will enhance the educational experiences of trainees as well as practitioners who were trained in contexts where sufficient education in these areas was nonexistent or inadequate.

This is partially in response to demographic changes that have resulted in greater ethnic, racial, and cultural diversification in the United States. The helping professions have been increasingly committed to training practitioners to work within a multicultural counseling framework. Further, because there is significant overlap between the cultural experiences of ethnic and racial minorities and of sexual minorities, sexual minority issues are increasingly integrated into counselor education and training (Carroll & Gilroy, 2001) along with other aspects of diversity, including disabilities, social class, and religion. A multicultural counseling framework specifies the competencies that culturally competent practitioners must attain (Sue, Arredondo, & McDavis, 1992; Sue et al., 1982; Sue & Sue, 1999): (1) specific knowledge and information about the worldviews of the culturally different, including their life experiences, heritages, and historical backgrounds; (2) appropriate, relevant, and sensitive skills for use with culturally different clients; and (3) awareness of possible negative emotional and cognitive responses toward culturally different clients.

Sexual Minority Issues

Moderate levels of homophobia have been reported in samples of graduate trainees in social work, counseling, and psychology (Krieglstein, 2003; Snively, Kreuger, Stretch, Watt, & Chadha, 2004). Newman, Dannenfelser, and Benishek (2002) explored attitudes in their sample of 2,837 graduate social work and counseling students and reported that 6.5% (N = 184) expressed intolerant attitudes toward sexual minorities.

The object of one unique study was to examine the impact of counseling trainees' sex and gender identities on their countertransference responses to sexual minority clients (Korfhage, 2006). The study found that, while the sex of participants did not predict negative attitudes toward sexual minority clients, traditional gender identities did. As is consistent with research presented in Chapter 1, counseling trainees who maintained traditional conceptions of gender (men-masculine-heterosexual and women-feminine-heterosexual) were less accepting of their sexual minority clients.

Retrospective surveys of practitioners about their graduate training experiences have demonstrated that many practitioners perceived their training in sexual minority issues as inadequate. In 1996, Doherty and Simmons surveyed practicing marriage and family therapists regarding their level of preparation, both in graduate training and in postgraduate continuing education, to treat sexual minorities. Approximately one-half of their sample of 526 practitioners believed that they were adequately prepared to work with sexual minority clients.

Phillips and Fischer (1998) conducted a survey regarding doctoral-level training experiences in clinical psychology and found that the majority of their graduate-student respondents viewed themselves as ill prepared to work with lesbian and gay clients. The authors further reported that their respondents had even less training in bisexual issues. Phillips and Fischer concluded:

> It must be stated unequivocally that both counseling and clinical psychology need to ensure that graduate programs make more consistent and more concerted efforts to integrate LGB issues into their curricula if they are to produce psychologists that are competent to work with LGB clients. (p. 728)

The majority of graduate programs in the helping professions offer little formal training and specialized coursework in sexual minority issues (Fassinger & Richie, 1997; Krieglstein, 2003; Matthews et al., 2005; Phillips & Fischer, 1998; Snively et al., 2004). In one study, Murphy, Rawlings, and Howe (2002) randomly selected doctoral-level psychologists to participate in a survey of their training experiences. Murphy et al. reported that 56% of their sample of clinical psychologists had counseled a minimum of one sexual minority client in the past week. However, only 10% of their sample reported the availability of a graduate-level course specifically in sexual minority issues. Savage, Prout, and Chard (2004) surveyed 288 school psychologists regarding their practices and level of preparedness for working with sexual minorities. The majority (85%) of their respondents indicated that they had never received any specific education and training regarding sexual orientation in their graduate studies.

Some graduate programs—for example, doctoral-level counseling psychology programs accredited by the American Psychological Association (APA)—have lately begun to introduce content specific to sexual minorities in the context of multicultural counseling courses (Sherry, Whilde, & Patton, 2005). In many cases, however, the texts in graduate multicultural counseling are restricted to a single chapter about sexual minority issues (Atkinson & Hackett, 2004; Robinson & Howard-Hamilton, 2000; Sue & Sue, 2003; Vacc, DeVaney, & Brendel, 2003). As late as 1996, textbooks used in graduate-level counseling courses still viewed same-sex sexuality and bisexuality as pathological (Pilkington & Cantor, 1996).

Several studies have explored the extent to which graduate training programs in the helping professions have gay-supportive faculty–student mentor relationships. In 1996, Pilkington and Cantor surveyed graduate students in doctoral programs in psychology and reported that the students were subjected to heterosexist comments by their instructors. More recently, Messinger (2004) engaged in a series of in-depth interviews with gay and lesbian social work students about their clinical fieldwork experiences. In addition to experiencing heterosexist assumptions by fellow staff members, gay and lesbian interns expressed feelings of anxiety and a sense of being unsafe. Messenger concluded that in addition to improving the quality of training, it is imperative that interns and trainees experience the academic environment as welcoming and gay/les/bi/trans-affirmative.

Today there is often little support in graduate programs for research related to sexual and gender minority issues (Biaggio et al., 2003). Those who research topics related to sexual and gender minorities are frequently assumed to be gay, lesbian, or bisexual, and professionals who work predominately with sexual and gender minority clients are often assumed to be sexual and gender minorities. Voorhis and Wagner (2004) conducted a content analysis of four major social work journals published between 1988 and 1997. Approximately 4% of the total number of articles dealt with sexual minorities, and most of these articles focused on HIV and AIDS. Phillips, Ingram, Smith, and Mindes (2003) reported that in eight major counseling journals from 1990 to 1999, only 2.11% contained a focus on sexual minorities. Buhrke, Ben-Ezra, Hurley, and Ruprecht (1992) reported that a review of the literature contained in six major counseling psychology journals from 1978 to 1989 found not a single article focused exclusively on bisexuality. In their quantitative analysis of psychological research documented in the PsycInfo database and published over a 27-year period, Lee and Crawford (2007) reported that research incorporating gay and lesbian persons accounted for less than 1% of the total research and that bisexual persons accounted for less than 0.20% of the research. Sexual minority graduate students experience apprehension and concern about doing such research for fear of receiving negative evaluations and being discontinued in their respective programs (Biaggio et al. 2003).

To date, there has been little research regarding the degree to which counseling faculty members experience homophobia, biphobia, and/or gender phobia. In one of the few studies, Ben-Ari (2001) explored attitudes of faculty members in three departments—psychology, social work, and education—at five major universities in Israel. Ben-Ari reported "low-grade homophobia" among his sample of faculty members in social work and psychology, who exhibited significantly less homophobia than faculty members in education.

Gender Minority Issues

The extent to which gender minorities are omitted from graduate counseling training (Cole, Denny, Eyler, & Samons, 2000; Gainor, 2000) is distressing. While guidelines established by Division 44 APA's (2000) and the American Counseling Association's Association for Gay, Lesbian, and Bisexual Issues in Counseling (AGLBIC, 2003) did not included gender minorities, efforts are currently underway to address the counseling competencies that practitioners need to work with gender minority clients (APA, 2008). Mallon (1999) points out that despite the Council on Social Work Education's revision of accreditation standards in 1992 to include training related to sexual minorities, gender minority issues were not mentioned.

TRAINING RECOMMENDATIONS

Professional ethical codes and policies of counseling, psychology, and social work associations (i.e., the American Psychological Association, the National Association of Social Workers, and the Council on Social Work Education) specifically require professionals to obtain specialized training in sexual minority issues. Yet Bieschke, Paul, and Blasko (2007) caution that "trainees and professionals can sometimes profess to be affirmative without delving very deeply into what that means for them and how such attitudes may manifest in therapy" (p. 310). In the words of Bowers and Bieschke (2005):

> In light of the influence of homophobic and biphobic sentiment prevalent within mainstream U.S. culture, and the not-so-distant practice of diagnosing

and conceptualizing LGB sexual orientations as pathologically deviant, we recommend that psychologists engage in further training, supervision, and their own therapy to develop greater acuity in recognizing how they experience and assess clients of differing sexual orientations and how stereotypes about LGB people contribute to their reactions. (p. 102)

Two fairly recent studies (Godfrey, Haddock, Fisher, & Lund, 2006; Israel, Ketz, Detrie, Burke, & Shulman, 2003) employed the Delphi method, asking panels of experts to identify aspects of training programs considered essential to affirmative therapy practices with sexual minorities and their families. Experts view the need to cultivate openness and to explore values and biases as crucial. Godfrey et al. (2006) note that their panel of experts strongly endorsed the notion of training that incorporates personal explorations of one's own constructions of gender and sexual identity.

Several authors recommend the inclusion of speaker panels comprised of sexual and gender minorities and interview assignments (Biaggio et al., 2003). There is some evidence to suggest that, like the general population, therapists tend to feel more favorably toward their sexual minority clients when they have had a history of prior contact with sexual minorities outside the therapy context (Mohr & Rochlen, 1999). Others (e.g., Long & Serovich, 2003) recommend that biographical films and first-person narratives be used as a stimulus for counselor self-exploration. Particularly in the area of gender minorities, it is critical that counseling trainees and professionals hear the voices of transgender persons. In accordance with this view, this text offers a number of recommendations.

Attitudes Toward Sex

Self-examination is necessary if practitioners are to explore their personal conceptions of polyamory and nonmonogamy. Practitioners need to guard against the tendency to assume a traditionally negative view of extradyadic sexual relationships as undesirable and evidence of relationship instability or dysfunction in the primary relationship. There has been limited research on the impact of therapists' values and biases regarding various sexual practices (Ford & Hendrick, 2003). In their survey of 314 psychologists, Ford and Hendrick (2003) reported that male therapists were more accepting of sexual behaviors including sadomasochism and group sex than were women therapists. Studies have shown that sexual fidelity may not be as crucial a variable in the longevity and satisfaction of couples, particularly gay couples, as is the open communication between partners about the parameters of the relationship regarding sexual exclusivity (Peplau, Fingerhut, & Beals, 2004; Shernoff, 1995).

Practitioners also need to be especially open to self-examination regarding the atypical sexual behaviors that are practiced by sexual and gender minorities (Nichols, 2006). Atypical behaviors are defined as sexual behaviors including bondage/discipline/dominance/submission/sadism/masochism (BDSM), and many of them have been pathologized in psychiatry (Nichols, 2006). Nichols (2006) posits that in countertransference responses to BDSM, practitioners experience feelings such as shock, revulsion, and fear. According to Nichols, "when practitioners find themselves believing that their clients' pathology is self-evident despite no concrete evidence of harm, it is fairly certain that countertransference is present" (p. 286). Nichols suggests practitioners might borrow the term *squicked* from the BDSM community. Squicked refers to "having a strong negative emotional reaction to an activity while knowing that you do not actually 'judge' the activity as 'wrong' or 'bad' (p. 288).

The following recommendations are gleaned from a survey of the current literature and include suggestions for change in clinical training.

1. Include sexual and gender orientation in admission and recruitment materials (Biaggio et al., 2003; Long & Serovich, 2003; Phillips, 2000).
2. Provide visible faculty role models and mentors who are openly identified as sexual and gender minorities (Biaggio et al., 2003; Long & Serovich, 2003; Phillips, 2000).
3. Include sexual and gender minorities in nondiscrimination policies and hiring policies (Biaggio et al., 2003; Phillips, 2000).
4. Establish resource centers for sexual and gender minority students (Biaggio et al., 2003).
5. Include curriculum content in bisexuality (Phillips, 2000; Phillips & Fischer, 1998), polyamory (Weitzman, 2006), and gender minority issues (Gainor, 2000; Mallon, 1999), and adopt this content in courses other than those related to sexuality and multicultural classes (Long & Serovich, 2003).
6. Encourage student research—including theses, dissertations, and research agendas as new professionals—on sexual and gender minority issues (Biaggio et al., 2003).
7. Provide training to work with family members, spouses, friends, and relatives of gender minorities who seek assistance and support for dealing with their transgender loved ones (Gainor, 2000).
8. Include panels with sexual and gender minority persons (Biaggio et al., 2003; Godfrey et al., 2006).
9. Encourage readings and films with sexual and gender minority content and characters (Long & Serovich, 2003).

RELIGION AND THE PRACTICE OF AFFIRMATIVE PSYCHOTHERAPY

During a recent introductory counseling class, a student was wrestling with her conflict between her deeply held religious beliefs and the mandate to practice gay-affirmative counseling. During the class discussion, this student disclosed her intention to resolve her dilemma by referring her sexual minority clients to other practitioners. Imagine yourself in a similar context as a clinical supervisor or mentor. How might you have responded to this student's statement?

While this particular student seemed cognizant of the ethical and moral imperative that practitioners do no harm to their clients, there are many factors to consider in making clinical judgments such as this. For instance, one needs to consider that many sexual and gender minority clients are hesitant to self-disclose their sexual and gender identities until a trusting therapeutic relationship has been established (Morrow, 2000). Hence, therapists who refer out may well be in danger of generating feelings of rejection and abandonment in their clients. Additionally, there are many areas in the United States, including geographically isolated communities, where there are few counseling and support resources available for sexual and gender minorities. These areas offer extremely limited referral options.

In their chapter entitled "Perceived Conflicts Between Affirmation of Religious Diversity and Affirmation of Sexual Diversity: That's Perceived," Fischer and DeBord

(2007) apply an ethical decision-making model to help therapists consider the conflict between personal religious values and same-sex sexual orientations. Fischer and DeBord maintain that the moral imperative to do no harm overrides the temporary infringement on the right of the therapist to enact his or her own religious values in the professional arena.

WHEN THERAPISTS ARE SEXUAL OR GENDER MINORITIES

Research suggests that sexual minorities report more positive gain from therapy when therapists are female, gay, or lesbian (Jones et al., 2003; Liddle, 1996). Liddle (1996), for example, surveyed 392 lesbian and gay persons who rated their therapy experiences with their past and present therapists and provided information about each therapist's gender and sexual orientation. Participants rated their therapists, a total of 923, in terms of their perceived helpfulness. Participants rated their gay, lesbian, and heterosexual female therapists as significantly more helpful than their heterosexual male therapists. In one ambitious study of sexual minority therapy consumers, Jones et al. (2003) explored the impact of client–therapist matching on the perceptions of therapeutic benefit in a national nonprobability sample of 600 sexual minority participants. Predictors of benefit were the therapist's sex (female) and sexual orientation (gay or lesbian).

While practitioners who have similar identities in terms of sexual and/or gender orientation as their clients may appear to be at an advantage, this similarity can also pose difficulties for practitioners, as Spritz (2002), a gender minority therapist, noted:

> As a post-operative transsexual woman and psychiatrist, I have the distinction of having sat on both sides of the couch. What I've learned from working with trans clients is that we have to both treat the transgender/transsexual issue, and also treat the human being. Each client is unique, and his or her life experiences may share some similarities with mine, but there is so much variation that I can't take anything for granted. Even when the client presents with a story similar to my own, I have to investigate and question my own assumptions. (p. 15)

Sexual and/or gender minority psychologists, social workers, and practitioners are sometimes more susceptible to overidentifying with their clients. Another danger exists in terms of possible dual relationships, especially in smaller communities where therapists and clients may sometimes travel in similar social circles.

The Use of Self-Disclosure by Sexual and Gender Minority Therapists

The question of whether sexual and gender minority therapists should "come out" to their clients has resulted in an especially provocative debate. There are varying opinions within the psychotherapy field as to whether self-disclosure is beneficial to clients (Bashan, 2005; Satterly, 2006). Brown and Walker (1990), Kooden (1991), and Perlman (1991) conclude that sexual minority therapists' self-disclosure is especially desirable, given the scarcity of gay and lesbian role models. Some authors (i.e., Frost, 1998; Liddle, 1996) have argued that when sexual minority therapists "pass" as heterosexuals, their feelings of genuineness are affected, and the therapeutic process is negatively impacted.

Bernstein (2000) cautioned that sexual and gender minority therapists may be putting themselves at risk when they "out" themselves during preliminary telephone conversations with clients. Bernstein endorsed Pearlman's (1996) idea of routinely asking clients if they have thought about wanting to work with a gay therapist or a straight therapist.

Satterly (2006) conducted a qualitative study of gay male therapists on this issue of "coming out" to clients and reported that a number of his participants recommended that colleagues consider the potential damage that might be done to the therapeutic relationship as a result of self-disclosure. Many participants indicated that the possibility of seeing clients in gay-related social contexts outside of therapy situations led them to proactively disclose their orientation to their sexual minority clients (Satterly, 2006). Guthrie (2006) offered the following questions for therapists' self-reflection when the issue of their own sexual orientation arises in therapy:

a. Why is the subject coming up at this point in the therapy?
b. What meaning might the answer have to this particular patient?
c. How will knowing my sexual orientation facilitate or hamper the therapy?
d. Is more to be gained in delaying my response until a later time? (p. 47)

Summary

In our heterosexist culture, it is theoretically impossible for all practitioners, even those who are gender and sexual minorities, to be free of homophobia, biphobia, and gender phobia. However, given research evidence that sexual minorities are more likely to seek counseling than are nonminorities (Bieschke et al., 2000; Liddle, 1997), it is probable that you, as a future mental health professional, will encounter at least one sexual or gender minority client at some point in your professional career. Without sufficient training that encompasses acquisition of knowledge, attitudinal exploration, and skill building, you may be at risk of committing clinical errors. Even well-meaning therapists may engage in avoidance behaviors, not because of homophobic, biphobic, or transphobic beliefs but because of anxiety related to a fear of offending sexual and gender minority clients (Devine, Evett, & Vasquez-Suson, 1996).

Personal Reflection 1

In her autobiography *My Life So Far* (2005), film actor Jane Fonda describes her reaction to the news of Christine Jorgensen's sex change from male to female in the early 1950s:

I was obsessed by the story, feeling, like Jorgensen, that a mistake had been made with me: Perhaps I was a boy inside a girl's body.

Haunted by this, I would lie on the floor with my legs up on a chair, holding a mirror to see if there were any signs of a penis. (p. 90)

Fonda, then in high school, was unable to verbalize her questions and concerns about her gender identity to anyone. Fonda's shame mirrors the experiences of many transgendered people who learn fairly quickly that society has little tolerance for persons who threaten the gender binary. In many instances, transgender persons go to great lengths to suppress their inner feelings, while outwardly manifesting stereotypical gender attributes and behaviors.

In her text *My Husband Betty* (2003), Boyd writes about her husband's cross-dressing and the implications of his behavior for her own sexual identity:

> *In my early twenties I was hit on pretty frequently by women, and went through a time when I just didn't feel sure of my sexuality. Many people go through a period where they ask similar questions. What I resented, when faced with my husband's crossdressing, was feeling like I had to open a box I'd already shut years before. Being attracted to my husband when he was en femme didn't make it easier. I am convinced that when we go to a lesbian bar, the women there think I'm a closet case. I wonder if my friends think the same. (p. 61)*

Are Boyd's self-examination of her sexual orientation and Fonda's confusion regarding her gender identity difficult to understand and relate to? Alternately, will some readers identify closely with the personal experiences Fonda and Boyd describe? The process of self-exploration mainly entails questioning many taken-for-granted assumptions about ourselves, including our identities as gendered and sexual beings.

Self-Reflection Questions

1. Was there ever a time when you questioned your sexual orientation? Describe this experience.
2. Was there ever a time when someone expressed a concern about your sexual orientation or mistakenly assumed that you were a different sexual orientation? Describe this experience and your reaction to it.
3. Was there ever a time in your life when you questioned your gender identity? Describe this experience.
4. Was there ever a time when someone mistakenly assumed that you were a different sex? Describe this experience and your reaction to it.

Personal Reflection 2

In his article "Heterosexual Identity and the Heterosexual Therapist: An Identity Perspective on Sexual Orientation Dynamics in Psychotherapy," Mohr (2002) presents a model of heterosexual identity. He maintains that heterosexuality is determined by the following: (1) our early personal sexual experiences with others, (2) our fantasies and behaviors toward romantic partners, and (3) our experiences receiving social messages from others about sexual orientation. All of these variables enable us to develop working models or conceptual ways to think of ourselves in terms of our own sexual orientation. According to Mohr, one's sexual orientation is also impacted by core motivations. Mohr proposed two broad categories of motivations: the need for social acceptance by social reference groups and the need for a consistent sense of self.

The question "What causes a person to be gay, lesbian, or bisexual?" is a familiar one for most sexual minorities. Seldom are heterosexuals asked, "What caused you to become heterosexual?"

Self-Reflection Questions

1. In your opinion, what do you believe are the determinants of your own sexual orientation?
2. In your opinion, what do you believe are the determinants of your own gender orientation?

3. What attitudes and beliefs did you learn in your family about sexual minorities?
4. What attitudes and beliefs did you learn in your family about gender nonconformity?
5. Describe your previous personal contacts with sexual minorities, and evaluate your cognitive, affective, and behavioral responses to such persons.

6. Describe your previous personal contacts with gender minorities, and evaluate your cognitive, affective, and behavioral responses to such persons.

(Questions were modified from Dillon, Worthington, Savory, Rooney, Becker-Schutte, & Guerra, 2004; Lum, 1999).

Library, Media, and Internet Activities

Instructions: The following list contains labels that many sexual and gender minorities use to identify themselves. Read the list and consider which of these you are familiar with and which are unknown. Explore what meanings and connotations these labels have for you. What meanings are available in the general culture? Now, consult the Internet and other sources in order to define each term.

ACDC
Ambigendered
Androgyne
Bicurious
Bi dyke
Bigendered
Bisensual
Bisexual lesbian
Byke
Down low
Dyke
Faggot

Fairy
Femme
Gay bisexual
Genderqueer
Gender outlaw
Gender variant
Lesbian-identified bisexual
Lesbian who has sex with men
Metrosexual
Multisexual
Omnisexual
Polyamorous
Polyfidelitious
Polygendered
Polysexual
Queen
Queer
Trannyboy
Trannyfag
Transman
Trisexual
Two spirited

Group Activity

In the exercise below, you examine your attitudes toward and beliefs about sexual and gender minorities. This exercise is designed especially to create an open environment where people can safely explore their opinions. Take a few moments to write your responses to the statements below as honestly as you can. Do not put your name or any other identifying marks on your paper. It is important that your identity be kept anonymous. Papers will be shuffled and randomly distributed back to members of the class. Note the responses that are listed on your sheet. You will be asked to share and defend the answers on the sheet in front of you (not your own personal views).

1. I would be comfortable with an openly identified lesbian teaching history at my children's high school.
2. Same-sex couples should be permitted to adopt children and to serve as foster parents.
3. I would feel comfortable working with a transgender co-worker.
4. Same-sex couples ought to have the same legal right to marry as their heterosexual counterparts.
5. I would feel comfortable living next door to a same-sex couple.
6. I believe that the current "don't ask, don't tell" military policy should be abolished and sexual minorities should be permitted to serve in the U.S. armed services without fear of court martial or dishonorable discharge.
7. If my son or daughter decided to change sex, I would be supportive of that decision.

References

American Psychological Association (2008, August). Resolution on Transgender, gender identity, and gender expression non-discrimination. Retrived September 17, 2008, from http:/www.apa.org/pi/lgbc/policy/transgender.html

American Psychological Association Division 44, Committee on Lesbian, Gay, and Bisexual Concerns Joint Task Force. (2000). Guidelines for psychotherapy with lesbian, gay, and bisexual clients. *American Psychologist, 55,* 1440–1451.

Association for Gay, Lesbian and Bisexual Issues in Counseling. (2003). *Competencies for counseling gay, lesbian, bisexual and transgendered clients.* Retrieved May 29, 2007, from http://www.aglbic.org/resources/competencies.html.

Atkinson, D. R., & Hackett, G. (2004). *Counseling diverse populations.* Boston: McGraw Hill.

Bashan, F. (2005). Therapist self-disclosure of their sexual orientation: From a client's perspective (Doctoral dissertation, Wright Institute, 2005). *Dissertation Abstracts International, 65,* 12-B.

Ben-Ari, A. T. (2001). Homosexuality and heterosexism: Views from academics in the helping professions. *British Journal of Social Work, 31(1),* 119–131.

Bergh, N. D., & Crisp, C. (2004). Defining culturally competent practice with sexual minorities: Implications for social work education and practice. *Journal of Social Work Education, 40(2),* 221–238.

Berkman, C. S., & Zinberg, G. (1997). Homophobia and heterosexism in social workers. *Social Work, 42,* 319–332.

Bernstein, A. C. (2000). Straight therapists working with lesbians and gays in family therapy. *Journal of Marital & Family Therapy, 26(4),* 443–454.

Biaggio, M., Orchard, S., Larson, J., Petrino, K., & Mihara, R. (2003). Guidelines for gay/lesbian/bisexual-affirmative educational practices in graduate psychology programs. *Professional Psychology: Research & Practice, 34(5),* 548–554.

Bieschke, K. J., & Matthews, C. (1996). Career counselor attitudes and behaviors toward gay, lesbian, and bisexual clients. *Journal of Vocational Behavior, 48(2),* 243–255.

Bieschke, K. J., McClanahan, M., Tozer, R., Grzegorek, J. L., & Park, J. (2000). Programmatic research on the treatment of lesbian, gay and bisexual clients: The past, the present, and the course for the future. In R. M. Perez, K. A. DeBord, & K. J. Bieschke (Eds.), *Handbook of counseling and psychotherapy with lesbian, gay, and bisexual clients* (pp. 309–335). Washington, DC: American Psychological Association.

Bieschke, K. J., Paul, P. L., & Blasko, K. A. (2007). Review of empirical research focused on the experience of lesbian, gay, and bisexual clients in counseling and psychotherapy. In K. J. Bieschke, R. M. Perez, & K. A. DeBord (Eds.), *Handbook of counseling and psychotherapy with lesbian, gay, bisexual, and transgender clients* (2nd ed.) (pp. 293–315). Washington, DC: American Psychological Association.

Bockting, W., Knudson, G., & Goldberg, J. M. (2006). *Counselling and mental health care of transgender adults and loved ones.* Vancouver Canada: Vancouver

Coastal Health, Transcend Transgender Support & Education Society, and the Canadian Rainbow Health Coalition. Retrieved February 15, 2007, from http://www.vch.ca/transhealth

Bowers, A. M. V., & Bieschke, K. J. (2005). Psychologists' clinical evaluations and attitudes: An examination of the influence of gender and sexual orientation. *Professional Psychology: Research & Practice, 36(1)*, 97–103.

Boyd, H. (2003). *My husband Betty: Love, sex, and life with a crossdresser.* New York: Thunder's Mouth Press.

Brown, L. S., & Walker, L. E. A. (1990). Feminist therapy perspectives on self-disclosure. In G. Stricker & M. Fisher (Eds.), *Self-disclosure in the therapeutic relationship* (pp. 135–154). New York: Plenum Press.

Buhrke, R. A., Ben-Ezra, L. A., Hurley, M. E., & Ruprecht, L. J. (1992). Content analysis and methodological critique of articles concerning lesbian and gay male issues in counseling journals. *Journal of Counseling Psychology, 39(1)*, 91–99.

Carroll, L., & Gilroy, P. J. (2001). Teaching "outside the box": Incorporating queer theory in counselor education. *Journal of Humanistic Counseling, Education & Development, 40*, 49–57.

Carroll, L., & Gilroy, P. J. (2002). Transgender issues in counselor preparation. *Counselor Education & Supervision, 41(3)*, 233–242.

Cole, S. S., Denny, D., Eyler, A. E., & Samons, S. L. (2000). Issues of transgender. In T. Szuchman & F. Muscarella (Eds.), *Psychological perspectives in human sexuality* (pp. 149–195). New York: Wiley.

Cole, C. M., & Meyer, W. J., III. (1998). Transgender behavior and the *DSM–IV*. In D. Denny (Ed.), *Current concepts in transgender identity* (pp. 227–236). New York: Garland Press.

Corey, M., & Corey, G. (2007). *Becoming a helper* (5th ed.). Pacific Grove, CA: Brooks/Cole.

Crawford, I., McLeod, A., Zamboni, B. D., & Jordan, M. (1999). Psychologists' attitudes toward gay and lesbian parenting. *Professional Psychology: Research & Practice, 30(4)*, 394–401.

Crisp, C., & McCave, E. L. (2007). Gay affirmative practice: A model for social work practice with gay, lesbian, and bisexual youth. *Child & Adolescent Social Work Journal, 24(4)*, 403–421.

Devine, P. G., Evett, S. R., & Vasquez-Suson, K. A. (1996). Exploring the interpersonal dynamics of intergroup contact. In R. M. Sorrentine & E. T. Higgins (Eds.), *Handbook of motivation and cognition: The interpersonal context (Vol. 3).* New York: Guilford Press.

Dillon, F. R., Worthington, R. L., Savory, H. G., Rooney, S. C., Becker-Schutte, A., & Guerra, R. M. (2004). On becoming allies: A qualitative study of lesbian-, gay-, and bisexual-affirmative counselor training. *Journal of Counselor Education & Supervision, 43*, 162–178.

Doherty, W. J., & Simmons, D. S. (1996). Clinical practice patterns of marriage and family therapists and their clients. *Journal of Marital & Family Therapy, 22*, 9–26.

Dorland, J. M., & Fischer, A. R. (2001). Gay, lesbian, and bisexual individuals' perceptions: An analogue study. *Counseling Psychologist, 29(4)*, 532–547.

Ettner, R. (1999). *Gender loving care: A guide to counseling gender-variant clients.* New York: Norton.

Fassinger, R. E. (1991). The hidden minority: Issues and challenges in working with lesbian women and gay men. *Counseling Psychologist, 19*, 157–176.

Fassinger, R. E., & Richie, B. S. (1997). Sex matters: Gender and sexual orientation in training for multicultural counseling competency. In D. B. Pope-Davis & H. L. K. Coleman (Eds.), *Multicultural counseling competencies: Assessment, education and training, and supervision* (pp. 83–110). Thousand Oaks, CA: Sage.

Fischer A. R., & DeBord, K. A. (2007). Perceived conflicts between affirmation of religious diversity and affirmation of sexual diversity: That's perceived. In K. J. Bieschke, R. M. Perez, & K. A. DeBord (Eds.), *Handbook of counseling and psychotherapy with lesbian, gay, bisexual, and transgender clients (2nd ed.)* (pp. 317–339). Washington, DC: American Psychological Association.

Fonda, J. (2005). *My life so far.* New York: Random House.

Ford, M. P., & Hendrick, S. S. (2003). Therapists' sexual values for self and clients: Implications for practice and training. *Professional Psychology: Research & Practice, 34(1)*, 80–87,

Freud, S. (1959). Future prospects of psychoanalytic psychotherapy. In J. Strachey (Ed. & Trans.). *The standard edition of the complete psychological works of Sigmund Freud* (Vol. 11, pp. 139-151). London: Hogarth Press (Original work published 1910).

Frost, J. C. (1998). Counter-transference considerations for the gay male when leading psychotherapy groups for gay men. *International Journal of Group Psychotherapy, 48(1)*, 3–24.

Gagne, P., Tewksbury, R., & McGaughey, D. (1997). Coming out and crossing over: Identity formation and proclamation in a transgender community. *Gender & Society, 11*(4), 478–508.

Gainor, K. (2000). Including transgender issues in lesbian, gay, and bisexual psychology: Implications for clinical practice and training. In B. Greene & G. L. Croom (Eds.), *Education, research, and practice in lesbian, gay, bisexual, and transgendered psychology: A resource manual* (pp. 131–160). Thousand Oaks, CA: Sage.

Garnets, L., Hancock, K. A., Cochran, S. D., Goodchilds, J., & Peplau, L. A. (1991). Issues in psychotherapy with lesbians and gay men: A survey of psychologists. *American Psychologist, 46*(9), 964–974.

Gelso, C. J., Fassinger, R. E., Gomez, M. J., & Latts, M. G. (1995). Countertransference reactions to lesbian clients: The role of homophobia, counselor gender, and countertransference management. *Journal of Counseling Psychology, 42*(3), 356–364.

Godfrey, K., Haddock, S. A., Fisher, A., & Lund, L. (2006). Essential components of curricula for preparing therapists to work effectively with lesbian, gay, and bisexual clients: A Delphi study. *Journal of Marital & Family Therapy, 32*(4), 491–504.

Goetstouwers, L. (2006). Affirmative psychotherapy with bisexual men. *Journal of Bisexuality, 6*(1/2)12, 27–49.

Guthrie, C. (2006). Disclosing the therapist's sexual orientation: The meaning of disclosure in working with gay, lesbian, and bisexual patients. *Journal of Gay & Lesbian Psychotherapy, 10*(1), 63–77.

Hayes, J. A. (2004). The inner world of the psychotherapist: A program of research on countertransference. *Psychotherapy Research, 14*(1), 21–36.

Hayes, J. A., & Erkis, A. J. (2000). Therapist homophobia, client sexual orientation, and source of client HIV infection as predictors of therapist reactions to clients with HIV. *Journal of Counseling Psychology, 47*(1), 71–78.

Hayes, J. A., & Gelso, C. J. (1993). Male practitioners' discomfort with gay and HIV-infected clients. *Journal of Counseling Psychology, 40*, 86–93.

Israel, G. E., & Tarver, D. E., II. (1997). *Transgender care: Recommended guidelines, practical information and personal accounts.* Philadelphia: Temple University Press.

Israel, T., Ketz, K., Detrie, P. M., Burke, M. C., & Shulman, J. L. (2003). Identifying counselor competencies for working with lesbian, gay, and bisexual clients. *Journal of Gay & Lesbian Psychotherapy, 7*, 3–21.

Jones, M. A., Botsko, M., & Gorman, B. S. (2003). Predictors of psychotherapeutic benefit of lesbian, gay, and bisexual clients: The effects of sexual orientation matching and other factors. *Psychotherapy: Theory, Research, Practice, Training, 40*(4), 289–301.

Kooden, H. (1991). Self-disclosure: The gay male therapist as agent of social change. In C. Silverstein (Ed.), *Gays, lesbians, and their therapists* (pp. 143–154). New York: Norton.

Korell, S. C., & Lorah, P. (2007). An overview of affirmative psychotherapy and counseling with transgender clients. In K. J. Bieschke, R. M. Perez, & K. A. DeBord (Eds.), *Handbook of counseling and psychotherapy with lesbian, gay, bisexual, and transgender clients (2nd ed.)* (pp. 271–288). Washington, DC: American Psychological Association.

Korfhage, B. A. (2006). Psychology graduate students' attitudes toward lesbian and gay men. *Journal of Homosexuality, 51*(4), 145–159.

Krieglstein, M. (2003). Heterosexism and social work: An ethical issue. *Journal of Human Behavior in the Social Environment, 8*(2–3), 75–91.

Lee, I-C., & Crawford, M. (2007). Lesbians and bisexual women in the eyes of scientific psychology. *Feminism & Psychology, 17*(1), 109–127.

Liddle, B. J. (1996). Therapist sexual orientation, gender, and counseling practices as they relate to ratings of helpfulness by gay and lesbian clients. *Journal of Counseling Psychology, 43*(4), 394–401.

Liddle, B. J. (1997). Gay and lesbian clients' selection of therapists and utilization of therapy. *Psychotherapy: Theory, Research, Practice, Training, 34*(1), 11–18.

Long, J. K., & Serovich, J. M. (2003). Incorporating sexual orientation into MFT training programs: Infusion and inclusion. *Journal of Marital & Family Therapy, 29*(1), 59–67.

Lum, D. (1999). *Culturally competent practice: A framework for growth and action.* Monterey, CA: Brooks/Cole.

Mallon, G. P. (1999). Knowledge for practice with transgendered persons. *Journal of Gay & Lesbian Social Services, 10*(3/4), 1–8.

Martell, C. R., Safren, S. A., & Prince, S. E. (2004). *Cognitive-behavioral therapies with lesbian, gay, and bisexual clients.* New York: Guilford Press.

Mathy, R. M. (2001). A nonclinical comparison of transgender identity and sexual orientation: A framework for multicultural competence. *Journal of Psychology & Human Sexuality, 13*(1), 31–54.

Matthews, C. R., Selvidge, M. M. D., & Fisher, K. (2005). Addictions counselors' attitudes and behaviors toward gay, lesbian and bisexual clients. *Journal of Counseling & Development, 83*(1), 57–65.

Messinger, L. (2004). Out in the field: Gay and lesbian social work students' experiences in field placement. Field education in social work. [Special Section]. *Journal of Social Work Education, 40*(2), 187–204.

Mohr, J. J. (2002). Heterosexual identity and the heterosexual therapist: An identity perspective on sexual orientation dynamics in psychotherapy. *Counseling Psychologist, 30*(4), 532–566.

Mohr, J. J., Israel, T., & Sedlacek, W. E. (2001). Counselors' attitudes regarding bisexuality as predictors of counselors' clinical responses: An analogue study of a female bisexual client. *Journal of Counseling Psychology, 48*(2), 212–222.

Mohr, J. J., & Rochlen, A. B. (1999). Measuring attitudes regarding bisexuality in lesbians, gay male, and heterosexual populations. *Journal of Counseling Psychology, 46*(3), 353–369.

Morrow, S. L. (2000). First do no harm: Therapist issues in psychotherapy with lesbian, gay, and bisexual clients. In R. M. Perez, K.A. DeBord, & K. J. Bieschke (Eds.), *Handbook of counseling and psychotherapy with lesbian, gay, and bisexual clients* (pp. 137–156). Washington, DC: American Psychological Association.

Murphy, J. A., Rawlings, E. I., & Howe, S. R. (2002). A survey of clinical psychologists on treating lesbian, gay, and bisexual clients. *Professional Psychology: Research & Practice, 33*(2), 183–189.

Newman, B. S., Dannenfelser, P. L., & Benishek, L. A. (2002). Assessing beginning social work and counseling students' acceptance of lesbians and gay men. *Journal of Social Work Education, 38*(2), 273–288.

Nichols, M. (2006). Psychotherapeutic issues with "kinky" clients: Clinical problems, yours and theirs. *Journal of Homosexuality, 50*(2/3), 281–300.

O'Brien, J. M. (2005). Sexual orientation, shame and silence: Reflections on graduate training. In J. M. Croteau, J. S. Lark, M. A. Lidderdale, & Y. B. Chung (Eds.), *Deconstructing heterosexism in the counseling professions: A narrative approach* (pp. 97–102). Thousand Oaks, CA: Sage.

Pearlman, S. F. (1996). Lesbian clients/lesbian therapists: Necessary conversations. In N. D. Davis, E. Cole, & E. D. Rothblum (Eds.), *Lesbian therapists and their therapy: From both sides of the couch* (pp. 71–80). New York: Haworth.

Peplau, L. A., Fingerhut, A., & Beals, K. P. (2004). Sexuality in the relationships of lesbians and gay men. In J. H. Harvey, A. Wenzel, and S. Sprecher (Eds.), *The handbook of sexuality in close relationships* (pp. 349–369). Mahwah, NJ: Erlbaum.

Perlman, G. (1991). The question of therapist self-disclosure in the treatment of a married gay man. In C. Silverstein (Ed.), *Gays, lesbians, and their therapists* (pp. 201–209). New York: Norton.

Phillips, J. C. (2000). Training issues and considerations. In R. M. Perez, K. A. DeBord, & K. J. Bieschke (Eds.), *Handbook of counseling and psychotherapy with lesbian, gay, and bisexual clients* (pp. 337–358). Washington, DC: American Psychological Association.

Phillips, J. C., & Fischer, A. R. (1998). Graduate students' training experiences with lesbian, gay, and bisexual issues. *Counseling Psychologist, 26,* 712–734.

Phillips, J. C., Ingram, K. M., Smith, N. G., & Mindes, E. J. (2003). Methodological and content review of lesbian-, gay-, and bisexual-related articles in counseling journals: 1990–1999. *Counseling Psychologist, 31*(1), 25–62.

Pilkington, N. W., & Cantor, J. M. (1996). Perceptions of heterosexual bias in professional psychology programs: A survey of graduate students. *Professional Psychology: Research & Practice, 27,* 604–612.

Rachlin, K. (2002). Transgender individuals' experiences of psychotherapy [Electronic Version]. *International Journal of Transgenderism, 6,* 1. Retrieved June 22, 2005, from http://www.symposion.Com/ijt/ijtvo06no01_03.htm

Raj, R. (2002). Towards a transpositive therapeutic model: Developing clinical sensitivity and cultural competence in the effective support of transsexual and transgendered clients [Electronic Version]. *International Journal of Transgenderism, 6,* 2. Retrieved June 22, 2005, from http://www.symposion.Com/ijt/ijtvo06no02_04.htm

Resick, P. A., & Schnicke, M. K. (1993). *Cognitive processing therapy for rape victims: A treatment manual. Interpersonal violence: The practice series (Vol. 4).* Note: This is a text book.

Robinson, T. L., & Howard-Hamilton, M. F. (2000). *The convergence of race, ethnicity, and gender.* Upper Saddle River, NJ: Merrill.

Satterly, B. A. (2006). Therapist self-disclosure from a gay male perspective. *Families in Society : The Journal of Contemporary Social Services, 87 (2)*, 240–247.

Savage, T. A., Prout, T. H., & Chard, K. M. (2004). School psychology and issues of sexual orientation: Attitudes, beliefs, and knowledge. *Psychology in the Schools, 41(2)*, 201–210.

Shernoff, M. (1995). Male couples and their relationship styles. *Journal of Gay & Lesbian Social Services*, (2), 43–57.

Sherry, A., Whilde, M. R., & Patton, J. (2005). Gay, lesbian, and bisexual training competencies in American Psychological Association accredited graduate programs. *Psychotherapy: Theory, Research, Practice, Training, 42(1)*, 116–120.

Snively, C. A., Kreuger, L., Stretch, J. J., Watt, J. W., & Chadha, J. (2004). Understanding homophobia: Preparing for practice realities in urban and rural settings. *Journal of Gay & Lesbian Social Services, 17(1)*, 59–81.

Spritz, M. (2002). Holding up a mirror: In the therapy room with a trans therapist and her trans clients. *In the Family, 8(2)*, 15.

Stevens, C. L., Muran, J. C., & Safran, J. D. (2003). Obstacles or opportunities? A relational approach to negotiating alliance ruptures. In R. L. Leahy (Ed.), *Roadblocks in cognitive-behavioral therapy: Transforming challenges into opportunities for change* (pp. 274–294). New York: Guilford Press.

Sue, D. W., Arredondo, P., & McDavis, R. J. (1992). Multicultural counseling competencies and standards: A call to the profession. *Journal of Counseling & Development, 70*, 477–486.

Sue, D. W., Bernier, J. G., Durran, M., Feinberg, L., Pedersen, P., Smith, E., et al. (1982). Position paper: Cross-cultural counseling competencies. *Counseling Psychologist, 10*, 45–52.

Sue, D. W., & Sue, D. (1999). *Counseling the culturally different: Theory and practice* (3rd ed.). Hoboken, NJ: Wiley.

Sue, D. W., & Sue, D. (2003). *Counseling the culturally diverse: Theory and practice* (4th ed.). Hoboken, NJ: Wiley.

Vacc, N. A., DeVaney, S. B., & Brendel, J. M. (2003). *Counseling multicultural and diverse populations: Strategies for practitioners*. New York: Brunner-Routledge.

Voorhis, R. V., & Wagner, M. (2004). Among the missing: Content on lesbian and gay people in social work journals. *Social Work, 47(4)*, 345–354.

Weitzman, G. (2006). Therapy with clients who are bisexual and polyamorous. *Journal of Bisexuality, 6(1/2)*, 137–164.

Zandvliet, T. (2000). Transgender issues in therapy. In C. Neal & D. Davies (Eds.), *Issues in therapy with lesbian, gay, bisexual and transgender clients* (pp. 176–189). Philadelphia: Open University Press.

CHAPTER 5

Interwoven Identities: Race, Ethnicity, Class, Religion, and Disability

INTRODUCTION

Tania Israel is currently a counseling psychologist. She is also Chinese American/Jewish American who identifies herself as bisexual:

> Only recently did I realize that I am not half-Chinese and half-Jewish rather I am half–Chinese American and half–Jewish American. My homeland is neither China nor Israel, but rather California and New York. This is where I feel most at home. This is where I find people who are like me, who look Asian, or somewhat Asian, and understand my middle class American cultural references. Here are people who appreciate a good bagel and dim sum. And here is a place where people don't stare and strangers don't question my ethnicity. No wonder I can't relate to Margaret Cho's depiction of her mother. My Chinese American mother shops at Talbot, belongs to a book club, and is a rowdy college basketball fan. My Jewish American father teaches Chinese history, organized the neighborhood Christmas caroling, and loves to go camping. Even more accurately, I am not half anything. I embody the complexity of my family histories, the context of my upbringings, and my unique psychological makeup. (Israel, 2004, pp. 178–179)

Neely, an African-American lesbian, is currently an artist:

> My coming out, while nothing near as glorious as a debutante's ball was relatively easy compared to some stories I've heard. I was way, way out before I was reeled in. I didn't know that our brand of love was so scary and so powerful to

heterosexuals that it had to be hidden. I didn't learn that until I was nine years old. And then I resorted to doing what my people do in slavery times. I developed masks to wear for the oppressor and learned to switch pronouns with the swiftness of women wiping rouge over bruises. Doing that led to a severe case of multiple persona syndromes—a putting on of faces not fully one's own until habit overcomes bone structure and one is unlinked from one's self. This is a sickness easy to catch in America, particularly if you're Black, queer, and not sure there are other options for survival/living. (Neely, 1999, pp. 248–249)

Israel's and Neely's words capture the sense of alienation and emotional isolation that accompanies the experience of marginalization in our culture. In Israel's case, her coming out as bisexual in her late twenties helped her come to grips with her multiethnic heritage. The various aspects of her identity became more fully developed and integrated, perhaps as a result of her process of realizing and affirming herself as a bisexual woman. Her experiences are consistent with research observations. Rust (1996), for example, noted that bisexual persons with a mixed ethnic and racial heritage become accustomed to "straddling categories and thinking beyond bipolar categories" (p. 69). In contrast to Israel, Neely indicates that her efforts to cope with the racism she experienced as an African-American female enabled her to cope more effectively with the stress and stigmatization she experienced later after she came out as a lesbian.

A Preview of Chapter Contents

This chapter explores in depth how sexual and gender minority persons who are of color, poor, disabled, and non-Christian are vulnerable to hostility and discrimination on several fronts. These hostile responses come from their families; their ethnic, racial, and faith-based communities and the mainstream culture as well as from the gay community itself (Fukuyama & Ferguson, 2000; Greene, 1997; McLean, 2003; Raj, 2002; Walters, 1998).

Israel's and Neely's narratives reflect the tremendously complex nature of identity. Lester (2002) distinguished between mosaic and layered approaches to analyzing multiple identities. In the *mosaic approach*, researchers and practitioners study one distinct component of identity (e. g., race, ethnicity, or sexual orientation) at a time. This approach is relatively common. Most popular texts in multicultural counseling (e. g., Lee, Blando, Mizelle, & Orozco, 2007) include separate chapters on African Americans, Asian Americans, Hispanic Americans, and so on. While the mosaic approach is relatively straightforward, it tends to be overly simplistic.

In contrast, a *layered approach* allows an examination of several aspects of identity and the interrelationships of a client's identities. The downside to this method of analysis is that it can be confusing and difficult to understand. The next section takes a layered approach to describing the experiences of sexual and gender minority persons who are also minorities by virtue of their racial, ethnic, class, and disability statuses and their religious affiliations. The studies discussed

- Examine the ways in which sexual and gender minority persons integrate different aspects of their identities and the possible effects of multiple and interlocking oppressions.
- Explore the ways sexual and gender minority persons utilize their strengths to develop healthfully.

- Offer specific recommendations to aid practitioners in their work with clients whose identities are complex and interwoven.

EXPLORING IDENTITIES

According to Arredondo et al. (1996) and Arredondo (1999), every person's identity comprises a unique constellation of factors, including race/ethnicity, age, gender identity, sexual orientation, socioeconomic level, religious affiliation, and disability status. Each of these aspects of identity has a different rank and value in our society. Some identity configurations, like heterosexuality, are more privileged in Western culture than others (Croteau, Talbot, Lance, & Evans, 2002). Those who are minorities in more than one identity category are at risk for multiple forms of discrimination. A physically disabled African-American woman who identifies herself as bisexual is potentially vulnerable to multiple forms of oppression, including racism, sexism, biphobia, and ableism.

Ascribed Versus Achieved Identities/Visible Versus Invisible Identities

Garnets (2002) employed the term *ascribed* to refer to personal attributes or characteristics that are long-standing and enduring, such as ethnicity, race, and disability. An example of someone with an ascribed identity might be an African-American woman, Serena, who was born with cerebral palsy. Serena is like most racial and ethnic minority persons with ascribed identities, reared in familial and community contexts with others who supported and affirmed her identity as an African American (Israel & Selvidge, 2003). Her family and her community acted as buffers against racism. In terms of her disability, Serena was often subjected to teasing and name-calling by the other children in her neighborhood for the ways she walked and talked. So, of the two ascribed identities, both of which placed Serena in minorities, her disability provided the greater difficulty.

Alternately, Garnets (2002) applied the term *achieved identity* to denote attributes, such as sexual orientation, that arise after birth. Serena realized in late adolescence that she was attracted to other girls. She felt isolated and alone, as she knew no one in her small circle of friends was like her. The term *invisible* is often used to describe Serena's sexual orientation. Serena often tried to pass as heterosexual, joining in when the other girls talked about "cute guys." Serena's race and disability are clearly visible to others. Her sexual orientation is not.

There are instances where light-skinned African Americans may not be identified as such, and some disabilities are not readily apparent to others. There are also gender minority persons who have received hormonal replacement therapy and sex reassignment surgery and are capable of passing as their chosen gender without detection. The degree to which one's minority status is visible to others and the extent to which aspects of identity are acquired have implications for the kind and amount of stress that sexual and gender minorities experience.

Traditional Views of Identity Formation in Minorities

Historically, a number of identity development models have been created by psychologists to describe how minority persons develop a sense of themselves as marginalized groups. These theories "provide a conceptual framework for understanding identity attitudes related to reference group orientation, as well as the effects of oppression on both personal and ascribed identity development" (Fukuyama & Ferguson, 2000, p. 85). Most of these models focus on a singular aspect of identity, such as race or ethnicity, and assume that persons with fully developed, mature minority identities are those who achieve a holistic integration of various aspects of themselves. For example, Cross's Nigrescence Model (1971) described the processes that characterize the development of a sense of pride as a black person. Subsequent identity theories have been developed for different populations, including Asian Americans (Sodowsky, Kwan, & Pannu, 1995), Pilipino Americans (Nadal, 2004), and Mexican Americans (Bernal, Knight, Ocampo, Garza, & Cote, 1993).

Recognizing Complex Identities: A Contemporary Approach

Despite the proliferation and popularity of recent identity models, these have been criticized on several grounds. The first of these criticisms is that these models do not describe the complex, dynamic, and interwoven nature of identities. Many sexual and gender minority persons fit into several identity categories simultaneously and face the challenges associated with conflicting allegiances to different communities at different times (Garnets, 2002).

Researchers have begun to develop identity models that are more true to life (Croteau et al., 2002; Fukuyama & Ferguson, 2000; Williams, 2005). One example of such an approach was developed by Collins (2000) to describe the processes by which biracial persons develop a sense of identity. Collins recognized that in the past, biracial persons were depicted in social science research as troubled as a result of their mixed and/or marginal identities. In her research, Collins sampled a relatively small number of biracial Japanese Americans. She noted that the majority of her participants experienced a period of *confusion* about which community, either Euro-American or Japanese, to identify with. This period was followed by what Collins termed *suppression*, in which her participants felt compelled by others to choose one identity, while suppressing the other. In the third stage, *exploration*, Collins observed that her participants wanted to own all aspects of themselves, even those that had been heretofore suppressed. At the last stage, *resolution/ acceptance*, her respondents had more fully accepted all aspects of their identity. Collins also noted that the process of identity development for bisexual persons seemed to parallel the experiences of biracial persons. Her model was one of the first to capture the integration of multiple aspects of identity. Recently, other theoretical models have been developed to describe persons who hold dual identity statuses, such as racial and disability identities (Mpofu & Harley, 2006).

Researchers have begun to question the assumption that the goal of healthy identity development is synthesis. In their qualitative study of Orthodox Jewish gay men and lesbian women, Halbertal and Koren (2006) noted that their participants were not able to integrate their religious identities with their sexual identities; however, their participants did not abandon either. The researchers described a process of negotiation as men and women found their religion helpful in terms of understanding their homosexuality and vice versa.

Crocker, Luhtanen, Blaine, and Broadnax (1994) posited that identities are also social in nature. Their concept of *collective self-esteem* was used to describe the degree to which people positively assessed their cultural group. Studies with racial minorities have confirmed a connection between collective self-esteem and psychological adjustment (Crocker et al., 1994).

EXPLORING RACE AND ETHNICITY IN SEXUAL AND GENDER MINORITIES

Despite the current emphasis on diversity and multicultural issues in the counseling, psychology, and social work professions, there are significant gaps in the research, especially with regard to sexual and gender minority persons of color (Gainor, 2000; Holmes & Cahill, 2005; Korell & Lorah, 2007). Most studies of sexual and gender minorities do not include large enough samples of people of color to make reliable statistical comparisons (Croom, 2000; Hughes et al. 2006; Mays, Cochran, & Roeder, 2003). In fact, many researchers do not even include descriptions of their samples. For example, Phillips, Ingram, Smith, and Mindes (2003) reported that during the years 1990 to 1999, only 18% of the empirical studies that incorporated sexual minority participants included a description of the racial or ethnic composition of their samples.

There are a number of possible reasons for the scarcity of research with ethnically and racially diverse samples. Part of the difficulty is related to the hardships in recruiting research participants. Many ethnic and racial minorities have little to no experience in participating in research and may view researchers negatively, especially those inquiring about sexual behavior. Incidents such as the Tuskegee experiment, in which black men were exposed to syphilis and not treated in order for investigators to explore disease progression, have left lasting feelings of distrust (Cahill, Battle, & Meyer, 2003).

Other obstacles in research with minorities include language barriers. For example, Zea, Reisen, and Diaz (2003) noted that measures used in studies with Latinos are not developed for use with Latinos, and the cultural equivalence in translation is elusive. Another issue that makes research difficult is that race, like sexual orientation, is not easily defined and assessed. The categories used by the U.S. government to classify persons include four races—Alaskan Native, Asian or Pacific Islander, black, and white—and two ethnicities—Hispanic origin and not of Hispanic origin. Within the category of Asian or Pacific Islander, there are 25 different ethnic groups with different languages and religions (Chan, 1995). In effect, they are being forced to choose which part of them is most important and, perhaps worse, which part of them isn't.

The Interwoven Nature of Racial/Ethnic Identity, Sexual Orientation, and Gender Identity

One model that has attempted to capture the dynamic and interwoven nature of being both a sexual or gender minority and a racial or ethnic minority has been described in the joint works of Berry, Kim, Minde, and Mok (1987), Sedeno (1999), and Crawford, Allison, Zamboni, and Soto (2002). Using a 2 × 2 matrix with sexual orientation on one axis and racial/ethnic identification on the other, persons who have established a low level of sexual orientation identification, while simultaneously achieving a high level of racial/ethnic identification, are termed *assimilated*. According to Crawford et al., assimilated persons tend to have a strong sense of their racial/ethnic heritage but little sense of themselves as gay, lesbian, or bisexual. They may have little to no contact with the sexual minority culture. Persons who have achieved *integration* statuses are those who are high in both their sexual orientation identification and their racial/ethnic identification.

Those who are high in sexual orientation identification and low in racial/ethnic identification are categorized as *separated*. Persons in this category tend to be heavily invested in the gay community but have little to do with the political and social agendas in their racial or ethnic community. According to Greene (1997), "ethnic minority gay men and lesbians frequently experience a sense of never being part of any group completely, leaving them at risk for feelings of isolation and estrangement and thus increased psychological vulnerability" (p. 235). Persons of color who have little, if any, involvement in the gay community and do not have a strong sense of themselves as racial or ethnic minority persons are classified as *marginalized*. Crawford et al. (2002) explored the relationship between these racial/ethnic identity statuses and sexual orientation in a sample of African-American gay and bisexual men. Crawford and his colleagues found that participants who felt positive identifications both as African American and as gay (integrated) also had higher levels of self-esteem. They had stronger social support networks, greater levels of life satisfaction, lower levels of psychological distress, and were more responsible with HIV prevention measures.

For many racial and ethnic minorities, the realization that they are attracted to persons of the same sex poses "problems of identity integration" (Rust, 1996, p. 54). This realization means having to adjust to different social contexts and communities—a process that can be demanding and stressful. Boykin (1996) observed that in the struggle for unconditional acceptance, many sexual minority persons of color "compartmentalize themselves into multiple persons, seeking the comfort of different homes for different needs" (p. 122). Bing (2004) reported that for some people of color, being heterosexual may be one of the few sources of privilege they have.

Almost by definition, any minority individual, simply by being a minority, experiences stress. Adding more minorities to that individual compounds stress. Research has demonstrated that this is a reality for persons of color who are also gay, lesbian, or bisexual. In their national survey of 603 African-American women who self-identified as sexual minorities, Mays et al. (2003) reported that levels of psychological distress greatly exceeded the population norms for heterosexual African-American women.

In a bilingual study of male Latino sexual minorities in the United States, Diaz, Ayala, Bein, Henne, and Marin (2001) sampled over one thousand participants in Miami, Los Angeles, and New York. Results indicated that racism, poverty, and homophobia were experienced by a very large proportion of Latino gay men and that these experiences were significantly related to mental health outcomes. In a separate analysis of interview and survey data from this sample, Diaz, Bein, and Ayala (2006) reported that multiple experiences of social discrimination in the form of homophobia and racism were strongly correlated with financial hardship and suicidal ideation.

In 2006, Hughes et al. used the data set from the Chicago Health and Life Experiences of Women Study, which consisted of information from 447 lesbians whose ages ranged from 18 to 83 years (48% were white, 28% were black, 20% were Hispanic or Latino/a, and 4% were "other"—Asian/Pacific Islander, American Indian, or biracial). Hughes et al. reported that alcohol consumption rates and the incidence of alcohol treatment were high. Little variation in these dimensions was observed across racial/ethnic groups.

Homophobia, Biphobia, and Transphobia in Racial/Ethnic Communities

Sexual and gender minority persons of color must function in multiple worlds and must have the abilities necessary to "traverse many social and cultural boundaries and multiple social roles and expectations" (Walters, 1998, p. 51).

Most racial and ethnic minorities (e.g., African American, Asian American, Pacific Islander American, and Latino) are reared in communities where the family unit is highly valued (Greene, 1997; Holmes & Cahill, 2005). These minority families offer support and act as buffers against the racism and discrimination that exist in mainstream culture. Because most racial and ethnic minority cultures emphasize the necessity of fulfilling family roles via marriage and parenthood, same-sex sexuality is perceived as a threat to the perpetuation of family. For some, same-sex relationships are considered to be tantamount to rejection of one's family and one's race or ethnicity (Chan, 1992; Espin, 1987; Rust, 1996). When people of color identify themselves as gay, lesbian, bisexual, or transgender, they may be viewed by their families and communities as betraying their heritage, reflecting badly on their culture or religion, and trying to "pass" as white (Garnets & Kimmel, 1993).

African-American sexual minorities are, for example, seen by some in the African-American community as traitors to their families and to their race because same-sex sex does not lead to procreation (Adams & Kimmel, 1997; Boykin, 1996). Many African-American sexual minorities perceive homophobia within the African-American community as more intense than that outside (Greene, 1993).

Among some minority cultures, intergenerational family ties are highly stressed. In African-American families, intergenerational support from relatives is expected, with grandparents, particularly grandmothers, taking an active role in care-giving. Asian-American families also place a strong emphasis on maintaining the family name through generations (Matteson, 1997). The stress on family and respect for one's elders is evident in the Latina/o culture; for example, it is not unusual for many unmarried adult children to live at home with their parents and other family members into adulthood (Chernin & Johnson, 2003).

Racism in Sexual and Gender Minority Communities

As Bohan (1996) aptly states, gay communities are just as diverse as mainstream culture and contain persons who carry the same racist, classist, and ableist attitudes. This is evidenced in the literature, which verifies that sexual and gender minority persons of color and bisexual persons of color are sometimes excluded from gay culture (Diaz et al., 2006; Nemoto et al., 2003), in particular, gay events (Allman, 1996) and gay clubs (Boykin, 1996). One Puerto Rican male observed the following:

> Well, my experience in growing up in a gay world . . . it's kind of almost like if you are not Caucasian, you do not even deserve to be gay, in the sense of . . . you know, like what are you doing here in these kinds of clubs, and unless you go to a specific Hispanic club, I personally feel that you're not treated equally, not only as an individual, but because you are different, your race. You can also be homosexual, which I would think would be enough of a unity, [but] just because you are gay like someone else does not unify you to any kind of organization or group. It's not enough. I feel . . . it's almost a hindrance being Puerto Rican, to be accepted in the gay community. (Diaz, Bein, & Ayala, 2006, p. 213)

Many people of color perceive the gay, lesbian, bisexual, and transgender rights movement as white-focused (Human Rights Campaign, 2004).

Greene (1993) used the term *ethnosexual stereotyping* to describe the sexual objectification and stereotyping of persons of color that exist in the gay community. For example, Icard (1986) noted the existence of terms like "Super Stud" and "Miss Thing," which are used to describe the identities of African-American men in the gay male community. The Asian-American sexual minority community must contend with ethnosexist stereotypes within the white gay male community, like the term "rice queens," typically used to refer to white male partners pursuing Asian men, who are cast as playing female roles (Fukuyama & Ferguson, 2000). In their national survey of Latino gay men, Diaz, Bein, and Ayala (2006) reported that 62% of their sample indicated that they had experienced racism in the form of sexual objectification by other gay white men.

As previous chapters explained, bisexual persons have generally been viewed with suspicion and antagonism by other sexual and gender minority persons (Rust, 1996). Thus, the experience for bisexual racial/ethnic minority persons is rendered more difficult.

Little empirical research has explored the issue of racism in gender minority communities. Nonetheless, in many indigenous cultures, sexual and gender minority persons were perceived in positive ways. Anthropological and historical reports contain evidence of persons whose gender was other than male or female in many cultures. Among the Navajo tribe, the *Nadle* were not considered male or female, and in the Kaota tribe, such persons were called *Winkte* (Tafoya, 1997). In India, members of a religious sect called the *Hijras* were biological men who had their genitalia removed and lived as women. In Thailand, the term *Katoey* was used to refer to men who dressed and acted as women. Male-to-female transgender persons were once a familiar and accepted part of Polynesian culture, and the *Mahu* in Hawaii culture were once considered healers (Bopp, Juday, & Charter, 2005). Today Polynesian youth who come out as gay are often encouraged to adopt feminine behaviors and occupations because many Polynesians consider homosexuality less desirable than transgenderism (Bopp et al., 2005). Youth in Hawaii are more apt than those in the continental United States to identify themselves as a third gender rather than a female trapped in a male body (Bopp et al., 2005). Bopp et al. observed that transgender persons in Hawaii typically begin gender transition during adolescence, in contrast to practices in the continental United States.

In terms of contemporary Western culture, Israel and Tarver (1997) noted that gender minorities of color are subject to exclusion from the "white dominant culture" of gender and sexual minority communities. The transphobia in gay communities is ironic, given that the gay rights movement was born in a gay bar, the Stonewall Inn, in New York City in 1969. Tired of being harassed by the police for years, a frustrated group of drag queens fought back (Haldeman, 2007).

Transgender issues were purposefully excluded from the Human Rights Campaign's Employment Non-discrimination Act until August 2004 for fear of losing congressional representatives' support for its passage (Human Rights Campaign, 2004). Lev (2007) noted that it has taken approximately thirty years for gender minority persons to assume a more prominent place in the larger gay rights movement. Among gender minority youth of color, most feel disconnected from the larger gay community, which is perceived to be mostly white and nonsupportive of gender minorities (Garofalo, Deleon, Osmer, Doll, & Harper, 2006).

EXPLORING CLASS IN SEXUAL AND GENDER MINORITIES

Socioeconomic status has generally been ignored in psychology and counseling research, particularly in relation to sexual and gender minorities (Frable, 1997; Greene, 2003, 2007; Sue & Lam, 2002). Yet income affects almost all aspects of life, including access to and quality of health care, housing, and education (Sue & Lam, 2002). In particular, socioeconomic status has a significant bearing on whether gender minorities are able to afford hormonal and surgical reassignment surgery, especially since fewer and fewer insurance companies are covering the costs associated with transitioning (Lombardi & Davis, 2006). Income also places limitations on the assistive technologies of physically disabled persons regardless of sexual or gender orientation (Fassinger & Arseneau, 2007; Liddle, 2006). Income affects the degree to which sexual and gender minorities are able to enter the places and attend the events where other sexual and gender minorities are likely to socialize (Fassinger & Arseneau, 2007; Liddle, 2007). As Greene (2007) observed, "socializing at such venues usually requires some level of disposable income" (p. 189).

Race, gender, gender identity, and socioeconomic status are interwoven (Harley, Jolivette, McCormick, & Tice, 2002; Sue & Lam, 2002). African Americans are disproportionately poorer than white Americans (Wyche, 1996), and African-American women remain concentrated in low-wage occupations (Harley et al., 2002). White gay men are seen as affluent (Greene, 2003). Gates (1993) refers to a phenomenon known as *blacklash* in the gay community. This is a perception that the impact of heterosexism that white gay persons experience is not as harsh as the impact of racism for gay persons of color. Within the gender minority community, biological females who identify as and transition to males report more power, status, and income than do those who are born as biological males and transition to females (Paxton, Guentzel, & Trombacco, 2006). Even gay men who are perceived to be effeminate are economically disadvantaged in terms of earning power (Diaz et al., 2006).

EXPLORING DISABILITY IN SEXUAL AND GENDER MINORITIES

Persons with disabilities face a number of disparate conditions, including physical, mental, cognitive, and learning disabilities (Alexander, 2006; Saad, 1997; Thompson, 1994). Other variables besides the nature of the disability itself that are important to consider in this population are the age of onset, severity, and identification as a "disabled person" (Lee et al., 2007).

Multiple Forms of Oppression

Persons with disabilities face challenges similar to those confronting sexual and gender minorities. Perhaps the greatest challenge is attempting to develop a sense of positive identity in the face of discrimination and marginalization. Like sexual and gender minorities, persons with disabilities are not always given the emotional, physical, and financial support of their families. They are often the sole disabled person in their families and are not encouraged by family members to connect with other persons with disabilities and with the disability culture (Olkin, 1999). They have no role models and are not always taught by their loved ones how to cope with discrimination (Olkin, 2007). Also, in those cases where the nature of the disability may not be readily apparent or noticeable to others, they must face decisions about disclosure and identity management just as sexual and gender minorities do.

As with sexual and gender minorities, negative stereotypes about persons with disabilities persist. Many perceive parents who are disabled as unfit for or inadequate in their roles as parents (Olkin, 1999). And many sexual and gender minority persons with disabilities are likely to be older and have low incomes, and are, therefore, more likely to experience multiple forms of discrimination, including homo/bi/transphobia, ableism, ageism, and classism (Vernon, 1999). Harley, Hall, and Savage (2000) indicated that "the combination of being gay or lesbian with a disability subjects the individual to multiple oppressions resulting in isolation and distress" (p. 6).

Homophobia, Biphobia, and Transphobia in the Disability Community

The climate within disability rights organizations can be characterized as one of "rampant heterosexism" (O'Toole & Bregante, 1993). In O'Toole's (2000) interviews with lesbians who are disabled, her participants discussed the painful stereotypes that continue to exist in the disability community. One lesbian with disabilities that O'Toole interviewed stated:

> The one myth that bothers me the most is the idea that we sleep with women because we have no other choice. I have actually had straight crip women tell me that the only reason crip women sleep with women is they cannot find a man. Give me a break. Maybe we sleep with women because that is who we fell in love with or because women make us hot or because the sex is much better; in other words, the same reason women without disabilities sleep with women. The problem with this myth is that it is just a derivation of the idea that disabled women are asexual. (p. 209)

Many of O'Toole's participants were in couple relationships and noted the unique and extensive psychosocial stressors that accompany their relationships, particularly for those couples in which one member has a disability and the other does not. O'Toole's interviewees indicated that often family members and friends view these relationships with suspicion. The popular conception among many people is that persons with disabilities must form relationships with any available potential partner (O'Toole & Brown, 2003). Family and friends question the sincerity of the nondisabled partner's choice of a person with a disability. The nondisabled partner often feels forced to take on the disability discrimination or to compensate for the lack of access often experienced by persons with disabilities.

Ableism in Sexual and Gender Minority Communities

The term *ableism* is used here to refer to the negative stereotypes and discrimination targeted at persons with disabilities. Historically, they have been depicted in one of three ways: as "child-like" (Whitney, 2006), "asexual," or "oversexed" (Hunt, Matthews, Milsom, & Lammel, 2006). Ironically, although the lesbian community has long been a pioneer in providing accommodations such as wheelchair seating and sign language interpreters at some major community events since the early 1970s (O'Toole, 2000), many person with disabilities feel rejected by the gay community (Whitney, 2006). In their convenience sample of 43 gay and lesbian participants with deafness or hearing impairments, LeBlanc and Tully (2001) reported that approximately half said they chose not to affiliate with the gay community in their respective geographic areas.

The emphasis in the gay men's communities on muscular bodies, dancing, recreational drug use, and glamour often preclude involvement of disabled persons (Shakespeare, 1996). In addition to ableism, gay men with disabilities have noted the existence of "lookism" or discrimination based on physical appearance (Saad, 1997). Information in an accessible format (e.g., Braille) about resources, bars, and clubs is often not available to sexual and gender minorities who are disabled (Butler, 2001).

EXPLORING RELIGION IN SEXUAL AND GENDER MINORITIES

Religion is one of the most powerful social institutions in the United States (Morrow, 2003) and has had a significant impact on public perceptions of homosexuality (Morrow & Tyson, 2006). Approximately 72% of Americans cite religion and spirituality as the most important influences in their lives (Bergin & Jensen, 1990). Many religions view homosexuality as sinful and immoral. Most religious organizations prohibit sexual and gender minorities to marry, to minister, and to assume leadership positions in their places of worship (Morrow & Tyson, 2006). In mainstream churches, sexual minority persons report negative interpretations of scriptures and teachings, unwelcoming climates, and fear of exposure as gay or lesbian (Shuck & Liddle, 2001). Religious organizations, including faith-based treatment centers, actively aid in the conversion of persons from homosexual to heterosexual. For example, Exodus International, an ex-gay Christian ministry, has local ministries all over the globe (Shidlo & Schroeder, 2002).

Sexual minority persons who experience religious-based prejudice are likely to internalize their churches' negative messages about homosexuality. In some cases, the psychological fallout has been likened to the symptoms associated with posttraumatic stress disorder. For those who have experienced this religious-based trauma, the damaging psychological effects can include depression, low self-esteem, and poor health (Hancock, 2000; Rosario, Yali, Hunter, & Gwadz, 2006; Yakushko, 2005).

Because religious sexual minority persons often experience inner conflict, they feel forced to choose between their same-sex sexual orientation and their religious affiliation (Rodriguez & Ouellette, 2000). Many try to resolve this conflict by engaging in prayer, suppressing their sexuality, and/or seeking church-based conversion programs in order to change their sexual orientation (Morrow, 2003). Rodriguez and Ouellette (2000) identified several strategies that sexual minority persons use in order to cope with the negative and rejecting messages they receive from their churches and faith communities. One strategy is *compartmentalizing*, which refers to the need to achieve a complete segregation of one's religious orientation from one's sexual identity. In Rodriguez and Ouellette's survey of sexual minority persons who were members of a gay-affirmative church, 25% of their participants reported they had not fully integrated their sexual orientation with their religious identity.

There has also been some research to suggest that religious institutions that espouse full acceptance of homosexuality can have positive impact on sexual minority persons, including fostering social support and higher self-esteem in their gay and lesbian congregation (Hancock, 2000; Yakushko, 2005).

There has been little research concerning the interwoven nature of ethnicity, religion, and sexual and gender identities (Davidson, 2000). For ethnic and racial minorities, affiliation with a faith-based community is often extremely important. Many authors (e.g., Boykin, 1996) have noted the significance of the church within the African-American community. Empirical evidence suggested that African Americans, as a group, hold conservative religious views, which contribute significantly to their negative views of homosexuality and bisexuality (Crawford et al., 2002). Catholicism, a major institution within the Latino culture, is thought to play a large part in the condemnation of same-sex sexuality (Chernin & Johnson, 2003).

A STRENGTHS/RESILIENCY PERSPECTIVE

A common theme in discussions of identity development is the sense of conflict that can result when people hold simultaneous memberships in several minority groups (Akerlund & Cheung, 2000). Typically, the emphasis in research has been on the pathology inherent in sexual and gender minority persons who are also members of other marginalized groups (Akerlund & Cheung, 2000; O'Toole, 2000; Walters, 1998).

However, some writers have adopted what is known as a *strengths perspective* (Saleebey, 1994), in which the focus is on ways that minority persons cope effectively and survive multiple forms of oppression. In 1922, Du Bois introduced the concept of *double consciousness* to refer to the consequences of learning to convert obstacles presented by racism into opportunities. Mayo (1982) introduced the concept of *positive marginality* to denote the fact that people who are marginalized in our society have the capacity to develop unique strengths and coping mechanisms. After analyzing the experiences of black women who were forced by slavery and the labor market to perform domestic work for white families, Collins (1990) noted that such women developed a unique ability to be the "outsider-within," thus permitting them to experience oppression from a different vantage point. Croom (2000) asserted that sexual and gender minority persons of color develop a greater sense of flexibility and fluidity as a result of having to abide by multiple allegiances. Other strengths that can emerge as a result of experiences associated with marginalization include the abilities to detach psychologically from destructive situations and to maintain self-identity and not be influenced by the opinions of others (Greene, 2000). O'Toole (2000) noted a similar phenomenon in her sample of racially diverse lesbians with disabilities. Hall and Fine (2005) identified two aspects of positive marginality: (1) critical watching and (2) reframing. According to Hall and Fine, the subversion of social institutions requires engagement with social institutions (critical watching) with the aim of exploiting what is useful and living lives of meaning (reframing).

Croteau et al. (2002) engaged in a qualitative analysis of interview content in order to explore the interaction of racial/ethnic and sexual orientation statuses. In particular, they were interested in the simultaneous interplay of oppressed and privileged identity statuses. Participants reported that having a "privileged status sometimes lessened the effects of oppression, lessened the participants' recognition of their oppression, or lessened the acceptance by others of the participants as part of an oppressed group" (p. 252). Participants also reported that their experiences of oppression helped them to have greater empathy toward others who were socially marginalized.

Sue and Constantine (2003) and Constantine and Sue (2006) described the strengths that people of color who must navigate living in two cultures experience: (1) heightened perceptual wisdom, (2) the ability to rely on nonverbal and contextual meanings, and (3) bicultural flexibility. According to Constantine and Sue (2006), people of color must adapt to the dominant white European-American context, and in order to do so, they must become good at discerning the "thoughts and actions of White Americans" (p. 237). Living in two cultural worlds also enables people of color to see other people's points of view and to exercise behavioral flexibility.

Abes and Jones (2004) were intrigued by the suggestion (Kegan, 1982; Fassinger, 1998) that increased cognitive complexity may result from being a sexual minority. In their qualitative study of meaning making in lesbians' development of multiple identities, Abes and Jones noted that many participants experienced cognitive dissonance when their self-perceptions didn't fit with external expectations of others, thus "early and constant experiences with dissonance might be the impetus for cognitive development" (p. 627).

Rust (2000) maintained that the skills that racial and ethnic minorities use to manage their marginality can be applied in the case of bisexual women who must cope with being marginalized for their sexuality. "Biracial sexual minority women face challenges that reflect significant similarity to the challenges bisexual women of all racial and ethnic backgrounds face when intimately involved in predominantly lesbian women's communities" (Firestein, 2007, p. 96). In other words, biracial persons are sensitized to question bipolar thinking by virtue of their socialization experiences (Rust, 1996).

It is important to remember that many white gay men do not experience the marginalization and oppression that persons of color are routinely subjected to until such time as they come to acknowledge that they might be gay or bisexual. This may actually mean for some that there have been fewer opportunities to develop the kinds of survival strategies that many sexual minority persons of color are forced to cultivate.

COUNSELING CULTURALLY DIVERSE SEXUAL AND GENDER MINORITIES

Recent models have accurately mirrored the complexities of sexual and gender minority identities and have important implications for helping professionals. Practitioners need to acquire knowledge and skills to work with culturally diverse sexual and gender minority persons. However, the very systems of knowledge they acquire can sometimes block their ability to see the individuality inherent in each client. This demands that the practitioner, though trained and grounded in the research, still assume the stance of "informed not knowing" (Shapiro, 1996). In this process, the counselor leaves "behind her own cultural biases and pre-understandings, to enter the experience of the other" (Laird, 1999, p. 75).

Several helping professionals (Appleby, 2001; Bing, 2004; Hays, 2008; Israel, 2004) recommend that practitioners be direct in addressing identity issues with their clients. This means discussing together the realistic challenges the clients face:

- How to integrate the sometimes divergent aspects of identity (e.g., ethnicity, race, social class, disability, religious affiliation)
- How to understand the impact such identities have on their relationships with others

- How to grasp a sense of pride and privilege at being a member of a particular group
- How to get clients to ask directly about any concerns they might feel at working with therapists who are in either a minority or a majority culture

Bowman (2003) cautions therapists against responding to clients purely on the basis of visible or ascribed identities like their color or disability status, while simultaneously ignoring sexual and gender issues. Practitioners also do their clients a disservice by fixating on the achieved identity statuses of their clients (i.e., sexual orientation, gender identity), especially when this tendency overshadows everything else. Hays (2008) recommended that helping professionals use the acronym ADRESSING (aging, disabilities, religion, ethnicity, socioeconomic status, sexual orientation, indigenous heritage, nationality, and gender) as a conscious reminder to consider the multiple aspects of personal identity.

Practitioners should not assume that clients' sexual orientation labels and behaviors are necessarily aligned.

For example, in some Latin American cultures, there is a distinction between receptive and insertive partners in anal intercourse among men. Latino men who assume "top" or insertive anal sex positions in same-sex sexual relationships are considered "straight" (Rosario, 2004), while anally receptive partners label themselves as "gay" (Fassinger & Arseneau, 2007). The assumption on the part of a counselor that the insertive partner is in denial of his bisexuality would be tantamount to imposing cultural bias (Almaguer, 1993; Rust, 1996).

Hancock (2000) argues that expertise in sexual and gender orientation issues does not automatically equip practitioners to work with ethnic minority issues. For example, therapists who are sexual minorities themselves may sometimes assume that their experiences of oppression or homophobia are the same as the racist and oppressive experiences persons of color encounter (Croteau et al., 2002). The next section of this chapter explores the dispositions, knowledge, and skills needed to work with culturally diverse sexual and gender minority persons.

Understanding Ourselves

According to Sue et al.'s (1982) and Sue and Sue's (1999) multicultural counseling competencies, practitioners need to be aware of any possible negative emotional and cognitive responses toward their culturally different clients. Practitioners, social workers, and psychologists must be willing to uncover their blind spots and hot buttons. This process will likely entail exploring the ways practitioners have been privileged by virtue of membership in particular cultural groups. Just like their clients, practitioners must exhibit cognitive complexity and behavioral flexibility when dealing with sexual and gender minority clients with multiple minority identities.

Greene (2003) wrote:

There is the potential for oppressive behavior in anyone who holds societal privilege and the power that accompanies it. Because of that potential, it is important in our work as psychologists to determine the nature of our own multiple identities, where along the spectrum of privilege and disadvantage those identities place us, as the research scientist, therapist, supervisor or teacher, in what dimensions. It is important to locate and acknowledge our own locus of social advantage and its impact on our perceptions in our professional work. It is equally important to acknowledge the effect of our own membership in groups that may be marginalized on our view of the client, student, research participant, or supervisee. This process often provokes anxiety. (p. 392)

RACE/ETHNICITY   Beginning practitioners are sometimes hesitant to raise, and uncomfortable in discussing, issues related to race and sex in therapy (Bing, 2004). One danger is imposing their own personal frames of reference and values systems on the sexual behaviors and identities of sexual and gender minorities of color. Boykin's (2005) analysis of a highly publicized story about African-American men on the "down low" illustrates the pervasive and deep-seated nature of racism. Boykin noted that, without sufficient scientific evidence, the increased incidence of HIV among African-American heterosexual women was attributed to African-American men who were in heterosexual relationships but were having sex with other men in secret. Boykin argued that the expression "on the down low" has been part of popular culture for decades and that it was used to refer to any clandestine behavior. He noted that this expression was borrowed expressly to refer to African-American men who were having sex with other men and then returning home to engage in sex with their female partners. Boykin contended that this was done on the basis of anecdotal evidence rather than scientific data.

DISABILITY   Helping professionals need to be open to exploring their countertransference reactions not only to persons on the basis of sexual and gender orientation but also to persons with varying disabilities. Avoidance of discussion about either disability or sexual orientation sends messages that having a disability and being gay or lesbian is shameful (O'Toole & Brown, 2003).

Smart and Smart (2006) observed that many helping professionals consciously or unconsciously adopt a "Biomedical Model" of disabilities, which emphasizes the medical and dysfunctional aspects of having a disability. Therapists who do this tend to hold lowered expectations for, respond with pity instead of empathy to, foster dependence of, and refrain from giving honest feedback to their clients who are disabled (Smart & Smart, 2006). Therapists must be cognizant that persons with disabilities often view their disabilities as an integral and valued aspect of their identities (Smart & Smart, 2006).

One area that might be particularly problematic in terms of countertransference concerns the exploration of sexual issues in persons with disabilities who identify as sexual and gender minorities. As Fraley, Mona, and Theodore (2007) observed, there is a "doubling effect" of negative stereotypes and social perceptions about the sexuality of sexual and gender minorities and about persons with disabilities when practitioners, social workers, and psychologists consider issues related to sexuality.

RELIGION   Practitioners must be aware of their own values and religious beliefs about homosexuality, bisexuality, and gender variance and should seek consultation and supervision specifically related to these issues (Lease & Shulman, 2003; Richards & Bergin, 1997). It is critical that therapists cultivate self-knowledge regarding personal biases against organized religion as well as alternative or New Age spirituality (Davidson, 2000).

Creating Climates of Safety

According to Miville and Ferguson (2004), counseling with culturally diverse sexual and gender minority clients must "encompass a space for safe dialogues without fear of being pathologized or subtly rejected by the therapist" (p. 769). Given the sense of suspicion and distrust many minority groups have felt toward the mental health establishment, a client-centered therapeutic approach is especially appropriate in the initial stages of therapy. Crucial clinical skills for working with diverse people include listening, empathizing, and providing a safe zone. The repeated validation of feelings is of paramount importance to the therapy because of the discrimination and negative stigma that await clients outside the therapy room. It is also essential that counseling trainees feel at ease asking clarifying questions when they lack information about or experience with a particular issue.

RACE/ETHNICITY   Gutierrez (1997) encouraged therapists to be sensitive to the issues that may confront sexual minority people of color who seek out psychotherapy, since such a decision may run counter to cultural norms that encourage help seeking from family members or religious leaders.

Walters (1998) suggested the use of positive reframes with gay people of color. She cites the work of Anzaldua (1987), who recommended that multiple-status persons develop a "border" consciousness, meaning they affirm the marginal parts of themselves and integrate their varying identity statuses. "As a practitioner, one can reframe this intermediary position not as a problem, but, rather, as an opportunity to grow and teach" (Walters, 1998, p. 69). Walters emphasized that counseling practitioners need to be cognitively flexible in order to tolerate and manage complexity and contradiction in their clients.

Loiacano (1993) recommended that therapists explore the nature of the social messages that persons of color receive from their communities about the compatibility of their racial/ethnic identities and homosexuality. Constantine (2002) argued that understanding clients from the standpoint of racial, ethnic, and gender identity issues increased the potential for diagnostic validity.

It is also vitally important that practitioners be sensitive to and attentive in their use of inclusive language (e.g., significant other, partner) and gender-specific pronouns. Many persons in the African-American sexual and gender minority communities prefer the term *same-gender-loving* over labels such as "gay," "lesbian," or "bisexual" (Human Rights Campaign, 2004). Bieschke and Matthews (1996) advocate that practitioners make sure such organizational or environmental issues as the office climate, the terminology contained on the intake forms, and the books and magazines available in the waiting room are affirmative of ethnically and racially diverse sexual and gender minority persons.

CLASS   As counseling trainees and professionals, we need to explore our own economic privilege relative to our sexual and gender minority clients (Greene, 2003; Lott, 2002: Smith, 2005). Stereotypes like poor families are dysfunctional and poor persons are lazy, unmotivated and responsible for their poverty (Greene, 2003; Lott, 2002; Smith 2005) are classist. These beliefs predispose psychologists, counselors, and social workers to discount the "strengths, skills and wisdom" (Lott, 2005; p. 108) in poor individuals and families.

Lott (2002) notes that psychologists, counselors and social workers are apt to distance themselves emotionally and cognitively from those without economic privilege and to render poor and working-class persons as the "other." She views distancing feelings and behaviors in helping professionals as reflective of the middle class lifestyles that accompany our choice of professions and our incomes.

Counseling trainees and professionals also need to guard against the common assumption that sexual minorities, particularly gay man, are affluent. This stereotype can often lead to negative counter-transference responses when therapists encounter clients whose appearance deviates from the metro-sexual look.

DISABILITY One way for practitioners to provide affirmative therapy for sexual and gender minority clients with disabilities is to make therapy itself accessible (Olkin, 2007). Smart and Smart (2006) recommended that practitioners be attentive to issues of power in therapeutic relationships, particularly if clients have disabilities and therapists do not. Practitioners who either minimize clients' disabilities or allow their perception of their clients to be dominated by their disabilities will likely be ineffectual in establishing climates of safety and trust (O'Toole & Brown, 2003).

RELIGION Religion and spirituality have been traditionally taboo topics in counseling. However, practitioners may need to let their sexual and gender minority clients know directly and early on in the therapy that they are open to exploring religious issues (Lease & Shulman, 2003). It is recommended that practitioners introduce the topic of religion during the initial psychosocial assessment process by asking about both damaging and protective aspects of clients' religious affiliations (Yakushko, 2005; Zinnbauer & Pargament, 2000).

Developing Knowledge and Skills

A culturally competent counselor possesses specific knowledge and information about the worldviews of the culturally different, including life experiences, heritage, and historical background. And as a consequence, helping professionals will employ appropriate, relevant, and sensitive skills (Sue, Arredondo, & McDavis, 1992; Sue et al., 1982; Sue & Sue, 1999).

RACE/ETHNICITY While it is important that neophyte practitioners become familiar with diverse cultures (African American, Latino/a, Hispanic, etc.), there is a danger that such exposure will lead to stereotyping of a different nature.

Each cultural group is distinguished by variables such as language, socioeconomic status, length of time after migration, sociopolitical history, and identity development, all of which need to be considered and have an impact on the identities and practices of various minority groups (Garnets, 2002; Israel & Selvidge, 2003). In her work with black-white biracial lesbians, Bing (2004) advised therapists to be aware of historical issues relative to black and white relationships. For example, she suggested that practitioners be aware of the "one drop rule," which defines a person as black by virtue of a single drop of black blood. This rule was used to control and oppress black persons. The therapist also needs to explore the clients' current feelings about interracial relationships and what it means for the children of black and white parents to be lighter skinned. Exploring such issues can permit clients freedom to explore possible feelings of "guilt for approximating the appearance of a White person or concerns about looking 'too Black' and, therefore, not adequately representing the other half of her heritage" (p. 197).

Models like those devised by Crawford et al. (2002), which conceptualize dual identity (sexual orientation and racial/ethnic) processes, are helpful therapeutic tools for practitioners to open up discussion with clients who are struggling with multiple minority issues.

CLASS   Poor and working class sexual and gender minority persons are missing in counseling research. Historically, our information and our models of sexual and gender minority persons' lives were constructed on the basis of a small segment of this population (Barrett & Pollack, 2005; Greene, 2003). Historically, samples used in research consisted of persons who were "out" as homosexual and/or transgender. These research participants were also likely to be white and middle class and to have the economic resources needed to socialize in gay communities, live in gay-friendly cities, and vacation at gay-friendly resorts (Barrett & Pollack, 2005).

DISABILITY   The issues that confront sexual and gender minorities with disabilities are missing from the curriculum of traditional training programs in counseling, psychology, and social work. Such work is often relegated to rehabilitation practitioners (O'Toole, 2000). One accessible text for practitioners is Olkin's *What Psychotherapists Should Know About Disability* (1999). Persons with disabilities should not be expected to educate their practitioners about disability issues (O'Toole, 2000). Mental health issues that are particularly salient are depression and suicide, particularly among disabled women (O'Toole & Brown, 2003).

RELIGION   Morrow and Tyson (2006) offered valuable suggestions for those practitioners who work with sexual and gender minority clients:

- Assess the possibility of religious trauma by exploring clients' history of involvement in organized religion.
- Explore any ways in which religious messages have impeded clients' self-esteem (Morrow, 2003).
- Look for evidence of guilt and shame related to same-sex feelings or behaviors.
- Assess symptoms of depression, suicidality, and substance abuse in clients.
- Help clients go through the grieving process over the losses associated with religious trauma (Morrow & Tyson, 2006).

The Healing Power of Personal Narrative

One important way for clients to facilitate exploration of attitudes and beliefs is through the use of biographies, novels, and films. When our personal stories are shared with others, they help normalize our experiences and limit the isolation that many sexual and gender minority persons with multiple identity statuses experience (Cerbone, 1997).

RACE/ETHNICITY   Some excellent texts that capture the authentic voices of sexual minority persons of color include *Freedom in the Village: Twenty-Five Years of Black Gay Men's Writing* (Harris, 2005); *Brother to Brother: New Writings by Black Gay Men* (Hemphill, 2007); *Loving in the War Years* (Moraga & Moraga, 2001); *The Very Inside: An Anthology of writings by Asian and Pacific Islander Lesbians* (Lim-Hing, 1998); *Piece of My Heart: A Lesbian of Colour*

Anthology (Silvera, 1991); and *A Lotus of Another Color: An Unfolding of the South Asian Gay and Lesbian Experience* (Ratti, 1993).

CLASS   Some texts that might enable readers to explore the meaning of class and its intersections with race, ethnicity, disability and religion include: *Working Class Lesbian Life: Classed Outsiders* (Taylor, 2007); *Working Class Gay and Bisexual Men* (Appleby, 2000); *Queerly Classed. Gay Men and Lesbians Write about Class*, (Raffo, 1997), and *Stone Butch Blues* (Feinberg, 1993).

DISABILITY   Some resources that might enable readers to better understand the worldview of persons who both have disabilities and are sexual/gender minorities include *Bent: Journal of Cripgay Voices* (http://www.bentvoices.org); *Eyes of Desire: A Deaf Gay and Lesbian Reader* (Luczak, 1993); and *Queer Crips: Disabled Gay Men and Their Stories* (Guter & Killacky, 2003).

RELIGION   The following texts help readers understand the inner conflicts that present themselves for persons who are sexual and gender minorities and committed to their religions: *Stranger at the Gate: To Be Gay and Christian in America* (White, 1994); *Like Bread on the Seder Plate: Jewish Lesbians and the Transformation of Tradition* (Alpert, 1997); and *Wrestling with the Angel: Faith and Religion in the Lives of Gay Men* (Bouldrey, 1995).

Rethinking the Meaning of Coming Out

Several authors have cautioned therapists against placing undue pressure on their sexual minority clients to come out to family, friends, and communities (Liddle, 2007; Rust, 1996). Many of the assumptions about coming out have been gleaned from research whose subjects consist predominantly of white persons (Smith, 1997). Thus, it is likely that practitioners who are not culturally informed are not cognizant of the pressure within certain cultures to be straight. Israel and Selvidge (2003) emphasized that sexual minorities need to develop stigma management skills to ensure that they are not risking personal safety and protection in coming out in various contexts. The reality is that overzealous encouragement to have a client come out can have disastrous results.

RACE/ETHNICITY   Liddle (2007) cautioned therapists against minimizing the risks that often accompany self-disclosure by persons of color within their ethnic communities. In instances where ethnic minorities have recently migrated from other countries to the United States, their financial and emotional ties with their families and ethnic communities may be particularly important, and any affiliation with the gay community would be perceived as a threat to these support systems (Firestein, 2007). Brauner (2000), a psychotherapist, wrote:

> Coming out to their family was, for a number of my white male clients, crucial to their psychological health and, for a number of my black clients it was equally crucial to psychological health not to come out to their families. For the latter it was more important to maintain their closeness to their community and racial identities and to continue to fight racism, rather than address homophobia

within the community and the wider society. . . . It is important not to pathologize such choices. (p. 17)

Smith (1997) reconceptualized coming out in African-American families as "taking in"; in other words, African-American families may provide a positive response without formal acknowledgment of and reference to such terms as *gay* and *lesbian*. She noted that "clients of color often feel pressured, pigeonholed, or not understood by white friends and lovers. White clients may report feeling abandoned by their Black, Asian, or Latino partners or counterparts to fight homophobia alone" (Smith, 1997, p. 282). Smith recommended that therapists consider asking their clients to tell stories about their positive experiences as a result of the different ways their family and friends have been supportive rather than focusing on acts of resistance by family and friends. The emphasis according to Smith should be on helping the clients develop other supportive networks.

CLASS   Economic power and issues of self-disclosure of sexual orientation and gender identity are intertwined. Sexual minorities who come out in blue collar employment settings risk employment termination and/or loss of benefits. Gender minorities who transition on the job risk employment termination and/or loss of benefits. The economic burden even with health insurance for gender minorities who decide to transition—through hormonal and surgical interventions—is prohibitive.

DISABILITY   Therapists need to be sensitive to the possibility that for some sexual and gender minority persons with disabilities, their disability identity and affiliation with the disability culture are more salient and important than their identification as a sexual and/or gender minority. For example, in research with sexual minority persons with disabilities, Whitney (2006) and Shakespeare (1999) reported that participants tended to view the identity that developed first as the more positive and powerful aspect of their overall identity. In her qualitative interviews of sexual minority women with disabilities, Axtell (1999) reported that her participants stressed the importance of being perceived as a whole person rather than being defined by their disabilities.

For many persons with disabilities, the ability to connect with other sexual and/or gender minorities with disabilities is more problematic than for sexual and gender minority persons without disabilities. Typical venues for meeting others like bars are not likely to be accessible. On the other hand, the use of the Internet as a tool for dating has permitted persons with disabilities to meet other sexual and gender minorities and socialize without fear of rejection (Fraley et al., 2007).

RELIGION   Until recently, therapists were afraid of dealing with spiritual and religious issues in therapy. Yet, as the research shows, this can be a tremendous source of self-esteem, support, and existential meaning in the lives of sexual and gender minorities (Rosario et al., 2006). The ability and willingness on the part of the therapist to serve as a conduit to nonjudgmental clergy who are willing to minister to clients are important (Rosario et al., 2006).

Resources

RACE/ETHNICITY   Fukuyama and Ferguson (2000) recommend that counselors help sexual minorities find support systems that are separate from the white gay community. For example, Those We Love is a program for African-American families of sexual and gender minorities. Parents, Families, and Friends of Lesbians and Gays (PFLAG) has formed a Families of Color Network, which addresses issues of racism and the barriers that exist for sexual and gender minorities within communities of color. Another national organization, Men of All Colors Together (MACT), is "a social and educational organization whose major purpose is for men of different ethnicities to meet one another" (Chernin & Johnson, 2003, p. 41). Other resources include Llego—National Latina/o Lesbian, Gay, Bisexual, and Transgender Organization (www.LLEGO.org); African American Lesbians United (www.celebratesisterhood.org); Asian Equality (www.asianequality.com); and Native Out (for American Indians, www.nativeout.com).

CLASS   Resources which address economic equality and discrimination issues for sexual and gender minorities include the following: Human Rights Watch—Lesbian, Gay, Bisexual, and Transgender Human Rights Watch (http://hrw.org/doc/?t=lgbt) and National Center for Transgender Equality (http://www.nctequality.org/About/about.asp)

DISABILITY   Because it can be challenging for disabled persons to find role models and communities (O'Toole, 2000), practitioners can help. Resources include Rainbow Alliance of the Deaf, a national organization with chapters in the United States and Canada (www. rad.org); Blind Friends of Lesbians and Gays (www.bflag.org); and Deaf Queer Resources Center (www.deafqueer.org).

RELIGION   It is vitally important that practitioners be aware of alternative resources for religious and spiritual support and gay-affirming religious communities (Morrow & Tyson, 2006; Yakushko, 2005). Some examples are Rainbow Baptists (http://www.rainbowbaptists.org); Integrity (Episcopalian Church, http://www.integrityusa.org); Lutherans Concerned/North American Lutheran Church (http://lcna.org); Metropolitan Community Church (Christian-based, http://www.mccchurch.org); Dignity (Catholic Church, http://www. dignityusa. org); Affirmation (United Methodist Church, http://www.umaffirm.org); and United Church of Christ Coalition for LGBT Concerns (http://www.ucccoalition.org).

Serving as Advocates

Our traditional psychological paradigm says that practitioners and psychologists interpret emotional and behavioral problems as intrapsychically or interpersonally generated and maintained. This orientation makes it difficult to view many of the issues that diverse sexual and gender minorities face as the social consequences of their experiences. And treatment is wholly inadequate if it fails to address the social dimensions of this problem. While Chapter 11 covers issues related to practitioners as advocates, there are many things that practitioners as professionals and private citizens can do.

Race/Ethnicity

- Support coalition-building. This helps create understanding between various segments of the sexual and gender minority communities and political and faith leaders in communities of color.
- Offer educational programming for religious and political leaders of communities of color.
- Write letters to the editors of local newspapers.

CLASS The growing trend towards privatization of social services and the expanding use of faith-based social service programs negatively impacts sexual and gender minorities (Blackwell & Dziegielewski, 2005). Because of religious beliefs, faith based organizations are more apt to discriminate against sexual and gender minorities. These organizations can legally exclude sexual and gender minority clients from services and from hiring consideration as helping personnel (Blackwell & Dziegielewski, 2005). This threat as well as the shrinking public funding for social services makes it imperative that helping professionals develop the skills to advocate for laws and public policies that protect sexual and gender minorities. The social services and health care needs of gender minorities are especially acute given evidence of housing, employment, and educational discrimination (Spade, 2006).

Disability

- Intervene to support clients with disabilities (Smart & Smart, 2006).
- Ensure that all facilities are accessible.
- Help clients gain access to the health care and social services that they need (Hunt et al., 2006). Do not require that clients be seen only in the agency offices (O'Toole & Brown, 2003).
- Provide a sliding fee scale that takes into account disability-related expenses such as transportation.
- Help provide written or electronic materials in accessible formats (e.g., Braille, accessible websites, accessible consent forms).
- Advocate for additional research. Make others aware of the dearth of empirical studies dealing with disabilities in the sexual and gender minority population (Fraley et al., 2007; Hunt et al., 2006; LeBlanc & Tully, 2001; O'Toole & Brown, 2003).

Religion

- Address spiritual and religious issues on a broader, systemic level (Bridges, Selvidge, & Matthews, 2003). This will help offset possible negative messages from organized religious institutions.
- Practitioners affiliated with religious institutions may work inside their own places of worship to be more welcoming to and supportive of sexual and gender minority congregants.

Summary

How minority persons are able to integrate differing aspects of their identities has been the topic of increasing interest. Garnets (2002) wrote that rather than making assumptions about clients based purely on a singular attribute like ethnicity or race, "[a]ll psychologists need to open their minds to individuals' multiple identities and the full range of diversity" (p. 126).

Sexual and gender minority persons of color and those who are poor or have disabilities are vulnerable to hostility and discrimination from three sources: (1) mainstream culture, which is predominantly white, middle class, Christian, and able-bodied; (2) their own communities, including their families; and (3) sexual and gender minority communities (Fukuyama & Ferguson, 2000; Greene, 1997; McLean, 2003; Raj, 2002; Walters, 1998).

Rather than focusing exclusively on the negative repercussions that result from interwoven identities and multiple oppressions, researchers are beginning to focus on the positive outcomes associated with these phenomena. For example, sexual and gender minority persons of color often develop a greater sense of flexibility and fluidity as a result of having to abide by multiple allegiances (Croom, 2000). Additionally, many gain the ability to detach psychologically from destructive situations; that is, to maintain their self-identities and not be influenced by opinions of others (Greene, 2000; O'Toole, 2000).

It is further recommended that therapists pursue the following course of action:

- Engage in dialogues that focus pointedly on client self-definition.
- Talk with clients about issues that have frequently been ignored or even considered taboo (Appleby, 2001; Bing, 2004; Israel, 2004).
- Help clients examine how various aspects of their identities—ethnicity, race, social class, disability, and religious affiliation—have an impact on their relationships with others.
- Initiate discussions on how clients have tried to integrate differing aspects of their identities.
- Look beyond visible identities and facilitate clients' continued efforts at self-definition (Bowman, 2003).

Personal Reflection 1

In Carbado's (2005) essay entitled "Privilege," he describes how white privilege operates for him in a trip to a department store:

My individual identity is lost in the social construction of black manhood. I can try to adopt race-negating strategies to challenge this dignity-destroying social meaning. I can work my identity (to attempt) to repudiate the stereotype. I might, for example, dress "respectable" when I go shopping. There is, after all something to the politics of dress, particularly in social contexts in which race matters, that is, in every American social context. Purchasing an item, especially something expensive, immediately on entering the store is another strategy I can employ to disabuse people of my blackness. This sort of signaling strategy will reveal to the department store's security personnel what might not otherwise be apparent because of my race and gender: that I am a shopper. If I am in the mood to dress up and I do not want to spend any money, there is a third strategy I can employ: solicit the assistance of a white sales associate. This too, must be done early in the shopping experience. A white salesperson would not be suspected of facilitating or contributing to black shoplifting and can be trusted to keep an eye on me. Finally, I might simply whistle Vivaldi as I move among the merchandise: only a good (safe, respectable) black man would know Vivaldi or whistle classical music. (p. 193)

Directions

An important component of multicultural counseling training involves self-knowledge and the use of experiential techniques to explore biases that result from privilege (Greene & Sanchez-Hucles, 1997). This process will likely entail exploring ways in which we have been privileged by virtue of our membership in one or more cultural groups. For example, a white lesbian is privileged in some but not all ways: possibly privileged with respect to race but not sexual orientation or gender. Think about the ways in which you are privileged. Take into account the dimensions of race, class, gender, gender identity, sexual orientation, religion, and disability status. Complete the following sentence: I am privileged in _____ but not in _____. How has being privileged in these ways affected you in the past and at present? How might these sources of privilege impact your counseling relationships with those who are not privileged?

Personal Reflection 2

In her graduate-level experiential exercise, Tania Israel, a biological female, was asked to dress as a man and to assume the role of a male. In the narrative below, she describes this experience:

> I am 23 years old, in my masters program in Human Sexuality Education, and the course I'm taking requires us to come to class one day dressed as the other gender. I am excited about the idea of dressing as a man. I don't just want to wear the jeans and button down shirt that I, as a woman, can freely don without challenging my gender role. No, I want to "pass." I raid my male friends' closets, and they coach me on how to walk, talk, and sit "like a guy." I'm psyched to go to class the next day. I even wear the clothes home that night. I know I'm doing well when I have trouble offering a friend of mine a ride home because he thinks it's a car full of fraternity men harassing him because he's gay. Not only can I pass for a man, but I can pass for a homophobic fraternity brother! I feel very powerful. Then I get home and look in the mirror, expecting to see reflected back my image of myself as powerful and male. What I see, though, is an Asian man. No, no, that's not at all what I want to be. Asian men are emasculated in this society. No one sees them as powerful. I thought I'd see a white man in the mirror, further proof of my denial of my own ethnicity. This incident is a poignant reminder that I'm not a member of the powerful group. I am marginalized and

> can't change that simply by changing my clothing and the way I sit. It's more indelible than that. (Israel, 2004, pp. 175–176)

Directions

1. Select a partner for this exercise. Each of you will take a few moments to silently select salient aspects of identity discussed in this chapter (gender, gender identity, sexual orientation, race/ethnicity, disability status, religious/spiritual status, and socioeconomic status).
2. Print each word you've selected on a separate 3" × 3" sized piece of paper.
3. Select one person, partner A, to mix up the slips of paper and place them face down so that the words are not showing.
4. Partner B will select one slip of paper and read this word silently. Whatever word is selected by partner B describes an aspect of partner A's identity. Whatever this characteristic is, it is the single defining element in partner A's identity. Dismiss or ignore any other aspects of the client's identity—even ones that may be visibly evident like gender and skin color.
5. Partner A will now assume the role of a client and partner B will be the therapist. Using a real-life issue, partner A will engage in a therapeutic dialogue with partner B for approximately 15 minutes. Describe your reactions to this exercise and how this might impact your future work as a counselor.

Library, Media, and Internet Activity

Check your local video/DVD store for three important films.

Ethan Mao (Lee, 2004)

Ethan Mao is an 18-year-old Chinese American who was kicked out of his home by his father and stepmother for being gay. Ethan lives on the streets and becomes a street hustler to survive. He is befriended by 19-year-old Remigio, a fellow street hustler and drug dealer. Ethan asks his younger brother for the security code, and he and Remigio enter Mao's family home while his family is away on Thanksgiving. When his family returns home unexpectedly, chaos ensues.

Discussion Questions

1. Ethan alludes to the fact that his father's actions during the robbery of their family restaurant were upsetting to him. What are your thoughts about this, and how might you facilitate a dialogue between Ethan and his father about this incident?
2. From the perspective of the research, how does Ethan's father's response to his son's homosexuality compare with research? How might you work with the Mao family after this incident? What do you anticipate will happen as a result of this incident?
3. What does the research say about the experiences of ethnic youth? How do Ethan's and Remigio's stories compare with those in the literature?

Brother to Brother (Evans, 2004)

Perry Williams is an African-American art student who befriends a homeless man named Richard Bruce Nugent. He soon discovers that Bruce was a rather well known artist during the Harlem Renaissance period in the 1920s. Bruce and his fellow artists—Langston Hughes, Wallace Thurman, and Nora Zeale Hurston—lived together for a short period and wrote a magazine called *Fire*, a literary magazine for African-American men. Through the use of black-and-white documentary-style scenes, Perry discovers what the world was like for gay African-American men.

Discussion Questions

1. The film switches back and forth between the events of the 1920s and the present. What similarities exist between the plights of gay African-American men then and now? Do you agree with Evans's portrayal of the plight of contemporary African-American men?
2. How does the research presented in this chapter compare to the depiction of gay black men in this film?
3. How do the lives of gay black youth of today compare with those of Hughes, Nugent, and Thurman?

Saving Face (Wu, 2005)

Hwei-Lan, a 48-year-old widow, becomes pregnant and will not disclose the identity of the baby's father to anyone. After Hwei-Lan's father banishes her from their home in disgrace, Hwei-Lan comes to live with her daughter Wil, a young doctor who works in Manhattan. Meanwhile, Wil falls in love with Vivian, a dancer, and keeps their relationship a secret.

Discussion Questions

1. Describe the relationship between mother and daughter.
2. What was your reaction to Wil's disclosure to her mother that she was gay?
3. How does Wil feel about being gay? Why couldn't Wil kiss Vivian at the airport?

Case Study

Lisa is a 29-year-old social worker. She comes to the counseling center on her own volition. She has had difficulty sleeping and has experienced a decrease in appetite and lost several pounds over the past six months. She is the younger of two siblings. Lisa's brother is 11 years older and has lived on the West Coast for several years with his wife and two children. Lisa currently resides at home with her mother. Lisa's father died of complications due to alcoholism when she was 12 years old. Lisa excelled in school and attended the local university in her area.

She has been an active member of her church and is currently a Sunday school teacher. Lisa attributes her sleeplessness and weight loss to "stress from work," but you suspect there is more to her story. Lisa tells you at the end of her third session that she has strong feelings for a fellow social worker at her agency. She tells you that she sees no way to pursue this relationship, given her affiliation with the church. She tells you that pursuing a same-sex relationship is clearly against the teachings of the Bible and of her church. She says she went to her church pastor a few months ago when she first began having romantic feelings toward her friend. She and her pastor prayed together, and on her last visit, he told her she must "choose between her faith and her homosexuality." He stated she "couldn't have it both ways."

Discussion Questions

1. What additional information would you like to obtain from Lisa?
2. How might you proceed with Lisa in counseling?
3. What sorts of countertransference issues might arise for you when working with Lisa?

References

Abes, E. S., & Jones, S. R. (2004). Meaning-making capacity and the dynamics of lesbian college students' multiple dimensions of identity. *Journal of College Student Development, 45*(6), 612–632.

Adams, C. L., & Kimmel, D. C. (1997). Exploring the lives of older African American gay men. In B. Greene (Ed.), *Ethnic and cultural diversity among lesbians and gay men* (pp. 132–151). Thousand Oaks, CA: Sage.

Akerlund, M., & Cheung, M. (2000). Teaching beyond the deficit model: Gay and lesbian issues: African Americans, Latinos, and Asian Americans. *Journal of Social Work Education, 36,* 279–290.

Alexander, N. (2006). Gender identity, cross-dressing and gender reassignment and people with learning disabilities. *Learning Disability Review, 11*(2), 12–15.

Allman, K. M. (1996). (Un)natural boundaries: Mixed race, gender, and sexuality. In M. P. Root (Ed.), *The multiracial experience: Racial border as the new frontier* (pp. 275–290). Thousand Oaks, CA: Sage.

Almaguer, T. (1993). Chicano men: A cartography of homosexual identity and behavior. In H. Abelove, M. A. Barale, & D. M. Halperin (Eds.), *The lesbian and gay studies reader* (pp. 255–273). New York: Routledge.

Alpert, R. (1997). *Like bread on the seder plate: Jewish lesbians and the transformation of tradition.* New York: Columbia University Press.

Anzaldua, G. (1987). *Borderlands/la frontera: The new Mestiza.* San Francisco: Spinsters/Aunt Lute Foundation.

Appleby, G. A. (2001). Framework for practice with working class gay and bisexual men. *Journal of Gay & Lesbian Social Services, 12* (3/4), 5–46.

Appleby, G. A. (Ed.) (2001). *Working-class gay and bisexual men.* New York: Routledge.

Arredondo, P. (1999). Multicultural counseling competencies as tools to address oppression and racism. *Journal of Counseling & Development, 77*(1), 102–108.

Arredondo, P., Toporek, R., Brown, S. P., Jones, J., Locke, D. C., Sanchez, J., et al. (1996). Operationalization of the multicultural competencies. *Journal of Multicultural Counseling & Development, 24*(1), 42–78.

Axtell, S. (1999). Disability and chronic illness identity: Interviews with lesbians and bisexual women and their partners. *Journal of Gay, Lesbian, & Bisexual Identity, 4*(1), 53–72.

Barrett, D. C. & Pollack, L. M. (2005). Whose gay community? Social class, sexual self-expression, and gay community involvement. *The Sociological Quarterly 46,* 437–456.

Bergin, A. E., & Jensen, J. (1990). Religiosity of psychotherapists: A national survey. *Psychotherapy, 27*(1), 3–7.

Bernal, M. E., Knight, G. P., Ocampo, K. A., Garza, C. A., & Cote, M. K. (1993). Development of Mexican-American identity. In M. D. Bernal &

G. P. Knight (Eds.), *Ethnic identity: Formation and transmission among Hispanics and other minorities* (pp. 31–46). Albany, NY: SUNY.

Berry, J. W., Kim, U., Minde, T., & Mok, D. (1987). Comparative studies of acculturative stress. *International Migration Review 21*(3), 491–511.

Bieschke, K. J., & Matthews, C. (1996). Career counselor attitudes and behaviors toward gay, lesbian, and bisexual clients. *Journal of Vocational Behavior, 48*(2), 243–255.

Bing, V. (2004). Out of the closet but still in hiding: Conflicts and identity issues for a black-white biracial lesbian. *Women & Therapy, 27*(1/2), 185–201.

Blackwell, C. W. & Dziegielewki, S. F. (2005). The privatization of social services from public to sectarian: Negative consequences for America's gays and lesbians. *Journal of Human Behavior in the Social Environment, 11*(2), 25–41.

Bohan, J. S. (1996). *Psychology and sexual orientation: Coming to terms.* New York: Routledge.

Bopp, P. J., Juday, T. R., & Charter, C. W. (2005). A school-based program to improve life skills and to prevent HIV infection in multicultural transgendered youth. In J. T. Sears (Ed.), *Gay, lesbian and transgendered issues in school based programs, policies and practices* (pp. 147–165). New York: Harrington Park Press.

Bouldrey, B. (Ed.). (1995). *Wrestling with the angel: Faith and religion in the lives of gay men.* New York: Riverhead Books.

Bowman, S. L. (2003). A call to action in lesbian, gay, and bisexual theory building and research. *Counseling Psychologist, 31*(1), 63–69.

Boykin, K. (1996). *One more river to cross: Black and gay in America.* New York: Bantam Doubleday Dell.

Boykin, K. (2005). *Beyond the down low: Sex, lies, and denial in America.* New York: Carroll & Graf.

Brauner, R. (2000). Embracing difference: Addressing race, culture and sexuality. In C. Neal & D. Davies (Eds.), *Issues in therapy with lesbian, gay, bisexual and transgender clients* (pp. 7–21). Philadelphia: Open University Press.

Bridges, S., Selvidge, M. M. D., & Matthews, C. R. (2003). Lesbian women of color: Therapeutic issues and challenges. *Journal of Multicultural Counseling & Development, 31*(2), 113–130.

Butler, R. (2001). A break from the norm: Exploring the experiences of queer crips. In K. Backett-Milburn & L. McKie (Eds.), *Constructing gendered bodies* (pp. 224–242). New York: Palgrave.

Cahill, S., Battle, J., & Meyer, D. (2003). Partnering, parenting, and policy: Family issues affecting black lesbian, gay, bisexual, and transgender (LGBT) people. *Race & Society, 6*(1), 85–98.

Carbado, D. W. (2005). Privilege. In E. P. Johnson & M. G. Henderson (Eds.), *Black queer studies: A critical anthology* (pp. 190–212). Durham, NC: Duke University Press.

Cerbone, A. R. (1997). Symbol of privilege, object of derision: Dissonance and contradictions. In B. Greene (Ed.), *Ethnic and cultural diversity among lesbian and gay men* (pp. 117–131). Thousand Oaks, CA: Sage.

Chan, C. S. (1992). Cultural considerations in counseling Asian American lesbians and gay men. In S. H. Dworkin & F. J. Gutierrez (Eds.), *Counseling gay men and lesbians: Journey to the end of the rainbow* (pp. 115–124). Alexandria, VA: American Association for Counseling and Development.

Chan, C. S. (1995). Issues of sexual identity in an ethnic minority: The case of Chinese American lesbians, gay men and bisexual people. In A. R. D'Augelli & C. J. Patterson (Eds.), *Lesbian, gay and bisexual persons over the lifespan: Psychological perspectives* (pp. 87–101). New York: Oxford University Press.

Chernin, J. N., & Johnson, M. R. (2003). *Affirmative psychotherapy and counseling for lesbians and gay men.* Thousand Oaks, CA: Sage.

Collins, J. F. (2000). Biracial-bisexual individuals: Identity coming of age. *International Journal of Sexuality & Gender Studies, 5*(3), 221–253.

Collins, P. H. (1990). *Black feminist thought.* New York: Routledge.

Constantine, M. G. (2002). The intersection of race, ethnicity, gender, and social class in counseling: Examining selves in cultural contexts. *Journal of Multicultural Counseling & Development, 30*(4), 210–215.

Constantine, M. G., & Sue, D. W. (2006). Factors contributing to optimal human functioning in people of color in the United States. *Counseling Psychologist, 34*(2), 228–244.

Crawford, I., Allison, K. W., Zamboni, B. D., & Soto, T. (2002). The influence of dual-identity development on the psychosocial functioning of African-American gay and bisexual men. *Journal of Sex Research, 39*(3), 179–189.

Crocker, J., Luhtanen, R., Blaine, B., & Broadnax, S. (1994). Collective self-esteem and psychological well-being among white, black, and Asian college students. *Personality & Social Psychology Bulletin,* 20(5), 503–513.

Croom, G. L. (2000). Lesbian, gay, and bisexual people of color: A challenge to representative sampling in empirical research. In B. Greene & G. L. Croom (Eds.), *Lesbian, gay, bisexual and transgender psychology: A resource manual* (pp. 263–281). Thousand Oaks, CA: Sage.

Cross, W. E., Jr. (1971). The negro-to-black conversion experience. *Black World, 20*(9), 13–27.

Croteau, J. M., Talbot, D. M., Lance, T. S., & Evans, N. J. (2002). A qualitative study of the interplay between privilege and oppression. *Journal of Multicultural Counseling & Development, 30*(4), 239–258.

Davidson, M. G. (2000). Religion and spirituality. In R. M. Perez, K. DeBord, & K. J. Bieschke (Eds.), *Handbook of counseling and therapy with lesbians, gays, and bisexuals* (pp. 409–433). Washington, DC: American Psychological Association.

Diaz, R. M., Ayala, G., Bein, E., Henne, J., & Marin, B. V. (2001). The impact of homophobia, poverty, and racism on the mental health of gay and bisexual men: Findings from three U.S. cities. *American Journal of Public Health, 91*(6), 927–932.

Diaz, R. M., Bein, E., & Ayala, G. (2006). Homophobia, poverty, and racism: Triple oppression in mental health outcomes in Latino gay men. In A. M. Omoto & H. S. Kurtzman (Eds.), *Sexual orientation and mental health: Examining identity and development in lesbian, gay, and bisexual people* (pp. 207–224). Washington, DC: American Psychological Association.

DuBois, W. E. B. (1922). *Souls of black folks.* New York: First Vintage Books.

Espin, O. M. (1987). Issues of identity in the psychology of Latina lesbians. In Boston Lesbian Psychologies Collective (Eds.), *Lesbian psychologies: Explorations and challenges* (pp. 35–55). Urbana: University of Illinois Press.

Evans, R. (Producer/Director). (2004). *Brother to brother* [Motion picture]. United States: Wolfe Releasing.

Fassinger, R. E. (1998). Lesbian, gay, and bisexual identity and student development theory. In R. L. Sanlo (Ed.), *Working with lesbian, gay, bisexual, and transgender college students: A handbook for faculty and administrators* (pp. 13–22). Westport, CT: Greenwood Press.

Fassinger, R. E., & Arseneau, J. R. (2007). "I'd rather get wet than be under that umbrella": Differentiating the experiences and identities of lesbian, gay, bisexual, and transgender people. In K. J. Bieschke, R. M. Perez, & K. A. DeBord (Eds.), *Handbook of counseling and psychotherapy with lesbian, gay, bisexual, and transgender clients* (2nd ed., pp. 19–49). Washington, DC: American Psychological Association.

Feinberg, L. (1993). *Stone butch blues.* Ithaca, NY: Firebrand Books.

Firestein, B. A. (2007). Cultural and relational contexts of bisexual women: Implications for therapy. In K. J. Bieschke, R. M. Perez, & K. A. DeBord (Eds.), *Handbook of counseling and psychotherapy with lesbian, gay, bisexual, and transgender clients* (2nd ed., pp. 91–118). Washington, DC: American Psychological Association.

Frable, D. E. S. (1997). Gender, race, ethnic, sexual, and class identities. *Annual Review of Psychology, 48*, 139–162.

Fraley, S. S., Mona, L. R., & Theodore, P. S. (2007). The sexual lives of lesbian, gay, and bisexual people with disabilities: Psychological perspectives. *Sexual Research & Social Policy: Journal of NSRC, 4*(1), 15–26.

Fukuyama, M. A., & Ferguson, A. D. (2000). Lesbian, gay, and bisexual people of color: Understanding cultural complexity and managing multiple oppressions. In R. M. Perez, K. DeBord, & K. J. Bieschke (Eds.), *Handbook of counseling and therapy with lesbians, gays, and bisexuals* (pp. 81–106). Washington, DC: American Psychological Association.

Gainor, K. A. (2000). Including transgender issues in lesbian, gay and bisexual psychology. In G. Greene & G. L. Croom (Eds.), *Education, research and practice in lesbian, gay, bisexual and transgendered psychology: A resource manual* (pp. 131–160). Thousand Oaks, CA: Sage.

Garnets, L. D. (2002). Sexual orientations in perspective. *Cultural Diversity & Ethnic Minority Psychology, 8*(2), 115–129.

Garnets, L. D., & Kimmel, D. C. (1993). Cultural diversity among lesbians and gay men. In L. D. Garnets & D. C. Kimmel (Eds.), *Psychological perspectives on lesbian and gay male experiences* (pp. 331–337). New York: Columbia University Press.

Garofalo, R., Deleon, J., Osmer, E., Doll, M., & Harper, G. W. (2006). Overlooked, misunderstood and at-risk of ethnic minority male-to-female transgender youth. *Journal of Adolescent Health, 38*, 230–236.

Gates, H. L., Jr. (1993, May 17). Blacklash. *New Yorker, 69*(13), 42–44.

Greene, B. (1993). Stereotypes of African American sexuality: A commentary. In S. Rathus, J. Nevid, & L. Rathus-Fichner (Eds.), *Human sexuality in a world of diversity* (p. 257). Allyn & Bacon.

Greene, B. (1997). Ethnic minority lesbians and gay men: Mental health and treatment issues. In B. Greene (Ed.), *Ethnic and cultural diversity among lesbians and gay men* (pp. 216–239). Thousand Oaks, CA: Sage.

Greene, B. (2000). Beyond heterosexism and the cultural divide. In B. Greene & G. L. Croom (Eds.), *Lesbian, gay, bisexual and transgender psychology: A resource manual* (pp. 1–45). Thousand Oaks, CA: Sage.

Greene, B. (2003). Beyond heterosexism and across the cultural divide—Developing an inclusive lesbian, gay, and bisexual psychology: A look to the future. In L. Garnets & D. C. Kimmel (Eds.), *Psychological perspectives on lesbian, gay and bisexual experiences* (pp. 357–400). Washington, DC: American Psychological Association.

Greene, B. (2007). Delivering ethical psychological services to lesbian, gay, and bisexual clients. In K. J. Bieschke, R. M. Perez, & K. A. DeBord (Eds.), *Handbook of counseling and psychotherapy with lesbian, gay, bisexual, and transgender clients* (2nd ed., pp. 181–199). Washington, DC: American Psychological Association.

Greene, B., & Sanchez-Hucles, J. (1997). Diversity: Advancing an inclusive feminist psychology. In J. Worrell & N. G. Johnson (Eds.), *Shaping the future of feminist psychology: Education, research, and practice* (pp. 173–202). Washington, DC: American Psychological Association.

Guter, B., & Killacky, J. R. (2003). *Queer crips: Disabled gay men and their stories.* Binghamton, NY: Harrington Park Press.

Gutierrez, F. J. (1997). Culturally sensitive HIV treatment. In M. F. O'Connor (Ed.), *Treating the psychological consequences of HIV* (pp. 165–193). San Francisco: Jossey-Bass.

Halbertal, T. H., & Koren, I. (2006). Between "being" and "doing": Conflict and coherence in the identity formation of gay and lesbian orthodox Jews. In D. P. McAdams, R. Josselson, & A. Lieblich (Eds.), *Identity and story: Creating self in narrative* (pp. 37–61). Washington, DC: American Psychological Association.

Haldeman, D. C. (2007). The Village People: Identity and development in the gay male community. In K. J. Bieschke, R. M. Perez, & K. A. DeBord (Eds.), *Handbook of counseling and psychotherapy with lesbian, gay, bisexual, and transgender clients* (2nd ed., pp. 71–89). Washington, DC: American Psychological Association.

Hall, R. L., & Fine, M. (2005). The stories we tell: The lives and friendship of two older black lesbians. *Psychology of Women Quarterly, 29*(a), 177–187.

Hancock, K. (2000). Lesbian, gay, and bisexual lives: Basic issues in psychotherapy training and practice. In B. Greene & G. L. Croom (Eds.), *Lesbian, gay, bisexual and transgender psychology: A resource manual* (pp. 91–130). Thousand Oaks, CA: Sage.

Harley, D. A., Hall, M., & Savage, T. A. (2000). Working with gay and lesbian consumers with disabilities: Helping practitioners understand another frontier of diversity. *Journal of Applied Rehabilitation Counseling, 31*(1), 4–11.

Harley, D. A., Jolivette, K., McCormick, K., & Tice, K. (2002). Race, class, and gender: A constellation of positionalities with implications for counseling. *Journal of Multicultural Counseling & Development, 30*(4), 216–238.

Harris, E. L. (Ed.). (2005). *Freedom in the Village: Twenty-five years of black gay men's writing.* New York: Carroll & Graff.

Hays, P. A. (2008). *Addressing cultural complexities in practice: Assessment, diagnosis, and therapy* (2nd ed.). Washington, DC: American Psychological Association.

Hemphill, E. (Ed.). (2007). *Brother to brother: New writings by black gay men.* Washington, DC: RedBone Press.

Holmes, S. E., & Cahill, S. (2005). School experiences of gay, lesbian, bisexual, and transgender youth. In J. T. Sears (Ed.), *Gay, lesbian, and transgender issues in education. Program, policies, and practices* (pp. 63–76). New York: Harrington Park Press.

Hughes, T. L., Wilsnack, S. C., Szalacha, L. A., Johnson, T., Bostwick, W. B., Seymour, R. , et al. (2006). Age and racial/ethnic differences in drinking and drinking-related problems in a community sample of lesbians. *Journal of Studies on Alcohol, 67*(4), 579–590.

Human Rights Campaign. (2004). *Human Rights Campaign adopts policy supporting modernized workplace legislation.* Retrieved October 10, 2006, from http://www.hrc.org

Hunt, B., Matthews, C., Milsom, A., & Lammel, J. A. (2006). Lesbians with physical disabilities: A qualitative study of their experiences with counseling.

Journal of Counseling & Development, 84(2), 163–173.

Icard, L. (1986). Black gay men and conflicting social identities: Sexual orientation versus racial identity. *Journal of Social Work & Human Sexuality, 4*(1/2), 83–92.

Israel, G. E., & Tarver, E. E. (1997). *Transgender care: Recommended guidelines, practical information, and personal accounts.* Philadelphia: Temple University Press.

Israel, T. (2004). Conversations, not categories: The intersection of biracial and bisexual identities. *Women & Therapy, 27*(1/2), 173–184.

Israel, T., & Selvidge, M. M. D. (2003). Contributions of multicultural counseling to counselor competence with lesbian, gay, and bisexual clients. *Journal of Multicultural Counseling & Development, 31*(2), 84–98.

Kegan, R. (1982). *The evolving self: Problem and process in human development.* Cambridge, MA: Harvard University Press.

Korell, S. C., & Lorah, P. (2007). An overview of affirmative psychotherapy and counseling with transgender clients. In K. J. Bieschke, R. M. Perez, & K.A. DeBord (Eds.), *Handbook of counseling and psychotherapy with lesbian, gay, bisexual, and transgender clients* (2nd ed., pp. 271–288). Washington, DC: American Psychological Association.

Laird, J. (1999). Gender and sexuality in lesbian relationships: Feminist and constructionist perspectives. In J. Laird (Ed.) *Lesbians and lesbian families* (pp. 47–89). New York: Columbia University Press.

Lease, S. H., & Shulman, J. L. (2003). A preliminary investigation of the role of religion for family members of lesbian, gay male, or bisexual male and female individuals. *Counseling & Values, 47*(3), 195–209.

LeBlanc, J. M., & Tully, C. T. (2001). Deaf and hearing-impaired lesbians and gay males: Perceptions of social support. *Journal of Gay & Lesbian Social Services, 13*(3), 57–84.

Lee, Q. (Director). (2004). *Ethan Mao* [Motion picture]. United States: Margin Films.

Lee, W. M., Blando, J. A., Mizelle, N. D., & Orozco, G. L. (2007). *Introduction to multicultural counseling for helping professionals.* New York: Routledge.

Lester, T. (2002). *Gender nonconformity, race, and sexuality.* Madison: University of Wisconsin Press.

Lev, A. I. (2007). Transgender communities: Developing identity through connection. In K. J. Bieschke, R. M. Perez, & K. A. DeBord (Eds.), *Handbook of counseling and psychotherapy with lesbian, gay, bisexual, and transgender clients* (2nd ed., pp. 147–175). Washington, DC: American Psychological Association.

Liddle, B. J. (2007). Mutual bonds: Lesbian women's lives and communities. In K. J. Bieschke, R. M. Perez, & K. A. DeBord (Eds.), *Handbook of counseling and psychotherapy with lesbian, gay, bisexual, and transgender clients* (2nd ed., pp. 51–70). Washington, DC: American Psychological Association.

Lim-Hing, S. (1998). *The very inside: An anthology of writings by Asian and Pacific Islander lesbians.* Toronto: Sister Vision.

Liu, W. M. & Ali, S. R. (2005). Addressing social class and classism in vocational theory and practice: Extending the emancipator communitarian, approach. *The Counseling Psychologist, 33*(2), 189–196.

Loiacano, D. (1993). Gay identity issues among black Americans. In L. D. Garnets & D. C. Kimmel (Eds.), *Psychological perspectives on lesbian and gay male experiences* (pp. 364–375). New York: Columbia University Press.

Lombardi, E., & Davis, S. M. (2006). Transgender health issues. In D. F. Morrow & L. Messinger (Eds.), *Sexual orientation and gender expression in social work practice: Working with gay, lesbian, bisexual, and transgender people* (pp. 343–363). New York: Columbia University Press.

Lott, B. (2002). Cognitive and behavioral distancing from the poor. *American Psychologist, 57*(2), 100–110.

Luczak, R. (Ed.). (1993). *Eyes of desire: A deaf gay and lesbian reader.* Boston: Alyson.

Matteson, D. R. (1997). Bisexual and homosexual behavior and HIV risk among Chinese-, Filipino- and Korean-American men. *Journal of Sex Research, 34*(1), 93–104.

Mayo, C. (1982). Training for positive marginality. *Applied Social Psychology Annual, 3*, 57–73.

Mays, V. M., Cochran, S. D., & Roeder, M. R. (2003). Depressive distress and prevalence of common problems among homosexually active African American women in the United States. *Journal of Psychology & Human Sexuality, 15*(2/3), 27–46.

McLean, R. (2003). Deconstructing black gay shame: A multicultural perspective on the quest for a healthy ethnic and sexual identity. In G. Roysircar, D. S. Sandhu, & V. E. Bibbins (Eds.), *Multicultural competencies: A guidebook of practices* (pp. 109–118).

Alexandria, VA: Association for Multicultural Counseling and Development.

Miville, M., & Ferguson, A. D. (2004). Impossible "choices": Identity and values at a crossroads. *Counseling Psychologist, 32* (5), 760–770.

Moraga, C., & Moraga, C. (2000). *Loving in the war years* (2nd ed.). Cambridge, MA: South End Press.

Morrow, D. F. (2003). Cast into the wilderness: The impact of institutionalized religion on lesbians. *Journal of Lesbian Studies, 7*(4), 109–123.

Morrow, D. F., & Tyson, B. (2006). Religion and spirituality. In D. F. Morrow & L. Messinger (Eds.), *Sexual orientation and gender expression in social work practice* (pp. 384–404). New York: Columbia University Press.

Mpofu, E., & Harley, D. A. (2006). Racial and disability identity: Implications for the career counseling of African Americans with disabilities. *Rehabilitation Counseling Bulletin, 50*(1), 14–23.

Nadal, K. L. (2004). Pilipino American identity development model. *Journal of Multicultural Counseling & Development, 32*(1), 45–62.

Neely, L. (1999). Always coming. In J. Larkin (Ed.), *A woman like that: Lesbian and bisexual writers tell their coming out stories* (pp. 248–256). New York: HarperCollins.

Nemoto, T., Operario, D., Soma, T., Bao, D., Bajrabukka, A., & Crisostomo, V. (2003). HIV risk and prevention among Asian/Pacific islander men who have sex with men: Listen to our stories. *AIDS Education & Prevention, 15*(1), 7–20.

Olkin, R. (1999). *What psychotherapists should know about disability.* New York: Guilford Press.

Olkin, R. (2007). Persons of color with disabilities. In M. G. Constantine (Ed.), *Clinical practice with people of color: A guide to becoming culturally competent* (pp. 162–179). New York: Teachers College Press.

O'Toole, C. J. (2000). The view from below: Developing a knowledge base about an unknown population. *Sexuality & Disability, 18*(3), 207–224.

O'Toole, C. J., & Bregante, J. L. (1993). Disabled lesbians: Multicultural realities. In M. Nagler (Ed.), *Perspectives on disabilities* (2nd ed., pp. 261–271). Palo Alto CA: Health Markets Research.

O'Toole, C. J., & Brown, A. A. (2003). No reflection in the mirror: Challenges for disabled lesbians accessing mental health services. *Journal of Lesbian Studies, 7*(1), 35–49.

Paxton, K. C., Guentzel, H., & Trombacco, K. (2006). Lessons learned in developing a research partnership with the transgender community. *American Journal of Community Psychology, 37* (3–4), 349–356.

Phillips, J. C., Ingram, K. M., Smith, N. G., & Mindes, E. J. (2003). Methodological and content review of lesbian-, gay-, and bisexual-related articles in counseling journals: 1990–1999. *The Counseling Psychologist, 31*(1), 25–62.

Raffo, S. (1997). *Queerly classed. Gay men and lesbians write about class.* Cambridge, MA: South End Press.

Raj, R. (2002). Towards a transpositive therapeutic model: Developing clinical sensitivity and cultural competence in the effective support of transsexual and transgendered clients [electronic version]. *International Journal of Transgenderism, 6*(2). Retrieved April 7, 2005, from http://www. symposion.com/ijt/ijtvo06no02_04.htm

Ratti, R. (Ed.). (1993). *A lotus of another color: An unfolding of the South Asian gay and lesbian experience.* New York: Alyson.

Richards, P. S., & Bergin, A. F. (1997). *A spiritual strategy for counseling and psychotherapy.* Washington, DC: American Psychological Association.

Rodriguez, E. M., & Ouellette, S. C. (2000). Gay and lesbian Christians: Homosexual and religious integration in the members and participants of a gay-positive church. *Journal for the Scientific Study of Religion, 39*(3), 333–348.

Rosario, M., Yali, A. M., Hunter, J., & Gwadz, M. V. (2006). Religion and health among lesbian, gay, and bisexual youths: An empirical investigation and theoretical explanation. In A. M. Omoto & H. S. Kurtzman (Eds.), *Sexual orientation and mental health: Examining identity and development in lesbian, gay, and bisexual people* (pp. 117–140). Washington, DC: American Psychological Association.

Rosario, V. A. (2004). "Que joto bonita!": Transgender negotiations of sex and ethnicity. *Journal of Gay & Lesbian Psychotherapy, 8*(1/2), 89–97.

Rust, P. C. (1996). Managing multiple identities: Diversity among bisexual men and women. In B. Firestein (Ed.), *Bisexuality: The psychology and politics of an invisible minority* (pp. 53–83). Thousand Oaks, CA: Sage.

Rust, P. C. R. (2000). Alternatives to binary sexuality: Modeling bisexuality. In P. C. R. Rust (Ed.), *Bisexuality in the United States* (pp. 33–54). New York: Columbia University Press.

Saad, S. C. (1997). Disability and the lesbian, gay man, or bisexual individual. In M. L. Sipski &

C. J. Alexander (Eds.), *Sexual function in people with disability and chronic illness* (pp. 413–427). Gaithersburg, MD: Aspen.

Saleebey, D. (1994). Culture, theory, and narrative: The intersection of meanings in practice. *Social Work, 39*(4), 351–361.

Sedeno, A. (1999). *The relationship between acculturation attitudes, acculturative minority stress, and the use of academic support services among Latino undergraduates.* Unpublished master's thesis, Loyola University of Chicago.

Shakespeare, T. (1996). Power and prejudice: Issues of gender, sexuality and disability. In L. Barton (Ed.), *Disability and society: Emerging issues and insights.* New York: Longman.

Shakespeare, T. (1999). Coming out and coming home. *Journal of Gay, Lesbian, and Bisexual Identity, 4*(1), 39–51.

Shapiro, V. (1996). Subjugated knowledge and the working alliance: The narratives of Russian Jewish immigrants. *In Session: Psychotherapy in Practice, 1,* 9–22.

Shidlo, A., & Schroeder, M. (2002). Changing sexual orientation: A consumer's report. *Professional Psychology: Research & Practice, 33*(3), 249–259.

Shuck, K. D., & Liddle, B. J. (2001). Religious conflicts experienced by lesbian, gay, and bisexual individuals. *Journal of Gay & Lesbian Psychotherapy, 5*(2), 63–83.

Silvera, M. (1991). *Piece of my heart: A lesbian of colour anthology.* Toronto: Sister Vision.

Smart, J. F., & Smart, D. W. (2006). Models of disability: Implications for the counseling profession. *Journal of Counseling & Development, 84,* 29–40.

Smith, A. (1997). Cultural diversity and the coming-out process: Implications for clinical practice. In B. Greene (Ed.), *Ethnic and cultural diversity among lesbians and gay men* (pp. 279–300). Thousand Oaks, CA: Sage.

Smith, L. (2005). Psychotherapy, classism, and the poor. Conspicuous by their absence. *American Psychologist 60*(7), 687–696.

Sodowsky, G. R., Kwan, K. K., & Pannu, R. (1995). Ethnic identity of Asians in the United States. In J. G. Ponterotto, J. M. Casas, L. A., Suzuki, & C. M. Alexander (Eds.), *Handbook of multicultural counseling* (pp. 123–154). Thousand Oaks, CA: Sage.

Spade, D. (2006). Compliance is gendered: Struggling for gender self-determination in a hostile economy. In P. Currah, R. M. Juang, S. P. Minter (EDs.),

Transgender rights (pp. 217–241). Minneapolis: University of Minnesota Press.

Sue, D. W., Arredondo, P., & McDavis, R. J. (1992). Multicultural counseling competencies and standards: A call to the profession. *Journal of Counseling & Development, 70,* 477–486.

Sue, D. W., Bernier, J. G., Durran, M., Feinberg, L., Pedersen, P., Smith, E., et al. (1982). Position paper: Cross-cultural counseling competencies. *Counseling Psychologist, 10,* 45–52.

Sue, D. W., & Constantine, M. G. (2003). Optimal human functioning in people of color in the United States. In W. B. Walsh (Ed.), *Counseling psychology and optimal human functioning* (pp. 151–169). Mahwah, NJ: Erlbaum.

Sue, D. W., & Sue, D. (1999). *Counseling the culturally different: Theory and practice* (3rd ed.). New York: Wiley.

Sue, S., & Lam, A. G. (2002). Cultural and demographic diversity. In S. Stanley (Ed.), *Psychotherapy relationships that work: Therapist contributions and responsiveness to patients* (pp. 401–421). New York: Oxford University Press.

Tafoya, T. (1997). Native gay and lesbian issues: The two-spirited. In B. Greene (Ed.), *Ethnic and cultural diversity among lesbians and gay men* (pp. 1–10). Thousand Oaks, CA: Sage.

Taylor, Y. (2007). *Working class lesbian life: Classed outsiders.* Basing stoke, UK: Palgrave Macmillan.

Thompson, D. (1994). The sexual experiences of men with learning disabilities having sex with men—Issues for HIV prevention. *Sexuality & Disability, 12*(3), 221–242.

Vernon, A. (1999). The dialectics of multiple identities and the disabled people's movement. *Disability & Society, 14*(3), 385–398.

Walters, K. L. (1998). Negotiating conflicts in allegiances among lesbians and gays of color: Reconciling divided selves and communities. In G. P. Mallon (Ed.), *Foundations of social work practice with lesbian and gay persons* (pp. 47–75). New York: Haworth Press.

White, M. (1994). *Stranger at the gate: To be gay and Christian in America.* New York: Simon & Schuster.

Whitney, C. (2006). Intersections in identity—Identity development among queer women with disabilities. *Sexuality & Disability, 24*(1), 39–52.

Williams, C. B. (2005). Counseling African American women: Multiple identities—Multiple constraints. *Journal of Counseling & Development, 83*(3), 278–283.

Wu, A. (Director & Producer). (2005). *Saving face* [Motion picture]. United States: Sony Pictures Classics.

Wyche, K. F. (1996). Conceptualization of social class in African-American women: Congruence of client and therapist definitions. *Women & Therapy, 18*(3/4), 35–43.

Yakushko, O. (2005). Influence of social support, existential well-being, and stress over sexual orientation on self esteem of gay, lesbian, and bisexual individuals. *International Journal for the Advancement of Counselling, 27*(1), 131–143.

Zea, M. C., Reisen, C. A., & Diaz, R. M. (2003). Methodological issues in research on sexual behavior with Latino gay and bisexual men. *American Journal of Community Psychology, 31*(3/4), 281–291.

Zinnbauer, B. J., & Pargament, K. I. (2000). Working with the sacred: For approaches to religious and spiritual issues in counseling. *Journal of Counseling & Development, 78*(2) 162–171.

CHAPTER 6

Sexual and Gender Minority Youth

INTRODUCTION

Joelle Ruby Ryan is currently enrolled in graduate school and working on her second graduate degree. In her story below, you will learn of both the pain and the resiliency so often found in the narratives of sexual and gender minority youth.

I partially enabled my own survival by applying to private school. For four years I attended one of the most elite prep schools in the country, relying on a scholarship, student loans and work study to cover the cost of tuition. My dad's barbershop was located a stone's throw from the school's campus. I continued to wear my hair long but my androgynous dress from junior high was curtailed by the academy's dress code policy. I was expected to wear a sports coat, shirt and tie, or a turtleneck, to class each day, six days a week. I opted for a Warholesque black turtleneck (every day, including 100 degree ones) and either skipped the sports coat or carried one crumpled up in my bag in case they required me to produce it. Halfway through my freshman year the woman deemed my "Adviser" called a meeting about me with my therapist and my other instructors because I was not seen as "thriving" in my new academic community, despite the fact that my grades were top notch. Shortly thereafter my parents were called and my adviser expressed concern about my appearance, my inability to fit in, and my lack of friends. To me now the translation is simple: your son is too queer and needs to cut his hair, dress like everyone else and learn to toe the line. I remained steadfast in my resolve to buck the system right up until the end.

During my freshman year at a public university I not only continued to wear my hair long but began to experiment with jewelry, make up and feminine clothing. I was still living at home and so it was an ongoing struggle to hide my gender expression from my parents. I would stuff different blouses, makeup, and jewelry into my school bag and dodge into a gender-neutral bathroom to feminize myself. One time when I got home I had taken off my makeup but forgotten to take off my feminine blouse and all my many brightly-colored beaded necklaces. My parents looked at me disdainfully when I removed my overcoat. Rather than rush to take it off I sat down and looked down into my lunch plate: a soupy mass of Howard and Johnson's macaroni and cheese. "What, do you want to be a woman or something?" My father's angry red face glowered at me. Well, here was an opening if ever there was one. "Yes, I do." There. I said it. I eyed the mac-and-cheese the whole time, my fork tracing paths through the orange glob. I said it softly and meekly, but I said it. "I AM A TRANSSEXUAL." The fall-out was strongest in the months following my declaration of gender queerness, but it continues right up to the present day.

My parents were upset by my gender transgression for many reasons. One of their strongest concerns was: what would the neighbors think? Unlike many gays and lesbians, who can conceal their sexual orientation, transgendered and cross-dressing people get noticed, big time, when they step out of the front door. As a 6'6", feminine, cross-dressing, trans, genderqueer, there was literally no bushel basket big enough for me to hide in. My parents feared my reality and the harsh judgments I was going to encounter in my life, and they feared that my non-traditional identity would reflect badly on them. Did they cause this? If they had been "better" parents would I have been straight and gender-traditional? My mother in particular had anxiety that she had done something to cause my femininity, a false notion reinforced by my father. "You always babied him way too much. You were too easy on him. You made a girl out of him." It was not uncommon to hear these mother-blaming remarks both before and after I came out as trans. My father advised me that I was just setting myself up for a long life of misery and it would be easier to conform. This was similar to my mother's frequent refrain: "I can't help how the world is." (*Source*: From *Sargent Camp* [unpublished manuscript] by Joelle Ruby Ryan, 2006. Used with permission.)

Because Ryan's minority status was visible to others, she became a target of harassment and abuse. In some cases, gender minority youth are more secretive about their gender nonconformity, which no doubt saves them from harassment and abuse. But they may feel even more isolated and estranged from others, also a high price to pay.

A Preview of Chapter Contents

This chapter explores the lives of sexual and gender minority youth from a social constructionist perspective. Minority youth of today differ from previous cohorts, and these differences are due, in large measure, to changing social contexts. Today's youth are coming of age decades after Stonewall and the birth of gay liberation. As a result, they are often more aware of sexual and gender diversity and the broad range of sexual and gender expressions than was the case in previous generations. However, while these youth are more visible than ever before, they often live in social environments that are not welcoming, affirmative, or even tolerant. This chapter looks at their lives and answers the following questions:

- What are the issues that confront sexual and gender minority youth?
- What is the impact of minority stress on the lives of sexual and gender minorities?
- What are the current research findings regarding mental health issues, such as depression, suicide, and substance abuse, in samples of sexual and gender minority youth?
- What are some of the controversies surrounding the diagnosis and treatment of gender-nonconforming children and adolescents?
- What are the counseling interventions currently in use with sexual and gender minority youth?

SEXUAL AND GENDER MINORITIES TODAY: A NEW BREED?

Research shows that youth are beginning to question their sexual identities at earlier ages, acknowledging their same-sex sexual attractions to themselves and others at earlier ages than was true of previous cohorts (D'Augelli, 2006; D'Augelli & Grossman, 2001; Grov, Bimbi, Nanin, & Parsons, 2006; Peplau & Beals, 2004; Ryan, 2001; Savin-Williams, 2005). Increasing numbers of youth describe themselves as questioning and/or refusing to label themselves at all (Diamond, 2006; Russell, Seif, & Truong, 2001; Ryan & Futterman, 1998; Williams, Connolly, Pepler, & Craig, 2005).

Today's youth also seem to be more accepting of bisexuality than was true just 20 years ago (Herdt, 2001). Some (Murdock & Bolch, 2005) even suggest that the interest and experimentation with bisexuality, or "bi-curiosity," is a current fad among youth today. In general, more and more youth appear "gender ambiguous" due in part to unisex clothing styles and the increasing popularity of body modification practices, including tattoos and body piercings (Herdt, 2001).

Gender minorities are becoming more visible. Many have been depicted in television shows and in popular films, such as *The Crying Game* (Jordan, 1992), *Midnight in the Garden of Good and Evil* (Eastwood, 1997), and *Transamerica* (Tucker, 2005). While the research on gender minority youth is not as plentiful as it is for sexual minority youth, many (e.g., Burgess, 1999; Fish & Harvey, 2005; Hansbury, 2004; Pazos, 1999) believe there are increasing numbers of youth who are coming out as gender minorities. Some of these do not want surgery and do not seek services from gender reassignment programs (Eyler & Wright, 1997). Others, and increasing numbers of them, "find their lives unbearable without hormonal interventions" (Cohen-Kettenis & Pfafflin, 2003, p. 140).

Transgender activists and their allies are increasingly vocal in campaigning for significant changes in the medical and psychiatric care of infants who are born with intersex or sexual development disorders. Numerous medical professionals, bioethicists, and advocacy groups such as the Intersex Society of North America are working together to change the medical and psychiatric care of infants who are born with intersex or sexual development disorders. Many members of these organizations are particularly critical of past practices where children and families were deceived by physicians. Some have also experienced surgical complications, including impairments in sexual functioning and fertility rates (Lev, 2006).

Sadly, but perhaps not surprisingly, while the visibility of sexual and gender minorities has grown, signs of backlash and intensified hatred are also more evident. The impact of societal intolerance is particularly dramatic in the case of sexual and gender minority youth who, unlike adults, are dependent emotionally and financially on their parents and other adults. Trends toward earlier self-recognition are equated with increased vulnerability to harassment and violence (Friedman, Marshal, Stall, Cheong, & Wright, 2007). Sexual and gender minority youth are enrolled in schools, attend places of worship, and join social organizations (e.g., Boy Scouts) that are often less than welcoming and supportive. As was illustrated in Chapters 2 and 4, even practitioners with the best intentions are often intolerant and/or ill equipped to work with sexual and gender minority youth. According to Ryan (2001), "with few exceptions, counseling and clinical care professionals have not kept pace with the rapidly changing experiences of today's generation of LGB youths" (p. 224).

THE DEVELOPMENT OF SEXUAL ORIENTATION

The psychological and social processes inherent in the formation of a same-sex sexual orientation have captivated researchers for decades. The period from 1970 through 1990 witnessed a proliferation of stage models that depicted the developmental pathways to the establishment of a healthy gay or lesbian identity. Cass (1979, 1984), Coleman (1982), and Troiden (1979), among others, described these developmental processes similarly: all proposed a sequence of events beginning with awareness of same-sex attraction, followed by a period of sexual experimentation and confusion. Eventually, individuals emerge from this turmoil with an internal sense of themselves as gay or lesbian. Usually, this involves labeling oneself as gay or lesbian, followed by self-disclosure to others. The final developmental milestone in this process is the achievement of a sense of pride. Thus, over time, sexual orientation shifts from being the dominant aspect of one's identity to one component in a constellation of aspects that make up one's identity.

Research on bisexual identity development has been slower in coming, perhaps because of the tenacity of negative stereotypes and beliefs about bisexuality. Recent models by Brown (2002) and Bradford (2004) propose that bisexual persons experience a period of initial confusion and anxiety, followed by further exploration, an active search for support from others, and eventual self-acceptance, pride, and activism (Potoczniak, 2007).

Alternative Developmental Models

Although stage models like those proposed by Cass and Coleman have been widely cited in the literature, they have also been criticized on several grounds (Diamond, 2006; Savin-Williams, 2005). Many researchers believe that conventional stage theories are too simplistic to account for the complex nature of sexuality and sexual identity and that they do not adequately reflect the extent to which sexual attractions, behaviors, and identities fluctuate throughout adolescent and adult development. Psychologists Diamond and Savin-Williams are among the critics of same-sex identity stage theories. Each espouses a more social constructionist view of sexual orientation that takes into account the impact of social forces in the making of identities. Savin-Williams (2005) argued that "unless a sexual identity model explicitly rejects universalism and includes contextual, cultural, and historic considerations it is doomed as an obsolete relic of a time when development was perceived as predetermined and universal" (p. 81). Savin-Williams (2001, 2005) proposed an alternative construct to the developmental stage models to better capture the process of sexual orientation termed *differential developmental trajectories.*

Savin-Williams cited examples in which people's real-life experiences don't seem to "fit" the theoretical models that have been proposed. For example, Dube's (2000) research suggested that some men identify themselves as gay or bisexual without ever having had same-sex sexual experiences. Dube distinguished between gay and bisexual men who label themselves after having sexual experiences with other men (*sex-centered*) and those who identify themselves before having sexual contact with other men (*identity-centered*). Schindhelm and Hospers (2004) found confirmatory evidence of this in their sample of gay men.

Diamond (2006, 2008) has conducted longitudinal studies of young sexual minority women over the period of a decade. She found evidence of variation and fluidity in the self-reports of women about their sexuality and identities. In her 10-year follow-up in 2008, Diamond found that more women embraced a "bisexual" label or "no label" over time than claimed a "lesbian" label. As a result of her research findings, Diamond (2006, 2008) has provocatively argued against some of the stereotypes, many of which have been embedded in the research on sexual orientation:

- The nature of sexual attraction is dichotomous, exclusively oriented to either the same or the opposite sex.
- People question their sexual orientation only once during what could be tantamount to a life "crisis."
- Bisexuality is just a phase on the way to becoming exclusively same-sex oriented.
- Embracing a "label" is necessary in order to achieve a healthy outcome.

In conclusion, Diamond (2006) recommended overhauling our views on sexuality and identity and eliminating the use of categories to describe sexual identities. She recommended that researchers explore "how specific personal-context interactions shape diverse manifestations of same-sex sexuality over time" (p. 87).

Gender Nonconformity and the Development of Sexual Orientation

Gender variance and homosexuality are assumed to be the same thing. As a matter of fact, gender nonconformity is so often associated with pre-homosexuality in children that many anxious parents seek psychiatric treatment for their children. D'Augelli, Grossman, Salter et al. (2005) note that, "gender-atypical behavior provokes parents' concern that the youth might be lesbian or gay, and some parents react with efforts to diminish or suppress these behaviors to thwart homosexuality, especially for males" (p. 658). According to Haldeman (2000), parents are mistakenly convinced that the "additional masculinization of their boys or the increased feminization of their girls will ward off any latent or obvious tendencies toward same-sex erotic attraction" (p. 197).

In actuality, research supports the perception that sexual minority youth often adopt gender-nonconforming behaviors. Retrospective studies of adults report that large percentages of sexual minority adults had childhood histories of gender-atypical interests and behaviors. In Green's (1987) longitudinal research, as many as two-thirds of gender-nonconforming male children ultimately grow up to identify themselves as gay or bisexual in adulthood. Cross-sectional studies also report that sexual minority adult males recall more cross-gendered behaviors, such as dressing as girls, than do heterosexual males (Bailey & Zucker, 1995; Savin-Williams, 1998). One recent study—by Rieger, Linsenmeier, Gygax, and Bailey (2008)—addressed the issue of gender identification through the analysis of childhood home movies of both heterosexual and gay and lesbian participants. Raters who were unaware of the participants' sexual orientations judged gay and lesbian participants' behaviors in films as significantly more gender nonconforming than were those of nongay participants.

Gender nonconformity is a central concept in Bem's (1996) theory of the origin of same-sex sexual orientation. In his theory, Exotic Becomes Erotic (EBE), he posited that gender identity precedes and helps determine sexual orientation. Bem's assumption is not a novel idea. Developmental theorists have long been interested in the processes involved in gender identity. Many have hypothesized that gender identity emerges early in life and probably precedes the formation of sexual identity. Kohlberg (1966), for example, argued that an understanding of gender as a permanent aspect of one's identity is acquired somewhere between three and five years of age. Conceptions of gender are thought to remain fairly stable thereafter.

According to Bem's EBE theory, children's temperaments predispose them to preferences for certain kinds of play activities. Children whose preferences entail same-sex activities and same-sex friends were termed by Bem as *gender conforming* and those whose interests were in opposite-sex activities and opposite-sex friends were said to be *gender nonconforming*. Bem theorized that the experience of physiologically based arousal typically ensues when human beings encounter the unfamiliar. Feelings of arousal occur when gender-nonconforming girls are in the presence of girls, with whom they spend little time. The same is true when gender-nonconforming boys are in the presence of the "other"—in this case, other boys. This arousal becomes equated with erotic attraction toward the same sex. While there are many competing theories of the origin of same-sex sexual orientation, this particular approach emphasizes the extent to which gender nonconformity exists among sexual minority youth.

THE DEVELOPMENT OF GENDER MINORITY IDENTITIES

The following section focuses on research efforts to describe the developmental trajectories associated with the creation of gender minority identities.

Describing Developmental Pathways

Few empirically based studies have explored the developmental trajectories of gender minorities. Most of our information about the early childhood and adolescent experiences of gender minorities has been gleaned from qualitative studies, interviews, case studies, and autobiographical accounts of gender minority adults.

The work of Gagne and his colleagues represents one of the few empirical explorations of the perceptions of gender minority adults and their childhoods. Gagne, Tewksbury, and McGaughey (1997) and Gagne and Tewksbury (1998) undertook extensive interviews with gender minority persons to obtain retrospective accounts of their childhoods. The researchers interviewed 65 participants, all biological males. Interviewees noted that they learned early in childhood that cross-dressing and feminine behavior were considered "deviant." As children, they experienced anxiety and shame when they observed the reactions of others, including family members, neighbors, and peers, when they played with other girls, engaged in cross-dressing, and wore make-up. "Boys were scolded, shamed, beaten, and sent to psychiatrists for wanting to do feminine things" (Gagne & Tewksbury, 1998, p. 87). One interviewee noted: "I would paint my toenails on occasion. My father caught me one time and beat the hell out of me for it" (1998, p. 87). The majority of their participants recalled trying hard to repress feminine interests and engaging in hypermasculine activities. Beginning in late childhood and early adolescence, most participants reported cross-dressing in secret. Youth who were caught cross-dressing were humiliated; some continued in secret, and some suppressed this behavior completely until adulthood when the behavior resurfaced. For most, it was contact with other gender minority adults through either the Internet or support groups that facilitated their coming out as transgendered.

Other reports from therapists who have worked extensively with gender minority clients are fairly consistent with the descriptions given by Gagne and Tewksbury's interviewees. Several authors (Anderson, 1998; Brown & Rounsley, 1996; Israel & Tarver, 1997; Pazos, 1999) indicated that their clients were conscious of their gender atypicality at very early ages. This awareness was experienced by gender minority clients in different ways. Some felt a strong sense that they would eventually become their desired sex by puberty, some felt as though they *were* the opposite sex despite outward physical appearances, and some simply believed they should have been born the opposite sex (Brown & Rounsley, 1996).

In response to this early recognition of gender atypicality, many gender minority youth engaged in compensatory activities. In cases involving biological females, many engaged in magical thinking, tried to adopt penises by using socks or toys, urinated standing up, and refused to wear bathing suit tops or shirts during the summer (Pazos, 1999). Many recalled wanting short hair, wanting to play only with boys, and taking on male roles in imaginary play activities. Depending on parental attitudes to nonconforming behaviors, these children were forced to join organizations that reinforced their female status, such as Girl Scouts.

By most accounts, gender minority adults spent their childhood feeling isolated and estranged from their peers (Anderson, 1998; Brown & Rounsley, 1996; Grossman, D' Augelli, & Salter, 2006). Many described being harassed verbally and physically by peers and developing solitary interests to protect themselves against social ostracism. Many also tried to suppress their feelings and adopted a desire to please others and to conform to others' expectations of what they should be (Brown & Rounsley, 1996).

The onset of puberty constituted a crisis for many gender minority youth (Brown & Rounsley, 1996; Burgess, 1999; Fish & Harvey, 2005; Israel & Tarver, 1997). The emergence of secondary sex characteristics at puberty was associated with feelings of betrayal and disgust and negative body images. Many (e.g., Brown & Rounsley, 1996) described this as the sense that their bodies had betrayed them. Many biological females attempted to alter their appearances by binding their breasts, and biological males often used surgical tape to tape the penis down or hid their testicles by pushing them back into the inguinal canal (Brown & Rounsley, 1996). Other males attempted autocastration and injected silicone in their lips, chest, buttocks, and/or thighs (Burgess, 1999). "Gender variant people go through this crucial developmental period struggling with the dissonance between what the culture tells them they are and whom they feel themselves to be internally" (Fish & Harvey, 2005, p. 85). School-based rites of passage, such as dating, the prom, and athletics, furtherly acerbated the alienation that these gender minority youth experienced.

Research on the developmental trajectories of gender minorities is only just beginning. Most gender minorities employ the term *coming out* to describe the developmental process of acknowledging one's gender minority status. Based on his extensive personal experiences and interviews with female-to-male transgenders, Devor (2004), a sociologist, developed a model consisting of 14 stages to depict the developmental process for persons who adopt a transsexual identity and who elect to transition to the opposite sex. This model was adapted from Cass's (1979, 1984) stages of homosexual identity formation. As in Cass's model, gender minorities progress from anxiety about their gender identities to discovery of their transsexualism. This discovery is followed by a period of anger, confusion, tolerance, and acceptance of transsexual identity. Once the sex reassignment surgery is over and the transition is complete, the final stage of identity formation is pride.

MENTAL HEALTH ISSUES IN SEXUAL AND GENDER MINORITY YOUTH

Research initiated nearly thirty years ago suggests that sexual minority youth are more likely than their nonminority peers to experience difficulties with depression and suicide, lower self-esteem, difficulties in academic functioning, and substance abuse (Russell, 2006; Williams et al., 2005). Unfortunately, this focus on negative symptoms or "pathology" led researchers to ignore other research topics, such as those related to resilience and resourcefulness in this population. Some researchers (e.g., Cole, Denny, Eyler, & Samons, 2000) are now more interested in exploring how external pressures associated with homophobia, biphobia, and transphobia symptoms may lead to depression, substance abuse, dropping out of school, homelessness, and increased risk for HIV and sexually transmitted diseases. The next section reviews current research findings regarding mental health issues in sexual and gender minority youth.

Research Challenges

The first empirical study of sexual minority youth was published by Roesler and Deisher in 1972 in the *Journal of the American Medical Association* (noted by Savin-Williams, 2005). The 1980s were a time of intense research productivity, particularly in the areas of same-sex sexual identity development, suicide, and HIV. The bulk of the research incorporated convenience samples of sexual minority youth who sought mental health services or who attended social, recreational, or educational programs specifically for sexual minorities (Savin-Williams, 2005).

Most studies employed retrospective or cross-sectional designs and lacked uniform and well-defined questions. Sexual orientation was assessed using single items such as the following: "Are you gay, lesbian, bisexual, heterosexual?" "Have you had sex with males, females, or both?" (D'Augelli, Grossman, Salter et al., 2005). Because of the negative stigma associated with homosexuality, researchers were hard-pressed to capture youth who covertly thought of themselves as gay or lesbian but were not open with others about their identities (Anhalt & Morris, 2003). Ethnic minorities were typically underrepresented in these samples (Diamond, 2006). Bisexual youth were usually omitted from consideration or grouped together with gay- and lesbian-identified participants and mislabeled as such (Russell & Seif, 2002). The research on gender minority children and adolescents was largely based on the autobiographical accounts of gender minority adults and the case reports of practitioners who worked in clinical settings with gender minority youth, many of whom were diagnosed with gender identity disorder (GID). Many researchers also relied on the retrospective recall of adults, many of whom were affiliated with gay or transgender organizations.

Recent advances in research design and methodology have permitted investigators to develop more-sophisticated research agendas. Some of these include the use of multiple recruitment strategies like the Internet to reach stigmatized populations (Cochran & Mays, 2006; Savin-Williams, 2005). Others use alternative measures of sexual orientation, including questions to assess same-sex sexual behaviors and attractions (Savin-Williams, 2005). Still others use existing data sets on comprehensive national health issues (Cochran & Mays, 2006).

Suicide

SEXUAL MINORITY YOUTH   Suicide among sexual minorities has been a hotly debated and well-researched issue. In 1989, the U.S. Department of Health and Human Services (DHHS) released a report in response to what was perceived to be an epidemic of suicides in children and adolescents. The report indicated that gay and lesbian youth were two to three times more likely than their peers to attempt and succeed in committing suicide (Gibson, 1989). In a later response to the report, the Secretary of the DHHS, Dr. Louis W. Sullivan, repudiated this section of the report, stating "I am strongly committed to advancing traditional family values. . . . In my opinion, the views expressed in the paper run contrary to that aim" (Sullivan, 1989).

Despite the controversy over this report, a limited number of states (e.g., Massachusetts, Vermont, and Washington) began including sexual minority youth as part of the Youth-Risk Behavior Surveillance Surveys administered in public and private secondary schools. Thus far, results of these surveys have been remarkably consistent with the information reported by Gibson in 1989 (Morrison & L'Heureux, 2001).

In 2005, D'Augelli, Grossman, Salter et al. attempted to address methodological problems associated with prior research by distinguishing among three groups. First, they looked at sexual minority youth who had never attempted suicide, then those who reported suicide attempts related to their sexual orientation, and finally those whose suicide attempts were unrelated to sexual orientation.

D'Augelli and his colleagues also addressed the effect of several risk factors associated with suicide, including age of self-recognition and self-disclosure, victimization experiences, and childhood history of gender nonconformity. Significant determining factors among those who attempted suicide were greater psychological abuse from parents and more childhood gender-atypical behavior, especially for males. Similar results were reported by Friedman et al. (2007). Using data from the Urban Men's Study, Friedman et al. reported that early gay-related harassment was related to depression, attempted suicide, and HIV seropositivity in adulthood.

GENDER MINORITY YOUTH   Estimates of attempted suicides by gender minorities range from a low of 17% (Brown & Rounsley, 1996) to a high of 50% (Israel & Tarver, 1997). DiCeglie, Freedman, McPherson, and Richardson (2002) conducted an audit of 124 cases seen in their gender clinic since 1989. The mean age at referral was 11 years. DiCeglie et al. reported that incidents of harassment and persecution were significantly more common in boys than in girls. Older children were more likely to report dislike of bodily sex characteristics than were younger children. DiCeglie et al. observed that their patients experienced "considerable difficulties with their relationships with adults and peers which may lead to significant isolation." Girls in their sample reported more depression than boys and high rates of depression. DiCeglie et al. concluded that "gender identity disorder represents a high suicide risk."

Results from a convenience sample of 54 gender minorities between 15 and 24 years of age were consistent with those observed in DiCeglie's et al. clinical sample. Grossman and D'Augelli (2007) reported that 50% of their sample had serious thoughts about suicide and 25% had made at least one attempt. Verbal and physical abuse by parents and lower body esteem were significantly correlated with suicide attempts by these youth.

Swann and Herbert (1999) noted that transgender youth are at risk for self-harm, as many were apt to self-mutilate in order to bring about their own cross-gender body modification. Many engaged in self-destructive activities, such as cutting their breasts.

Harassment and Victimization

SEXUAL MINORITY YOUTH   Sexual minority youth reported higher rates of harassment, bullying, and victimization in schools than did their heterosexual counterparts (Bontempo & D'Augelli, 2002). Garofalo, Wolf, Kessel, Palfrey, and DuRant (1998) reported that one-third of their sample indicated they had been threatened with a weapon at school, in contrast to 7% of their heterosexual counterparts. The Gay, Lesbian, and Straight Education Network (GLSEN), a national advocacy organization, indicated that among its national sample of sexual and gender minority youth, 42% had been physically harassed in school (GLSEN, 2001). Both national and regional studies (Murdock & Bolch, 2005; Peters, 2003) found that sexual minority youth were subjected to verbal harassment on a daily basis in school.

GENDER MINORITY YOUTH   Chapter 2 addressed the disproportionate violence and abuse that gender minority persons experienced for their failure to conform to gender norms. In the case of gender minority children and adolescents, the abuse was experienced at home, in school, and on the playground. In schools, children who are gender nonconforming are regarded as disruptive and are often punished or expelled (Israel & Tarver, 1997). In Devor's (1994) interviews with 45 female-to-male transgender adult participants, 60% indicated that they had been psychologically, physically, or sexually abused in their childhood. Gagne and Tewksbury (1999) described the childhood experiences of their gender minority interviewees: as feminine males, they were "stigmatized, ostracized, beaten, cajoled, corrected, scolded, punished and otherwise socially pressured to be masculine males" (p. 78).

Grossman et al. (2006) conducted interviews with 31 male-to-female transgender youth ranging in age from 15 to 21 years regarding gender expression milestones in development and experiences of verbal, physical, and sexual victimization. All participants reported feeling "different," being told they were "different" during their middle childhood years, and being called derogatory names like "sissies." Most considered themselves to be transgendered or transsexual and disclosed this to someone else in their late adolescent years. All reported being the recipients of verbal abuse. Gehring and Knudson (2005) explored the incidence of abuse among 42 adult participants who were referred by their family physicians to outpatient clinics for the treatment of GID. Of these participants, 77% reported verbal abuse, 81% were insulted, 55% were embarrassed in front of others,

58% were made to feel guilty, and 55% reported being embarrassed by one of their parents before the age of 15.

The brutality of the violence against gender minority youth is illustrated in the following two incidents. In the first, Fred C. Martinez, Jr., a Native American student of Navajo ancestry at Montezuma-Cortez High School in Colorado, was attacked and beaten to death in June 2001. His assailant was a teenage male who bragged about the attack, saying he beat a "fag" (Moser, 2005). The second incident occurred in October 2002 and was the subject of a recent television movie titled *A Girl Like Me* (Holland, 2006). Gwen Araujo, a 17-year-old biological male, expressed a desire to be female at an early age and started to live as a woman while in school. Gwen stopped attending Neward Memorial High School in California in response to the harassment she received. Later she was attacked while attending a party. Her skull was bashed in with a pan and a barbell; she was strangled with a rope and buried in a shallow grave in a remote wooded area. None of her attackers was charged with a hate crime.

Lack of Familial Support

SEXUAL MINORITY YOUTH   D'Augelli (2006) explored developmental processes in a sample of over 500 sexual minority youth who attended community-based gay-friendly social organizations. The data for this study were collected over a 10-year period. Twenty-four percent of the sample described their mothers as "intolerant" or "rejecting" of their sexual orientation, in contrast to 37% of their fathers. Their mothers were described as more positive and more knowledgeable than their fathers. Thirty percent of the participants feared verbal harassment at home, while 13% feared physical attack from family members. Studies that have compared the rates of verbal and physical abuse in the families of disclosing and nondisclosing youths reported that victimization acts as a strong deterrent to coming out to family members (D'Augelli, Hershberger, & Pilkington, 1998). It is estimated that 50% of homeless youth are struggling with sexual orientation issues (Little, 2001).

GENDER MINORITY YOUTH   Rejection by families and schools prompts many gender minority teens to drop out of school and leave home, ending up on the streets (Oggins & Eichenbaum, 2002). Many homeless gender minority youth seek out sex work because it is a source of self-worth and validation and because it is an important means of financing expensive cosmetic and sex reassignment surgery (Oggins & Eichenbaum, 2002).

Substance Abuse

SEXUAL MINORITY YOUTH   Early studies reported that self-identified sexual minority youth were at higher risk for substance use and abuse than were their heterosexual counterparts (Remafedi, 1987). A recent meta-analysis of several studies continues to demonstrate that sexual minority youth are more vulnerable to substance use disorders (Marshal et al., 2008). The reasons for this are numerous. Drugs and alcohol may be used as a means of rationalizing same-sex sexual activities; fitting into the gay and lesbian subculture, which in many places is organized around bars (Jordan, 2000); and coping with the minority stress.

Recent studies have used population-based surveys to explore substance abuse. Youth-Risk Behavior Surveillance Surveys were administered in Massachusetts and Vermont to a sample of 9,188 students in 9th through 12th grade. The students were asked to select a label to describe their sexual orientation and then were asked a series of questions about health risk behaviors such as substance use, sexual risk, and at-school victimization. Sexual minority youth reported significantly higher rates of cigarette, alcohol, and marijuana use than did nonminority youth (Garofalo et al., 1998).

The National Longitudinal Study of Adolescent Health (ADD Health) was the first nationally representative study of adolescents in the United States to incorporate questions related to sexual orientation. The study was initiated in 1995 and covered a period of two "waves," which incorporated over 90,000 youths in grades 7 through 12. Data were collected during the second wave through the use of the audio computer-aided self-interview (Audio-CASI), during which adolescents listened to audiotaped questions and used a laptop computer to respond. Adolescents were questioned about their romantic attractions but not their sexual behaviors in this study. Adolescents who reported same-sex romantic attractions were more likely to abuse alcohol (Russell & Joyner, 2001).

A cross-sectional study using a national data set of early and middle adolescent youths ages 9 to 14 reported that girls who described themselves as "mostly heterosexual" or "lesbian/bisexual" were at elevated risk for alcohol-related behaviors, compared to heterosexual girls (Ziyadeh et al., 2007).

There is some recent evidence to suggest that youth who report relationships with both sexes may have more difficulties with substance abuse than do those whose orientation is more exclusively same-sex (Marshal et al., 2008; Russell, 2006). One study found that teens who reported bisexual attractions were at greater risk for alcohol abuse than were those who reported heterosexual attractions (Russell, Driscoll, & Truong, 2000). And bisexual girls seem at particular risk for substance abuse (Russell, 2006).

GENDER MINORITY YOUTH   In a recent study (Garofalo, Deleon, Osmer, Doll, & Harper, 2006) of 51 self-identified ethnic minority male-to-female transgender youth aged 16 to 25 years, high rates of risky sexual behavior were reported. All participants indicated they had sex with men, 47% self-identified as gay, 26% referred to themselves as heterosexual, 16% identified as bisexual and 11% unlabeled. High rates of substance use were reported and alcohol and drugs were used as a coping strategy to deal with numerous psychosocial stressors, including limited familial support, unstable housing, economic hardships, and little access to competent health care. The use of hormones purchased on the streets or through the Internet with no input from doctors or other adults was high. Of 61% of youth reporting the use of feminizing hormones, only 29% received hormones from their medical providers. Twenty-nine percent of gender minority youth reported lifetime use of injection silicone. These findings are consistent with other anecdotal and survey data of gender minority youth (Dean et al., 2002).

The risks associated with the use of illegal hormones include the possibility that these hormones are not pharmaceutically pure or taken in the correct dosage (Jennings, 2003). Bodily changes caused by the hormones are irreversible even after the hormones are withdrawn (Cole et al., 2000). For example, facial hair continues to grow even without continued testosterone injections, and electrolysis would be necessary to stop this. However, youth who undergo hormonal transitions and take testosterone injections are not at the same risk level as adults for elevated cholesterol and coronary artery disease (Cole et al., 2000). Journalist Cris Beam, in her book *Transparent* (2007), chronicled the experiences of several teenage gender minorities, many of whom live temporarily on the streets in Los Angeles. Beam described the practice among these youth who are desperate to transition.

Without family or financial support, they turn to black market hormones and the practice of "pumping" or shooting loose silicone directly into the body to make parts of the body look fuller and more feminine (Beam, 2007).

MINORITY STRESS AND SEXUAL AND GENDER MINORITY YOUTH

Chapter 3 introduced Meyer's (1995) concept of *minority stress*, a term employed to describe the emotional distress associated with verbal and physical harassment and discrimination. Most researchers now view symptoms such as depression, anxiety, and suicidal impulses as artifacts of the cumulative stress associated with being marginalized and oppressed (Williams et al., 2005).

Williams et al. (2005) explored the impact of minority stress, victimization, and social support on the mental health of high school students in a Canadian city. They reported that depression and other symptoms resulted largely from victimization experiences and lack of social support rather than from sexual orientation alone. Rutter and Soucar (2002) and Hershberger and D'Augelli (1995) also reported similar results. In contrast, Rosario, Schrimshaw, Hunter, and Gwadz (2002) employed a longitudinal design to explore gay-related stress, depression, anxiety, and conduct problems and found there to be no association between gay-related stress and emotional distress.

Gender nonconformity is a significant and common factor in the violence that sexual and gender minority youth experience (Horn, 2007). Previous chapters explored the concept of *gender policing* and described this as the social processes that exist to punish those in society who do not conform to standard notions of gender expression. The penalties for boys who exhibit interest in traditionally feminine activities or who display feminine traits ("sissyboys") are particularly harsh. Girls who exhibit interest in traditionally masculine play preferences and activities ("tomboys") are more tolerated than are "sissyboys." However, when tomboyism in girls extends past puberty, these attributes become less acceptable.

Wood (2004) and others argued that the trauma associated with "gender oppression" has even more profound effects than the trauma associated with homophobia. Fitzpatrick, Euton, Jones, and Schmidt (2005) found that cross-gender role behaviors predicted suicidal symptoms more than did sexual orientation. Research (Feder, Levant, & Dean, 2007; Rottnek, 1999; Savin-Williams, 1995; Waldo, Hesson-McInnis, & D'Augelli, 1998) has shown, for example, that sexual minority youth who are gender atypical are subject to greater levels of harassment and violence than are sexual minority youth who are gender conforming. Childhood gender atypicality, especially among gay and bisexual males, has been found to be significantly related to suicidality (D'Augelli, Grossman, Salter et al., 2005; Friedman, Koeske, Silvestre, Korr, & Sites, 2006), or at the least to loneliness and fewer friends (Young & Sweeting, 2004).

In a recent study, D'Augelli, Grossman, and Starks (2005) incorporated a sample of 293 sexual minority youth, the first wave of a longitudinal study of youth aged 15 to 19 years. One-third of their sample had parents who did not know that they were sexual minorities. Youth whose parents knew about their sexual orientation at the time of the study described themselves as more gender atypical during childhood. These youth experienced significantly more antigay comments by parents than did youth who were gender conforming. D'Augelli et al. hypothesized that parents who suspected their children of being gay made more antigay comments, which, in turn, may have led to finding out that their children were gay.

Some psychologists hypothesize that adolescence and young adulthood are developmental periods in which social norms about gender and sexual identity become salient and that these play a significant role in peer acceptance (Horn, 2007). Adolescents who exhibit gender-atypical behaviors, gestures, and appearances are sanctioned or policed by means of harassment and other forms of victimization (Horn, 2007).

COUNSELING SEXUAL AND GENDER MINORITY YOUTH

Sexual and gender minority youth seldom seek therapy of their own accord. Most are referred for therapy by their parents, teachers, school practitioners, and other adults because of issues unrelated to their sexual orientation and gender expressions. Youth often present themselves for counseling with symptoms such as depression, anxiety, substance abuse, academic failure, and family conflicts (Holman & Goldberg, 2006). For that reason, it is recommended that practitioners routinely screen for their sexual orientation/gender identity concerns (Holman & Goldberg, 2006). Holman and Goldberg recommended the use of a simple statement and a probe: "Many people struggle with gender [sexual orientation]. Is this an issue for you?"

The exploration of sexual feelings and behaviors is considered a developmentally appropriate task of adolescents. Sexual and gender minority youth are particularly interested in exploring their sexual and/or gender feelings and expressions. For this reason, it is imperative that practitioners who work with youth understand the fluidity and diversity of sexual and gender expressions and identifications that characterize this population. Many practitioners are already familiar with Klein's Sexual Orientation Grid (Klein, Sepekoff, & Wolf, 1985; Klein, 1990), which conceptualizes sexual orientation in terms of arousal, fantasy, sexual behaviors, and social and emotional preferences over time. The grid requires persons to rate themselves on each dimension, using a seven-point heterosexual-bisexual-homosexual scale for each dimension.

Another tool that helps youth and family members think beyond a dichotomous view of gender is Eyler and Wright's (1997) nine-point gender continuum. This psychoeducational tool helps increase awareness and appreciation of the complexities of gender identities and expressions. With the support of helping professionals, youth evaluate each point to determine those that seem most relevant:

1. *Female*—I have always considered myself to be a woman (or girl).
2. *Female-maleness*—I currently consider myself to be a woman, but at times I have thought of myself as really more of a man (or boy).
3. *Genderblended-female predominant*—I consider myself gender-blended because I consider myself female predominantly (in some significant way to be both a woman and a man, but somehow more of a women).
4. *Othergendered*—I am neither a woman nor a man, but a member of some other gender.
5. *Ungendered*—I am not a woman, a man, or a member of any other gender.
6. *Bigendered*—I consider myself bigendered because sometimes I feel (or act) more like a woman and other times more like a man, or sometimes like both a woman and a man.
7. *Genderblended-male predominantly*—I consider myself gender-blended because I consider myself male predominantly (in some significant way to be both a man and a woman, but somehow more of a man).

8. *Male-femaleness*—I currently consider myself to be a man, but at times I have thought of myself as really more of a woman (or girl).

9. *Male*—I have always considered myself to be a man (or boy) (Eyler & Wright, 1997).

This tool is meant to serve as a catalyst for further dialogue and as a way of normalizing the concept of gender diversity.

Support a Questioning Stance

Adolescence is perceived as a period in which young people begin to question authority as well as other aspects of their self-definitions, including spiritual beliefs, values, and goals. It is no surprise then that increasing numbers of youth are identifying more closely with the term *questioning* with regard to sexual identity (Diamond, 2006; Russell et al., 2001; Williams et al., 2005).

Some adolescents need reassurance that it is okay to "question" and healthy to refuse labels. Practitioners can be helpful by clearly conveying the message that it is natural to be confused about one's sexual orientation and it is okay for youth to abstain from sexual relationships (Hunter & Mallon, 2000). It might be necessary to point out that sexual orientation is not determined by having "slept with one or even a few members of the same or other sex" (Owens, 1998, p. 179). Many sexual minority youth know what their sexual orientation is prior to actual same-sex sexual contact, and many are engaged in heterosexual sexual contact while labeling themselves as sexual minorities.

Hunter and Mallon's (2000) advice is also pertinent to gender minority youth who are exploring and experimenting with gender expression. Gender minority youth are often thrown into crisis, however, at the emergence of secondary sex characteristics in puberty and are apt to respond with a great deal of urgency about pursuing gender reassignment. Practitioners have to be prepared to explore options and aid these youth in managing feelings of anxiety.

Some sexual and gender minority youth may be less comfortable with labels than were previous generations and are less apt to categorize their gender identities and sexual orientations in binary or dichotomous terms (Herdt, 2001; Savin-Williams, 2005). Therefore, therapists should be tentative in the use of such labels as "gay," "lesbian," "bisexual," and "transgendered" (Hart & Heimberg, 2001).

Provide Affirmation/Validation

The experiences of sexual and gender minority youth are similar in many respects. The most striking of these commonalities is the sense of isolation and shame that is experienced. Feelings of shame add to a deeper sense of isolation, which contributes to co-morbid symptoms such as anxiety, depression, suicidal ideation, and behavioral problems (Rosenberg, 2002). Any and all therapeutic interventions with these youth must, therefore, include at a minimum the communication of affirmation and validation (Lemoire & Chen, 2005; Rosenberg, 2002; Swann & Herbert, 1999). Frequently, practitioners constitute one of the few sources, and perhaps the only source, of support available to these youth (Fish & Harvey, 2005; Owens, 1998).

As in the research outlined above, great numbers of sexual minority children and gender minority children engage in gender-defiant behaviors. Lev (2004) advocated that treatment "should, first and foremost, normalize children's gender expression" (p. 335).

What this means is that practitioners must affirm the range of gender variation expressed by the client (Raj, 2002).

The alliance between gender minority persons and psychiatry has been an uneasy one, primarily because mental health professionals operated as gatekeepers. In effect, they had power over which persons were eligible for sex reassignment under the Standards of Care (Meyer et al., 2001). This dynamic has been problematic and has sometimes inhibited gender minorities from being totally honest with their therapists. Because gender minority persons were viewed as pathological, practitioners need to be especially sensitive to the difficulties inherent in establishing trusting therapeutic relationships with gender minority clients. Raj (2002) advocated that practitioners avoid using psychiatric language that is stigmatizing, such as gender identity disorder (vs. gender discomfort), hermaphrodite (vs. intersex), and transvestite (vs. cross-dresser). Practitioners should also refer to gender minority clients by their preferred names and pronouns in cases when birth-assigned names and pronouns are not reflective of clients' gender identities (Gainor, 2000; Israel & Tarver, 1997).

Assess for Suicide Risk

In addition to the individual risk factors for suicide in the general population (availability of a lethal method, family history of suicide), research has identified risk factors specifically for sexual and gender minority youth. Practitioners will need to be especially watchful when youth exhibit one or more of the following:

- Keeps one's sexual orientation a secret from everyone (Morrison & L'Heureux, 2001)
- Exhibits gender-nonconforming behaviors during childhood (D'Augelli, Grossman, Salter et al., 2005)
- Presents strong inner conflict about one's sexual orientation (D'Augelli, Hershberger, & Pilkington, 2001)
- Becomes self-aware of one's sexual orientation at an early age (Remafedi, Farrow, & Deisher, 1991)

Morrison and L'Heureux (2001) also recommended conducting a risk assessment based on systemic variables:

- Does the school that the sexual or gender minority youth attends have a nondiscrimination policy?
- Does this policy include sexual and gender minorities?
- Does it provide diversity training to staff and students?
- Are sexual and gender minorities represented in the school's curriculum?
- What are the values and practices of other institutions (this includes places of worship, helping resources, and social organizations) that the youth and his or her family are affiliated with?

Assess for Trauma-Related Symptoms and Concurrent Disorders

When working with sexual and gender minority youth, practitioners should be mindful of the elevated possibility that their clients have experienced significant trauma related to their sexual and/or gender identities. Traumatic events are defined as those that are unanticipated, exceed an individual's coping strategies, and disrupt one's internal frame of reference (McCann & Pearlman, 1990). For example, Wood (2004) advocated that practitioners focus on the issue of gender oppression, particularly when working with gay male adolescents, given the likelihood that they have experienced wounding associated with effeminacy.

Because of the minority stress associated with sexual and gender minority youth, there may be many concomitant symptoms present in these youth, such as substance abuse. Finnegan and McNally (2002) also raised the possibility that sexual and gender minorities who abuse substances or are dependent on substances are "doubly traumatized" as a result of their addiction and the discrimination they experience as stigmatized minorities. As Ryan and Futterman (1998) point out, it is important to assess motivations of sexual and gender minority youth who use substances.

Teach Stigma Management Skills

Practitioners who work with sexual and gender minority youth are ideally situated to provide guidance related to managing stigma and making decisions about self-disclosure. Commenting on a pervasive bias among practitioners, Hunter and Mallon (2000) cautioned practitioners against the tendency to pressure sexual minority youth to disclose their sexual orientation to family members. When counseling sexual minority youth who want to disclose their sexual orientation to family members, it is advisable that practitioners help them explore the possible risks and benefits of doing so (Hunter & Mallon, 2000). In a similar vein, Owens (1998) recommends that practitioners complete a "danger assessment" with their adolescent clients in order to determine how safe it is for the adolescent to come out. He suggests that practitioners aid their adolescent clients in exploring reasons for wanting to come out. Following are some possible questions that might be explored:

- Do your parents want to know?
- Are your parents intimately involved in your life?
- Are your parents actively avoiding any possibility that you have same-sex attractions?
- Have they ignored all of your hints so far? (Owens, 1998, p. 192).

While gender minority youth may be already outwardly expressing their inner sense of their gender identity within their families, it is appropriate for practitioners to engage in similar sorts of risk assessments. Israel and Tarver (1997) encourage their gender minority clients to adopt an androgynous appearance in places where it may not be safe to crossdress. The same is true with adopting an androgynous name until they are old enough to be certain they want to change permanently.

Help Youth Become Connected

Helping professionals need to encourage sexual and gender minority youth to participate in support groups and connect with positive role models (Cole et al., 2000; Fish & Harvey, 2005; Hershberger & D'Augelli, 2000). McDaniel, Purcell, and D'Augelli (2001) advocate that practitioners focus on strength and resilience as well as maladaptive behaviors, such as substance abuse. They also recommend peer-based prevention and treatment programs, which incorporate resilient sexual and gender minority youth as role models.

It is important that helping professionals familiarize themselves with social and recreational opportunities for sexual and gender minority youths and assist youths in accessing these. In some geographic areas, resources and role models for sexual and gender minority youth may be in short supply. In such cases, first-person narratives or fictional works are an important source of the affirmation that these youth need. Some possible examples of these include *Two Teenagers in Twenty: Writings by Gay and Lesbian Youth* (Heron, 1994); *Am I Blue? Coming Out from the Silence* (Bauer, 1995); *Annie on My Mind* (Garden, 1992); *Dare Truth or Promise* (Boock, 1999); *Rainbow Boys* (Sanchez, 2001); *Geography Club* (Hartinger, 2003); *Trans Forming Families: Real Stories About Transgendered Loved Ones* (Boenke, 1999); *Finding the Real Me: True Tales of Sex and Gender Diversity* (O'Keefe, 2003); *Luna* (Peters, 2005); and *Transparent: Love, Family, and Living the T with Transgender Teenagers* (Beam, 2007).

The growing visibility in the media of sexual and gender minorities and the growing access to these communities on the Internet have equipped young people with increased options for self-definition. Ringo (2002) suggested that the media and Internet function as facilitators for youth who are developing their gender identities. While the Internet may hold potential dangers for youth, it also is the site of opportunities. Some particularly useful sites for sexual and gender minority youth and questioning youth include Soc. support.youth.gay-lesbian-bi, a moderated discussion forum for GLBT and questioning youth (http://www.ssyglb.org); OutProud, resources for queer and questioning youth (http://www.outproud.org); Oasis magazine, where LGBT youth can post and chat (http://oasismag.com); YouthResource, online sexual health information by peer educators (http://www.YouthResource.com); and GayTeens, support and information for GLBT and questioning youth (http://www.gayteens.org).

Adapt an Anticipatory Guidance Approach

In *Lesbian & Gay Youth: Care & Counseling* (1998), authors Ryan and Futterman recommend adopting an anticipatory guidance approach with sexual minority youth. This approach requires therapists to provide psychoeducational information related to practicing safe sex, building healthy relationships, and developing access to support systems within the sexual minority community.

One area where an anticipatory guidance approach might be especially appropriate for sexual minority youth concerns dating and forming romantic relationships. Hershberger and D'Augelli (2000) note this is problematic for many sexual minority youth. "Because same-sex dating is essentially culturally prohibited until adulthood, sexual activity for LGB youth may occur less often with peers and more often with older partners" (p. 238). D'Augelli (1998) termed the lack of dating among sexual minority adolescents a *developmental opportunity loss*. He advised practitioners to discuss without judgment what risks might ensue when dating older persons and engaging in sexual activities.

The need for practitioners to provide accurate, reliable information related to gender minority issues is particularly urgent. Israel and Tarver (1997) asserted that the needs of gender minorities differ, depending on their unique identities. It is important that practitioners, psychologists, and social workers communicate to youth and their families that not all gender minorities will want to conform to a transsexual model. In other words, not every adolescent or adult wants to undergo hormonal therapy and gender reassignment surgery. Some choose hormonal therapy only or hormonal therapy plus cosmetic surgery only, to name two options. The following sources provide in-depth information about the procedures, risks, and benefits associated with hormonal and surgical interventions: *Transgender Care* (Israel & Tarver, 1997); *Transgender Emergence* (Lev, 2004); "Clinical Management of Gender Dysphoria in Adolescents" (De Vries, Cohen-Kettenis, & Delemarre-van de Waal, 2006b) and "Counseling and Mental Health Care of Transgender Adults and Loved Ones" (Bockting, Knudson, & Goldberg, 2006).

CURRENT PROTOCOLS AND CONTROVERSIES IN CHILD AND ADOLESCENT GENDER TRANSITIONING

Many adolescents are adamant about their desire to undergo a partial or complete gender transition (De Vries, Cohen-Kettenis, & Delemarre-van de Waal, 2006a). In one recent survey of gender minority adolescents, 68% of the sample indicated that they had or were currently taking hormones (Grossman et al., 2006). Treatment protocols continue to emerge for gender transitioning in youth (e.g., the Gender Identity Research and Education Society's guidelines on hormonal medication for adolescents, 2005). The most well-established guidelines were those crafted by the Harry Benjamin International Gender Dysphoria Association, or HBIGDA (now known as the World Professional Association for Transgender Health). This group of multidisciplinary professionals from around the world was formed in 1980. The WPATH established the Standards of Care (SOC) in order to provide minimal criteria for determining how and when to recommend interventions like hormone therapy and sex reassignment surgery to gender minorities. The current SOC (Meyer et al., 2001) contains guidelines specifically for the treatment of children and adolescents with GID.

The SOC for adult treatment are often referred to as a triadic therapy because these consist of hormone therapy, real-life experience, and sex reassignment surgery. Generally, all candidates for sex reassignment are required to have a written endorsement from mental health providers as a requirement for access to hormonal therapy and surgery. For those who are born biological male, an evaluation is required by an experienced therapist to verify the diagnosis of GID. Then they can begin taking feminizing hormones, which cause loss of muscle, redistribution of fatty tissue, and softening of the skin. The next step is the real-life experience in which the client begins living as a woman. If sex reassignment surgery is desired, the client must have two letters of documentation, one of which must be from a doctoral-level mental health specialist. Electrolysis and cosmetic procedures may follow.

In the case of a biological woman, a psychological evaluation is required before testosterone can be administered. Once testosterone is given, the patient typically experiences an increase in muscle mass, body and facial hair growth, voice lowering, and acne. Two separate recommendations are needed before a bilateral mastectomy can be performed. This usually occurs before the real-life experience. Penile constructive surgeries may be performed, although they are not regarded as fully successful (Seil, 2004).

The SOC (Meyer et al., 2001) for children and adolescents contain recommendations for two different forms of treatment interventions. The first category, termed *psychological/social*, refers to interventions that involve providing parents with support for managing the child's gender expression. For example, practitioners might help parents identify areas that are most problematic in terms of the child's gender nonconformity and "help the family establish some rules they can all live with about ways to act, dress, and behave at home and in public" (Fish & Harvey, 2005, p. 83).

The second category, *physical intervention*, includes three options. The first option is fully reversible interventions, including lutein hormone releasing hormone (LHRH) agonists. These hormones prevent the development of physical characteristics that have to be removed later. The second option is partially reversible interventions. The third is irreversible or surgical procedures. Adolescents may be eligible for partially reversible interventions at the age of 16. According to the SOC, surgical procedures are not to be employed until the age of 18, and this should include a real-life experience of at least two years.

Current Controversies: Hormone Therapy

The idea of giving hormone therapy to persons who are little more than children is highly controversial and deemed by many to be unethical. Several writers (Fish & Harvey, 2005; Swann & Herbert, 1999) have discussed such complexities in working with gender minority youth and their families. One of the major challenges concerns the pursuit of options for gender transition when the youth is below the age of consent. Swann and Herbert (1999) suggest that the use of hormonal therapy with persons under 18 years of age raises several ethical questions. Their article "Ethical Issues in the Mental Health Treatment of Gender Dysphoric Adolescents" advises practitioners to be cautious with underaged clients and their caregivers and to be sure to explain the options and risks associated with this therapy. Because hormone treatment raises complex issues, some practitioners (Fish & Harvey, 2005) recommend adhering to the World Professional Association of Transgender Health (WPATH) SOC. Israel and Tarver (1997) suggest that a qualified senior gender specialist evaluate individuals on a case-by-case basis in order to determine whether hormones should be administered. They also recommend a two-year wait for transgender youth before hormone administration.

Griggs (1998), a proponent of hormonal therapy in adolescence, argues that youth should be permitted to transition on the grounds that the therapy would retard secondary sex characteristics and eliminate the need for cosmetic surgery in the future. Cohen-Kettenis and van Goozen (1997) and Cohen-Kettenis and Pfafflin (2003) have treated adolescent transsexual patients at their medical clinic. With some, they advocate the use of puberty-delaying hormones such as LHRH agonists. These hormones are used to prevent the development of physical characteristics that have to be removed later. This early intervention can help prevent the stress and discomfort of waiting until adulthood to begin the transition process. For example, hormones that block the development of facial hair and lowered voices would help young biological males pass more easily. De Vries et al. (2006b) argue that this treatment may be appropriate in cases when youth have just entered puberty and have had intense cross-gender identities since early childhood. Familial consent and support are also necessary. They also recommend the use of partially reversible feminizing or masculinizing hormones in cases involving youth over 16 years of age.

Current Controversies: Gender Identity Disorder

Youth who are referred to therapy specifically for issues related to sexual orientation and gender identity are often diagnosed and treated for gender identity disorder. Treatment approaches for children diagnosed with GID are based on the assumption that such children will grow to adulthood and become homosexual and/or transsexual (Haldeman, 2000; Lev, 2004).

The inclusion of GID in the *Diagnostic and Statistical Manual of Mental Disorders (DSM)* has become increasingly controversial. GID and transsexualism first appeared in the 1980 edition of the *DSM*, seven years after the removal of homosexuality. In the 1994 edition, the diagnosis of transsexualism was replaced by the more generic GID. Although the diagnosis of GID was not to be confused with sexual orientation, the current edition of the *DSM* includes "specifiers" that practitioners use to denote sexual orientation in "mature individuals." In the current edition of the *DSM*, the *DSM–IV–TR* (American Psychiatric Association, 2000), the criteria for GID in children include the following:

A. A strong and persistent cross-gender identification (not merely a desire for any perceived cultural advantages of being the other sex). The disturbance is manifested by four (or more) of the following:

   1. repeatedly stated desire to be, or insistence that he or she *is* the other sex;
   2. in boys, the preference for cross-dressing or simulating female attire; in girls, insistence on wearing only stereotypically masculine clothing;
   3. strong and persistent preferences for cross-sex roles in make believe play or persistent fantasies of being the other sex;
   4. intense desire to participate in the stereotypical games and pastimes of the other sex;
   5. strong preference for playmates of the other sex.

Adolescents and adults: GID is manifested by such symptoms as: (1) a stated desire to be the other sex; (2) the conviction that one has the typical feelings and reactions of the other sex; (3) a desire to live or be treated as the other sex; (4) frequent passing as the other sex.

A. Persistent discomfort with his or her sex or sense of inappropriateness in the gender role of that sex.
B. The disturbance is not concurrent with a physical intersex condition.
C. The disturbance causes clinically significant distress or impairment in social, occupational, or other important areas of functioning. (pp. 581–582)

Under the current diagnostic guidelines, children who are gender nonconforming but do not want to be the opposite sex and do not have an aversion to their own biological sex can meet the criteria for GID, provided there is evidence of clinically significant distress.

Not all children who are diagnosed with GID will grow up and become sexual and gender minorities in adulthood (Fish & Harvey, 2005). However, Cohen-Kettenis, a leading gender specialist in the Netherlands, argues that there are more children with GID who undergo sex reassignment surgery in adulthood than had been previously assumed. Research estimates of children diagnosed as GID who elect to transition in adulthood range from a low of 6% (Zucker & Bradley, 1995) to a high of 23% (Cohen-Kettenis & Pfafflin, 2003).

WHAT PROPONENTS SAY   Proponents of the diagnosis argue that GID is a biopsychosocially determined disorder (DiCeglie et al., 2002; Seil, 2004). They state that in many cases the GID diagnosis is required in adulthood in order to secure third-party reimbursement for services associated with hormonal therapy and sex reassignment surgery (Dean et al., 2000; Haldeman, 2000; Schrock, Reid, & Boyd, 2005). Others (e.g., Cole et al., 2000) note that many insurance companies exclude coverage of psychiatric and medical services related to GID.

In response to demands for refinement of the GID diagnostic criteria, Rekers (1995) recommended that mental health professionals make a distinction between gender role behavior disturbance, characterized by children who exhibit cross-gender behavior but do not have a stated desire to change sex, and cross gender identification disturbance, in which children exhibit cross-gender behavior and want to change sex.

WHAT OPPONENTS SAY   Those who disagree with the inclusion of GID in the *DSM* (e.g., Bartlett, Vasey, & Bukowksi, 2000; Spade, 2006; Tarver, 2002) argue that it pathologizes gender-atypical children. These opponents recommend revision, if not deletion, of the disorder and its criteria. Spade (2006) argues:

> The diagnostic criteria for GID produce a fiction of natural gender, in which normal, non-transsexual people grow up with minimal to no gender trouble or exploration, do not cross-dress as children, do not play with the wrong gendered kids, and do not like the wrong kinds of toys or characters. This story isn't believable, but because medicine produces it through a generalized account of the transgression, and instructs the doctor/parent/teacher to focus on the transgressive behavior, it establishes a surveillance and regulation effective for keeping both nontransexuals and transsexuals in adherence to their roles. In order to get authorization for body alteration, this childhood must be produced, and the GID diagnosis accepted, maintaining an idea of two discrete gender categories that normally contain everyone but occasionally are wrongly assigned, requiring correction to reestablish the norm. (p. 321)

Current Controversies: The Treatment of Gender Identity Disorder

Rekers, Coates, and Zucker are considered leading proponents of what Raj (2002) called *rehabilitative treatment* of GID. A rehabilitative treatment objective in GID cases means to put the child "on track" in terms of his or her gender role behaviors. Ultimately, the treatment also helps defend against the negative effects of the social ostracism that gender-nonconforming children typically experience. Most reparative treatment approaches incorporate behavioral techniques (e.g., Rekers, 1995; Zucker & Bradley, 1995) and have been the subject of criticism (e.g., Burke, 1996).

Tarver (2002) recommends eliminating gender dysphoria, transsexualism, and transvestism as diseases and limiting treatment to recovery from the traumas people encounter at the hands of an intolerant culture. As Lev (2004) asserts, the assumption that such gender-nonconforming behaviors are not problematic means that the whole focus of treatment is radically altered. Recent examples of alternative interventions for children have been the focus of intense media attention. In a 2008 radio broadcast, parents described how, with the help of psychologists, they were able to support their son's cross-gender identification by enrolling him in kindergarten as a girl (Spiegel, 2008).

Treatment Protocols for Use with Intersex Youth

In recent years, the treatment protocols for infants who are born intersexed have changed radically. The Consortium on the Management of Disorders of Sex Development has created clinical guidelines that call for a multidisciplinary team to work with parents in making decisions about the sex assignment of their child (Intersex Society of North America, 2006). The consortium comprises clinical specialists who work with patients diagnosed with disorders of sexual development (DSDs), adults with DSDs, and parents of children with DSDs. Its guidelines now call for honest disclosure by physicians and other personnel and emphasize the child's right to make decisions about the preferred gender at a time when he or she is developmentally able to do so.

ADVOCATE FOR SEXUAL AND GENDER MINORITY YOUTH

Several authors (Anderson, 1998; Ettner, 1999; Morrow, 2004; Raj, 2002) recommend that therapists advocate for the rights of sexual and gender minority youth by extending the therapists' work outside the therapy room and into the schools and the community. It is generally agreed that all schools should take the following measures:

- Include sexual and gender minorities in school nondiscrimination policies
- Provide in-service training for school personnel on sexual and gender minority issues
- Expand the curriculum to include sexual and gender minority issues
- Employ sexual and gender minority role models (Fish & Harvey, 2005; Morrow, 2004)

Practitioners employed in full-service schools can help educate school personnel about the ways in which all children, not just sexual and gender minorities, are damaged by gender policing practices. Practitioners need to join with politically active members of the intersex community who are now demanding that intersexed persons have the right to define themselves without doctor or parental interference. Accordingly, sex assignment and genital surgery should at least be delayed until the child is old enough to make such decisions (Kessler, 1990, 1998). Gainor (2000) also addressed the need for advocacy efforts related to intersex youth who are sometimes subject to unnecessary testing and research, given the fact that they are unable to speak for themselves.

Summary

Research suggests that sexual minority youth are beginning to question their sexual identities and the labels used to describe these at earlier ages than was true of previous cohorts. While some sexual minority youth may have greater access to resources, role models, and support systems, the vast majority exist in social institutions like families, schools, and places of worship that can be hostile, rejecting, and unwelcoming.

Despite researchers' proliferation of stage models that describe developmental pathways to the establishment of a healthy gay or lesbian identity, more-recent critiques have emphasized the role of contextual, cultural, and historical variables in identity development. The developmental trajectories of gender minorities suggest that many gender minority youth recognize their gender atypicality at an early age and engage in compensatory activities, such as cross-dressing. The onset of puberty constitutes a crisis for many gender minorities, who experience puberty as the body's betrayal (Israel, 2005).

Sexual minority youth experience elevated rates of depression, substance abuse, and homelessness and are at increased risk of HIV and sexually transmitted diseases, when compared to their nonminority peers (D'Augelli, 2006; Russell & Joyner; 2001; Ryan, 2001; Safren & Heimberg, 1999; Safren & Pantalone, 2006). The experiences of gender minority youth are much like those of sexual minority youth in terms of their exposure to prolonged minority stress and their concomitant vulnerability to depression, suicidality, substance abuse, and HIV and sexually transmitted diseases (Dean et al., 2000).

Continued research is necessary to explore the experiences of youth who identify as bisexual, particularly given recent findings that suggest bisexual youth experience poorer social adjustment and are at even greater risk for substance abuse and suicide than lesbian and gay youth (Hershberger, Pilkington, & D'Augelli, 1997; Marshal et al., 2008; Russell, 2006; Russell et al., 2001).

Gender-atypical children are often diagnosed with gender identity disorder, a diagnosis associated with controversy. Supporters of GID argue that in many cases the GID diagnosis is required in order to satisfy the WPATH Standards of Care and to secure third-party reimbursement for services associated with hormonal therapy and sex reassignment surgery (Dean et al., 2000; Haldeman, 2000; Schrock et al., 2005). Critics of GID and its treatment argue that GID pathologizes gender-atypical children and recommend that treatment be limited to recovery from the traumas gender minority youth experience in an intolerant culture.

Therapists who work with sexual and gender minority youth are likely to see a broad range of sexual and gender expressions. Counseling professionals may see youth who are perhaps questioning and exploring their sexual orientations and gender identities. And at the other end of the spectrum, they will work with those who have self-labeled and already disclosed themselves to others. In the case of gender minority youth, it is important that helping professionals realize not all gender minority youth will want to conform to a transsexual model. In other words, not every client wants to undergo hormonal therapy and gender reassignment surgery. Regardless of whatever options clients choose, it is imperative for practitioners to demonstrate unconditional positive regard for these youth. True supportive psychotherapy requires that the therapist do the following:

- Adopt an anticipatory guidance approach
- Adopt a questioning or "not knowing" stance
- Acquire up-to-date knowledge of community supports
- Participate in advocacy efforts to expand the civil and human rights of sexual and gender minorities
- Teach stigma management skills
- Assess trauma and suicidal risk

Library, Media, and Internet Activities

Check your local video/DVD store for three important films depicting the experiences of sexual minority youth.

Latter Days (Cox, 2003)

This film depicts the story of Aaron Davis, a young Mormon missionary from Utah, who shares an apartment with his fellow missionaries across the way from Christian Markelli. Christian, a waiter and party boy, begins to fall in love with Aaron. Their exposure as a couple brings disastrous consequences.

Discussion Questions

1. This film contains depictions of same-sex sexual relationships that are seldom seen in mainstream cinema or television. What were your thoughts and feelings while viewing these scenes? What might your response have been if these scenes were between two female characters?
2. Place yourself in the role of a counselor and imagine how you might have intervened with Aaron once he returned home to face his family and church? How might you have facilitated a dialogue between Aaron and his mom when Aaron comes home and is excommunicated from the Mormon Church? As Aaron's counselor, how might you aid him in finding his place in a faith community? Using the Internet and other resources, what faith communities, churches, and temples do you find that engage in special outreach to sexual and gender minorities?
3. According to the research presented in this chapter on sexual minority youth suicide, how would you assess Aaron's level of risk for suicide?

But I'm a Cheerleader (Babbit, 1999)

This film tells the story of Megan Bloomfield, a 17-year-old high school cheerleader. Her parents suspect she is a lesbian and they send her to True Directions, a rehabilitation camp for homosexuals.

Discussion Questions

1. What therapy techniques did the rehabilitation program at True Directions use to con-vert youth? How did these compare with reparative or conversion therapy practices described in Chapter 2?
2. Identify several examples in this film of the confounding of gender and sexual orientation.
3. Assume the role of Megan's therapist during Megan's family meeting with Nancy and Peter Bloomfield, and describe how you might intervene when Megan's parents warn her that if she chooses to be a lesbian, she will be kicked out of the house.

Camp (Graff, 2003)

This film depicts the experiences of several young people attending a musical theater camp during summer break. Several themes, including sexual orientation, family dysfunction, obesity, and cross-dressing, are dealt with in this film in a humorous and lighthearted way.

Discussion Questions

1. In the opening scene of *Camp*, Michael attends the junior prom attired in women's formal wear with disastrous consequences. Assume the role of a school counselor who is called in to consult with the administrators. What might you recommend to them in terms of dealing with this incident?
2. What common beliefs and assumptions about homosexuality did Vlad voice to Michael? How many of these were consistent with your personal beliefs and assumptions?
3. How does the camp depicted in this film compare to your personal experience in camp?

Group Activity 1

"How do you know you want rhinoplasty, a nose job?" he inquires, fixing me with a penetrating stare.

"Because," I reply, suddenly unable to raise my eyes above his brown wing-tips, "I've always felt like a small-nosed woman trapped in a large-nosed body."

"And how long have you felt this way?" He leans forward, sounding as if he knows the answer and needs only to hear the word.

"Oh, since I was five or six, doctor, practically all my life."

"Then you have rhino-identity disorder," the shoe tops state flatly. My body sags in relief. "But first," he goes on, "we want you to get letters from two psychiatrists and live as a small-nosed woman for three years ... just to be sure."

The excerpt above is from Richi Anne Wilchins's book *Read My Lips: Sexual Subversion and the End of Gender* (1997). Wilchins humorously attempted to highlight one of the frequently voiced criticisms of the process dictated by the World Professional Association of Transgender Health (WPATH) Standards of Care. The WPATH Standards of Care require candidates for sex reassignment surgery to have a diagnosis of GID and written endorsement from mental health providers in order to receive hormonal therapy and gender reassignment surgery. Wilchins and others (e.g., Califia, 1997) argued

that adults who elect to get cosmetic surgery, such as breast enhancement and laser vaginal reconstruction, are able to do so without a psychiatric evaluation. Wilchins called for a conceptual shift from seeing transsexual surgery as a way to fix a disorder to viewing it as a way to fix the client's body to suit his or her image, as one can do with cosmetic surgery.

Critics of the SOC argued that mental health professionals who work with gender minorities are cast in a gatekeeping role, one that is not familiar to or comfortable for many practitioners.

Discussion Questions

1. What are your reactions to Wilchins's viewpoint?
2. How might you react if an adolescent client came to you expressly for the purpose of acquiring a letter needed for a sex reassignment procedure under the WPATH Standards of Care?

Group Activity 2

In her article titled: "Judicial Child Abuse: The Family Court of Australia, Gender Identity Disorder, and the 'Alex' Case," Jeffreys (2005) condemned a judgment of the Australian Family Court in 2004. In this case, Chief Justice Nicholson of the Australian Family Court ordered that a 13-year-old girl be permitted, in accordance with her wishes, to begin the process of transition by taking hormones to suppress menstruation. The court also ordered that she not be permitted to begin sex reassignment surgery before the age of 18. Jeffreys (2005) questioned the existence of gender identity disorder (GID) and argued that it is based on a socially constructed view of traditional gender roles. She posited that the underlying assumption that GID is a biological condition has not been properly substantiated by empirical research. She warned that the side effects of

androgen therapy for those transitioning from female to male, the health risks associated with surgical procedures (including irreversibility and scarring) and the possible reduction in the number of relationship partners make this process grounds for "judicial child abuse."

Discussion Questions

1. If possible, read a copy of Jeffreys' article for a more detailed outline of her position. After reading the article and/or the discussion presented in this chapter, clarify your own thoughts about providing hormones to persons under the age of 18. What is your opinion about the use of puberty-delaying hormones? How does this compare to your opinion on the use of irreversible hormones during adolescence? What do you think of

Jeffreys' position about Alex's case being one of "judicial child abuse"? Where do you stand on this issue?

2. At what age are people competent to make their own decisions regarding hormonal therapy and surgical procedures such as breast augmentation and genital reconstruction? Should adolescents be permitted to assume a cross-gender identification through means other than hormonal or surgical intervention (e.g., name change or dress)?

CASE STUDY 1

You are a therapist in private practice, and you receive a telephone call from an anxious parent looking for your professional advice about her 15-year-old son. The caller tells you that her son came out to her as "gay" several months ago. At that time, she sought counseling for her son and was contacted by the local chapter of PFLAG. While she tells you that she has come to accept her son's same-sex sexual orientation, she is increasingly anxious about his school performance and deteriorating grades over the last several months. She tells you that his falling grades coincide with his spending increasing amounts of time on the Internet, and she believes that he is going online to look at gay porn. She tells you that she believes that despite the limits on the amount of time he spends online, he is finding other ways to access the computer. She is very worried about his behavior and asks what she should do.

Discussion Questions

1. What additional information would you like to acquire from the caller? Specifically, what questions would you ask of her?
2. How do you view the caller's son's interest in gay porn?
3. What recommendations might you make to the caller?

CASE STUDY 2

Justin's mother, Mrs. Alexander, brings 15-year-old Justin in for treatment. She expresses concern that he might be depressed as he has become increasingly withdrawn and isolative. Without his mother present, Justin reveals to you that he has been "surfing the Net" and found sites dealing with the topic of transsexualism. He tells you that he loathes his male body and knows that he was truly meant to be a woman. He intends to have a sex-change operation and is currently saving money to afford this. He tells you that he is 100% sure about this decision and has even contemplated finding a way to get hormones off the Internet. Select a partner from your group and set up a role play in which one of you assumes the role of Justin and the other his therapist.

Discussion Questions

1. What were your feelings as you assumed these roles?
2. Given professional ethical codes and laws in your state, how might you handle the issue of confidentiality in this case?

CASE STUDY 3

You are a guest speaker at a local community education series lecture. Your topic is communication and conflict resolution within families. After the question-and-answer period, you notice that one of the audience members stays in her seat until everyone has left the room. She approaches you and begins to share a personal concern that she has with her four-year-old son. She tells you that her son has always had a strong preference for playing with his older sister's dolls, especially Barbie. He is enamored with princess playthings and insisted on dressing as a princess this past Halloween. She tells you that, at first, she gave in to his insistence for girls' toys, but now she is beginning to get worried. She has tears in her eyes and wonders where she can go to get her son "tested."

Discussion Questions

1. How might you respond to her concerns?
2. What might you advise her or a similar parent who presents her child for therapy?

References

American Psychiatric Association. (2000). *Diagnostic and statistical manual of mental disorders—Text revision* (4th ed.). Washington, DC: Author.

Anderson, B. F. (1998). Therapeutic issues in working with transgendered clients. In D. Denny (Ed.), *Current concepts of transgender identity* (pp. 215–226). New York: Garland Press.

Anhalt, K., & Morris, T. L. (2003). Developmental and adjustment issues in gay, lesbian, and bisexual adolescents: A review of the literature. In L. D. Garnets & D. C. Kimmel (Eds.), *Psychological perspectives in lesbian, gay, and bisexual experiences* (pp. 571–601). New York: Columbia University Press.

Babbit, J. (Director). (1999). *But I'm a cheerleader* [Motion picture]. United States: Lions Gate.

Bailey, J. M., & Zucker, K. J. (1995). Childhood sex-types behavior and sexual orientation: A conceptual analysis and quantitative review. *Developmental Psychology, 31*(1), 43–55.

Barlett, N. H., Vasey, P. L., & Bukkowki, W. M. (2000). Is gender identity disorder in children a mental disorder? *Sex Roles 43* (11–12), 753–785.

Bauer, M. D. (1995). *Am I blue?: Coming out from the silence.* New York: HarperTrophy.

Beam, C. (2007). *Transparent: Love, family, and living the T with transgender teenagers.* Orlando, FL: Harcourt.

Bem, D. J. (1996). Exotic becomes erotic: A developmental theory of sexual orientation. *Psychological Review, 103,* 320–335.

Bockting, W. O., Knudson, G., & Goldberg, J. M. (2006). *Counselling and mental health care of transgender adults and loved ones.* Vancouver, Canada: Vancouver Coastal Health, Transcend Transgender Support & Education Society, and Canadian Rainbow Coalition. Retrieved February 1, 2007, from http://www.vch.ca/transhealth

Boenke, M. (Ed.). (1999). *Trans forming families: Real stories about transgendered loved ones.* Imperial Beach, CA: Walter Trook.

Bontempo, D. E., & D'Augelli, A. R. (2002). Effects of at-school victimization and sexual orientation on lesbian, gay, or bisexual youths' health risk behavior, *Journal of Adolescent Health, 30*(5), 364–374.

Boock, P. (1999). *Dare truth or promise.* New York: Houghton Mifflin.

Bradford, M. (2004). The bisexual experience: Living in a dichotomous culture. *Journal of Bisexuality, 4* (1–2), 7–23.

Brown, M. L., & Rounsley, C. A. (1996). *True selves: Understanding transsexualism—For families, friends, coworkers, and helping professionals.* San Francisco: Jossey-Bass.

Brown, T. (2002). A proposed model of bisexual identity development that elaborates on experiential differences of women and men. *Journal of Bisexuality, 2*(4), 67–91.

Burgess, C. (1999). Internal and external stress factors associated with the identity development of transgendered youth. *Journal of Gay & Lesbian Social Services. 10*(3–5), 35–47.

Burke, P. (1996). *Gender shock.* New York: Doubleday.

Califia, P. (1997). *Sex changes: The politics of transgenderism.* San Francisco: Cleis Press.

Cass, V. C. (1979). Homosexual identity formation: A theoretical model. *Journal of Homosexuality, 4*(3), 219–235.

Cass, V. C. (1984). Homosexual identity formation: Testing a theoretical model. *Journal of Sex Research, 20*(2), 143–167.

Cochran, S., & Mays, V. M. (2006). Estimating prevalence of mental and substance-using disorders among lesbians and gay men from existing national health data. In A. M. Omoto & H. S. Kurtzman (Eds.), *Sexual orientation and mental health: Examining identity and development in lesbian, gay, and bisexual people* (pp. 143–165). Washington, DC: American Psychological Association.

Cohen-Kettenis, P. T., & Pfafflin, F. (2003). *Transgenderism and intersexuality in childhood and adolescence.* Thousand Oaks, CA: Sage.

Cohen-Kettenis, P. T., & van Goozen, S. H. M. (1997). Sex reassignment of adolescent transsexuals: A follow-up study. *Journal of the American Academy of Child & Adolescent Psychiatry, 36*(2), 263–271.

Cole, S. S., Denny, D., Eyler, A. E., & Samons, S. L. (2000). Issues of transgender. In T. Szuchman & F. Muscarella (Eds.), *Psychological perspectives in human sexuality* (pp. 149–195). New York: Wiley.

Coleman, E. (1982). Developmental stages of the coming out process. *Journal of Homosexuality, 7,* 31–43.

Cox, C. J. (Director). (2003). *Latter days* [Motion picture]. United States: TLA Releasing.

D'Augelli, A. R. (1998). Developmental implications of victimization of lesbian, gay, and bisexual youths. In G. M. Herek (Ed.), *Stigma and sexual orientation: Understanding prejudice against lesbians, gay men, and bisexuals* (pp. 187–210). Thousand Oaks, CA: Sage.

D'Augelli, A. R. (2006). Developmental and contextual factors and mental health among lesbian, gay, and bisexual youths. In A. M. Omoto & H. S. Kurtzman (Eds.), *Sexual orientation and mental health: Examining identity and development in lesbian, gay, and bisexual people* (pp. 37–53). Washington, DC: American Psychological Association.

D'Augelli, A. R., & Grossman, A. H. (2001). Disclosure of sexual orientation, victimization, and mental health among lesbian, gay, and bisexual older adults. *Journal of Interpersonal Violence, 10,* 1008–1027.

D'Augelli, A. R., Grossman, A. H., Salter, N. P., Vasey, J. J., Starks, M. T., & Sinclair, K. O. (2005). Predicting the suicide attempts of lesbian, gay, and bisexual youth. *Suicide & Life-Threatening Behavior, 35*(6), 646–660.

D'Augelli, A. R., Grossman, A. H., & Starks, M. T. (2005). Parents' awareness of lesbian, gay, and bisexual youths' sexual orientation. *Journal of Marriage & Family, 67,* 474–482.

D'Augelli, A. R., Hershberger, S. L., & Pilkington, N. W. (1998). Lesbian, gay, and bisexual youths and their families: Disclosure of sexual orientation and its consequences. *American Journal of Orthopsychiatry, 68,* 361–371.

D'Augelli, A. R., Hershberger, S. L., & Pilkington, N. W. (2001). Suicidality patterns and sexual orientation-related factors among lesbian, gay, and bisexual youths. *Suicide & Life-Threatening Behavior, 31,* 250–264.

Dean, L., Meyer, I. H., Robinson, K., Sell, R. L., Sember, R., Silenzio, V. M. B., et al. (2000). Lesbian, gay, bisexual, and transgender health: Findings and concerns. *Journal of the Gay & Lesbian Medical Association, 4*(3), 101–150.

Devor, A. H. (2004). Witnessing and mirroring: A fourteen stage model of transsexual identity formation. *Journal of Gay & Lesbian Psychotherapy, 8*(1–2), 41–67.

Devor, H. (1994). Transsexualism, dissociation and child abuse: An initial discussion based on nonclinical data. *Journal of Psychology & Human Sexuality, 6*(3), 49–72.

De Vries, A. L. C., Cohen-Kettenis, P. T., & Delemarre-van de Waal, H. (2006a). *Caring for transgender adolescents in BC: Suggested guidelines.* Vancouver, Canada: Vancouver Coastal Health, Transcend Transgender Support & Education Society, and Canadian Rainbow Health Coalition. Retrieved April 11, 2007, from http://www.vch.ca/transhealth

De Vries, A. L. C., Cohen-Kettenis, P. T., & Delemarre-van de Waal, H. (2006b). Clinical management of gender dysphoria in adolescents [Electronic version]. *International Journal of Transgenderism, 9*(3/4), 83–94. Retrieved on April, 11, 2007, from http://ijt.haworthpress.com

Diamond, L. M. (2006). What we got wrong about sexual identity development: Unexpected findings from a longitudinal study of young women.

In A. M. Omoto & H. S. Kurtzman (Eds.), *Sexual orientation and mental health: Examining identity and development in lesbian, gay, and bisexual people* (pp. 73–94). Washington, DC: American Psychological Association.

Diamond, L. M. (2008). Female bisexuality from adolescence to adulthood: Results from a 10-year longitudinal study. *Developmental Psychology, 44*(1), 5–14.

DiCeglie, D., Freedman, D., McPherson, S., & Richardson, P. (2002). Children and adolescents referred to a specialist gender identity development service: Clinical features and demographic characteristics [Electronic version]. *International Journal of Transgenderism, 6*(1). Retrieved September 16, 2005, from http://www.symposion.com/ijt/ijtvo06no01_01.htm

Dube, E. M. (2000). The role of sexual behavior in the identification process of gay and bisexual males. *Journal of Sex Research, 37*(2), 123–132.

Eastwood, C. (Director). (1997). *Midnight in the garden of good and evil* [Motion picture]. United States: Warner Brothers.

Ettner, R. (1999). *Gender loving care: A guide to counseling gender-variant clients.* New York: Norton.

Eyler, A. E., & Wright, K. (1997, July–September). Gender identification and sexual orientation among genetic females with gender-blended self-perception in childhood and adolescence [Electronic version]. *International Journal of Transgenderism, 1*(1). Retrieved May 20, 2001, from http://www.symposion.com/ijt/ijtc0102.htm

Feder, J., Levant, R. F., & Dean, J. (2007). Boys and violence: A gender-informed analysis. *Professional Psychology: Research & Practice, 38*(4), 385–391.

Finnegan, D. G., & McNally, E. B. (2002). *Counseling lesbian, gay, bisexual, and transgender substance abusers: Dual identities.* New York: Haworth Press.

Fish, S. L., & Harvey, R. G. (2005). *Nurturing queer youth: Family therapy transformed.* New York: Norton.

Fitzpatrick, K. K., Euton, S. J., Jones, J. N., & Schmidt, N. B. (2005). Gender roles, sexual orientation and suicide risk. *Journal of Affective Disorders, 87*(1), 35–42.

Friedman, M. S., Koeske, G. F., Silvestre, A. J., Korr, W. S., & Sites, E. W. (2006). The impact of gender-role nonconforming behavior, bullying, and social support on suicidality among gay male youth. *Journal of Adolescent Health 38*(5), 621–623.

Friedman, M. S., Marshal, M. P., Stall, R., Cheong, J., & Wright, E. R. (2007). Gay-related development, early abuse and adult health outcomes among gay males. *AIDS and Behaviors,* DOI 10.1007/s1046-007-9319-3 (online journal).

Gagne, P., & Tewksbury, R. (1998). Conformity pressure and gender resistance among transgendered individuals. *Social Problems, 45*(1), 81–102.

Gagne, P., & Tewksbury, R. (1999). Knowledge and power, body and self: An analysis of knowledge systems and the transgendered self. *Sociological Quarterly, 40*(1), 59–83.

Gagne, P., Tewksbury, R., & McGaughey, D. (1997). Coming out and crossing over: Identity formation and proclamation in a transgender community. *Gender & Society, 11*(4), 478–508.

Gainor, K. A. (2000). Including transgender issues in lesbian, gay and bisexual psychology. In G. Greene & G. L. Croom (Eds.), *Education, research and practice in lesbian, gay, bisexual, and transgendered psychology: A resource manual* (pp. 131–160). Thousand Oaks, CA: Sage.

Garden, N. (1992). *Annie on my mind.* New York: Farrar, Straus & Giroux.

Garofalo, R., Deleon, J., Osmer, E., Doll, M., & Harper, G. W. (2006). Overlooked, misunderstood and at-risk: Exploring the lives and HIV risk of ethnic minority male-to-female transgender youth. *Journal of Adolescent Health, 38*(3), 230–236.

Garofalo, R., Wolf, R., Kessel, S., Palfrey, J., & DuRant, R. (1998). The association between health risk behaviors and sexual orientation among a school based sample of adolescents. *Pediatrics, 101*, 895–902.

Gay, Lesbian, and Straight Education Network. (2001). *2001 National School Climate Survey.* New York: Author.

Gehring, D., & Knudson, G. (2005). Prevalence of childhood trauma in a clinical population of transsexual people. *International Journal of Transgenderism, 8*(1), 23–30.

Gender Identity Research and Education Society. (2005). *Hormonal medication for adolescents: Developing guidelines for endocrinological intervention in the gender identity development treatment of adolescents.* Retrieved April 11, 2007, from http://www.gires.org.uk/Web_Page_Assets/Hormonal_Medication.htm

Gibson, P. (1989). Gay male and lesbian youth suicide. In *Alcohol, Drug Abuse, and Mental Health Administration, Report of the Secretary's Task Force on Youth Suicide* (DHHS Publication No. ADM 89–1623, Vol. 3, pp. 110–142). Washington, DC: U.S. Government Printing Office.

Graff, T. (Director). (2003). *Camp* [Motion picture]. United States: MGM.

Green, R. (1987). *The "sissy boy syndrome" and the development of homosexuality.* New Haven, CT: Yale University Press.

Griggs, C. (1998). *S/he: Changing sex and changing clothes.* Oxford, England: Berg.

Grossman, A. H., & D'Augelli, A. R. (2007). Transgender youth and life-threatening behaviors. *Suicide & Life-Threatening Behavior, 37*(5), 527–537.

Grossman, A. H., D'Augelli, A. R., & Salter, N. P. (2006). Male-to-female transgender youth: Gender expression milestones, gender atypicality, victimization and parents' responses. *Journal of GLBT Family Studies, 21*(1), 71–92.

Grov, C., Bimbi, D. S., Nanin, J. E., & Parsons, J. T. (2006). Race, ethnicity, gender, and generational factors associated with the coming-out process among gay, lesbian, and bisexual individuals. *Journal of Sex Research, 43*(3), 115–122.

Haldeman, D. C. (2000). Gender atypical youth: Clinical and social issues. *School Psychology Review, 29*(2), 192–200.

Hansbury, G. (2004). Transgender subjectivities: A clinician's guide. *Journal of Gay & Lesbian Psychotherapy, 8*(1/2), 7–18.

Hart, T. A., & Heimberg, R. G. (2001). Presenting problems among treatment-seeking gay, lesbian, and bisexual youth. *JCLP/In Session: Psychotherapy in Practice, 57*(5), 615–627.

Hartinger, B. (2003). *Geography club.* New York: HarperTempest.

Herdt, G. (2001). Social change, sexual diversity, and tolerance for bisexuality in the United States. In A. R. D'Augelli & C. J. Patterson (Eds.), *Lesbian, gay, and bisexual identities and youth* (pp. 267–283). New York: Oxford University Press.

Heron, A. (Ed.). (1994). *Two teenagers in twenty: Writings of gay and lesbian youth.* Boston: Alyson.

Hershberger, S. L., & D'Augelli, A. R. (1995). The impact of victimization on the mental health and suicidality of lesbian, gay and bisexual youth. *Developmental Psychology, 31*, 65–74.

Hershberger, S., & D'Augelli, A. R. (2000). Issues in counseling lesbian, gay, and bisexual adolescents (pp. 225–247). In R. M. Perez, K. A. DeBord, & K. J. Bieschke (Eds.), *Handbook of counseling and psychotherapy with lesbian, gay, and bisexual clients.* Washington, DC: American Psychological Association.

Hershberger, S. L., Pilkington, N. W., & D'Augelli, A. R. (1997). Predictors of suicide attempts among gay, lesbian, and bisexual youth. *Journal of Adolescent Research, 12*(4), 477–497.

Holland, A. (Producer). (2006, June 19). *A girl like me* [Television broadcast]. LifeTime.

Holman, C. W., & Goldberg, J. M. (2006). *Social and medical advocacy with transgender people and loved ones: Recommendations for BC practitioners.* Vancouver, Canada: Vancouver Coastal Health, Transcend Transgender Support & Education Society, and Canadian Rainbow Health Coalition. Retrieved April 11, 2007, from http://www.vch.ca/transhealth

Horn, S. S. (2007). Adolescents' acceptance of same-sex peers based upon sexual orientation and gender expression. *Journal of Youth & Adolescence, 36*(3), 363–371.

Hunter, J., & Mallon, G. P. (2000). Lesbian, gay and bisexual adolescent development: Dancing with your feet tied together. In B. Greene & G. L. Croom (Eds.), *Research and practice in lesbian, gay, bisexual, and transgender psychology: A resource manual* (pp. 226–243). Thousand Oaks, CA: Sage.

Intersex Society of North America. (2006). *Clinical guidelines for the management of disorders of sex development in childhood.* Retrieved April 11, 2007, from http://www.dsdguidelines.org

Israel, G. E. (2005). Translove: Transgender persons and their families. *Journal of GLBT Family Studies, 1*(1), 53–67.

Israel, G. E., & Tarver, D. E. (1997). *Transgender care.* Philadelphia: Temple University Press.

Jeffreys, S. (2005). Judicial child abuse: The family court of Australia, gender identity disorder, and the "Alex" case. *Women's Studies International Forum, 29*(1), 1–12.

Jennings, K. (2003). *Always my child: A parent's guide to understanding your gay, lesbian, bisexual, transgendered or questioning son or daughter.* New York: Fireside.

Jordan, K. (2000). Substance abuse among gay, lesbian, bisexual, transgender, and questioning adolescents. *School Psychology Review, 29*(2), 201–207.

Jordan, N. (Director). (1992). *The crying game* [Motion picture]. United States: Miramax Films.

Kessler, S. (1990). The medical construction of gender: Case management of intersexed infants. *Signs, 16*, 3–26.

Kessler, S. (1998). *Lessons from the intersexed*. New Brunswick, NJ: Rutgers University Press.

Kitts, R. L. (2005). Gay adolescents and suicide: Understanding the association. *Adolescence, 40*, 621–628.

Klein, F. (1990). The need to view sexual orientation as a multivariable dynamic process: A theoretical perspective. In D. P. McWhirter, S. A. Sanders, & J. M. Remisch (Eds.), *Homosexuality/heterosexuality: Concepts of sexual orientation* (pp. 277–282). New York: Oxford University Press.

Klein, F., Sepekoff, B., & Wolf, T. J. (1985). Sexual orientation: A multi-variable dynamic process. *Journal of Homosexuality, 11*(1/2), 35–50.

Kohlberg, L. (1966). A cognitive-developmental analysis of children's sex-role concepts and attitudes. In E. E. Maccoby (Ed.), *The development of sex differences* (pp. 82–173). Stanford, CA: Stanford University Press.

Lemoire, S. J., & Chen, C. P. (2005). Applying person-centered counseling to sexual minority adolescents. *Journal of Counseling and Development, 83*(2), 146–154.

Lev, A. I. (2004). *Transgender emergence: Therapeutic guidelines for working with gender-variant people and their families*. New York: Haworth Press.

Lev, A. I. (2006). Intersexuality in the family: An unacknowledged trauma. *Journal of Gay & Lesbian Psychotherapy, 10*(2), 27–56.

Little, J. N. (2001). Embracing gay, lesbian, bisexual, and transgendered youth in school-based settings. *Child & Youth Care Forum, 30*(2), 99–110.

Marshal, M. P., Friedman, M. S., Stall, R., King, K. M., Miles, J., Gold, M. A., et al. (2008). Sexual orientation and adolescent substance use: A meta-analysis and methodological review. *Addiction, 103*, 546–556.

McCann, L., & Pearlman, L. A. (1990). *Psychological trauma and the adult survivor: Theory, therapy, and transformation*. New York: Brunner/Mazel.

McDaniel, J. S., Purcell, D., & D'Augelli, A. R. (2001). The relationship between sexual orientation and risk for suicide: Research findings and future directions for research and prevention. *Suicide & Life-Threatening Behavior, 31*, 84–105.

Meyer, I. H. (1995). Minority stress and mental health in gay men. *Journal of Health & Social Behaviors, 36*, 38–56.

Meyer, W., Bockting, W., Cohen-Kettenis, P., Coleman, E., DiCeglie, D., Devor, H., et al. (2001). The standards of care for gender identity disorders, sixth version [Electronic version] . *International Journal of Transgenderism, 5*(1). Retrieved April 17, 2005, from www.symposion.com/ijt/soc_.05.htm

Morrison, L. L., & L'Heureux, J. (2001). Suicide and gay/lesbian/bisexual youth: Implications for practitioners. *Journal of Adolescence, 24*(1), 39–49.

Morrow, D. F. (2004). Social work practice with gay, lesbian, bisexual, and transgender adolescents. *Families in Society, 85*(1), 91–99.

Moser, B. (2005, February 10). The murder of a boy named Gwen [Electronic version]. *Rolling Stone*. Retrieved July 14, 2006, from http://www.rollingstone.com/news/story/6959159/the_murder_of_a_boy_named_gwen

Murdock, T. B., & Bolch, M. B. (2005). Risk and protective factors for poor school adjustment in lesbian, gay, and bisexual (LGB) high school youth: Variable and person-centered analyses. *Psychology in the Schools, 42*(2), 159–172.

Oggins, J., & Eichenbaum, J. (2002). Engaging transgender substance users in substance use treatment [Electronic version]. *International Journal of Transgenderism, 6*(2). Retrieved from http://www.symposion.com/ijt/ijtvo06no02_03.htm

O'Keefe, T. (Ed.). (2003). *Finding the real me: True tales of sex and gender diversity*. New York: Jossey-Bass.

Owens, R. E. (1998). *Queer kids: The challenge and promise for lesbian, gay, and bisexual youth*. Binghamton, NY: Haworth Press.

Pazos, S. (1999). Practice with female-to-male transgendered youth. *Journal of Gay & Lesbian Social Services, 10*(3/4), 65–82.

Peplau, L. A., & Beals, K. P. (2004). The family lives of lesbians and gay men. In A. L. Vangelisti (Ed.), *Handbook of family communication* (pp. 233–248). Mahwah, N.J.: Erlbaum.

Peters, A. J. (2003). Isolation or inclusion: Creating safe spaces for lesbian and gay youth. *Families in Society: The Journal of Contemporary Human Services, 84*(3), 331–337.

Peters, L. A. (2005). *Luna*. New York: Little, Brown.

Potoczniak, D. J. (2007). Development of bisexual men's identities and relationships. In K. J. Bieschke, R. M. Perez, & K. A. DeBord (Eds.), *Handbook of counseling and psychotherapy with lesbian, gay, bisexual, and transgender clients* (2nd ed., pp. 119–145). Washington, DC: American Psychological Association.

Raj, R. (2002). Towards a transpositive therapeutic model: Developing clinical sensitivity and cultural competence in the effective support of transsexual and transgendered clients [Electronic version]. *International Journal of Transgenderism, 6*(2), Retrieved April 7, 2005, from http://www.symposion.com/ijtvo06no02_04.htm.

Rekers, G. A. (1995). Assessment and treatment methods for gender identity disorders and transvestism. In G. A. Rekers (Ed.), *Handbook of child and adolescent sexual problems* (pp. 272–289). New York: Lexington Books.

Rekers, G., & Lovass, I. (1974). Behavioral treatment of deviant sex-role behaviors in a male child. *Journal of Applied Behavior Analysis, 7*(2), 173–190.

Remafedi, G. (1987). Male homosexuality: The adolescent's perspective. *Pediatrics, 79*(3), 326–330.

Remafedi, G., Farrow, J. A., & Deisher, R. W. (1991). Risk factors for attempted suicide in gay and bisexual youth. *Pediatrics, 87*(6), 869–875.

Rieger, G., Linsenmeier, J. W., Gygax, L., & Bailey, M. J. (2008). Sexual orientation and childhood gender nonconformity: Evidence from home videos. *Developmental Psychology, 44*(1), 46–58.

Ringo, P. (2002). Media roles in female-to-male transsexual and transgender identity formation [Electronic version]. *International Journal of Transgenderism, 6*(3). Retrieved June 9, 2006, from http://www.symposion.com/ijt/ijtvo06no03_01.htm

Roesler, T., & Deisher, R. W. (1972, February 21). Youthful male homosexuality: Homosexual experience and the process of developing homosexual identity in males aged 16 to 22 years. *Journal of the American Medical Association, 219*(8), 1018–1023.

Rosario, M., Schrimshaw, E. W., Hunter, J., & Gwadz, M. (2002). Gay-related stress and emotional distress among gay, lesbian, and bisexual youths: A longitudinal examination. *Journal of Consulting & Clinical Psychology, 70*(4), 967–975.

Rosario, V. A. (2004). "Que joto bonita!": Transgender negotiations of sex and ethnicity. *Journal of Gay & Lesbian Psychotherapy, 8*(1/2), 89–97.

Rosenberg, M. (2002). Children with gender identity issues and their parents in individual and group treatment. *Journal of the American Academy of Child & Adolescent Psychiatry, 41*(5), 619–621.

Rottnek, M. (1999). *Sissies and tomboys: Gender nonconformity and homosexual childhood.* New York: New York University Press.

Russell, S. T. (2006). Substance use and abuse, and mental health among sexual-minority youths: Evidence from ADD Health. In A. M. Omoto & H. S. Kurtzman (Eds.), *Sexual orientation and mental health: Examining identity and development in lesbian, gay, and bisexual people* (pp. 13–35). Washington, DC: American Psychological Association.

Russell, S. T., Driscoll, A. K., & Truong, N. L. (2002). Adolescent same sex romantic attractions and relationships: Implications for substance use and abuse. *American Journal of Public Health, 92*(2), 198–202.

Russell, S. T., & Joyner, K. (2001). Adolescent sexual orientation and suicide risk: Evidence from a national study. *American Journal of Public Health, 91*(8), 1276–1281.

Russell, S. T., & Seif, H. M. (2002). Bisexual female adolescents: A critical review of past research, and results from a national study. *Journal of Bisexuality, 2*, 73–94.

Russell, S. T., Seif, H. M., & Truong, N. L. (2001). School outcomes of sexual minority youth in the United States: Evidence from a national study. *Journal of Adolescence, 24*(1), 111–127.

Rutter, P. A., & Soucar, E. (2002). Youth suicide risk and sexual orientation. *Adolescence, 37* (146), 289–299.

Ryan, C. (2001). Counseling lesbian, gay, and bisexual youths. In A. R. D'Augelli & C. J. Patterson (Eds.), *Lesbian, gay, and bisexual identities and youth* (pp. 224–250). New York: Oxford University Press.

Ryan, C., & Futterman, D. (1998). *Lesbian & gay youth: Care & counseling.* New York: Columbia University Press.

Ryan, J. R. (2006). *Sargent camp.* Unpublished manuscript.

Safren, S. A., & Heimberg, R. G. (1999). Depression, hopelessness, suicidality and related factors in sexual minority and heterosexual adolescents. *Journal of Consulting & Clinical Psychology, 67*, 859–886.

Safren, S. A., & Pantalone, D. W. (2006). Social anxiety and barriers to resilience among lesbian, gay, and bisexual adolescents (pp. 55–71). In A. M. Omoto & H. S. Kurtzman (Eds.), *Sexual orientation and mental health: Examining identity and development in lesbian, gay, and bisexual people.* Washington, DC: American Psychological Association.

Sanchez, A. (2001). *Rainbow boys.* New York: Simon & Schuster Children's Publishing.

Savin-Williams, R. C. (1995). Lesbian, gay male, and bisexual adolescents. In A. R. D'Augelli & C. J. Patterson (Eds.), *Lesbian, gay, bisexual identities over the lifespan: Psychological perspectives* (pp. 165–189). New York: Oxford University Press

Savin-Williams, R. C. (1998)."…*and then I became gay: Young men's stories.*" New York: Routledge.

Savin-Williams, R. C. (2001). *Mom, Dad, I'm gay.* Washington, DC: American Psychological Association.

Savin-Williams, R. C. (2005). *The new gay teenager.* Cambridge, MA: Harvard University Press.

Schindhelm, R. K., & Hospers, H. J. (2004). Sex with men before coming-out: Relation to sexual activity and sexual risk-taking behavior. *Archives of Sexual Behavior, 33*(6), 585–591.

Schrock, D., Reid, L., & Boyd, E. (2005). Transsexuals' embodiment of womanhood. *Gender & Society, 19*(3), 317–335.

Seil, D. (2004). The diagnosis and treatment of trans-gendered patients. *Journal of Gay & Lesbian Psychotherapy, 8*(1/2), 99–116.

Spade, D. (2006). Mutilating gender. In S. Stryker & S. Whittle (Eds.), *The trans studies reader* (pp. 315–332). New York: Routledge.

Spiegel, A. (Executive Producer). (2008, May 7). Two families grapple with their son's gender preferences. [Radio broadcast]. New York and Washington, DC: National Public Radio.

Swann, S., & Herbert, S. E. (1999). Ethical issues in the mental health treatment of gender dysphoric adolescents. *Journal of Gay & Lesbian Social Services, 10*(3/4), 19–34.

Tarver, D. E. (2002). Transgender mental health: The intersection of race, sexual orientation, and gender identity. In B. E. Jones & M. J. Hill (Eds.), *Mental health issues in lesbian, gay, bisexual, and transgender communities* (pp. 93–108). Washington, DC: American Psychiatric Association.

Troiden, R. R. (1979). Becoming homosexual: A model of gay identity acquisition. *Psychiatry, 42*(4), 362–373.

Tucker, D. (Director). (2005). *Transamerica* [Motion picture]. United States: Weinstein Co.

Waldo, C. R., Hesson-McInnis, M. S., & D'Augelli, A. R. (1998). Antecedents and consequences of victimization of lesbian, gay, and bisexual young people: A structural model comparing rural university and urban samples. *American Journal of Community Psychology, 26*(2), 307–335.

Wilchins, R. (1997). *Read my lips: Sexual subversion and the end of gender.* Ithaca, NY: Firebrand.

Williams, T., Connolly, J., Pepler, D., & Craig, W. (2005). Peer victimization, social support, and psychosocial adjustment of sexual minority adolescents. *Journal of Youth & Adolescence, 34*(5), 471–482.

Wood, M. J. (2004). The gay male gaze: Body image disturbance and gender oppression among gay men. *Journal of Gay & Lesbian Social Services, 17*(2), 43–62.

Young, R., & Sweeting, H. (2004). Adolescent bullying, relationships, psychological well-being, and gender-atypical behavior: A gender diagnosticity approach. *Sex Roles, 50*(7/8), 525–537.

Ziyadeh, N. J., Prokop, L. A., Fisher, L. B., Rosario, M., Field, A. E., Camargo, C. A., et al. (2007). Sexual orientation, gender and alcohol use in a cohort study of U.S. adolescent girls and boys. *Drug & Alcohol Dependence, 87* (2–3), 119–130.

Zucker, K. J., & Bradley, S. J. (1995). *Gender identity disorder and psychosexual problems in children and adolescents.* New York: Guilford Press.

CHAPTER 7

Sexual and Gender Minority Couples

INTRODUCTION

In the narrative below, our anonymous author describes her often painful struggle to accept her husband's decision to change sex. Although her marriage appears to have remained intact, such a situation would constitute an insurmountable crisis for most couples. Now reflect how you might respond to a partner's intention to change sex—or how, as a helping professional, you would work with this couple and others who might be at that critical juncture in their lives. Here is her poignant story:

Why shouldn't I be hurt? Why couldn't I cry about it? Was my heart not broken by his words? He wanted to be a woman; not my male lover anymore but my female lover. I just couldn't understand and so I grieved for myself.

After holding all my questions and feelings in, I finally broke down. I began bombarding my husband with every question I could think of regarding his thoughts, feelings, and past history. It took days to get all the questions out and some were still unanswered, but now he understood my feelings and fears and I understood his. This opened up our hearts and allowed us to be honest with each other. It also helped me to finally comprehend his position and how it affected him. His hope that it could work out became mine. I truly believe that because we were honest with each other, we were able to get through it all.

I know that, no matter what, the person I love loves me, and that whatever the outward appearance, it's the inner personality that truly matters. I now find great joy in teaching my spouse what it is to be my sex. We have a great time together shopping for clothing and shoes. We look through women's magazines, discuss hair styles, and even dress each other up. I feel that now I have a friend, as well as a lover, in my spouse. This closeness of sharing and being an active part of my spouse's new life has made what was once dreadful and depressing now a wonderfully new and exciting experience. The more I saw him as her, the more used to it I became. I know now I couldn't see her any other way. (*Source:* From "A Partner Speaks" by Anonymous (1999). In L. Hubschman (Ed.), *Transsexuals: Life from Both Sides* (pp. 87–89). Darby, PA: Diane Publishing. Reprinted with permission.)

A Preview of Chapter Contents

This chapter looks at such challenges—personal and professional—in depth as it covers the following:

- The empirical research on questions and issues that seem to have captivated investigators for over 25 years: How do heterosexual, gay, and lesbian couples compare on a number of relationship dynamics, including communication, conflict resolution, sexual functioning, relationship satisfaction, and duration? Are the dynamics that contribute to intimate partner violence comparable to those that characterize battering in heterosexual couples?
- The literature that explores the impact of gender variance on intimate relationships and the issues that arise for heterosexual couples when partners decide to transition after their relationships have been established.
- Counseling guidelines and interventions that are germane to the needs of sexual and gender minority couples.

COMPARING DYADIC ADJUSTMENT IN SEXUAL MINORITY AND HETEROSEXUAL COUPLES

A Caveat

Before surveying the research, the reader should be cautioned that as is often the case with stigmatized populations, investigators have had to rely on volunteer convenience samples consisting predominantly of white, urban, and well-educated participants (Peplau, Fingerhut, & Beals, 2004; Peplau & Spalding, 2003). In the past, the most efficient mode of collecting data on sexual minority persons was to distribute questionnaires at gay community organizations and events. When these samples were contrasted with samples of heterosexuals, researchers often failed to match both groups on demographic characteristics (Kurdek, 2004) and to distinguish couples who are casually dating from those who are in long-term, committed relationships (Todosijevic, Rothblum, & Solomon, 2005). Researchers also relied too heavily on self-reports of participants (Gottman et al., 2003) and on measures that lacked established psychometric properties (Kurdek, 2004).

More recently, some investigators (i.e., Solomon, Rothblum, & Balsam, 2004) have begun the practice of eliciting participation from sexual minorities who have, in turn, recruited their heterosexual siblings for comparison purposes. Still others (Roisman, Clausell, Holland, Fortuna, & Elieff, 2008) employ multiple methods, such as self-report measures, recorded laboratory observations of couples, and physiological measures of partners during couple interactions.

However, there still remains a gap in the research on couples where one or both partners are self-identified as bisexuals. Empirical research incorporating the full spectrum of gender minorities is scarce. This would include gender minority couples who express their gender identities without the use of surgical and hormonal intervention or who consider themselves to be gender variant.

The bulk of the literature on gender minority couples comprises observations made by therapists who have worked in clinical settings with persons who are interested in transitioning from male to female (MTF) (Brown & Rounsley, 1996). Much of this published work on gender minority couples was written from a psychopathological perspective. As a case in point, women who were married to male cross-dressers were portrayed in the literature as "masochists" and "malicious male haters" (Stoller, 1967). Brown (1998), a psychiatrist, observed:

> One could make the case that the existing literature was potentially damaging to these couples in its inappropriate generalizations and unsupported conclusions and did nothing to facilitate the process of communication and self-disclosure so vital to these relationships. (p. 354)

"American Couples": Then and Now

In the early 1980s, sociologists Blumstein and Schwartz undertook an extensive exploration of couples, the first of its kind to incorporate cohabitating lesbian, gay, and heterosexual couples. Blumstein and Schwartz assessed 12,000 couples (including 788 lesbian and 969 gay male couples). Their research explored several dimensions of couple relationships, including relationship satisfaction, division of household labor, finances, sexual frequency and monogamy, and communication and conflict resolution skills. Their findings were published in the classic text *American Couples* (1983). Blumstein and Schwartz discovered that couples did not differ on overall relationship satisfaction. Compared to heterosexual couples, lesbian and gay male couples were more egalitarian in terms of the division of household labor and financial arrangements and were less likely to experience conflicts over these issues. Gay couples, particularly those in short-term relationships, reported having sex more often than did other couples, and lesbian couples reported having sex less often than gay and heterosexual couples. Most heterosexual and lesbian couples were monogamous, while gay couples were predominately nonmonogamous. Among couples who had been together 10 years, breakup rates over the 18 months of the study were highest for lesbians (6%), gay couples (4%), and married couples (4%).

Approximately 22 years after the publication of Blumstein and Schwartz's work, Solomon, Rothblum, and Balsam (2005) replicated their study. Solomon et al. included a unique sample of sexual minority couples, those whose relationships were legalized through civil unions in Vermont. For the first time in history, researches were able to compare legally married heterosexual couples and same-sex couples in civil unions who were, therefore, "matched" in terms of their level of relationship commitment. Solomon et al. adapted Blumstein and Schwartz's original questionnaire, which included items related to division of finances, household chores, sexual and relationship maintenance behaviors, and conflict. Their sample consisted of 336 gay and lesbian members of civil unions in Vermont, 238 members of same-sex couples not in civil unions, and 413 married heterosexual couples. Gay and lesbian couples who were in civil unions and those who were not in civil unions were more egalitarian than were heterosexual couples in terms of finances and relationship maintenance behaviors. Women in heterosexual couples reported performing more household tasks than did their partners, while lesbian and gay couples in civil unions and not in civil unions shared household activities equally. Gay, lesbian, and heterosexual couples reported similar levels of sexual satisfaction. However, lesbian couples reported having sex less often than did gay and heterosexual couples. Overall, their results seemed fairly comparable to those of Blumstein and Schwartz over 20 years earlier.

In the years after the publication of *American Couples* in 1983, other researchers explored numerous dimensions of same-sex relationships. Chief among these is psychologist Lawrence Kurdek, who has been especially prolific in terms of his work on couples. The following sections cover more about his work as well as the efforts of others who have explored such relationship dynamics as relationship duration, satisfaction, autonomy and intimacy, communication and conflict resolution, relational validation and social support, and sexuality.

Relationship Satisfaction and Duration

According to several researchers (Blumstein & Schwartz, 1983; Kurdek, 1991a; Kurdek & Schmitt, 1986; Metz, Rosser, & Strapko, 1994), heterosexual, gay, and lesbian couples report similar levels of relationship satisfaction. Because most of these studies were based on single assessments of relationship satisfaction, Kurdek (1998) decided to follow heterosexual, gay, and lesbian couples longitudinally and reported that same-sex partners did not differ from heterosexual partners in perceived relationship satisfaction over a five-year period. Kurdek also found that the breakup rates between couples were comparable to those reported by Blumstein and Schwartz (1983), with gay and lesbian couples being more likely than heterosexual couples to end their relationships over the five-year period.

Intimacy and Autonomy

Kurdek (1998) had also followed married heterosexual couples and gay and lesbian cohabiting couples over a five-year period with regard to intimacy ("merging the self and the other") and autonomy ("maintaining a sense of self separated from the relationship") (p. 554). At the one-year point, lesbian couples reported significantly higher levels of intimacy than did gay and heterosexual couples. However, by the fifth year there were no differences in reported levels of intimacy among couples. Lesbian and gay partners reported consistently higher levels of autonomy than did heterosexual partners.

In 2004, Kurdek compared sexual minority couples who were cohabitating without children with married heterosexual couples with and without children. In all cases, sexual minority partners reported higher levels of autonomy than did heterosexual couples with children. This was not so when they were compared to heterosexual couples without children.

Communication and Conflict Resolution

Studies exploring relational conflict have found no differences in areas of conflict (Kurdek, 1994), frequency of conflict (Kurdek, 1994; Metz et al., 1994), and use of constructive problem solving (Kurdek, 1994) between same-sex and heterosexual partners. In contrast, Metz et al. (1994) reported that women in lesbian relationships reported significantly greater hope of conflict resolution and more effective conflict-resolution styles than did either gay male couples or heterosexual couples.

John Gottman, who is a relationship expert, has been especially prolific while pursuing his innovative research agenda, combining self-report measures, measures of physiological arousal, and videotapes of interactions between heterosexual and same-sex couples. Gottman and his colleagues identified communication patterns and emotions that seem to predict the viability of relationships. Their work (Gottman Institute, 2004) also integrated self-report measures, videotaped interactions, and interviews with 21 gay, 21 lesbian, and 42 heterosexual couples over a 12-year period. Gottman noted that gay and lesbian couples remained more positive after disagreements and tended to use more affection and humor when they dealt with a disagreement than did their heterosexual counterparts. They were less belligerent and domineering than were heterosexual couples. They also took disagreements less personally than did heterosexual couples. Lesbian couples seemed more emotionally expressive than were gay male couples, as they showed more anger, more excitement, and more interest in their partners than gay male couples did (Gottman Institute, 2004).

The capacity of lesbian couples to stay emotionally engaged was also supported in a study by Roisman et al. (2008) in which lesbian dyads had significantly more relational skills in laboratory couple interactions than did persons in gay male and heterosexual couples.

Social Support and Barriers to Leaving

Research (Bryant & Demian, 1994; Kurdek & Schmitt, 1987) has generally been consistent in suggesting that sexual minorities receive less social support, specifically from family members, for their relationships. In surveys of same-sex couples, most report that other sexual minorities are their greatest source of social support. For example, in one national survey, same-sex couples ranked their heterosexual friends and co-workers ahead of their mothers and fathers in terms of social support (Bryant & Demian, 1994). In 2001, Kurdek explored gay and lesbian couples, heterosexual couples who were parents, and heterosexual nonparent couples at various time intervals on a number of dimensions, including social support. The differences among the types of couples were minimal with the exception of social support from family members. As anticipated, lesbian and gay couples reported receiving less social validation and support for their relationships than did heterosexual couples. Heterosexual partners reported more barriers to leaving their relationships than did lesbian and gay partners (Kurdek, 1998). Barriers were defined as "anything that increases the psychological, emotional, or financial costs of ending the relationship" (Peplau & Spalding, 2003, p. 463).

In his longitudinal study of cohabiting heterosexual, gay, and lesbian couples published in 2004, Kurdek compared couples on several measures of relationship functioning. On most measures, there were no differences between couples. When differences were found, the majority (78%) indicated that gay or lesbian partners functioned better than did their heterosexual counterparts. The only area in which lesbian and gay couples were functioning below heterosexual partners was that of social support. Specifically, sexual minorities received less support for their relationships from family members.

Todosijevic et al. (2005) explored stressors in 313 sexual minority couples who were in civil unions in Vermont and reported that lesbian couples experienced more stress related to family members' reactions to their sexual orientation than did gay male couples. In contrast, gay male couples reported more stress associated with HIV/AIDS and violence/harassment based on sexual orientation.

Sexual Intimacy

Comparative studies (i.e., Blumstein & Schwartz, 1983; Kurdek, 1991b; Solomon et al., 2005) of gay, lesbian, and heterosexual couples find similar levels of sexual satisfaction. However, lesbian couples reported having sex less often than did gay and heterosexual couples. Gay male couples were found to be less monogamous than were lesbian partners or married heterosexual men and women (Solomon et al., 2005). Surveys conducted after the onset of the AIDS epidemic continued to suggest that monogamy rates among gay men were lower than for lesbian and heterosexual couples (Bryant & Demian, 1994).

A Synthesis of Research Findings

The research outlined above suggests that sexual minority couples and heterosexual couples are alike in many respects. Both experience similar rewards as well as stresses in their relationships, including decisions about parenting and child rearing, career issues and employment concerns, family of origin issues, household chores, and finances (Bepko & Johnson, 2000; Long, Burnett, & Thomas, 2006). Yet there are also some general differences between same-sex and straight couples. For example, same-sex partners, especially lesbians, seem to prioritize equality in their relationships and divide finances and household tasks in a more egalitarian fashion than do heterosexual couples (Kurdek, 1995). Same-sex couples generally perceive family members as less supportive of their relationships than do heterosexual couples, which may account for the more active role that ex-partners play in the lives and friendship networks of sexual minorities (Bohan, 1996; Harkless & Fowers, 2005). In general, sexual minority couples tend to terminate their relationships more frequently than do their married heterosexual counterparts (Kurdek, 1998).

Lesbian and gay male couples also differ in certain aspects of their relationships. Lesbian couples tend to value the expression of emotion. Gay male couples were found to be less monogamous than were lesbian partners or married heterosexual men and women (Kurdek, 1995; Solomon et al., 2005).

Competing Hypotheses

A number of competing hypotheses have been offered to explain the findings outlined above. One view is that cultural forces concomitant with heterosexism leave sexual minority couples lacking in legal, social, and religious support for their relationships. As a case in point, many blame the more frequent relationship dissolutions in sexual minority couples on the lack of legal protection and family support.

Harkless and Fowers (2005) have written about how the lack of family support impacts sexual minority couples. While noting the importance of ex-partners in the lives of sexual minorities, they also observed that such involvements can pose unique emotional challenges to subsequent partners and may also evoke feelings of jealousy and competition among partners. Harkless and Fowers considered the ability to maintain friendships with ex-partners as mostly positive evidence of relational boundaries that are fluid. They found this phenomenon among sexual minority couples to be consistent with the view that discrimination and oppression from society foster emotional intimacy in these couples. Discrimination and lack of societal support and validation can cause partners in sexual minority relationships to adopt a "two against the world" perspective and isolate themselves from the outer world.

Others view the patterns of differences, as well as similarities, between same-sex and heterosexual couples as a byproduct of the fact that same-sex couples comprise two partners who have experienced similar gender-role socialization. Several authors and practitioners have noted that when two people of the same sex are intimately involved with one another, the resulting dynamics between them will likely reflect the compounding effects of socialization. Ossana (2000) termed this phenomenon *socialization squared*.

The idea that various aspects of lesbian relationships, such as autonomy and sexuality, might differ as result of the duplicative gender-role socialization was originally popularized in the now-classic article published in 1980 by Krestan and Bepko titled "The Problem of Fusion in the Lesbian Relationship." The authors argued that merger, defined as a condition in which two partners in a relationship think, feel, or act as if they were the same, is more pervasive among lesbian couples than gay or heterosexual couples. Krestan and Bepko (1980) accounted for this phenomenon by reminding readers of the gender socialization experiences for women, which emphasize relational skills and prioritize relationships over autonomy. Research has also suggested that lesbian partners tend to be overly dependent on and enmeshed with one another (Bohan, 1996; Burch, 1982; Krestan & Bepko, 1980; Scrivner & Eldridge, 1995; Slater & Mencher, 1991) and have difficulty asserting their individual needs. Researchers attributed lower rates of sexual contact between lesbian partners to the impact of gender-role socialization, which leads women to repress sexual feelings and experience difficulty being sexually assertive (Green & Mitchell, 2002; Peplau et al., 2004).

In a similar manner, researchers have looked at relationship difficulties experienced by gay male couples. These studies typically concerned issues of intimacy, emotional expression, and competion with one another in terms of salaries and initiation of sex (Green, Bettinger, & Zacks, 1996; Green & Mitchell, 2002). The research attributed these difficulties to the impact of male gender-role socialization, which emphasizes autonomy and achievement.

An obvious problem with the socialization squared hypothesis is that it presumes that gender-role socialization has not changed in the last 20–30 years. However, women, in particular, have seen huge changes in their earning potentials, career options, childbearing options, and so on.

An alternative explanation for the emotional dynamics commonly noted among gay male couples combines both psychodynamic and sociocultural factors. Alonzo (2005), Greenan and Tunnell (2003), and Mohr (1999) incorporated John Bowlby's work on attachment to account for relational distancing in gay male couples. Bowlby theorized that infants form internal working models of how relationships will be, based on their early experiences with primary caregivers. Even if those models are positive, the emerging sense of same-sex attraction, which occurs for many in adolescence, may threaten these models. In other words, the attachment process, which begins in infancy, may be disrupted in adolescence as children start to perceive themselves as different from their parental caregivers and parents are not able to validate them. Children may move into adulthood feeling ambivalence or avoiding intimacy. Greenan and Tunnell (2003), both practitioners, believe that gay men are ambivalent about closeness partly because of their socialization experiences as males and partly because of their early childhood experiences. Many learn from a young age to repress or deny their own internal experiences and to adopt a "false self" (p. 33) in order to gain the acceptance and approval of others. "A gay male often learns it is not safe to turn to others when feeling vulnerable, particularly to other males" (p. 33).

Debate continues in terms of which factor, heterosexism or gender-role socialization, is more influential in determining relationship dynamics in sexual minority couples (Harkless & Fowers, 2005). To add further confusion, it is conceivable that research findings are also partly an artifact of methodological and conceptual limitations. For example, with reference to the finding of lower rates of sexual frequency among lesbian couples, sometimes referred to as "lesbian death bed" (Iasenza, 2002), one might also consider this to be an artifact of the way in which sexual activity is defined and operationalized by researchers (Sandfort & de Keizer, 2001). Tolman and Diamond (2001) raised similar issues in their critique of sexuality research, saying that it tends to focus on tabulating sex acts, especially those that are genitally focused. This has significance for the assessment of sexual activities in lesbian couples, who report more nongenital sexual contact such as kissing and hugging (MacDonald, 1998).

Bisexual Couples

Empirical research on relational dynamics between couples comprised of one or more bisexual partners is relatively sparse (Buxton, 2004; Ossana, 2000). Much of the limited research on bisexual couples has focused on issues of sexual monogamy and HIV. For example, in one of the most frequently cited studies of bisexual couples, Weinberg, Williams, and Pryor (1994) interviewed bisexual men and women in San Francisco in the 1980s and reported that the majority of their participants were in sexually nonmonogamous relationships.

In a more recent study, Rust (2003) surveyed 577 gay, lesbian, bisexual, and heterosexual respondents. The bisexual men and women in her sample were more likely than the lesbians, gay men, and heterosexuals to form polyamorous relationships or simultaneous sexual involvements with two or more partners. Rust noted a number of different types of polyamorous relationships in her sample, including:

- "Nonsexual lovers"
- "Cuddle bunnies" (partners experience varying degrees of sexual activity and emotional involvement)
- "Fuck buddies" (partners experience sexual activity with one another)
- Acquaintance or stranger sexual relationships

Rust (2003) also reported that bisexual women and men most often preferred having a "primary" relationship with a partner and a "secondary partner(s)" with whom they had encounters of a sexual, romantic, or emotional nature. A similar pattern has been observed in gay male couples (Bettinger, 2006).

Mixed Orientation Couples

Mixed orientation couples are defined as those comprised of one partner who is heterosexual and another partner who is gay, lesbian, or bisexual (Buxton, 2006). Buxton, who is executive director of the Straight Spouse Network (SSN), has been prolific in terms of her research with these couples. Buxton estimates that approximately one-third of mixed orientation couples dissolve shortly after one partner is discovered or comes out. The period following discovery is usually tumultuous for both partners. Often upon discovering their partners are attracted to same-sex persons, spouses experience feelings of shock, confusion, betrayal, and inadequacy related to their sexual performance as well as their gender and sexual orientation (Buxton, 2006). When couples resolve to stay together, there are several strategies that lend themselves to the continuation of these relationships, according to Buxton (2004). In her sample of couples, where male partners were heterosexual and their female partners were either lesbian or bisexual, the most helpful coping strategy in keeping their relationships together was honest communication.

COUNSELING SEXUAL MINORITY COUPLES

The task of counseling sexual minority couples requires that helping professionals critically explore their attitudes and behaviors. Basham (1999) introduced the notion of alpha and beta biases in counseling. *Alpha bias* refers to the tendency to exaggerate the differences between opposite-sex and same-sex couples. For example, therapists might assume that couples consisting of two women are exempt from partner violence, since women are generally socialized to be passive and nonviolent (Basham, 1999). Alternately, *beta bias* refers to the tendency to minimize the differences between opposite- and same-sex couples. Therapists may be guilty of exhibiting beta bias when they assume there are no differences between same-sex and heterosexual relationships. Likewise, therapists may be guided by beta bias when they put undue pressure on partners to self-disclose their orientation to their families of origin. This may actually expose their clients to potential harm (Basham, 1999). Basham (1999) advised:

> Each clinician should walk very carefully along the path of respectful acceptance of diversity without exaggerating differences (where the risk is polarization and bigotry) or ignoring important similarities (where the risk is the illusion of homogeneity and the disqualifying of unique experience). (pp. 143–144)

Assess Homophobia and Biphobia

In order to avoid errors associated with alpha and/or beta bias, the first task in therapy with sexual minority couples is to assess whether or not the couples' issues are related to the unique challenges of being gay, lesbian, or bisexual (Green & Mitchell, 2002). As discussed in Chapter 3, sexual minorities must deal with multiple stressors associated with their status as stigmatized minorities. There are a myriad of ways in which homophobia affects relationship dynamics in sexual minority couples. Here are some examples of the difficulties or challenges sexual minority couples experience as a result of homophobia:

1. Difficulty in meeting new romantic partners because of the comparatively smaller pool of potential partners and limited ways to meet potential partners (Peplau & Spalding, 2003; Sanders, 2000)
2. Fewer available role models (Alonzo, 2005; Ossana, 2000; Sanders, 2000; Spitalnick & McNair, 2005) on which to pattern healthy relationships
3. Lack of validation and ongoing support from families of origin (Bepko & Johnson, 2000)
4. Lack of legal validation and all that this implies about monogamous relationships: finances, caring for each other and each other's families during serious illnesses and old age, and health care powers of attorney in times of medical emergency (Green & Mitchell, 2002; Spitalnick & McNair, 2005)

5. Discrepancies between partners in relationships in the extent to which each is out to others—these have negative consequences for the overall quality of relationships (Jordan & Deluty, 2000)
6. Lack of rituals to celebrate and publicly validate couple relationships (Ossana, 2000)
7. Increased likelihood of socializing with former partners, given the comparatively small size of the gay community (Marvin & Miller, 2000; Sanders, 2000). While this may be viewed from a positive perspective, it can also engender more complex emotional dynamics, including competition and jealousy among partners

Sanders (2000) suggested that therapists actively "name what is traditionally not commented on in therapy" (p. 228)—that is, the impact of homophobia. Green and Mitchell (2002) suggested interviewing both partners about the various messages they received while growing up about homosexuality and about gender roles from their respective families, schools, churches, neighborhoods, and the media. The following questions developed by Sanders (2000) can be used as a means of stimulating dialogue:

1. How has society's antigay bias affected you as a couple and as individuals?
2. How much have you been able to escape the effects of that bias to date?
3. How much does the bias still trip you up?
4. How much do you worry that I, as your therapist, will fall victim to heterosexist assumptions as we work together? Is this something you as a couple have discussed?
5. If you feel that I am acting in ways that collude with an antigay bias, would you be comfortable in telling me?
6. If not, can you help me understand how come not? (p. 228)

In reviewing some of the common clinical issues that bisexual couples experience, Bradford (2004) noted that most of these stem from biphobia—that is, the common negative stereotypes and misconceptions about bisexuality that are prevalent in our culture. Buxton (2004, 2006) warned against the therapists' tendency to view mixed sexual orientation couples as "doomed."

Martell, Safren, and Prince (2004) recommended the use of cognitive-behavioral therapy with couples in which one or both partners identify as bisexual. For example, partners of bisexual persons in same-sex relationships often experience fear that their bisexual partners will abandon them for the privileged status of other-sex relationships. Often partners also experience trepidation about whether or not their bisexual partners will receive acceptance and validation from the gay and lesbian community. Therapists can provide valuable assistance, helping couples explore the nature of biphobic stereotypes and the assumptions associated with bisexuality. Further, therapists can help couples communicate clearly about their level of relationship commitment and their desire for monogamy/nonmonogamy.

Therapists should also explore the extent to which each partner has internalized homophobia and/or biphobia because, in point of fact, sexual minority couples can sabotage their own relationships as a result of having internalized negative beliefs about homosexuality. The ways this sabotage expresses itself can be both broad and subtle:

• Keeping separate households and finances because of the belief that homosexual relationships don't last
• Using the pronoun "I" rather than "we," even when talking about experiences that involved a partner (Kleinberg & Zorn, 1998)

- Insisting on "passing" as heterosexual despite the lack of risk in coming out
- Suppressing public displays of affection with the partner despite being affectionate with friends and family (Alonzo, 2005)
- Devaluing one's partner because he is too feminine (in the case of gay couples) or she is too masculine (in the case of lesbian couples)
- Hastily ending relationships with their partners before "alternatives can be explored" (Alonzo, 2005)

Another issue that therapists need to assess is the degree of self-disclosure or the degree to which each partner in the relationship is out to others (Green & Mitchell, 2002; McVinney, 1998). For same-sex and bisexual couples, the developmental stage in terms of the individual's sexual identity is a significant variable in counseling. If one partner has only recently come to discover his or her same-sex sexual orientation, this may pose additional challenges and stresses on the relationship.

Assess the Nature and Extent of Social Support/External Validation

Most practitioners agree that it is important to inquire about how each partner perceives his or her current support network. The therapist will need to be thorough, even explicitly asking about issues such as the couple's exact practices to prevent HIV transmission.

1. What does it mean to you that you are a "couple"?
2. What has been your history as a couple?
3. How did your becoming a couple affect your relationships with family members, friends, the lesbian/gay community, and the straight community?
4. What are the rules in your relationship regarding monogamy versus sex outside the relationship? What are the rules in terms of safer sex practices with each other and/or with others?
5. What are your agreements with each other about monthly finances, current or future debts, pooling versus separation of financial resources, ownership of joint property, and other financial planning matters?
6. Who does what tasks in the relationship and in the household, and how is this division or sharing of tasks decided? Are you satisfied with the current division or sharing of these tasks?
7. What do you see as your obligations to each other in terms of caring for each other in the event of illness, injury, or disability?
8. Are you viewing this relationship as a lifetime commitment? If so, have you prepared legal health-care power of attorney documents and wills to protect each other's interests in case of serious illness or death? (Green & Mitchell, 2002, pp. 555–556)

Genograms and/or sociograms can be used to summarize interview material and to provide a visual representation of the social support networks of same-sex couples (Green & Mitchell, 2002). On a cautionary note, however, in their work with lesbian-headed families, Swainson and Tasker (2006) found that the traditional genogram format was not sufficient to capture the presence and significance of nontraditional relationships in these families, including sperm donors, ex-partner relationships, and other family members of choice. When the traditional genogram is reformatted, the exercise of developing modified genograms can be a helpful tool for families to explore the impact of heterosexism and homophobia on their lives (Swainson & Tasker, 2006).

Provide Relationship Validation in the Context of Therapy

Marvin and Miller (2000), Martell et al. (2004), and Rust (2003) argued that therapists can provide a vital means of external support and relationship validation that is often missing for sexual minority couples. Greenan and Tunnell (2003) advanced a number of ideas for affirming the relationships of gay male couples that can be used with any sexual minority couples. These include posing the following questions:

- In what ways, if any, has your relationship been recognized and respected by family and friends?
- Do you have an anniversary date, and how has this date typically been celebrated in the past?
- Have you or will you have a commitment ceremony?
- Do you have children? If not, do you intend on having children?

Along with validating the relationship, therapists can serve as catalysts for couples by proactively discussing potential issues that may arise in the context of the relationship. Often such issues like pooling finances, relocating together when career advancements are offered, and caring for one another in the case of serious illnesses are not automatically expected or assumed and typically are not dealt with until the couple faces a crisis situation (Green & Mitchell, 2002).

Aid Couples in Establishing Rituals That Validate Their Relationships

Many therapists (Marvin & Miller, 2000; Sanders, 2000; Sussal, 1999) emphasized the role of ritual, and specifically the role of commitment ceremonies, in the lives of sexual minority couples. Kleinberg and Zorn (1998) described the use of relationship affirmation in the context of couples groups. They begin their gay and lesbian couples workshops with the "brag exercise," in which partners introduce each other to the group by providing a one-minute description of how he or she is the perfect partner. They terminate the workshop with a candle ceremony, a ritual in which a large candle is lighted to represent the "light and energy of all gay relationships" (p. 146).

Consider the Use of Alternative Therapeutic Approaches

If the therapist ascertains that a couple's issues are not related to homophobia, Green and Mitchell (2002) believe that interventions commonly used with straight couples are appropriate. The use of interventions that have been shown to have strong empirical support, such as behavioral marital therapy and emotionally focused therapy, is recommended (Baucom, Shoham, Mueser, Daiuto, & Stickle, 1998; Johnson & Lebow, 2000). The work of Gottman and his colleagues (1998) is especially useful. This research underscores the negative impact of traditional gender roles. It illustrates certain harmful interaction patterns, such as those characterized by criticism, and it looks at the negative effects of distancing and stonewalling. Emotional distancing seems also to be more detrimental to the health of relationships than are angry interactions.

Two contemporary counseling approaches, imago relationship therapy and narrative therapy, have value for same-sex relationships precisely because they focus on what is often missing for sexual minority couples: empowerment and validation. Imago theory was developed by Hendrix and described in detail in his text *Getting the Love You Want*

(1988). Hendrix employs the Latin word *imago* ("image") to refer to the images we each construct of our ideal romantic partner. These images are based on the positive and negative attributes of our primary caregivers. As adults, we are most attracted to partners based on their degree of resemblance to our imagoes. Given this reality, we are also likely to experience some of the same conflicts and emotional wounds in our significant relationships that we experienced as children. Lest this theory sound overly negative and deterministic, Hendrix proposed that if partners are committed to each other and each is capable of communicating, they can help heal each other's inner wounds.

Children whose sexual and gender identities don't conform to social imperatives are generally rejected by their families, schools, churches, and peers. As a result, sexual and gender minorities must often place undue pressure on their relationship partners to provide affirmation, validation, and mirroring. The consequence is that same-sex couples can often be perceived as too close or merged. The lack of affirmation for many sexual and gender minorities also results in the suppression of feelings and the creation of false, inauthentic selves (Kleinberg & Zorn, 1998). The lack of honesty and authenticity with others has implications for the quality of intimacy in same-sex relationships. Fearing rejection, many same-sex couples refrain from spontaneous signs of affection. The suppression of such behavior may have consequences for couples, including difficulties "loving spontaneously in private as well" (Kleinberg & Zorn, 1998, p. 143).

Imago relationship therapy involves the use of techniques such as a communication exercise called the intention couples dialogue (ICD). This technique is especially effective with sexual and gender minorities who suffer the consequences of lack of validation and mirroring (Kleinberg & Zorn, 1998). ICD consists of three phases: mirroring, validation, and empathy. The role play at the end of this chapter will provide readers with an opportunity to practice this approach.

Hall (2001), Laird (1999, 2000), Sanders (2000), and Green and Mitchell (2002) advocated the use of narrative therapy with sexual minority couples. Hall (2001) maintained that narrative therapy is especially suitable for use with sexual minority couples because they may have already had to redefine themselves in terms of their sexual identities. In addition, narrative therapy offers "specific strategies necessary to rehabilitate widely discredited identities" (p. 280). For example, techniques such as externalizing the problem enable persons who are marginalized to feel a greater sense of control in their lives.

Laird (1999) advocated that therapists assume an "informed not knowing" stance, meaning that they shed their own cultural and personal assumptions and biases and retain, but shelve, professional theories and skills in order to listen to those underlying themes of the clients' story that are inherent in the larger cultural context. The process of deconstruction involves the use of questions by the therapist in order to help clients identify limiting or damaging narratives.

Hall (2001) and Sanders (2000) have identified some of the dominant cultural narratives that lesbian and gay males bring into their intimate relationships with one another. Hall (2001) maintained that among lesbian partners, the expectation that they will form "permanent partnerships" becomes a "central legitimizing strategy" (p. 281). Lesbian partners who are not able to achieve long-lasting relationships are likely to feel a tremendous sense of failure. Therapists have the potential to help lesbian partners by reframing shorter unions as passages and opportunities for growth. Lesbians also tend to prize equality between partners and may have to be reminded that seldom are both partners equal in terms of sexual desire and willingness to be the initiator in a sexual encounter.

Hall also observed that lesbians are predisposed to fuse sex and passion. The therapist might reframe sexual activity as a form of relaxation, diversion, and individuality. Lesbian couples tend to view sex as something that occurs spontaneously and resist the notion that it may have to involve a conscious prioritizing.

Sanders (2000), a sex therapist, identified cultural narratives that seem to apply to straight men as well as gay men. Using the term *genitalization of the heart*, he observed: "many of my male clients, either gay or straight, appear to be 'diving for their hearts with their genitals'" (p. 251). Sanders proposed that "by linguistically separating the problematic ideas from the person, I invite the client into experiencing greater choice over whether the idea participates in his or her life. This allows the person to have more conscious choice concerning what ideas and what values guide his or her life" (p. 229).

Assist Couples in Establishing Relational Boundaries

Many researchers have noted the greater fluidity of relational boundaries in sexual and gender minority relationships than in heterosexual relationships. This is evidenced in the number of ongoing relationships with ex-partners and former lovers. Therapists can play an instrumental role by validating this norm and at the same time acknowledging its complications for couples in relationships (Marvin & Miller, 2000).

Assess the Impact of Socialization Squared on Relational Boundaries

Practitioners who work with lesbian and gay male couples should be cognizant of the fact that because of their common socialization experiences, they may be prone to develop certain relationship patterns. However, practitioners must guard against taking an overly stereotyped and negative view of these patterns. It is perhaps facile to assume that when same-sex couples stay engaged with their ex-partners, it is a failure to set boundaries. In reality, it may be evidence of the need to maintain supportive networks in situations where family members and others are anything but supportive.

Assist Couples in Establishing Relational Structure and Communicating About Sexuality

Practitioners who work with same-sex couples, bisexual couples, and mixed orientation couples may be called on to aid partners in working through issues regarding monogamy or polyamory in their relationships (Goetstouwers, 2006; LaSala, 2001; Peplau et al., 2004). First, practitioners need to guard against the tendency to assume a traditionally negative view of extradyadic sexual relationships as undesirable and evidence of relationship instability or dysfunction in the primary relationship. Studies have shown that monogamy is not related to relationship satisfaction in gay men (Kurdek, 1988, 1991a) and that extradyadic sex is often perceived as primarily recreational (Blumstein & Schwartz, 1983; Ossana, 2000). Shernoff (1995) noted that for many gay male couples, the "emotional primacy of the relationship" (p. 45) is more important than sexual fidelity in terms of relationship satisfaction.

Perhaps the most critical variable seems to be the agreement between partners about exclusivity versus openness of the relationship (Peplau et al., 2004). Therapists can aid partners in negotiating contracts regarding extradyadic sexual encounters. As a therapist, it is important to determine if the partners have previously set rules for outside sexual behavior. Often these rules serve the purpose of preventing extradyadic sexual behavior from interfering with their primary relationships. "Inquiring about rules and getting the partners to talk to each other about them is a way to help couples create or modify existing guidelines to fit their particular preferences and circumstances" (LaSala, 2001, p. 610). Rust (2003) provides a number of useful guidelines to aid in this process:

1. Are outside sexual liaisons permitted?
2. What kinds of sexual activities are permitted? When? Where?
3. What kinds of outside partners (e.g., gender) are permitted?
4. Should outside sexual liaisons be disclosed?
5. Should the nature of the primary relationships be disclosed to friends and family members?

It seems evident that a variety of extradyadic sexual arrangements may be possible in relationships, but for such relationships to succeed, partners must be on the same page.

Therapists should also be cognizant of the possibility that one or both partners may have histories of sexual abuse and that these histories may exacerbate their problems.

Encourage Political Activism

Green and Mitchell (2002) encourage their clients to participate in some form of political activism within the sexual minority community. These involvements represent "a form of subversion of the status quo and legitimization of the self, implicitly naming society's homophobia (rather than the self) as the problem that needs to be eliminated" (p. 551).

INTIMATE PARTNER VIOLENCE IN SEXUAL AND GENDER MINORITY COUPLES

Intimate partner violence (also known as domestic violence) among sexual and gender minority couples has been a taboo issue for quite some time. The research continues to be sparse, and prevalence rates vary largely as a result of methodological flaws. These include difficulties in finding representative samples and the use of diverse definitions of what constitutes intimate partner (Greenwood et al., 2002; McKenry, Serovich, Mason, & Mosack, 2006).

A primary focus for researchers and practitioners is whether the dynamics that contribute to intimate partner violence in sexual and gender minority couples are comparable to those that characterize battering in heterosexual couples. A number of authors (i.e., McLaughlin & Rozee, 2001; Ristock, 2002; VanNatta, 2005) have been critical of contemporary theory, research, and treatment approaches, arguing that these do not seem to fit the "lived" experiences of sexual and gender minority couples. The popular feminist analysis of domestic violence assumes that the male partner is the perpetrator and the female partner is the victim (McLauglin & Rozee, 2001). In an interesting study that sought to assess this, Blasko, Winek, and Bieschke (2007) explored family therapists' assessments of domestic violence. The authors constructed different scenarios. One was an ambiguous scenario in that the perpetrator and victim were purposefully left vague. Another scenario manipulated the sexual orientation of the couple (heterosexual vs. lesbian vs. gay men). As Blasko et al. (2007) predicted, the prototypical stereotype of man as perpetrator and woman as victim prevailed when participants rated the heterosexual scenario. This contrasted to the ratings of the gay and lesbian scenarios where both partners were viewed as perpetrator and victim.

The impact of homophobia/biphobia is another important factor distinguishing the dynamics of same-sex intimate partner violence from those associated with heterosexual intimate partner violence. Sexual and gender minority victims of intimate partner violence frequently avoid reporting incidents or approaching attorneys and other professionals for a number of reasons, including the negative stigma associated with homosexuality/bisexuality (Bryne, 1996; McClennen, Summers, & Vaughan, 2002). Police officers have been dismissive when reported incidents involved two women or two men. Even worse, they have often either failed to arrest or arrested the wrong partner (Peterman & Dixon, 2003). Law enforcement, social service, and medical personnel are often guilty of providing inadequate support to sexual and gender minorities (Ofreneo, 2006). Current domestic violence laws, organizations, shelters, and services are directed toward women in heterosexual relationships (Peterman & Dixon, 2003). For one thing, as more than half of the states have laws making sodomy an offense, calls for help mean having to confess a criminal offense (McClennen, 2005). Gay and bisexual men are rarely accepted at domestic violence shelters (Peterman & Dixon, 2003). Many sexual and gender minority victims of intimate partner violence do not use domestic shelters out of fear of discrimination. Some fear encountering shelter personnel or other victims closely connected to their own gay communities (VanNatta, 2005). Most depend primarily on the support of friends instead of helping professionals or family members (McClennen et al., 2002; Renzetti, 1992).

Internalized homo/bi/transphobia has also been at the center of analyses of intimate partner abuse (Balsam & Szymanski, 2005). A controlling tactic used by perpetrators of intimate partner violence is outing. Abusers threaten to tell others, including family members, friends, employers, landlords, and the like, about their partner's same-sex sexual orientation, gender identity, and/or HIV status. Other tactics include perpetrators' assertions that the abuse is deserved because of their partners' same-sex sexual orientation/gender identity.

In a recent study of same-sex domestic violence among lesbian partners, Balsam and Szymanski (2005) assessed experiences of discrimination among their participants and internalized homophobia. Their sample included 272 self-identified lesbian and bisexual women. Balsam and Szymanski found support for their hypothesis that minority stress and discrimination were significantly associated with domestic violence and relationship quality.

Tiegert (2001) argued that sexual minorities experience internalized homophobia and ongoing traumatization throughout their daily lives as a result of cultural oppression. She argued that shame is a central emotion in the lives of sexual minorities and that "attacking the self" and "attacking the other" are defenses against shame (see Nathenson, 1992). Tiegert cites her clinical experiences with lesbian batterers, who sometimes report that they felt as though they were attacking themselves when hitting their partners. Sometimes the use of power and control, as well as attacks, enables one to feel less inferior to others.

Lesbian Partnerships

Analyses of intimate partner violence in lesbian couples have focused on a number of variables. These relate primarily to the individual and developmental attributes of both perpetrators and victims. The bulk of research has focused on dependency and power imbalances between partners (Lockhart, White, Causby, & Isaac, 1994; Miller, Greene, Causby,

White, & Lockhart, 2001; Renzetti, 1992), childhood history of abuse (Girshick, 2002), and alcohol use (Renzetti, 1992).

Gay Men's Partnerships

Analyses of intimate partner violence in gay men's relationships have focused primarily on issues related to HIV, age, and substance abuse. Using a national probability sample of 2,881 men from four urban areas who had self-identified as gay or bisexual or had reported sexual behavior with other men, Greenwood et al. (2002) asked about different forms of abuse, including psychological, physical, and sexual abuse. Of their sample, 34% reported psychological violence, 22% reported physical violence, and 5% reported sexual violence. The researchers concluded intimate partner violence among urban men was "a very serious public health problem" (p. 1967). The demographic factors of age, HIV-serostatus, and education were correlated with victimization. In another national sample of HIV-positive adults, 11% of gay and bisexual men reported intimate partner violence since their diagnosis, and nearly half of these men believe it was their HIV serostatus that prompted the attack (Zierler et al., 2000).

In their study of gay and bisexual men, Merrill and Wolfe (2000) reported that their participants suffered patterns, forms, and frequencies of physical, emotional, and sexual abuse similar to those documented among lesbians and heterosexual women. However, like heterosexual women and lesbians, gay and bisexual men in their sample reported that a significant variable in their commitment to staying in the abusive relationships was their own and their partners' HIV status.

In Stanley, Bartholomew, Taylor, Oram, and Landolt's (2006) study of gay and bisexual men who were chosen from a randomly selected community sample, the majority of domestic violence incidents were a response to unmet needs for closeness with their partners and frustration over lack of commitment and monogamy. Of abuse incidents, only 2% were motivated by the need for domination or control. The majority of these incidents were motivated instead by the perpetrators' sense of having no control in their relationships (Stanley et al., 2006).

Gender Minority Partnerships

Very few studies have explored the issue of intimate partner violence in the gender minority population. Domestic violence has, however, been identified as a symptom of distress in couples in which one partner self-discloses either his or her gender variance or the desire to transition (Lev, 2006; Lev & Lev, 1999).

Counseling Implications

Pitt and Dolan-Soto (2001) recommend that intake forms and interviews routinely include at least one question about intimate partner abuse, one about psychological abuse in relationships, and one about perpetrating violence in the context of a family relationship:

- Have you ever been kicked, punched, or otherwise hurt by your intimate partner or family member?
- Have you ever been controlled by, or made to feel afraid of, your intimate partner or a family member?

- Have you ever been or are you now concerned about hurting an intimate partner or a family member? (p. 167)

Therapists should guard against applying the same treatment procedures used with heterosexual survivors of partner violence to same-sex partners. They need to take into account the role that homophobia/heterosexism plays in same-sex partner abuse. As Tiegert (2001) reported, one way this may manifest itself is when others minimize the abusive situation because it involves two persons of the same sex. Family members and friends don't acknowledge the true nature of the relationship and so ignore the danger.

McLaughlin and Rozee (2001) provided some helpful guidelines, urging practitioners to familiarize themselves with community resources and to not assume that violence in lesbian relationships is less intense than that experienced in heterosexual relationships.

The reality is that law enforcement and helping professionals have had trouble differentiating perpetrators and victims in cases of same-sex and gender minority intimate partner violence. Pitt and Dolan-Soto (2001) and Ristock (2001) emphasize the need to conduct an assessment to determine who is abusing whom.

Education and Advocacy

On a systemic level, practitioners, social workers, and psychologists need to advocate for policies and laws that provide sexual and gender minorities the same protections currently afforded heterosexual persons. They are also aptly poised to implement recommendations for improving domestic violence services. These include

- Training on sexual and gender minority issues for shelter staff personnel and practitioners
- A commitment to more programs especially for gay and bisexual men, transgender persons, and lesbians of color (Ristock, 2001; VanNatta, 2005)
- The use of nongender-specific language in all outreach materials and intake interviews

DYADIC ADJUSTMENT, SEXUAL ORIENTATION, AND SEXUALITY IN GENDER MINORITY COUPLES

Empirical research that explores the dynamics of gender minority relationships is scarce. Most of the literature comes from observations of therapists working in clinical settings with persons interested in transitioning either male-to-female (MTF) or female-to-male (FTM) and their partners. Current data may also be tainted because preoperative transsexuals likely present themselves in ways to convince their therapists to recommend desired professional services (Bolin, 1988). As long as gender minorities are viewed as persons with psychopathological conditions and helping professionals are viewed basically as gatekeepers, this may continue to be the case.

Partners of Gender Minorities

In Brown and Rounsley's (1996) extensive work with family members and spouses of persons who are engaged in the transition process, they found that a higher percentage of transitioning MTFs were married than were FTMs. A large percentage of FTMs were in relationships with female partners. In some cases, these female partners were bisexual and able to adjust to their partners' use of hormonal and surgical procedures.

Spouses and/or partners, especially female partners, face tumultuous emotional upheaval when they discover their partner's gender issues. Their responses may include shame; curiosity; anxiety; fear; sexual arousal; sexual dysfunction; aversion; feelings of abandonment, self-blame, and competition; and decreased self-esteem or body image (Cole, 1998). Spouses/partners might also voice the following:

- Dismissal of the partner's desire to transition as a temporary "phase"
- Fears that the partner is mentally ill
- Perceptions of inadequacies in the body morphology that might make passing difficult (Israel, 2004)

Feelings of disbelief are also common, given that in most cases gender minority persons have had a history of being extremely closeted about their feelings (Brown & Rounsley, 1996).

It is also not uncommon for spouses/partners to assume that their transitioning spouses/partners are gay or bisexual. This can cause them to question their own gender identities and/or sexual orientations, particularly if they experience sexual attraction to their partners' transitional status (Boyd, 2007).

Some common stressors for couples who are trying to preserve their relationships include the great financial costs of initiating hormonal therapy, undergoing cosmetic and genital surgeries, and coming out to others (Israel, 2004). Also, postoperatively, couples are faced with the difficult challenge of redefining their sexual intimacy (Israel, 2004).

There are variables that seem to be correlated with relationship stability and satisfaction. These include timing and the extent to which gender minority partners have been honest with their partners about their dissatisfaction with their biological sex (Cole, 1998; Cole, Denny, Eyler, & Samons, 2000; Nuttbrock, Rosenblum, & Blumenstein, 2002).

Cole (1998), who has had extensive experience as a lecturer, group facilitator, and therapist with MTF transsexuals and their spouses, observed that the earlier in the relationship the disclosure, the better. If the relationship is terminated, the breakup is more likely to occur soon after the partner discloses his or her identity and intention to transition. A relationship that is long established seems more susceptible to relationship dysfunction and termination. The relationship partner experiences feelings of betrayal and lack of trust in her partner. The ongoing survival of the relationship depends on the nature of the emotional investment and commitment. The gender minority spouse/partner may have engaged in distancing behaviors, and the couple may have experienced sexual difficulties.

The female spouse/partner often exerts enormous pressure to keep her spouse's gender status a secret. The urge to keep the secret is often motivated by fears of abandonment by church, family, and community. The sense of responsibility and the stressors associated with these experiences often leave the spouse vulnerable to mental and physical health problems. Cole (1998) writes:

> If [the spouse] remains in the relationship, she will usually assume the largest, most comprehensive responsibility for managing the secret (his, hers, and theirs). This additional task is not always easily accommodated by her. She predictably will experience a wide range of emotions which may go unnoticed by both her and her partner, who is primarily focused on his own gender complexities. (p. 374)

A common complaint of MTF gender minorities about their spouses/partners is the setting of limits regarding feminizing procedures (Cole, 1998). Female spouses/partners may limit body shaving or other feminizing procedures that are serious desires of their partners. They may set conditions under which they will "allow" or "permit" cross-dressing. Sexual minority partners sometimes refer to these circumstances with the same descriptive language, such as "I am allowed" and "She permits me" (Cole, 1998, p. 382). They appear to have agreed that their spouses/partners are responsible and have the power to determine such things. Ironically, a common complaint of many female partners is that they resent the burden and responsibility of having to set all the boundaries, and yet their partners complain that they appear to be inconsistent and too restrictive about the rules (Cole, 1998).

The presence of children has a strong impact on couple dynamics. Many couples with children face a whole series of issues regarding their ability to adjust to a parent's changing gender status. And the children's adjustment is greatly influenced by how the members of the couple act toward one another. According to Cole (1998), the "presence and age of children will directly influence the female partner's ability to explore and integrate transgender expression into the relationship" (p. 377).

Research (Kockott & Fahrner, 1988; Lewins, 2000; Tully, 1992) has suggested that FTMs seem more successful at sustaining stable partnerships than are MTFs. Stable relationships are defined as sexual liaisons with cohabitating partners characterized by longevity (Lewins, 2000). Interestingly, as Kockott & Fahrner (1988) observed, this finding is true despite the fact that "reassignment surgery for MTFs offers a closer approximation of the desired genitalia than it does for FTMs; the latter have more stable relationships in spite of unfavorable anatomical conditions" (p. 544). Lewins (2000) noted in his sample of gender minorities a preponderance of female partners among the FTMs and male partners among the MTFs. Lewins offered a theory to account for his finding that seems rather like the socialization squared hypothesis discussed earlier. He argued that the legacy of socialization is not forgotten and that in the case of the FTM transsexual, there is a greater emphasis on expressive qualities and emotional connection for women in relationships. When an FTM establishes a heterosexual relationship with a woman, both bring their histories of female socialization. In contrast, the social histories of boys and men tend to emphasize appearance and the physical capacity for intercourse.

Cross-Dressing Partners

Within the cross-dressing population, studies have found the majority describe themselves as heterosexual (Docter & Prince, 1997). In Docter and Prince's (1997) survey of 1,032 cross-dressers, 87% described themselves as heterosexual and 83% had been married.

Brown's (1998) study encompassed 106 spouses of cross-dressers from 25 different states. Of this sample, 40% knew of their husband's cross-dressing before committing to the relationship. The mean duration of the relationships was 13.1 years. Statistically within the relationships, the study found

- 48% of the women indicated that their partner was cross-dressed during at least one sexual encounter during the relationship
- 32% of the women stated that they had "seriously considered" divorce or separation from their partner based on his cross-dressing
- 44% thought they should be more accepting of their spouse's cross-dressing
- 42% thought that no change was needed in their current level of acceptance

Brown commented on the wide range of acceptance behaviors reported by the women in this sample and noted that a key variable associated with this acceptance was the degree to which their partners had been honest with them about their cross-dressing activities.

Sexual Intimacy in Gender Minority Relationships

The topic of sexual intimacy among couples with one or more gender minority partners is largely based on small nonrandom clinical samples—namely, partners who are either in the process of or have completed surgical gender reassignment. The bulk of publications focus on the sexual orientations of partners; less attention has been paid to such variables as sexual behaviors and sexual frequency of couples.

Usually, practitioners and researchers define a gender minority partner's sexual orientation according to the gender of preference, not to the gender assigned at birth. For example, a gender minority person who was identified as an anatomical male at birth and presently identifies and is living as a woman is described as a lesbian if she is sexually attracted to other women. By contrast, a person who was identified as an anatomical female at birth and presently identifies and is living as a man is described as gay if he is sexually attracted to other men (Tarver, 2002).

Research conducted during the early 1970s found that MTFs were heterosexual in their sexual orientations after transition (Devor, 1998; Pauly, 1998). However, more recent reports show a greater incidence of FTMs and MTFs who identify themselves as bisexual or homosexual after their transitions are completed (Coleman, Bockting, & Gooren, 1993). In her in-depth interviews with 46 self-defined FTMs, Devor (1998), a sociologist, reported a 275% increase in the number of FTMs who, after completing transition, found gay men sexually attractive. Devor noted many of these participants had not taken the step toward surgical construction of penises, called phalloplasties. Phalloplastic surgeries have not changed significantly since the 1960s, and many FTMs call phalloplasties "frankendicks" because of significant and unattractive scarring that occurs as a result of this surgery (Cromwell, 1999). As Cromwell (1999) noted, most FTMs choose to forgo such surgical procedures. For the majority of Devor's (1998) sample, sexual behavior and orientation were also based on the attributions made by potential partners. "Those who successfully established relationships in the preferred SOID (sexual orientation identity) did so with support of partners who shared their images of themselves as bona fide men with a physical problem which medical technology could fix" (p. 272). These individuals averaged 7.4 years after transitioning before they found gay men sexually attractive.

Israel (2004) observed that 50% of persons who had completed their transitions to a different gender reconsidered their sexual orientation, and many have relationships with other gender minorities. In a similar vein, Erhardt (2007) and Boyd (2007) noted that a high number of heterosexually identified men who transition to women move through a period of sexual exploration with men and eventually return to sexual relationships with women. While more research is needed, it appears as though the gender minorities are somewhat fluid in their sexuality and sexual orientations.

Brown and Rounsley (1996) noted that gender minority partners in committed relationships tend to engage in sexual behavior less frequently than do non–gender minority partners. Frequently, sexual activities are accompanied by sexual fantasies of being the other partner or sex. They also note that many gender minority persons who are in the transitioning process either don't date or will set limits on sexual contact, preferring instead to spend time on computer chat lines or socialize in gay and lesbian communities. For some, their genitals are off limits until after surgical interventions, but for others, this is not the case (Cole et al., 2000). Cole et al. (2000) note that in the latter samples, partners of gender variant persons frequently experience depression and posttraumatic stress disorder.

COUNSELING GENDER MINORITY COUPLES

The beginning of the chapter told the story of the woman whose husband discloses after several years of marriage that he wants to change his sex. The prospect of encountering such a situation in counseling may seem overwhelming. The partner who wishes to transition in this case will have a myriad of needs, including a referral to a qualified gender therapist, sex or gender information hotlines and computer online services, and other supportive services. The nontransitioning partner in this couple will also need support throughout this process, and couples therapy might be considered as a possible adjunctive service for gender minorities and their partners. Practitioners often need to attend to broader relationship issues, not just to issues related specifically to gender transitioning.

It may come as no surprise to discover that many of the recommendations that were given above regarding counseling same-sex couples are relevant in working with couples in which at least one partner is differently gendered.

Avoid Labeling

Cole (1998) warned practitioners against rigidly and permanently classifying or labeling clients as "transvestites," "transsexuals," and so on. "The transgender experience is fluid and can evolve, fluctuate, and/or change in relationship to the couple, family situation, work, and community environment" (Cole, 1998, p. 388). Practitioners will also need to aid partners in understanding this fluidity and help guard against the tendency to make stereotyped assumptions about their gender minority partners. Yet it is a confusing new era. For example, nonminority partners might automatically assume that their spouses' cross-dressing behaviors will progress to the point at which they will choose surgical reassignment. They might further assume that because their partners are gender minorities, they are also gay, lesbian, or bisexual. Practitioners can advise nonminority partners that while some cross-dressers do transition and many gender minorities discover that their sexual orientation has changed after transitioning (Brown & Rounsley, 1996), this is not always the case.

Practitioners can also provide clients who elect to transition with information about what to expect throughout the transitioning process. For example, if the postoperative person begins to date and to establish intimate relationships after transitioning, this can often be a turbulent time, one of experimentation often likened to a second adolescence (Brown & Rounsley, 1996).

Actively Confront Personal Transphobia

Perhaps the most important attribute of any practitioner who counsels gender minority clients and their partners is the capacity to be nonjudgmental. This is especially crucial in light of the hatred and ridicule that gender minorities experience outside the therapy room. Therapists must be attentive to their use of labels and avoid terms that are pathologizing, such as *gender dysphoria* (Cole, 1998). They must also be personally aware of any stereotyped assumptions they may have about gender minorities, including the assumption that they are really gay, lesbian, or bisexual, and any visceral reactions associated with the physical appearance of gender minority clients whose external body morphology and physical features may not seem to match their stated gender identity. One important, but simple, rule for therapists is to inquire at the start of therapy about the gender minority client's preferred name.

Assess Support Services for Non–Gender Minority Partners

Cole (1998) makes several useful recommendations to therapists regarding the needs of partners of transgendered persons, including peer support and competent professional support (Cole, 1998). Practitioners need to encourage partners of gender minority persons to focus on their own needs and guard against the tendency to neglect their health and other issues. It is not uncommon for spouses of gender minority persons to feel emotionally isolated and to assume that they are alone in feeling as they do (Brown, 1998).

As it tends to be a well-guarded secret, the therapist is often the first to know about a partner's cross-dressing (Dzelme & Jones, 2001). Given the negative stigma associated with cross-dressing, it is imperative that practitioners depathologize cross-dressing and reduce the sense of emotional isolation that the couple may feel. The literature on cross-dressing suggests that these behaviors are often more problematic for the partners of cross-dressers than for the cross-dressers themselves (Dzelme & Jones, 2001). For example, partners of cross-dressers typically voice concerns that their spouse's behavior may progress to the point of choosing surgical reassignment (Brown, 1998). Some possible resources that might be offered to cross-dressers and their partners are *Head over Heels: Wives Who Stay with Cross-Dressers and Transsexuals* (Erhardt, 2007), an anthology of stories of women whose spouses are cross-dressers and MTFs, and *My Husband Betty: Love, Sex, and Life with a Crossdresser* (Boyd, 2003), which chronicled the author's personal journey as she confronted her husband's cross-dressing. Boyd's next book, *She's Not the Man I Married: My Life with a Transgender Husband* (2007), describes her adjustment to her husband's desire to transition from a biological male to a female.

Provide Relationship Validation

As is true of sexual minority couples, the quality and duration of gender minority relationships are dependent on the degree to which their desired gender identities and relationships are supported and validated by others (Nuttbrock et al., 2002). Practitioners can play an important role in validating the strengths and coping skills that gender minority clients and their partners have exercised in the face of a largely transphobic culture.

Assist Couples in Establishing Boundaries

Trust is a major issue for the partners of many gender minority persons. Because timing and the context of self-disclosure are such important variables in the relationship quality, honesty must be deemed a priority. The partner of a transgendered person is typically fearful that he or she may be withholding or hiding other personal information.

Provide Education and Advocacy

Therapists are uniquely positioned to advocate for gender minorities and their partners. Today gender minorities and their partners lack basic legal rights and protections in terms of their partnerships and families (Lombardi & Bettcher, 2006). Chapter 11 provides readers with a number of ideas for how practitioners, social workers, and psychologists can advocate for broader legal reforms and institutional changes in order to help create a more affirmative climate for gender minority couples. Above all, helping professionals need to encourage their gender minority clients and partners to take part in some form of political activism. Research has demonstrated the importance of collective organizing and political action in strengthening the self-esteem and validation of gender minorities (Carroll, Gilroy, & Ryan, 2002; Lombardi, 1999).

Summary

For years, researchers have been fascinated by the extent to which same-sex and heterosexual couples were alike or different on various relationship dimensions. After over twenty-five years of ongoing research, it seems that same-sex couples share much in common with their straight counterparts. They face the same stressors, including finances, decisions about parenting and child rearing, career decisions and job concerns, and family of origin issues. Yet sexual minority couples appear distinct and different from straight couples by virtue of the lack of social validation of their relationships as well as the compounding effects of having both partners with similar gender-role socialization.

In contrast to gay and lesbian couples, comparatively little empirical research has explored relational dynamics and sexual intimacy in the lives of couples in which at least one partner is bisexual, is transgendered, or engages in cross-dressing.

The prevalence of intimate partner violence or same-sex domestic violence in sexual minority couples is a neglected area of research. However, estimates of the rates of violence are equal to those in heterosexual relationships (Balsam, Rothblum, & Beauchaine, 2005; McClennen, 2005; Merrill & Wolfe, 2000). Future research is needed to explore the dynamics of abuse in these relationships as well as in those of gender minority couples.

Most of the existing literature on gender minority couples comprises observations of therapists working in clinical settings with transsexuals—that is, persons transitioning from either male-to-female (MTF) or female-to-male (FTM)—and their partners. Unfortunately, empirical research addressing the full spectrum of gender minorities is scarce. Ideally, this research would cover couples comprised of partners who express their gender identities without the use of surgical and hormonal intervention or who consider themselves to be gender variant.

There were approximately 1.2 million sexual minority couples in America as of 2003 (Sue & Sue, 2003). It is likely that as helping professionals, you will encounter such couples with relationship conflicts. Many of the counseling guidelines appropriate for same-sex couples are relevant when counseling gender minority couples. This includes exploring the role of internalized beliefs in couple dynamics. But probably the single most important benefit helping professionals offer is to approach sexual and gender minority couples without bias or judgment and to validate and affirm their relationships. This means exercising caution, guarding against reflexively pathologizing such phenomena as extradyadic sexual activities. Practitioners who work with gender minorities must also be cautious about rigidly and permanently classifying or labeling clients as "transvestites" and "transsexuals" (Cole, 1998). "The transgender experience is fluid and can evolve, fluctuate, and/or change in relationship to the couple, family situation, work, and community environment" (Cole, 1998, p. 388). Practitioners must be able to focus on broader relationship issues, not just on the gender identity issues.

In the words of psychologist Brown (1995): "same sex relationships model new possibilities for intimate couple relationships that go beyond the paradigms generated by heterosexuality" (p. 289). Indeed, research cited in this chapter seems to support this claim. Because same-sex partners cannot fall back on traditional gender-linked expectations about such issues as the division of household labor and responsibilities (Green & Mitchell, 2002), they are called on to invent new possibilities and decision-making models. This is a lesson that might well benefit many heterosexual couples, whose female partners often feel overburdened with domestic chores and child care (Dempsey, 2002).

Personal Reflection 1

John, aged 42, and Paul, aged 36, come to you for couples counseling. They have been living together as partners for the past seven years. About five years ago, they began to cruise for men together at a popular gay bar with the intention of having sexual experiences with other men in the form of "three-ways." Initially, Paul resisted the idea, but John felt that this was an important means of "keeping our relationship with one another alive" and "adding some variety and excitement" to their sexual lives. Paul finally acquiesced but has been becoming more and more dissatisfied with their three-way experiences.

Self-Reflection Questions

1. What were your initial thoughts and personal feelings as you read about John and Paul's sexual encounters?
2. How might you view John and Paul's sexual encounters, given the research presented in this chapter?
3. How would you respond to John and Paul as their therapist?

Personal Reflection 2

Sharon, aged 47, has dinner with Theresa, her former lover for 12 years, every Thursday evening and often confides in her about relationship problems she is having with her current partner of six months. Your supervisor tells you that this is "not healthy" and that Sharon and Theresa are "enmeshed with one another." During your next session with Sharon, you prepare to confront her about her relationship with Theresa.

Self-Reflection Questions

1. What is your reaction to the supervisor's comment? Do you agree with her assessment of Sharon and Theresa's friendship as "unhealthy"?
2. Are there alternative ways of thinking about the nature of Sharon and Theresa's current relationship with one another?
3. What might you say to your supervisor?

Library, Media, and Internet Activities

Check your local video/DVD store for the HBO film *Normal* (Anderson, 2003). *Normal* is set in a farming community in rural Illinois. As the film begins, Roy and Irma Appleton are celebrating their 25th wedding anniversary together. Shortly thereafter, Roy tells Irma that he wants a sex change operation. As Roy prepares himself for surgical reassignment, he begins the process by ingesting hormones, while Irma and their children attempt to come to grips with his decision and its consequences.

Discussion Questions

1. Roy and Irma sought counseling from their church pastor, Reverend Muncie, after Roy faints at his and Irma's 25th wedding anniversary party. What were your reactions to Reverend Muncie's attempts to help Roy and Irma?

2. Imagine yourself in the role of a counselor meeting with Roy and Irma for the first time. How might you have responded following Roy's self-disclosure? Formulate a tentative plan for your next session with Roy and Irma.

3. As Roy and Irma's therapist, discuss any personal countertransference issues that might arise for you as you work with this couple.

4. Bearing in mind that Roy and Irma live in rural Illinois, what resources and/or referrals might you recommend for them? Be as specific as possible.

5. Describe the process depicted in the film for Irma as she accompanies Roy on his personal journey through the transition process. Did the dynamics of their relationship change over time? If so, how? How do their experiences compare with the research presented in this chapter?

6. Try to place yourself in Irma's shoes. How might you have reacted to Roy's decision to change sex?

7. Jane Anderson, who is the author and director of *Normal*, describes this film as a "wacky love story." Do you agree with this assessment?

Group Activity

Laurie, a master's-level intern at a community mental health agency, asked for some assistance with a client she had recently been assigned. She indicated that Walter, aged 32, had been experiencing a number of depressive symptoms. She told her fellow interns that as she probed further, she determined that Walter's depression was largely a consequence of relationship conflicts he had been experiencing with his partner of five years, Keith. When she discussed the possibility of doing couples counseling with the two men, Walter seemed enthusiastic about the idea. As she prepared for her first joint session with Walter and Keith, Laurie felt herself becoming increasingly anxious. She asked her professor and fellow interns for guidance and support. Pete, a fellow classmate, was quick to point out to Laurie: "Gay couples are no different from straight couples." Pete assumes that all relationships are basically similar in terms of their dynamics and that most counseling approaches are appropriate and applicable regardless of sexual orientation. Based on the information presented earlier in the chapter:

- Do you personally agree with Pete's opinion? Why or why not?
- According to the material presented in the chapter, do you think that Pete is demonstrating alpha or beta bias?
- What support and information would you provide Laurie in preparation for her session with Walter and Keith?
- Which counseling models and techniques might be particularly relevant and effective in her work with Walter and Keith?

Role-Play Activity

In this chapter, it was suggested that imago relationship therapy (IRT) might be especially useful in counseling sexual and gender minority couples. The narrative below was written by Joe Kort, a psychotherapist and author of a popular self-help book titled *10 Smart Things Gay Men Can Do to Improve Their Lives* (2003). Kort is a licensed clinical social worker in private practice.

He is also a certified imago therapist. Below he describes the valuable personal insights he had derived about himself and his relationships from his professional training in IRT.

From what I've learned in IRT, I now understand why I was drawn to bullies. First, while I was growing up, boys in school taunted and humiliated me. I never stood up for myself because I didn't know how. I just took it. . . . My parents divorced when I was 3, and because of my father's absence and neglect, I was left with just my mother, who was the more dominant of the two. At home, her motto was "my way or the highway." Again, I chose to acquiesce. My sister didn't and our mother punished her regularly for not complying. So these narcissistic types I dated were quite right: Yes, I was angry. But they didn't deserve my anger, because it wasn't meant for them. It was unresolved rage toward my mother and father and those childhood bullies. In my case, if any of those self absorbed men I dated had been willing to say, "Joe, sorry I disappointed you. I can see your point and am willing to consider your needs more" then I could have started to heal the pain from my childhood. Mike, my partner, was the first man I dated who finally did this and he grabbed my heart. (Kort, 2003, pp. 172–173)

In his work as a psychotherapist, Kort makes use of a popular communication exercise from IRT called the intention couples dialogue (ICD). This technique is especially effective with sexual and gender minorities who suffer the consequences of lack of validation and mirroring (Kleinberg & Zorn, 1998). ICD consists of three phases: mirroring, validation, and empathy.

In the exercise below, you will have the opportunity to familiarize yourself in an experiential fashion with the ICD technique. Read the case study of Tim and Steve, and follow the instructions below:

Tim and Steve have been in a relationship with one another for approximately 13 years.

They live in a small, conservative town in southeastern Pennsylvania. Both are closeted and are out to only a small group of friends, all of whom are female and heterosexual. Recently, Tim and Steve sought counseling related to Steve's problem with alcohol. During one session, Steve disclosed a painful childhood memory when, at the age of six, his father came home from work earlier than expected while Steve was "playing house" and wearing his mother's dress and heels. Following this discovery, Steve's father punished him severely. Tim listened to this story in horror and afterward asked Steve why he had not shared this story with him before. Tim turned to the counselor and exclaimed: "I can't believe after 13 years together you never told me about this. It makes me wonder what else you're keeping from me." Steve shrugged his shoulders and replied, "I didn't see the point. It happened so long ago."

As a consequence of this incident and his upbringing throughout his childhood, Steve learned to suppress parts of himself. Realizing at an early age that he was gay, he compensated by developing a "macho" persona. He worked hard to bulk up and for a time was involved in competitive weight lifting. In high school, he was popular among his peers, dated the same girl for all four years of high school, and was on the football team.

Tim was the youngest of three boys. His older brother was the favored son, and because Tim was considered "effeminate" by his peers, he often felt lonely and unpopular. He had a somewhat distant relationship with his father, resulting largely because of his lack of interest in activities that his father and brothers seemed to enjoy, like fishing and lacrosse.

Instructions

Gather in groups of three. Select one person to assume the role of Tim (partner A), one to role-play Steve (partner B), and one to role-play the therapist in this case.

In the mirroring phase of ICD, partner A uses "I" statements, while partner B listens without interruption. Partner B reflects these statements back to partner A, followed by these questions: "Did I get it? Is there more?"

    In the validation phase, partner B validates what he or she heard: "I can see why you'd think this way."

During the empathy phase, partner B validates partner A's feelings. Still staying with the same issue, partners A and B now switch roles, and partner B begins with an "I" statement.

References

Alonzo, D. J. (2005). Working with same-sex couples. In M. Harway (Ed.), *Handbook of couples' therapy* (pp. 370–384). Hoboken, NJ: Wiley.

Anderson, J. (Director). (2003). *Normal* [Motion picture]. United States: HBO.

Balsam, K. F., Rothblum, E. D., & Beauchaine, T. P. (2005). Victimization over the lifespan: A comparison of lesbian, gay, bisexual and heterosexual siblings. *Journal of Consulting & Clinical Psychology, 73*(3), 477–487.

Balsam, K. F., & Szymanski, D. M. (2005). Relationship quality and domestic violence in women's same-sex relationships: The role of minority stress. *Psychology of Women Quarterly, 29*(3), 258–269.

Basham, K. K. (1999). Therapy with a lesbian couple: The art of balancing lenses. In J. Laird (Ed.), *Lesbians and lesbian families: Reflections on therapy and practice* (pp. 143–177). New York: Columbia University Press.

Baucom, D. H., Shoham, V., Mueser, K. T., Daiuto, A. D., & Stickle, T. R. (1998). Empirically supported couple and family interventions for marital distress and adult mental health problems. *Journal of Consulting & Clinical Psychology, 66*(1), 53–88.

Bepko, C., & Johnson, T. (2000). Gay and lesbian couples in therapy: Perspectives for the contemporary family therapist. *Journal of Marital & Family Therapy, 26*(4), 409–419.

Bettinger, M. (2006). Polyamory and gay men: A family systems approach. In J. Bigner (Ed.), *An introduction to GLBT family studies* (pp. 161–181). Binghamton, NY: Haworth Press.

Blasko, K. A., Winek, J. L., & Bieschke, K. J. (2007). Therapists' prototypical assessment of domestic violence situations. *Journal of Marital & Family Therapy, 33*(2), 258–269.

Blumstein, P., & Schwartz, P. (1983). *American couples: Money, work, sex.* New York: Morrow.

Bohan, J. S. (1996). *Psychology and sexual orientation: Coming to terms.* New York: Routledge.

Bolin, A. (1988). *In search of Eve: Transsexual rites of passage.* South Hadley, MA: Bergin & Garvey.

Boyd, H. (2003). *My husband Betty: Love, sex, and life with a crossdresser.* New York: Thunder's Mouth Press.

Boyd, H. (2007). *She's not the man I married: My life with a transgender husband.* Emeryville, CA: Seal Press.

Bradford, M. (2004). Bisexual issues in same-sex couple therapy. In J. J. Bigner & J. L. Wetchler (Eds.), *Relationship therapy with same-sex couples* (pp. 43–52). Binghamton, NY: Haworth Press.

Brown, G. R. (1998). Women in the closet: Relationships with transgendered men. In D. Denny (Ed.), *Current concepts in transgender identity* (pp. 353–371). New York: Garland.

Brown, L. (1995). Therapy with same-sex couples: An introduction. In N. S. Jacobson & A. S. Gurman (Eds.), *Clinical handbook of couple therapy* (pp. 274–294). New York: Guilford.

Brown, M. L., & Rounsley, C. A. (1996). *True selves: Understanding transsexualism—For families, friends, coworkers, and helping professionals.* New York: Jossey-Bass.

Bryant, A. S., & Demian (1994). Relationship characteristics of American gays and lesbians: Findings from a national survey. *Journal of Gay & Lesbian Social Services, 1,* 101–117.

Bryne, D. (1996). Clinical models for the treatment of gay male perpetrators of domestic violence. In C. M. Renzetti & C. H. Miley (Eds.), *Violence in gay and lesbian domestic partnerships* (pp. 107–116). Binghamton, NY: Haworth Press.

Burch, B. (1982). Psychological merger in lesbian couples: A joint ego psychological and systems approach. *Family Therapy, 9,* 201–208.

Buxton, A. P. (2004). Works in progress: How mixed-orientation couples maintain their marriages after the wives come out. *Journal of Bisexuality, 4*(1/2), 57–82.

Buxton, A. P. (2006). When a spouse comes out: Impact on the heterosexual partner [special issue]. *Sexual Addiction & Compulsivity, 13*(2/3), 317–332.

Carroll, L., Gilroy, P. J., & Ryan, J. (2002). Counseling transgendered, transsexual, and gender-variant clients. *Journal of Counseling & Development, 80*(2), 131–139.

Cole, S. S. (1998). The female experience of the femme: A transgender challenge. In D. Denny (Ed.), *Current concepts in transgender identity* (pp. 373–389). New York: Garland.

Cole, S. S., Denny, D., Eyler, A. E., & Samons, S. L. (2000). Issues of transgender. In T. Szuchman & F. Muscarella (Eds.), *Psychological perspectives in human sexuality* (pp. 149–195). New York: Wiley.

Coleman, E., Bockting, W. O., & Gooren, L. (1993). Homosexual and bisexual identity in sex-reassigned female-to-male transsexuals. *Archives of Sexual Behavior, 22*(1), 37–50.

Cromwell, J. (1999). *Transmen and FTMs: Identities, bodies, genders, and sexualities.* Urbana: University of Illinois.

Dempsey, K. (2002). Who gets the best deal from marriage: Women or men? *Journal of Sociology, 38*(2), 91–110.

Devor, H. (1998). Sexual-orientation identities, attractions, and practices of female-to-male transsexuals. In D. Denny (Ed.), *Current concepts of transgender identity* (pp. 249–275). New York: Garland.

Doctor, R. F., & Prince, V. (1997). Transvestism: A survey of 1032 cross-dressers. *Archives of Sexual Behavior, 26*(6), 589–605.

Dzelme, K., & Jones, R. A. (2001). Male cross-dressers in therapy: A solution-focused perspective for marriage and family therapists. *American Journal of Family Therapy, 29*(4), 293–305.

Erhardt, V. (2007). *Head over heels: Wives who stay with cross-dressers and transsexuals.* Binghamton, NY: Haworth Press.

Girshick, L. B. (2002). No sugar, no spice: Reflections on research on woman-to-woman sexual violence. *Violence Against Women, 8,* 1500–1520.

Goetstouwers, L. (2006). Affirmative psychotherapy with bisexual men. *Journal of Bisexuality, 6*(1/2), 27–49.

Gottman Institute. (2004). *Twelve-year study of gay and lesbian couples.* Retrieved November 30, 2005, from http://www.gottman.com/research/projects/gaylesbian

Gottman, J. M., Levenson, R. W., Cross, J., Frederickson, B. L., McCoy, K., Rosenthal, L., et al. (2003). Correlates of gay and lesbian couples' relationship satisfaction and relationship dissolution. *Journal of Homosexuality, 45*(1), 23–43.

Green, R.-J., Bettinger, M., & Zacks, E. (1996). Are lesbian couples fused and gay male couples disengaged? Questioning gender straightjackets. In J. Laird & R.-J. Green (Eds.), *Lesbians and gays in couples and families: A handbook for therapists* (pp. 185–230). San Francisco: Jossey-Bass.

Green, R.-J., & Mitchell, V. (2002). Gay and lesbian couples in therapy: Homophobia, relational ambiguity, and social support. In A. S. Gurman & N. E. Jacobson (Eds.), *Clinical handbook of couple therapy* (3rd ed., pp. 546–568). New York: Guilford.

Greenan, D. E., & Tunnell, G. (2003). *Couple therapy with gay men.* New York: Guilford.

Greenwood, G. L., Relf, M. V., Huang, B., Pollack, L. M., Canchola, J. A., & Catania, J. A. (2002). Battering victimization among a probability-based sample of men who have sex with men. *American Journal of Public Health, 92*(1/2), 1964–1969.

Hall, M. (2001). Beyond forever after: Narrative therapy with lesbian couples. In P. J. Kleinplatz (Ed.), *New directions in sex therapy: Innovations and alternatives* (pp. 279–301). Philadelphia: Brunner-Routledge.

Harkless, L. E., & Fowers, B. J. (2005). Similarities and differences in relational boundaries among heterosexuals, gay men, and lesbians. *Psychology of Women Quarterly, 29*(2), 167–176.

Hendrix, H. (1988). *Getting the love you want: A guide for couples.* New York: Holt.

Hubschman, L. (Ed.). *Transsexuals: Life from both sides.* Darby, PA: Diane Publishing.

Iasenza, S. (2002). Beyond "lesbian death bed": The passion and play in lesbian relationships. *Journal of Lesbian Studies, 6*(11), 111–120.

Israel, G. E. (2004). Supporting transgender and sex reassignment issues: Couple and family dynamics. In J. J. Bigner & J. L. Wetchler (Eds.), *Relationship therapy with same-sex couples* (pp. 53–63). Binghamton, NY: Haworth Press.

Johnson, S., & Lebow, J. (2000). The "coming of age" of couple therapy: A decade review. *Journal of Marital & Family Therapy, 26*(1), 23–38.

Jordan, K. M., & Deluty, R. H. (2000). Social support, coming out, and relationship satisfaction in lesbian couples. *Journal of Lesbian Studies, 4*(1), 145–164.

Kleinberg, S., & Zorn, P. (1998). Multiple mirroring with lesbian and gay couples: From Peoria to P-Town. In W. Luquet & M. T. Hannah (Eds.),

Healing in the relational paradigm (pp. 135–150). Bristol, PA: Taylor & Francis.

Kockott, G., & Fahrner, E. M. (1988). Male-to-female and female-to-male transsexuals. *Archives of Sexual Behavior, 17*(6), 539–546.

Kort, J. (2003). *10 smart things gay men can do to improve their lives.* Los Angeles: Alyson.

Krestan, J. A., & Bepko, C. S. (1980). The problem of fusion in the lesbian relationship. *Family Process, 19,* 277–289.

Kurdek, L. A. (1988). Relationship quality of gay and lesbian cohabiting couples. *Journal of Homosexuality, 15*(3–4), 93–118.

Kurdek, L. A. (1991a). Correlates of relationship satisfaction in cohabiting couples. *Journal of Personality & Social Psychology 61,* 910–922.

Kurdek, L. A. (1991b). Sexuality in homosexual and heterosexual couples. In K. McKinney & S. Sprecher (Eds.), *Sexuality in close relationships* (pp. 177–191). Hillsdale, N.J.: Erlbaum.

Kurdek, L. A. (1993). Lesbian and gay couples. In A. R. D'Augelli & C. J. Patterson (Eds.), *Lesbian, gay and bisexual identities over the life span: Psychological perspectives* (pp. 243–261). New York: Oxford University Press.

Kurdek, L. A. (1994). Areas of conflict for gay, lesbian, and heterosexual couples: What couples argue about influences relationship satisfaction. *Journal of Marriage & the Family, 56*(4), 923–934.

Kurdek, L. A. (1995). Assessing multiple determinants of relationship commitment in cohabitating gay, cohabitating lesbian, dating heterosexual, and married heterosexual couples. *Family Relations, 44*(3), 261–266.

Kurdek, L. A. (1998). Relationship outcomes and their predictors: Longitudinal evidence from heterosexual married, gay cohabiting, and lesbian cohabiting couples. *Journal of Marriage & the Family, 60*(3), 553–568.

Kurdek, L. A. (2001). Differences between heterosexual-nonparent couples and gay, lesbian, and heterosexual-parent couples. *Journal of Family Issues, 22*(6), 727–754.

Kurdek, L. A. (2004). Are gay and lesbian cohabiting couples *really* different from heterosexual married couples? *Journal of Marriage & the Family 66*(4), 880–900.

Kurdek, L. A., & Schmitt, J. P. (1986). Relationship quality of partners in heterosexual married, heterosexual cohabiting and gay and lesbian relationships. *Journal of Personality & Social Psychology, 51,* 711–720.

Kurdek, L. A., & Schmitt, J. P. (1987). Perceived emotional support from family and friends in members of homosexual, married, and heterosexual cohabiting couples. *Journal of Homosexuality, 14*(3–4), 57–68.

Laird, J. (1999). Gender and sexuality in lesbian relationships: Feminist and constructionist perspectives. In J. Laird (Ed.), *Lesbians and lesbian families* (pp. 47–89). New York: Columbia University Press.

Laird, J. (2000). Gender in lesbian relationships: Cultural, feminist, and constructionist reflections. *Journal of Marital & Family Therapy, 26*(4), 455–467.

LaSala, M. C. (2001). Monogamous or not: Understanding and counseling gay male couples. *Families in Society, 82,* 605–611.

Lev, A. I. (2006). Transgender emergence within families. In D. F. Morrow & L. Messinger (Eds.), *Sexual orientation and gender expression in social work practice* (pp. 263–283). New York: Columbia University Press.

Lev, A. I., & Lev, S. S. (1999). Sexual assault in the lesbian, gay, bisexual, and transgendered communities. In J. C. McClennen & J. Gunther (Eds.), *A professional guide to understanding gay and lesbian domestic violence: Understanding practice interventions* (pp. 35–62). Lewiston, NY: Edwin Mellen.

Lewins, F. (2002). Explaining stable partnerships among FTMs and MTFs: A significant difference [Electronic version]. *Journal of Sociology, 38*(1), 76–88. Retrieved November 11, 2005, from http://find.galegroup.com/itx/informer.do?type=retrieve&tablD=Too2&prodiD=EAIM&source=gale&srcprod=Eim&userGroupName=Jack91990+version=1.0>

Lockhart, L. L., White, B. N., Causby, V., & Isaac, A. (1994). Letting out the secret: Violence in lesbian relationships. *Journal of Interpersonal Violence, 9*(4), 469–492.

Lombardi, E. L. (1999). Integration within a transgender social network and its effect upon members' social and political activity. *Journal of Homosexuality, 37*(1), 109–124.

Lombardi, E., & Bettcher, T. (2006). Lesbian, gay, bisexual, and transgender/transsexual individuals. In B. S. Levy & V. W. Sidel (Eds.), *Social injustice* (pp. 130–144). New York: Oxford University Press.

Long, L. L., Burnett, J. A., & Thomas, R. V. (2006). *Sexuality counseling: An integrative approach.* Upper Saddle River, NJ: Pearson/Merrill/Prentice Hall.

MacDonald, B. J. (1998). Issues in therapy with gay and lesbian couples. *Journal of Sex & Marital Therapy, 24*, 165–190.

Martell, C. R., Safren, S. A., & Prince, S. E. (2004). *Cognitive-behavioral therapies with lesbian, gay, and bisexual clients.* New York: Guilford.

Marvin, C., & Miller, D. (2000). Lesbian couples entering the 21st century. In P. Papp (Ed.), *Couples on the faultline: New directions for therapists* (pp. 257–283). New York: Guilford.

McClennen, J. C. (2005). Domestic violence between same-gender partners: Recent findings and future research. *Journal of Interpersonal Violence, 20*(2), 149–154.

McClennen, J. C., Summers, B., & Vaughan, C. (2002). Gay men's domestic violence: Dynamics, help-seeking behaviors, and correlates. *Journal of Gay & Lesbian Social Services, 14*(1), 23–49.

McKenry, P. C., Serovich, J. M., Mason, T. L., & Mosack, K. (2006). Perpetration of gay and lesbian partner violence: A disempowerment perspective. *Journal of Family Violence, 21*(4), 233–243.

McLaughlin, E. M., & Rozee, P. D. (2001). Knowledge about heterosexual versus lesbian battery among lesbians. *Women & Therapy, 23*(3), 39–58.

McVinney, L. D. (1998). Social work practice with gay male couples. In G. P. Mallon (Ed.), *Foundations of social work practice with lesbians and gay persons* (pp. 209–227). Binghamton, NY: Haworth Press.

Merrill, G. S., & Wolfe, V. A. (2000). Battered gay men: An exploration of abuse, help seeking and why they stay. *Journal of Homosexuality, 39*(2), 1–30.

Metz, M. E., Rosser, B. R. S., & Strapko, N. (1994). Differences in conflict-resolution styles among heterosexual, gay, and lesbian couples. *Journal of Sex Research, 31*(4), 293–308.

Miller, D. H., Greene, K., Causby, V., White, B. W., & Lockhart, L. L. (2001). Domestic violence in lesbian relationships. *Women & Therapy, 23*(3), 107–127.

Mohr, J. J. (1999). Same-sex romantic attachment. In J. Cassidy & P. R. Shaver (Eds.), *Handbook of attachment: Theory, research, and clinical applications* (pp. 378 -393). New York: Guilford.

Nathenson, D. L. (1992). *Shame and pride: Affect, sex, and the birth of the self.* New York: Norton.

Nuttbrock, L., Rosenblum, A., & Blumenstein, R. (2002). Transgender identity affirmation and mental health [Electronic version]. *International Journal of Transgenderism, 6*(4). Retrieved June 6, 2005, from http://www.symposion.com/ijt/ijtvo06no04_03.htm

Ofreneo, M. A. P. (2006). When thinking straight is detrimental to health. *Women in Action, 1*, 90–99.

Ossana, S. (2000). Relationship and couples counseling. In R. M. Perez, K. A. DeBord, & K. J. Bieschke (Eds.), *Handbook of counseling and psychotherapy with lesbian, gay, and bisexual clients* (pp. 275–302). Washington, DC: American Psychological Association.

Pauly, I. B. (1998). Gender identity and sexual orientation. In D. Denny (Ed.), *Current concepts in transgender identity* (pp. 237–247). New York: Garland.

Pearlman, S. F. (1989). Distancing and connectedness: Impact on couple formation in lesbian relationships. *Women & Therapy, 8*(1/2), 78–89.

Peplau, L. A., Fingerhut, A., & Beals, K. P. (2004). Sexuality in the relationships of lesbians and gay men. In J. H. Harvey, A. Wenzel, & S. Sprecher (Eds.), *The handbook of sexuality in close relationships* (pp. 349–369). Mahwah, NJ: Erlbaum.

Peplau, L. A., & Spalding, L. R. (2003). The close relationships of lesbians, gay men, and bisexuals. In L. D. Garnets & D. C. Kimmel (Eds.), *Psychological perspectives on lesbian, gay, and bisexual experiences* (pp. 449–474). New York: Columbia University Press.

Peterman, L. M., & Dixon, C. G. (2003). Domestic violence between same-sex partners: Implications for counseling. *Journal of Counseling & Development, 81*(1), 40–47.

Pitt, E., & Dolan-Soto, D. (2001). Clinical considerations in working with victims of same-sex domestic violence. *Journal of the Gay & Lesbian Medical Association, 5*(4), 163–169.

Renzetti, C. (1992). *Violent betrayal: Partner abuse in lesbian relationships.* Newbury Park, CA: Sage.

Ristock, J. L. (2001). Decentering heterosexuality: Responses of feminist practitioners to abuse in lesbian relationships. *Women & Therapy, 23*(3), 59–72.

Ristock, J. L. (2002). *No more secrets: Violence in lesbian relationships.* New York: Routledge.

Roisman, G. I., Clausell, E., Holland, A., Fortuna, K., & Elieff, C. (2008). Adult romantic relationships as contexts of human development: A multimethod comparison of same-sex couples with opposite-sex dating, engaged, and married dyads. *Developmental Psychology, 44*(1), 91–101.

Rust, P. C. (1995). *The challenge of bisexuality to lesbian politics: Sex, loyalty, and revolution.* New York: New York University Press.

Rust, P. C. (2003). Monogamy and polyamory: Relationship issues for bisexuals. In L. D. Garnets &

D. C. Kimmel (Eds.), *Psychological perspectives on lesbian, gay, and bisexual experiences* (pp. 475–496). New York: Columbia University Press.

Sanders, G. (2000). Men together: Working with gay couples in contemporary times. In P. Papp (Ed.), *Couples on the faultline: New directions for therapists* (pp. 222–256). New York: Guilford.

Sandfort, T. G. M., & de Keizer, M. (2001). Sexual problems in gay men: An overview of empirical research. *Annual Review of Sex Research, 12*, 93–120.

Scrivner, R., & Eldridge, N. S. (1995). Lesbian and gay family psychology. In R. H. Mikesell, D. D. Lusterman, & S. H. McDaniel (Eds.), *Integrating family therapy: Handbook of family psychology and systems therapy* (pp. 327–346). Washington, DC: American Psychological Association.

Shernoff, M. (1995). Male couples and their relationship styles. *Journal of Gay & Lesbian Social Services, 2*, 43–57.

Slater, S., & Mencher, J. (1991). The lesbian family life cycle: A contextual approach. *American Journal of Orthopsychiatry, 61*, 372–382.

Solomon, S. E., Rothblum, E. D., & Balsam, K. F. (2004). Pioneers in partnership: Lesbian and gay male couples in civil unions compared with those not in civil unions and married heterosexual siblings. *Journal of Family Psychology, 18*(2), 275–286.

Solomon, S. E., Rothblum, E. D., & Balsam, K. F. (2005). Money, housework, sex, and conflict: Same-sex couples in civil unions, those not in civil unions and heterosexual married siblings. *Sex Roles, 52*(9/10), 561–575.

Spitalnick, J. S., & McNair, L. D. (2005). Couples therapy with gay and lesbian clients: An analysis of important clinical issues. *Journal of Sex & Marital Therapy, 31*(1), 43–56.

Stanley, J. L., Bartholomew, K., Taylor, T., Oram, D., & Landolt, M. (2006). Intimate violence in male same-sex relationships. *Journal of Family Violence, 21*(1), 31–41.

Stoller, R. (1967). Transvestites' women. *American Journal of Psychiatry, 124*, 89–95.

Sue, D. W., & Sue, D. (2003). *Counseling the culturally diverse: Theory and practice* (4th ed.). New York: Wiley.

Sussal, C. M. (1999). Object relations couples therapy with lesbians. In J. Laird (Ed.), *Lesbians and lesbian families: Reflections on therapy and practice,* (pp. 179–194). New York: Columbia University Press.

Swainson, M., & Tasker, F. (2006). Genograms redrawn: Lesbian couples define their families. In J. J. Bigner (Ed.), *An introduction to GLBT family studies* (pp. 89–115). Binghamton, NY: Haworth Press.

Tarver, D. E. (2002). Transgender mental health: The intersections of race, sexual orientation, and gender identity. In B. E. Jones & M. H. Hill (Eds.), *Mental health issues in lesbian, gay, bisexual, and transgender communities* (pp. 93–108). Washington, DC: American Psychiatric Publishing.

Tiegert, L. M. (2001). The power of shame: Lesbian battering as a manifestation of homophobia. *Women & Therapy, 23*(3), 73–85.

Todosijevic, J., Rothblum, E. D., & Solomon, S. E. (2005). Relationship satisfaction, affectivity, and gay-specific stressors in same-sex couples joined in civil unions. *Psychology of Women Quarterly, 29*(2), 158–166.

Tolman, D. L., & Diamond, L. M. (2001). Desegregating sexuality research: Cultural and biological perspectives on gender and desire. *Annual Review of Sex Research, 12*, 33–74.

Tully, B. (1992). *Accounting for transsexualism and trans homosexuality: The gender identity careers of over 200 men and women who have petitioned for surgical reassignment.* Oxford, England: Whiting & Birch.

VanNatta, M. (2005). Constructing the battered woman. *Feminist Studies, 31*(2), 416–443.

Weinberg, M. S., Williams, C. J., & Pryor, D. W. (1994). *Dual attraction—Understanding bisexuality.* New York: Oxford University Press.

Zierler, S., Cunningham, W. E., Andersen, R., Shapiro, M. F., Bozzette, S. A., Nakazono, T., et al. (2000). Violence victimization after HIV infection in a U.S. probability sample of adult patients in primary care. *American Journal of Public Health, 90*, 208–215.

CHAPTER 8

Sexual and Gender Minority Families

INTRODUCTION

The narratives below offer a glimpse of just some of the challenges that confront sexual and gender minority families. In the first excerpt, from the best-selling autobiography *She's Not All There: A Life in Two Genders* (2003), Colby College professor Jennifer Finney Boylan recalls her conversation with her six-year-old son, Luke. Boylan has begun hormone therapy as part of her transition from a biological man to a woman and is preparing Luke for the change as well:

> One day Luke said, "We need to come up with a better name for you than Daddy, if you're going to be a girl."
>
> "Okay," I said, "Well what name do you think would work? You know I use the name 'Jenny,' when I'm a girl."
>
> "Jenny!" Luke, said, bursting into laughter. "That sounds like the name of a little old lady!"
>
> Trying not to be hurt, I said, "Okay, well what else can you think of?"
>
> Luke thought about it for a moment and then he said, "How about 'Maddy?' You know, like half Mommy and half Daddy?" (Boylan, 2003, p. 135)

In the second narrative, Michael Galluccio recalls his conversation with his biological parents about his intention to adopt a child with his male partner:

> I had a long talk with my family alone, over dinner one night in my parents' big formal dining room. When I told them that Jon and I were thinking of adopting, my mother removed her gaze from the chandelier above the table, glanced at my younger sister, and then burst into tears. My father, looking stony, got up from the tall mahogany chair at the head of the table and said, "You need to know that I don't approve of this." His face was serious and sincere beneath his shock of salt and pepper hair as he walked into the kitchen, staring down at the floor the entire way.

"Dad, I understand," I called after him. "But you need to understand that I'm not asking for approval. I just thought you needed to know."

I couldn't raise a child surrounded by shame I told them. . . . My parents would have to look upon my children and not have their warmest feelings stymied by embarrassment. It would have to be that way if they were to be included in my kids' upbringing. (Galluccio, Galluccio, & Groff, 2001, p. 23)

Galluccio's words voice an expectation that his parents move beyond tacit acceptance of his relationship with his partner to one of affirmation and support. Ironically, Galluccio and his partner were to challenge the boundaries of acceptance on a wide scale, as they were the first gay couple to adopt a baby in the state of Virginia.

A Preview of Chapter Contents

Imagine yourself as a helping professional employed in a community mental health clinic. You are asked to work with families whose compositions are like those above. What kind of knowledge and skills might be necessary in order to counsel these families? Specifically, how might you support transitioning parents in their dialogues with their children about their gender identities? How might the age and developmental level of children impact this process? How might you help children of sexual and gender minority parents deal with issues of disclosure both within and outside of the family context? This chapter covers key aspects in counseling sexual and gender minority families as it:

- Examines some of the challenges and the rewards that sexual and gender minorities experience as they create and sustain family life
- Reviews the research on sexual minority parents who come out as gay, lesbian, bisexual, or transgender after conceiving children in the context of heterosexual relationships
- Reviews the research on sexual and gender minority couples who have children through biological means or through adoption
- Explores some of the common clinical issues that arise for therapists working with sexual and gender minority families

ADOPTING A RESILIENCE FRAMEWORK

Historically, the bulk of the literature on sexual and gender minority families has been written from a psychopathological perspective, which emphasizes the dysfunctional symptoms or behaviors within families. This perspective neglects the majority of sexual and gender minority families who cope effectively and who find meaning even in the most difficult of circumstances. A resilience approach necessitates that helping practitioners:

- Appreciate the resourcefulness that families demonstrate
- Accept that some family problems are the natural consequences of living in a homophobic, biphobic, and transphobic culture
- Normalize the stress that sexual and gender minority families experience
- Affirm their determination to maintain loving family relationships (Walsh, 2002)

THE FAMILIES WE CHOOSE

In most cultures, families are portrayed as hierarchically structured groups of persons who are tied to one another by blood. Families who don't seem to fit this definition are considered to be "unnatural" and, as a result, are viewed with suspicion. It is not uncommon for people to assume that harm will befall children who are reared by sexual minority parents. Gay male parents are suspect in some instances because of the deep-seated belief that the majority of sexual predators are gay men (Patterson, 2003). It is assumed that children reared by lesbian mothers will experience disturbances in their sexual functioning and/or sexual and gender identities because of the lack of male/father figures (Bos, van Balen, & van den Boom, 2004; Patterson, 2003). Even those who are supportive of gay civil rights often experience discomfort with the issue of gay parenting because of fears that children will suffer from emotional and physical abuse by their peers.

It is necessary to explore ways in which sexual minorities create family connections, especially in instances where relationships between blood kin have become strained or severed because of sexual orientation. The term *families of choice* (Weston, 1991) was coined in order to describe families that are created outside of legal marriage. Families of choice comprise "a partner, adopted or biological children, and an extended network of friends, usually not exclusively lesbian and gay, who perform functions similar to those of close, extended biological families" (Laird, 1998, p. 198). According to Ryan, Pearlmutter, and Groza (2004), there are two categories of families of choice. The first, labeled "secondary" families, comprises those in which one or both adult partners have children from previous heterosexual relationships. The second category is called "planned" because it refers to families that consist of adult partners who decide to conceive children through natural or artificial means or to adopt. The next section explores the empirical research that has addressed various aspects of secondary families.

SECONDARY SEXUAL MINORITY FAMILIES

Research began in the late 1970s, largely in response to the controversies created when women who were in heterosexual marriages came out as lesbians and were involved in divorce proceedings. At that time, lesbian mothers frequently lost custody of their children because it was assumed that their sexual orientation would negatively impact their children (Bos et al., 2004; MacCallum & Golombok, 2004; Tasker, 2005). As a result of several controversial custody cases, social scientists felt compelled to evaluate judicial decisions regarding child custody. The focus of these investigations was the potential impact of mothers' same-sex sexual orientation on the social and psychological adjustment, sexual orientation, and gender roles of their children. Typically, researchers sampled comparative groups of children who grew up in households with single divorced lesbian mothers, two lesbian mothers, single heterosexual mothers, and two heterosexual parents. These samples were predominantly white and well educated. Participants were often recruited from support groups such as Parents, Families, and Friends of Lesbians and Gays (PFLAG) and were usually aware of the nature of the researchers' objectives and hypotheses (Tasker, 2005). Gay or bisexual male parents were often missing from the research. Investigators relied heavily on self-report questionnaires, and little, if any, research explored the long-term implications of sustained interactions in families when loved ones were out (Laird, 1998; Peplau & Beals, 2004).

Single Lesbian Mothers Vs. Single Heterosexual Mothers

One of the earliest studies of children of lesbian mothers was published in Great Britain in 1983 by Golombok and her colleagues. Thirty-seven children of divorced lesbian mothers were compared with a group of children in divorced heterosexual female-headed households on a variety of standardized measures. The children who participated in this study were all of school age and had lived with their fathers during their early childhood years. Based on their analysis, Golombok and her colleagues found that the children in both groups were comparable in terms of their psychological adjustment; however, children of lesbian mothers were more likely to be living with their mother's subsequent romantic partner and to have more contact with their biological fathers than were children of heterosexual mothers (Golombok, Spencer, & Rutter, 1983). Additional research throughout the 1980s (e.g., Green, Mandel, Hotvedt, Gray, & Smith, 1986) explored the psychological adjustment of children of single heterosexual and lesbian mothers and reported no differences between these groups.

One of the first studies to incorporate children raised in lesbian-headed households in which their biological fathers were never present was conducted by Golombok, Tasker, and Murray in 1997. The researchers recruited 30 families headed by single lesbian mothers and 42 families headed by single heterosexual mothers and compared them with 41 two-parent heterosexual families. The children in these families were approximately six years of age. Although there were no differences in the incidence of emotional and behavioral problems among children in single heterosexual mother, single lesbian mother, and two-parent families, children in father-absent homes perceived themselves as less cognitively and physically competent than did those in families with a father present.

Approximately seven years later, MacCallum and Golombok (2004) recontacted the same families who participated in their earlier study. Participants from the original study were now adolescents. In interviews with families headed by single lesbian mothers, single heterosexual mothers, and two-parent heterosexuals, a number of instruments were administered, including measures of school and peer adjustment and emotional and behavioral functioning. There were no differences among single lesbian mother, single heterosexual mother, and two-parent families in terms of the children's social and emotional development. MacCallum and Golombok also found no evidence to support the concern that children of lesbian mothers would experience more teasing and bullying in their relationships with their peers. The earlier finding that at age six children in both forms of father-absent households perceived themselves as less cognitively and physically competent than did those in father-present households appeared to have washed out by adolescence.

Same-Sex Partnered Households Vs. Two-Parent Heterosexual Households

Numerous studies (Bailey, Bobrew, Wolfe, & Mikach, 1995; Bigner & Jacobsen, 1989; Brewaeys, Ponjaert, Van Hall, & Golombok, 1997; Chan, Raboy, & Patterson, 1998; Perry et al., 2004) have compared levels of psychological functioning of children in secondary two-parent same-sex families and two-parent heterosexual families. In 1997, Tasker and Golombok compared children who resided in two-partner lesbian households and those in married heterosexual families. Children in lesbian households described more positive relationships with their mothers' new partners than did those in heterosexual families. The female partners exercised greater flexibility in terms of roles than did the male partners in heterosexual relationships. The lesbian partners were more likely to enter the family without clearly defined roles and to permit these roles to slowly evolve based on the individual needs and circumstances of the family. Chan et al. (1998) reported that lesbian mothers shared parenting more equally with their partners than did heterosexual mothers and fathers.

In one of the few studies to explore adolescent-age children in secondary families, Wainright, Russell, and Patterson (2004) reviewed data gleaned from a recent comprehensive national study of 12- to 18-year-old adolescents parented by same-sex and heterosexual couples. Both groups were carefully matched on demographic characteristics. No differences emerged on a variety of measures assessing school and personal adjustment. Regardless of which family type adolescents came from, those who were reared in warm, caring relationships with parents were more positively adjusted.

"No Differences": An Artifact of Research Bias?

In the studies described above, researchers reported no differences between children reared in two-parent sexual minority households and those reared in two-parent heterosexual households. Like many highly visible endeavors, the research process is influenced by politics. As mentioned earlier, this research was initially undertaken in response to controversial child custody decisions wherein judges frequently deemed lesbian mothers unfit to raise their children. Accordingly, social scientists were motivated to refute or support the notion that children reared by homosexuals were harmed by this experience.

In their article published in *American Sociological Review* in 2001, Stacey and Biblarz posited that the politically sensitive nature of the gay parenthood issue has led some researchers to be hesitant in acknowledging instances where they did indeed find differences between sexual minority and nonminority families. Stacey and Biblarz reviewed 21 data-based studies that compared children reared in lesbian families with those reared in heterosexual families during the period 1981 through 1998. In contrast to the assertion of "no differences" by previous researchers, Stacey and Biblarz concluded that there are instances in which the "sexual orientations of these parents matter somewhat more for their children than the researchers claimed" (p. 167). They argued that daughters of lesbian mothers were less conforming to sex-typed cultural norms in terms of both recreational interests and occupational preferences. Young female adults raised by lesbian mothers were significantly more likely to report being open to a broader range of sexual possibilities and being more sexually adventurous. Sons were somewhat less sexually adventurous. The researchers concluded that such discrepancies seem easily understandable, given that two female parents would exhibit less stereotypic gender-role behaviors and be more open to questions about sexuality.

Stacey and Biblarz noted that research findings continue to have enormous implications in terms of the legal rights of sexual minorities and their ability to adopt and foster children and to have access to fertility services. But they also argued that "the case for granting equal rights to nonheterosexual parents should not require finding their children to be identical to those reared by heterosexuals" (p. 178).

COUNSELING SECONDARY SEXUAL MINORITY FAMILIES

Sexual minority parents face the same stresses all parents face. But in addition, they must deal with a unique set of challenges:

- When and how to self-disclose their sexual orientation to their own children
- How to guide their children through the process of making decisions about disclosing their parents' sexual orientation to others
- How to help children cope with the potential reactions of their peers, the parents of peers, their teachers, and so on (Barrett & Tasker, 2001)

Research suggests that children of sexual minority parents have their own set of psychosocial stressors. For example, Garner's (2004) extensive interviews with children of sexual minority parents suggest that the children feel burdened by a responsibility to present themselves as "model" children to a world that looks at them with a certain scrutiny and suspicion. This burden may even be more deeply felt when the children of sexual minority parents are also gay, lesbian, or bisexual. Garner observed that such children are also stigmatized in the gay/lesbian/bisexual (GLB) community because of fears that their visibility will reinforce stereotypes. The remainder of the section focuses on these and other challenges in sexual minority families and offers practical advice to helping professionals who endeavor to assist such families.

Prepare Parents for Planned and Deliberative Self-Disclosure

A basic issue for sexual minority parents is whether to tell their children about their sexual identities and relationships and, if so, how and when. Historically, family systems theorists (e.g., Beeler & DiProva, 1999; LaSala, 2000; Rostosky et al., 2004) have been adamantly against the notion of family members keeping "secrets" from one another. Many family therapy practitioners believe that not disclosing one's sexual orientation can have a dramatic impact on children, generating anxiety and confusion (Murray & McClintock, 2005). Green (2000) noted, for example, the tendency among many family therapists to exercise undue pressure on parents to self-disclose:

> In many family therapy circles (Bowenian circles) the decision to keep a major secret like this from your family is almost inconceivable because family therapists typically value open communication, differentiation of self, and authenticity so highly in family life. (p. 279)

Future practitioners may need to guard against this bias and exercise caution when discussing the issue of self-disclosure with parents. It is perhaps advisable for therapists to first explore with parents where they are in their own identity development as gay, lesbian, or bisexual, since this may have important implications for their ability to discuss their sexual orientation (Barret & Logan, 2002). Parents who are struggling with their own homophobic or biphobic feelings may not have the emotional energy necessary to deal with similar responses in their children. The ages and development stages of children are important considerations in determining how and when parents might initiate conversations about their same-sex sexual orientation. Certainly, most guidelines stress the importance of preparing ahead of time and providing accurate education and reassurance.

Practitioners can play a vital role in coaching sexual minority parents through the process. Planned self-disclosures tend to be more effective than those that are undertaken impulsively in the heat of the moment (Morrow, 2006). Parents can actively prepare for disclosure by establishing a private time and space to talk to their children and by writing down points in the conversation ahead of time (*Tips for Coming Out to Your Kids*, n.d.). Next, it is a good idea to encourage parents to ask what their children already know or have heard from others about being "gay," "lesbian," "bisexual," and/or "queer."

Common emotional reactions in children once parents self-disclose include anger, shame, confusion, and shock (Gottlieb, 2003; Robinson, Walters, & Skeen, 1989), responses that are frequently associated with the grieving process. Children may feel as though they have lost the parent they thought they knew. They may experience a loss of status in their community and with their peers. They may feel a loss of certainty about the world (Gottlieb, 2003). Some children experience the fear that they could become gay as well as contracting AIDS (Garner, 2004). Practitioners can help provide children with safe places to mourn as well as much needed education about the nature of sexual orientation and the transmission of HIV.

It is vital to provide reassurance that children are loved regardless of sexual orientation and gender identity. It is also advisable to offer children the option of talking with their own counselor and/or other adults and to invite further conversations. In addition, practitioners can recommend numerous books for children that talk of having a gay, lesbian, or bisexual parent: *Heather Has Two Mommies* (Newman, 1991); *Felicia's Favorite Story* (Newman, 2002); *Daddy's Roommate* (Wilhoite, 1991); and *My Dad Has HIV* (Alexander, Rudin, Sejkora, & Shipman, 1996). A number of additional recommendations for childrens' and adolescents' books about sexual and gender minority parents are available on the website of Children of Lesbians and Gays Everywhere (COLAGE) (www.colage.org).

Because sexual minority parents are especially concerned with the possibility that their children may be teased and harassed by their peers (Johnson & O'Connor, 2002), practitioners can help parents in preparing children with important decision-making skills. Specifically, children will need to decide if, when, and how information about their family structure should be shared with others outside the family. In situations where sexual minority parents are selectively open about their identities, children may well experience heightened anxiety about letting this information accidentally slip out. These concerns may and often do prevent children from inviting peers into their homes (Adams, Jaques, & May, 2004; Lamme & Lamme, 2001). There are certain contexts where children might not wish to disclose their parents' sexual identities. It's important that parents not internalize this or take it personally. In instances where parents are open with their identities, their children may also be in danger of internalizing pressure to defend and protect their parents (Garner, 2004; Lamme & Lamme, 2001).

Recognize and Validate

Therapists are ideally situated to provide families with the external support and validation often missing in social contexts. This validation is crucial, as sexual minorities often internalize societal disapproval of their sexual orientation and their family structure (O'Dell, 2000). There are many ways to offer such validation:

- Use inclusive language within counseling sessions.
- Make sure all written communication and policies use inclusive statements.
- Choose images, photos, magazines, and décor in the office that reflect this validation. (Adams et al., 2004)

Helping professionals who work with sexual minority families must be well acquainted with the resources within their own community, such as support groups like COLAGE.

It is a fact that sexual minority families sometimes feel themselves invisible even within gay communities. Bigner (1996) explored the specific challenges that await gay fathers whose children were born in heterosexual marriages, noting that the singles-oriented gay subculture is a major issue for gay fathers, as are divided personal identities.

The issues of validation and recognition are especially important in blended families, families where one partner is the biological mother or father and the other is not. Mitchell (1996) cautioned family therapy practitioners who work with sexual minority families not to assign the biological mother or father the role of "primary" parent and relegate the non-biological partner as the "secondary" parent. She argued that this view only compounds the invisibility of nonbiological parents, who are often not recognized as such beyond the realm of immediate family members (Mitchell, 1996). This is especially true in states where adoption laws permit only one parent to adopt, often leaving the other partner feeling discounted and invisible.

Based on her intensive interviews with 35 stepfamilies, the majority of whom had children from previous heterosexual relationships, Lynch (2004) made a number of compelling observations. She noted that sexual minorities typically lose their status as parents within same sex relationships. Their abilities as parents are questioned in the context of a heterosexist culture. The stepparenting role is particularly problematic. It is poorly defined and has no legal or social underpinnings. In Lynch's sample, gay stepfathers reported feeling less accepted in both the heterosexual and the gay communities than did lesbian stepmothers. She noted that most stepfathers in her sample coped with the sense of rejection they felt from the gay male community by surrounding themselves with other gay men who were parents. Taken together, the research seems to suggest that when practitioners focus almost exclusively on the biologically or legally adoptive parent, they are in effect contributing to the invalidation of the other parent. This is yet another area where practitioners need to develop awareness and sensitivity.

In order to aid practitioners in working with reconstituted or blended families, Ariel and McPherson (2000) recommended that therapists consider the following issues:

1. How supportive is the heterosexual former spouse?
2. How comfortable with his or her own sexual orientation is the new gay or lesbian partner?
3. What is the attitude toward the children of the lesbian or gay parent's new partner and the former spouse's new partner, if there is one?
4. Do the adults share their definition of family and parenting with the children, or is it kept secret?
5. How much communication is there in general between the biological parents, and how safe do the children feel talking to either or both parents?
6. How is the extended family involved within the family dynamic?
7. Should extended family members be told, and how supportive will they be? (p. 423)

Identify Family Strengths

Researchers, as well as practitioners, have typically focused on dysfunctional symptoms in sexual minority families and ignored the strengths that such families exhibit. There are one or two notable exceptions. In one study, Litovich and Langhout (2004) sought to identify aspects of resiliency within their sample of sexual minority families. They observed that lesbian mothers in their sample began communicating with their children at very early ages about the kinds of discrimination they might conceivably experience in the future. They taught their children terminology to help them develop an intellectual understanding, and they helped create an environment where their children would feel comfortable discussing their experiences. They provided their children with knowledge about diverse kinds of family forms and taught them that the discrimination they might experience was not directed at them personally but at the "demographic they represented" (p. 431). Mitchell (1998) reported that children of sexual minority parents develop greater affective expressiveness than do children in nonminority samples and value social diversity to a greater extent than do their counterparts.

It is important to bear in mind that some of the ideas and practices presented in this and the previous chapters are in direct contradiction to those presented only a decade or so ago. In their text *Nurturing Queer Youth*, family therapists Fish and Harvey (2005) observed, for example, that the field of marriage and family counseling has adopted a stance of "tolerance" with regard to homosexuality. "It is one thing to hold liberal views of sexuality or even to be accepting of sexual minorities, but it is quite another to intentionally and purposefully help our children grow up gay" (p. 26). Fish and Harvey distinguish between helpers who are accepting of sexual and gender minority youth and those who affirm and celebrate them.

Practitioners who work with sexual minority families must be mindful of how few sources of affirmation are available to such families and consciously note possible strengths these families possess, such as increased emotional openness and expressiveness and greater cognitive and gender-role flexibility.

Help Families Develop Rituals

As discussed, heterosexism and homophobia can have substantial impact on the lives and relationships of sexual minority couples. Like their sexual minority parents, children are faced with having to continually manage their identities in the wake of nonaffirming and/or hostile social environments. Research has shown that sexual minority parents worry about the possibility that their children will be the recipients of harassment and/or injury from their peers. Most teach their children stigma management strategies in order to minimize the risks of harassment. Tradition and family rituals help combat any invalidation or invisibility sexual minority families may experience. Family rituals often range from "patterned routines," like mealtimes, to celebrations, like birthdays or holidays (Kiser, Bennett, Heston, & Paavola, 2005). Therapists can aid families in developing rituals (Muzio, 1996), including creating baby books and photo albums to record memories and milestones (Roberts, 1999) and holding commitment ceremonies.

PLANNED SEXUAL MINORITY FAMILIES

Researchers posit that planned families are becoming more prevalent; many think we are in the midst of a "gay baby boom" in which gay men and lesbians are choosing to have children through adoption, foster care, surrogacy arrangements, and donor insemination (Johnson & O'Connor, 2002). A recent national survey by Johnson and O'Connor in 2002 was partly designed to assess the different methods that sexual minorities employ to either conceive or adopt children in planned families. Their sample consisted of planned families (70 gay fathers and 336 lesbian mothers) from 34 states. The majority of lesbian couples (88%) in their sample chose to conceive their children. The majority of gay couples (85%) elected to adopt their children.

Donor Insemination

In the late 1980s, research began to assess the family lives of sexual minorities who choose to create families through adoption, foster care, surrogacy arrangements, and donor insemination. The National Lesbian Family Study (NLFS) was initiated in 1986 in the United States in order to develop a database on the first generation of families whose children were conceived by donor insemination. Donor insemination involves inseminating sperm from a known or unknown donor into the uterus of a female. Insemination can entail self-insemination or insemination with the assistance of physicians. The NLFS is now on its fourth phase. During the first phase, 84 mothers who identified themselves as lesbian were interviewed extensively. Half of this group had selected donors who were known to them, and half had selected anonymous donors (Gartrell al et., 1996). At the initial interview, 70 households had a birth mother and a co-mother, and 14 were headed by a single mother. Most mothers formed parenting groups and were involved in sharing information and networking with one another.

The second interview phase was conducted when the children were two years old (Gartrell et al., 1999). In most families with co-parents, the child-rearing responsibilities were shared equally. At five years of age, the children of lesbian mothers were considered to be as healthy and psychologically well adjusted as their counterparts were (Gartrell et al., 2000). By the time phase four of the study was completed, 78 of the original 84 families remained in the study (Gartrell, Deck, Rodas, Peyser, & Banks, 2005). A series of questionnaires and semistructured interviews was conducted with mothers, co-mothers, and children. In terms of social and psychological development, the NLFS children, who were 10 years of age at the time, were comparable to children in normative samples of children raised in heterosexual families. No differences were found on any measures between children whose donors were known and those whose donors were permanently unknown. Fifty-seven percent of the children reported that they had disclosed their mothers' sexual orientation to most people, and 39% had disclosed to some people. Forty-three percent of the children reported experiencing homophobic responses from others.

Adoption

Van Voorhis and Wagner (2002) conducted a content analysis of 12 prominent social work journals covering a 12-year period and found there that were no articles dealing with sexual minorities as adoptive or foster parents. Sexual minorities pursue international adoption singly, and frequently, their partners legally adopt in the United States through the "second parent adoption process" (Connolly, 1996). Adoption applications by gay men and lesbians are prohibited in China, Thailand, and Guatemala (Brodzinsky, 2002). It is suspected that most sexual minority parents choose to conceal their sexual orientation out of fear of being denied the possibility of adoption (Ricketts & Achtenberg, 1990). In a national adoption survey, approximately 25% of respondents surveyed indicated that the birth parents either objected to the placement or specifically requested that their child not be placed with sexual minorities (Brodzinsky, 2003). Florida is the only state that prohibits adoption by sexual minorities. Only four states—California, Massachusetts, New Jersey, and Vermont—and the District of Columbia allow joint adoptions by gay and lesbian couples (Ryan, Pearlmutter, & Groza, 2004). Typically, the adoption process entails an assessment of the prospective parent's personal background and a home study by the Department of Children and Family Services.

Brooks and Goldberg (2001) conducted semi-structured interviews with 10 key staff members of a social services agency and a focus group of adoptive parents. The critical variable in whether or not a foster or adoption placement is made with gay men and lesbians is the institutional climate of the agency, including its formal policies and informal attitudes of its personnel. Brooks and Goldberg concluded that "an agency's attitude toward placements with gay men and lesbians can have profound implications for recruitment and placement practices of individual workers" (p. 152).

Leung, Erich, and Kanenberg (2005) explored factors that contribute to how a family functions. They looked at families headed by sexual minority parents and by heterosexual parents and families who had children with special needs. Results indicated that family functioning worsened as the age of the child at the time of adoption increased. No negative effects on family functioning were associated with the sexual orientation of the adoptive parents.

Many lesbians adopt children internationally because they perceive the domestic adoption system to be antigay (Alperson, 1997). Bennett (2003) interviewed 15 such lesbian couples and noted they experienced postadoption stress to the same degree as heterosexual couples. Many of their respondents perceived the main challenge as the child's acceptance of their nontraditional family structure. What's more, as only single applications are accepted for international adoption, this frequently caused power struggles within these sexual minority families. The majority of the couples also noted initial ambivalence related to the adoption on the part of extended family members regarding conflicts with religious beliefs and cultural standards.

Mitchell (1996) describes the common pattern in planned two-mother lesbian families as dual-career and nonhierarchical, with household responsibilities equally divided. Often the nonbiological parent is considered by others to be less significant or legitimate than the biological parent (Mitchell, 1996). Some therapists are guilty of making this assumption as well, thereby jeopardizing the therapeutic alliance and perhaps reinforcing situations in couples where this dynamic is already present.

Co-parenting Issues

Patterson (1998) conducted research on lesbian parenting constellations that involved artificial inseminations. She noted that the biological mothers spent more time in child-care activities and less time in employment than did the nonbiological mothers. The biological mothers also reported more contact with their extended family members than did the nonbiological mothers.

Brewaeys et al. (1997) studied lesbian partners and heterosexual partners who had had donor inseminations and compared them to heterosexual partners whose children were naturally conceived. Social or nonbiological mothers in the lesbian families interacted more with their children than did fathers in the donor insemination and naturally conceived families. There were no differences between social and biological mothers in the parent–child interactions.

Patterson (2003) also designed the Bay Area Families Study to explore variables related to child development and family functioning in lesbian and heterosexual parent families. Eligibility requirements for participation by lesbian families included the presence of at least one child in the household between four and nine years of age, either born to or adopted by a lesbian mother or adopted by both mothers. She observed that children of lesbian mothers reported healthier reactions to stress and a greater sense of well-being. There was an equal division of household and family tasks in lesbian couples, compared to heterosexual couples. And generally, research seemed to suggest that variables like the quality of the parent–child interaction is more meaningful than the family structure in determining the psychological adjustment of children in donor insemination families (Chan et al., 1998; Murray & Golombok, 2005).

The Impact of Parenthood on Families of Origin

Sexual minorities electing to have children frequently have to renegotiate their relationships with their families of origin (Muzio, 1996). Persons who are not out to their families of origin often find concealment less feasible once children enter the picture. As Michael Galluccio described at the start of the chapter, when he told his biological parents about his intention to adopt a child with his same-sex partner, their reaction was not a positive one.

Johnson and O'Connor (2002) noted that approximately 50% of the lesbian parents and 25% of the gay male parents they studied reported that they had faced negative reactions from their own parents regarding their decision to have children.

COUNSELING PLANNED SEXUAL MINORITY FAMILIES

Sexual minorities face a number of issues in contemplating parenthood:

- Choosing parenting options
- Addressing health concerns, including prenatal care and preparation for birth
- Finding support networks and resources (Patterson, 1998)

Chabot and Ames (2004) chose to articulate the sorts of questions and issues faced by lesbian couples who choose parenthood through donor insemination. Based on their qualitative analysis of extensive interviews, they noted that several key questions guided couples' decision-making processes:

- Do we want to become parents?
- Where do we access information and support?
- How will we become parents?
- Who will be the biological mother?
- How do we decide on a donor?
- How do we incorporate inclusive language?
- How do we negotiate parenthood within the larger heterosexist context?

As a helping professional, you may be called on to assist sexual minority clients in answering these as well as other questions and concerns. Excellent bibliographic resources for you and for prospective same-sex parents include *The Queer Parent's Primer* (Brill, 2001); *The Essential Guide to Lesbian Conception, Pregnancy, and Birth* (Toevs & Brill, 2002); *The Ultimate Guide to Pregnancy for Lesbians* (Pepper, 2005); *A Gay Couple's Journey Through Surrogacy* (Menichiello, 2006), *Fatherhood for Gay Men: An Emotional and Practical Guide to Becoming a Gay Dad* (McGarry, 2003) and *A Legal Guide for Lesbian and Gay Couples* (Curry, Clifford, & Hertz, 2005).

Advocate for Sexual Minority Families

An important role for helping professionals who work with sexual minority families is that of advocacy. If we are to afford sexual minority parents and children the same opportunities and rights as nonminority families, there is much work to be done in changing local and state adoption laws and policies regarding foster care.

SEXUAL MINORITIES AND THEIR FAMILIES OF ORIGIN

Sexual minorities face a myriad of issues as they relate to their families of origin. The next chapter explores in more detail the experiences of youth who have questioned their sexual orientation or who have come out as sexual minorities. In this section, however, the focus is specifically on the issues that confront other family members, particularly parents, as they relate to their sexual minority kin.

Responses to Self-Disclosure by Family Members

In a recent survey, 50% of lesbians and 32% of gay men reported that one or more family members had refused to accept them because of their sexual orientation (Kaiser Foundation, 2001). A number of researchers and practitioners liken the responses of family members following a relative's disclosure of homosexuality to those associated with the grieving process. Kubler-Ross's (1969) stages of grieving (shock, denial, sadness, anger, and eventual acceptance) have been widely applied to describe the reactions of parents following their child's disclosure (Robinson et al., 1989). Yet some researchers (i.e., Savin-Williams, 2001; Savin-Williams & Dube, 1998) question the applicability of this model. Crosbie-Burnett, Foster, Murray, and Bowen (1996) developed an alternative stage model to depict family members' responses. This includes periods of questioning whether to disclose the news to others; feeling blame, guilt, anger, and confusion; and finally, deciding about how to disclose to others both inside and outside the family.

However, most researchers and practitioners agree that parents respond to their sexual minority children in varying ways. Some react negatively to the realization that their daughter or son is gay. They blame themselves and feel at fault. They fear for the physical and psychological well-being of their children. And they worry about the reactions of friends, relatives, and neighbors (Goldfried & Goldfried, 2001). Some move beyond negative responses to a level of tolerance that might be similar to a "don't ask–don't tell" policy, in which parents know their children are gay, lesbian, or bisexual but try to minimize the salience of this through silence (Tremble, Schneider, & Appathurai, 1989). Lastly, some are able to fully embrace and accept their children and their children's partners.

In Beeler and DiProva's (1999) extensive interviews with families of sexual minorities, the majority of parents reported feelings of loss related to missed opportunities for weddings and grandchildren. Many sought information from the gay community and from gay-positive sources and went through their own parallel coming out process in terms of deciding to whom they might reveal information about the family member's sexual orientation. One common response from the parents of expectant couples is fear of disclosure to others.

Research suggests parents' attitudes toward their children's homosexuality improve over time (LaSala, 2000), and parental attitudes may sometimes differ on the basis of their child's gender and age. For example, Herdt and Koff (2000) found that parents had more difficulty dealing with a daughter's sexual orientation than with that of a son. Saltzburg's (2004) qualitative study of parent responses to adolescent children's disclosure of sexual orientation states that many parents seem to develop an early awareness of their child as different from others, and there is often a a sense of emotional detachment following the self-disclosure. Many parents are especially fearful of becoming estranged from their children, and many ultimately find support and mentoring relationships to assist with their adjustment process.

COUNSELING SEXUAL MINORITIES AND THEIR FAMILIES OF ORIGIN

Guide Families Through the Self-Disclosure Process

Family systems therapists (e.g., Beeler & DiProva, 1999; LaSala, 2000; Rostosky et al., 2004) should not exert undue pressure on children to self-disclose their sexual orientation to their families of origin. Noting the extent to which sexual minority persons develop alternative support systems, Green (2000) advocates that therapists aid their sexual minority clients in conducting a cost–benefit analysis to determine the advisability of coming out to their families of origin.

LaSala (2000) offers a number of useful suggestions to family therapy practitioners on ways to assist family members during the coming out process. He advises therapists to coach parents on noncombative communication styles to use with their children following disclosure. He observed that family members often instinctively impose reactive distance following disclosure partly because of the intense emotional reactions they experience. He, therefore, encourages parents and children to have brief and limited contacts with each other. He further suggests separate sessions for parents and children, which would allow both to express the intense feelings they are experiencing in a safe atmosphere. When parents reject their child, it is important for therapists "to sit with the client's grief or anger and validate the loss" (Muzio, 1996, p. 364).

Recommend Support Groups

Saltzburg (2004) recommends developing gay and lesbian adult mentors and peer support groups of parent volunteers with gay or lesbian children. "For parents who have not had contact with the gay community, a mentoring relationship can bring about the first realization that being gay is not synonymous with deviance or immorality" (p. 116). Support groups such as PFLAG are adjunctive means of support for parents and can circumvent the sense of emotional isolation that many family members experience. An activity at the end of this chapter provides information on PFLAG chapters as well as geographic locations and services for sexual minority persons and their families.

The message basic to family therapy literature (e.g., Herdt & Koff, 2000) is that heterosexual parents experience a crisis when their children come out as gay, lesbian, or bisexual. The emphasis is twofold: the sense of loss that parents experience and the process of renegotiation and readjustment that must take place. Historically, the focus in therapy training and practice has been on helping family members cope rather than finding ways to celebrate their child's same-sex sexual orientation (Fish & Harvey, 2005). Beeler and DiProva (1999) emphasized the therapist's role as helping families of origin tell their stories about how they learned of a family member's homosexuality. They argue that these "finding out" stories are as meaningful and significant to family members as "coming out" stories are to their homosexual family members.

GENDER MINORITY FAMILIES

Gender minority parents and their children face tremendous social, economic, and legal barriers. In a transphobic culture, gender minority parents who undergo transitions after their children are conceived often lose custody and visitation rights in civil and family courts in the United States (Flynn, 2006; Lev, 2006).

As noted repeatedly throughout this text, the helping professions have extensive histories of both pathologizing gender variance and ignoring the needs of gender minority families (Lev, 2006; Zamboni, 2006). Yet helping professionals are ideally situated to offer validation and support to such families. This section reviews the empirical research and discusses the implications of this literature in terms of counseling interventions for use with gender minority parents and their family members.

The Lack of Research

In contrast to the quantities of research on sexual minority parents and their children, the research on gender minority families is sparse (Lesser, 1999; Lev, 2004; White & Ettner, 2004; Liren, 2002). Much of what has been written is by physicians or psychotherapists who specialize in gender identity issues, and their insights have been gleaned largely from their gender reassignment patients. Most of this work also pertains exclusively to secondary families, those families made up of gender minority parents whose children were conceived prior to coming out as gender minorities or initiating gender transitions. As with early research on sexual minority families, most researchers and family practitioners assumed that children exposed to the truth about the gender orientation of their parents would be psychologically damaged, harassed by their peers, and confused about their own gender identities (Green, 1998). The little empirical research that does exist assesses the impact of parents' gender minority status on children's psychological adjustment, especially their gender and sexual identities.

In one of the few empirically based studies of children of gender minority parents, Green (1978) compared 37 children raised by either lesbian parents or transsexual parents. Green reported that the children did not appear to be conflicted about their own gender identities and that the majority described themselves as heterosexual. Almost twenty years later, Green (1998) revisited this topic. He explored the nature of peer relationships and gender identity of the children of gender minority parents. He interviewed 18 youths who were between the ages of 5 and 16 and who either resided with or had extensive contact with their gender minority parents. Green found no evidence of gender identity disorder (GID) in his sample. He described most of the sexual minority parent–child relationships as "warm" and found no indication that youths were experiencing interpersonal difficulties with peers. Green noted that one of the most significant determinants of children's psychological adjustment was the non–gender minority parent's attitude toward and acceptance of his or her gender minority partner.

White and Ettner (2004) attempted to identify factors that correlated with children's adjustment to their parents' gender minority status. They surveyed a sample of psychotherapists whose clinical specialty was working with gender minority clients and their families. Their total sample consisted of 10 therapists with an average of 14.2 years of clinical experience and a combined total of 4,768 clients. About half of their clients had undergone sex reassignment surgery: 64% male-to-female (MTF) and 36% female-to-male (FTM). Survey respondents were asked to rank a list of possible factors that White and

Ettner had identified as the risk factors that placed children at the greatest risk for adjustment problems. Respondents identified the following factors, in order of significance:

- An abrupt separation from either parent
- A spouse who was extremely opposed to the transition
- A personality disorder in the transitioning parent
- The presence of parental conflict regarding the transition
- A personality disorder in the nontransitioning parent

Participants were also asked to rank the following protective factors in order of helpfulness:

- A close emotional tie between the child and the nontransitioning parent
- Cooperation between the parents regarding the children
- Extended family support
- A close emotional relationship between the child and the transitioning parent
- Ongoing contact with both parents

Adolescent-age children appeared to have the most difficulty with their parents' gender transitions, and preschool-age children seemed to fare the best. White and Ettner (2004) also noted that the gender minority clients who fared the best during the transition process were in families where the amount of pretransition conflict was minimal. This is consistent with a large body of research on resiliency in children that identifies factors leading to successful adaptation. Chief among these are accepting and supportive relationships with parents.

Gender Minority Parents and Self-Disclosure

In the excerpt at the beginning of this chapter, Boylan (2003), a male-to-female transsexual, tried to explain to her six-year-old son about the numerous physical changes that had occurred as she transitioned from a biological man to a woman. The mere prospect of entering into such a communication with a six-year-old may seem daunting, especially for the transitioning adult who already has a myriad of issues to deal with. Assume you are Boylan's therapist. Is her attempt to talk with someone so young about such a complex issue advisable?

According to Brown and Rounsley (1996), "until around fifteen years ago, therapists used to suggest that transsexual parents disappear forever from their young children's lives" (p. 187). Lev (2004) is a psychotherapist with extensive clinical experience with gender minority clients and their families. She observes that practitioners continue to advise gender minority parents not to share information related to their gender identity with children. Yet many practitioners have observed that young children are often better able to adjust to their parents' gender transitions than are adolescents and adults (Israel, 2005).

The prospect of communicating about gender variance and gender transitioning may be overwhelming for most gender minority parents. White and Ettner (2004) noted that many gender minorities never reveal themselves to anyone. Some self-disclose but only in the context of therapy. Others present themselves for counseling when their impulses to cross-dress become more powerful or when their gender identity issues are exposed either intentionally or unintentionally. When gender identity issues are exposed, it is not uncommon for spouses or partners to express concerns about the well-being of their children or to forbid their partners to self-disclose to their children. Often gender minority parents instinctively believe that they should keep their gender minority status a secret from their children. What they don't realize is that children sense emotional disturbance and are aware something in the family is amiss (White & Ettner, 2004). And children who sense something is amiss also generally assume it is their fault. A number of gender minority parents choose to wait until their children are adults to express their true gender identity and/or transition with the aid of hormones and surgical interventions (White & Ettner, 2004).

There are distinct variables that seem significant for a parent deciding whether to self-disclose:

- The ages and maturity levels of the children (Lev, 2004)
- The level of acceptance and support provided by the transitioning person's partner (Brown & Rounsley, 1996; Lev, 2004)
- The degree to which the gender minority parent is comfortable with his or her own gender minority status (Lev, 2004)
- The gender minority parent's prior relationships and experiences with self-disclosure in his or her family of origin (Lev, 2004)

Brown and Rounsley (1996) observed that young children grow up hearing stories about people and animals whose forms and appearances change regularly. They further note that children do accept their gender minority parents if their relationships with both parents are loving and supportive. Older children, particularly adolescents, tend to experience shame and embarrassment. Lev (2004) advised parents to provide assurance that any desire to transition gender is not caused by the child and does not mean that he or she dislikes others of the same gender.

GENDER MINORITIES AND THEIR FAMILIES OF ORIGIN

Many troubling issues confront gender minorities and their families of origin. While Chapter 6 focused exclusively on the experiences of gender minority youth, the issues that arise for parents when their children identify as gender minorities are formidable. Unfortunately, few helping professionals are equipped with the sensitivity and training necessary to work effectively with distressed parents (Israel & Tarver, 1997; Zamboni, 2006). In *Always My Child* (2003), Jennings emphasized that many of the issues parents of gender minority youth face are similar to those parents of sexual minorities deal with. The exception is the issue of visibility. The appearance of gender minority youth often makes them more visible to the rest of the world. They are sometimes more averse to gender-stereotyped activities. They may want to change their name to one that is more androgynous. When parents develop a sense that their child is different from other children, they often assume their child is gay or lesbian. Yet in many instances, the awareness of a child's status may come as a complete surprise. In that case, parents initially feel shock, betrayal, and anger, immediately followed by labile emotional reactions (Israel & Tarver, 1997; Lev, 2004; Pearlman, 2006; Zamboni, 2006), symptoms considered to be comparable to those associated with posttraumatic stress (Cole, Denny, Eyler, & Samons, 2000).

Mothers in particular experience betrayal and fears related to the impact of the gender minority child on other siblings in the family. They often feel shame, blame themselves (Israel & Tarver, 1997; Lesser, 1999; Pearlman, 2006) and fear rejection by extended family and friends (Ellis & Eriksen, 2002). Many parents attempt to keep their child's gender minority status a secret (Pearlman, 2006; Rosenberg, 2002), even in cases where their child's "cross-gender behaviors were obvious to even the most casual observer" (Rosenberg, 2002, p. 620). Some parents and family members exhibit extreme reactions to their gender variant children, which they express as emotional, verbal, and physical abuse (Burgess, 1999). According to Miller in *Counseling in Genderland* (1996), parents also experience concerns over the physical safety of their gender minority children at the hands of their peers.

Many practitioners (Ellis & Eriksen, 2002; Emerson & Rosenfeld, 1996; Lev 2004) depict the affective reactions of parents of gender minorities as resembling Kubler-Ross's (1969) stages of denial, anger, bargaining, depression, and acceptance. Lev (2004) poses an alternative model to account for parental responses. Lev asserts that parental responses are characterized by the following series of stages, which is not necessarily linear: discovery and disclosure, turmoil, negotiation, and balance. Lev (2004) notes that sometimes parents and other family members may be supportive until obvious outward changes in appearance and identity are evident. For some parents in the turmoil stage, the prospect of using a different first name to refer to their child is tantamount to a sense of betrayal (Zamboni, 2006). In the subsequent period of time when family emotions become less intense, what Lev called the "negotiation" period, family members, usually spouses, try to put limits on the kinds of changes that are acceptable to them and their partners as well as the degree of privacy or secrecy that is needed. In the balance stage, "the family is now ready to integrate the transgendered person—as a transgendered person—back into the normative life of the family" (Lev, 2004, p. 291).

For parents, such an emotional upheaval understandably breeds all manner of reactions, including denial, belief that their child is going through a phase, and assumptions of mental illness. They may well discount the reality because their child's body morphology doesn't seem to coincide with the desired gender identity (Brown & Rounsley, 1996). In some instances, the gender minority child becomes the family scapegoat. He or she is the cause of everything that seems to go wrong in the family of origin (Grossman, D'Augelli, & Salter, 2006).

There are few studies of families who were able to work toward actively accepting their gender minority members. In one qualitatively based study, Wren (2002) explored instances in which parents engaged in clinical treatment were accepting of their children's nontraditional gender identities. Wren looked at the communication patterns in families through the use of qualitative interviews with parents of gender minority adolescents. Wren posited that parental acceptance of their children's gender minority status is closely connected to the interpretive framework they used to understand their children's nonconforming gender status. She noted that the desire to stay in "strong empathic connection with the child" (p. 389) often propelled parents to develop a framework for understanding. She also noted that the majority of the parents in her sample experienced strong feelings of loss that accompanied their ultimate awareness of their child's gender minority status. The next pages describe some of the similar themes inherent in the experiences of parents who are supportive and accepting of their gender minority children. These themes emerged not only through my own qualitative research but from the research of Wren (2002) and Pearlman (2006). Box 8.1 provides background context for this study.

BOX 8.1

Notes from the Field

Because there is such a dearth of research, especially research from a "strengths-based" perspective, I undertook a series of interviews with several mothers of gender minority children (Carroll, 2003). A strengths-based approach goes beyond the negative ways that a child's gender minority status may affect families. Instead, it places the focus on the positive aspects and the resiliency that such families exhibit. In these interviews, I specifically focused on the positive behavioral and attitudinal strategies mothers employed in order to cope with the possible stress and confusion that come from parenting a gender minority child. The mothers who participated in this research were all affiliated with a local chapter of PFLAG. For purposes of this study, the term *transgendered* was defined as including preoperative and postoperative transsexuals, intersex persons, and persons who are disinterested in "passing" and thereby fitting into the gender bipolarity. Each of my interviews lasted approximately one hour. The research explored two primary themes within the context of the interviews. The first was the cognitive and emotional processes mothers employed in their own transitions from early awareness of their children's gender nonconformity, to learning of the transgendered status, to acceptance. The second theme was the cognitive frameworks employed by mothers for understanding transgenderism as well as the nature of their own gender identity.

The experience was particularly beneficial in that it gave me new insights and a proactive approach to help others.

Early Recognition

Consistent with Wren's and Pearlman's research, the parents in this study (Carroll, 2003) described how their expectations for a typical boyhood or girlhood for their children were dismantled early on and how their children's current gender identity seemed to make sense in light of these past behaviors. A 48-year-old biological mother of an 18-year-old FTM preoperative transsexual, Ms. B., told the following story about her experience with her then one-and-a-half-year-old daughter:

> My husband and I took a trip to Martha's Vineyard, where they have bicycle paths, or was it Cape Cod . . . I forget . . . but we had a lovely week and the child was maybe 18 months. . . . and at that age there was always a preference to wear a baseball cap and to always wear it backward . . . it was just something that was always on her head and we thought we had a great woman's libber on our hands and encouraged her; flexing her muscles. . . . that's my most vivid picture of the whole vacation she had a preference for red t-shirts and overalls and a dislike for dressy dresses . . . . no dolls. The first dolls were really more action-figures. If it was a choice between a he-man and a she-doll, the he-man was definitely the only toy. She thought those were for somebody else.

Later this mother recollects another instance when her daughter was seven years old:

> So I had her join a Brownie troop and she had a little Valentine's, father-daughter dance at this Brownie troop and my husband would say to me, can't

you do anything to make her look less frumpy! Can't you make her *walk*, right—she doesn't *walk* like a girl! You know, and it was embarrassing for him, he'd be, he wanted to be the dad of his little girl, but here is this girl who is just messy, shirt was just coming out, the walk was clump, clump, clump you know, and there were all the other little girls, you know, in their little dresses, and just sitting right, with their hands folded and all the ways that and I don't know, he thought it was something that I should teach her—it was like, this is something innate. And I don't know, I don't remember being taught myself, I don't know how to go about teaching her to be, that's kind of foreign ground.

Consistent with Jennings's (2003) observation that parents of gender minority youth often notice that there is something different about their child, one 52-year-old biological mother of a 19-year-old "trans" person (born biologically female), Ms. P., also described a time when she consciously sensed that her daughter was different from other biological females:

Probably, when she was maybe six or seven. . . . Seven that I know for sure. That's when she wanted to be on, be on the tee-ball team, she wanted to wear boys' clothes; she did not want to wear pink anymore. And that's when I first noticed that Laura was different. And then it escalated into, into . . . now. The way she looks now. And um . . . yeah. And Laura was such a tiny, feminine little girl. That's, I think part of what made it kind of hard to deal with. That she was so pretty and delicate. And with her long blonde hair and her hair got shorter and shorter as time went on she . . . she, you know. So I knew, but I'm not sure. I know now, at the time I didn't know why it bothered me that she wanted to wear boys' clothes, but I know now at this present time, it's a fear that people won't accept her, won't understand, at this point in time at her age now, it's dangerous for her to be different, to look different. To want to be . . . to look male.

Biological View of Causation

Uniformly, all of the interviewees struggled to develop a framework for understanding their child's gender nonconformity (Carroll, 2003). All of the mothers seemed to subscribe to an essentialist or biological explanation for why their children were transgendered, and this explanation seemed to mediate the sense of guilt that has often been reported in the literature (Israel & Tarver, 1997; Lesser, 1999; Pearlman, 2006).

Use of Supportive Alliances and Emotional Cutoffs to Foster Parental Acceptance

All the participants in this study noted the extent to which their personal involvements in support groups such as Parents and Friends of Lesbians and Gays (PFLAG) had been helpful. One mother found her ongoing dialogues with an MTF transsexual who was also a parent to be especially helpful. Personal involvement in support groups and the use of Internet resources appear to be effective strategies for alleviating the burden of isolation and shame many parents of gender minority children feel (Beeler & DiProva, 1999).

Two mothers described experiences of being rejected by family members because of their children. One mother eventually distanced herself from family in an effort to avoid further rejection. One interviewee relayed a story about how she changed churches because she felt that her church held negative views about homosexuality.

Parental Acceptance as Contingent on Willingness to Engage in Self-Reflection

Some of the interviewees described how having a gender minority child had somehow prompted them to reflect more on their own personal sense of gender and sexual identity. One mother indicated:

> [T]here's, on a scale from one to ten, and if one is being very feminine and ten is being very male, that you could really be anywhere on the spectrum and still be physically identified as being male or female. . . . When I had to rate myself as that, I had to rate myself as a seven with maleness, or six. But definitely not a one or two, I mean (long pause) . . . . so that's how I identified as gender, you know, just an essence, not so much the physical.

Ms. P. indicated that she was about to have gastric bypass surgery and drew a parallel between her desire to have a thin body that matched her sense of herself as she appeared physically 20 years ago and her daughter's desire to have her body fit the internal image of herself as male.

Acceptance as an Act of Unconditional Love

It was clear that the parents interviewed experienced a wide range of emotions in response to their gender minority children (Carroll, 2003). In particular, many remarked on the process of working through feelings of sadness and loss. While many considered this an ongoing journey of acceptance, most described what might be deemed "unconditional love" for their children. For example, one mother described her recent struggle over the summer as she watched her son, who came home from college during the summer, as he began taking hormones:

> Yeah, it sucks . . . (laughs). Every once-in-a-while I grieve because I lost my daughter and you know, it's like my child is high on steroids and you see the other little mothers and daughters, and you know you're never going to get that, you know, that's gone. I think I've got a beautiful son instead—the kid's just been a really good kid, so the spirituality and the character is just A-1-A and that's what I concentrate on . . . (laughs).

Ms. C. conveyed a similar sense of being able to see beyond her grandchild's morphology to her inner essence:

> Well, I just *love* [*with emphasis*] her as the person. I don't, I'm not, I guess I don't . . . I think of her as my grandchild. I love her as my grandchild and I don't necessarily, maybe put what I think or what I want on the forefront.

It is clear that the parents who participated in these interviews struggled to connect, accept, and affirm their children. As Ms. B. dealt with the reality of hormonal injections, she openly admitted "it's disgusting!"

> Even before the hormones, he came home and he had hairy legs and you know, I was just really tense. I know who you are, but the . . . it was just a hard thing. Then one time he said, "I'll shave my legs!" And I said, "Don't you dare, because then you'll be doing it for me and you'll hate me and I don't want you to do that!" Of course, he did. Now the arms are all hairy and there's pubic hair on his belly. The hormones and the face changes [and her voice trails off] the fatty deposits on the face. . . .

For the parents, understanding and acceptance of their children's identity is an ongoing process, made all the more difficult for these parents in the context of a transphobic culture. Many of the themes that emerged in the interviews were similar to those obtained in Beeler and DiProva's (1999) interviews with family members of sexual minorities. For example, accurate information and supportive contacts with other family members and persons in the gender minority community were therapeutically important in working through feelings of sadness and loss, enabling healing and even survival.

It is worth noting the great sense of vulnerability and risk that many participants felt at the prospect of participating in this research. Many had experienced the same sense of judgment and nonacceptance in the gay community as they had experienced in the context of the larger culture. In many cases, the reluctance to engage with me stemmed from past experiences with nontransgendered others who had exploited them or victimized them. Yet it is clear thus far that these families have much to teach us about the true nature of resiliency.

COUNSELING GENDER MINORITIES AND THEIR FAMILIES OF ORIGIN

Psychologists, practitioners, and social workers who work with gender minority clients need to be aware of the importance of recognizing and addressing other family members' concerns and issues (Lev, 2004). Not only must therapists be informed about gender and sexual minority issues, but also they must be knowledgeable of and skilled in family system dynamics (Lev, 2004). According to Lev (2004):

> Families will need support to grieve their assumptions and hopes as to who their child would become, skill development to address extended family members, siblings, and school officials, and assistance in incorporating their child's needs into the daily flow of family life so that the child does not become the focal point of family "pathology." (p. 332)

Validate and Recognize

Lev's (2004) model depicting the developmental progression that many families experience in coming to terms with their loved one's emergence as a gender minority person can be a useful therapeutic tool. Lev (2004, 2006) recommends that practitioners take into account the particular stage of transition that a parent or other family member is in when designing therapeutic interventions. She noted that during the initial stages, after finding out about the gender minority identity of their loved ones, emotions and conflict may be extremely intense, and therapists need to guard against prematurely deciding that "the family situation is irresolvable." The transitioning person may also need help in understanding that family members need time to adjust to changes (Lev, 2006). Pearlman (2006) notes that therapists must assume "two non-contradictory empathic locations" (p. 118). The first of these is related to the need for support and validation of parents who feel a sense of disappointment and loss at not having gender-typical children (Pearlman, 2006; Rosenberg, 2002). Israel (2005), a noted clinician and writer who was disowned by her biological family for being transgendered, emphasized how important it is for the counselor to assume a "caretaking" role, meaning to "contain the family members' shock and distress" (p. 54). Parents need assurance that they are not responsible for their child's gender identity issues (DiCeglie, 1998; Lev, 2006). Regardless of the sequence and process of reactions that parents and other family members experience in relation to their gender minority loved ones, therapists need first and foremost to recognize and normalize these responses. Beyond this, therapists must also be knowledgeable advocates for transgender issues and help parents make sense of their children's gender identity and transition (Pearlman, 2006).

Rosenfeld and Emerson (1998) recommended that families develop rituals to mark their loved one's transition process. Examples of possible family rituals include a re-birthday celebration on the anniversary of one's sexual reassignment surgery and a "naming" ceremony to mark the occasion of assuming another name (Muzio, 1996).

Educate

Educating parents and family members about gender minority issues is considered to be a key component of therapy by many practitioners (e.g., Lev, 2004; Zamboni, 2006). For example, Zamboni (2006) has designed a seminar for significant others, friends, and family members that provides definitions of important vocabulary terms and an overview of research data on gender minority issues. Education for parents and family members might encompass skill-building experiences. Parents might be coached in ways to talk with school personnel and others about their child's gender identity. Parents can also be coached on how to engage in dialogues with children around the issue of safety. Specifically, practitioners can help parents develop safety plans for children who may be dealing with peer harassment, such as teasing and bullying (Jennings, 2003; Rosenberg, 2002). And parents may benefit from developing increased negotiation and conflict resolution skills. Israel and Tarver (1997) emphasized the use of compromise when working with parents of gender minority youth. This may mean that parents permit children to dress androgynously for everyday activities and dress in conforming ways for formal events. Parents may also need to be prepared to deal with issues related to possible changes in the sexual orientation of their gender minority children. According to Israel (2005), a majority of gender minority clients who transition will reexamine their sexual orientation. And finally, every practitioner must emphasize the need for parents to express unconditional love of their children.

Use Support Groups

Several authors (Ellis & Eriksen, 2002; Rosenberg, 2002; Wren, 2002; Zamboni, 2006) advocate the use of support groups for parents and other family members. Ellis and Eriksen (2002) observed that eventually parents may seek out support from others with similar experiences and begin the journey toward greater acceptance. Some may ultimately even experience a feeling of pride and a desire to educate others. A number of variables determine the parents' reactions to the dramatic changes in the lives of their children. These include the resources of the family, their social support network, and their belief systems (Wren, 2002). Family members can receive support and validation through bibliotherapy. Reading about the experiences of other families can bring much needed validation and lessen the sense of isolation; suggested are *Trans-forming Families: Real Stories About Transgendered Loved Ones* (Boenke, 1999) and *Out of the Ordinary: Essays on Growing Up with Gay, Lesbian, and Transgender Parents* (Howey & Samuels, 2000). Exercises at the end of this chapter include some excellent resources for use with families.

Advocate for Sexual Minority Families

Advocacy is an important role for psychologists, social workers, and family practitioners who work with gender minorities. As the research presented in Chapter 3 clearly demonstrated, gender minorities are vulnerable to harassment and abuse. There is an urgent need for a more affirmative social environment for gender minorities with regard to personal safety, health care, employment, education, and housing. Fish and Harvey (2005) emphasized the need for practitioners and therapists to become advocates for their gender minority clients, particularly the youth. As therapists, they often attended meetings with school personnel such as teachers and administrators to address problems or issues that arose for their gender minority youth.

Summary

Legal cases in which lesbian mothers lost custody of their children because of the belief that homosexuality would have deleterious effects on the children (MacCallum & Golombok, 2004) were the impetus for studies of sexual minority families. Many of these early studies were methodologically flawed because researchers used small convenience samples, the majority of which were white, middle class, and well educated (Brooks & Goldberg, 2001; Tasker, 2005). However, despite these flaws, the bulk of the researchers reported no differences between children raised by sexual minority parents and those reared by heterosexual parents. Recently, however, investigators have questioned these "no difference" findings. Stacey and Biblarz (2001), in particular, determined that children from sexual minority families were more flexible than those with heterosexual parents in terms of gender-role behaviors and were more open to the possibility of sexual experiences with same-sex partners. Future research is needed to explore developmental outcomes of children who are reared in families of gender minority persons, bisexual persons, and gay male couples who elect to have children in the context of same-sex relationships (Tasker, 2005).

Sexual minority families face numerous challenges, perhaps beyond those experienced by nonminority families, including decisions about parenting options and financial and legal arrangements. Family members must decide how open to be with persons outside the family, including peers, relatives, school personnel, and doctors (Matthews & Lease, 2000). Given the increasing numbers of sexual minorities who are pursuing parenthood through adoption and donor insemination (Patterson, 1995), it is likely that such families will become increasingly visible in counseling settings.

In contrast to sexual minority families, research on the family lives of gender minorities is sorely lacking. In one of the few empirical explorations of gender minority parents and their children, White and Ettner (2004) identified two factors that are most significant in determining children's adjustment to their parents' gender minority status: (1) the degree to which the nonminority parent has accepted his or her partner's gender minority status and (2) the degree of conflict between the gender minority and nonminority parents. Given these findings and the recommendations of practitioners (e.g., Miller, 1996), there is truly a unique opportunity to help by working closely with parents to explore fully their options and feelings associated with telling their children about their gender minority status.

Research efforts have failed to address the experiences of parents and other family members who successfully come to terms with the nontraditional sexual and gender orientations of their children. A *resilience framework* stresses the range of coping strategies in sexual and gender minority families. Resilient families are able to mobilize active coping responses and develop the capacity to find meaning even in difficult circumstances. For example, Boxer, Cook, and Herdt (1991) noted that parents who dealt with their children's homosexuality did so with a renewed sense of growth and enlightment.

Most guidelines for practitioners focus more on assisting family members in their efforts to cope than to celebrate the sexual orientation of family members. Probably the single most important thing helping professionals can do is to approach gender minority parents without bias or judgment and to validate and affirm their identities. To do this requires awareness and a degree of caution because reflexively pathologizing the client, as has been the case historically, is harmful. Most mental health professionals have been taught in graduate schools that gender dysphoria is indicative of a classifiable mental disorder known as gender identity disorder. Family practitioners were taught to encourage parents of gender minority children to suppress their children's cross-gender behaviors through behavioral means (Israel & Tarver, 1997).

Personal Reflection

Rich, an influential author, poet, and lesbian activist, was married in 1953 at the age of 24. She describes in the excerpt below how the cultural narratives concerning women's roles and their relationships led her to a sense that there were few options available to her as a woman beyond heterosexual marriage and children:

> I have a very clear, keen memory of myself the day after I was married: I was sweeping a floor. Probably the floor did not really need to be swept; probably I simply did not know what else to do with myself. But as I swept that floor I thought: "Now I am a woman. This is an age-old action; this is what women have always done." I felt I was bending to some

> ancient form, too ancient to question. This is what women have always done. (1976, p. 25)

Like Rich, Muzio (1996) suggested that the dominant cultural narratives for lesbians and gay men during the 1960s and 1970s held few options, especially in the area of parenthood outside the bonds of heterosexual marriage. It has only been in the past 15 to 20 years that sexual minorities have begun to consider the option of parenting. Muzio wrote:

> As women's stories are listened to with increasing attention and respect, notions of what a family is or should be are becoming radically

altered. *The notion of healthy families existing independent of heterosexual relationships has emerged. . . .*

Indeed, it is only within the very recent past that lesbian mothers have begun to be spoken of at all in the popular culture or that language has even encompassed the idea of lesbian mothers. (pp. 359–360)

Now more and more single and partnered sexual minorities are exploring the possibility of becoming parents to an extent that is significant enough to be termed a *gayby boom* (Garner, 2004, p. 5).

On the other hand, gender minorities have thought little about options for parenting. However, reproductive techniques now allow in vitro fertilization and sperm freezing and insemination. De Sutter, Kira, Verschoor, and Hotimsky (2002) advocated that those transitioned surgically and hormonally from male to female should be routinely offered the opportunity to freeze their sperm, allowing them the option for parenting in the future.

Self-Reflection Questions

1. Think back to the cultural messages or narratives that circulated about gender roles and sexual orientation as you were growing up.

   a. Was homosexual parenting tolerated, condoned, or affirmed?
   b. Specifically what messages did you receive about this?
   c. How did these messages impact your thinking?

2. What is your opinion about De Sutter et al's. position regarding parenthood options for persons who complete the transition process and, therefore, lose their capacity to have children once the transition is complete?

   a. What cultural narratives dominated your childhood and adulthood?
   b. How did these messages impact your thinking and your views about gender minority parents?

Library, Media, and Internet Activities 1

Check your local video/DVD store for three important films depicting the experiences of gay men and lesbians as they deal with their families of origin and choice.

The Big Eden (Bezuena, 2000)

This heartwarming film tells the story of Henry, an artist who leaves New York City and returns to his hometown to take care of his ailing grandfather.

Discussion Questions

1. How realistic a depiction of lesbian and gay life in small-town America was this?
2. How is the theme of families of choice dealt with?
3. Does Henry's grandfather know about Henry's homosexuality? How might you have facilitated a dialogue between the two? Was it necessary for Henry to tell his grandfather?

The Incredibly True Adventure of 2 Girls in Love (Maggenti, 1995)

This film tells the story of Randy Dean, a 17-year-old high school student who lives with her aunt and her aunt's female partner. Randy is an out lesbian who is attracted to Evie, a popular student in her high school.

Discussion Questions

1. How is the theme of families of choice dealt with?
2. How realistic is Randy's portrayal of a lesbian teen? What stereotypes are depicted in this film?

3. How does each character deal with her or his homosexuality?

My Mother Likes Women (Paris & Fejerman, 2005)

This film depicts the story of Sofia, a concert pianist and mother of three adult daughters. The film opens as Sofia introduces her new love, Eliska, a fellow pianist, to her daughters. In the comedy of errors that ensues, Sol, Jimena, and Elvira try to engineer the breakup of their mother's relationship.

Discussion Questions

1. How do Sol, Jimena, and Elvira react to their mother's disclosure? How do their responses compare to the research observations?
2. What stereotypes or assumptions are embedded in terms of their reactions to their mother?
3. Does this film accurately and realistically depict the experiences of children whose parents come out as gay, lesbian, and bisexual? What is a family?

Library, Media, and Internet Activities 2

This list contains a selection of popular books about "true-to-life" experiences of sexual and gender minorities and their families. After reading at least one selection below, take some time to reflect on this story on a personal level. What were your feelings as you read about the personal struggles of various characters? How do the experiences of sexual and gender minorities and their families depicted in the story you read compare with those observations reported in the research presented in this chapter? What implications does this book have for practitioners, social workers, and psychologists in-training?

Aarons, L. (1995). *Prayers for Bobby: A mother's coming to terms with the suicide of her gay son.* New York: HarperCollins.

Bohjalian, C. (2000). *Trans-sister radio.* New York: Vintage.

Dew, R. F. (1995*). The family heart: A memoir of when our son came out.* New York: Ballantine Books.

Fricke, A., & Fricke, W. (1991). *Sudden strangers: The story of a gay son and his father.* New York: St. Martin's Press.

Howey, N. (2002). *Dress codes: Of three girlhoods— My mother's, my father's, and mine.* New York: St. Martin's Press.

Leavitt, D. (1987). *The lost language of cranes.* New York: Bantam Books.

Selvadurai, S. (1997). *Funny boy.* New York: Morrow.

Library, Media, and Internet Activities 3

The World Wide Web has become an important resource for sexual and gender minorities and their families. The list below includes selected Web-based resources for sexual and gender minority families. In small groups, assign students the task of researching one or two of these organizations and reporting their findings to the group. Be sure to note if there are chapters of these organizations and/or similar kinds of resources in your specific geographic location.

1. Children of Lesbians and Gays Everywhere
2. Families Like Ours
3. FamilyNet—Human Rights Campaign
4. Family Pride Organization
5. Gay and Lesbian Alliance Against Defamation
6. International Foundation for Gender Education
7. Parents, Families, and Friends of Lesbians and Gays
8. Lambda Legal
9. National Center for Lesbian Rights
10. Transparentcy

References

Adams, L., Jaques, J. D., & May, K. M. (2004). Counseling gay and lesbian families: Theoretical considerations. *Family Journal: Counseling & Therapy for Couples & Families, 12*(1), 40–42.

Alexander, E., Rudin, S., Sejkora, P., & Shipman, R. W. (1996). *My dad has HIV.* Minneapolis, MN: Fairview Press.

Alperson, M. (1997). *The international adoption handbook:* How to make foreign adoption work for you. New York: Holt.

Ariel, J., & McPherson, D. (2000). Therapy with lesbian and gay parents and their children. *Journal of Marital & Family Therapy, 26*(4), 421–432.

Bailey, J. M., Bobrew, D., Wolfe, J., & Mikach, S. (1995). Sexual orientation of adult sons of gay fathers. *Developmental Psychology 31*(1), 124–129.

Barret, R. L., & Logan, C. (2002). *Counseling gay men and lesbians: A practice primer.* Pacific Grove, CA: Brooks/Cole.

Barrett, H., & Tasker, R. (2001). Growing up with a gay parent: Views of 101 gay fathers on their sons' and daughters' experiences. *Educational & Child Psychology, 18*(1), 62–77.

Beeler, J., & DiProva, V. (1999). Family adjustment following disclosure of homosexuality by a member: Themes discerned in narrative accounts. *Journal of Marital & Family Therapy, 25*(4), 445–459.

Bennett, S. (2003). International adoptive lesbian families: Parental perceptions of the influence of diversity on family relationships in early childhood. *Smith College Studies in Social Work, 74*(1), 73–91.

Bezuena, T. (Director). (2000). *The Big Eden* [Motion picture]. United States: Chaiken Films.

Bigner, J. J. (1996). Working with gay fathers: Developmental, postdivorce parenting, and therapeutic issues. In J. Laird & R.-J. Green (Eds.), *Lesbians and gays in couples and families: A handbook for therapists* (pp. 370–402). San Francisco: Jossey-Bass.

Bigner, J. J., & Jacobsen, R. B. (1989). Parenting behaviors of homosexual and heterosexual fathers. *Journal of Homosexuality, 18*(1/2), 173–186.

Boenke, M. (Ed.). (1999). *Transforming families: Real stories about transgendered loved ones.* Imperial Beach, CA: Walter Trook.

Bos, H. M. W., van Balen, F., & van den Boom, D. C. (2004). Lesbian families and family functioning. *Patient Education & Counseling, 59*(3), 263–275.

Boxer, A. M., Cook, J. A., & Herdt, G. (1991). Double jeopardy: Identity transitions and parent-child relations among gay and lesbian youth. In K. Pillemer & K. McCarney (Eds.), *Parent-child relationships throughout life* (pp. 59–92). Hillsdale, NJ: Erlbaum.

Boylan, J. F. (2003). *She's not there: A life in two genders.* New York: Broadway Books.

Brewaeys, A., Ponjaert, I., Van Hall, E. V., & Golombok, S. (1997). Donor insemination: Child development functioning in lesbian mother families. *Human Reproduction, 12*(6), 1349–1359.

Brill, S. (2001). *The queer parent's primer: A lesbian and gay families' guide to navigating the straight world.* Oakland, CA: New Harbinger Publications.

Brodzinsky, D. (2003). *Adoption by lesbians and gays: A national survey of adoption agency policies, and attitudes.* New York: Evan B. Donaldson Adoption Institute.

Brooks, D., & Goldberg, S. (2001). Gay and lesbian adoptive and foster care placements: Can they meet the needs of waiting children? *Social Work, 46*(2), 147–157.

Brodzinsky, D. Patterson, C. J., & Vasiri, M. (2002). Adoption agency perspectives on lesbian and gay prospective parents: A national study. *Adoption Quarterly, 5*(3), 5–23.

Brown, M. L., & Rounsley, C. A. (1996). *True selves: Understanding transsexualism—For families, friends, coworkers, and helping professionals.* San Francisco: Jossey-Bass.

Burgess, C. (1999). Internal and external stress factors associated with the identity development of transgendered youth. *Journal of Gay & Lesbian Social Services, 10*(3/4), 35–47.

Carroll, L. (2003, March). *Trans-families: Profiles in resiliency.* Paper presented at the annual meeting of the Association of Women in Psychology, Jersey City, NJ.

Chabot, J. M., & Ames, B. D. (2004). "It wasn't 'let's get pregnant and go do it'": Decision making in lesbian couples planning motherhood via donor insemination. *Family Relations, 53*(4), 348–356.

Chan, R. W., Raboy, B., & Patterson, C. J. (1998). Psychosocial adjustment among children conceived via donor insemination by lesbian and heterosexual mothers. *Child Development, 69*(2), 443–457.

Cole, S. S., Denny, D., Eyler, A. E., & Samons, S. L. (2000). Issues in transgender. In L. T. Szuchman & F. Muscarella (Eds.), *Psychological perspectives on human sexuality* (pp. 149–195). New York: Wiley.

Connolly, C. (1996). An analysis of judicial opinions in same-sex visitation and adoption cases. *Behavioral Sciences & the Law, 14*(2), 187–203.

Crosbie-Burnett, M., Foster, T. L., Murray, C. I., & Bowen, G. L. (1996). Gays' and lesbians' families-of-origin: A social-cognitive-behavioral model of adjustment. *Family Relations, 45*(4), 397–403.

Curry, H., Clifford, D., Hertz, F., & Leonard, R. (2005). *A legal guide for lesbian and gay couples.* Berkeley, CA: Nolo.

De Sutter, P., Kira, K., Verschoor, A., & Hotimsky, A. (2002). The desire to have children and the preservation of fertility in transsexual women: A survey. [Electronic version]. *International Journal of Transgenderism, 6*(3). Retrieved January 20, 2006, from http://www.symposion.com/ijt/ijtvo06no03_02.htm

Di Ceglie, D. (1998). Reflections on the nature of the "atypical gender identity organization." In. D. DiCeglie (Ed.), *A stranger in my own body: Atypical gender identity development and mental health* (pp. 9–25). London: Karnac.

Ellis, K. M., & Eriksen, K. (2002). Transsexual and transgenderist experiences and treatment options. *Family Journal: Counseling & Therapy for Couples & Families, 10*(3), 289–299.

Emerson, S., & Rosenfeld, C. (1996). Stages of adjustment in family members of transgender individuals. *Journal of Family Psychotherapy, 7*(3), 1–12.

Fish, S. L., & Harvey, R. G. (2005). *Nurturing queer youth: Family therapy transformed.* New York: Norton.

Flynn, T. (2006). The ties that (don't) bind: Transgender family law and the unmaking of families. In P. Currah, R. M. Juang, & S. P. Minter (Eds.), *Transgender rights* (pp. 32–50). Minneapolis: University of Minnesota Press.

Galluccio, J., Galluccio, M., & Groff, D. (2001). *An American family.* New York: St. Martin's Press.

Garner, A. (2004). *Families like mine: Children of gay parents tell it like it is.* New York: HarperCollins.

Gartrell, N., Banks, A., Hamilton, J., Reed, N., Bishop, H., & Rodas, C. (1999). The National Lesbian Family Study: 2. Interviews with mothers of toddlers. *American Journal of Orthopsychiatry, 69*(3), 362–369.

Gartrell, N., Banks, A., Reed, N., Hamilton, J., Rodas, C., & Deck, A. (2000). The National Lesbian Family Study: 3. Interviews with mothers of five-year-olds. *American Journal of Orthopsychiatry, 70*(4), 542–548.

Gartrell, N., Deck, A., Rodas, C., Peyser, H., & Banks, A. (2005). The National Lesbian Family Study: 4. Interviews with the 10-year-old children. *American Journal of Orthopsychiatry, 75*(4), 518–524.

Gartrell, N., Hamilton, J., Banks, A., Mosbacher, D., Reed, N., Sparks, C., et al. (1996). The National Lesbian Family Study: 1. Interviews with prospective mothers. *American Journal of Orthopsychiatry, 66*(2), 272–281.

Goldfried, M. R., & Goldfried, A. P. (2001). The importance of parental support in the lives of gay, lesbian and bisexual individuals. *Journal of Clinical Psychology, 57*(5), 681–693.

Golombok, S., Spencer, A., & Rutter, M. (1983). Children in lesbian and single-parent households: Psychosocial and psychiatric appraisal. *Journal of Child Psychology & Psychiatry, 24*(4), 551–572.

Golombok, S., Tasker, F., & Murray, C. (1997). Do parents influence the sexual orientation of their children? Findings from a longitudinal study of lesbian families. *Developmental Psychology, 32*(1), 3–11.

Gottlieb, A. R. (2003). *Sons talk about their gay fathers: Life curves.* New York: Harrington Park Press.

Green, R. (1978). Sexual identity of 37 children raised by homosexual or transsexual parents. *American Journal of Psychiatry, 135*, 692–697.

Green, R. (1998). Transsexuals' children [Electronic version]. *International Journal of Transgenderism, 2*(4). Retrieved February 20, 2006, from http://www.symposion.com/ijt/ijtc0601.htm

Green, R. J. (2002). Coming out to family . . . in context. In E. Davis-Russell (Ed.), *The California School of Professional Psychology handbook of multicultural education, research, intervention, and training* (pp. 277–284). San Francisco: Jossey-Bass.

Green, R., Mandel, J. B., Hotvedt, M. E., Gray, J., & Smith, L. (1986). Lesbian mothers and their children: A comparison with solo parent heterosexual mothers and their children. *Archives of Sexual Behavior, 15*(2), 167–184.

Grossman, A., D'Augelli, A. R., & Salter, N. P. (2006). Male-to-female transgender youth: Gender expression milestones, gender atypicality, victimization, and parents' responses. *Journal of GLBT Family Studies, 21*(1), 71–92.

Herdt, G., & Koff, B. (2000). *Something to tell you: The road families travel when a child is gay.* New York: Columbia University Press.

Howey, N., & Samuels, E. (2000). *Out of the ordinary: Essays on growing up with gay, lesbian, and transgender parents.* New York: St. Martin's Press.

Israel, G. E. (2005). Translove: Transgender persons and their families. *Journal of GLBT Family Studies, 1*(1), 53–67.

Israel, G. E., & Tarver, D. E. (1997). *Transgender care: Recommended guidelines, practical information, and personal accounts.* Philadelphia: Temple University Press.

Jennings, K. (2003). *Always my child: A parent's guide to understanding your gay, lesbian, bisexual, transgendered or questioning son or daughter.* New York: Fireside Books.

Johnson, S. M., & O'Connor, E. (2002). *The gay baby boom: The psychology of gay parenthood.* New York: New York University Press.

Kaiser Family Foundation. (2001, November). *Inside-out: A report on the experiences of lesbians, gays and bisexuals in America and the public view on issues and policies related to sexual orientation.* (Pub. 3191). Menlo Park, CA: Author.

Kiser, L. J., Bennett, L., Heston, J., & Paavola, M. (2005). Family ritual and routine: Comparison of clinical and non-clinical families. *Journal of Child & Family Studies, 14*(3), 357–372.

Kubler-Ross, E. (1969). *On death and dying.* New York: Macmillan.

Laird, J. (1998). Invisible ties: Lesbians and their families of origin. In C. J. Patterson & A. R. D'Augelli (Eds.), *Lesbian, gay, and bisexual identities in families* (pp. 197–228). New York: Oxford University Press.

Lamme, L. L., & Lamme, L. A. (2001). Welcoming children from gay families into our schools. *Educational Leadership, 59*(4), 65–69.

LaSala, M. C. (2000). Lesbians, gay men, and their parents: Family therapy for the coming-out crisis. *Family Process, 39*(1), 67–81.

Lesser, J. G. (1999). When your son becomes your daughter: A mother's adjustment to a transgender child. *Families in Society, 80*(2), 182–189.

Leung, P., Erich, S., & Kanenberg, H. (2005). A comparison of family functioning in gay/lesbian, heterosexual and special needs adoptions. *Children & Youth Services Review, 27*(9), 1031–1044.

Lev, A. I. (2004). *Transgender emergence: Therapeutic guidelines for working with gender-variant people and their families.* Binghamton, NY: Haworth Clinical Practice Press.

Lev, A. I. (2006). Transgender emergence within families. In D. F. Morrow & L. Messinger (Eds.), *Sexual orientation and gender expression in social work practice* (pp. 263–283). New York: Columbia University Press.

Litovich, M. L., & Langhout, R. D. (2004). Framing heterosexism in lesbian families: A preliminary examination of resilient coping. *Journal of Community & Applied Social Psychology, 14*(16), 411–435.

Lynch, J. M. (2004). The identity transformation of biological parents in lesbian/gay stepfamilies. *Journal of Homosexuality, 47*(2), 91–107.

MacCallum, F., & Golombok, S. (2004). Children raised in fatherless families from infancy: A follow-up of children of lesbian and single heterosexual mothers at early adolescence. *Journal of Child Psychology & Psychiatry, 45*(8), 1407–1419.

Maggenti, M. (Director). (1995). *The Incredibly True Adventure of 2 Girls in Love* [Motion picture]. United States: Fine Line Features.

Matthews, C. R., & Lease, S. H. (2000). Focus on lesbian, gay, and bisexual families. In R. M. Perez, K. A. DeBord, & K. J. Bieschke (Eds.), *Handbook of counseling and psychotherapy with lesbian, gay, and bisexual clients* (pp. 249–273). Washington, DC: American Psychological Association.

McGarry, K. (2003). *Fatherhood for gay men: An emotional and practical guide to becoming a gay dad.* Binghamton, NY: Haworth Press.

Menichiello, M. (2006). *A gay couple's journey through surrogacy: Intended fathers.* New York: Harrington Park Press.

Miller, N. (1996). *Counseling in genderland: A guide for you and your transgendered client.* Boston: Different Path Press.

Mitchell, V. (1996). Two moms: Contribution of the planned lesbian family to the deconstruction of gendered parenting. In J. Laird & R.-J. Green (Eds.), *Lesbians and gays in couples and families: A handbook for therapists* (pp. 343–357). San Francisco: Jossey-Bass.

Mitchell, V. (1998). The birds, the bees . . . and the sperm banks: How lesbian mothers talk with their children about sex and reproduction. *American Journal of Orthopsychiatry, 68*(3), 400–409.

Morrow, D. F. (2006). Coming out as gay, lesbian, bisexual and transgender. In D. F. Morrow and L. Messinger (Eds.), *Sexual orientation and gender expression in social work practice* (pp. 129–149). New York: Columbia University Press.

Murray, C., & Golombok, S. (2005). Going it alone: Solo mothers and their infants conceived by donor insemination. *American Journal of Orthopsychiatry, 75*(2), 242–253.

Murray, P. D., & McClintock, K. (2005). Children of the closet: A measurement of the anxiety and self-esteem of children raised by a non-disclosed homosexual or bisexual parent. *Journal of Homosexuality, 49*(1), 77–95.

Muzio, C. (1996). Lesbians choosing children: Creating families, creating narratives. In J. Laird & R.-J. Green (Eds.), *Lesbians and gays in couples and families: A handbook for therapists* (pp. 358–369). San Francisco: Jossey-Bass.

Newman, L. (1991). *Heather has two mommies*. Los Angeles: Alyson.

Newman, L. (2002). *Felicia's favorite story*. Ridley Park, PA: Two Lives.

O'Dell, S. (2000). Psychotherapy with gay and lesbian families: Opportunities for cultural inclusion and clinical challenge. *Clinical Social Work Journal, 28*(2), 171–182.

Paris, I. & Fejerman, D. (Directors). (2002). *My Mother Likes Women* [Motion picture]. Spain: Fernando Colomo Producciones Cimatograficas, S.L.

Patterson, C. J. (1995). Lesbian mothers, gay fathers and their children. In A. R. D'Augelli & C. J. Patterson (Eds.), *Lesbian, gay and bisexual identities over the life-span: Psychological perspectives* (pp. 262–290). Oxford, England: Oxford University Press.

Patterson, C. J. (1998). The family lives of children born to lesbian mothers. In C. J. Patterson & A. R. D'Augelli (Eds.), *Lesbian, gay, and bisexual identities in families* (pp. 154–176). New York: Oxford University Press.

Patterson, C. J. (2003). Children of lesbian and gay parents. In L. D. Garnets & D. C. Kimmel (Eds.), *Psychological perspectives on lesbian, gay, and bisexual experiences* (pp. 497–548). New York: Columbia University Press.

Pearlman, S. F. (2006). Terms of connection: Mother-talk about female-to-male transgender children. *Journal of GLBT Family Studies, 2*(3/4), 93–122.

Peplau, L. A., & Beals, K. P. (2004). The family lives of lesbians and gay men. In A. L. Vangelisti (Ed.), *Handbook of family communication* (pp. 233–248). Mahwah, N.J.: Erlbaum.

Pepper, R. (2005). *The ultimate guide to pregnancy for lesbians* (2nd ed.). San Francisco: Cleis Press.

Perry, B., Burston, A., Stevens, M., Steele, H., Golding, J., & Golombok, S. (2004). Children's play narra-

tives: What they tell us about lesbian-mother families. *American Journal of Orthopsychiatry, 74*(4), 467–479.

Rich, A. (1976). *Of women born*. New York: Norton.

Ricketts, W., & Achtenberg, R. (1990). Adoption and foster parenting for lesbians and gay men: Creating new traditions in family. In F. W. Bozett & M. B. Sussan (Eds), *Homosexuality and family relationships* (pp. 83–118). Binghamton, New York: Haworth Press.

Roberts, J. (1999). Beyond words: The power of rituals. In D. J. Wiener (Ed.), *Beyond talk therapy: Using movement and expressive techniques in clinical practice* (pp. 55–78). Washington, DC: American Psychological Association.

Robinson, B., Walters, I., & Skeen, P. (1989). Response of parents to learning that their child is homosexual and concern over AIDS: A national study. *Journal of Homosexuality, 18*(1–2), 59–79.

Rosenberg, M. (2002). Children with gender identity issues and their parents in individual and group treatment. *Journal of the American Academy of Child & Adolescent Psychiatry, 41*(5), 619–621.

Rosenfeld, C., & Emerson, S. (1998). A process model of supportive therapy for families of transgender individuals. In D. Denny (Ed.), *Current concepts in transgender identity* (pp. 391–400). New York: Garland.

Rostosky, S. S., Korfhage, B. A., Duhigg, J. M., Stern, A. J., Bennett, L., & Riggle, E. D. B. (2004). Same-sex couple perceptions of family support: A consensual qualitative study. *Family Process, 43*(1), 43–57.

Ryan, S. D., Pearlmutter, S., & Groza, V. (2004). Coming out of the closet: Opening agencies to gay and lesbian adoptive parents. *Social Work, 49*(1), 85–95.

Saltzburg, S. (2004). Learning that an adolescent child is gay or lesbian: The parent experience. *Social Work, 49*(1), 109–118.

Savin-Williams, R. C. (2001). *Mom, Dad, I'm gay: How families negotiate coming out*. Washington, DC: American Psychological Association.

Savin-Williams, R. C., & Dube, E. M. (1998). Parental reactions to their child's disclosure of a gay/lesbian identity. *Family Relations, 47*(1), 7–13.

Stacey, J., & Biblarz, T. J. (2001). (How) does the sexual orientation of parents matter? *American Sociological Review, 66*(2), 159–183.

Tasker, F. (2005). Lesbian mothers, gay fathers, and their children: A review. *Journal of Developmental & Behavioral Pediatrics, 26*(3), 224–241.

Tasker, F. L., & Golombok, S. (1997). *Growing up in a lesbian family: Effects on child development.* New York: Guilford.

Tips for coming out to your kids. (n.d.). Retrieved January 20, 2006, from http://www.colage.org/kids

Toevs, K., & Brill, S. (2002). *The essential guide to lesbian conception, pregnancy and birth.* Los Angeles: Alyson.

Tremble, B., Schneider, M., & Appathurai, C. (1989). Growing up gay or lesbian in a multicultural context. *Journal of Homosexuality, 17*(3/4), 253–267.

Van Voorhis, R., & Wagner, M. (2002). Among the missing: Content on lesbian and gay people in social work journals. *Social Work, 47*(4), 345–354.

Wainright, J. L., Russell, S. T., & Patterson, C. J. (2004). Psychosocial adjustment, school outcomes, and romantic relationships of adolescents with same-sex parents. *Child Development, 75*(6), 1886–1898.

Walsh, F. (2002). A family resilience framework: Innovative practice applications. *Family Relations, 51*(2), 130–137.

Weston, K. (1991). *Families we choose.* New York: Columbia University Press.

White, T., & Ettner, R. (2004). Disclosure, risks, and protective factors for children whose parents are undergoing gender transition. *Journal of Gay & Lesbian Psychotherapy, 8*(1/2), 129–145.

Wilhoite, M. (1990). *Daddy's roommate.* Los Angeles: Alyson.

Wren, B. (2002). "I can accept my child is transsexual but if I ever see him in a dress I will hit him": Dilemmas in parenting a transgendered adolescent. *Clinical Child Psychology and Psychiatry, 7*(3), 377–397.

Zamboni, B. (2006). Therapeutic considerations in working with the family, friends and partners of transgendered individuals. *Family Journal, 14*(2), 174–179.

CHAPTER 9

Sexual Health and Substance Use in Sexual and Gender Minorities

INTRODUCTION

In the excerpt below, Garrett provides a personal account of his experiences at his university's health center.

Waiting around at the student health center is probably the last thing on my list of things I would like to be doing on a Tuesday afternoon, but I had to do something about this illness that hasn't gone away for four months. Now, logically, if you're sick for more than a few weeks you go and see a doctor, but when you're terrified of them like I am, avoiding seeking medical help seems completely logical.

It's not needles or anything like that; hell, I give myself testosterone injections once a week and have been doing so for almost three years. I am not scared that I have some sort of horrible disease; I survived cancer at a young age already and if I can deal with gender identity disorder I can handle any type of disease/disorder.

What I can't stand, what makes me never want to go see a doctor (other than my endocrinologist who handles my hormone dosage) is the way I get treated. The constant probing and questioning like I am some sort of medical experiment irritates me to no end. I should not have to be everyone's learning experience when it comes to transgender people.

This time is no different. I had this barking cough that would not go away for three months. All my roommates and my girlfriend were worried about my health and I still refused to go to the doctor until they dragged me there. I would have been kicking and screaming had I felt better, but even someone as stubborn as me was willing to meet defeat and finally get healthy again. I checked in by handing the woman at the front desk my student ID and waited. . . .

My name had been legally changed since my second year of college. With our school IDs the number on the chart, regardless of name, would always be the same. Since I had once visited Student Health my freshmen year, they still had my birth name on file. When the nurse called my birth name out, you bet I was completely mortified. After the nurse called it again I went up to her and explained that she was calling me. Before I could quietly explain my situation to her while avoiding all the staring eyes of other sick students, she said with the same loud voice, "Child are you trying to tell me you're a girl?"

Maybe mortified isn't the best word, maybe something like "fearing for my safety" or "so embarrassed I wanted to run of out of there and deal with being sick," would better describe how I was feeling. After clearing up the name situation by going over to student records to get a copy of my name change form, the nurse finally let me into the exam room. As my luck would have it, the same nurse who was so shocked by my birth name turned out to be the one elected to take my temperature (which had hit 102 after running around in the rain to get my paper work) and other vital information. Of course she then had to ask who knows how many embarrassing questions while I had a disposable thermometer in my mouth, such as how I had sex and what did my genitalia look like.

After three hours of this and countless embarrassing questions, I was FINALLY able to go home with a bottle of antibiotic and a hurt pride. People wonder why I'll do things like let a little sore throat become a full blown infection or why I insisted on not going to the doctor when I got into a car accident. If you had to go through all this every time, you'd hate going to the doctor too. (*Source:* From *To the Health Center* [unpublished manuscript] by Garrett, 2005. Used with permission.)

What feelings were evoked in response to reading about Garrett's personal account? If shock made your list of reactions, reflect on this: Virtually every gender minority person shares Garrett's experiences. Clearly, the medical personnel who dealt with Garrett demonstrated a lack of sensitivity and an inability to respect his desired gender identity. And Garrett will continue to avoid health care until he's in a crisis situation. But putting aside how he was treated, Garrett, like many other gender and sexual minorities in the United States and Canada, including the poor and people of color, generally lacks access to health care (Heck, Sell, & Gorin, 2006). Not only that, but also they tend to be at risk for sexually transmitted infections, substance abuse, and other medical syndromes (Julien & Chartrand, 2005).

A Preview of Chapter Contents

Chapter 3 explored the numerous ways in which homophobia, biphobia, and transphobia adversely impact the mental health of sexual and gender minorities in this country. This chapter examines the impact of discrimination on medical practices, policies, and research, especially as they are related to the sexual health of sexual and gender minorities. Sexual health is defined as follows: "A state of physical, emotional, mental, and social well-being related to sexuality; it is not merely the absence of disease, dysfunction, or infirmity" (World Health Organization, 2000). This topic is arguably a life-and-death matter for your future clients. Therefore, this chapter covers the following in some depth:

- Research on sexually transmitted infections (STIs)
- Current research on the human immunodeficiency virus (HIV) and the disease it causes, acquired immunodeficiency syndrome (AIDS)

- The impact of substance use on the sexual behaviors of sexual and gender minorities
- The barriers that sexual and gender minorities experience while in substance abuse recovery
- Counseling techniques and models for the prevention of HIV and the treatment of substance abuse among sexual and gender minorities
- Recommendations and resources to empower readers and to work toward collective action at the systemic level

BARRIERS TO SEXUAL HEALTH RESEARCH, CARE, AND POLICY FOR SEXUAL AND GENDER MINORITIES

Sexual Health: Practice Barriers

National health studies have consistently reported that certain segments of the U.S. population, including sexual and gender minorities, lack access to and quality of health care (Kenagy, 2005; Wilkinson, 2006). In 2000, the U.S. Department of Health and Human Services (DHHS) developed a 10-year nationwide plan to promote health care delivery and prevention. This plan, published in *Healthy People 2010,* specifically identified sexual minorities as one of six U.S. population groups affected by disparities in health care prevention and treatment (U.S. Department of Health and Human Services, 2000).

Why such inequity in access to and quality of medical care? There are a number of explanations: A significant one relates to economic issues. The fact is that many sexual and gender minorities are without health insurance and spousal health benefits (Cochran, Mays, Bowen, & Gage, 2001; Klitzman & Greenberg, 2002; Marrazzo, Coffey, & Bingham, 2005; Marrazzo, Koutsky, Kiviat, Kuypers, & Stine, 2001).

Health experts also blame the deeply rooted homophobic, biphobic, and transphobic nature of the health-care system itself. Most medical personnel assume that their patients are heterosexual and, accordingly, practice heterosexual sex. This leads to "incomplete or inaccurate assumptions," and the medical personnel who make these assumptions deliver "inadequate care" (Hutchinson, Thompson, & Cederbaum, 2006, p. 399).

Sexual and gender minority patients are faced with having to decide whether to self-disclose their sexual practices and/or identities to each and every health care provider they see (Daley, 1998; Stevens, 1995). Surveys reveal that 70–90% of sexual minority patients (Allen, Glicken, Beach, & Naylor, 1998; Brogan, 1997) report that their health-care providers have never inquired about their sexual orientation. Many physicians do not discuss safe sex with their male patients who have sex with other men (MSM) and their gay and bisexual male patients who are HIV-positive (Wolitski, 2005). Among gay and bisexual men, 25% of the participants in one survey reported that their current health-care providers had never talked to them about safe sex despite the fact that they were all HIV-positive (Wolitski, Parsons, & Gomez, 2004).

Many medical professionals lack sufficient knowledge and skill in treating the sexual health issues of their sexual and gender minority patients. They often mistakenly assume lesbians and bisexual women are immune to STIs and HIV and, therefore, ignore them in the research, education, and prevention programs (Cochran et al., 2001; Goldstein, 1997). Research also indicates that medical personnel routinely show hostility toward and discriminate against lesbians and bisexual women (Barbara, Quandt, & Anderson, 2001; Bauer & Welles, 2001; Eliason & Schope, 2001; Lehmann, Lehmann, & Kelly, 1998; van Dam, Koh, & Dibble, 2001). A majority of health care professionals lack adequate knowledge and training in clinical care issues that are of concern to gender minorities (Clements, Wilkinson, Kitano, & Marx, 1999; Sperber, Landers, & Lawrence, 2005). Negative experiences with health-care providers are also reported in the anecdotal stories of bisexual men and women (Dobison, MacDonnell, Hampson, Clipsham, & Chow, 2005; Miller, Andre, Ebin, & Bessonova, 2007).

Sexual Health: Research, Policy, and Prevention Barriers

The reality is that we live in a culture whose institutions preserve dichotomous assumptions of sexual orientation (homosexual versus heterosexual) and of gender identity (male versus female). So perhaps it shouldn't be surprising that research protocols, policies, treatment procedures, and prevention practices do not adequately address the needs and identities of sexual and gender minorities. For example, during the early days of HIV/AIDS, researchers and health prevention experts made assumptions about the sexual behaviors of women and men on the basis of their self-reported identities (Gonzales, Washienko, Krone, & Chapman, 1999; Sell & Petrulio, 1996). This practice proved to be problematic because many men and women who engaged in sexual relations with persons of the same sex were reluctant to use labels such as "gay" or "lesbian" and those who had sex with both men and women were uncomfortable ascribing the label "bisexual" to themselves. As a result, many of these people were omitted from HIV research and prevention programs (Cochran & Cauce, 2006; Mays, Cochran, & Zamudio, 2004; Miller et al., 2007). Studies of sexual behavior also revealed that women who identified themselves as lesbian had had sex with men, and women who self-identified as heterosexual had had sex with women (Gonzales et al., 1999; McCabe, Hughes, & Boyd, 2004).

In their more recent efforts to improve the efficacy of HIV/AIDS prevention, researchers and prevention specialists have developed descriptors based solely on sexual behaviors: women who have sex with women (WSW), men who have sex with men (MSM), women who have sex with men and women (WSMW), men who have sex with men and women (MSMW). Yet not all researchers and prevention specialists have been satisfied with these categories. For example, Bell, Ompad, and Sherman (2006) argue that the categories of WSW and MSM are too broad and complex to be useful. They advocate that risk profiles and health interventions include consideration of a number of factors, including sexual identity, sexual behaviors, childhood history, current living situation, and gender of partner. Transgender activists have also critiqued this approach to identification and categorization because it is based on one's sexual anatomy rather than on one's subjective sense of identity (Miller et al., 2007). Some male-to-female (MTF) transsexuals who are sexually and romantically involved with men refer to themselves as "heterosexual women" and not "transgender." Reback, Lombardi, Simon, & Frye (2005) and Operario, Burton, Underhill, and Sevelius (2008) observed that in the past, health researchers have categorized MTF transsexual research participants as men who have sex with men (MSM). This practice is problematic, and the interventions that are developed as a result of these studies "are more likely to alienate rather than educate transgendered women" (Reback et al., 2005, p. 19).

The research, policy, and prevention programs designed for the sexual health of gender and sexual minorities are also plagued by other problems. It is difficult to obtain representative samples of sexual minorities and gender minorities, and researchers have relied heavily on self-report measures. Also, researchers have often compromised their data sets by collapsing bisexual women and lesbian participants into single groups for purposes of statistical analysis (McCabe et al., 2004). Bisexual persons have felt excluded from HIV prevention programs, which typically focus on gay men and same-sex behaviors (Miller et al., 2007).

The inclusion of large probability samples in recent national health surveys that address sexual health issues is beginning to rectify some of the sampling problems (Julien & Chartrand, 2005). These surveys are sponsored by federal agencies to study a number of health issues in the general population. However, there are still significant gaps in sexual health research, policy, and prevention programs for gender minorities, bisexual women, and sexual minority persons of color.

This is particularly disturbing in the case of gender minorities because their health care needs exceed the norm. The reality is that persons who elect to transition hormonally and/or surgically must interact extensively with medical personnel and often need a second set of health-care professionals for their routine health-care issues. The Standards of Care (SOC) that were established by the Harry Benjamin International Gender Dysphoria Association (now the World Professional Association for Transgender Health) also continue to situate mental health professionals in regulatory roles. The controversy surrounding this dynamic is the subject of discussion and debate (Bockting & Kirk, 2001; Lombardi & van Servellen, 2000).

SEXUAL HEALTH ISSUES IN SEXUAL MINORITY MEN

The topic of barebacking (see below) is not only controversial but also provocative—and to many, baffling. Many sexual minority men battle self-destructive tendencies. Particularly with this group of clients, helping professionals can quite literally save lives.

BOX 9.1

Anecdote from the Field

I was speaking at an HIV/AIDS workshop. Afterward a mental health professional attending the workshop came up to me. She was outraged and disgusted. "Barebacking? How crazy is that? Men who do that have a total death wish." In this workshop, I took the term "barebacking" to mean, in Wolitski's (2005) words, "intentional anal sex without a condom." During my talk, I had used terms like *bug chasers*, which refers to gay men who are HIV-negative yet actively try to get infected with HIV, and *gift givers*, which describes HIV-positive gay men who are willing to knowingly infect others. Shernoff wrote about both terms in 2005, and I had purposely used the street language familiar to this community of clients. Looking at the faces of several in the group, I could see expressions of revulsion, and I wondered how they could possibly be effective in trying to help a client who admitted to such practices.

Questions: How would you have responded to the woman who was disgusted by the practice of *barebacking?* How would you react to a client who professed to be a *bug chaser*"?

Sexually Transmitted Infections and HIV

While the incidence of STIs among sexual minority men had sharply declined in 1980, recent research seems to suggest a reversal of this trend (Fox et al., 2001). Among MSM, gonorrhea has increased (Fox et al., 2001) as has syphilis (Adam, Husbands, Murray, & Maxwell, 2005; Bellis, Cook, Clark, Syed, & Hoskins, 2002) and chlamydia (Makadon, 2006).

Particularly among gay men and MSM, HIV/AIDS prevention programs conducted over the course of the last 20 years were considered to be fairly effective (Wolitski, 2005). But recent evidence suggests that unprotected sex among gay men and MSM is on the increase and growing numbers are not consistently maintaining safer sex practices (Halkitis, Wolitski, & Gomez, 2005; Wolitski, 2005). Men who have sex with men, particularly men of color, accounted for 45% of all new HIV infections in 2003 (Centers for Disease Control and Prevention, 2004; McKee, Picciano, Roffman, Swanson, & Kalichman, 2006).

Rates of high-risk sex practices, particularly unprotected anal intercourse, among HIV-positive MSM have increased since 2000 (van Kesteren, Hospers, & Kok, 2007). These high-risk sexual behaviors increase the likelihood of contracting STIs. Those persons who are HIV-positive also risk being reinfected with other strains of HIV (called "HIV superinfection").

Several possible factors may account for the reported increase in unprotected sex among gay men and MSM. Highly active antiretroviral therapy (HAART) and improved prophylaxis have prevented most fatal AIDS-related infections from occurring (Shernoff, 2006). Many gay men and MSM now view HIV/AIDS as a treatable condition rather than a fatal disease, a phenomenon known as *AIDS optimism* (Adams et al., 2005).

Other medical advances—in particular, the use of viral load testing—allow frequent blood tests to examine viral load and CD4 levels (T-helper cells) to see if the anti-HIV drugs are working effectively (Shernoff, 2006). The use of weight training, testosterone, and steroids by people who are HIV-positive has helped supplant media images of HIV/AIDS sufferers as wasted and sickly (Shernoff, 2006). Even pharmaceutical advertisements for antiretroviral drugs depict men and women engaged in strenuous physical activity, such as biking and mountain climbing (Shernoff, 2006). Complacency about safe sex—and specifically the use of condoms, a phenomenon known as *condom fatigue* (Adam et al., 2005; Race, 2003)—has also contributed to changing patterns of safe sex among gay men and MSM.

Over the years, researchers have attempted to identify factors that contribute to the use or nonuse of safe sex practices by sexual minority men and MSM. A number of variables have been identified. These include relationship status (Carballo-Dieguez, Remien, Dolezal, & Wagner, 1997), self-esteem issues (Martin & Knox, 1997; Preston et al., 2004; Stokes & Peterson, 1998), sexual compulsivity (Parsons, Kelly, Bimbi, Muench, & Morgenstern, 2007), and drug and alcohol use (Halkitis, Parson, & Stirratt, 2001; Kelly & Kalichman, 1998).

COUNSELING SEXUAL MINORITY MEN

Recognize Countertransference

The role of practitioners' personal attitudes and beliefs about homosexuality, bisexuality, and transgenderism was covered in some detail in Chapter 3. Personal responses are likely to surface even in the most liberal-minded practitioners who engage in frank discussions with their sexual minority clients about sexual health matters. During these dialogues, practitioners are faced rather directly with several issues, all of which are stigmatized in our culture. These include same-sex sexual behaviors (often graphically described), HIV/AIDs, multiple sexual partners (nonmonogamy or polyamory), illegal drug use, and alcohol abuse (Lee, Kochman, & Sikkema, 2002).

Negative countertransference reactions are not uncommon. They arise for any practitioner, helping professional, and psychologist working with clients who engage in risky sexual behaviors. Cheuvront (2002) recommended that therapists assess how they think and feel about risk-taking sexual behavior and be aware of how these reactions might impact their clients. Shernoff, a prolific writer and psychotherapist, has written extensively about sexual risk behaviors, HIV/AIDS, and sexual minority men. He noted:

> Even today, mental health professionals often fail to question clients about areas where they themselves feel uncomfortable or about which they are ignorant or biased. The result is that clients may be engaging in risky sexual behavior that is ignored or overlooked by therapists because of unrecognized countertransference. (2006, p. 44)

Therapists must feel comfortable discussing any and all forms of sexual behavior and take care not to pathologize sexual risk-takers (Shernoff, 2005). Indeed, most of our clinical literature and media images portray sexual risk-takers as deeply damaged and character flawed. In addition to responding judgmentally to their clients, therapists may exhibit countertransference responses, such as becoming overly involved with clients or emotionally distancing themselves from clients. Lastly, therapists can experience "vicarious erotic titillation as a result of listening to graphic descriptions of clients' sexual encounters" (Shernoff, 2006, p. 137).

Cheuvront (2002) addressed these countertransference issues in his article in the *Journal of Gay & Lesbian Psychotherapy*. He suggested that therapists reframe intentionally unsafe sexual behavior in situational terms so as to move beyond marginalizing the risk-taker. For example, many gay men perceive condoms as barriers that prevent them from feeling emotionally close to their partners (Hoff et al., 2004; Shernoff, 2005). Forstein (2002) proposed that for some gay men and MSM, the exchange of semen through anal sex is a sacred, even if momentary, bonding experience. "In the intimate exchange of semen lies perhaps a defiance that protests the unrelenting experience of gay men of being outlawed, made invisible, and devalued by society's institutions, values and laws" (p. 40).

Therapists who work with sexual minority men either individually or in couples need to ask about safe sex (Shernoff, 2005): Are their clients practicing it? How did they arrive at decisions regarding safe sex? And how does each regard the level of safety they practice? This line of questioning is particularly helpful as a means of determining a client's characteristic communication style with his sexual partner(s).

In their manual *Asking the Right Questions 2: Talking with Clients About Sexual Orientation and Gender Identity in Mental Health, Counselling and Addiction Settings* (2007), Barbara and Doctor advocate that helping professionals ask questions early on related to HIV and AIDS: "HIV is such a big concern for a lot of people. Can you tell me in what ways this may be true for you?" (p. 34). Following are other questions that practitioners might include:

- Are there times when you thought a lot about or worried about HIV or AIDS?
- Are you concerned about your own HIV status?
- Are you concerned about a loved one's HIV status? (p. 35)

Assess for Sexual Compulsivity

While guarding against the tendency to pathologize same-sex sexual behaviors, helping professionals should be aware that unsafe sexual behaviors and elevated risk for HIV and sexually transmitted infections often co-occur with various addictions (Shernoff, 2005). While alcohol and drug abuse and its treatment are discussed in greater detail below, sexual addiction is thought to be especially problematic for gay and bisexual men. Alternatively termed *sexual compulsivity*, this refers to engaging excessively in sexual activities, masturbating, using the Internet and pornography, cruising steam rooms and adult bookstores, and developing romantic obsessions. Some studies report higher incidences of such behaviors in gay and bisexual men than in nonminority persons (Parsons et al., 2007; Schneider, 2004; Weiss, 2004). Tools like the Sexual Compulsivity Scale (Kalichman & Rompa, 1995) are recommended to help therapists complete more-thorough assessments. Helping professionals should also assist clients in identifying events that can trigger their sexual compulsivity, such as relationship turmoil, and their contextual triggers, including specific persons and locations (Parsons et al., 2007). Treatment recommendations for sexual compulsivity include the use of cognitive-behavioral techniques such as a sexual boundary plan (Weiss, 2004) and active participation in Sexual Compulsives Anonymous (*www.sex-recovery.org/index.htm*), a 12-step program that is especially welcoming of sexual minorities.

Be Knowledgeable

Practitioners need to be familiar with the language used by sexual minority men to describe sex practices. And they must have up-to-date information about HIV/AIDS and STIs. With the advent of HIV, new categories of sexual practices and concomitant labels to describe these have emerged in gay men's culture (Yep, Lovaas, & Pagonis, 2002). Gay men and MSM are categorized in terms of sexual practices ("vanilla," "kinky," "raunchy"), sexual types ("bear," "daddy," "surfer," "cowboy"), and serostatus ("HIV-positive," "HIV-negative") (Shernoff, 2005). These terms fluctuate in popularity. Practitioners need to stay current in their language.

Therapists need to know about sex practices and such safer sex practices as changing condoms frequently during extended periods of sex, reapplying lubrication frequently to keep condoms from breaking, checking penises for sores, and checking mouths during extended periods of oral sex. There are also several behavioral modifications that are considered risk-reduction or harm-reduction strategies. Some of these strategies include

- Negotiated safety (Kippax, Crawford, Rodden, & Dowsett, 1993)
- Strategic sexual positioning (Van de Ven et al., 2002)
- Dipping (anal insertion for one or two strokes without a condom) (Parsons et al., 2004).

In Australia, the practice of *negotiated safety* (Crawford, Rodden, Kippax, & Van de Ven, 2001) is popular as a safer sex strategy. According to Wolitski (2005), five conditions must be met in a negotiated safety relationship:

1. The sexual partners are in an ongoing primary relationship;
2. The sexual partners are HIV-negative and aware of each other's negative status;
3. The sexual partners have reached a clear and unambiguous agreement about the types of sexual behaviors that will be practiced within and outside of their relationship;

4. The agreement is that sex outside of the relationship is safe with regard to HIV transmission; and

5. The agreement is kept by all partners. (p. 13)

Gay and bisexual men who use the harm-reduction technique known as *strategic sexual positioning* are aware of each other's HIV status and adjust their behavior accordingly: HIV-positive men are "receptive" during anal intercourse, and HIV-negative men are "insertive" partners (Parsons, 2005b). When using the harm-reduction strategy known as *serosorting*, gay and bisexual men engage in risky sex only with those partners who are believed to be of a similar or concordant HIV status (Parsons, 2005b; Suarez & Miller, 2001).

Obviously, for such approaches to be effective in promoting safer sex, sexual partners need to be honest in disclosing or exchanging information about their serostatus. But for some, that degree of honesty is difficult. This is where trained practitioners are ideally qualified to employ assertiveness and social skill training to help their sexual minority clients use these strategies. In addition, role plays of sexual encounters help clients rehearse communication skills needed to negotiate safer sex.

Be Aware of Internalized Stigmas

Therapists need to be aware of indications that their sexual minority clients have internalized the stigmas associated with homosexuality and HIV/AIDS:

No gay man grows up immune to the insidious and overt messages that his sexual desire is in itself fundamentally wrong and unacceptable. By the time a conscious awareness of homoerotic desire emerges, countless negative images and beliefs have been foisted upon the developing self. (Forstein, 2002, p. 39)

Research demonstrates that the negative stigma associated with HIV/AIDS is related to the health behaviors of gay men themselves. Using data from the Seropositive Urban Men's Study (SUMS), Wolitiski et al. (2004) explored gay men's attitudes toward other HIV-positive men. Participants had been diagnosed with HIV for an average of 6.8 years (SD = 4.0). HIV-seropositive participants perceived negative attitudes from other members of their gay community as a result of their health status. Those who perceived higher levels of HIV/AIDs stigma in the gay community were more likely to seek out sexual partners in such places as sex parties and sex clubs, often putting themselves and others at further risk.

Counseling Sexual Minority Men Who Are HIV-Positive

Medical advances in HIV treatment include the development of highly active antiretroviral therapy (HAART) and viral load testing. The latter entails frequent blood tests, which enable physicians to examine viral load and CD4 levels (T-helper cells) to see if the anti-HIV drugs are working effectively (Shernoff, 2006). These advancements have created a paradigm shift from viewing AIDS as a death sentence to a manageable disease. According to Rose (1998), "the language and assumptions of hope have been firmly incorporated into the vocabulary of the epidemic" (p. 198).

Sexual minorities who are HIV-positive and who have access to services now face a number of complex treatment decisions related to their HIV status (Dilley, 1998). As Dilley

(1998) notes, for those who are responsive to antiviral medications, the focus is on sustaining difficult treatment regimens, which typically involve doctors' appointments and adherence to strict medication schedules. For those who are not responding to antiviral medications, the focus of therapy shifts to coping with declining health and a future that may involve treatment possibilities as well as disappointments (Dilley, 1998). Providing support and helping clients find meaning in catastrophe will continue to be part of the psychotherapists' task (Dilley, 1998).

O'Connor (1997) noted that, as pharmacological interventions now enable HIV-positive clients to be asymptomatic for prolonged periods with little to no outward manifestation of their illness to others, "this experience often recapitulates the gay man's earlier struggle with sexual orientation and 'coming out'" (p. 126). The HIV-positive client is now faced with similar sorts of dilemmas, such as when to tell, who to tell, and "What then?" Given this, O'Connor (1997) noted:

> it is not unusual for a gay man to review the traumatic events of his developmental history in the course of psychotherapeutic treatment. That history is likely to include experiences of teasing, denigration, and disappointment from parents, adults, and peers and of marginality and oppression. (p. 128)

In terms of dating and forming relationships, Harmon and Voker (1995) observed that sexual minorities frequently seek out partners whose serostatuses are the opposite of theirs. HIV-negative partners may be motivated to date HIV-positive partners out of a desire to "rescue" their partners. Alternatively, some HIV-positive persons seek HIV-negative partners who will care for them. It has also been noted that in serodiscordant partners, it is the HIV-negative partner who is prone to the experience of "survivor guilt" (Chernin & Johnson, 2003). Given these issues, a number of therapists (e.g., Chernin & Johnson, 2003) recommend the use of support groups made up of serodiscordant partners.

Several psychosocial stressors—including family, employment, finance, and health-related issues—confront HIV-positive couples (Chernin & Johnson, 2003). Therapists working with such couples need to address these issues and help them prepare for the possibility of opportunistic infections and the need for additional social supports.

HIV Prevention Models for Sexual Minority Men

Prevention models for sexual minority men have evolved from a "condoms only" stance to the use of support group–based and community-based interventions, with some programs being offered in gay bathhouses and bars (Johnson et al., 2005). Many HIV prevention programs are based on the health belief model (Becker, 1984) and the theory of planned behavior (Ajzen & Madden, 1986), both of which presume that people are rational creatures. Practitioners now recommend alternatives to "rational" and "fear-based" models of prevention. For example, the Drag Initiative to Vanquish AIDS (DIVA) is perhaps a unique outreach effort. DIVA sends out educators attired in wigs and matching outfits who approach men in bars and distribute safer sex kits with lighthearted conversation about HIV prevention (Parsons, 2005b). Another San Francisco-based prevention program incorporates the use of an STFree Card, a driver's license–sized card with a photograph and a code that permits sexual partners to retrieve the cardholder's HIV status from a hotline number (*www.stfree.com*).

In addition, new intervention programs are now being launched on the Internet. Since large numbers of gay men and MSM already use computer technology to meet sex partners, Internet-based HIV prevention programs are a viable and affordable way to reach large numbers of gay men and MSM (Bowen, Horvath, & Williams, 2007). There are Internet sites that allow users to keep track of their sex partners so that, if they should test positive for STIs, their partners would be notified via online postcards (*www.itrick.org*). Other web-based resources for gay men and MSM can be found at *www.aids.infonet.org* (harm-reduction fact sheets), *www.gmhc.org* (Gay Men's Health Crisis programs and information), and *www.thefenwayinstitute.org* (Fenway Community Health's information on HIV and STIs).

SEXUAL HEALTH AND SEXUALLY TRANSMITTED INFECTIONS AMONG SEXUAL MINORITY WOMEN

Lesbians frequently assume that they are at a reduced risk for STIs, compared with heterosexual and bisexual women. For example, Morrow and Allsworth (2000) reported that 84% of their lesbian respondents believed they were at "zero risk" of HIV or STI infection through sexual activity and 61% believed they were at "no risk" over their lifetime. As a result of this assumption, lesbians are less likely to seek or be referred by their primary care physicians for routine gynecological screenings (Hutchinson et al., 2006; Van Dam et al., 2001) and PAP tests (Marrazzo et al., 2001).

Despite the widespread myth that lesbians do not contract STIs, studies have shown that 13–17% of them do contract STIs (Fethers, Marks, Mindel, & Estcourt, 2000). Lesbians and WSW engage in sexual activities that involve the exchange of bodily fluids, exposure to blood, and genital and anal stimulation (Bauer & Welles, 2001; Diamant, Schuster & Lever, 2000). Penetrative sexual practices such as digital-vaginal and digital-anal contact and the use of insertive sex toys are plausible means of contracting sexually transmitted diseases (Marrazzo et al., 2005). Lesbians and WSW have a high rate of bacterial vaginosis, which results from a shift in the vagina's microbial ecosystem with an overgrowth of harmful bacteria (Marrazzo et al., 2005). Lesbians also contract human papillomavirus (HPV) (Marrazzo, Koutsky, & Stine, 1998), trichmoniasis, and anogenital warts (Carroll, Goldstein, Lo, & Mayer, 1997).

In 1999, the Institute of Medicine concluded that lesbians are at higher risk for cervical cancer and breast cancer (Solarz, 1999). O'Hanlan's (1995) review of research concluded that breast, ovarian, and endometrial cancers are more frequent among lesbians than among heterosexual women. The risks of breast and endometrial cancer are higher among lesbians for several reasons. These include their lower use of oral contraceptives (O'Hanlan, 1995; Sadovsky, 2000), lower pregnancy rates (Bybee, 1990), increased prevalence of smoking (Sadovsky, 2000), greater consumption of alcohol, and higher rates of obesity (Aaron, Markovic, Danielson, & Honnold, 2001; Cochran et al., 2001).

HIV in Sexual Minority Women, WSW, and WSMW

Lesbians have been omitted from HIV-related medical research, health prevention programs, and other public health interventions (Cochran et al., 2001; Goldstein, 1997) in part because they are believed to be immune to HIV/AIDs. Goldstein (1997) posited that the Centers for Disease Control and Prevention's (CDC) HIV reporting procedures have "obscured" the rate or cause of infection among WSW.

The widely held assumption that women who engage in sexual relations with women are immune from HIV infection has been challenged in several case reports of infected lesbians who have reported sex exclusively with other women (Kwakwa & Ghobrial, 2003; Monzon & Capellan, 1987); however, the CDC has neither confirmed these cases nor included them in their databases (CDC, 2006). In 2003, Kwakwa and Ghobrial described a case of female-to-female transmission of HIV in a 20-year-old African-American woman and her bisexual female partner. The transmission of HIV in this case was attributed to vigorous use of sex toys and exchange of blood-tinged body fluids.

COUNSELING SEXUAL MINORITY WOMEN, WSW, AND WSMW

Recognize Countertransference Issues

Therapists may experience a number of emotional responses at the prospect of discussing sexual health and sexual behaviors with their sexual minority clients. Sexual behaviors between women partners are often eroticized or sensationalized and may leave practitioners feeling uncomfortable about raising such issues in the therapy room. Others may feel inadequately prepared. And still others may find themselves wondering, "What do two women/men do in bed together?" That said, it is nonetheless important that therapists be prepared to discuss sexual health issues with their clients in affirmative and constructive ways. Even those who do not wish to acquire specialized training in sex counseling must be prepared to discuss issues of sexuality and sexual health.

Be Knowledgeable

Therapists who work with sexual minority women need to transmit accurate information about STIs and HIV and about risk-reduction options. Specifically, therapists can help dispel the myth that sexual minority women are somehow immune to STIs and HIV. Therapists may need to reinforce the necessity of partners checking for cuts or sores in the mouths or genitals of their sexual partners, using dental dams (squares of plastic wrap or latex condoms cut open and spread flat) during oral sex, and disinfecting sex toys and vibrators before and after sexual contact. Web-based resources about STIs and HIV for lesbians and WSW are available at *www.lesbianSTD.com*, *www.lesbianhealthinfo.org*, *www.Avert.org*, and *www.superdyke.com*.

Counseling Sexual Minority Women, WSW, and WSMW Who Have STIs

An STI diagnosis in one or both partners can cause feelings of shame, guilt, embarrassment, anger, and anxiety as well as problems in the relationship. Often reactions are exacerbated by each partner's religious and cultural background as well as societal messages about the manner in which STIs and HIV are transmitted. Practitioners can help partners explore the impact of the STIs on their relationships and their issues of fidelity, communication skills, and coping skills to deal with the medical management of their symptoms (Long, Burnett, & Thomas, 2006).

HIV/STI Prevention Models for Sexual Minority Women, WSW, and WSMW

Prevention programs for sexual minority women, WSW, and WSMW do not appear to be as numerous and inventive as those which exist for sexual minority men. Specialized health clinics in metropolitan areas such as the Fenway Clinic (*http://www. fenway-health.org*) in Massachusetts and the Whitman-Walker Clinic (*http://www.wwc. org*) in Washington, DC provide community outreach, peer support groups, and educational programs on the prevention of STIs and HIV. Yet in most areas, prevention programs for lesbians, bisexual women, WSW, and WSMW are largely dependent on Internet-based information. Two noteworthy examples of informative Web-based programs include the following: *http://www.Lesbianstd.com*, which contains bibliographic resources and opportunities for browsers to pose questions about STIs and *http://www.girl2girl. info/cms/index.phb?page=what_can_i_catch&images=on*, a resource especially geared to WSW and WSMW.

According to HIV-prevention experts, effective educational programs are generally ones that recognize that people's sexual behaviors are distinct from their identities. Because some women do not identify with the term *lesbian* or *bisexual*, prevention programs should consider offering support and education without the labels (Miller et al., 2007). One way to provide support as well as HIV education to WSW and WSMW is through the use of support groups that incorporate the label "bi-curious" (Miller et al., 2007).

SEXUAL HEALTH IN GENDER MINORITY PERSONS

In a recent survey of gender minorities in the Philadelphia area, 25% of the respondents indicated that they had been denied medical services because of their gender minority status (Kenagy, 2005). It does seem incomprehensible that anyone would be denied potentially life-saving medical intervention, yet consider the details of the story of Tyra Hunter, a male-to-female transgender person who was injured in an automobile accident in 1995. Tyra was denied life-saving medical intervention after the Washington, DC, Fire Department's emergency medical technicians discovered that underneath Tyra's female clothing she had a penis! The attendants uttered epithets and stopped working on her for 5–7 minutes. Tyra died shortly after she was taken to a local hospital. Tyra's mother received a $2 million settlement after a jury found the District of Columbia guilty of negligence and malpractice (Gender Public Advocacy Coalition, 1998).

The next section explores ways in which transphobia impacts the health care, particularly the sexual health care, of gender minorities.

STIs and HIV in Gender Minority Persons

The bulk of research on STIs and HIV in the gender minority population is based on convenience sampling, primarily in large metropolitan areas such as San Francisco, Los Angeles, and New York City. The majority of these studies (e.g., Bockting, Robinson, Forberg, & Scheltema, 2005; Bockting, Robinson, & Rosser, 1998; Bockting, Rosser, & Coleman, 1999; Clements-Nolle, Marx, Guzman, & Katz; 2001; Kenagy, 2005; Kenagy & Hsieh, 2005; Lombardi & van Servellen, 2000) report that gender minorities are at greater risk, compared with non–gender minorities, for STIs and HIV. Among MTF transgender persons in particular, the risk of HIV infection is thought to surpass that of bisexual men and gay men (Lombardi & van Servellen, 2000). Clements-Nolle et al. (2001) studied the HIV prevalence among 392 MTF and 123 FTM persons. Of these, 35% of MTFs reported positive HIV test results, while 2% of FTMs tested positive for HIV.

In their study of MTF transgender persons of color in San Francisco, Nemoto, Operario, Keatley, Han, and Soma (2004) interviewed 48 participants and distributed surveys to an additional 332 participants. The majority of their sample identified themselves as preoperative transgenders or preoperative transsexuals. Of their respondents, 26% reported being HIV-positive and 14% reported testing positive for STIs during the past year. In addition, 12% reported unprotected anal intercourse with partners in the past 30 days.

Commercial sex workers form a subgroup within the gender minority community thought to be particularly at risk for HIV infection (Bockting et al., 1998; Oggins & Eichenbaum, 2002; Pisani et al., 2004). For gender minorities, sex work provides a means to supplement lower levels of income related to lower levels of education (Nemoto, Luke, Mamo, Ching, & Patria, 1999). It also bridges periods of unemployment and helps defray medical costs associated with sex reassignment (Bockting et al., 1998). Bockting et al. (1998) identified several risk factors that are often found among gender minority sex workers, including multiple sexual partners, frequent anal receptive sex, irregular condom use, and drug and injecting drug use and needle sharing.

Melendez et al. (2006) designed a unique study to compare access to health care and the actual health status between HIV-positive MTF and HIV-positive nontransgendered persons. They found that both groups were similar in health status. Both had similar viral loads and numbers of AIDS-related symptoms. There were no differences in terms of visits to a health-care provider and health-care coverage between the two groups. However, fewer MTF participants than nontransgendered persons reported currently taking highly active antiretroviral therapy despite the fact that this therapy has been "associated with prolonged life" (Melendez et al., 2006, p. 1036).

COUNSELING GENDER MINORITIES WITH STIS AND HIV/AIDS

Recognize Countertransference Issues

The stories of gender minorities included in this chapter painfully demonstrate the intensity of fear and hostility that can emerge when people, even trained medical personnel, encounter patients who transgress gender. If practitioners are going to work with gender minorities, they must confront their own transphobia as well as the negative stigmas associated with HIV/AIDS, sex work, and drug use (Lee et al., 2002). Lastly, because the sexual orientation of gender minorities is more fluid and many engage in same-sex sexual behaviors, practitioners must deal with their own homophobic and biphobic responses.

Recognize Internalized Stigmas

Therapists also need to be aware of indications that gender minority clients have internalized the stigmas associated with gender variance, same-sex sexuality, and HIV/AIDS. In much the same way as sexual minorities are taught that same-sex desire is fundamentally wrong and unacceptable, gender minorities must deal with trauma associated with growing up as a gender-nonconforming person.

Some gender minority persons experience discomfort, including anxiety and depression, when discussing their genitals and their sexual functioning (Bockting, Knudson, & Goldberg, 2006). They may talk about their genitals in terms that are nontraditional but consistent with their subjective sense of themselves. Some biological females may describe their clitoris as a "phantom penis" (Bockting et al., 2006). Practitioners must be sensitive to these issues and realize that some intersexed and gender minorities may have physically different genitals (O'Brien, 2003). For example, some gender minority persons who take testosterone develop enlarged clitorises, sometimes called "dicklits" (O'Brien, 2003).

Prevent STIs/HIV in Gender Minorities

Therapists who work with gender minority persons either individually or in couples need to ask whether their clients are having safe sex, how they arrived at their decisions regarding safe sex, and how each feels about the level of safety they practice (Shernoff, 2005).

Prevention programs dealing with STIs and HIV often fail to meet the unique needs and circumstances of gender minorities (Bockting et al., 1998). The reasons are numerous. Bockting, who has been particularly prolific in his work on HIV prevention in the gender minority population, maintains that the ineffectiveness of these efforts is due to the inability of health-care professionals to appreciate the broad spectrum of ways in which people express their gender identities. On one end of this continuum are those who wish to fully transition to their desired gender and who want to pass as their desired gender. The possibility of being "read" or identified as transsexual is not acceptable, nor do they feel the need for sexual health information and HIV prevention education. Hence, Bockting sees the desire to pass as transsexual as a risk factor in prevention education.

Bockting et al. (1998) illustrate that prevention efforts in the gender minority population are often impeded because many do not see themselves as actually engaging in high-risk sexual behaviors. The need to blend in and to hide one's transgender identity can motivate the use of dangerously high dosages of hormones, sometimes beyond those prescribed. Many gender minorities obtain black market hormones and inject these intramuscularly in order to feminize or masculinize their bodies. Worse, they sometimes share their needles. Yet many who engage in these practices do not consider themselves "drug users," nor do they feel at risk for HIV by virtue of their needle sharing. According to Bockting et al., HIV prevention programs must target the specific risk factors within this population, promote the responsible use of hormones, and improve access to specialized Medicare.

Bockting et al. (1998) additionally note that the unique physical characteristics of MTF persons change the nature of safe sex information. For example, the neovagina of MTF transsexuals does not lubricate. It may also be constructed with delicate colon tissue, thus making vaginal penetration riskier. Assumptions are often made that safe sex is not applicable to "men with breasts and penises, men with vaginas, women penetrating men as well as women" (p. 521). For example:

> Whereas male to female transsexuals attracted to men may prefer the receptive role in intercourse, female impersonators and drag queens may assume the insertive role in anal and vaginal intercourse. Male crossdressers often have penis-vagina intercourse in sexual relationships with their female partners, while engaging in receptive anal sex with their male sex partners. (Bockting et al., 1998, p. 521)

REMOVE SYSTEMIC BARRIERS TO SEXUAL HEALTH IN SEXUAL AND GENDER MINORITIES THROUGH ADVOCACY

The global HIV/AIDS health crisis during the 1980s galvanized many gay activists and their allies to advocate aggressively for improved and responsive HIV/AIDS treatment. As a result, many public health researchers, practitioners, and policy makers shifted from the purely biomedical aspects of HIV and other diseases to a health and human rights perspective (Parker et al., 2004). Many argued that access to competent and compassionate health care is not a privilege; rather, it is a basic human right. Now health researchers, practitioners, and policy makers are becoming more involved in the political struggles for reproductive rights, sexual health, human rights, and justice around the globe (Parker et al., 2004). Helping professionals can work with their peers to advocate for improved training on and sexual health services for sexual and gender minorities. Sexual and gender minority persons must receive quality health-care services and culturally relevant education in the prevention of disease. Helping professionals can also work to make health insurance more widely available to gender minorities and help establish outreach programs on HIV and STI prevention that are targeted at gender minorities.

SUBSTANCE ABUSE IN SEXUAL AND GENDER MINORITIES

Much has been written about the abuse of substances in sexual minority communities, and certainly, gay bars figure prominently in the gay and lesbian life. There is valuable research pertaining to substance abuse in sexual and gender minorities, and in particular, the association between substance use and sexual risk behaviors. This section also discusses two treatment strategies that may be especially appropriate for use with sexual and gender minorities.

Substance Use in Sexual Minority Women and WSW

Research findings consistently show that the rates of alcohol-related problems and other substance abuse problems seem to be higher in sexual minority women than in heterosexual women (Bradford, Ryan, & Rothblum, 1994; Cochran & Mays, 2000; Gilman et al., 2001; Lombardi & Bettcher, 2006; McCabe, Boyd, Hughes, & d'Arcy, 2003; McCabe et al., 2004; Ryan & Gruskin, 2006). Using a state-maintained database of over 20,000 clients who sought state-funded treatment over an 18-month period, Cochran and Cauce (2006) reported that participants who identified themselves as sexual minorities had greater frequencies of substance use than did heterosexual participants.

However, some of the earlier research may have overestimated the extent to which substance abuse is problematic for this population. Many of the early studies incorporated convenience samples of sexual minority women who were often recruited directly from gay bars (Cabaj, 2000). Current research also yields contradictory findings. For example, Gilman et al. (2001) and Cochran, Sullivan, and Mays (2003) conducted national health surveys and reported no significant differences in substance use disorders in sexual minorities, compared with heterosexual men and women. Hughes, Wilsnack, and Johnson (2006) were principal investigators in a study comparing three groups of women: lesbians and heterosexual women residing in Chicago and a sample of U.S. women. There were no significant differences in overall levels of drinking. However, significantly more lesbians than heterosexual women worried about developing a drinking problem.

Club drug use among gay and bisexual men is a topic of extensive research and prevention efforts (Parsons, Kelly, & Wells, 2006). Yet sexual minority women have received little attention. Drugs such as cocaine, methamphetamine, ecstasy, GHB (gamma-hydroxybutyrate), and ketamine are labeled "club drugs" because of their association with gay dance clubs, bars, circuit parties, and rave scenes in the 1990s. In their study of over 1,000 sexual minority and heterosexual women, Parsons et al. found that sexual minority women were significantly more likely to use cocaine, methamphetamine, and LSD over a lifetime than were heterosexual women.

Substance Use and Sexual Risk Behaviors in Sexual Minority Men and MSM

While rates of alcohol use in gay and heterosexual men are comparable, drug use among gay men is higher than in the straight community (Stall et al., 2001). In the past decade, there has been a dramatic increase in poly-substance use in the gay and bisexual men's communities (Gorman, Nelson, Applegate, & Scrol, 2004; Halkitis et al., 2001; Kurtz, 2005; Mansergh et al., 2001).

For gay men and MSM, there is a definite association between the use of alcohol and recreational drugs and high-risk sexual behaviors (Chiasson et al., 2005; Parsons, Kutnick, Halkitis, Punzalan, & Carbonari, 2005; Stueve et al., 2002). For example, the online expression "chem friendly" is used by sexual minority men to refer to the desire to have sex while using methamphetamines (Shernoff, 2005).

Parsons et al. (2005) conducted a longitudinal study with 253 HIV-positive gay men who were enrolled in an intervention program called Positive Choices from 1997 to 2002. The majority of participants met the *Diagnostic and Statistical Manual for Mental Disorders* (DSM–IV; American Psychiatric Association, 1994) criteria for alcohol dependence or alcohol abuse. The research noted that 94.3% of the sample used alcohol before or during sex, possibly promoting a drop in inhibitions and an increase in unprotected anal sex. The use of alcohol before or during sex was significant when men engaged in risky sex. There was also a clear relationship between HIV-risk behaviors and the use of other drugs, including marijuana, stimulants, hallucinogens, opiates, and inhalants.

Research findings point to a strong association between club drugs and high-risk sexual behavior and the transmission of HIV (Gorman et al., 2004; Kurtz, 2005; Wilton, Halkitis, English, & Roberson, 2005). One common club drug, methamphetamine (referred to as "crystal" or "tina"), is often used by gay men to enhance and extend sexual encounters (Halkitis, Parsons, & Wilton, 2003). The popularity of crystal meth is also tied to feelings of sexual disinhibition and to the strong feelings of attractiveness and sexual desirability it creates (Kurtz, 2005). Other motivators identified by researchers are cognitive escapism (McKirnan, Ostrow, & Hope, 1996) and the avoidance of thoughts about their HIV status. Methamphetamine impacts neurons that release serotonin, norepinephrine, and dopamine. And depending on the amount taken, its effects, including hypersexuality, euphoria, and increased self-confidence, can last from 8 to 24 hours. Long-term use of methamphetamines is linked to induced psychosis (Ellenhorn, Schonwald, Ordog, & Wasserberger, 1997). In high doses, it can lead to peripheral effects, including the inability to obtain a partial or full erection; this is sometimes referred to as "crystal dick" (Whitfield, 1996).

Ross and Williams (2001) reviewed several hypotheses to explain the connection between substance use and high-risk sexual behaviors. They saw a causal relationship, where drugs serve as an aphrodisiac, causing people to engage in high-risk sexual behaviors.

Other hypotheses are that drugs reduce inhibitions and that drugs are a key component in sensation seeking. Lastly, Ross and Williams saw a more complex relationship involving multiple factors: the biochemical interactions, the situational contexts of drug use, and the specific types of drugs used.

Substance Use in Gender Minorities

Surveys conducted in metropolitan areas throughout the United States, such as New York City (Valentine, 1998), Washington, DC (Xavier, 2000), and Boston (Marcel, 1998), consistently report high levels of drug and alcohol abuse in gender minority participants. For example, investigators have found that rates of abuse range from 27.1% for alcohol abuse and 23.6% for drug abuse in New York City to 34% for alcohol abuse and 36% for drug abuse in Washington, DC (Valentine, 1998; Xavier, 1998).

Mathy (2002) compared the use of alcohol and drugs and suicidality among several groups using an online survey of matched samples of gender minorities, nontransgendered males and females, gay men and lesbians, and traditionally gendered heterosexual males and females. No differences were found among the groups. Among the gender minority sample, those who had attempted suicide were significantly more likely to use alcohol and drugs excessively, compared to gender minorities who had not attempted suicide.

Substance Use and HIV in Gender Minorities

Nemoto et al. (1999) observed that transgender sex workers often use methamphetamines to cope with life on the street. The strong need for affirmation and for validation as sexually desirable often overrides the desire to practice safe sex.

Reback et al. (2005) compared HIV seroprevalence and risk behaviors among persons who exchanged sex for money, drugs, shelter, or food, using data from the Los Angeles Transgender Health Study. In the study, which interviewed 244 transgendered women, those who exchanged sex were more likely to be under 30 years of age, be Latina, and use condoms during either receptive or insertive anal intercourse. According to Reback et al., the use of alcohol and/or drugs was found to be the "greatest behavioral predictor of HIV infection, as was being African-American and having a low socioeconomic status" (p. 18).

In a survey of gender minorities in San Francisco, Nemoto et al. (2004) reported that being HIV-positive and having sex under the influence of drugs were two predictors of unprotected receptive anal intercourse with a casual partner. Research by Reback et al. (2005) also links the use of substances to high-risk sexual activities and the increased likelihood of HIV infection.

COUNSELING SEXUAL AND GENDER MINORITIES WHO ENGAGE IN SUBSTANCE ABUSE

Recognize Countertransference Issues

Little attention has been given to substance abuse treatment within sexual and gender minority populations (Cochran & Cauce, 2006; Finnegan & McNally, 2002).

What little research exists is focused predominately on the attitudes of addictions practitioners who work with sexual minority clients. For example, Eliason (2000) assessed knowledge and attitudes of substance abuse practitioners toward their sexual and gender minority clients. Of those who participated, 50% reported that they had no instruction about gay and bisexual issues, and 80% claimed no instruction about transgender issues. However, most indicated that they were accepting of sexual and gender minorities.

In their sample of addictions practitioners, Matthews, Selvidge, and Fisher (2005) found that women practitioners reported more affirmative behavior toward their sexual minority clients than did men practitioners. The study further stated that the organizational climate within the treatment facility itself was the most significant variable creating an affirmative treatment environment for sexual and gender minority clients.

In their qualitative analysis of interviews with recovering sexual minority substance abusers, Matthews, Lorah, and Fenton (2006) asked their interviewees about their treatment experiences for drug and alcohol addiction and had them evaluate these in terms of what was therapeutic and what was not. One theme that emerged from their analysis of interview data was the recommendation that substance abuse practitioners "address sexual orientation directly rather than waiting for clients to raise these issues" (p. 117). The tendency among substance abuse practitioners to avoid dealing with sexual orientation in the recovery process was also reported by Finnegan and McNally (2002), who noted that, despite the fact that most treatment programs routinely incorporate psychosocial histories, few practitioners ask about their clients' sexual orientation or gender identity.

Assess for Trauma

Trauma is defined as a sudden, unexpected, or non-normative event whose demands exceed a person's perceived ability to meet them; thus, it disrupts the person's frame of reference and other central psychological needs (McCann & Pearlman, 1990). Many sexual and gender minorities are dually traumatized: first, by the oppression often inherent with their identities and second, by the substance abuse itself (Finnegan & McNally, 2002). In *Counseling Lesbian, Gay, Bisexual and Transgender Substance Abusers (2002),* they describe the work of addictions practitioners as helping clients establish positive identities:

> When practitioners (among others) are supportive and empathetic, LGBT substance abusers have their best chance to recover. If, however, practitioners are homo/bi/transphobic or are prejudiced against substance abusers—or both—then they may well compound the damage already done by these dual traumas. (p. 22)

The presence of posttraumatic stress disorder symptomatology and the escalation of symptoms associated with this are a possible occurrence throughout therapy.

Implement Substance Abuse Treatment Strategies

There are a myriad of treatment approaches that are used in psychotherapy with substance-addicted sexual and gender minorities. Helping professionals must be able and willing to confront clients who are in denial about their substance abuse. They must be able to recognize when clients are "bullshitting" and being manipulative and must be able to challenge these behaviors when necessary. Participation in 12-step programs is especially appropriate (*www.gayalcoholics.com*).

This chapter focuses on the use of motivational interviewing (MI), harm reduction, and relapse prevention (RP). All of these approaches have been recommended for use with sexual and gender minorities (Martell, Safren, & Prince, 2004; Parsons, 2005a; Shernoff, 2006). Their benefit is that rather than reinforcing "shame"-based messages about addiction, they espouse a positive view of clients and their abilities to make changes. This is a particularly important message to convey to sexual and gender minority persons, most of whom have been marginalized and stigmatized because of their identities (Martell et al., 2004). And as many sexual and gender minorities have also been rejected by organized religions, they may not be initially antagonistic to the spiritual aspects of 12-step programs (Martell et al., 2004).

MI was developed by Miller and Rollnick in 1991. It is grounded in the belief that people have the natural capacity to find the resources they need to change their problematic behaviors. MI has been shown in several outcome studies to be especially effective in the treatment of substance abuse (Miller & Rollnick, 2002). The second edition of Miller and Rollnick's text, entitled *Motivational Interviewing*, contains general guidelines and case examples that illustrate how to implement MI principles with various clients (Miller & Rollnick, 2002). Interested readers are urged to consult this text for more detailed information.

Typically, therapists begin the MI process by adopting an open, empathic, and accepting posture with regard to their clients' feelings of resistance or ambivalence about changing their substance use behaviors. This can be a challenging process for therapists, particularly because they know the many life-damaging consequences that can result from unsafe sex practices and from drug and alcohol addictions. During the *empathy* stage, clients are clearly directed to explore their ambivalence and to focus on the good things associated with drinking/drugging. Therapists also help clients articulate their values and goals in life. Using the next principle, *developing discrepancy*, therapists underscore the contradictions within clients between their life goals and their current behaviors. Miller and Rollnick described *rolling with resistance* as the opposite of confronting or opposing the clients' reluctance to change their behaviors. Finally, therapists engage in the process of *supporting clients' self-efficacy*, or their belief in their own abilities to make changes they desire.

One tool used in the process of evaluating clients' readiness for change is stage-of-change theory. The Prochaska, DiClemente, and Norcross (1992) stage model was specifically adapted for use with addictions. According to Prochaska et al., the stages include precontemplation, contemplation, preparation, action, and change maintenance. Ideally, practitioners assess the stage clients are in and develop strategies to aid the person in working through the subsequent stages of change.

Shernoff (2006) recommends the use of harm reduction methods as an alternative to the widely accepted abstinence-based approach to treating substance abuse. In his treatment of HIV-positive men who use crystal meth, for example, Shernoff (2006) incorporated the following harm reduction suggestions in the treatment of clients who were planning on using crystal:

a. Purchase a pocket-sized medicine case that can be programmed to beep when it is time for them to take a dose of their antiretroviral medication.
b. Disclose their HIV status to prospective sex partners.
c. Stay hydrated in order to minimize bodily damage.
d. Carry protein bars or other nutritionally complete and portable sources of nutrition they can easily eat while partying at a club, the baths, a sex party, etc. (p. 130)

Other ideas about harm reduction interventions related to drug use and HIV/STIs may be found on the Harm Reduction Coalition website at *www.harmreduction.org*.

Relapse prevention is a cognitive-behaviorally based approach that was developed in 1985 by Marlatt. The approach is designed to prevent relapses, aid clients in identifying the triggers or cues that often promote a relapse into destructive behaviors, and help clients manage their behaviors through the use of cognitive-behavioral coping responses once relapse has occurred (Marlatt, 1985; Marlatt & Donovan, 2005). Relapses are defined as setbacks, which are reframed by therapists as learning opportunities rather than failures (Marlatt & Donovan, 2005).

When working specifically with gender minorities, Bockting et al. (2006) recommend an integrated approach to treatment. The idea is to permit clients with co-occurring gender issues to undergo treatment while simultaneously engaging in treatment for substance abuse.

Assess High-Risk Sex Behaviors and Co-occurring Substance Use

Given the connection between high-risk sex behaviors and substance abuse, practitioners (e.g., Shoptaw & Forsch, 2000) recommend that substance abuse treatment programs address issues of sexuality. Given research about the co-occurrence of sexual compulsivity and substance abuse among gay and bisexual men, it is important to accurately assess and treat both forms of addiction. It is also advocated that HIV prevention programs for sexual and gender minorities routinely include substance abuse screening protocols and procedures for substance abuse treatment (Reback, et al., 2005).

Based on his clinical observations, Guss (2000) noted that many of his gay male patients reported greater high-risk sexual behaviors while high on crack cocaine. Most felt a greater sense of attractiveness and sexual desirability while high on crack; these feelings were quite different from their developmental experiences of feeling unmasculine and undesirable. Guss also noted that many of these patients used weight training as a compensatory activity. Therapy should, therefore, address issues related to body image and self-esteem.

Therapy may be particularly challenging with sexual and gender minority clients who are HIV-positive and who are diagnosed with multiple co-morbid disorders, including substance abuse and other mental illnesses. Treatment often requires providers to interact with a variety of practitioners from the medical, mental health, and substance abuse treatment fields.

Advocate

A number of systemic changes in addictions treatment are necessary to address the kinds of inadequacies identified in the surveys of sexual and gender minorities' experiences with health care:

- Use inclusive language in agency mission statements and other agency publications, including intake forms (Cochran & Cauce, 2006).
- Hire sexual and gender minority staff who are open about their sexual orientation and gender identities (Matthews et al., 2006; Matthews et al., 2005; Oggins & Eichenbaum, 2002).
- Create community resource guides that help sexual and gender minorities locate sensitive health care and substance abuse treatment (Saulnier, 2002), and make

written resources available for and about sexual and gender minorities (Cochran & Cauce, 2006; Finnegan & McNally, 2002; Matthews et al., 2006; Matthews et al., 2005).

- Offer Internet-related resources and web-based programs dealing with sexual health issues.
- Expand definitions of family to include same-sex partners and others in treatment (Finnegan & McNally, 2002).
- Make use of 12-step support groups that are welcoming of sexual and gender minorities (Cabaj, 2000).
- Provide regular training and continuing educational opportunities for staff members on sexual and gender minority treatment issues (Finnegan & McNally, 2002; Lombardi & Bettcher, 2006; Oggins & Eichenbaum, 2002).
- Enact a "no tolerance" policy on homophobic, biphobic, and transphobic remarks by clients and staff (Finnegan & McNally, 2002; Lombardi & Bettcher, 2006).
- Make housing accommodations for gender minorities in residential treatment programs that are safe and affirmative (Lombardi & van Servellen, 2000; Oggins & Eichenbaum, 2002).
- Establish written policies about confidentiality related to sexual orientation and gender identity, and provide staff with training about federal confidentiality regulations (Substance Abuse and Mental Health Services Administration, 2001).

Summary

Sexual and gender minorities, like other marginalized minorities, experience significant barriers to their access to sexual health care. Research shows that those homophobic, biphobic, and transphobic attitudes and behaviors reflected in the general population are also mirrored in the health-care professions. Gender minority persons, in particular, are omitted from health-care research, treatment, and prevention programs and are often treated by health-care professionals with hostility and disdain.

While HIV prevention programs in the gay men's community have been remarkably effective, recent evidence suggests that unprotected sex among gay men is increasing and that growing numbers of MSM are not maintaining safer sex practices (Halkitis, Wolitski, & Gomez, 2005; Wolitski, 2005). Gender minorities are omitted from HIV-related medical research, education, and prevention programs (Cochran et al., 2001; Goldstein, 1997; Namaste, 2000).

Helping professionals need to be knowledgeable about HIV risk indicators and risk reduction options for sexual and gender minorities. All helping professionals must explore possible countertransference issues that might impede discussions about sexual behaviors with their sexual and gender minority clients. It is especially important that medical and mental health professionals ask questions and promote dialogue about HIV and STIs without evaluating or pathologizing those who intentionally take sexual risks (Shernoff, 2005).

Sexual and gender minorities have received little attention in the research on substance abuse treatment and training programs. This is despite research findings that show higher rates of abuse among sexual minority women, compared to heterosexual women (Bradford, Ryan, & Rothblum, 1994; Cochran & Mays, 2000; Gilman et al., 2001; Lombardi & Bettcher, 2006; McCabe et al., 2003; McCabe et al., 2004). Recommendations to improve the effectiveness of substance abuse treatment programs for sexual and gender minorities include employing staff persons who are out about their sexual and/or gender orientations and providing organizational climates that are gay-, lesbian-, bisexual-, and trans-affirmative.

Personal Reflection

Part I

Directions

As you read the following vignettes, take your "emotional temperature." What visceral reactions do you have to each situation? To help you clarify your responses, assess your reactions using the scale below:

> 1 = strongly disapprove
> 2 = somewhat disapprove
> 3 = neutral
> 4 = somewhat approve
> 5 = strongly approve

Vignettes

1. Frank, age 38, and Matt, age 32, have been together 10 years. Both are committed to their monogamous relationship. Frank is a firefighter and Matt teaches at the local high school. Because their jobs put them in the public service arena, both men are relatively closeted about being gay, and only a handful of close friends and family members know about their relationship. Both are HIV-negative and have decided not to use condoms when having sex.

2. Jorge is a Latino who works at a manufacturing facility in a large industrial park. He's married with two young children and another on the way. He has a monthly struggle to make ends meet. One night he finishes his shift and stops by a bar that he knows is frequented by gay men. He catches the eye of a man standing at the bar, he takes out a condom, and the two go and engage in intercourse. Jorge has never been tested for HIV, and going to this bar has now become a weekly habit.

3. Laney, age 42, is a lesbian who is HIV-positive. She occasionally hooks up with another lesbian for basically a one-night stand. However, she is careful about any exchange of bodily fluids with her partner.

4. Paul and Kurt have been in a monogamous relationship with one another for 18 years. They share a beautiful home and are out to family and friends. Both share the same bed but rarely have sex. Approximately five years ago, they decided by mutual agreement to have an "open" relationship. Their agreement stipulates that sexual contacts with other men are fine, provided they don't see one partner more than once, use a condom each time, and never have sexual contacts with other men in their own home. Both are HIV-negative and are tested every few months at the local health clinic.

5. Carlo is a diminutive, strikingly attractive black man in his early twenties. He has a lucrative career as a sex worker, responding on call to a fairly steady client list of closeted and successful older men. He has just discovered that he is HIV-positive. He decides not to tell any of his clients but to be sure to wear a condom in all future assignations.

6. Jeff and Steve have lived together for three years. By mutual agreement, both men are free to have sexual contacts outside their relationship. The details of their encounters are never disclosed to one another, including whether or not they engage in safe sex practices with their respective partners.

7. Tim and Michael have been dating each other for several months. Both have decided to move slowly into the sexual phase of their relationship. Both assume that the other is HIV-negative and have never discussed their HIV status.

Part II

Directions

From the standpoint of research findings about safe sex, reread each vignette and assess the level of risk for HIV infection for each partner. Now compare your visceral reaction ratings with the risk level ratings you've assigned. Do you notice any patterns in terms of your responses? Compare your ratings to those of other members in your group. What insights did you derive about yourself as result of completing this exercise?

Library, Media, and Internet Activities

Check your local video/DVD store for three important films that deal with HIV/AIDS.

Days (Muscardin, 2001)

This controversial Italian film deals with HIV, sexuality, relationships, and responsibility. The protagonist, Claudio, is a 35-year-old banker who has been HIV-positive for 10 years. On a daily regimen of medications and in a long-term relationship with his partner, Dario, Claudio's life is controlled and predictable until he has a casual sexual encounter with a young waiter, Andrea.

Discussion Questions

1. What were your reactions when Andrea had sex with Claudio without a condom?
2. How might you explain Andrea's behavior in light of the literature presented in this chapter about men who take sexual risks with other men?
3. Assume that Andrea is your client and that he has described to you the nature of his sexual activities with Claudio. How might you respond to his disclosure? What would you say?

Loggerheads (Kirkman, 2005)

This film was based on actual events and chronicles the seemingly parallel but interconnected lives of four characters: a North Carolina minister, Robert, and his wife, Beth; their HIV-positive adopted son, Mark, who ran away from home at the age of 17; and Grace, who is searching for the son she was forced to give up for adoption, when she was 17.

Discussion Questions

1. In what ways were bigotry and prejudice portrayed in this film, and what were your responses to these depictions?
2. This film deals with the themes of loss, rejection, shame, and saving face. In your view, why did the author/director include images of loggerhead turtles, and how does this fit with the themes of the film? Explain this statement by Beth's neighbor Ruth: "That's your solution to everything—move it to the backyard."
3. What was your reaction to Mark's decision not to engage in treatment for HIV? How might you relate to Mark if he were your client and he chose not to be treated for HIV?

The 24th Day (Piccirillo, 2004)

This powerful film tells the story of twenty-something Tom. Tom meets Dan at a bar one night and brings him home to his apartment for a sexual encounter. Suddenly, Dan remembers that he was in Tom's apartment several years ago and that he had a sexual encounter with him while he was somewhat drunk. What happens next between these men may surprise you.

Discussion Questions

1. Dan insists, "I just know I am HIV-negative. I would know if I had it." How might you relate to a client like Dan, who has not been tested for HIV but who insists he is HIV-negative? He says, "I can tell by looking at someone if he is HIV-positive or not." What might you hypothesize could be going on with Dan on an intraphysic level? How might you relate to Dan if he were your client?

2. Tom and Dan each give voice to a number of sentiments that are widely circulated in our culture about people who are HIV-positive, including the belief that there are people who are HIV-positive who are innocent victims and those who are more deserving or are to blame for their fate. Where do you stand in terms of your own beliefs on this issue? How might these beliefs impact your work with clients like Tom and Dan?

3. On the 26th day, Tom removes the plywood from the window. What needs to happen next for these men? How might you work clinically with each man as he is at the end of the film? What are their needs at that point from the standpoint of psychosocial intervention?

Group Activity

This chapter suggests that the sexual health issues of sexual and gender minorities are not adequately addressed. Recent evidence indicates that the rates of HIV and STIs in sexual minority men and MSM, which had been dropping, may be reversing (Rosser et al., 2002). Given this evidence, it is clear that more-effective prevention programs are needed. This exercise is intended to provide you with the opportunity to discover firsthand the unique challenges and rewards involved in developing a community-wide intervention program to address sexual health issues.

Directions

Divide the class into groups of four to six members. Each group should select a segment of the sexual and gender minority population (i.e., gay men, bisexual men, MSM, MSWM, lesbians, bisexual women, WSW, WSMW, MTF transsexuals, FTM transsexuals, and trannies). Each group must then design an STI/HIV/AIDS prevention program that could be delivered in your community. Be sure to consult this chapter, websites, and other resources to discover as many models of prevention programs as you possibly can. Be creative and remember that research suggests that the effectiveness of these programs is greatly dependent on the delivery of information to meet the HIV/STI preventions needs of specific groups. Your assignment:

1. Design advertisements and promotional materials for your educational workshop or program.

2. Develop an outline for your educational workshop or program. Be sure to include a module on substance use and sexual risk behaviors.

3. Develop a list of resources to distribute to workshop participants and a list of "affirmative" medical practitioners in your geographic area who are knowledgeable about sexual health issues in your target population.

Role-Play Activity

Motivational interviewing (MI) is suitable for use when counseling sexual and gender minority persons. In particular, many therapists (e.g., Parsons, 2005a; Shernoff, 2006) use MI with sexual and gender minorities who engage in high-risk sexual behaviors and drug use.

In the exercise below, you will have the opportunity to familiarize yourself in an experiential fashion with MI. Read the case study of Kai and follow the instructions below.

Instructions

(a) Gather in groups of three. Select one member to assume the role of Kai and another member to play the therapist in this case; the third will act as observer/recorder.

(b) Conduct a 15-minute role play. The person who assumes the therapist role should be sure to incorporate the steps of expressing empathy, developing discrepancy, rolling with resistance, and supporting the client's self-efficacy. The recorder should note specifically the presence of these interventions and record them verbatim.

(c) Now discuss the experience. The observer/recorder should provide verbatim examples of expressing empathy, developing discrepancy, rolling with resistance, and strengthening self-efficacy. The therapist and Kai should provide feedback about these.

(d) Take time to script out possible alternative statements for expressing empathy, developing discrepancy, rolling with resistance, and supporting self-efficacy.

Case Information

Kai is a 19-year-old white male who was recently referred to the University Counseling Center by his resident advisor, who had become concerned about Kai's late-night partying and recurrent cutting of classes. Kai was a high-achieving high school student who is attending the university on an academic scholarship. Kai had suspected that he might be gay early on in high school but was not about to act on his feeling until he could get away from his hometown. College in the big city gave him the freedom and courage to experiment with his sexuality. Kai became immediately enthralled with the gay club scene and the readily available drugs. During his first counseling session, Kai breaks down and tells the therapist that he is afraid he has missed so many classes this term that he is in danger of failing at least 2 of 6 courses and thereby losing his scholarship. Kai admits to trying a number of drugs, including methamphetamine ("crystal"), speed, and cocaine; however, the therapist suspects that Kai's drug use is more serious than he lets on. Kai says that he is basically "shy" and loves the feeling of being high and hence more sociable. He also says that he has had a number of sexual encounters with men he has met at the club.

References

Aaron, D. J., Markovic, N., Danielson, J. E., & Honnold, J. A. (2001). Behavioral risk factors for disease and preventive health practices among lesbians. *American Journal of Public Health, 91*(6), 972–975.

Adam, B. D., Husbands, W., Murray, J., & Maxwell, J. (2005). AIDS optimism, condom fatigue, or self-esteem? Explaining unsafe sex among gay and bisexual men. *Journal of Sex Research, 42*(3), 238–248.

Ajzen, I., & Madden, T. J. (1986). Prediction of goal-directed behavior: Attitudes, intentions, and perceived behavioral control. *Journal of Experimental Social Psychology, 22*(5), 453–474.

Allen, L. G., Glicken, A. D., Beach, R. K., & Naylor, K.E. (1998). Adolescent health care experience of gay, lesbian, and bisexual young adults. *Journal of Adolescent Health 23*(4), 212–220.

American Psychiatric Association (1994). *Diagnostic and statistical manual of mental disorders: DSM-IV* (4th ed.). Washington, DC: Author.

Barbara, A. M., & Doctor, F. (2007). *Asking the right questions 2: Talking with clients about sexual orientation and gender identity in mental health, counselling and addiction settings.* Toronto, Canada: Centre for Addiction and Mental Health.

Barbara, A. M., Quandt, S. A., & Anderson, R. T. (2001). Experiences of lesbians in the health care environment. *Women & Health, 34*(1), 45–62.

Bauer, G. R., & Welles, S. L. (2001). Beyond assumptions of negligible risk: Sexually transmitted diseases and women who have sex with women. *American Journal of Public Health, 91*(8), 1282–1286.

Becker, M. H. (Ed.). (1984). *The health belief model and personal health behavior.* Thorofare, NJ: Slack.

Bell, A. V., Ompad, D., & Sherman, S. G. (2006). Sexual and drug risk behaviors among women who have sex with women. *American Journal of Public Health, 96*(6), 1066–1072.

Bellis, M. A., Cook, P., Clark, P., Syed, Q., & Hoskins, A. (2002). Re-emerging syphilis in gay men: A case-control study of behavioural risk factors and HIV status. *Journal of Epidemiology and Community Health, 56*(3), 235–236.

Bobbe, J. (2002). Treatment of lesbian alcoholics: Healing shame and internalized homophobia for ongoing sobriety. *Health & Social Work, 27*(3), 218–222.

Bockting, W. O., & Kirk, S. (Eds.). (2001). *Transgender and HIV: Risks, prevention, and care.* New York: Haworth Press.

Bockting, W. O., Knudson, G., & Goldberg, J. M. (2006). *Counselling and mental health care of transgender adults and loved ones.* Vancouver, Canada: Vancouver Coastal Health, Transcend Transgender Support & Education Society and Canadian Rainbow Health Coalition. Retrieved February 1, 2007, from *http://www.vch.ca/ transhealth*.

Bockting, W. O., Robinson, B. E., Forberg, J., & Scheltema, K. (2005). Evaluation of a sexual health approach to reducing HIV/STD risk in the transgender community. *AIDS Care, 17*(3), 289–303.

Bockting, W. O., Robinson, B. E., & Rosser, B. R. S. (1998). Transgender HIV prevention: A qualitative needs assessment. *AIDS Care, 10*(4), 505–525.

Bockting, W. O., Rosser, S., & Coleman, E. (1999). Transgender HIV prevention: Community involvement and empowerment [Electronic Version]. *International Journal of Transgenderism, 3*(1/2). Retrived July 30, 2006, from *http://www. symposion. com/ijt/ hiv_risk/bockting.htm*

Bowen, A. M., Horvath, K., & Williams, M. L. (2007). A randomized control trial of Internet-delivered HIV prevention targeting rural MSM. *Health Education Research, 22*(1), 120–127.

Bradford, J., Ryan, C., & Rothblum, E. D. (1994). National lesbian health care survey: Implications for mental health care. *Journal of Consulting & Clinical Psychology, 62*, 228–242.

Brogan, M. (1997). Healthcare for lesbians: Attitudes and experiences. *Nursing Standard, 11*(45), 39–42.

Bybee, D. (1990). *Michigan lesbian survey* (Report to the Michigan Organization for Human Rights and the Michigan Department of Public Health). Detroit: Michigan Department of Health and Human Services.

Cabaj, R. P. (2000). Substance abuse, internalized homophobia, and gay men and lesbians: Psychodynamic issues and clinical implications. *Journal of Gay & Lesbian Psychotherapy, 3*(3/4), 5–23.

Carballo-Dieguez, A., Remien, R. H., Dolezal, C., & Wagner, G. (1997). Unsafe sex in the primary relationships of Puerto Rican men who have sex with men. *AIDS & Behavior, 1*(1), 9–17.

Carroll, N., Goldstein, R. S., Lo, W., & Mayer, K. H. (1997). Gynecological infections and sexual practices of Massachusetts's lesbian and bisexual women. *Journal of the Gay & Lesbian Medical Association, 1*, 15–23.

Centers for Disease Control and Prevention (2004). *Cases of HIV infection and AIDS in the United States, 2003*, HIV/AIDS Surveillance Report, Vol. 15. Atlanta, GA: Author.

Centers for Disease Control and Prevention. (2006). *HIV/AIDS among women who have sex with women* (CDC HIV/AIDS Fact Sheet). Atlanta, GA: Author.

Chernin, J. N., & Johnson, M. R. (2003). *Affirmative psychotherapy and counseling for lesbians and gay men.* Thousand Oaks, CA: Sage.

Cheuvront, J. P. (2002). High-risk sexual behavior in the treatment of HIV-negative patients. *Journal of Gay & Lesbian Psychotherapy, 6*(3), 7–26.

Chiasson, M. A., Hirshfield, S., Humberstone, M., DiFilippi, J., Koblin, B. A., & Remien, R. H. (2005). Increased high risk sexual behavior after September 11 in men who have sex with men: An Internet survey. *Archives of Sexual Behavior, 34*(5), 527–535.

Clements, K., Wilkinson, W., Kitano, K., & Marx, R. (1999). HIV prevention and health services needs of the transgender community in San Francisco [Electronic version]. *International Journal of Transgenderism, 3*(1/2). Retrieved July 30, 2006 from *http://www.symposion.com/ijt.hiv_risk/ clements. htm*

Clements-Nolle, K., Marx, R., Guzman, R., & Katz, M. (2001). HIV prevalence, risk behaviors, health care use, and mental health status of transgender persons: Implications for public health intervention. *American Journal of Public Health, 91*(6), 915–921.

Cochran, B. N., & Cauce, A. M. (2006). Characteristics of lesbian, gay, bisexual, and transgender individuals entering substance abuse treatment. *Journal of Substance Abuse Treatment, 30*(2) 135–146.

Cochran, S. D., & Mays, V. M. (2000). Relations between psychiatric syndromes and behaviorally defined sexual orientation in a sample of the U.S. population. *American Journal of Epidemiology, 151*(5), 516–523.

Cochran, S. D., Mays, V. M., Bowen, D., & Gage, S. (2001). Cancer-related risk indicators and preventive screening behaviors among lesbians and bisexual women. *American Journal of Public Health, 91*(4), 591–597.

Cochran, S. D., Sullivan, J. G., & Mays, V. M. (2003). Prevalence of psychiatric disorders, psychological distress, and treatment utilization among lesbian, gay, and bisexual individuals in a sample of the U.S. population. *Journal of Consulting & Clinical Psychology, 71*, 53–61.

Crawford, J. M., Rodden, P., Kippax, S., & Van de Ven, P. (2001). Negotiated safety and other agreements between men in relationships: Risk practice redefined. *International Journal of STD & AIDS, 12*(3), 164–171.

Daley, A. (1998). Lesbian invisibility in health care services. *Canadian Social Work Review, 15*, 57–71.

Diamant, A., Schuster, M., & Lever, J. (2000). Receipt of preventive health care services by lesbians. *American Journal of Preventive Medicine, 19*(3), 141–148.

Dilley, J. W. (1998). Epilogue: The psychotherapist and HIV disease. In J. W. Dilley & R. Marks (Eds.), *The UCSF AIDS health project guide to counseling* (pp. 389–396). San Francisco: Jossey-Bass.

Dobison, C., MacDonnell, J., Hampson, E., Clipsham, J., & Chow, K. (2005). Improving the access and quality of public health services for bisexuals. *Journal of Bisexuality, 5*(1), 39–78.

Eliason, M. J. (2000). Substance abuse counselor's attitudes regarding lesbian, gay, bisexual, and transgendered clients. *Journal of Substance Abuse, 12*, 311–328.

Eliason, M. J., & Schope, R. (2001). Does "don't ask don't tell" apply to health care? Lesbian, gay, and bisexual people's disclosure to health care providers. *Journal of the Gay and Lesbian Medical Association, 5*(4), 125–134.

Ellenhorn, M. J., Schonwald, S., Ordog, G., & Wasserberger, J. (1997). *Ellenhorn's medical toxicology: Diagnosis and treatment of human poisoning* (2nd ed.). Baltimore, MD: Williams & Wilkins.

Fethers, K., Marks, C., Mindel, A., & Estcourt, C. S. (2000). Sexually transmitted infections and risk behaviors in women who have sex with women. *Sexually Transmitted Infections, 76*, 345–351.

Finnegan, D. G., & McNally, E. B. (2002). *Counseling lesbian, gay, bisexual and transgender substance abusers: Dual identities.* Binghamton, NY: Haworth Press.

Forstein, M. (2002). Commentary on Cheuvront's "High-risk sexual behavior in the treatment of HIV-negative patients." *Journal of Gay & Lesbian Psychotherapy, 6*(6), 35–43.

Fox, K. K., del Rio, C., Holmes, K. K., Hook, E. W., Judson, F. N., & Knapp, J. S. (2001). Gonorrhea in the HIV era: A reversal in trends among men who have sex with men. *American Journal of Public Health, 91*(6), 959–964.

Garrett (2005). *To the health center.* Unpublished manuscript.

Gender Public Advocacy Coalition. (1998, December 11). *Jury finds District of Columbia guilty of negligence and malpractice in Tyra Hunter's death.* Retrieved August 25, 2006, from ***http://www.gpac.org/archive/news/notitle.html?cmd=view&archive=news&msgnum=0049***

Gilman, S. E., Cochran, S. D., Mays, V. M., Hughes, M., Ostrow, D., & Kessler, R. C. (2001). Prevalence of DSM–III–R disorders among individuals reporting same-gender sexual partners in the National Comorbidity Survey. *American Journal of Public Health, 91*, 933–939.

Goldstein, N. (1997). Lesbians and the medical profession: HIV/AIDS and the pursuit of visibility. In N. Goldstein & J. L. Manlowe (Eds.), *The gender politics of HIV/AIDS in women* (pp. 86–110). New York: New York University Press.

Gonzales, V., Washienko, K. M., Krone, M. R., & Chapman, L. I. (1999). Sexual and drug-use risk factors for HIV and STDs: A comparison of women with and without bisexual experiences. *American Journal of Public Health, 89*(12), 1841–1846.

Gorman, E. M., Nelson, K. R., Applegate, T., & Scrol, A. (2004). Club drug and poly-substance abuse and HIV among gay/bisexual men: Lessons gleaned from a community study. *Journal of Gay & Lesbian Social Services, 16*(2), 1–1.

Guss, J. R. (2000). Sex like you can't even imagine: "Crystal," crack and gay men. *Journal of Gay & Lesbian Psychotherapy, 3*(3/4), 105–122.

Halkitis, P. N., Parsons, J. T., & Stirratt, M. J. (2001). A double epidemic: Crystal methamphetamine drug use in relation to HIV transmission among gay men. *Journal of Homosexuality, 41*(2), 17–35.

Halkitis, P. N., Parsons, J. T., & Wilton, L. (2003). Barebacking among gay and bisexual men in New York City: Explanations for the emergence of intentional unsafe behaviors. *Archives of Sexual Behavior, 32*(4), 351–357.

Halkitis, P. N., Wolitski, R. J., & Gomez, C. A. (2005). Understanding the sexual lives of HIV-positive gay and bisexual men: An overview of the seropositive urban men's study. In P. N. Halkitis, C. A. Gomez, & R. J. Wolitski (Eds.), *HIV + Sex: The psychological and interpersonal dynamics of HIV-seropositive gay and bisexual men's relationships* (pp. 3–19). Washington, DC: American Psychological Association.

Harmon, L., & Volker, M. (1995). HIV-positive people, HIV-negative partners. *Journal of Sex & Marital Therapy, 21*(2), 127–140.

Heck, J. E., Sell, R. L., & Gorin, S. S. (2006). Health care access among individuals involved in same-sex relationships. *American Journal of Public Health, 96*(6), 1111–1118.

Hoff, C. C., Gomez, C., Faigeles, B., Purcell, D. W., Halkitis, P. N., Parsons, J. T., et al. (2004). Serostatus of primary partner impacts sexual behavior inside and outside the relationship: A description of HIV-positive MSM in primary relationships. *Journal of Psychology & Human Sexuality, 16*(4), 77–95.

Hughes, T. L., Wilsnack, S. C., & Johnson, T. P. (2006). Investigating lesbians' mental health and alcohol use: What is an appropriate comparison group? In A. M. Omoto & H. S. Kurtzman (Eds.). *Sexual orientation and mental health: Examining identity and development in lesbian, gay, and bisexual people* (pp. 167–184). Washington, DC: American Psychological Association.

Hutchinson, M. K., Thompson, A. C., & Cederbaum, J. A. (2006). Multisystem factors contributing to disparities in preventive health care among lesbian women. *Journal of Obstetric, Gynecological, & Neonatal Nursing, 35*(3), 393–402.

Johnson, W. D., Holtgrave, D. R., McClellan, W. M., Flanders, W. D., Hill, A. N., & Goodman, M. (2005). HIV intervention research for men who have sex with men: A 7-year update. *AIDS Education & Prevention, 17*(6), 568–589.

Julien, D., & Chartrand, E. (2005). Review of studies using a probability sample on the health of gays, lesbians and bisexuals. *Canadian Psychology, 46*(4), 235–250.

Kalichman, S. C., & Rompa, D. (1995). Sexual sensation seeking and sexual compulsivity: Reliability, validity, and predicting HIV risk behavior. *Journal of Personality Assessment, 65*(3), 586–601.

Kelly, J. A., & Kalichman, S. C. (1998). Reinforcement value of unsafe sex as a predictor of condom use and continued HIV/AIDS risk behavior among gay and bisexual men. *Health Psychology, 17*(4), 328–335.

Kenagy, G. P. (2005). Transgender health: Findings from two needs assessment studies in Philadelphia. *Health & Social Work, 30*(1), 19–26.

Kenagy, G. P., & Hsieh, C. M. (2005). The risk less known: Female-to-male transgender persons' vulnerability to HIV infection. *AIDS Care, 17*(2), 195–207.

Kippax, S., Crawford, J., David, M., Rodden, P. & Dowsett, G. (1993). Sustaining safe sex: A longitudinal study of a sample of homosexual men. *AIDS, 7,* 257–263.

Kirkman, T. (Director). (2005). *Loggerheads* [Motion picture]. United States: Strand.

Klitzman, R. I., & Greenberg, J. D. (2002). Patterns of communication between gay and lesbian patients and their health care providers. *Journal of Homosexuality, 42*(4), 65–75.

Kurtz, S. P. (2005). Post-circuit blues: Motivations and consequences of crystal meth use among gay men in Miami. *AIDS & Behavior, 9*(1), 63–72.

Kwakwa, H. A., & Ghobrial, M. W. (2003). Female-to-female transmission of human immunodeficiency virus [Electronic version]. *Clinical Infectious Diseases, 36.* Retrieved March 14, 2003, from *http://www.journal.uchicago.dud/CID/journl/issues/v36n3/20886/20886.text.html*

Lee, R. S., Kochman, A., & Sikkema, K. J. (2002). Internalized stigma among people living with HIV–AIDS. *AIDS & Behavior, 6*(4), 309–319.

Lehmann, J. B., Lehmann, C. U., & Kelly, P. J. (1998). Development and health care needs of lesbians. *Journal of Women's Health, 7*(3), 379–387.

Lombardi, E. L., & Bettcher, T. (2006). Lesbian, gay, bisexual, and transgender/transsexual individuals. In B. S. Levy & V. W. Sidel (Eds.), *Social injustice and public health* (pp. 130–144). New York: Oxford University Press.

Lombardi, E. L., & van Servellen, G. (2000). Correcting deficiencies in HIV/AIDS care for transgendered individuals. *Journal of the Association of Nurses in AIDS Care, 11*(5), 61–69.

Long, L. L., Burnett, J. A., & Thomas, R. V. (2006). *Sexuality counseling: An integrative approach.* Upper Saddle River, NJ: Pearson Education.

Makadon, H. J. (2006). Improving health care for the lesbian and gay communities. *New England Journal of Medicine, 354*(9), 895–898.

Mansergh, G., Colfax, G., Marks, G., Rader, M., Guzman, R., & Buchbinder, S. (2001). The circuit party men's health survey: Findings and implications for gay and bisexual men. *American Journal of Public Health, 91*(6), 953–958.

Marcel, A. D. (1998). *Determining barriers to treatment for transsexuals and transgenders in substance abuse programs.* Boston: Transgender Education Network, Justice Resource Institute.

Marlatt, G. A. (1985). Relapse prevention: Theoretical rationale and overview of the model. In G. A. Marlatt & J. R. Gordon (Eds.), *Relapse prevention: Maintenance strategies in the treatment of addictive behaviors* (pp. 3–70). New York: Guilford.

Marlatt, G. A., & Donovan, D. M. (Eds.). (2005). *Relapse prevention: Maintenance strategies in the treatment of addictive behaviors.* New York: Guilford.

Marrazzo, J. M., Coffey, P., & Binghan, A. (2005). Sexual practices, risk perception and knowledge of sexually transmitted disease risk among lesbian and bisexual women. *Perspectives on Sexual & Reproductive Health, 37*(1), 6–12.

Marrazzo, J. M., Koutsky, L. A., Kiviat, N. B., Kuypers, J. M., & Stine, K. (2001). Papanicolaou test screening and prevalence of genital human papillomavirus among women who have sex with women. *American Journal of Public Health, 91*(1), 947–952.

Marrazzo, J., Koutsky, L., & Stine, K. (1998). Genital human papillomavirus infection in women who have sex with women. *Journal of Infectious Disease, 178*, 1604–1609.

Martell, C. R., Safren, S. A., & Prince, S. E. (2004). *Cognitive-behavioral therapies with lesbian, gay, and bisexual clients.* New York: Guilford.

Martin, J. I., & Knox, J. (1997). Self-esteem instability and its implications for HIV prevention among gay men. *Health & Social Work, 22*(4), 264–273.

Mathy, R. M. (2002). Transgender identity and suicidality in a nonclinical sample: Sexual orientation, psychiatric history, and compulsive behaviors. *Journal of Psychology & Human Sexuality, 14*(4), 47–65.

Matthews, C. R., Lorah, P., & Fenton, J. (2006). Treatment experiences of gays and lesbians in recovery from addiction: A qualitative inquiry. *Journal of Mental Health Counseling, 28*(2), 110–132.

Matthews, C. R., Selvidge, M. M. D., & Fisher, K. (2005). Addictions counselors' attitudes and behaviors toward gay, lesbian and bisexual clients. *Journal of Counseling & Development, 83*(3), 57–65.

Mays, V. M., Cochran, S. D., & Zamudio, A. (2004). HIV prevention research: Are we meeting the needs of African American men who have sex with men? *Journal of Black Psychology, 30*(1), 78–105.

McCabe, S. E., Boyd, C. B., Hughes, T. L., & d'Arcy, H. (2003). Sexual identity and substance abuse among undergraduate students. *Substance Abuse, 24*(2), 77–91.

McCabe, S. E., Hughes, T. L., & Boyd, C. (2004). Substance use and misuse: Are bisexual women at greater risk? *Journal of Psychoactive Drugs, 36*(2), 217–225.

McKee, M. B., Picciano, J. F., Roffman, R. A., Swanson, F., & Kalichman, S. C. (2006). Marketing the "sex check": Evaluating recruitment strategies for a telephone-based HIV prevention project for gay and bisexual men. *AIDS Education & Prevention, 18*(2), 116–131.

McKirnan, D., Ostrow, D., & Hope, B. (1996). Sex, drugs, and escape: A psychological model of HIV-risk sexual behaviors. *AIDS Care, 8*(6), 655–669.

Melendez, R. M., Exner, T. A., Ehrhardt, A. A., Dodge, B., Remien, R. H., Rotheram-Borus, M. J., et al. (2006). Health and health care among male-to-female transgender persons who are HIV positive. *American Journal of Public Health, 96*(5), 1034–1037.

Miller, M., Andre, A., Ebin, J., & Bessonova, L. (2007). *Bisexual health: An introduction and model practices for HIV/STI prevention programming.* New York: National Gay and Lesbian Task Force Policy Institute, Fenway Institute at Fenway Community Health, and BiNet USA.

Miller, W. R., & Rollnick, S. (2002). *Motivational interviewing: Preparing people to change addictive behavior* (2nd ed.). New York: Guilford.

Monzon, O.T., & Capellan, J. M. B. (1987). Female-to-female transmission of HIV. *Lancet, 2*, 40–41.

Morin, S. F., Vernon, K., Harcourt, J. J., Steward, W. T., Volk, J., & Riess, T. H., et al. (2003). Why HIV infections have increased among men who have sex with men and what to do about it: Finding from California focus groups. *AIDS & Behavior, 7*(4), 353–362.

Morrow, K. M., & Allsworth, J. E. (2000). Sexual risk in lesbians and bisexual women. *Journal of the Gay & Lesbian Medical Association, 4*(4), 159–165.

Muscardin, L. (Director). (2001). *Days* [Motion picture]. Italy: Movie Factory.

Namaste, V. K. (2000). *Invisible lives: The erasure of transsexual and transgendered people.* Chicago: University of Chicago Press.

Nemoto, T., Luke, D., Mamo, L., Ching, A., & Patria, J. (1999). HIV risk behaviors among male-to-female transgenders in comparison with homosexual or bisexual males and heterosexual females. *AIDS Care, 11*(3), 297–312.

Nemoto, T., Operario, D., Keatley, J., Han, L., & Soma, T. (2004). HIV risk behaviors among male-to-female transgender persons of color in San Francisco. *American Journal of Public Health, 94*(7), 1193–1199.

O'Brien, M. (2003). *Keeping it real: Transgender inclusion in safe sex—Notes for risk reduction educators and outreach workers.* Retrieved February 1, 2007, from *http://www.deadletters.biz/real.html*

O'Connor, M. F. (1997). Treating gay men with HIV. In M. F. O'Connor & I. D. Yalom (Eds.), *Treating the psychological consequences of HIV* (pp. 117–163). San Francisco: Jossey-Bass.

Oggins, J., & Eichenbaum, J. (2002). Engaging transgender substance users in substance use treatment [Electronic version]. *International Journal of Transgenderism, 6*(2). Retrieved May 12, 2006, from *http://www.symposion.com/ijt/ijtvo06no02_03.htm*

O'Hanlan, K. A. (1995). Lesbian health and homophobia: Perspectives for the treating obstetrician/gynecologist. *Current Problems in Obstetrics, Gynecology, & Fertility, 18*(4), 97–133.

Operario, D., Burton, J., Underhill, K., & Sevelius, J. (2008). Men who have sex with transgender women: Challenges to category-based HIV prevention. *AIDS and Behavior, 12*(1), 18–26.

Parker, R., di Mauro, D., Filiano, B., Garcia, J., Munoz-Laboy, M. & Sember, R. (2004). Global transformations and intimate relations in the 21st century: Social science research on sexuality and the emergence of sexual health and sexual rights frameworks. *Annual Review of Sex Research, 15*, 362–398.

Parsons, J. T. (2005a). Motivating the unmotivated: A treatment model for barebackers. *Journal of Gay & Lesbian Psychotherapy, 9*(3/4), 129–148.

Parsons, J. T. (2005b). HIV-positive gay and bisexual men. In S. C. Kalichman (Ed.), *Positive prevention: Reducing HIV transmission among people living with HIV/AIDS* (pp. 99–133). New York: Kluwer.

Parsons, J. T., Kelly, B. C., Bimbi, D. S., Muench, F., & Morgenstern, J. (2007). Accounting for the social triggers of sexual compulsivity. *Journal of Addictive Diseases: The Official Journal of the American Society of Addiction Medicine, 26*(3), 5–16.

Parsons, J. T., Kelly, B. C., & Wells, B. E. (2006). Differences in club drug use between heterosexual and lesbian/bisexual females. *Addictive Behaviors, 31*, 2344–2349.

Parsons, J. T., Kutnick, A. H., Halkitis, P. N., Punzalan, J. C., & Carbonari, J. P. (2005). Sexual risk behaviors and substance use among alcohol abusing HIV-positive men who have sex with men. *Journal of Psychoactive Drugs, 37*(1), 27–36.

Parsons, J., Wolitski, R., Purcell, D., Gomez, C., Schrimshaw, E., Halkitis, P., et al. (2004, November 12). *Use of harm reduction strategies in New York City and San Francisco.* Presentation at the 5th National Harm Reduction Conference, New Orleans, LA.

Piccirillo, T. (Director). (2004). *The 24th Day* [Motion picture]. United States: Warner Brothers.

Pisani, F., Girault, P., Gultom, M., Sukartini, N., Kumalawati, J., Jazan, S., et al. (2004). HIV, syphilis infection, and sexual practices among transgenders, male sex workers, and other men who have sex with men in Jakarta, Indonesia. *Sexually Transmitted Infections, 80*(6), 536–540.

Preston, D. B., D'Augelli, A. R., Kassab, C. D., Cain, R. E., Schulze, F. W., & Starks, M. T. (2004). The influence of stigma on the sexual risk behavior of rural men who have sex with men. *AIDS Education & Prevention, 16*(4), 291–303.

Prochaska, J., DiClemente, C., & Norcross, J. (1992). In search of how people change. Applications to addictive behavior. *American Psychologist, 47*(9), 1102–1114.

Race, K. D. (2003). Revaluation of risk among gay men. *AIDS Education & Prevention, 15*(4), 369–381.

Reback, C. J., Lombardi, E. L., Simon, P. A., & Frye, D. M. (2005). HIV seroprevalence and risk behaviors among transgendered women who exchange sex in comparison with those who do not. *Journal of Psychology & Human Sexuality 17*(1/2), 5–22.

Rose, A. (1998). HIV disease over the long haul: Hope, uncertainty, grief, and survival. In J. W. Dilley & R. Marks (Eds.), *The UCSF AIDS health project guide to counseling* (pp. 197–208). San Francisco: Jossey-Bass.

Ross, M. W., & Williams, M. L. (2001). Sexual behavior and illicit drug use. *Annual Review of Sex Research, 12*, 290–310.

Rosser, B. R. S., Bockting, W. O., Rugg, D. L., Robinson, B. E., Ross, M. W., Bauer, G., et al. (2002). A randomized controlled intervention trial of a sexual health approach to long-term HIV risk reduction for men who have sex with men: Effects of the intervention on unsafe sexual behavior. *AIDS Education & Prevention, 14*(3) (Suppl. A), 59–71.

Ryan, C., & Gruskin, E. (2006). Health concerns for lesbians, gay men, and bisexuals. In D. F. Morrow & L. Messinger (Eds.), *Sexual orientation and gender expression in social work practice* (pp. 307–342). New York: Columbia University Press.

Sadovsky, R. (2000). Sexual orientation and associated health care risks. *American Family Physician, 62*(12), 12–13.

Saulnier, C. F. (2002). Deciding who to see: Lesbians discuss their preferences in health and mental health care providers. *Social Work, 4*(4), 355–365.

Schneider, J. P. (2004). Understanding and diagnosing sex addiction. In R. H. Coombs (Ed.), *Handbook of addictive disorders: A practical guide to diagnosis and treatment* (pp. 208–232). Hoboken, NJ: Wiley.

Sell, R. L., & Petrulio, C. (1996). Sampling homosexuals, bisexuals, gays, and lesbians for public health research: A review of the literature from 1990 to 1992. *Journal of Homosexuality 30*(4), 31–47.

Shernoff, M. (2005). Condomless sex: Considerations for psychotherapy with individual gay men and male couples having unsafe sex. *Journal of Gay & Lesbian Psychotherapy, 9*(3/4), 149–169.

Shernoff, M. (2006). *Without condoms: Unprotected sex, gay men and barebacking.* New York: Routledge.

Shoptaw, S., & Frosch, D. (2000). Substance abuse treatment as HIV prevention for men who have sex with men. *AIDS & Behavior, 4*(2) 193–203.

Solarz, A. (1999). *Lesbian health: Current assessment and directions for the future.* Washington, DC: National Academies Press.

Sperber, J., Landers, S., & Lawrence, S. (2005). Access to health care for transgendered persons: Results of a needs assessment in Boston. *International Journal of Transgenderism, 8*(2–3), 75–91. Retrieved May 12, 2006, *http://www.haworthpress.com*.

Stall, R., Paul, J. P., Greenwood, G., Pollack, L. M., Bein, E., Crosby, G. M., et al. (2001). Alcohol use, drug use, and alcohol-related problems among men who have sex with men: The Urban Men's Health Study. *Addiction, 96*, 1589–1601.

Stevens, P. E. (1995). Structural and interpersonal impact of heterosexual assumptions on lesbian health care clients. *Nursing Research, 44*(1), 25–30.

Stokes, J. P., & Peterson, J. L. (1998). Homophobia, self-esteem, and risk for HIV among African Americans who have sex with men. *AIDS Education & Prevention, 10*(3), 278–292.

Stueve, A., O'Donnell, L., Duran, R., Doval, A. S., Geier, J., & Community Intervention Trial for Youth Study Team. (2002). Being high and taking sexual risks: Findings from a multi-site survey of urban young men who have sex with men. *AIDS Education & Prevention, 14*(6), 482–495.

Suarez, T., & Miller, J. (2001). Negotiating risks in context: A perspective on unprotected anal intercourse and barebacking among men who have sex with men—Where do we go from here? *Archives of Sexual Behavior, 30*(3), 287–300.

Substance Abuse and Mental Health Services Administration, U. S. Department of Health and Human Services. (2001). *A provider's introduction to substance abuse treatment for lesbian, gay, bisexual, and transgender individuals.* Retrieved March 30, 2007, from *http://www.samhsa.gov*

U.S. Department of Health and Human Services (2000). *Health People 2010: Understanding and Improving Health,* (2nd ed.) (2 volumes). Washington, DC: U.S. Government Printing Office.

Valentine, D. (1998). *Gender identity project: Report on intake statistics, 1989–April 1997.* New York: Lesbian and Gay Community Services Center.

van Dam, M. A. A., Koh, A. S., & Dibble, S. L. (2001). Lesbian disclosure to health care providers and delay of care. *Journal of the Gay & Lesbian Medical Association, 5*(1), 11–19.

Van de Ven, P., Kippax, S., Crawford, J., Rawstorne, P., Prestage, G., Grulich, A., et al. (2002). In a minority of gay men, sexual risk practice indicates strategic positioning for perceived risk reduction rather than unbridled sex. *AIDS Care, 14*(4), 471–480.

Van Kesteren, N. M. C., Hospers, H. J., & Kok, G. (2007). Sexual risk behavior among HIV-positive men who have sex with men: A literature review. *Patient Education and Counseling, 65*, 5–20

Weiss, R. (2004). Treating sex addiction. In R. H. Coombs (Ed.), *Handbook of addictive disorders: A practical guide to diagnosis and treatment* (pp. 233–272). Hoboken, NJ: Wiley.

Whitfield, C. (1996, November). Crystal and the gay men of L. A. *Sexvibe, 13*, 16–32.

Wilkinson, W. (2006). Public health gains of the transgender community in San Francisco: Grassroots organizing and community-based research. In P. Currah, R. M. Juang, & S. P. Minter (Eds.), *Transgender rights* (pp. 192–214). Minneapolis: University of Minnesota Press.

Wilton, L., Halkitis, P. N., English, G., & Roberson, M. (2005). An exploratory study of barebacking, club drug use, and meanings of sex in black and Latino gay and bisexual men in the age of AIDS. *Journal of Gay & Lesbian Psychotherapy, 9*(3/4), 49–72.

Wolitski, R. J. (2005). The emergence of barebacking among gay and bisexual men in the United States: A public health perspective. *Journal of Gay & Lesbian Psychotherapy, 9*(3/4), 9–34.

Wolitski, R. J., Parsons, J. T., & Gomez, C. A. (2004). Prevention with HIV-seropositive men who have sex with men: Lessons from the Seropositive Urban Men's Study (SUMS) and the Seropositive Urban Men's Intervention Trial (SUMIT). *Journal of Acquired Immune Deficiency Syndromes, 37*(Suppl. 2), S101–S109.

World Health Organization. (2000). *Gender and reproductive health glossary*. Retrieved May 12, 2006, from ***http://www.who.int/reproductive-health/gender/glossary.html***

Xavier, J. M. (2000). *The Washington, DC transgender needs assessment survey: Final report for phase two*. Washington, DC: Administration for HIV/AIDS, Department of Health of the District of Columbia Government.

Yep, G. A., Lovaas, K. E., & Pagonis, A. V. (2002). The case of "riding bareback": Sexual practices and the paradoxes of identity in the era of AIDS. *Journal of Homosexuality, 42*(2), 1–14.

CHAPTER 10

Career and Workplace Issues in Sexual and Gender Minorities

INTRODUCTION

Donovan's story below reflects the hardships that so many gender minority persons face.

> I would like to begin by telling you some things about myself. I am a woman, 61 years old and transgender. I have lived the last 27 years as a woman, much to the chagrin of my parents and some friends. They just did not understand the nature of my struggles since early childhood. I knew all along that I was female, not a male. When I revealed this information to my parents, my father said I was "nuts" and my mother cried. They both thought that my gender identification was a result of their failing to raise me in the correct way. In truth, my father was an alcoholic and very abusive to me. But, it is impossible to really know all the ways this experience has affected my life and the lives of my brother and sister. Being transgender, however, has had a very clear effect on my life and on my ability to find work, housing, and other forms of security. Whenever I looked for employment, though I was willing and eager, people did not usually want to employ "someone like me." Because the jobs that I could get were usually at gay bars, working as a bartender "off the books," I have nothing in my social security account, which means that when I turn 65 I will have no financial security. As a result of the discrimination that I have experienced, I have often had to depend on public assistance like welfare to allow me to survive. I was 37 years old before I had enough money to have my own place. Until then I had to sleep on the beds, couches, or floors in friends' apartments. Occasionally, I even had to sleep on streets and subways. (*Source:* From "Being Transgender and Older: A First-Person Account" by T. Donovan (2001). *Journal of Gay & Lesbian Social Services, 13*(4), 20. Reprinted with permission.)

Donovan's status as a gender minority clearly impacted her employment opportunities and economic livelihood. Take a moment and assume that Donovan is your client.

How might you begin your first session with Donovan? How much emphasis might you place on work-related issues with Donovan? How does her age influence your views about this? How do her experiences of discrimination compare to those of other gender minorities whose transformation is less obvious? Or to those of sexual minorities? What challenges might you face as a counselor in working with Donovan?

A Preview of Chapter Contents

First, examine the following two real-life scenarios. How might you regard the two individuals?

> *Scenario 1:* A graduate counseling intern contemplated a semester-long internship at a gay men's health center located in an urban area. He was looking forward to the internship but had concerns about how this experience might impact his opportunities for future employment after graduation. Would prospective employers assume that he was gay? Would this experience marginalize him and make it difficult for him to be a candidate for other positions with different populations?
>
> *Scenario 2:* A student approached his counselor with a question related to his scholarship application for college. The student wondered if he should include his volunteer experience as a peer educator at a local gay community center's HIV prevention program for gay teens. If so, would this hurt or help his application for the scholarship?

Assume the role of these students' counselor. How might you respond to their concerns?

Chapter 3 outlined some of the harsh realities that gender minority persons like Donovan face, including unemployment, underemployment, and employment discrimination (Prentiss & McAnulty, 2002). This chapter takes an unjaundiced and realistic view of the workplace and addresses the range of concerns presented in the cases described above. To what degree does prejudice exist? And as helping professionals, will you be tainted by even trying to help these communities? The next pages cover the following:

- The degree to which contemporary career development theories and practices have addressed the needs and life experiences of sexual and gender minorities
- Research on the incidence of workplace discrimination and its psychological effects on sexual and gender minorities
- How sexual and gender minorities manage their identities at work
- Counseling approaches that are especially relevant to the career and employment issues that sexual and gender minorities face

A REVIEW OF CONTEMPORARY CAREER DEVELOPMENT THEORIES AND RESEARCH

Career development theories and practices have been criticized for a number of reasons. For starters, many practitioners who focus on career exploration and planning naively believe that everyone has equal access to opportunities and that we all have the potential to choose freely the kind of work we will do. Blustein (2006), an articulate critic of vocational psychology, argues that the values of autonomy and individualism are so embedded in career counseling theories that these theories reflect "a linear career path with predictable stages of promotion—a life narrative led by a young, able-bodied, middle-class white man in the United States" (Blustein, McWhirter, & Perry, 2005, p. 143). This is not necessarily the case—not by a long shot. Blustein et al. recommend that vocational psychologists focus more on persons who are marginalized, underemployed, and unemployed or who are in jobs that are not necessarily satisfying.

Another criticism addresses the practice of *matching*. Practitioners who are defined as "experts" collect data about their clients' interests, aptitudes, and skills and attempt to match them to particular careers based on the fit (Brott, 2001; Brown & Brooks, 1996; Herr, 1997). This process has also been described as "positivist" (Brott, 2001) and as seeking "person–environment fit" (Patton & McMahon, 1999). Typically, these processes are performed in a context separate from personal counseling. Savickas (1993) is a critic of the artificial separation of career from personal issues in counseling, arguing that "career is personal" (p. 212).

Career development theories are faulted (e.g., Ragins, 2004) for a lack of attention and a lack of relevancy to the lives of sexual and gender minorities. Most of these theories were based on the work lives of heterosexual persons. Sexual minorities were seldom the focus of vocational research until the 1990s (Pope et al., 2004). And the preponderance of the research that does exist is based on convenience samples that consisted largely of gay employees who are out at work (Badgett, 2003; Ragins, 2004). Researchers relied almost exclusively on self-report surveys to assess self-disclosure in the workplace and workplace discrimination. Ragins (2004) noted these methods tend to either over- or underestimate actual discrimination. The career development and workplace experiences of bisexual persons and gender minority persons were, and continue to be, noticeably absent from this body of research (Croteau, Anderson, Distefano, & Kampa-Kokesch, 2000; Hash & Ceperich, 2006). Researchers have also neglected to examine the effects of multiple identity statuses, including race, ethnicity, sexual orientation, and gender identity, on workplace experiences (Ragins, Cornwell, & Miller, 2003).

Career development theories routinely ignore two critical issues. The first is the impact of environmental variables such as homophobia and biphobia on career decision making and workplace satisfaction (Barrio & Shoffner, 2005; Hash & Ceperich, 2006; Pope, 2003; Ragins, 2004); the second is the dynamic and mutually interdependent nature of career and sexual identity (Driscoll, Kelley, & Fassinger, 1996; Lev, 2004; Ritter & Terndrup, 2002).

EXPLORING THE IMPACT OF HOMOPHOBIA AND BIPHOBIA IN THE WORK LIVES OF SEXUAL AND GENDER MINORITIES

There are theoretical approaches that have been praised for their applicability to sexual minority persons. In his "Theory of Circumscription, Compromise, and Self-Creation" (2002), Gottfredson observed that children as young as three to nine years of age learn the gender stereotypes as to which careers/jobs are appropriate for males and which are appropriate for females. By the age of six to eight, they are already ruling out certain occupations (called *circumscription*) based on these stereotypes. Later on variables such as individual interests and abilities come into play. But nonetheless, at a remarkably early age, each person has developed a "social space" of occupations or "zone of acceptable occupational alternatives." This process ultimately involves compromising and developing a sense of how feasible it would be to obtain a particular job, given one's aptitude, educational requirements, availability, family responsibilities, and notion of "life niche," which refers to how one's cultural context supports or affirms one's abilities.

Gottfredson's ideas are relevant to sexual and gender minorities who often avoid certain careers because these are linked to either male or female gender roles (Fassinger, 1995). Some gay and bisexual men choose to avoid occupations that are considered effeminate, like hair styling or interior design, for fear that they will be marginalized (Ritter & Terndrup, 2002). In a similar fashion, lesbians are reluctant to seek careers that are considered masculine, like athletics, because of the common assumption that women who participate in certain sports (e.g., softball, basketball) are likely to be lesbians (Woods, 1992). Women who participate in professional sports are often "feminized" before games because of fears that "she will look like a dyke, or even worse, be one" (Griffin, 2002, p. 196). Croteau et al. (2000) also noted that lesbians are frequently assumed to have gender-nontraditional occupational interests. As a result, they don't get the support to pursue their real career interests.

The theory of work adjustment (TWA) is an empirically supported approach commended for its applicability to sexual and gender minorities (Lyons, Brenner, & Fassinger, 2005). The TWA maintains that there is a relationship between person–environment (P–E) fit and workplace outcome variables, such as job satisfaction (Dawis, England, & Lofquist, 1964). In their study based on this theoretical model, Lyons et al. (2005) incorporated data from the National Gay and Lesbian Experiences Study, which acquired participants from electronic lists, word of mouth, advertisements, and so on. The results confirmed that approximately half of the sexual minority employees' job satisfaction is accounted for by the degree to which they feel they fit with their environment. Lyons et al. concluded that sexual minorities may be more attuned to and influenced by their environments than nonminorities when making judgments about workplace outcomes.

EXPLORING THE INTERSECTION OF SEXUAL/GENDER AND CAREER IDENTITIES

Savickas's (2002, 2005) theory of career construction has also been considered to be especially applicable to the sexual and gender minority population. This approach is an expansion of Super's work on career development. Super (1990) proposed that there are five life-span developmental periods: growth, exploration, establishment, maintenance, and disengagement. These phases intersect with different life roles (student, citizen, parent, child, and spouse). Persons may occupy several roles simultaneously, and these roles affect one another. Savickas posits that most people "construct" their career orientations in response to the impact that social forces have on their identities.

Schmidt and Nilsson (2006) suggest that Savickas's ideas about career development are ideally suited to the life experiences of sexual minorities. The view that adolescent career development is a result of the interplay between internal struggles and external factors, such as environmental support, seems especially germane to sexual minority youth.

Hetherington (1991) coined the term *bottleneck effect* to describe a phenomenon in adolescence when psychic energy is consumed by issues of sexual identity rather than possible vocation choices. According to Hetherington, sexual minority career choice issues are temporarily derailed during adolescence.

Sexual minority persons who are aware of their same-sex orientation in adolescence report that their sexual orientation affected their career choices. This is in direct contrast with those who self-identify much later in life (Morgan & Brown, 1993). Those who come to acknowledge their same-sex sexual orientation later in adulthood may be faced either with "changing careers or with learning to integrate their sexual orientation within the careers they have previously chosen" (p. 278).

Most traditional psychological theories assumed that gender identity is acquired in early childhood and is stable throughout life and that sexual orientation issues are resolved in early adulthood. Yet evidence indicates that self-awareness of sexual orientation occurs at different ages. Consider, for example, a thirty-something man who has established a career in the military before realizing that he is attracted to men as well as women (Chung, 1995; Prince, 1995).

Boatwright, Gilbert, Forrest, and Ketzenberger (1996) empirically explored the connection between Super's vocational-oriented developmental tasks and the stages of sexual minority identity development. They interviewed 10 self-identified lesbians who described their sexual identity development as a "personally demanding" process that tended to "delay, disrupt and in some cases seriously derail their vocational lives" (p. 210).

Schmidt and Nilsson (2006) decided to assess the bottleneck hypothesis in their sample of nearly 100 sexual minority youth whose ages ranged from 15 to 19 years, most of whom were in high school. Participants were given several measures assessing dimensions such as sexual identity, career decision, career maturity, and social support. Results supported the bottleneck hypothesis and indicated that sexual minority adolescents who reported higher levels of inner sexual identity conflict had lower levels of social support and career maturity and higher levels of career indecision.

WORKPLACE DISCRIMINATION AGAINST SEXUAL AND GENDER MINORITIES

According to the research, the workplace discrimination against sexual and gender minority persons is pervasive, and its effects are detrimental (Chung, 2001; Dovidio & Gaertner, 2000; Griffith & Hebl, 2002; Hebl, Foster, Mannix, & Dovidio, 2002; Tejeda, 2006). Whitcomb, Wettersten, and Stolz (2006) defined workplace discrimination as "negative behavior targeted at persons who are deemed to not 'belong' within the organization" (p. 397). In their review of publications dealing with the career experiences of gay men and lesbians during the 16-year period from 1980 to 1996, Croteau et al. (2000) noted that the topic of workplace discrimination was most often the focus of research attention. It is necessary to understand these studies as well as those that show how stigmatized identities are managed in the workplace and what strategies are employed by sexual and gender minority employees in order to survive in the workplace.

Types of Discrimination

DIRECT VERSES NONDIRECT DISCRIMINATION   Several authors (Ragins, 2004; Whitcomb et al., 2006) have differentiated between direct and indirect forms of discrimination. *Direct discrimination* involves behaviors such as failure to provide merit pay or salary increases, job termination, and the like. *Indirect discrimination* refers to discriminatory behaviors (e.g., avoiding or snubbing the employee or practicing dismissive nonverbal behaviors) that have a negative impact on sexual minorities even when these actions are not aimed at a specific person (Ragins, 2004). One example of indirect discrimination is found when homophobic jokes are told in a group, as if the assumption existed that everyone is heterosexual. Ragins (2004) noted that sexual minorities who are closeted at work are more likely to experience indirect discrimination than are those who are out. The obvious reason is that co-workers are less likely to censor negative comments or stereotypes.

ACCESS-RELATED VERSES TREATMENT-RELATED DISCRIMINATION   According to Greenhaus, Parasuraman, and Wormley (1990), discrimination can be *access-related*, when members of a stigmatized group are prevented from entering organizations, or *treatment-related*, when members of a stigmatized group are blocked from being promoted or receiving the rewards they have earned.

DISPARATE TREATMENT, ADVERSE IMPACT, AND SOCIAL DISCRIMINATION   Ragins (2004) referred to the existence of three forms of discrimination targeted at sexual minority employees: disparate treatment, adverse impact, and social discrimination. *Disparate treatment* occurs when employees are purposefully treated differently on the basis of group membership. *Adverse impact* occurs when a supposedly neutral employment practice adversely affects employees belonging to a particular group. *Social discrimination* is typically more subtle and involves differential access to social networks, relationships, and activities that can improve an employee's job performance. Sexual minority persons face social discrimination in the form of "exclusion from valuable mentoring and networking relationships irrespective of whether or not they have disclosed their sexual identity in the workplace" (Ragins, 2004, p. 44).

WORKPLACE BULLYING   Recently, the phenomenon of *workplace bullying* has captured the attention of the popular media (Fox & Stallworth, 2005). Research into this area was initiated in the early nineties by Scandinavian investigators Weingarten and Leyman (Jones, 2006). Workplace bullying is also known as *workplace aggression* and *workplace incivility*. Bullying typically consists of offending or excluding someone or disrupting their work assignments. "Bullying is an escalating process in the course of which the person confronted ends up in an inferior position and becomes the target of systematic negative social acts" (Einarsen, Hoel, Zapf, & Cooper, 2003, p. 15). To be considered bullying, the offense or exclusion must be more than an isolated incident and it must involve two people who are not equal in standing (Einarsen et al., 2003).

Bullying behaviors are generally viewed as more subtle than those associated with workplace harassment and include such acts as the importance of unreasonable deadlines and workloads, excessive monitoring or supervision, and persistent teasing and/or criticism (Einarsen et al., 2003). The effects of workplace bullying can range from depression, shame, and lack of self-confidence to the total destruction of a career (Lewis, Coursol, & Wahl, 2002).

The possibility that bullying may be as noxious in its impact as direct forms of employment discrimination needs to be widely explored, particularly in light of Fox and Stallworth's (2005) suggestion that overt forms of racism in the workplace have been replaced by more subtle, covert bullying behaviors. A number of researchers (Berdahl, Magley, & Waldo, 1996; Jones, 2006; Stockdale, Visio, & Batra, 1999) have noted the existence of *gendered bullying*, referring to specific instances where male employees are harassed for exhibiting "feminine" behaviors in the workplace.

The Prevalence of Workplace Discrimination

The bulk of empirical research on the topic of workplace discrimination has been based on either surveys of sexual minority employees or analogue studies, which are experimental in design.

SURVEY RESULTS   In 1996, Croteau indicated that 24–66% of sexual minority employees reported discrimination at work based on their sexual orientation. In their national study of 534 gay and lesbian professionals, Ragins & Cornwell (2001b) reported that over 33% had faced verbal or physical harassment in their prior positions because of their sexual orientation, 36% had faced discrimination because others suspected or assumed they were gay, and 12% had left their last job because of discrimination.

ANALOGUE RESULTS   In an experimental study, 236 undergraduate students were asked to rate "fake" resumes supposedly submitted by applicants for a technical writer position (Horvath & Ryan, 2003). The resumes were identical except for one thing. All information related to the sexual orientation and the sex of the applicants had been changed. In one version, Horvath and Ryan included a listing of the applicant's membership in organizations specifically for gay men and lesbians. Another version included either a common first name for a female or a common first name for a male. Again, all other employment and background information on these fictional resumes was identical. Perhaps not surprisingly, the results reflected that the heterosexual male applicant was rated significantly more favorably than lesbian or gay male applicants.

Hoye and Lievens (2003) asked over one hundred employee selection personnel to read and rate candidate profiles. These candidate profiles contained manipulated content related to the sexual orientation of the candidate:

- Gay or living together with a man
- Heterosexual or living together with a woman
- Single or living alone

Participants rated the hirability of the profiles using a Likert rating scale. The sexual orientation of the job candidates did not influence their evaluations.

Hebl et al. (2002) elicited the aid of actors to pose as either a heterosexual or a gay applicant for sales positions at several stores. They then evaluated the feedback of the interviewers. Which applicants would they call back? Which would they likely hire? Conversations with prospective employers were recorded. No differences were found on measures of formal discrimination between straight and gay applicants. However, employers were perceived as more standoffish, nervous, and hostile and as less interested in and helpful to gay applicants than with nongay applicants.

The Impact of Multiple Identity Statuses on Workplace Discrimination

Workplace discrimination has been shown to result from a variety of personal attributes including sex, age, race, ethnicity, disability status, and sexual orientation. For example, a large body of scholarly research reports that women are slower to advance, lack appropriate mentors, and are less well compensated (Beatty & Kirby, 2006; Fassinger & Arsenal, 2007; Schilt, 2006).

According to feminist psychologists double jeopardy is the right term to describe the cumulative impact of being a woman and a sexual minority in the workplace. Degges-White and Shoffner (2002) and Fassinger and Arseneau (2007) state that workplace discrimination against sexual minority women is compounded by the lower status of women in general and their depressed earnings relative to men. Boatwright et al. (1996) observed that lesbians experience more obstacles in career advancement than do heterosexual women and take longer to achieve their career goals.

To date, few researchers have examined the effects of multiple identity statuses on employment experiences. And there are only a handful of studies that explore the impact of triple minority memberships or triple jeopardies in the workplace. One such study of 534 sexual minority employees showed that persons of color were less likely to disclose their same-sex sexual orientations in the workplace compared to their white counterparts (Ragins et al., 2003).

Persons with HIV/AIDS and Workplace Discrimination

Protease inhibitors have greatly reduced the mortality rates of persons with AIDS (Barrio & Shoffner, 2005), diminished their symptoms (Martin, Arns, Chernoff, & Steckart, 2004), and improved their quality of life (Sansone & Frengley, 2000). Yet there is a dearth of research on the career and workplace experiences of sexual and gender minority persons living with HIV/AIDS (Barrio & Shoffner, 2005). For one thing, persons of color may already have experienced discrimination based on race, so why subject themselves to more by disclosing the fact that they're gay? Now that HIV is no longer considered a terminal illness, greater numbers of persons infected with HIV are returning to the workplace (Chung, 2003). This is a good thing, as employment is a significant contributing factor to the overall emotional well-being of persons with HIV/AIDS (McReynolds, 2001).

However, these individuals face a number of challenges. Persons with HIV/AIDS are vulnerable to health problems, such as opportunistic infections and fatigue, that often can affect their job performance and attendance and result in higher insurance premiums for their employers (Hash & Ceperich, 2006). Persons living with HIV are often in a "Catch-22" situation. They need to work because they need health insurance benefits. But their employers may withdraw these benefits because of their health status (Barrio & Shoffner, 2005; Glenn, Ford, Moore, & Hollar, 2003; Hunt, Jaques, Niles, & Wierzalis, 2003).

Sexual and gender minorities must deal with the stigmas associated with having a same-sex sexual orientation and/or gender identity and being HIV-positive. Certainly, people with HIV/AIDS face discrimination in all facets of life (Glenn et al., 2003; Hunt et al., 2003)—but perhaps especially in the workplace. Sexual and gender minority persons who live with HIV/AIDS are another population, doubly "stigmatized." In their qualitative investigation of gay men with HIV/AIDS, Hunt et al. (2003) found concerns about how to accommodate medical treatment in the workplace. Sometimes multiple medications are ingested throughout the day. Some must be taken on an empty stomach and some with food (Glenn et al., 2003). Many of these medications must also be refrigerated (Glenn et al., 2003). This area is a minefield. Should they explain to supervisors and co-workers? Or would doing so subject them to further discrimination?

CONSEQUENCES OF WORKPLACE DISCRIMINATION

Research shows that workplace discrimination has tremendously negative effects on the physical and emotional health of sexual and gender minority employees. In 1996, Driscoll et al. reported that workplace climate was related to occupational stress and coping in their sample of lesbian employees. In 1999, Waldo examined heterosexism in the workplace in two community samples. For sexual minority employees, heterosexism was positively related to psychological distress and health problems and negatively related to satisfaction with life and self-esteem. Smith and Ingram (2004) reported that workplace heterosexism was found to be positively related to depression and psychological distress in their sample of approximately 100 sexual minority employees.

While there has been little systematic empirical research on the impact of workplace discrimination on the gender minority population, anecdotal evidence suggests that it is just as detrimental. Based on their extensive involvement with child welfare systems, Mallon and DeCrescenzo (2006) report that severe employment discrimination particularly affects gender minority youth who are homeless or who have run away and turn to sex work to pay the extensive costs associated with hormones, electrolysis, and cosmetic and sex reassignment surgeries.

THE USE OF JOBS/CAREERS AS SAFE HAVENS

Several authors (Chung, 2001; Chung & Harmon, 1994; Ragins, 2004) note that sexual minorities anticipate workplace discrimination and use career choice as a strategy to avoid it. Levine and Leonard (1984) applied the label *job tracking* to a phenomenon in which sexual minority employees deliberately choose to work in careers and jobs that attract sexual and gender minority persons. Sexual and gender minority employees often apply for positions in businesses they know are owned and operated by other sexual and gender minorities or those that they know hire sexual and gender minority employees. Avoiding discrimination has been the impetus behind many sexual minority persons becoming entrepreneurs and establishing their own businesses. Ragins (2004) referred to a similar dynamic, the *safe haven hypothesis*, meaning that sexual and gender minorities selected careers and workplaces on the basis of their anticipation that such workplaces would be gay-positive and supportive. Ragins (2004) introduced the notion of safe havens to denote those "occupations, organizations and work groups that provide protection against discrimination and support the development of a gay identity" (p. 102). Safe havens would seem to have an enormous influence on sexual minority persons' entry and retention in employment positions. However, sexual minorities may pay a steep price. Ryan and Gruskin (2006) observed that by selecting jobs in areas that are more tolerant of sexual and gender minorities, sexual and gender minorities may receive lower salaries and no health insurance, pensions, or retirement benefits. They may also pay an additional price: By entering professions more tolerant of sexual and gender minorities, they may sacrifice their real job potential and deny their true talents and passions to pursue different professions.

VISIBILITY, IDENTITY MANAGEMENT, AND SELF-DISCLOSURE IN THE WORKPLACE

To be visible or invisible—that is the question. For sexual and gender minorities, managing their identities in the workplace poses many real issues.

Sexual and Gender Minorities and Self-Disclosure in the Workplace

Whether to reveal one's sexual orientation and/or gender identity is probably one of the most important decisions that a sexual or gender minority person can make, and perhaps one of the most stressful (Ragins, 2004; Ward & Winstanley, 2005). Self-disclosure at work has been a consistent theme in the literature on career counseling with sexual minorities since the mid-1970s (Pope et al., 2004). Typically, many sexual and gender minorities assess the organizational climate in the place of employment before coming out (Ward & Winstanley, 2005). Also, sexual minorities are motivated to self-disclose based on a need to be honest and maintain personal integrity and to educate others (Humphrey, 1999).

According to Ragins (2004), "the most disturbing and potentially stressful case of loss of control over the disclosure process involves LGB employees who are involuntarily 'outed' by others at work" (p. 63). The idea of *disclosure disconnects* describes a situation where incongruence exists between the ways that gay, lesbian, and bisexual identities are managed at home versus at work (Ragins, 2004). The notion of *sexual identity conflict* means "the LGB worker discloses his or her sexual identity in one domain but not in another" (Ragins, 2004, p. 66). In contrast, *congruent sexual identity* "involves a consistency in the degree of sexual identity disclosure across work and home domains" (p. 66). Ragins posits that sexual identity strain involved at least a moderate degree of disclosure disconnect.

Several studies have attempted to explore the relationship between self-disclosure and workplace adjustment in the sexual minority population. For example, Day and Schoenrade (1997) assessed the impact of self-disclosure of sexual orientation on work attitudes, organizational commitment, managerial support, and job satisfaction in a convenience sample. Their results revealed that communication about sexual orientation predicted work attitudes. Their results revealed that employees who were more open with others about their same-sex orientation were more committed and satisfied with their jobs than those were more closeted.

In their study of self-disclosure at work, Sandfort, Bos, and Vet (2006) explored the idea of burnout, defined as "a syndrome of emotional exhaustion, depersonalization, and reduced sense of personal competence" (p. 229) that results from a burdensome workload. Using a convenience sample, they recruited members of the lesbian and gay interest group of a Dutch labor union comprising health care, social work, and other service-related fields. They distributed surveys assessing bullying, formal and informal discrimination, and three dimensions of burnout (emotional exhaustion, depersonalization, and reduced personal competence) to their participants. They did not find that formal and informal discrimination was based on sexual orientation.

Kirby (2006) conducted a qualitative study of gay and lesbian officers in gay, lesbian, bisexual, and transgender (GLBT) student organizations on college campuses throughout the country. Students expressed concerns about disclosing their involvements with GLBT organizations on their resumes, and most anticipated those references would be negatively perceived by potential employers.

Visibility and Identity Management in Sexual Minority Employees

Ragins (2004) argued that unlike race and gender, sexual orientation is not usually outwardly visible in the workplace. Despite this, same-sex and bisexual identity categories are negatively stigmatized in Western culture, and most sexual minority persons experience challenges that other stigmatized minority groups do not. Sexual minority persons must decide how to manage their minority identities. In a sense, they must learn information management strategies and make repeated decisions about how much of themselves to reveal to their co-workers/supervisors and when (Beatty & Kirby, 2006). They must deal with the challenge of not having complete control over the disclosure process as well as the possible disparities between levels of openness at home and at work and the resulting strain this may generate (Ragins, 2004).

A number of researchers (Chrobot-Mason, Button, & DiClementi, 2002; Griffin, 1992; McNaught, 1993; Woods & Lucas 1993) have empirically explored the issue of workplace identity or stigma management strategies. Griffin (1992) developed a model to account for the identity management strategies that are used by sexual minority employees in the workplace. This model encompassed four strategies: passing (fabricating to appear heterosexual), covering (censoring information to prevent detection as gay or lesbian), being implicitly out (being honest about being gay or lesbian but not labeling oneself as "gay" or "lesbian"), and being explicitly out (being out and using the label of "lesbian" or "gay").

Wood and Lucas (1993) noted similar types of strategies, including the notion of counterfeiting, which involves trying to pass as heterosexual and sometimes involves lies or deception. Passing was defined by Leary (1999) as "a cultural performance whereby one member of a denied social group masquerades as another in order to enjoy the privileges afforded to the dominant group" (p. 85).

Lidderdale, Croteau, Anderson, Tovar-Murray, and Davis (2007) developed a comprehensive model, workplace sexual identity management (WSIM), to describe the complex process through which sexual minorities manage their identities at work. The WSIM model starts with the premise that every person has inputs or attributes, such as gender, race, ethnicity, sexual orientation, and so on, and what Lidderdale et al. termed *distal contextual affordances*, which include messages about family and community regarding education, sexual orientation, and diversity. Experiences guide the development of a sense of self-efficacy regarding the use of identity management strategies (i.e., concealing, covering, being implicitly out, and being explicitly out) and the expectations of outcomes. Self-efficacy and outcome expectations related to sexual identity management, in turn, lead ultimately to a repertoire of identity management strategies that are used in a particular workplace. According to Lidderdale et al. (2007), *proximal contextual factors* are factors such as work roles and tasks, organizational climate, and the like that also impact the use of particular identity strategies in the workplace.

Regardless of which strategies sexual minorities use to cope in the workplace, they all require a good deal of psychological energy. They tend to generate stress and encourage a sense of isolation (McNaught, 1993; Ragins, 2004; Woods & Lucas 1993). Decisions regarding self-disclosure for most sexual minority employees are seldom an "all or nothing" phenomenon; rather, most use a combination of approaches in the workplace (Chrobot-Mason et al., 2002).

Visibility and Identity Management in Gender Minority Employees

There are those gender minority persons who engage in identity management strategies and who conceal their gender minority identity statuses from others. For example, some cross-dressers typically avoid cross-dressing in their places of employment for fear of being outed (Israel & Tarver, 1997). However, people with visibly stigmatizing identities, like those who are gender nonconforming or those who are gender variant, typically do not have stigma management options such as passing or concealing.

Concealment is not an option for gender minority persons who wish to pursue sex reassignment while employed at the same workplace (Barclay & Scott, 2006). Previous chapters discussed the Standards of Care (Meyer et al., 2001) developed by the Harry Benjamin International Gender Dysphoria Association (now known as World Professional Association for Transgender Health (WPATH) (*www.wpath.org*), which require gender minorities who wish to transition to live for a period of at least one year as their preferred gender. Living as their preferred gender may require those wishing to transition to come out to their employers and transition while on the job. Without legal protection, many who attempt to make transitions while on the job are frequently harassed, terminated, or eventually forced to resign.

Gender minority persons who have completed the gender reassignment process often fear that their histories prior to transition will be discovered (Israel & Tarver, 1997). While research hasn't explored this area, it is assumed that many engage in passing and counterfeiting strategies so as not to be the target of discrimination.

Research that explores the experiences of gender minority persons in the workplace affords rare opportunities to explore the topic of workplace discrimination. As Schilt (2006) notes, gender minority persons who have completed the hormonal and surgical sex reassignment procedures are uniquely situated to assume "an outsider within" perspective. Sociologists Gagne and Tewksbury (1998) used in-depth interviews to explore the experiences, including the workplace experiences, of 65 masculine-to-feminine transgendered persons. Among their participants who left jobs in order to begin the transition process, those who secured new employment experienced a concomitant drop in pay, prestige, and security. Schilt (2006) noted that "transmen," those who have transitioned from biological females to males, are in a unique position. They lived as women and now find themselves potentially experiencing the advantages that come with being male in the workplace. Schilt conducted a series of interviews with participants who were biological females at birth and were currently living and working as men or open "transmen." Two-thirds of her respondents reported experiencing posttransition advantages, such as gaining authority, gaining recognition at work, gaining "body privilege," and gaining economic opportunities.

> By undergoing a change in gender attribution, transmen can find that the same behavior, attitudes, or abilities they had as females bring them more reward as men. This shift in treatment suggests that gender inequality in the workplace is not continually reproduced only because women make different education and workplace choices than men but rather because coworkers and employers often rely on gender stereotypes to evaluate men and women's achievements and skills. (p. 487)

THE ROLE OF POLICY IN WORKPLACE DISCRIMINATION

No federal legislation currently protects sexual and gender minorities from workplace discrimination. Title VII of the Civil Rights Act of 1964 prohibits workplace discrimination based on sex. But the term *sex* was not intended to mean sexual orientation or gender identity. Although the Employment Nondiscrimination Act (ENDA) was first introduced in 1994, it has been repeatedly blocked in Congress (Cahill, 2005). It is estimated that 53% of the population in the United States lives in a jurisdiction in which no job or housing protection is provided for sexual minorities (Cahill, 2005).

The Impact of Nondiscrimination Policies

Where organizations have policies that affirm and protect sexual and gender diversity, there does seem to be less discrimination. The general assumption is that nondiscrimination policies communicate to all employees that their sexual and gender minority colleagues are valued and should be treated equitably (Button, 2001). In their review of literature, Lidderdale et al. (2007) reported that job policies that were supportive of sexual minorities correlated with more openness and support and less discrimination.

In their random national survey of 768 employees, Ragins and Cornwell (2001a) reported that supportive organizational policies have a positive effect on employee retention, work attitudes, and work commitment. Companies with affirmative policies generally compensated their employees better and had fewer reports of discrimination when compared to organizations without discrimination policies.

Tejeda (2006) surveyed a sample of 65 gay males, all of whom held management-level positions. Of these, 55% reported that their companies did not have nondiscrimination policies that explicitly incorporated sexual orientation. Those participants who were employed in organizations with nondiscrimination policies reported greater satisfaction with work and better supervisor–supervisee relationships. However, workplace hostility was higher in organizations with nondiscrimination policies. Gay men who had come out to their supervisors reported significantly greater workplace hostility than did those that had not disclosed. Furthermore, not disclosing to a supervisor was related to higher promotion opportunities and higher turnover intentions. It was Tejeda's conjecture that straight employees in workplaces with nondiscrimination policies might have felt more threatened. And gay workers might have felt more stigmatized by the very policies designed to protect them, thus generating a more hostile working environment. Tejeda concluded by advocating that sexual minority employees "be particularly judicious about sexual orientation disclosure regardless of how 'gay friendly' organizational policies may be" (p. 56).

The Impact of Policy on Sexual Minorities in the Military

The employment harassment and violence against sexual minorities who serve in the military are especially disconcerting. The 1982 policy that explicitly banned sexual minorities from entry into the military was amended in 1993 with the adoption of the Don't Ask, Don't Tell, Don't Pursue policy. Under the new guidelines, the military was barred from asking candidates or recruits about their sexual orientation. A person's suitability for the military was to be judged strictly on the basis of conduct (Moradi, 2006). The Don't Ask, Don't Tell, Don't Pursue policy has been heavily criticized. The American Psychological Association Task Force on Sexual Orientation and Military Service passed a resolution against it on the grounds that military personnel continue to be harassed and unfairly treated. Two thousand military employees have been discharged from the military on the basis of sexual orientation as of the year 2000 (Evans, 2000). Also in 2000, a survey of 71,000 military personnel on military bases had disturbing results: 80% reported hearing offensive jokes and demeaning remarks, and 37% had either been witness to or been the target of harassment, including unfair discipline, overt threats related to sexual orientation, and diminished career opportunities (Myers, 2000). In her comparative random sample of nearly 200 civilians and 200 military personnel, Moradi (2006) reported that both groups were comparable on measures of perceived sexual orientation harassment. The only major difference between the samples concerned the role of senior personnel.

A larger portion of military personnel reported that senior personnel perpetrated sexual orientation harassment.

CAREER COUNSELING AND SEXUAL AND GENDER MINORITY PERSONS

There are a number of different kinds of career counseling programs in business, industry, and other settings, including employee assistance programs (EAPs), employee enhancement programs (EEPs), and outplacement counseling programs (Nugent & Jones, 2005). There are also a number of professionals (i.e., employment practitioners, vocational rehabilitation practitioners, school practitioners, mental health practitioners and counseling psychologists) with different training experiences, credentials, and professional affiliations whose practice involves providing career counseling. This next section explores individual counseling interventions and programmatic interventions that may be used across a variety of these settings and disciplines. It is important to note that regardless of one's setting and orientation, career and workplace issues are interwined with sexual and gender minority identity issues. Career services with this population are not limited to just testing and interpretation issues (Tomlinson & Fassinger, 2003).

Help Define the Relationship Between Work and Life

Helping professionals need to integrate workplace issues within the context of therapy with sexual and gender minority clients. In his text *The Psychology of Working* (2006), Blustein notes that our jobs serve a number of important functions in our lives. They provide us with relationship connections, opportunities for self-determination, and a means of survival. Given that work is such a significant domain of human existence, it seems odd that traditional models of psychotherapy pay it so little attention. Blustein advocates that practitioners routinely integrate questions about work into the intake procedure as a way of "opening up space" (p. 276) in the therapeutic relationship to explore work-related issues:

1. How would you describe your current working life?
2. Tell me the story of how you moved from school to your current working life.
3. What sorts of struggles and psychological pain do you experience at work?
4. How do you balance your family and caregiving responsibilities with work in the paid labor market? (p. 277)

Explore and Evaluate Identity Management Issues

Career counseling interventions that focus solely on career issues without exploring the related processes of identity formation in gender and sexual minorities are inadvisable (Okun & Ziady, 2005; Schmidt & Nilsson, 2006). For clients who are in the job search process, practitioners should attend to the issue of fit between clients and particular organizations. In order to accomplish this, Lyons et al. (2005) recommend that practitioners explore sexual minority clients' values and help identify careers or workplace environments that are compatible. For example, practitioners can ask questions that encourage reflection:

• How important is it for you to be out to others at the job?
• Are job security and status more important than being out to others at the job?
• How would a homophobic atmosphere affect job performance?

Practitioners can also help their sexual and gender minority clients identify jobs where discrimination is less likely to occur.

Most sexual and gender minority clients are challenged to develop ways to manage their sexual and gender identities in their workplaces (Lidderdale et al., 2007; Tejeda, 2006). One tool that can help explore and evaluate workplace climates is the LGBT Climate Inventory (Liddle, Luzzo, Hauenstein, & Schuck, 2004). This 20-item inventory applies a Likert scale to statements such as "Non-LGBT employees are comfortable engaging in gay-friendly humor with LGBT employees (for example, kidding them about a date)" and "LGBT employees feel free to display pictures of a same-sex partner." Another way of beginning an exploration of sexual identity management issues with clients is to present the WSIM theory developed by Lidderdale et al. (2007). This model is a helpful conceptual tool that enables sexual and gender minority clients to think self-reflectively and critically of their past, current, and future workplace behaviors.

Anderson, Croteau, Chung, and DiStefano (2001) developed the workplace sexual identity management measure (WSIMM). This measure includes different strategies that sexual minorities might use to come out in the workplace and serves as a great stimulus for sexual minority employees who are wrestling with issues of self-disclosure (Pope et al., 2004).

Lay Groundwork with Adolescents

Almost by definition, adolescence is a time of turmoil. The combination of hormones, new challenges, and competition make focusing on possible academic and career choices difficult. Add to that the additional conflicts of grappling with sexual identity, and any kind of focus seems elusive. The phenomenon of bottlenecking mentioned earlier is particularly important for those who work with adolescents and young adults. Practitioners need to be mindful that sexual and gender identity issues are likely to overshadow issues associated with career choice and academic success. Gay and lesbian students do report receiving less direction and support from their academic advisors than do heterosexual students (Nauta, Saucier & Woodard, 2001). This makes it all the more important that these issues be explored in counseling.

Clients who are returning to college or entering college for the first time should be advised to explore the Princeton Review website (*www.princetonreview.com*). This website lists colleges that are most accepting of sexual and gender minority students, that have resource centers for sexual and gender minority students, and that have student organizations and support groups for sexual and gender minority students. Prince (1995) advocates beginning counseling sessions with routine questions about the client's developmental history regarding sexual orientation as naturally as one might ask about other issues, including gender, race, ethnicity, or religion. The same can be said for practitioners who work with gender minority clients.

As clients become comfortable acknowledging their sexual/gender orientation, they become more accepting of directional guidance about possible career fits and the higher education to help them reach new goals.

Assess Supplemental Support and Information

Practitioners can help clients assess their employment options by helping them investigate whether workplaces have antidiscrimination policies that protect sexual and gender minorities and whether domestic partnership benefits are offered (Chung, 2001).

Given the dearth of sexual and gender minority career role models and the significance of mentors for the careers of sexual and gender minorities (Nauta et al., 2001), practitioners should work toward developing mentor programs for sexual and gender minority employees. A number of valuable programmatic recommendations have been offered to make career counseling more effective with sexual minorities:

- Look for externships or cooperative education placements in gay- or lesbian-owned businesses (Hetherington & Orzcek, 1989).
- Establish mentorship programs (Elliott, 1993).
- Arrange career shadowing with gay and lesbian professionals (Belz, 1993).

Counseling Gender Minority Employees Who Transition on the Job

Despite the enormity of challenges that confront gender minorities in the workplace, career practitioners receive little to no information about these issues (Chung, 2003). The bulk of applicable literature focuses on gender minorities who are already employed and who are planning on transitioning while on the job. Gender minorities who do not elect hormone replacement therapy and/or surgical intervention and those who are gender variant are seldom addressed in the career counseling literature.

Several practitioners (i.e., Hash & Ceperich, 2006; Israel & Traver, 1997; Korell & Lorah, 2007) recommend that helping professionals work with their gender minority clients to determine if staying in the same employment setting while they are transitioning is a good idea. It is important for practitioners to help clients assess the level of risk related to self-disclosure in their workplace. Israel and Tarver (1997) note that changing jobs and/or careers may pose a number of difficulties and should be considered carefully. For one thing, the expenses associated with transitioning are enormous, and many employees feel compelled to remain in their current positions. Hash and Ceperich (2006) estimated the cost of hormones exceeds $200 a month and genital surgery is a minimum of $25,000.

Many gender minority persons who seek employment after transition are faced with the difficult dilemma of whether or not to disclose their status as a transsexual. If they choose not to disclose, then they must determine how to present their work history (Brown & Rounsley, 1996).

A number of resources are available to gender minority persons who elect to transition while employed in the same workplace, including *Transsexual Workers: An Employer's Guide* (Walworth, 1998). The websites of the Human Rights Campaign (*www.hrc.org/worknet*) and Transgender at Work (*www.tgender.net/taw*) contain information and resources to download on transitioning in the workplace.

Several authors have made valuable suggestions for transitioning in the workplace. Barclay and Scott (2006) advocate the organization of a transition team comprising a human resources person, a top manager, an EAP person, a union representative, and the transitioning employee. Where clear policies and procedures do not exist, they need to be developed, and employee training should be adapted. Policies can extend to the use of toilets and changing rooms, since this is probably one of the most frequently mentioned concerns of co-workers and generally a source of contention in the workplace (Barclay & Scott, 2006; Brown & Rounsley, 1996). Walworth (1998) suggests that gender minority employees meet with employee assistance or human resource professionals and supervisors to discuss the gender transition process. It is recommended that information about an employee's transition be disseminated in writing to others in the workplace. Letters from employee assistance and/or human resource professionals and employers should refer to gender minority employees by their desired names and pronouns, offer support, instructions about restroom issues, and stress the importance of workplace civility (Brown & Rounsley, 1996; Israel & Tarver, 1997). Brown and Rounsley (1996) also recommend using photographs and new business cards as tools to help employees and supervisors accommodate more easily to the transition employee's appearance and desired gender identity.

Addressing Workplace Discrimination in Counseling with Sexual and Gender Minorities

Practitioners who work with sexual and gender minority clients need to be sensitive to even the most subtle biases that their clients face in the workplace and actively address them (Smith & Ingram, 2004). Obviously, some subtle forms of discrimination and workplace bullying are better defined as an organizational problem than as one that can be explained purely on interpersonal grounds (Lewis, 2006). And practitioners can help clients understand, "It's not you. It's the corporation." But where possible, practitioners can work with workplace organizations to be more proactive in terms of recognizing discrimination and preventing it. Practitioners in particular have an important role to play in providing training and information about bullying to employers (Lewis, 2006). Given the empirical evidence that suggests that workplace bullying is the consequence of extended periods where patterns of behavior are not addressed (MacIntosh, 2006), it makes sense that early detection is advisable. It is also highly advisable for employers to gain a heightened awareness of bullying and put "no tolerance" policies firmly in place.

MacIntosh (2006) recommends the use of learning circles as an action-research method (Gagnon & Collay, 2001) for data collection as well as experiential learning. Learning circles, made up of sexual and gender minority participants, constitute an excellent means by which participants can reduce their isolation and enhance their insights. According to MacIntosh (2006): "Employers were most successful in limiting bullying when they promoted Employee Assistance Programs (EAPs), used policies that prevented bullying, enforced those policies with consequences, and used policies that encouraged freedom to discuss work place issues" (p. 675).

Practitioners can play an important role in helping people who work with abusive co-workers and supervisors. For sexual and gender minority employees trying to cope with workplace bullying, Lewis et al. (2002) recommended the use of bibliotherapy. There are several excellent resources that address workplace discrimination, bullying, and other issues: *Transgender Americans: A Handbook of Understanding* (Moulton & Seaton, 2005); *The State of the Workplace for Gay, Lesbian, Bisexual and Transgender Americans 2005–2006* (Human Rights Campaign Foundation, 2006); and *Out at Work* (Lambda Legal, n.d.). The following websites contain information and resource that can be downloaded, including lists of companies that provide affirmative workplace climates for their sexual and gender minority employees: *www.lambdalegal.org; www.hrc.org/worknet; www.gendersanity.com*, and *www.ntac.org/ employ. html*.

Support groups can help clients feel less isolated. These groups can also help clients develop coping strategies for dealing with workplace heterosexism and transphobia (Smith & Ingram, 2004). Employee resource groups (ERGs) have been fairly effective in providing much-needed resources and support, particularly for sexual minority employees (Gore, 2000). In her survey of 200 respondents, Gore (2000) reported, however, that almost 90% of the ERG members said these were typically established by an individual rather than resulting from efforts of top management.

Working with Sexual and Gender Minorities with HIV/AIDS

Sexual and gender minority persons living with HIV/AIDS have employment issues similar to those of persons who have physical and psychological disabilities. These include dealing with social stigmatization, managing multiple roles, living with strained finances, and obtaining needed resources. Sexual and gender minorities who live with HIV/AIDS may need to shift career goals and make determinations about whether to disclose their HIV status to their employers and co-workers (Hunt et al., 2001). Practitioners can aid clients in these decision-making processes and assist them with stigma management.

Many clients lack basic information about their rights as persons with disabilities in the workplace (Brooks & Klosinksi, 1999; Glenn et al., 2003). Practitioners need to be aware of legal issues related to HIV/AIDS. While there is no federal law to protect sexual and gender minority persons from workplace discrimination, many who live with HIV/AIDS do benefit from other federal legislation, including the Americans with Disabilities Act of 1990 (ADA), the Occupational Safety and Health Act (OSHA), the Vocational Rehabilitation Act, and the Privacy Act of 1974. The ADA requires employers to make "reasonable accommodations" for persons who are disabled. In many cases, requests for accommodations are denied, and when they are denied, the disclosure of status may generate negative consequences (Barrio & Shoffner, 2005). Even though persons with HIV/AIDS are entitled to reasonable accommodations under the ADA, discrimination does occur (O'Brien & Koerkenmeier, 2001).

Practitioners can advocate for the accommodations that persons with HIV/AIDS sometimes need, including modified work schedules, liberal sick leave, and access to refrigerators, food, and water (Glenn et al., 2003). Practitioners should also refer clients to support groups for persons with HIV who are planning on returning to work (Brooks & Klosinski, 1999).

Dual-Career Couple Issues in Counseling

Whitcomb et al. (2006) noted a number of salient career issues that can arise for same-sex couples:

- Discrepant incomes
- Degrees of outness between partners
- The possible relocation of one partner
- The lack of role models
- Employee social functions
- Employee benefits

All of these issues may potentially require exploration in therapy.

Practitioners who work with lesbian couples need to be mindful of the stress associated with economic discrimination. This frequently results in dual-career lesbian couples earning less than comparable heterosexual or gay male couples (Hacker, 2003). Lower incomes for sexual and gender minority women can pose a significant hardship in terms of rearing children (Okun & Ziady, 2005).

The Use of Postmodern Counseling Interventions

The storied approach to career counseling is an alternative counseling approach based on postmodern theories, including constructivist and narrative therapies. The client in this general framework is viewed as a "self-organizing" "meaning-maker" (Peavy, 1997). Narrative therapy approaches are those in which sexual and gender minorities are encouraged to tell their stories. The exercise at the end of the chapter provides you with a first-hand opportunity to practice a narrative technique that can be used in career counseling with sexual and gender minority clients.

Education and Advocacy

Approximately 14 states ban antigay discrimination in private and public workplaces (Lambda Legal, n.d.), and 300 companies in the United States have nondiscrimination policies that include provisions for gender identity (Heller, 2006). While this is encouraging, it is clear that more needs to be accomplished in terms of policy development at the organizational level to protect both sexual and gender minority employees. Practitioners, social workers, and psychologists can and must assume an active role in the fight for equal rights. There are a number of specific policy issues that concern the rights of sexual and gender minority employees, including domestic partner benefits, the protection of sexual and gender minority military personnel, health insurance reforms for persons with HIV/AIDS who are transitioning back to work, and the passage of federal nondiscrimination laws like the Employment Nondiscrimination Act (ENDA). Important preconditions for these policies to be effective are the support of top management personnel (Day & Schoenrade, 2000) and the implementation of enforcement strategies as well as transparent hiring processes and promotion decisions (Clair, Beatty & MacLean, 2005).

Beginning in the 1990s, the role of EAPs broadened to include employee issues besides substance abuse and addictions. Now EAPs are also concerned with enhancing the overall work culture through preventive health and intervention services, midlife and retirement support, critical incident interventions, and violence prevention (Emener, 2003). Another important function for practitioners, social workers, and psychologists is the provision of diversity workshops. The last chapter of this text focuses more extensively on the kinds of skills needed for practitioners to serve as public policy advocates.

Summary

This chapter was guided by two underlying assumptions. The first is that each person's career development is influenced by a variety of factors, including contextual and ecological factors. Second, career and identity development are mutually interactive processes (Driscoll et al., 1996).

A sizeable body of evidence suggests that sexual and gender minority persons are the victims of workplace discrimination (Dovidio & Gaertner, 2000; Griffith & Hebl, 2002; Hebl et al., 2002; Tejeda, 2006) and that such discrimination negatively impacts the physical and emotional health of these sexual and gender minority employees (Smith & Ingram, 2004). While there is no national legislation prohibiting discrimination against sexual and gender minority employees, nondiscrimination legislation has been enacted in some states, counties, and municipalities. It has been estimated, for example, that one-third of sexual minority persons reside in areas that offer this protective legislation (Ragins, 2004). The majority of gender minority persons are without basic legal protections in the workplace, and "without jobs and without income it is impossible for gender minority persons to attain equal status in society" (Ohle, 2004, p. 264). Gender minority youth are especially likely to suffer employment discrimination and are, therefore, more apt than nongender minority youth to be homeless (Mallon & DeCrescenzo, 2006). Research that explores the experiences of gender minority persons in the workplace offers investigators rare opportunities to explore the topic of workplace discrimination from "an outsider within" perspective (Schilt, 2006).

Because sexual orientation is not outwardly visible, sexual minority employees must decide how to manage their minority identities. In a sense, they must learn information management strategies and make repeated decisions about how much of themselves to reveal to their co-workers/supervisors and when (Beatty & Kirby, 2006). Besides passing and concealing their sexual and gender minority status, persons may choose careers where they are more likely to receive environmental support.

Gender minority persons who are contemplating transitioning may need assistance in deciding whether to complete their transitions while employed or to seek new employment after their transition is complete. Interventions recommended for gender minority persons who wish to make transitions while employed include the following:

- Photographs to show employees and employers
- Business cards to use with co-workers with the new name
- Letters of introduction written by the employer to be distributed to employees expressing support of the person's transition (Israel & Tarver, 1997)

Brown and Rounsley (1996) recommend that practitioners schedule meetings with the transitioning client's co-workers to answer questions. They also recommend the presentation of letters to the immediate supervisor, co-workers, and human resources employees.

This chapter looked at a number of career counseling practices with sexual minority clients, including the use of postmodern approaches to career counseling. The chapter also offered recommendations for programmatic interventions, including making policy and establishing employee resource groups. An important role for practitioners is assisting their gender and sexual minority clients in assessing the level of risk related to self-disclosure in their workplaces. Regardless of which strategies sexual minorities use to cope in the workplace, they all require a good deal of psychological energy, generate stress, and encourage a sense of isolation (McNaught, 1993; Ragins, 2004; Woods, 1992).

Future research is needed to explore the unique identity management issues that arise for bisexual persons in the workplace when the gender of their partners changes over time (Fassinger & Arseneau, 2007).

Personal Reflection 1

The storied approach to career counseling is an alternative counseling approach based on postmodern theories, including constructivism and narrative therapy. The client in this general framework is viewed as a "self-organizing" "meaning-maker" (Peavy, 1997). As outlined by Brott (2001, 2004), the counseling process consists of three interwoven stages: (1) co-construction, (2) deconstruction, and (3) construction. The clients reveal their lives by telling personal stories—in this case, those relevant to their jobs and career interests and abilities. These stories are deconstructed or unpacked so that clients can explore their experiences from different perspectives. Questions are asked by therapists to help clients explore these experiences from different vantage points. Then clients are asked to complete stories about their personal futures. Practitioners are also encouraged to use qualitative means of gathering data about their clients, including autobiographies, early recollections, genograms, life lines, structured interviews, life roles, and card sorts (Patton & McMahon, 1999).

Directions

In this exercise, you will be asked to form dyads. One partner in the dyad will be the interviewee and the other the interviewer. Read the guidelines below and note that a more detailed description of this exercise is contained in Brott (2004).

1. Place a piece of newsprint and several colored pencils in front of your interviewee.
2. Provide the following instructions to your interviewee:

   To help me better understand and remember what has been important to you in your life's story, I am going to ask you to work on a life line that will be represented on this paper. You can choose the color of pen that best reflects your responses to my questions. You may begin by drawing a line through the center of the paper. (Brott, 2004, pp. 191–192)

3. Ask the client to draw the line from left to right with an arrow facing the right-hand edge of the paper. Write the client's birthdate on the left end and today's date on the right end. Ask the client to fill in on the line important transition points.
4. Ask the interviewee to share a specific memory from each transition point. Use facilitative questions in order to encourage your interviewee to reflect on feelings and experiences from different vantage points (e.g., the perspective of a friend or family member).
5. Place another piece of newsprint in front of your interviewee and ask him or her to extend the life line with today's date on the left edge of the paper. Ask the interviewee to point to a place on the line when he or she reaches a personal goal.
6. Process the exercise with your interviewee.

Personal Reflection 2

Deirdre McCloskey is a nationally renowned economist and Distinguished Professor at the University of Illinois at Chicago. She chronicles in her book *Crossing: A Memoir* (1996) the story of her transition from a biological male to female. McCloskey recounts how during her transition, her sister and a former associate twice tried to persuade judges to involuntarily commit her to mental hospitals (Wilson, 1996). When asked to describe her work experiences as an economist and professor in higher education after transitioning from a biological male to female, McCloskey (2002) responded with the following:

I can't ever have had the experience of having been a girl and young woman, facing the blank lack of understanding, and often enough hostility, of a male-dominated profession. Until age 53 I was a guy in a guy's field, a pretty tough and macho guy (alas). I have the advantage of coming into my womanhood in precisely the decade that other women come into their power, my 50s. Up until then I had all the advantages of income and smooth career that men have. . . .

I've just started to get the treatment that women get. In a way I expect discrimination, either for being a woman or for not being one, if you see what I mean: Either the discrimination comes to all women in our culture, or the discrimination against weird people that comes to the crossgendered. I remember well the first time, during a beginning transition year in Holland teaching at Erasmus University of Rotterdam, when I was the sole woman in a group of a half-dozen economists and I made a point and no one took notice and a few minutes later George made the same point and the men said, "That's a great point, George!" I gave myself a mental high-five: "Yes! They're treating me like a woman!" Believe me; the joy has drained out being dismissed as not speaking: Now like other women I just find the experience extremely annoying.

Self-Reflection Questions

1. Compare McCloskey's anecdotal observation of her job-related experiences with the research presented in this chapter.
2. After reading this passage from McCloskey's essay, imagine your body transformed into a different sex. How might you imagine your work life to be if you were to change sex? What challenges might you imagine experiencing? What rewards?
3. Further details about McCloskey's experiences as a faculty member are described in her memoir. Compare her experiences to those of other gender minorities like Tina Donovan, whose story you read at the beginning of this chapter.

Library, Media, and Internet Activities

Check your local video/DVD store for three important films that deal with a variety of issues.

Gypo (Dunn, 2005)

This film depicts the story of a conflicted family whose lives are impacted by two Czech refugees seeking asylum in the United Kingdom. The film deals with a number of themes, including prejudice, economic hardship, and exploitation of illegal aliens. The story is told from the perspective of the three main characters: Helen, Paul, and Tasha, a Czech refugee.

Discussion Questions and Activities

1. One might say that all the characters in this film yearn for a different life in terms of both their personal and their employment situations. How do their work lives relate to their current emotional struggles? As a counselor, how might you approach career counseling with each?
2. This film depicts several kinds of prejudices. Discuss the role of visibility in the many

forms of discrimination that were depicted in this film.
3. Assume the role of a career counselor for one of the central characters: Helen, Paul, or Tasha. Describe how you might adopt a postmodern approach to counseling your client.

Innocent (a.k.a. Ji oi mak sun yen) (Chung, 2005)

This coming-of-age film depicts the struggles of 17-year-old Eric, whose family moves from Hong Kong to Canada to begin a new life. As Eric's parents' marriage unravels, Eric deals with unrequited love, anal sex, school harassment, and deception.

Discussion Questions and Activities

1. How do the developmental tasks of sexual minority adolescents intersect with career development? Does Hetherington's (1991) concept of the bottleneck effect seem to fit Eric's case? If yes, why? If no, why not?

2. Assume a postmodern perspective with Eric and describe how you might work with Eric as his guidance counselor in developing a plan for a future career.

3. Assume the role of Eric's guidance counselor. How might you approach the climate in Eric's high school? How might you handle the incident in which Eric's classmates ostracize him?

Philadelphia (Demme, 1993)

In this critically acclaimed film, Andrew Beckett, an attorney in a prestigious law film in Philadelphia, is fired because he has AIDS. He hires a fellow attorney, Joe Miller, to represent him in a wrongful termination lawsuit. Joe must come to grips with his own homophobia and ignorance about HIV/AIDS, as must the jury members.

Discussion Questions and Activities

1. What are the overt and underlying assumptions that the characters in this film have about HIV/AIDS? Are these assumptions still present in our culture and in your own community more than a decade following the making of this film?

2. Imagine that Andy Beckett's law firm had an EAP and that he came to you as an EAP counselor for assistance immediately following the "lost file" incident? He tells you then that he thinks he is being set up to be fired. How might you approach his situation with him? And would approaching this situation openly place your own job at risk?

3. If Andy were alive now and receiving medical treatment to manage his HIV, how might you approach your work with him as his counselor?

CASE STUDY

You are a counselor in a community counseling center in a semirural area. Jude is a 52-year-old white male who comes to you for counseling. Jude recently retired after serving 30 years in the army. He is currently employed as a computer programmer in a small industry. He is tall and thin. His hair is shoulder length and graying. His dress is casual and androgynous. Jude discloses to you during the first session that he intends on getting a sex change operation. He tells you that he has found a doctor in another town who is willing to administer hormone injections. He shares with you his future plans to cash in his investments and to use all of his available savings to pay for sex reassignment surgery in Thailand.

Jude tells you that he has come to counseling because recently he has been harassed by several of his co-workers. He tells you that he tries to keep a low profile at work but that he has already confided in a co-worker about his plans to transition from male to female. He tells you that the human resources department in his company is very small, and he expresses little faith in its ability to deal with his transition. He tells you that he is quite fearful about the possibility that he may be fired from his current job and that he really needs the income for medical expenses associated with his transition.

Discussion Questions

1. Place yourself in the role of Jude's counselor. How capable would you feel to offer counseling to Jude? What might be some possible issues for you on a personal and on a professional level in working with Jude?

2. Suppose that Jude requested that you go with her to speak to the human resources director at her workplace. How might you approach this request? If you did agree to meet with a human resources department representative, how might you prepare yourself for such a meeting? What would the agenda be?

3. Develop a comprehensive bibliography of Internet resources and websites to share with Jude and with the human resources department representative.

4. As was recommended in the literature on transitioning in the workplace, assume the role of Jude and write letters to Jude's supervisor, human resources personnel, and co-workers.

5. Conduct a search on the Internet to find out what laws or policies exist in your jurisdiction and your state that provide employment discrimination protection for gender and sexual minorities.

References

Anderson, M. Z., Croteau, J. M., Chung, Y. B., & Distefano, T. M. (2001). Developing an assessment of sexual identity management for lesbian and gay workers. *Journal of Career Assessment, 9*(3), 243–260.

Badgett, M. V. L. (2003). Employment and sexual orientation: Disclosure and discrimination in the workplace. In L. D. Garnets & D. C. Kimmel (Eds.), *Psychological perspectives on lesbian, gay, and bisexual experiences* (2nd ed.) (pp. 327–348). New York: Columbia University Press.

Barclay, J. M., & Scott, L. J. (2006). Transsexuals and workplace diversity: A case of "change" management. *Personnel Review, 35*(4), 487–502.

Barrio, C. A., & Shoffner, M. F. (2005). Career counseling with persons living with HIV: An ecological approach. *Career Development Quarterly, 53*(4), 325–336.

Beatty, J. E., & Kirby, S. L. (2006). Beyond the legal environment: How stigma influences invisible identity groups in the workplace. *Employee Responsibilities & Rights Journal, 18*(1), 29–44.

Belz, J. R. (1993). Sexual orientation as a factor in career development. *Career Development Quarterly, 41*(3), 197–200.

Berdahl, J. L., Magley, V. J., & Waldo, C. R. (1996). The sexual harassment of men: Exploring the concept with theory and data. *Psychology of Women Quarterly, 20*(4), 527–547.

Blustein, D. L. (2006). *The psychology of working: A new perspective for career development, counseling, and public policy.* Mahwah, NJ: Erlbaum.

Blustein, D. L., McWhirter, E. H., & Perry, J. C. (2005). An emancipatory communitarian approach to vocational development theory, research, and practice. *Counseling Psychologist, 33*(2), 141–179.

Boatwright, K. J., Gilbert, M. S., Forrest, L., & Ketzenberger, K. (1996). Impact of identity development upon career trajectory: Listening to the voices of lesbian women. *Journal of Vocational Behavior, 48*(2), 210–228.

Brooks, R. A., & Klosinski, L. E. (1999). Assisting persons living with HIV/AIDS to return to work: Programmatic steps for AIDS service organizations. *AIDS Education & Prevention, 11*(3), 212–223.

Brott, P. E. (2001). The storied approach: A postmodern perspective for career counseling. *Career Development Quarterly, 49*(4), 304–313.

Brott, P. E. (2004). Constructivist assessment in career counseling. *Journal of Career Development, 30*(3), 189–200.

Brown, D., & Brooks, L. (1996). *Career choice and development* (3rd ed.). San Francisco: Jossey-Bass.

Brown, M. L., & Rounsley, C. A. (1996). *True selves: Understanding transsexualism—For families, friends, coworkers, and helping professionals.* San Francisco: Jossey-Bass.

Button, S. B. (2001). Organizational efforts to affirm sexual diversity: A cross-level examination. *Journal of Applied Psychology, 86*(1), 17–28.

Cahill, S. (2005). *The glass nearly half full.* Washington, DC: National Gay and Lesbian Task Force Policy Institute.

Chrobot-Mason, D., Button, S. B., & DiClementi, J. D. (2002). Sexual identity management strategies: An exploration of antecedents and consequences. *Sex Roles, 45*(5/6), 321–336.

Chung, S. (Director). (2005). *Innocent (a.k.a. Ji oi mak sun yen)* [Motion picture]. Hong Kong: Ying E. Chi.

Chung, Y. B. (1995). Career decision making of lesbian, gay, and bisexual individuals. *Career Development Quarterly, 44*(2), 178–203.

Chung, Y. B. (2001). Work discrimination and coping strategies: Conceptual frameworks for counseling lesbian, gay, and bisexual clients. *Career Development Quarterly, 50*, 33–44.

Chung, Y. B. (2003). Career counseling with lesbian, gay, bisexual, and transgendered persons: The next decade. *Career Development Quarterly, 52*(1), 78–86.

Chung, Y. B., & Harmon, L. W. (1994). The career interests and aspirations of gay men: How sex-role orientation is related. *Journal of Vocational Behavior, 45*(2), 223–239.

Clair, J. A., Beatty, J. E., & MacLean, T. L. (2005). Out of sight but not out of mind: Managing invisible social identities in the workplace. *Academy of Management Review, 30*(1), 78–95.

Croteau, J. M. (1996). Research on the work experiences of lesbian, gay, and bisexual people: An integrative review of methodology and findings. *Journal of Vocational Behavior* [Special/issue: Vocational issues of lesbian women and gay men], *48*(2), 195–209.

Croteau, J. M., Anderson, M. Z., Distefano, T. M., & Kampa-Kokesch, S. K. (2000). Lesbian, gay, and bisexual vocational psychology: Reviewing foundations and planning construction. In R. M. Perez, K. A. DeBord, & K. J. Bieschke (Eds.), *Handbook of counseling and psychotherapy with lesbian, gay and bisexual clients* (pp. 383–408). Washington, DC: American Psychological Association.

Dawis, R. V., England, G., & Lofquist, L. H. (1964). *A theory of work adjustment* (Minnesota Studies in Vocational Rehabilitation No. XV). Minneapolis: University of Minnesota, Industrial Relations Center.

Day, N. E., & Schoenrade, P. (1997). Staying in the closet versus coming out: Relationships between communication about sexual orientation and work attitudes. *Personnel Psychology, 50*(1), 147–163.

Day, N. E., & Schoenrade, P. (2000). The relationship among reported disclosure of sexual orientation, anti-discrimination policies, top management support and work attitudes of gay and lesbian employees. *Personnel Review, 29*(3), 346–363.

Degges-White, S., & Shoffner, M. F. (2002). Career counseling with lesbian clients: Using the theory of work adjustment as a framework. *Career Development Quarterly, 51*(1), 87–96.

Demme, J. (Director). (1993). *Philadelphia* [Motion picture]. United States: TriStar Pictures.

Donovan, T. (2001). Being transgender and older: A first person account. *Journal of Gay & Lesbian Social Services, 13*(4), 19–22.

Dovidio, J. F., & Gaertner, S. L. (2000). Aversive racism and selection decisions: 1989 and 1999. *Psychological Science, 11*(4), 315–319.

Driscoll, J. M., Kelley, F. A., & Fassinger, R. E. (1996). Lesbian identity and disclosure in the workplace: Relation to occupational stress and satisfaction. *Journal of Vocational Behavior, 48*, 229–242.

Dunn, J. (Director). (2005). *Gypo* [Motion picture]. United States: Wolfe Pictures.

Einarsen, S., Hoel, H., Zapf, D., & Cooper, C. L. (2003). *Bullying and emotional abuse in the workplace: International perspectives in research and practice.* New York: Taylor & Francis.

Elliott, J. E. (1993). Career development with lesbian and gay clients. *Development Quarterly, 41*(3), 210–226.

Emener, W. G. (2003). The preparation and development of employee assistance program professionals. In W. G. Emener, W. S. Hutchison, & M. A. Richard (Eds.), *Employee assistance programs* (3rd ed., pp. 171–182). Springfield, IL: Charles C. Thomas.

Evans, R. (2001). *U.S. military policies concerning homosexuals: Development, implementation, and outcomes.* Santa Barbara, CA: Center for the Study of Sexual Minorities in the Military.

Fassinger, R. E. (1995). From invisibility to integration: Lesbian identity in the workplace. *Career Development Quarterly, 44*(2), 148–167.

Fassinger, R. E., & Arseneau, J. R. (2007). "I'd rather get wet than be under that umbrella": Differentiating the experiences and identities of lesbian, gay, bisexual, and transgender people. In K. J. Bieschke, R. M. Perez, & K. A. DeBord (Eds.), *Handbook of counseling and psychotherapy with lesbian, gay, bisexual and transgender clients* (2nd ed.) (pp. 19–49). Washington, DC: American Psychological Association.

Fox, S., & Stallworth, L. E. (2005). Racial/ethnic bullying: Exploring links between bullying and racism in the US workplace. *Journal of Vocational Behavior, 66*(3), 438–456.

Gagne, P., & Tewksbury, R. (1998). Conformity pressures and gender resistance among transgendered individuals. *Social Problems, 45*(1), 81–100.

Gagnon, G. W., & Collay, M. (2001). *Designing for learning: Six elements in constructivist classrooms.* Thousand Oaks, CA: Corwin.

Glenn, M. K., Ford, J. A. , Moore, D., & Hollar, D. (2003). Employment issues as related by individuals living with HIV or AIDS. *Journal of Rehabilitation, 69*(1), 30–36.

Gore, S. (2000). The lesbian and gay workplace: An employee's guide to advancing equity. In B. Greene & G. L. Croom (Eds.), *Education, research & practice in lesbian, gay, bisexual and transgender psychology: A resource manual* (pp. 282–302). Thousand Oaks, CA: Sage.

Gottfredson, L. S. (2002). Gottfredson's theory of circumscription, compromise, and self-creation. In D. Brown & Associates (Eds.), *Career choice and development* (4th ed., pp. 85–148). San Francisco: Jossey-Bass.

Greenhaus, J. H., Parasuraman, S., & Wormley, W. M. (1990). Effects of race on organizational experiences, job performance evaluations, and career outcomes. *Academy of Management Journal, 33*(1), 64–86.

Griffin, P. (1992). From hiding out to coming out: Empowering lesbian and gay educators. In K. M. Harbeck (Ed.), *Coming out of the classroom closet* (pp. 167–196). Binghamton, NY: Harrington Park Press.

Griffin, P. (2002). Changing the game: Homophobia, sexism and lesbians in sport. In S. Scratton & A. Flintoff (Eds.), *Gender & sport: A reader* (pp. 193–208). London: Routledge.

Griffith, K. H., & Hebl, M. R. (2002). The disclosure dilemma for gay men and lesbians: "Coming out" at work. *Journal of Applied Psychology, 87*(6), 1191–1199.

Hacker, A. (2003). *Mismatch.* New York: Scribner's.

Hash, K., & Ceperich, S. D. (2006). Workplace issues. In S. F. Morrow & L. Messinger (Eds.), *Sexual orientation & gender expression in social work practice* (pp. 405–426). New York: Columbia University Press.

Hebl, M. R., Foster, J. B., Mannix, L. M., & Dovidio, J. F. (2002). Formal and interpersonal discrimination: A field study of bias toward homosexual applicants. *Personality & Social Psychology Bulletin, 28*(6), 815–825.

Heller, M. (2006). More employers broadening nondiscrimination polices to include transgender workers. *Workforce Management, 85*(12), 62–63.

Herr, E. L. (1997). Career counseling: A process in process. *British Journal of Guidance & Counselling, 25,* 81–93.

Hetherington, C. (1991). Life planning and career counseling with gay and lesbian students. In N. J. Evans & V. A. Wall (Eds.), *Beyond tolerance: Gays, lesbians and bisexuals on campus* (pp. 131–146). Alexandria, VA: American College Personnel Association.

Hetherington, C., & Orzcek, A. M. (1989). Career counseling and life planning with lesbian women. *Journal of Counseling & Development, 68*(1), 52–57.

Horvath, M., & Ryan, A. M. (2003). Antecedents and potential moderators of the relationship between attitudes and hiring discrimination on the basis of sexual orientation. *Sex Roles, 48*(3/4), 115–130.

Hoye, G. V., & Lievens, F. (2003). The effects of sexual orientation on hirability ratings: An experimental study. *Journal of Business & Psychology, 18*(1), 15–30.

Human Rights Campaign Foundation. (2006). *The state of the workplace for gay, lesbian, bisexual and transgender Americans 2005–2006.* Washington, DC: Author.

Humphrey, J. C. (1999). Organizing sexualities, organized inequalities: Lesbians and gay men in public service occupations. *Gender, Work & Organization, 6*(3), 134–151.

Hunt, B., Jaques, J., Niles, S. G., & Wierzalis, E. (2003). Career concerns for people living with HIV/AIDS. *Journal of Counseling & Development, 81,* 55–60.

Israel , G. E., & Tarver, D. E. (1997). *Transgender care: Recommended guidelines, practical information, and personal accounts.* Philadelphia: Temple University Press.

Jones, C. (2006). Drawing boundaries: Exploring the relationship between sexual harassment, gender and bullying. *Women's Studies International Forum, 29*(2), 147–158.

Kirby, S. (2006). American gay and lesbian student leaders' perceptions of job discrimination. *Equal Opportunities International, 25*(2), 126–140.

Korell, S. C., & Lorah, P. (2007). An overview of affirmative psychotherapy and counseling with transgender clients. In K. J. Bieschke, R. M. Perez, & K. A. DeBord (Eds.), *Handbook of counseling and psychotherapy with lesbian, gay, bisexual, and transgender clients* (2nd ed., pp. 271–288). Washington, DC: American Psychological Association.

Lambda Legal. (n.d.). *Out at work.* Retrieved January 20, 2005, from ***http://www.lambdalegal.org/lambda_pdf***

Leary, K. (1999). Passing, posing, and "keeping it real." *Constellations, 6,* 85–96.

Lev, A. I. (2004). *Transgender emergence: Therapeutic guidelines for working with gender-variant people and their families.* Binghamton, NY: Haworth Press.

Levine, M. P., & Leonard, R. (1984). Discrimination against lesbians in the work force. *Signs: Journal of Women in Culture and Society, 9,* 700–710.

Lewis, J., Coursol, D., & Wahl, K. W. (2002). Addressing issues of workplace harassment: Counseling the targets. *Journal of Employment Counseling, 39*(3), 109–116.

Lewis, S. (2006). Recognition of workplace bullying: A qualitative study of women targets in the public sector. *Journal of Community & Applied Social Psychology, 16*(2), 119–135.

Lidderdale, M. A., Croteau, J. M., Anderson, M. Z., Tovar-Murray, D., & Davis, J. M. (2007). Building lesbian, gay and bisexual vocational psychology: A theoretical model of workplace sexual identity management. In K. J. Bieschke, R. M. Perez, & K. A. DeBord (Eds.), *Handbook of counseling and psychotherapy with lesbian, gay, bisexual and transgender clients* (2nd ed., pp. 245–270). Washington, DC: American Psychological Association.

Liddle, B. J., Luzzo, D. A., Hauenstein, A. L., & Schuck, K. (2004). Construction and validation of the lesbian, gay, bisexual, and transgendered climate inventory. *Journal of Career Assessment, 12*(1), 33–50.

Lyons, H. Z., Brenner, B. R., & Fassinger, R. E. (2005). A multicultural test of the theory of work adjustment: Investigating the role of heterosexism and fit perceptions in the job satisfaction of lesbian, gay, and bisexual employees. *Journal of Counseling Psychology, 52*(3), 537–548.

MacIntosh, J. (2006). Tackling work place bullying. *Issues in Mental Health Nursing, 27,* 665–679.

Mallon, G. P., & DeCrescenzo, T. (2006). Transgender children and youth: A child welfare practice perspective. *Child Welfare, 85*(2), 215–241.

Martin, D. J., Arns, P. G., Chernoff, R. A., & Steckart, M. J. (2004). Working with HIV/AIDS: Who attempts workforce reentry following disability? *Journal of Applied Rehabilitation Counseling, 35*(3), 28–38.

McCann, L. & Pearlman, L. A. (1990). Vicarious traumatization: A theoretical framework for understanding the psychological effects of working with victims. *Journal of Traumatic Stress, 3,* 131–149.

McCloskey, D. (1996). *Crossing: A memoir.* Chicago: University of Chicago Press.

McCloskey, D. (2002). Crossing economics [Electronic version]. *International Journal of Transgenderism, 4*(3). Retrieved January 1, 2007, from *http://www.symposion.com/ijt/gilbert/mccloskey.htm*

McNaught, B. (1993). Gay issues in the workplace. New York: St. Martin's Press.

McReynolds, C. J. (2001). The meaning of work in the lives of people living with HIV disease and AIDS. *Rehabilitation Counseling Bulletin, 44*(2), 104–115.

Meyer, W., Bockting, W., Cohen-Kettenis, P., Coleman, E., DiCeglie, D., Devor, H., et al. (2001). The standards of care for gender identity disorders, sixth version [Electronic version]. *International Journal of Transgenderism, 5*(1). Retrieved May 1, 2004, from *http://www.symposion.com/ijt/soc_2001/index.htm*

Moradi, B. (2006). Perceived sexual-orientation-based harassment in military and civilian contexts. *Military Psychology, 18*(1), 39–60.

Morgan, K. S., & Brown, L. S. (1993). Lesbian career development, work behavior, and vocational counseling. In L. D. Garnets & D. C. Kimmel (Eds.), *Psychological perspectives on lesbian & gay male experiences. Between men—between women: Lesbian and gay studies* (pp. 267–286). New York: Columbia University Press.

Moulton, B., & Seaton, L. (2005). *Transgender Americans: A handbook of understanding.* Washington, DC: Human Rights Campaign Foundation.

Myers, S. L. (2000, March 25). Survey of troops finds antigay bias common in service. *The New York Times,* pp. AI, A10.

Nauta, M. M., Saucier, A. M., & Woodard, L. E. (2001). Interpersonal influences on students' academic and career decisions: The impact of sexual orientation. *Career Development Quarterly, 49*(4), 352–362.

Nugent, F. A., & Jones, K. D. (2009). *Introduction to the profession of counseling* (5th ed.). Upper Saddle River, NJ: Pearson Prentice Hall.

O'Brien, G. V. & Koerkenmeier, M. (2001). Persons with HIV/AIDS in the workplace: Implications for Employee Assistance Professionals [Electronic version]. *Employee Assistance Quarterly, 16*(3), 9–23. Retrieved September 17, 2008, from *http://www.haworthpress.com*

Ohle, J. M. (2004). Constructing the trannie: Transgender people and the law. *Journal of Gender, Race, & Justice, 8*(7), 237–280.

Okun, B. F., & Ziady, L. G. (2005). Redefining the career ladder: New visions of women at work. In

M. P. Mirkin, K. L. Suyemoto, & B. F. Okun (Eds.), *Psychotherapy with women: Exploring diverse contexts and identities* (pp. 215–236). New York: Guilford.

Patton, W., & McMahon, M. (1999). *Career development and systems theory: A new relationship.* Pacific Grove, CA: Brooks/Cole.

Peavy, R. V. (1997). A constructive framework for career counseling. In T. L. Sexton & B. L. Griffin (Eds.), *Constructivist thinking in counseling practice, research, and training* (pp. 122–140) (Counseling and Development Series No. 3). New York: Teachers College Press.

Pope, M. (2003). Career counseling in the twenty-first century: Beyond cultural encapsulation. *Career Development Quarterly, 52*(1), 54–60.

Pope, M., Barret, B., Szymanski, D. M., Chung, Y. B., Singaravelu, H., McLean, R., et al. (2004). Culturally appropriate career counseling with gay and lesbian clients. *Career Development Quarterly, 53*(2), 158–176.

Prentiss, C., & McAnulty, R. (2002). Gender identity disorder in the workplace. In L. Diamant & J. Lee (Eds.), *The psychology of sex, gender, and jobs: Issues and solutions* (pp. 171–184). Westport, CT: Praeger.

Prince, J. P. (1995). Influences on the career development of gay men. *Career Development Quarterly, 44*(2), 168–177.

Ragins, B. R. (2004). Sexual orientation in the workplace: The unique work and career experiences of gay, lesbian, and bisexual workers. *Research in Personnel & Human Resources Management, 23,* 35–120.

Ragins, B. R., & Cornwell, J. M. (2001a). Pink triangles: Antecedents and consequences of perceived workplace discrimination against gay and lesbian employees. *Journal of Applied Psychology, 86*(6), 1244–1261.

Ragins, B. R., & Cornwell, J. M. (2001b, August). *Walking the line: Fear and disclosure of sexual orientation in the workplace.* Paper presented at the meeting of the National Academy of Management, Washington, DC.

Ragins, B. R., Cornwell, J. M., & Miller, J. S. (2003). Heterosexism in the workplace: Do race and gender matter? *Group & Organization Management, 28*(1), 45–74.

Ritter, K. Y., & Terndrup, A. I. (2002). *Handbook of affirmative psychotherapy with lesbians and gay men.* New York: Guilford.

Ryan, C., & Gruskin, E. (2006). Health concerns for lesbians, gay men, and bisexuals. In D. F. Morrow & L. Messinger (Eds.), *Sexual orientation and gender expression in social work practice: Working with gay, lesbian, bisexual, and transgender people* (pp. 307–342). New York: Columbia University Press.

Sandfort, T. M., Bos, H., & Vet, R. (2006). Lesbians and gay men at work: Consequences of being out. In A. M. Omoto & H. S. Kurtzman (Eds.), *Sexual orientation and mental health: Examining identity and development in lesbian, gay, and bisexual people* (pp. 225–244). Washington, DC: American Psychological Association.

Sansone, G. R., & Frengley, J. D. (2000). Impact of HAART on causes of death of persons with late stage AIDS. *Journal of Urban Health, 77*(2), 166–175.

Savickas, M. L. (1993). Career counseling in the postmodern era. *Journal of Cognitive Psychotherapy: An International Quarterly, 7*(3), 205–215.

Savickas, M. L. (2002). Career construction: A developmental theory of vocational behavior. In D. Brown & Associates (Eds.), *Career choice and development* (4th ed., pp. 149–205). San Francisco: Jossey-Bass.

Savickas, M. L. (2005). The theory and practice of career construction. In D. Brown & R. W. Lent (Eds.), *Career development and counseling* (pp. 42–70). Hoboken, NJ: Wiley.

Schilt, K. (2006). Just one of the guys? How transmen make gender visible at work. *Gender & Society, 20*(4), 456–490.

Schmidt, C. K., & Nilsson, J. E. (2006). The effects of simultaneous developmental processes: Factors relating to the career development of lesbian, gay, and bisexual youth. *Career Development Quarterly, 55*(1), 22–37.

Smith, N., & Ingram, K. M. (2004). Workplace heterosexism and adjustment among lesbian, gay, and bisexual individuals: The role of unsupportive social interactions. *Journal of Counseling Psychology, 51*(1), 57–67.

Stockdale, M. S., Visio, M., & Batra, L. (1999). The sexual harassment of men: Evidence for a broader theory of sexual harassment and sex discrimination. *Psychology, Public Policy & Law, 5,* 630–664.

Super, D. E. (1990). A life span, life-space approach to career development. In D. Brown, L. Brooks, & Associates (Eds.), *Career choice and development* (2nd ed., pp. 197–261). San Francisco: Jossey-Bass.

Tejeda, M. J. (2006). Nondiscrimination policies and sexual identity disclosure: Do they make a difference in employee outcomes? *Employee Responsibilities & Rights Journal, 18*(1), 45–59.

Tomlinson, M., & Fassinger, R. E. (2003). Career development, lesbian identity development, and campus climate among lesbian college students. *Journal of College Student Development, 44*(6), 845–860.

Waldo, C. R. (1999). Working in a majority context: A structural model of heterosexism as minority stress in the workplace. *Journal of Counseling Psychology, 46*(2), 218–232.

Walworth, J. (1998). *Transsexual workers: An employer's guide.* Westchester, CA: Author.

Ward, J., & Winstanley, D. (2005). Coming out at work: Performativity and the recognition and renegotiation of identity. *Sociological Review 53*(3), 447–475.

Whitcomb, D. H., Wettersten, K. B., & Stolz, C. L. (2006). Career counseling with gay, lesbian, bisexual, and transgender clients. In D. Capuzzi & M. D. Stauffer (Eds.), *Career counseling: Foundations, perspectives, and applications* (pp. 386–411). Boston: Allyn & Bacon.

Wilson, R. (1996, February 16). Leading economist stuns field by deciding to become a woman. *Chronicle of Higher Education.* Retrieved September 20, 2008, from ***http://chronicle.com/che-data/ articles. dir/art-42.dir/issue-23.dir/23a01701.htm***

Woods, J. D. & Lucas, J. H. (1993). *The corporate closet: The professional lives of gay men in America.* New York: The Free Press.

Woods, S. E. (1992). Describing the experiences of lesbian physical educators: A phenomenological study. In A. C. Sparkes (Ed.), *Research in physical education and sport: Exploring alternative visions* (pp. 90–117). London: Palmer Press.

Social Justice for Sexual and Gender Minorities

INTRODUCTION

In this excerpt from her article "The Missing Vagina Monologue . . . and Beyond" (2006), Ester Morris Leidolf provides a glimpse of just some of the challenges that confront gender minority persons. Leidolf was born with Mayer–Rokitansky–Kuster–Hauser Syndrome (MRKH), an intersex condition (also known as a disorder of sexual development) that affects 1 in 1,500 infants (Consortium on the Management of Disorders of Sex Development, 2006). Infants with MRKH are born with "normal" external genitalia but do not have vaginas, fallopian tubes, cervixes, or uteruses. Leidolf's medical condition was not discovered until she was 13 years of age. She subsequently underwent three corrective surgeries by the age of 15 in order to create what the doctors termed a "functional" vagina, which was defined by her doctors as "one that will be able to accept a normal size penis" (p. 80). While in her forties, she obtained her hospital records and learned of her diagnosis for the first time.

> Curious to learn what other women were talking about, I read the *Vagina Monologues* (Ensler, 1998). I was not curious about the play, but the vaginas. I am a woman who was born (in 1956) without one. . . . Think of this as the Missing Vagina Monologue, or the Monologue of Missing Vaginas. Either way, this is a monologue that deserves more attention.
>
> I want people to understand that doing the "right thing" can often do more harm than good. The standard of normal for which we aim is imaginary. We are altering women's bodies when it is social and medical attitudes that need adjusting. Surgically correcting our genitals tells us that they are wrong. However, different is not wrong. Different is just different. Women should not have to endure so much emotional and physical pain just to perform one sexual act when other options are available. Yet, I understand why we do that as much as I resent it. I resent it because of the price we pay for society's lack of creative thinking. Women with MRKH should be treated as women with a syndrome rather than isolated with the label of "sexual dysfunction." My absence of a vagina posed less of a threat to my health than the parts of the syndrome that disabled me. So why was a vagina all that I was given to cope with a much greater loss? (Leidolf, 2006, p. 86)

After learning the truth about her condition, Leidolf went on to develop an online support group for women with MRKH. She continues to educate helping professionals about MRKH and to advocate for MRKH patients and their families. Her goal is to overcome the shame and secrecy that shroud this condition.

A Preview of Chapter Contents

Throughout this text, we have explored the extent to which conventional medical and psychiatric practices for intersex persons, or persons with disorders of sexual development (DSD), such as Leidolf have failed to provide compassionate and supportive treatment. We have also been sensitized to the myriad ways in which negative attitudes and discrimination toward sexual and gender minority persons continue to persist not only in our therapy offices but also in our schools, churches, hospitals, doctors' offices, workplaces, child welfare agencies, and homeless shelters. The policies and remedies to prevent discrimination and/or harassment in these settings are absent or wholly inadequate (Sandfort, Bos, & Vet, 2006). Despite empirical evidence showing that same-sex couples experience emotional dynamics and levels of satisfaction in their relationships similar to those of heterosexual couples (Herek, 2006) and that sexual minority parents are as competent and supportive in their parenting efforts as their nonminority counterparts (Herek, 2006), laws, policies, and decisions rendered in our courts often do not reflect these research findings (Fulcher, Sutfin, Chan, Scheib, & Patterson, 2006; Herek, 2006). In Chapter 3, readers learned about the concept of minority stress (Meyer, 2003), referring to the negative or ill effects that sexual and gender minority persons experience as a result of discrimination and marginalization in Western culture. Working to treat the symptoms associated with minority stress without addressing the underlying social causes seems foolhardy.

In a radical paradigm shift, psychologists and mental health practitioners (Arredondo & Perez, 2003; Donahue & McDonald, 2005; Goodman et al., 2004) have adapted a social justice perspective to counseling or adopted a sociopolitical framework for understanding emotional and behavioral problems. A social justice perspective means that many of the presenting issues that sexual and gender minorities bring to therapy are seen not as psychopathology but as byproducts of the consequences of their social experiences. Psychologists, practitioners, and social workers who work for social justice engage in "scholarship and professional action designed to change societal values, policies, and practices, such that disadvantaged or marginalized groups gain increased access to the tools of self-determination" (Goodman et al., 2004, p. 795).The call for helping professionals to expand their practices beyond the realm of service to individuals to become social change agents means a significant change in consciousness and in training procedures. Unfortunately, many helping professionals are ill prepared to work at changing the systems and structures that generate dysfunction in the lives of their clients (Goodman et al., 2004; Toporek & Liu, 2001). Many view their involvement in political affairs as separate from their professional lives (Fox, 2003) and are concerned that social science research and social services are being used to further political causes (Weinrach & Thomas, 1998). In their sample of graduate counseling trainees, Nilsson and Schmidt (2005) reported that participation in social advocacy efforts was low. Despite the call for helping professionals to advocate for social justice, most graduate programs provide very little training and preparation to serve in this capacity (Vera & Shin, 2006). This chapter will:

- Provide an overview of major theories of social justice and advocacy
- Describe strategies and skills that helping professionals will need in order to advocate effectively for sexual and gender minorities at the systemic level
- Suggest practical ways that helping professionals might advocate for sexual and gender minority persons

SOCIAL JUSTICE FOR SEXUAL AND GENDER MINORITIES

Mainstream approaches in counseling and psychotherapy have long emphasized treatment interventions with individuals at a micro practice level. The majority of helping professionals view themselves as advocates for their clients. Advocacy is defined as a "purposive effort to change specific existing or proposed policies or practices on behalf of or with a specific client or group of clients" (Ezell, 2001, p. 23). The recent call for helping practitioners (Arredondo & Perez, 2003; Donahue & McDonald, 2005; Goodman et al., 2004) to intervene within organizations and communities at the meso and macro levels to effect change in social policies and structures and to eliminate discriminatory social, legal, economic, and governmental policies is not entirely new (Goodman et al., 2004). Feminist and multiculturally oriented helping professionals have long criticized mainstream approaches on a number of grounds. They have argued that our theories and our practices focus on the promotion of individual autonomy and well-being, often to the exclusion of collective welfare (Toperek & Liu, 2001).

Social workers were among the first to establish a social justice agenda (Appleby & Anastas, 1998; Van Voorhis & Hostetter, 2006). One of the primary architects of the social work profession in the United States was Jane Addams, who was a powerful advocate for social justice and human rights. According to Saleebey (1990), social justice is a cornerstone of social work practice as well as the individual capacity to experience indignation, inquiry, compassion, and caring. Social justice figures prominently in the National Association of Social Workers (1999) Code of Ethics. While gender expression is not yet fully recognized in the ethical codes (Messinger, 2006), all social workers are expected to influence social policy, engage in social change, and advocate for disabled groups (Swenson, 1998).

In 1977, Berger, a social worker, proposed an advocate model of intervention specifically for use with sexual minorities. This model called for social workers to participate in organizations that support sexual minority persons, to lobby to change laws in order to extend protection to sexual minorities, and to conduct research and reeducation efforts to inform others about sexual orientation.

Feminist theorists have a long history of promulgating the connection between personal relationships and social systems. The popular slogan used by feminists, "the personal is political," embodied this connection. Feminist psychologists have a well-established and consistent concern with the obligations that therapists have toward society. For example, in 1990 the Feminist Therapy Institute established its Ethical Guidelines for Feminist Therapists that included advocacy. Rosewater (1990) contended that advocacy is one way for feminist psychologists to create meaningful change in the social structure and that such change is tantamount to an ethical imperative.

Multiculturalism is a social, intellectual movement that emphasizes the need to understand culturally diverse groups and to eliminate harmful practices in counseling and psychotherapy that perpetuate oppression of these groups (Fowers & Davidov, 2006). The Guidelines on Multicultural Education, Training, Research, Practice, and Organizational Change for Psychologists of the American Psychological Association (2003, p. 379) call for psychologists to contribute to social justice.

The goals of community counseling and psychology have also included the elimination of oppressive social conditions and the promotion of wellness (Prilleltensky, 2001). Community psychologist Prilleltensky (1997, 2001) has been particularly outspoken about the need for psychology and human service professionals to promote collective wellness, and specifically for professionals to help clients maintain a creative balance between personal and collective wellness. Prilleltensky (1997) advocated that counseling professionals assume what he termed an "emancipatory communitarian approach" to psychotherapy, meaning that therapists "seek not only to care for disadvantaged people but also to change the social and political conditions that perpetuate suffering" (p. 531).

HOW TO WORK FOR SOCIAL CHANGE: TECHNIQUES

Helping professionals face a significant challenge in terms of working toward the greater good, especially in a cultural context that emphasizes brief interventions and accountability. Before we define what social change strategies are, let's consider the following example.

> A first-year law student named Nancy went to her Contracts class with Professor Jay expecting nothing out of the ordinary. But somewhere between sessions on "promise" and "breach," between "expectation" and "reliance," she one day noticed something quite different about Professor Jay. Jay, who combined left-leaning politics and scholarship with a distinctly conservative fashion sense, usually sported short hair, penny loafers, and oxford cloth shirts. But today, Nancy noticed, Professor Jay was also wearing bright green nail polish.
>
> Unable to contain her curiosity, Nancy asked her professor about his new fashion statement. Jay explained that the day before, his young son Ted had come home in tears. On the playground that day, a group of children had encircled him with taunts about his "long messy hair." Noticing Ted's nail polish, they cruelly chided him for being "abnormal." Later, a teacher found Ted hiding under a piece of play equipment, crying because one of his harassers had finally slapped him.
>
> Professor Jay had taken the measures most parents would when faced with a beloved child in this state. He reassured Ted in every way possible. He called Ted's teacher as well as the principal of the school and sought assurances that the other children involved would be made to understand that their behavior was unacceptable. But that evening, Professor Jay went one step further—he took his young son in hand and went to the bathroom where the nail polish was stored. Did Professor Jay remove his son's nail polish at that point? No. He asked if Ted would like to paint his father's nails as well. How better, Jay asked, to convey to his son his solidarity and support? (*Source:* Ayres, Ian: *Straightforward.* © 2005 by Princeton University Press. Reprinted by permission of Princeton University Press.)

Professor Jay's actions might strike some as simply those of a loving and responsible parent. He tried to shield his son from the negative responses that often ensue for boys who dress or behave in ways that defy traditional gender roles. At the same time, Professor Jay also assumed a much greater personal risk by rendering himself "feminine" in order to advocate for the rights of others who are perceived as gender nonconforming. The act of painting his fingernails might also be considered an example of what feminist activist Gloria Steinem referred to in the title of her text *Outrageous Acts and Everyday Rebellions* (1995).

Social activists aid those who are disadvantaged or oppressed to collectively organize to bring about social justice (Alle-Corrlis & Alle-Corrlis, 1999). Readers will recall that it was the important work of gay activists that ultimately led to the removal of homosexuality as a diagnostic entity in the *Diagnostic and Statistical Manual of Mental Disorder* (American Psychiatric Association, 2000). During that time in the 1960s and 1970s, gay activists had employed a variety of what D'Emilio (1983) called "accommodationist" social change strategies, including attending the annual conventions of the American Psychiatric Association in conservative dress and demeanor so as to present themselves to its members as respectable and psychologically healthy citizens (Raeburn, 2004). After the riots that occurred in 1967 when several sexual and gender minorities were arrested during a police raid at a gay bar called the Stonewall Inn in New York City, social change strategies began to change. Tactics sometimes involved "zap" actions or direct actions of a more confrontational nature, such as the one that took place in 1972 at the American Psychiatric Association convention in Dallas. Risking censure from the association, Dr. John Fryer, a psychiatrist, donned an oversized tuxedo, cloak, and fright mask to hide his true identity and addressed the audience as "Dr. H. Anonymous" in order to educate his colleagues about homosexuality.

Social Change Strategies

Chronister and McWhirter (2006) noted several accommodationist social justice strategies that practitioners can use to create social change, including dialoguing, problem posing, and critical self-reflection. Goodman and colleagues (2004) also identified several skills or processes that professionals must employ if they are to serve as advocates for social justice: (1) exploring personal values and beliefs, (2) becoming sensitive to the issue of power and how professionals use power in relation to their clients, (3) helping people who have often been silenced or rendered invisible by societal oppression to tell their stories, (4) focusing on the strengths rather than just the weaknesses or deficiencies of clients, and (5) providing concrete tools and coping strategies that clients can use to further their own efforts at self-determination. In the next sections, we will explore some of these processes in more detail.

ENHANCE YOUR SELF-AWARENESS   In Chapter 4, we discussed the significance of exploring our own values and experiences in relation to gender identity, sexuality, and sexual orientation. Multicultural training efforts (Sue, Arredondo, & McDavis, 1992) typically encompass the three components of awareness, knowledge, and skills. Liberation psychologist Martín-Baró (1994) borrowed Brazilian educator Freire's (1970) notion of *concientizacao*, meaning to change one's awareness of oppression and take action against it. According to Freire (1970), dialogue with others is essential for a change in consciousness to take place.

ADOPT A SYSTEMIC PERSPECTIVE   In addition to exploration of the self, those working as advocates for sexual and gender minorities must, as a prerequisite, have an adequate understanding of systems theory (Alle-Corliss & Alle-Corliss, 1999; Kiselica & Robinson, 2001). Many practitioners and psychotherapists have had some exposure to systems theory in working with individuals and families. The systems approach was considered to be a revolutionary approach to working with families because of its emphasis on the complex nature of family life. According to systems theorists, families are made up of mutually interacting members whose emotional problems are the consequences of how members function not only with one another but also in society. Applying this to social change means that one must recognize all the persons who are influential in determining policy (Alle-Corliss & Alle-Corliss, 1999).

BUILD COALITIONS Perhaps the first step in working for social justice is to form alliances and coalitions, mobilize volunteers, and build communities of diverse allies. Del Castillo and Garcia (1995) delineated the tactics of social justice advocacy they deemed essential: mobilizing volunteers and building communities with diverse alliances. In a similar vein, Tully (2000) posited that helping professionals must be capable of building alliances and coalitions to support favorable legislation and defeat discriminatory legislation and policy.

ENHANCE COMMUNICATION AND TECHNOLOGY SKILLS A core requirement for social advocates is the ability to communicate effectively, especially through electronic means, including distribution lists, moderated and unmoderated discussion lists, bulletin boards, newsgroups, and Internet relay chat rooms (Freeman, 2005; Kiselica & Robinson, 2001).

During the 1990s, the use of the Internet as a tool for community organizing among gender minorities was especially effective (Lev, 2006b). Lev (2006b) noted: "Cyber communication cultivated the rise of political activism born of a newly emerging sense of social justice" (p. 164). Several authors (e.g., Denny, 1997; Gagne, Tewksbury, & McGaughey, 1997; Whittle, 1998) also attributed much of recent transgender activism to the increasing use of cyberspace. The plethora of websites and chat rooms has provided possibilities for gender minority persons to communicate and support one another with anonymity and without discrimination (Lev, 2006b). Many activists have been able to garner support for gender minorities through the use of the Internet. There has also been an explosion of websites and social networks developed for older sexual and gender minorities (e.g., Gay and Lesbian Association of Retired Persons (*www.gaylesbianretiring.org*). Persons who are oppressed have been widely described as "silenced," and the work of psychologists has been, therefore, termed as helping oppressed persons find their voices.

HELP THE SILENCED TELL THEIR STORIES McWhirter, Blustein, & Perry (2005) described the plight of the *arpilleristas* in Chile, who were the wives, mothers, and sisters of those who were murdered or tortured or who vanished during the dictatorship of General Augusto Pinochet. In an atmosphere of extreme censorship, these women gathered together to sew bits of cloth onto rough fabric and sold these as handicrafts. This was also an act of defiance because their work depicted the brutality of Pinochet's regime. The handicrafts were exported to other countries, thus telling the stories on cloth and letting the world know about what was happening in their country. In a similar vein, helping professionals must aid sexual and gender minorities in telling their stories. Being able to be recognized and having the capacity to tell their stories have been significant sources of healing.

In her work with participants in self-help groups for postpartum depression, Taylor (1996, 1999) argued that by telling personal stories or narratives, these mothers were able to appeal to the empathic emotions evoked from others as a deliberate tool for social change. In a similar fashion, the personal "coming out" stories that are told by sexual minorities in public contexts effectively reveal the "pain of exclusion" (p. 245) and serve as an important means of developing alliances with nongay persons (Raeburn, 2004).

Feminist political philosopher Fraser (2003) explored the distinction between the societal injustices that are based on an unequal distribution of resources and those that are associated with rendering others invisible. Morland (2005) posited that the latter is particularly germane in the cases of persons who are born as intersexed, or DSD. She criticized as an injustice the practice of interceding immediately after birth to "correct the mistake" of persons who are born with ambiguous genitalia. According to Morland, to recognize something is to do it justice. Indeed, many transgender activists have discussed the necessity of identifying themselves as "transgendered," even after having completed sexual reassignment surgery.

BOX 11.1

Anecdote from the Field

Several years ago I became an apprentice with a local community theater troupe called Playback Theatre. As a company, we have performed for those who are disempowered and/or marginalized in prisons, homeless shelters, and nursing homes. We've also performed for sexual and gender minority youth support groups and adults who are at risk for HIV/AIDS or who are living with HIV/AIDS (Carroll, 2005).

The concept for Playback Theatre was developed in 1974 by Jonathan Fox. It is a unique blend of drama therapy and community theater whose purpose is to promote community healing and social change (Fox, 1974; Salas, 2000).

In Playback Theatre performances, the actors ask audience members to share their personal stories, which the troupe members then act out. There are no scripts, no costumes, and no scenery changes—only a bare stage with several wooden boxes and a ladder placed in the upstage right corner with colored cloth draped over it. The playback process has five stages: (1) interviewing, (2) forming, (3) casting, (4) preparing, and (5) enacting.

The conductor may recommend a "form," which is a stylized way of portraying the story. Or the conductor may suggest a more conventional approach in which the teller's story is portrayed as a one-, two-, or three-act play. The "teller" or audience member is asked to select an actor from the troupe to represent him/her and various other actors to play additional characters in the story. Without conferring with one another, the actors set the scene, using pieces of cloth and wooden boxes found on the stage.

During the enactment stage, the actors may play intangible objects as well as characters. The actors approach the story without an agenda or script. In the fifth and final stage, the focus is back to the teller and the conductor. Depending on the feedback from the teller, the actors may need to do a "correction"—redo the scene. Or the actors may do a transformation where, with the teller's input, the scene is enacted with different outcomes.

In all cases, the enactment must be true to the essence of the teller's story. The audience members are asked to serve as supportive witnesses to these stories. Salas (1993) maintains that telling one's story in a community forum is a "way of bearing witness to the larger story behind the one being told. The audience becomes connected by emotions and life currents on a far deeper level" (p. 23).

Playback's approach to social change embodies narrative and feminist social constructionist principles. Playback embraces and validates multiple voices and permits persons to tell—and see—their own life stories. According to White and Epston (1990), the pioneers of narrative therapy, stories or narratives provide a framework for the organization for our life experiences. Like narrative therapy, Playback offers a safe space for participants to reflect on their experiences and to challenge basic assumptions. Almost all therapeutic interventions in narrative therapy are delivered in the form of questions. Narrative therapy involves deconstructing or questioning assumptions that have been made. In much the same way, the conductor in Playback Theatre is told to make use of questions to elicit the teller's point of view.

For helping professionals, Playback offers the potential to effect change in organizations and communities beyond the context of a one-to-one therapy session (Carroll, 2005). Playback is clearly successful in that it now has theater companies in over 30 countries (see www. playbacknet. org). Consider joining Playback or a similar organization in your community.

PARTICIPATE IN POLICY MAKING AND ENCOURAGE ACTIVISM IN OTHERS Because one of the most significant ways in which social system changes are created is through the "development and passage of public policy" (Tully, 2000, p. 185), it is necessary for helping professionals to be informed about every aspect of public policy as it relates to sexual and gender minorities and to encourage the involvement of others, including their clients. This is a difficult undertaking, as Messinger (2006) noted, primarily because public policy is "always in flux" (p. 427). Messinger observed that social welfare policies pertaining to sexual and gender minority issues include sodomy laws, hate crime laws, sex education in public schools, nondiscrimination laws, civil recognition of same-sex couples and gender minority couples, and adoption and foster care policies.

Sherraden, Slosar, and Sherraden (2002) observed that social policy in the United States has shifted from the federal to the state level. This means that opportunities to have impact and make a difference are more accessible and less time-consuming and expensive for novices. According to Sherraden et al., practitioners are on the frontlines and can more easily address issues that require policy changes by bringing "grassroots constituents to the table" (p. 213).

Ezell (2001) and Hayes and Mickelson (2003) identified other policy-related change strategies: joining political parties, participating in political action committees, conducting research that will be used to inform public policy, filing lawsuits and friend-of-the-court briefs, and engaging in legislative monitoring, lobbying, and committee testimony.

Learn About Social Change Strategies

Perhaps even without being fully cognizant of his actions, Professor Jay was resisting the natural order of things with regard to sex and gender. His actions might be characterized as a social change technique described by Ayres and Brown (2005) as ambiguation. *Ambiguation* is defined as deliberate actions a person performs that make his or her sexual orientation and gender identity ambiguous to others. When a person performs such actions, he or she temporarily calls into question his or her own sexual orientation and gender identity and thereby suspends or terminates any privileges that are associated with heterosexism and gender conformity. By having his fingernails painted, Professor Jay personally renounced the privileges associated with being a heterosexual and gender-conforming male.

Another social change strategy that destabilizes our notions of what ought to be with regard to the gender binary was described by Lorber (2005) as *degendering*. She refers to this as a deliberate form of resistance to "existing gendered social orders" (p. 33). These practices include (1) not assigning tasks in the home and workplace by gender, (2) not grouping children by gender in schools, (3) underplaying gender categories in language ("ladies and gentlemen" versus "colleagues and friends") (p. 33), and (4) eliminating sex-segregated public restrooms.

Grise-Owens, Vessels, and Owens (2004) described the strategies that were used to organize a successful campaign in Kentucky for sexual and gender minority rights. The multilevel grassroots organization that was created found several themes that seemed to facilitate its efforts. These also coincide with Alinsky's primer for social activism entitled *Rules for Radicals* (1972). Grise-Owens et al. (2004) provided this sound advice for aspiring social activists:

a. Small, but consistent steps lead to large, significant strides.
b. Significant change requires systemic intervention.

c. The personal is political and the political is personal.
d. Adaptation, patience, perseverance, planning, and a few lucky breaks bring success.
e. Success must be maintained with continued action.
f. Do not lose sight of the desired goal. (pp. 12–14)

WORKING FOR SOCIAL CHANGE: NEEDS AND CONTEXTS

Throughout the remainder of this chapter, we will focus on the myriad of social issues that confront sexual and gender minorities in this country. Following discussion of each, I will list ways that readers can begin their work as advocates for social justice.

Sexual and Gender Minorities in Mental Health Care Settings

As has been described in previous chapters, the current medically based approach to transsexuality has been contested over the past several years by a number of therapists, gender minorities, and activists (e.g., Lev, 2006a; Raj, 2002). Perhaps the strongest and most vocal criticism has resulted from the fact that mental heath care professionals, according to current standards, are required to render a psychiatric diagnosis to warrant further medical intervention. Ironically, the decision to view gender variance as psychopathology has been made on the basis of very little scientific evidence. There is little, if any, empirical evidence to suggest that gender dysphoria is pathological (Rivera, 2002). Transgender activists argue that it is necessary to confront members of the American Psychiatric Association to reevaluate the current classification of gender identity disorder and transvestic fetishism (Burgess, 1999). Many (e.g., Denny, 2004; Lev, 2005) believe that the removal of references to gender identity disorder and transgender fetishism in the text revision of the fourth edition of the *Diagnostic and Statistical Manual of Mental Disorders* (*DSM–IV–TR*; American Psychiatric Association, 2000) is necessary for gender minorities to achieve social and political equality with nonminorities. Gay activists (Drescher, 2002; Lev, 2005) attribute much of the progress that has been made in attaining gay rights to the elimination of homosexuality as a diagnosable mental disorder.

Others (e.g., Bockting & Ehrbar, 2005) question the strategy of eliminating the diagnosis of gender identity disorder because of the possibility that this will jeopardize medical coverage and legal recognition of transsexuals in some locales. For many, the lack of health insurance coverage for costs associated with transitioning has been a source of great consternation (Kirk & Kulkarni, 2006). Lombardi and Bettcher (2005) argued:

> Transgender/transsexual men and women need affordable and more reliable access to medical care that will enable them to better embody their gender identity. As such, legislative and other policies must prevent denial of public and private insurance coverage for such procedures, because doing so restricts people's ability to interact in society in their identified gender. (p. 138)

Gender minority activists are also critical of social service agencies that actively collude to enforce gender policing policies in community mental health agencies. It is commonplace for gender minority persons who have not had genital surgery to be classified according to their natal sex for purposes of residential substance abuse or other mental health treatment, prison housing, and homeless shelters. These practices often put such persons at risk for violence and discrimination (Messinger, 2006). Sexual and gender minority youth who are currently in foster or residential care are particularly vulnerable by virtue of past abuse and inadequate agency policies and procedures (Maccio & Doueck, 2002). Compared to nonminority youth, sexual and gender minority youth are more apt to experience multiple and unstable placements (Jacobs & Freundlich, 2006; Mallon, 2001), to be subjected to verbal harassment and gay-related abuse (Mallon, 2001), and to be denied appropriate mental health treatment (Estrada & Marksamer, 2006). Results from a sample of 45 sexual and gender minority youth in a study by Mallon, Aledort, and Ferrara (2002) showed the average number of placements was 6.35. Mallon (2001) attributed this instability to several factors, including the perception of staff members that these youth are management problems. "In the last few years, legal advocates have begun to bring lawsuits to address the serious abuses faced by GLBT youth in state care, and courts have begun to hold state agencies and professionals responsible for these abuses" (Estrada & Marksamer, 2006, p. 193).

Sexual and Gender Minorities in Medical Care Settings

Sexual minority persons, like gender minorities, face a lack of health-care access. Many public health concerns such as HIV and STIs, as well as noncommunicable diseases, affect gay and bisexual men disproportionately (Rhodes & Yee, 2006). The research findings presented in Chapter 8 illustrated the extent to which health-care providers hold negative attitudes and engage in discriminatory behaviors toward their sexual and gender minority patients. Many gender minorities do not seek routine medical evaluation and care out of fear that they will be rejected by their physicians (Kirk & Kulkarni, 2006). A number of researchers (e.g., Nemoto, Sausa, Operario, & Keatley, 2006) have discussed the need for health education programs for gender minorities who transition, particularly in the areas of HIV risk reduction and substance abuse.

The recent debate over how to intervene in the case of infants who are born with intersex conditions (DSD) is another area that needs to be addressed. Lev (2006a) observed that the professions of social work, counseling, and family therapy have been "silent" regarding the "therapeutic needs of people with intersex conditions and their families and there have been few clinical resources or informed advocates" (p. 28). There are numerous medical professionals, bioethicists, and advocacy groups, such as the Intersex Society of North America, that have been vocal about changing the medical protocols that are currently in use because of surgical complications, including impairments in sexual functioning and fertility rates (Lev, 2006a). Critics are particularly vocal about the use of deception and secrecy by physicians and family members. Lev recommended that interdisciplinary teams made up of social workers and other mental health experts be formed to serve as advocates. Adult persons who are intersexed (DSD) also need advocates in the medical system in order to track their medical records and converse with physicians, some of whom are still reluctant to fully disclose information about their patients' conditions (Lev, 2006a).

Recommendations

1. Challenge policies that discriminate on the basis of HIV status (Tully, 2000).
2. Educate current and future practitioners about current medical protocols for intersexed (DSD) infants and advocate for the use of full-service interdisciplinary teams

of mental health practitioners to educate families about intersex conditions (DSD) and future options (Lev, 2005).

3. Support a "strengths-based" approach to public health that incorporates lay health educators who are sexual and gender minorities of color and who can help build partnerships with formal health-care delivery systems (Rhodes & Yee, 2006).

4. Attend to the organizational climate in medical and social services facilities, including use of gender-sensitive terminology in official documents (Cochran & Cauce, 2006).

5. Ensure that gender minorities are given accommodations and adequate health care in the context of residential treatment programs, homeless shelters, and prisons (Minter, 2004).

Individuals in Communities

According to Messinger (2006), 14 states outlaw discrimination based on sexual orientation in employment, housing, and public accommodations. As of 2005, the number of cities, counties, and states that had enacted antidiscrimination laws addressing gender minorities was minimal, with coverage of approximately 29% of the U.S. population (National Gay and Lesbian Task Force, n.d.). Twenty-nine states have hate crime laws based on sexual orientation (Messinger, 2006), and seven states (California, Connecticut, Hawaii, Minnesota, Missouri, Pennsylvania, and Vermont) have hate crime laws that specifically include crimes motivated by bias based on gender identity and/or gender expression (Human Rights Campaign, n.d.).

One significant issue for persons who wish to seek gender reassignment concerns the right to achieve their desired gender legally. The availability of legal documents varies by locality, and in some places, little to no medical intervention is required to change one's legal sex or name, while in others, sex reassignment surgery is required (Lombardi & Bettcher, 2005).

Recommendations

1. Institute antidiscrimination laws for sexual and gender minorities or amend preexisting laws that do not include both sexual and gender minorities (Messinger, 2006; Morrow, 2004; Tully, 2000).

2. Repeal state sodomy laws (Messinger, 2006; Tully, 2000).

3. Provide educational programming for religious and political leaders (Tully, 2000).

4. Write letters to the editors of local newspapers on behalf of sexual and gender minority persons and issues (Ezell, 2001).

5. Develop community services, including retirement care facilities, to meet the needs of older sexual and gender minorities (Johnson, Jackson, Arnette, & Koffman, 2005; Tully, 2000).

6. Donate books and magazines featuring sexual and gender minority issues and persons to local libraries (Tully, 2000).

Couples and Families in Community Settings

There are hundreds of legal rights and benefits that married heterosexual couples receive that same-sex couples do not, including health and retirement benefits, the ability to file joint tax returns, and the right to make medical decisions for spouses in times of illness (Cahill,

Ellen, & Tobias, 2002). Without legal protection, it is possible that same-sex partners can be excluded from caring for their ailing and/or aging partners, having access to their loved ones in medical settings, taking part in and planning the funerals of their partners, and exercising inheritance and succession rights after death of their partners (Manthorpe, 2003).

The issue of marriage for gender minority persons, particularly transsexual persons, is more complex. Courts in Florida, Illinois, Kansas, Ohio, and Texas have refused to recognize marriages between gender minority persons on the basis of the view that these were unlawful marriages between same-sex persons (Human Rights Campaign Foundation, 2006). "There have been recent court cases with mixed responses to opposite-gender marriage of transsexual individuals, and all cases involved people who underwent some operative procedures as a requirement for changing legal sex designation" (Lombardi & Bettcher, 2006, p. 138). If one partner in a heterosexual marriage decides to change sex and remain in the relationship, the laws continue to view the transitioned partner as legal member of his or her birth sex (Minter, 2004). In 1999, for example, an appellate court in Texas invalidated a seven-year marriage between Christine Littleton, a transsexual woman, and her deceased husband. The case arose when Ms. Littleton brought a wrongful death suit for medical malpractice. The court denied that Ms. Littleton was legally married because it viewed her as genetically male. Transgender and transsexual parents commonly face tremendous discrimination in child custody and visitation decisions. Several courts have granted custody or visitation to transgender parents only when the parent has agreed to hide his or her transgender status. Other courts have restricted or denied visitation to transsexual parents.

Recommendations

1. Support same-sex marriages.
2. Join and support community-based family support groups and chapters of national organizations like Parents and Friends of Lesbians and Gays (PFLAG) (Tully, 2000).
3. Develop housing policies in jails and residential addictions treatment programs to provide safe housing for sexual and gender minorities (Silvestre & Arrowood, 2006).
4. Aggressively recruit staff members in mental health and other social service agencies through the creation and dissemination of advertisements in gay and lesbian publications (Silvestre & Arrowood, 2006).

Sexual and Gender Minority Youth in Schools and Universities

As we explored in Chapter 7, the needs of sexual and gender minority youth are greater than ever before. Research shows that youth are questioning their sexual identities at earlier ages and often coming out in their early or middle teens (McHaelen, 2006) in contexts (e.g., families, schools, and churches) that are frequently unwelcoming and unsupportive. Sexual and gender minority youth are a population at risk for substance abuse, depression, suicide, lower self-esteem, STIs, and HIV infection, as well as increased school dropout rates. Referrals for clinical services for these youth in middle schools have increased (McHaelen, 2006). When family conflicts arise over a child's sexual or gender orientation, there are few supportive resources. As a result, increasing numbers of youth are coming into contact with various child welfare services, including foster care, group homes, and juvenile detention centers (McHaelen, 2006).

Unfortunately, public schools are not safe havens for sexual and gender minority youth. Sex education policies are determined primarily at the state and local levels (Messinger, 2006). Not only do educators and administrators resist attending to sexual and gender identity in youth, but also they often punish colleagues who actually address these issues (Athanases & Larrabee, 2003). As gender minorities become more visible and aggressive in their bid for human rights, schools will have to develop policies related to the use of bathrooms, showers, gym classes, locker rooms, and dress codes (Holman & Goldberg, 2006).

According to research conducted by the Human Rights Campaign, as of June 2006, 562 universities had nondiscrimination policies related specifically to sexual orientation, and 74 had policies that included "gender identity and/or gender expression" (Human Rights Campaign Foundation, 2006).

Recommendations

1. Conduct training workshops and in-service programs in schools and other youth organizations for youth, teachers, administrators, and school board members about sexual and gender minority issues, including educational programs to prevent harassment (Elze, 2003; Fassinger, 2000; Morrow, 2004; Tully, 2000).
2. Establish school- and university-based support groups for sexual and gender minority students, staff members, teachers, and administrators (Broido, 2000; Elze, 2003).
3. Institute nondiscrimination policies and practices that affirm the basic rights of sexual and gender minority persons (Broido, 2000; Fassinger, 2000; Jacobs & Freundlich, 2006; Morrow, 2004; Tully, 2000).
4. Implement a gay/lesbian/bisexual-affirmative sex education curriculum (Fassinger, 2000).
5. Aggressively recruit openly gay, lesbian, bisexual, and gender minority staff members, teachers, and administrators (Fassinger, 2000; Jacobs & Freundlich, 2006; Morrow, 2004).
6. Transform the school curriculum to ensure that it is "gender-fair and gay-affirmative" (Fassinger, 2000, p. 370).
7. Revise the curriculum and requirements in teacher education and counselor education to include gender and sexuality (Fassinger, 2000; Jacobs & Freundlich, 2006).
8. Work within existing community organizations, such as churches, recreational facilities, and neighborhood associations, to dispel myths and stereotypes about sexual and gender minority youth, and organize community events with and for sexual and gender minority youth.
9. Include information and referral for sexual and gender minority teens in crisis through a gay-friendly crisis telephone hot line (Tully, 2000).
10. Provide educational programming and support services (e.g., housing for transgender students) for sexual and gender minorities in university settings (Beemyn, Curtis, Davis, & Tubbs, 2005).
11. Fund university-based research on sexual and gender minority issues (Broido, 2000).
12. Provide safe housing for sexual and gender minority foster children and others residing in group homes (Silvestre & Arrowood, 2006).
13. Provide training for staff, foster parents, and adoptive parents on sexual and gender minority issues (Silvestre & Arrowood, 2006).

14. Include sexual orientation and gender identification in the antidiscrimination practices and policies related to employment in foster and adoption agencies (Silvestre & Arrowood, 2006).

Sexual and Gender Minorities in Employment Settings

While there is no national legislation prohibiting sexual orientation discrimination, such legislation has been enacted in some states, counties, and municipalities. It is estimated that one-third of sexual minorities live in localities that offer protective legislation (Ragins, 2004).

Messinger's (2006) cursory review of employment law revealed that "most sexual and gender minority persons have no protection from harassment and discrimination in the workplace" (p. 449).

Recommendations

1. Require sensitivity training on sexual orientation and gender expression for employers and supervisors (Messinger, 2006; Winfeld & Spielman, 2001).
2. Hold workplace diversity training for employees (Messinger, 2006; Winfeld & Spielman, 2001).
3. Establish domestic partner benefits and spousal equivalency policies (Messinger, 2006; Winfeld & Spielman, 2001).
4. Ensure that antidiscrimination clauses are included in organizational documents (Messinger, 2006; Pope et al., 2004) and that sexual orientation and gender identity expression are included in equal employment opportunity policy statements.
5. Establish workplace networks for mentoring sexual minority employees (Messinger, 2006; Winfeld & Spielman, 2001) and employee resource groups.
6. Establish corporate giving policies for sexual and gender minority organizations.

WORKING FOR SOCIAL CHANGE: PERSONAL CHALLENGES AND REWARDS

The degree to which practitioners are willing to heed the call for social action is dependent on the nature of the personal, institutional, and systemic barriers they encounter. While there is little empirical research identifying possible obstacles that prevent practitioners from advocating for sexual and gender minority persons, Collison et al. (1999) identified several dimensions that are important for practitioners to consider when making personal decisions about their roles as advocates. These factors include (1) how well informed the counselor is about the particular issue, (2) the counselor's anticipation regarding the reactions of others to her/his activities, and (3) the counselor's self-efficacy as an advocate and social activist. These dimensions can also be viewed as barriers to advocacy. In our research, we reported that among our sample of counselor trainees, interest in advocating for sexual minorities was significantly lower than for other populations, including persons with psychiatric disabilities, victims of interpersonal violence, the elderly, and persons of color (Carroll, Gilroy, & Murra, 2000). In the same study, the counseling trainees' level of interest was even lower still for advocating for gender minorities.

Personal Consequences of Advocacy

Gainor (2005) recommended

> Engaging students and trainees in personal reflections and analyses regarding ways in which they have privilege in this society, what they fear they may lose if the oppressive system is eradicated, and how they may gain with such a transformation. (p. 183)

Russell's (2000) research on the experiences of gay rights activists in Colorado who campaigned against the passage of Colorado's Amendment II was one of the few explorations of the personal consequences of advocacy. This amendment would have excluded homosexuality from antidiscrimination laws in Colorado. Gay rights activists who were interviewed in her study reported significant difficulties with anxiety, depression, and posttraumatic stress. Several authors (e.g., Goodman et al., 2004; Kiselica & Robinson, 2001) have addressed similar issues in terms of the emotional costs that are associated with social justice work.

Other possible issues that might deter helping professionals include the possible dual-relationship dilemmas that may occur when clients and therapists work together in social or political settings (Stevenson, 2006). Another possible deterrent for practitioners in advocating on behalf of sexual and gender minority issues concerns the common misassumption by others that these advocates are homosexual (Stevenson, 2006).

The benefits of such work for professionals include opportunities to learn about political processes and to participate in structural change (Sherraden et al., 2002). The literature is replete with examples of how people who have advocated for social justice have been enriched. Studies of Holocaust survivors suggest that those who resisted their enemies, even quietly, often fared better after the war (Rose, 1996). Many persons who have lived with HIV have done so with the aid of their own activism (Rose, 1996).

Summary

The orientation most widely embraced in the education and training of psychologists and practitioners emphasizes a more traditional psychological paradigm—that is, one that interprets the cause of emotional and behavioral problems as intrapsychic and interpersonal. In a radical paradigm shift from this individualistic orientation, psychologists and mental health practitioners are increasingly being called on to adopt a sociopolitical understanding of emotional and behavioral problems and to serve as social change agents, transforming the cultural context in which sexual and gender minorities live. To assume a social justice perspective means that many of the presenting issues that sexual and gender minorities bring to therapy are seen not as evidence of individual psychopathology but as byproducts of the consequences of social experiences.

Unfortunately, most practitioners and psychologists are ill prepared to work at changing the systems and structures that generate dysfunction at the individual level (Goodman et al., 2004). As previously noted, many helping professionals are less well prepared to advocate for social change at the macro level.

Interestingly, much of what practitioners need to know about social activism can be gleaned from the literature and research associated with the practice of social work, feminist psychotherapy, multicultural counseling, and community and liberation psychology.

According to Goodman et al. (2004), social change can occur at three levels: micro (individuals, families), meso (communities, organizations), and macro (social structures, policies). Swenson (1998) suggested that we capitalize on ways that social justice is compatible with current managed care models: "planning comprehensive, continuous, and integrated community services; and supporting people to remain in the community" (p. 534).

The strategies that psychologists, practitioners, and social workers need for creating social change for sexual and gender minorities are numerous. Strategies that are used by social workers to achieve change at the macro level include joining political parties, becoming involved in political action committees, conducting research, filing lawsuits and friend-of-the-court briefs (Hayes & Mickelson, 2003), and influencing social policy.

Feminist activist Gloria Steinem (1995) once said: "no organizer should ever end a meeting or a book or article without ideas for practical action" (p. 384). So, just as she practiced making such deals with her audiences, I'd like to make a deal with readers to perform at least one "outrageous" act in the cause of social justice for sexual and gender minorities. This can range from challenging a homophobic joke to petitioning for a gender studies section in the local library. The exercises that follow provide you with some possible suggestions and ways for you to begin your journey as social activists.

Personal Reflection 1

Review the list of activities below, which were presented in the chapter, and assess your (a) interest, (b) knowledge, and (c) perceived self-efficacy associated with engaging in each activity. Use a 5-point Likert scale (1 = not at all and 5 = extremely) for each item.

1. Join a local chapter of a national organization (Gay, Lesbian and Straight Education Network, PFLAG, etc.) and regularly attend its meetings.
2. Write a letter to the editor of your local newspaper in support of a sexual or gender minority issue or person.
3. Present an educational workshop on an issue that affects sexual or gender minorities to members of your church, staff at work, students in your residence hall, or the like.
4. Write a work-related policy that specifically includes freedom of gender expression. Develop guidelines to handle violations of your policy.

Personal Reflection 2

Ayres and Brown (2005) decided to take advantage of the fact that heterosexual people who advocate for sexual minority issues are often assumed by others to be gay/lesbian/bisexual. They used the term *ambiguation* to describe a strategy that can be used both personally and collectively to bring about social change. Persons intentionally behave in such a way as to make their sexual orientation ambiguous to others and thereby temporarily suspend all privileges that accompany heterosexuality. An example of ambiguation can be found in stories during World War II when allies wore Jewish stars in order to confuse the enemy.

Directions

The items listed below describe some possible ways to effect social change through ambiguation of sexual orientation and/or gender identity. Select one activity that you can safely engage in and monitor your responses as well as those of others around you. Keep a log if necessary to record these reactions.

1. Wear a sticker or button with one of the following slogans: "Love Needs No Cure," "Silence = Death," "Out of the Closet and Into the Streets," "Who Are We to Judge," "United Against Hate," "Equal Rights Are Not Special Rights," "Value All Families," "The Quality of the Relationship Is More Important than the People in It," or "Proud to Be a Tran."
2. Hang a rainbow, transgender or bisexual pride flag in front of your house.
3. Hang a sticker or other sign at your workplace desk that says "Safe Zone" or "Trans Ally."
4. Affix a bumper sticker that is supportive of sexual and gender minority rights on the back bumper of your car.
5. Wear a t-shirt with a supportive slogan such as those listed above.
6. Join one of the following advocacy groups: Lambda Legal Defense, Human Rights Campaign, National Gay and Lesbian Task Force, Gay and Lesbian Alliance Against Defamation (GLAAD), National Lesbian Rights Center, Gay Men's Health Crisis.
7. Join one of the following advocacy groups for gender minorities: Intersex Society of North America, Transgender Advocacy Coalition, International Foundation for Gender Education, or National Center for Transgender Equality.
8. Tell someone you know about having joined one of the organizations listed above and describe to him or her the merits of membership in this organization.

Personal Reflection 3

Ayres and Brown (2005) also proposed the concept of *boycotting* as a social change strategy. According to Ayres and Brown, boycotting involves bestowing *rewards* on those who take positive action. For example, Ayres and Brown staged a "vacation pledge" in which people sign pledges that they will vacation in states that democratically choose to legalize same-sex marriage within three years of this legalization. They also proposed rewarding companies by doing business with them on the basis of their track record in advancing employment protections for sexual minorities.

Directions

*The Human Rights Campaign (HRC) has a Corporate Equality Index (**www.hrc.org/cei**) where it rates companies based on the existence of nondiscrimination policies for sexual and gender minorities, diversity training, same-sex domestic partner health insurance benefits, and charitable gifts to sexual and gender minority organizations. Visit the HRC website and find out more about the Corporate Equality Index project. Make a pledge to do business only with those corporations that promote equal rights for sexual and gender minorities. Talk a friend into doing the same.*

Library, Media, and Internet Activities 1

Check your local video/DVD store for three important films that deal with legal and social policies affecting the lives of sexual and gender minorities.

Tying the Knot (De Seve, 2004)

This documentary film deals with the current national debate over same-sex marriage. Among the stories and interviews featured in this documentary are those of Mickie and Sam, both of whom lost their long-time same-sex partners and were subsequently denied survivor benefits.

Discussion Questions and Activities

1. In a small group, discuss your personal position on legalizing same-sex marriages before watching this film. Did the retelling of Mickie's and Sam's stories impact your position? If so, how? If not, why?
2. What might you do if you were counseling clients like Mickie and Sam who had each been involved in a long-time relationship without benefit of legal protection? What might you advise them to do?
3. Locate three of the largest employers in your geographic area and investigate whether or not their nondiscrimination policies are inclusive of sexual and gender minority issues. Find out what, if any, benefits are available to partners of sexual and gender minority employees.

If These Walls Could Talk 2 (Anderson, 2000)

This film includes a trilogy of stories that debuted on Home Box Office. The first segment, which received critical acclaim, was set in the early 1960s and depicts the story of Edith, who must cope with the sudden death of her female partner of 50 years.

Discussion Questions and Activities

1. Keep a notebook on hand while you watch the first segment of this film. What kinds of emotions and thoughts arise for you while watching this film? How does Edith's experience in the 1960s compare with Mickie's and Sam's experiences approximately 35 years later in *Tying the Knot*?
2. Visit a local assisted living facility or nursing home in your geographic area. Does this facility accommodate its sexual and gender minority residents? If so, how? If not, what might you recommend to the facility in

terms of recognizing and meeting the needs of their sexual and gender minorities more effectively?
3. Assume that you have been invited to conduct training for staff members who work at the facility you visited. Design a two-hour workshop for staff members that would specifically provide them with the skills and behaviors necessary to address the needs of their aged sexual and gender minority residents.

Out of the Past (Dupre, 1998)

The documentary depicts the real-life story of Kelli Peterson, who fought to organize a Gay-Straight Alliance in her high school in Utah. Interwoven throughout the film are the stories of other sexual minority persons from the past, including a Puritan minister named Michael Wigglesworth and Bayard Rustin, a noted civil rights leader and colleague of Martin Luther King, Jr.

Discussion Questions and Activities

1. Does your local high school have a Gay-Straight Alliance (GSA). If yes, how might you assess its impact on the school and on the community? If no, how might you organize a GSA? Develop a detailed action plan delineating the process steps required to complete this project. How might you go about building a coalition of allies? What might be some of the obstacles you would anticipate encountering in your community?
2. Plan a program on gender minority youth issues for your local high school, residence hall, or agency. Prepare an agenda for the training and plan a series of activities in conjunction with the informational content you will be presenting.
3. Visit the guidance department of a local high school or the counseling center at your university. Conduct an assessment of the organizational climate in this setting. Are there pamphlets and other literature in waiting areas and on wall spaces that are inclusive of sexual and gender minorities?

Library, Media, and Internet Activities 2

Select a social issue discussed in this chapter, such as same-sex marriage or employee domestic partner benefits, and identify two political action or lobbying organizations who hold opposing positions on this issue. The list below contains some possible selections. Research and provide a description of each organization, including its funding sources, organizational structures and services, lobbying strategies, and staffing patterns. Be sure to include a statement of each organization's position on the issue you selected.

American Family Association
Christian Communication Network
Family Research Institute
Focus on Family

Gay and Lesbian Alliance Against
  Defamation
Gay Men's Health Crisis
Human Rights Campaign
Lambda Legal Defense
National Association for Research and
  Therapy for Homosexuality
National Gay and Lesbian Task Force
National Lesbian Rights Center
Parents and Friends of Ex-Gays
  and Gays
Positive Alternatives to
  Homosexuality

Group Activity 1

Earlier in this chapter, we explored the role of practitioners, psychologists, and social workers in helping sexual and gender minorities tell their own stories. Photovoice, a specific strategy that has proven particularly effective in facilitating change, was developed by Wang at the University of Michigan (Wang & Burris, 1997; Wang, Cash, & Powers, 2000). According to Hussey (2006), photovoice is a process by which people can "identify, present, and enhance their community through photographs and their related dialogue" (p. 133). People are given cameras and, as an example, asked to take photographs of their work- and health-related environments with the purpose of trying to record their community's strengths and weaknesses, generate dialogue, and impact policy makers (Wang & Burris, 1997). The photographs, when analyzed in a group context, become potential catalysts for change. Hussey (2006) used this technique to explore the experiences of transgendered persons in their health-care settings.

Hussey transcribed the sessions where transgendered participants discussed their photographs and analyzed the content. The results of her work are published in the article "Slivers of the Journey: The Use of Photovoice and Storytelling to Examine Female to Male Transsexuals' Experience of Health Care Access," published in the *Journal of Homosexuality*.

Directions

1. Conduct further research on the photovoice technique.
2. Select a particular social issue confronting sexual and gender minority persons discussed in this chapter and design and carry out a photovoice project.
3. Be sure to contact your university's Institutional Review Board (IRB) and to complete the necessary requirements to ensure the safety and confidentiality of those who participate in your project.

Group Activity 2

In their text entitled *Integrating Traditional Healing Practices into Counseling and Psychotherapy* (2005), Moodley and West advocated that psychotherapists consider integrating traditional healing methods like storytelling and ritual in order to expand their counseling practices into community settings. Brin (2004), a rabbi with training in counseling, uses ritual to help families deal with the pain of loss through miscarriage and stillbirth. She maintains that ritual "ameliorates pain, amplifies joy and enhances connection with the community" (p. 124).

> *The basic process of creating ritual is part of our continual search for meaning, and we do it all the time by repeating the stories we tell, elevating certain objects to having symbolic meanings, and associating songs and melodies with regular actions or special events"* (Brin, 2004, p. 125)

Rose (1996) posited that rituals help survivors of traumatic experiences stay connected to others who have gone through similar kinds of experiences, despite the fact that survivors often feel compelled to disconnect from these experiences in order to build new lives. Rose noted that some survivors may need to recount their stories to people who will listen with honor and respect. For example, the HIV epidemic has been documented in many creative ways through the use of oral and video history projects such as the NAMES Project Memorial Quilt.

Another wonderful example of how ritual can be used in a communal context to aid in healing was cited by Schwartzberg (1996). Schwartzberg recalled the Onion Cellar, a fictitious nightclub in Gunter Grass's postwar novel *The Tin Drum* (1962):

> *The Onion Cellar is an unusual place. It serves no food or drink, offers no conventional entertainment. Instead, well-heeled patrons sit at crude tables, where they are given cutting boards, paring knives, and onions. They wait obediently until the club owner instructs them to cut and peel the onions. They start timidly. But then they cut and peel with abandon. And they begin to cry. Their crying soon turns to wailing, a communal grief mirrored in a skein of individual tears. The patrons turn to their friends and to strangers, weeping and comforting each other. They confess their sins, their hurts, and their guilt. They use the onions to gain access to the pain they carry but cannot otherwise express. They come to the Onion Cellar to share this pain publicly, because the experience is less fulfilling if one cuts onion at home and cries alone. Some patrons come only once, others repeatedly, until exhausted of their tears. And somehow, in the process, they feel healed (pp. 218–219).*

Directions

In small groups, select a social issue for the sexual and gender minority population and develop a community ritual for healing like the one presented above.

References

Alinsky, S. (1972). *Rules for radicals: A pragmatic primer for realistic radicals.* New York: Random House.

Alle-Corliss, L., & Alle-Corliss, R. (1999). *Advanced practice in human service agencies: Issues, trends, and treatment perspectives.* Belmont, CA: Brooks/Cole.

American Psychiatric Association. (2000). *Diagnostic and statistical manual of mental disorders—Text revision* (4th ed.). Washington, DC: Author.

American Psychological Association. (2003). Guidelines on multicultural education, training, research, practice, and organizational change for psychologists. *American Psychologist, 58*(5), 377–402.

Anderson, J. (Director). (2000). *If these walls could talk 2* [Television broadcast]. New York: HBO.

Appleby, G. A., & Anastas, J. W. (1998). *Not just a passing phase: Social work with gay, lesbian, and bisexual people.* New York: Columbia University Press.

Arredondo, P., & Perez, P. (2003). Expanding multicultural competence through social justice leadership. *Counseling Psychologist, 31*(3), 282–289.

Athanases, S. Z., & Larrabee, T, G. (2003). Toward a consistent stance in teaching for equity: Learning to advocate for lesbian-and gay-identified youth. *Teaching & Teacher Education, 19*(2), 237–261.

Ayres, I., & Brown, J. G. (2005). *Straightforward: How to mobilize heterosexual support for gay rights.* Princeton, NJ: Princeton University Press.

Beemyn, B., Curtis, B., Davis, M., & Tubbs, M. J. (2005). Transgender issues on college campuses. *New Directions for Student Services, 11,* 49–60.

Berger, R. M. (1977). An advocate model for intervention with homosexuals. *Social Work, 22*(4), 280–283.

Bockting, W. O., & Ehrbar, R. D. (2005). Commentary: Gender variance, dissonance or identity disorder? *Journal of Psychology & Human Sexuality, 17*(3/4), 125–134.

Brin, D. J. (2004). The use of rituals in grieving for a miscarriage or stillbirth. *Women & Therapy, 27*(3/4), 123–132.

Broido, E. M. (2000). Ways of being an ally to lesbian, gay, and bisexual students. In V. A. Wall & N. J. Evans (Eds.), *Toward acceptance: Sexual orientation issues on campus* (pp. 345–370). Lanham, MD: University Press of America.

Burgess, C. (1999). Internal and external stress factors associated with the identity development of transgendered youth. *Journal of Gay & Lesbian Social Services, 10*(3/4), 35–47.

Cahill, S., Ellen, M., & Tobias, S. (2002). Family policy: Issues affecting gay, lesbian, bisexual, and transgendered families. New York; National Gay and Lesbian Task Force Policy Institute.

Carroll, L. (2005, February). *Playback Theatre: A feminist approach to collective healing and social change.* Paper presented at the annual meeting of the Association of Women in Psychology, Tampa, FL.

Carroll, L., Gilroy, P. J., & Murra, J. (2000). Advocating for gay, lesbian, bisexual and transgender persons: Overcoming barriers and resistances [Electronic version]. *Q: The Online Journal, 1*(1). Retrieved March 12, 2001, from http://www. aglbic.org/q/vol/num/Carroll.htm

Chronister, M. K., & McWhirter, E. H. (2006). An experimental examination of two career interventions with battered women. *Journal of Counseling Psychology, 53*(2), 151–164.

Cochran, B. N., & Cauce, A. M. (2006). Characteristics of lesbian, gay, bisexual, and transgender individuals entering substance abuse treatment. *Journal of Substance Abuse Treatment, 30*(2), 135–146.

Collison, B. B., Osborne, J. L., Gray, L. A., House, R. M., Firth, J., & Lou, M. (1999). Preparing practitioners for social action. In C. C. Lee & G. R. Walz (Eds.), *Social action: A mandate for counselors* (pp. 263–277). Alexandria, VA: American Counseling Association.

Consortium on the Management of Disorders of Sex Development. (2006). *Handbook for parents.* Rohnert Park, CA: Intersex Society of North America. Retrieved March 1, 2007, from http://www. dsdguidelines.org

Del Castillo, R. G., & Garcia, R. A. (1995). *Cesar Chavez—A triumph of spirit.* Norman: University of Oklahoma Press.

D'Emilio, J. (1983). *Sexual politics, sexual communities: The making of a homosexual minority in the United States, 1940–1970.* Chicago: University of Chicago Press.

Denny, D. (1997). Transgender: Some historical, cross-cultural, and contemporary methods of coping and treatment. In B. Bullough, V. L. Bullough, & J. Elias (Eds.), *Gender blending* (pp. 33–47). Amherst, NY: Prometheus Books.

Denny, D. (2004). Changing models of transsexualism. *Journal of Gay & Lesbian Psychotherapy, 8*(1/2), 25–40.

De Seve, J. (Director). (2004). *Tying the knot* [Motion picture]. United States: Independent Artists.

Donahue, P., & McDonald, L. (2005). Gay and lesbian aging: Current perspectives and future directions for social work practice and research. *Families in Society, 86*(3), 359–366.

Drescher, J. (2002). Editorial: In your face: Social activism and mental health. *Journal of Gay & Lesbian Psychotherapy, 6*(4), 1–7.

Dupre, J. (Director). (1998). *Out of the past* [Motion picture]. United States: Ardustry Home Entertainment.

Elze, D. (2003). Gay, lesbian, and bisexual youths' perceptions of their high school environments and comfort in school. *Children & Schools, 25*(4), 225–239.

Ensler, E. (1998). *The vagina monologues.* New York: Villard.

Estrada, R., & Marksamer, J. (2006). The legal rights of LGBT youth in state custody: What child welfare and juvenile justice professionals need to know. *Child Welfare, 85*(2), 171–194.

Ezell, M. (2001). *Advocacy in the human services.* Belmont, CA: Wadsworth.

Fassinger, R. (2000). Gender and sexuality in human development: Implications for prevention and advocacy in counseling psychology. In

S. D. Brown & R. W. Lent (Eds.), *Handbook of counseling psychology* (pp. 346–378). New York: Wiley.

Fowers, B. J., & Davidov, B. J. (2006). The virtue of multiculturalism: Personal transformation, character, and openness to the other. *American Psychologist, 61*(6), 581–594.

Fox, D. R. (2003). Awareness is good, but action is better. *Counseling Psychologist, 31*(3), 299–304.

Fox, J. (1994). *Acts of service: Spontaneity, commitment, and tradition in the nonscripted theatre.* New Paltz, NY: Tusitala.

Fraser, N. (2003). Social justice in the age of identity politics: Redistribution, recognition and participation. In N. Fraser & A. Honneth (Eds.), *Redistribution or recognition? A political-philosophical exchange* (pp. 7–109). London: Verso.

Freeman, I. C. (2005). Advocacy in aging: Notes for the next generation. *Families in Society, 86*(3), 419–423.

Freire, P. (1970). *Pedagogy of the oppressed.* New York: Continuum.

Fulcher, M., Sutfin, E. L., Chan, R. W., Scheib, J., & Patterson, C. (2006). Lesbian mothers and their children: Findings from the contemporary families study. In A. M. Omoto & H. S. Kurtzman (Eds.), *Sexual orientation and mental health: Examining identity and development in lesbian, gay, and bisexual people* (pp. 281–299). Washington, DC: American Psychological Association.

Gagne, P., Tewksbury, R., & McGaughey, D. (1997). Coming out and crossing over: Identity formation and proclamation in a transgender community. *Gender & Society, 11*(4), 478–508.

Gainor, K. A. (2005). Social justice: The moral imperative of vocational psychology, *Counseling Psychologist, 33*(2), 180–188.

Goodman, L. A., Liang, B., Helms, J. E., Latta, R. E., Sparks, E., & Weintraub, S. R. (2004). Training counseling psychologists as social justice agents: Feminist and multicultural principles in action. *Counseling Psychologist, 32*(6), 793–837.

Grass, G. (1962). *The tin drum* (Ralph Manheim, Trans.). London: Secker & Warburg.

Grise-Owens, E., Vessels, J., & Owens, L. W. (2004). Organizing for change: One city's journey toward justice. *Journal of Gay & Lesbian Social Services, 16*(3/4), 1–15.

Haynes, K. S., & Mickelson, J. S. (2003). *Affecting change: Social workers in the political arena* (5th ed.). Boston: Allyn & Bacon.

Herek, G. M. (2006). Legal recognition of same-sex relationships in the United States: A social science perspective. *American Psychologist, 61*(6), 607–621.

Holman, C. W., & Goldberg, J. M. (2006). *Social and medical advocacy with transgender people and loved ones: Recommendations for BC practitioners.* Vancouver, Canada: Vancouver Coastal Health, Transcend Transgender Support & Education Society, and Canadian Rainbow Health Coalition. Retrieved April 11, 2007, from http://www.vch.ca/transhealth

Human Rights Campaign. (n.d.). *Transgender, gender expression and identity issues.* Retrieved December 1, 2006, from http://www.hrc.org/Template.cfm?Section=Transgender_Issues1

Human Rights Campaign Foundation. (2006). *The state of the workplace for gay, lesbian, bisexual and transgender Americans.* Washington, DC: Authors.

Hussey, W. (2006). Slivers of the journey: The use of photovoice and storytelling to examine female to male transsexuals' experience of health care access. *Journal of Homosexuality, 51*(1), 129–158.

Jacobs, J., & Freundlich, M. (2006). Achieving permanency for LGBT youth. *Child Welfare, 85*(2), 299–316.

Johnson, M. J., Jackson, N. C., Arnette, J. K., & Koffman, S. D. (2005). Gay and lesbian perceptions of discrimination in retirement care facilities. *Journal of Homosexuality, 49*(2), 83–102.

Kirk, S. C., & Kulkarni, C. (2006). The whole person: A paradigm for integrating the mental and physical health of trans clients. In M. D. Shankle (Ed.), *The handbook of lesbian, gay, bisexual, and transgender public health: A practitioner's guide to service* (pp. 145–174). Binghamton, NY: Harrington Park Press.

Kiselica, M. S., & Robinson, M. (2001). Bringing advocacy counseling to life: The history, issues, and human dramas of social justice work in counseling. *Journal of Counseling & Development, 79*(4), 387–398.

Leidolf, E. M. (2006). The missing vagina monologue . . . and beyond. *Journal of Gay & Lesbian Psychotherapy, 10*(2), 77–92.

Lev, A. I. (2005). Disordering gender identity: Gender identity disorder in the *DSM–IV–TR. Journal of Psychology & Human Sexuality, 17*(3/4), 35–69.

Lev, A. I. (2006a). Intersexuality in the family: An unacknowledged trauma. *Journal of Gay & Lesbian Psychotherapy, 10*(2), 27–56.

Lev, A. I. (2006b). Transgender communities: Developing identity through connection. In K. J. Bieschke, R. M. Perez, & K. A. DeBord (Eds.), *Handbook of counseling and psychotherapy with lesbian, gay, bisexual, and transgender clients* (2nd ed.,) (pp. 147–175). Washington, DC: American Psychological Association.

Lombardi, E., & Bettcher, T. (2005). Lesbian, gay, bisexual, and transgender/transsexual individuals. In B. S. Levy & V. W. Sidel (Eds.), *Social injustice and public health* (pp. 130–144). New York: Oxford University Press.

Lorber, J. (2005). *Breaking the bowls: Degendering and feminist change.* New York: Norton.

Maccio, E. M., & Doueck, H. J. (2002). Meeting the needs of the gay and lesbian community: Outcomes in the human services. *Journal of Gay & Lesbian Social Services, 14,* 55–73.

Mallon, G. P. (2001). *Lesbian and gay youth issues: A practical guide for youth workers.* Washington, DC: CWLA Press.

Mallon, G. P., Aledort, N., & Ferrara, M. (2002). There's no place like home: Achieving safety, permanency, and well-being for lesbian and gay adolescents in out-of-home care settings. *Child Welfare, 81*(2), 407–439.

Manthorpe, J. (2003). Nearest and dearest? The neglect of lesbians in caring relationships. *British Journal of Social Work, 33*(6), 753–768.

Martin-Baro, I. (1994). *Writings for a liberation psychology* (A. Aron & S. Corne, Eds.). Cambridge, MA: Harvard University Press.

McHaelen, R. P. (2006). Bridges, barriers, and boundaries. *Child Welfare, 85*(2), 407–432.

McWhirter, E. H., Blustein, D. L., & Perry, J. C. (2005). Annunciation: Implementing an emancipatory communitarian approach to vocational psychology. *Counseling Psychologist, 33*(2), 215–224.

Messinger, L. (2006). Social welfare policy and advocacy. In D. F. Morrow & L. Messinger (Eds.), *Sexual orientation & gender expression in social work practice* (pp. 427–459). New York: Columbia University Press.

Meyer, I. H. (2003). Prejudice, social stress, and mental health in lesbian, gay, and bisexual populations: Conceptual issues and research evidence. *Psychological Bulletin, 129*(5), 674–697.

Minter, S. (2004). *Transgender persons and marriage: The importance of legal planning.* Retrieved December 1, 2006, from http://www.transgenderlaw.org/resources/transmarriage.pdf

Moodley, R., & West, W. (2005). *Integrating traditional healing practices into counseling and psychotherapy.* Thousand Oaks, CA: Sage.

Morland, I. (2005). The injustice of intersex: Feminist science studies and the writing of a wrong. *Studies in Law, Politics, & Society, 36,* 53–75.

Morrow, D. (2004). Social work practice with gay, lesbian, bisexual, and transgender adolescents. *Families in Society, 85*(1), 91–99.

National Association of Social Workers. (1999). *Code of ethics of the National Association of Social Workers.* Retrieved September 9, 2005, from http://www.socialworkers.org/pubs/code/code.asp

National Gay & Lesbian Task Force. (n.d.). *Year in review: State and local trans-inclusive legislation.* Retrieved December 1, 2006, from http://www.thetaskforce.org/downloads/trans/YearinReview2005.pdf

Nemoto, T., Sausa, L. A., Operario, D., & Keatley, J. (2006). Need for HIV/AIDS education and intervention for MTF transgenders: Responding to the challenge. *Journal of Homosexuality, 51*(1), 183–202.

Nilsson, J. E., & Schmidt, C. K. (2005). Social justice advocacy among graduate students in counseling: An initial exploration. *Journal of College Student Development, 46*(3), 267–279.

Pope, M., Barrett, B., Szymanksi, D. M., Chung, Y. B., Singarvelu, H., McLean, R., et al. (2004). Culturally appropriate career counseling with gay and lesbian clients. *Career Development Quarterly, 53*(1), 158–176.

Prilleltensky, I. (1997). Values, assumptions, and practices: Assessing the moral implications of psychological discourse and action. *American Psychologist, 52*(5), 517–535.

Prilleltensky, I. (2001). Value-based praxis in community psychology: Moving toward social justice and social action. *American Journal of Community Psychology, 29*(5), 747–778.

Raeburn, N. C. (2004). *Lesbian and gay workplace rights: Changing corporate America from inside out.* Minneapolis: University of Minnesota Press.

Ragins, B. R. (2004). Sexual orientation in the workplace: The unique work and career experiences of gay, lesbian, and bisexual workers. *Research in Personnel & Human Resources Management, 23,* 35–120.

Raj, R. (2002). Towards a transpositive therapeutic model: Developing clinical sensitivity and cultural competence in the effective support of transsexual and transgendered clients [Electronic version]. *International Journal of Transgenderism, 6*(2). Retrieved April 7, 2005, from http://www.symposion.com/ijt/ijtvo06no02_04.htm

Rhodes, S. D., & Yee, L. J. (2006). Public health and gay and bisexual men: A primer for practitioners, clinicians, and researchers. In M. D. Shankle (Ed.), *The handbook of lesbian, gay, bisexual, and transgender public health: A practitioner's guide to service* (pp. 119–143). Binghamton, NY: Harrington Park Press.

Rivera, M. (2002). Informed and supportive treatment for lesbian, gay, bisexual, and transgendered trauma survivors. *Journal of Trauma & Dissociation, 3*(4), 33–58.

Rose, A. (1996). HIV disease over the long haul: Hope, uncertainty, grief, and survival. In J. W. Dilley & R. Marks (Eds.), *The UCSF AIDS health project guide to counseling* (pp. 197–208). San Francisco: Jossey-Bass.

Rosewater, L. B. (1990). Public advocacy. In H. Lerman & N. Porter (Eds.), *Feminist ethics in psychotherapy* (pp. 229–238). New York: Springer.

Russell, G. M. (2000). *Voted out: The psychological consequences of antigay politics.* New York: New York University Press.

Salas, J. (1993). *Improvising real life: Personal story in Playback Theatre.* New Paltz, NY: Tusitala.

Salas, J. (2000). Playback Theatre: A frame for healing. In P. Lewis & D. R. Johnson (Eds.), *Current approaches in drama therapy* (pp. 288–302). Springfield, IL: Charles C. Thomas.

Saleebey, D. (1990). Philosophical disputes in social work: Social justice denied. *Journal of Sociology & Social Welfare, 27*(2), 29–40.

Sandfort, T., Bos, H., & Vet, R. (2006). Lesbians and gay men at work: Consequences of being out. In A. M. Omoto & H. S. Kurtzman (Eds.), *Sexual orientation and mental health: Examining identity and development in lesbian, gay, and bisexual people* (pp. 225–244). Washington, DC: American Psychological Association.

Schwartzberg, S. (1996). *A crisis of meaning: How gay men are making sense of AIDS.* New York: Oxford University Press.

Sherraden, M. S., Slosar, B., & Sherraden, M. (2002). Innovation in social policy: Collaborative policy advocacy. *Social Work, 47*(3), 209–221.

Silvestre, A. J., & Arrowood, S. H. (2006). Strategies for improving state, county and city government health and welfare services for LGBT people. In M. D. Shankle (Ed.), *The handbook of lesbian, gay, bisexual, and transgender public health: A practitioner's guide to service* (pp. 263–290). Binghamton, NY: Harrington Park Press.

Steinem, G. (1995). *Outrageous acts and everyday rebellions.* New York: Holt.

Stevenson, M. R. (2006). Public policy, mental health, and lesbian, gay, bisexual, and transgender clients. In K. J. Bieschke, R. M. Perez, & K. A. DeBord (Eds.), *Handbook of counseling and psychotherapy with lesbian, gay, bisexual, and transgender clients* (2nd ed., pp. 379–397). Washington, DC: American Psychological Association.

Sue, D. W., Arredondo, P., & McDavis, R. J. (1992). Multicultural counseling competencies and standards: A call to the profession. *Journal of Counseling & Development, 70*(4), 477–486.

Swenson, C. R. (1998). Clinical social work's contribution to a social justice perspective. *Social Work, 43,* 527–537.

Taylor, V. (1996). *Rock-a-by baby: Feminism, self-help, & postpartum depression.* New York: Routledge.

Taylor, V. (1999). Gender & social movements: Gender processes in women's self-help movements. *Gender & Society, 13*(1), 8–33.

Toporek, R., & Liu, W. M. (2001). Advocacy in counseling. Addressing race, class and gender oppression. In D. B. Pope-Davis & H. L. K. Coleman (Eds.), *The intersection of race, class and gender in multicultural counseling* (pp. 385–413). Thousand Oaks, CA: Sage.

Tully, C. T. (2000). *Lesbians, gays & the empowerment perspective.* New York: Columbia University Press.

Van Voorhis, R. M., & Hostetter, C. (2006). The impact of MSW education on social worker empowerment and commitment to client empowerment through social justice advocacy. *Journal of Social Work Education, 42*(1), 105–121.

Vera, E. M., & Shin, R. Q. (2006). Promoting strengths in a socially toxic world: Supporting resiliency with systemic interventions. *Counseling Psychologist, 34*(1), 80–89.

Wang, C., & Burris, M. (1997). Photovoice: Concept, methodology, and use for participatory needs assessment. *Health Education & Behavior, 24*(3), 369–387.

Wang, C., Cash, J. L., & Powers, L. (2000). Who knows the streets as well as the homeless? Promoting personal and community action through photovoice. *Health Promotion & Practice, 1*(1), 81–89.

Weinrach, S. G., & Thomas, K. R. (1998). Diversity-sensitive counseling today: A postmodern clash of values. *Journal of Counseling & Development, 76*(2), 115–122.

White, M., & Epston, D. (1990). *Narrative means to therapeutic ends.* New York: Norton.

Whittle, S. (1998). The trans-cyberian mail way. *Social & Legal Studies, 7*(3), 389–408.

Winfeld, L., & Spielman, S. (2001). *Straight talk about gays in the workplace.* Binghamton, NY: Harrington Park Press.

AUTHOR INDEX

SUBJECT INDEX